SOCIAL AND CULTURAL FORMS OF
MODERNITY

UNDERSTANDING MODERN SOCIETIES: AN INTRODUCTION

Series editor: Stuart Hall

Book 1   *Formations of Modernity*
edited by Stuart Hall and Bram Gieben

Book 2   *Political and Economic Forms of Modernity*
edited by John Allen, Peter Braham and Paul Lewis

Book 3   *Social and Cultural Forms of Modernity*
edited by Robert Bocock and Kenneth Thompson

Book 4   *Modernity and its Futures*
edited by Stuart Hall, David Held and Anthony McGrew

For general availability of all the books in the series, please contact your regular supplier or, in case of difficulty, Polity Press.

This book forms part of the Open University course D213 *Understanding Modern Societies*. Details of this and other Open University courses can be obtained from the Central Enquiry Service, PO Box 200, The Open University, Walton Hall, Milton Keynes, MK7 6YZ.

Cover illustration: John Tandy *Abstract composition* (*c.* 1930) Private Collection, London. Reproduced by courtesy of the Redfern Gallery, London, and by kind permission of Mrs Suzanne Tandy.
Photo: A.C. Cooper.

SOCIAL AND CULTURAL FORMS OF MODERNITY

EDITED BY ROBERT BOCOCK AND KENNETH THOMPSON

POLITY PRESS IN ASSOCIATION WITH THE OPEN UNIVERSITY

First published 1992 by Polity Press in association with Blackwell Publishers Ltd
and The Open University
Reprinted 1993, 1995

Editorial office:
Polity Press
65 Bridge Street,
Cambridge CB2 1UR, UK

Marketing and production:
Blackwell Publishers Ltd
108 Cowley Road,
Oxford OX4 1JF, UK

ISBN 0 7456 0963 5
ISBN 0 7456 0964 3 (pbk)

A CIP catalogue record for this book is available from the British Library.

Edited, designed and typeset by The Open University

Printed in Great Britain by Redwood Books, Trowbridge

CONTENTS

Understanding Modern Societies Course Team

Stuart Hall	Professor of Sociology and Course Team Chair
Maureen Adams	Secretary
John Allen	Senior Lecturer in Economic Geography
Margaret Allott	Discipline Secretary, Sociology
Robert Bocock	Senior Lecturer in Sociology
David Boswell	Senior Lecturer in Sociology
Peter Braham	Lecturer in Sociology
Vivienne Brown	Lecturer in Economics
Dianne Cook	Secretary
Robert Cookson	Senior Editor, Social Sciences
Helen Crowley	Lecturer in Women's Studies, North London Polytechnic
James Donald	Senior Lecturer in Cultural and Community Studies, University of Sussex
Paul du Gay	Post-graduate student, Sociology
Molly Freeman	Discipline Secretary, Sociology
Bram Gieben	Staff Tutor, Social Sciences
Peter Hamilton	Lecturer in Sociology
David Held	Professor in Politics and Sociology
Paul Lewis	Senior Lecturer in Politics
Vic Lockwood	Senior Producer, BBC
Anthony McGrew	Senior Lecturer in Politics
Gregor McLennan	Professor of Sociology, Massey University, NZ
David Scott-Macnab	Editor, Social Sciences
Graeme Salaman	Senior Lecturer in Sociology
Jane Sheppard	Graphic Designer
Paul Smith	Media Librarian
Keith Stribley	Course Manager
Kenneth Thompson	Professor in Sociology
Alison Tucker	Producer, BBC
Pauline Turner	Secretary
Diane Watson	Staff Tutor, Social Sciences
David Wilson	Editor, Book Trade
Chris Wooldridge	Editor, Social Sciences

Consultants

Harriet Bradley	Senior Lecturer, Sunderland Polytechnic
Tom Burden	Tutor Panel
Tony Darkes	Tutor Panel
Celia Lury	Lecturer in Sociology, University of Lancaster
Denise Riley	Researcher in political philosophy
Alan Scott	Lecturer in Politics, University of East Anglia
Jeffrey Weeks	Professor in Social Relations, Bristol Polytechnic
Geoffrey Whitty	Professor of Sociology of Education, Institute of Education, University of London
Steven Yearley	Professor of Sociology, University of Ulster

External Assessor

Bryan Turner	Professor of Sociology, University of Essex

PREFACE

Social and Cultural Forms of Modernity is the third book in a new series of sociology textbooks which aims to provide a comprehensive, innovative and stimulating introduction to sociology. The four books in the series, which is entitled *Understanding Modern Societies: An Introduction*, are listed on page ii. They have been written to suit students and readers who have no prior knowledge of sociology and are designed to be used on a variety of social science courses in universities and colleges. Although part of a series, each book is self-contained to facilitate use with students studying different aspects of the history, sociology and ideas of modern society and its international context.

The four books form the central part of an Open University course, also called *Understanding Modern Societies*. Open University courses are produced by an extensive course team consisting of academic authors and consultants, a panel of experienced tutors, an external academic assessor, editors and designers, BBC producers, academic administrators and secretaries. (The full course team responsible for this course is listed on the opposite page.) Every chapter has been subjected to wide-ranging discussion and improvement at each of several draft stages. The result is a unique series of textbooks which draw on the cumulative academic research and teaching experience of the Open University and the wider academic community.

All four books have three distinctive features. First, each chapter provides not only a descriptive, historical account of the key social processes which shaped modern industrial societies, and which are now, once again, rapidly transforming them, but also analysis of the key concepts, issues and current debates in the related academic literature. Secondly, each chapter includes a number of extracts from classic and contemporary books and articles, all of them pertinent to the chapter. These are printed conveniently at the end of the chapter in which they are discussed. They can be distinguished from the main text (and can thus be found easily) by the continuous line down the left-hand margin. The third important feature of the text is that it is *interactive*: every chapter contains specially designed exercises, questions and activities to help readers understand, reflect upon and retain the main teaching points at issue. From the long experience of Open University course writing, we have found that all readers will benefit from such a package of materials carefully designed for students working with a fair degree of independence.

While each book is free-standing, there are some cross-references to the other books in the series to aid readers using all the books. These take the following form: 'see Book 1 (Hall and Gieben, 1992), Chapter 4'. For further information on a writer or concept, the reader is sometimes referred to the *Penguin Dictionary of Sociology*. Full bibliographic details of this dictionary are provided where relevant at the end of each chapter, together with other references which suggest further reading which can be undertaken in each area.

In the long collaborative process by which Open University materials are made, the editors of such a volume are only the most obvious of those who have helped to shape its chapters. There are many others with responsibilities for the detailed and painstaking work of bringing a book with so many parts to completion. Our external assessor, Professor Bryan Turner, provided invaluable intellectual guidance, comment, advice, stimulus and encouragement at every stage of the production of these books. Our course manager, Keith Stribley, has done an excellent job of helping us all to keep to schedules, maintaining high standards of editorial consistency, and liaising between course team academics, editors and production. We owe special thanks to Molly Freeman, Maureen Adams, Pauline Turner, Dianne Cook and Margaret Allott for really marvellous secretarial support. Rarely in the history of word-processing can so many drafts have been produced so swiftly by so few. Our Open University editors, Chris Wooldridge, David Scott-Macnab, David Wilson and Robert Cookson, have improved each chapter with their insight and professionalism, usually under quite unreasonable pressures of time, and with unfailing good nature. Thanks also to Paul Smith, our media librarian, for his creative work in finding so many of the illustrations. Debbie Seymour, of Polity Press, has been a constant source of encouragement and good sense.

Finally, the chapter authors have borne stoically our innumerable criticisms and suggestions, and have managed to preserve the essence of their original creations through successive rounds of amendments and cuts. Their scholarship and commitment have made this book what it is.

Robert Bocock and Kenneth Thompson

INTRODUCTION

Robert Bocock and Kenneth Thompson

So far this series of books has examined the emergence of modern societies, from the period of their formation in Western Europe, at the close of the Middle Ages, through the rise of early capitalism, the age of exploration, and the eighteenth-century Enlightenment, to the culmination of the Industrial Revolution at the end of the nineteenth century. The first book, *Formations of Modernity*, traced the processes of formation in four major spheres — economic, political, social and cultural. The ways in which the West came to think of itself in relation to 'others' were then discussed.

After examining the emergence of modernity, we began to offer an analytic 'portrait' of western advanced industrial societies in the twentieth century. The main political and economic institutions and processes were the focus of Book 2, *Political and Economic Formations of Modernity*. In Book 3, we shall move on to examine the social and cultural spheres in order to complete the coverage of major components of modern social formations. At first sight this might appear to be the familiar ground of sociology textbooks. However, we believe our approach is innovatory and therefore challenging to more conventional approaches in several respects.

Rather than simply concentrating on contemporary British social structures and social relations, as is often the case in sociology, we have broadened the focus in a number of ways. Firstly, we give a great deal of attention to historical and comparative data in order to explain the different trajectories taken by modern societies. Consequently, although twentieth-century Britain is often the main focus, it is located within a broader framework. Secondly, we follow those new trends in social and cultural studies that emphasize the construction of cultural and social identities. This means that we are interested in the ways in which social relations are represented and the discourses about them as much as in analysing their structure or organization. At one level this is justified by the obvious fact that individuals' subjective definitions of situations affect how institutions operate. As the American sociologist William I. Thomas put it, 'If men [*sic*] define situations as real, they are real in their consequences'. However, this interest in subjectivity on the part of Thomas and his colleague Charles Horton Cooley has sometimes been portrayed as the preserve of a particular school of sociology, labelled 'symbolic interactionism', because it emphasized the subjective nature of social reality — the notion that society (its structure, institutions, normative patterns, etc.) exists in individuals' minds and feelings. But, although different schools may differ over the respective weights given to micro-social interaction or macro-social institutions, the emphasis on subjectivity need not be confined to any particular school. It was certainly present in the work of a 'founding father' of the sociological study of social institutions, Émile Durkheim, as shown by his comment that 'essentially social life is made up of representations' (Durkheim, 1951, p.312). Like Durkheim, we give a great deal of attention to the types and forms of social representation and signification, particularly where these processes enter into the construction of collective and individual identities. This leads on to the final distinctive characteristic of the approach followed in this book, which is the rejection of any boundary between the 'public' and 'private' spheres. We believe it cannot be emphasized too much that the 'social' is to be found in the most intimate and private spheres — gendered and ethnic identities, the household, consumption, health and sexuality — just as much as in class structure or large-scale organizations.

Having suggested some of the distinguishing characteristics of the approach adopted in this book, we can now outline its relevance for analysing the processes of reproduction of modern societies.

'Reproduction' may seem an odd word to use to designate a social process. Surely, one might think, reproduction is a biological, not a social, process? Well, it is both a biological and a social process. Here, the word 'reproduction' is used to connote, or to suggest, two major processes. The first is the way in which the process of conceiving and rearing human beings — biological reproduction — is affected by the social and cultural environment in which the basic biological acts take place. This may be called the social and cultural context of reproduction of the population. The word 'reproduction' can also be used to refer to the sustaining of cultural and social patterns over time. This second meaning of the word has been extended by some sociologists, significantly by Pierre Bourdieu, a French sociologist who wrote in the 1970s and 1980s. It came to mean the process — or political, social and cultural *processes* — by which the social structure and culture of a society was transmitted or reproduced from one year, from one decade, even from one century, to another.

These two meanings of 'reproduction' combine to highlight an important aspect of modern social formations. Advanced industrial societies have increasingly developed a consciousness of their need to ensure that they have an educated, healthy, reasonably fed and housed workforce. They know that this will not happen automatically, or by chance. The state, in such modern social formations, has to actively organize policies and organizations, or bureaucratic systems, to ensure that the majority of people are housed, whether in public housing or, encouraged through tax incentives, in private dwellings; that there is sufficient food; that people have access to health care; that they are provided for, at least minimally, when unemployed or in retirement; and that they have at least the minimum education to be able to undertake the various sorts of work required in a modern economy.

A society may find that these state practices not only reproduce a suitable workforce but also fulfil military requirements. Indeed, in some cases, including Britain at the time of the Second Boer War (1899–1902), the poor physical condition of many of the soldiers from the industrial areas led to policies by the state to improve the diet and health of the urban working classes. Out of the social mobilization to fight wars in the twentieth century came the recognition of the need to improve the food, health, even the housing conditions, of the workers. There were also political demands and trade union pressures for such improvements in health, housing, food and education/training throughout the twentieth century in Britain and in other modern industrial societies. The requirements of modern warfare for a better fed, well-nourished, fit and healthy, reasonably educated and technically trained set of armed services had coincided with the needs of modern industry, and with the political, even moral, demands of workers themselves for such basic physical, social and cultural advances and for their rights as citizens.

Here, then, the biological meaning of reproduction links with the social connotation of 'reproduction' in social science. Modern industrial societies have to 'reproduce' the labour power and citizenry they need — this has led to far more state welfare, health and education provisions being introduced in the twentieth century than rulers in the earlier decades of the nineteenth century ever imagined. The reasons for such state provisions being introduced have been complex. They have included the needs of the modern armed forces for healthy, fit and educable conscripts or recruits; the needs of modern industrial, technologically based production processes; and moral, political movements among working people who have struggled to achieve material, social and cultural advances for themselves. However, social formations such as 'nations' are not just economic or political entities; they are also composed of particular social and cultural patterns. These too have their hierarchies and unequal distributions of resources (e.g. Bourdieu refers to 'cultural capital', as in the case of the cultural assets that middle-class children bring to their education), which are frequently contested. Social reproduction processes are therefore not smooth and automatic, but rather are frequently characterized by struggles over means and ends, and even over the very discourses used to express these.

This book therefore provides analysis of a variety of processes, social practices and cultural activities which are involved in direct or indirect ways in reproducing the labour force and citizenry of a constantly changing modern industrial society. There are also analyses of reproduction in the broader sense, as it relates to social and cultural patterns, from the division of labour and the role of women in child-care to changes in the gender role of men too, including changes in definitions of femininity, masculinity and sexuality. Social and cultural activities such as consumption, health care, education, religious practices, entertainment, the mass media, and life in modern city areas — all these are discussed as aspects of the complex processes involved in reproduction in modern, urban, industrial, capitalist social formations.

Before you begin reading the chapters, it may be useful to think about the connections between this book, which is broadly focused on the social and the cultural processes, and the earlier books in the series.

Societies, or social formations, can be analysed as if they contain four major components, or zones: namely, the political, the economic, the social and the cultural. Book 1 examined all four of these in relation to the formation of modern, industrial, capitalist societies. In Book 2, the political and the economic were examined in more detail with regard to the twentieth century, especially the period since the end of the Second World War. Book 3 will examine the social and the cultural spheres, again taking the twentieth century, and in particular the last four or five decades, as a major focus of concern.

Just as the political and the economic can be separated from each other *analytically*, even though *empirically* they frequently are found intertwined, so in this book the social and the cultural will be separated *conceptually*, even though in many *concrete situations* they are linked together. Of course, this break between the political and the economic on the one hand, and the social and cultural on the other, should not be taken as a hard and fast one. There are not two main groups or sub-components in social formations — the political-economic and the social-cultural — with the result that other kinds of combination are ruled out. The social can be linked with the economic, as in the concept 'socio-economic class' which implies some complex set of relations between the economic structure of modern, industrial *capitalist* formations and social groups, such as status groups (often called 'classes'), as we shall see in Chapter 1, 'Changing social divisions: class, gender and race'. This particular example of linkage is important historically, in examining the interrelations between economic factors and status attributes such as gender and race.

The political sphere may also have important connections with the social and the cultural, as well as with economically powerful groups in a social formation. As you will see in the chapters on the *social* aspects of modern societies, changes and developments which originated in this zone we are calling 'the social' have had important political implications. For example, the changing role of women in paid work outside the home increased the influence of the voices of women demanding the right to vote in general and local elections. Their role in the First World War helped women over thirty to obtain the vote, but it took until 1928 for women to be given the same voting rights as men.

Thus, the economic and the social may be linked together, as may the political and the social. And as you will see, in the later chapters of this book, the cultural can be linked with the economic or the political too, not just with the social. The four components appear able to combine in all the logically possible combinations. And nothing suggests that any one component, or combination of two components, should be given any more weight in an analysis of a whole society than any other component, or combination. However, social theories have been advanced which do place more emphasis upon one or other of the components.

For example, some Marxists have held that the economic structure (i.e. capitalism in the case of Britain or the United States) is to be regarded as the major determinant of what occurs in the other three zones, at least in the long run. This view has been modified in the work of some later Marxists, such as Louis Althusser, the French social philosopher, to mean that the economic is the determinant of the other sectors *in the last instance*. This means that the state, or what are called here the political, the social and the cultural, have some considerable degree of autonomy from the economic structure, but that this autonomy is never complete; it is always relative to the economic in the last analysis. In other words, the economic does not determine every detailed feature of what goes on in the other spheres, but it does set the overall parameters of what can happen politically, socially or culturally.

Other social theorists have argued that military force is what frequently determines what happens in a given society, not the economic as Marx held. For example, Max Weber (1864–1920), the German sociologist, emphasized the importance of control over the means of violence as a basic power which some groups had in a social formation, although these groups may not necessarily be the major economic class group. This view was developed by Weber, of course, before the full effects of the Russian Revolution of 1917, or the rise of fascism and Nazism, or the development of 'Communist' regimes in Eastern Europe between the late 1940s and 1989–90 had been seen. However, some later social scientists have regarded these political events as examples which confirm Weber's main analytical point: namely, that control over the means of violence in a given territory can be crucial in determining what kind of economic, political, or social/cultural system is allowed to develop. Weber did not hold this to be the pre-eminent cause of all social developments of any significance. His position could be described as being eclectic, in that he also argued that social groups who were influenced by specific cultural values and world-outlooks could affect historical change, as was discussed in Book 1 in relation to Weber's analysis of religion and the emergence, or failure to emerge, of modern, rational forms of capitalism in particular societies.

Of course, cultural ideas and values do not cause major changes on their own — they have to be expressed in the lives of key *social* groups to have any influence at all. So the cultural alone does not seem able to cause change. Culture needs *social* groups to bear, articulate, or express ideas and values in order to have any effect on what happens. This leads to a distinct position which could be called the truly *sociological* position, for it emphasizes the *social* rather than the cultural, or the economic, or the political, alone. It may be seen as close to, if not identical with, the sociological position *par excellence* of Durkheim. For this reason, Durkheim is often seen as being the most social, or sociological, of the founders of modern social science.

Durkheim defined sociology as being the scientific, objective study of institutions, of their genesis and of their functioning. By 'institution' he meant a set of beliefs and practices that had become normative (obligatory) and that were focused on a recurrent or continuous social concern. The first book in the series focused on the genesis, or emergence, of modern institutions. This volume will concentrate on their functioning and adaptation in various circumstances. According to Durkheim, as institutions develop they tend to become more differentiated and elaborated, and at the same time self-sustaining and self-justifying (i.e. the tendency is for institutions to acquire relative autonomy from the original set of factors that brought them into existence). For this reason, Durkheim refused to give any privileged status to economic factors, even though he acknowledged that such factors may have been major determinants in the emergence of institutions. His main focus was on the normative character of institutions. The operation of norms was explained by Durkheim in terms of two processes:

1   the influence of positive or negative sanctions that are structural components of the norm; and

2   the legitimating effect produced by the prestige of the 'collective representations' (e.g. symbols) that give the norm an appearance of coming from a superior source standing above the individual.

Durkheim devoted less attention to the first type of compulsion — sanctions of punishment and reward — because it seemed to be more of a technical, calculative, or coercive constraint. Consequently, economic calculations and the coercive powers of the state did not feature much in his sociology, although he did offer some explanations for the development of the division of labour and of different attitudes towards crime and punishment in his book *The Division of Labour in Society* (1933). He had a greater theoretical interest in the second type of compulsion — that of a cognitive and moral nature. This, to him, was sociologically fundamental, as even economic activities and contracts could not occur without a prior cognitive and normative moral basis. He was fascinated by the way in which we internalize categories and norms so that they become our own, and yet have an authority over us that gives us a sense that they come from a superior source (God, Nature, the Nation, etc.). This book will examine the workings of these institutional processes in a number of spheres of social life.

Modernity is characterized by the differentiation of institutions, so that they enjoy a higher degree of autonomy than might have been the case in pre-industrial societies. However, this does not mean that there is no overall coherence or cohesion in society. Firstly, there are layers of culture that represent a shared inheritance in a society — language, symbols, values and practices — or, to put it in more negative terms, 'the past lies on the present like a dead weight'. Secondly, a certain level of cohesion may be secured due to the fact that, even in a so-called 'multicultural' society, not all cultures are equal. In its stark form of the 'Dominant Ideology Thesis', attributed to Marx, 'The ideas of the ruling class are in every epoch the ruling ideas'. This is a contentious thesis, as the discussion of it in Chapter 7 will make clear. Nevertheless, there would be general agreement with the broader thesis that the resources that offer the means to exercise power are not evenly distributed. Although Weber distinguished different sources of social stratification — market position, status, and political influence — he admitted that they frequently converge. Like Durkheim, he stressed that power is increasingly exercised impersonally through institutional norms in modern society. These norms may be formally set out in bureaucratic rules or may be implicit in the discourses and practices of various institutional spheres. Their authority may seem both rational and natural, when in fact they are the result of the exercise of power and processes of social construction. It is not surprising that this sociological perspective has often been unpopular with powerful groups in society. However, it is the kind of questioning that you will be encouraged to pursue in the chapters that follow.

In Chapter 1, 'Changing social divisions: class, gender and race', Harriet Bradley provides a link with the discussion of the emergence of the modern division of labour in Book 1 and with the analysis of recent developments in the state and the economy in Book 2. Class, gender and race are three important aspects of the pattern of stratification: that is, the structure of relationships between different social groups with differential command of various social resources. She traces the changing patterns of inequality in post-war Britain, showing that, whilst inequalities of class, gender and race are still very marked, the effect of post-war changes has been to produce a more fluid and complex social structure.

This theme is taken up by Helen Crowley in Chapter 2, 'Women and the domestic sphere', which is concerned with the growing diversity of families and households, and with changes in the sexual division of labour. Some of these changes are shown to have contradictory effects for women. The changes also represent the interesting process whereby an area of social life that has always been understood as 'natural' is slowly being recognized as 'socially constructed'. The combined effect of changes in patterns of marriage, cohabitation, divorce, family size, women's economic activity, types of family, and demographic trends appears to suggest that Britain is in a period of transition from the 'normative' family to a situation where diversity is the norm. However, Crowley maintains that the central feature of the family is still the sexual division of labour.

Another aspect of social stratification that is taken as an indicator of fundamental change is the increasing emphasis on consumption patterns and lifestyles rather than production processes. Is it the case that people are now free to choose their social identity through their decisions about what to purchase? Certainly the advertising industry is more interested now in classifying people in terms of consumption patterns and lifestyles rather than occupation. And, for many people, shopping is a major source of pleasure, fulfilment of desire, and a means of expressing their self-image. Robert Bocock examines some of these trends and different interpretations of their significance in Chapter 3, 'Consumption and lifestyles'.

The analysis of the processes through which the self is socially constructed is continued by David Boswell in Chapter 4, 'Health, the self and social interaction'. He outlines some of the key ideas of the social interactionist approach, which has been particularly prominent in the sociology of health. Within that approach, which was influenced by the ideas of social psychologists, there is an emphasis on taking account of the expectations of others in the formation of the concept of self and the performance of roles. Other sociologists, such as the structural-functionalist Talcott Parsons, sought to show how medical practice and the roles of patient and physician exemplified the functional interconnections of the social system and its methods for dealing with deviance from the norm, in this case sickness. A different approach is that of Goffman, who portrayed institutions in dramaturgical terms and also introduced the concept of 'spoiled identity', or 'stigma', seen in attitudes to the mental patient in the asylum. There is also discussion of the work of Foucault on the birth of the asylum and of Sontag on stigmatization of people with AIDs or cancer.

Another of Foucault's studies, this time of sexuality, is central to Chapter 5, 'The body and sexuality', by Jeffrey Weeks. Foucault insists that sexuality should not be thought of as something determined by nature, as it has been both in some theories and in 'common sense', but as a social and historical construct. Weeks examines historical and contemporary evidence suggesting that sexual identities are social and political definitions, subject to negotiation and change. Concern about sexuality, its regulation and control, has been a key element of political debate in modern society.

Social reproduction, regulation, and the construction of identity are processes that feature prominently in Chapter 6, 'Education, economy and national culture', by Geoffrey Whitty. Education was at the centre of the Enlightenment 'project', associated as it is with ideas about the triumph of reason, scientific progress, and the rational ordering of society. Universal education came to be accepted as a requirement for the reproduction of an industrial society. It has also been viewed as a 'civilizing' process by those anxious about the threat of social disorder from the lower classes. In post-war Britain there have been periodic attempts by government to introduce education policies that would answer the needs of the economy, as they defined them, and shape the consciousness of citizens to fit in with preferred ideas of national culture.

Issues of culture come to the fore in the next three chapters. Chapter 7, 'Religion, values and ideology', by Kenneth Thompson, begins with the question: How important is a shared culture in binding people together in a modern society? The Enlightenment project aimed to loosen the religious ties that were thought to have been a brake on progress and to replace such ties with a secular, rational-scientific culture. The 'secularization thesis' predicted that this process would proceed irreversibly as part of the more general process of social differentiation that characterized modernity. The thesis can be questioned on empirical and theoretical grounds. There is evidence that some cultural elements of religious origin are more enduring than was predicted. Religious beliefs and values are quite widely held, even in highly secularized societies like Britain. Some religious ideas and practices have influenced contemporary culture, as illustrated in Foucault's work on discourses and discursive practices such as sex and confession. Religious elements of culture also combine with other discourses to produce ideological effects when they give people a sense of identity as members of an imagined community, as in the case of civic symbolic events and rituals like the coronation and other royal events, which involve symbolic dramatizations of the nation. The struggles between the New Right and its opponents over the definition of national culture and its core values provide a further example of these processes.

The development of new technologies for the mass reproduction of cultural goods, starting with printing and then continuing in the mass media of broadcasting, seems to have provided even greater possibilities for ensuring social reproduction to meet the needs of the economy or a ruling class. However, in Chapter 8, 'Popular culture and the mass media', Celia Lury suggests that this is problematical. She sets out to explain a paradox that has frustrated some social scientists, according to which culture is always tied to power relations and at the same time is only recognizable as culture by its apparent distance from those same relations. Her focus in on the differentiation, or attempted autonomization, of the cultural sphere. A general question considered in this chapter is the nature of the relationship between production and reception — producers and audiences — of cultural goods. Examples range from the introduction of printing and struggles over literacy, to the development of the press, the novel, the distinction between high and low culture, and broadcasting as a means of cultural production and as a domestic medium.

Finally, James Donald's Chapter 9, 'Metropolis: the city as text', indicates some of the ways in which the concept of 'the city' has been deployed in arguments about modernization, modernity, and modernism. He pays special attention to questions of representation — not only what an author says, for example, when talking about the city, but also how (s)he says it. We can learn a lot about different views of modernity by studying how contemporary authors pictured great cities such as Manchester in the mid-nineteenth century, or Paris and Berlin at the end of the century. Furthermore, architects invest the city with meanings when they design buildings, and these too can be read like a text. Frequently, we can trace major economic and social transformations in great cities past and present by following the design and use of buildings and spaces. The city constitutes a symbolic landscape. Writers as diverse as Engels, Baudelaire, and Simmel have used the city to symbolize what they take to be the definitive character of modernity — whether it is viewed as the site of capitalist reproduction and regulation, or the space where the individual can express his or her uniqueness. It is significant that it is in the field of architecture and urban planning that some writers have identified an alleged clear break between modernism and post-modernism, and the end of the Enlightenment project involving rational planning based on grand theories. This issue is only touched on towards the end of this final chapter, but it will figure largely in the last book of this series, *Modernity and its Futures.*

References

Durkheim, E. (1933) *The Division of Labour in Society* (trans. George Simpson), New York, Macmillan (first published in French, 1893).

Durkheim, E. (1951) *Suicide: A Study in Sociology* (trans. George Simpson), Glencoe, Free Press (first published in French, 1897).

CHAPTER 1 CHANGING SOCIAL DIVISIONS: CLASS, GENDER AND RACE

Harriet Bradley

CONTENTS

INTRODUCTION

The patterns of gender and class inequalities which emerged along with industrialization, towards the end of the nineteenth century, tended to persist up to the onset of the Second World War. (See Book 1 (Hall and Gieben, 1992), Chapter 4 for a discussion of the development of these divisions of class and gender.) This chapter aims to bring the study of social divisions up to date by considering subsequent processes of change.

The post-war period brought many dramatic changes which have affected the social structure of Britain. These include the reconstitution of the economy after the war and the growth of consumer industries; the development of the welfare state and consequent growth of public-sector employment; the general expansion of the service sector; greater employment of women, especially in service jobs; increased immigration, including the settling in Britain of many former Commonwealth citizens, followed by a clampdown in the face of growing white hostility towards black immigrants; the consolidation of the mass education system and especially the expansion of higher education and its opening up to people from working-class backgrounds; and, more recently, the growing tendency for national economies to be more tightly integrated into an international capitalist order dominated by the giant multinational companies.

These changes have led to increased affluence for many groups in society, higher levels of social mobility and an increasingly open society, committed, at least in principle, to democracy and meritocracy. Indeed, it has been asserted at times that British society should now be seen as egalitarian and classless. Women's increased labour market participation, coupled with the regeneration in the 1970s of a militant feminist movement, has resulted in some recent claims that we now live in a 'post-feminist' era in which gender equality has also been achieved. However, my contention is that inequalities of class and gender are still marked, alongside a structure of racial inequalities fostered by post-war immigration policies. However, the cumulative effect of the changes listed above has been to produce a more fluid and complex social structure. One theme which will be elaborated in this chapter is that of *class fragmentation*: that is, the breaking up of each distinct class grouping into a number of different subgroups or *fractions*. Moreover, while early feminist analysis tended to be based on the assumption that women as a group faced common experiences, recent research has highlighted the differing situations of women from different classes and ethnic groups. If we add to this the plurality of different ethnic groups to be found in Britain in the 1980s, we end up with quite a bewildering picture. The idea of fragmentation embraces all these complexities.

Class, gender and race are three important aspects of the pattern of stratification, that is *the structure of relationships between different social groups with differential command of various social resources.*

These are, of course, not the only aspects. There is a considerable degree of age stratification in Britain, and the last two decades have seen an increase in regional disparities, such as that between North and South. Religious affiliation may also be a basis of differentiation and discrimination. However, class, gender and race have received more sustained attention and study from social scientists, so we shall concentrate on these aspects of stratification in this chapter.

I shall be concerned with tracing the changing patterns of inequality in post-war Britain, looking particularly at the last three decades. We shall consider some of the key concepts and theories developed by sociologists to explain these changes. We shall look at class, gender and race in turn, beginning with class; that is *not* because I consider class to be more important than the other two, but because the study of class has been central to sociology since its origination and is still considerably more developed within social science than the study of gender and race. However, there has been a growing awareness of how these factors interrelate. In this chapter we will consider how the dynamics of class, gender and race combine to produce the distinctive social formation of modern Britain.

1   CLASS AND CHANGE

1.1   THEORIZING CLASS: MARXIST AND WEBERIAN APPROACHES

Most social scientists accept that changes in the economy since 1945 have affected class relations; but there is considerable debate on how to interpret these effects. These debates must be viewed in the context of the theoretical disagreements between neo-Marxists and neo-Weberians, who have provided the two dominant perspectives in the analysis of the British class structure.

Marx analysed class in terms of the relations of production (see Book 1 (Hall and Gieben, 1992), Chapter 4), with the mechanism of exploitation at the core of the capitalist class structure. Although he recognized divisions within the working class ('the competition between the workers themselves' to quote from the *Communist Manifesto*), he believed that the unifying potential of the experience of exploitation and alienation would transcend them, and while he recognized the emergence of various 'fractions' of the middle class, he saw these groups as of marginal importance in comparison to the central antagonism between the bourgeoisie and the proletariat. By contrast, Weber saw divisions, within both the propertied and propertyless classes, as generated by the workings of the market; he emphasized that the fragmenting effects of these divisions would be supplemented by the overlapping of class with status and party-political groupings; he paid especial attention to the growth of the middle classes brought about by the spread of bureaucratic organization; and he believed that conflict would take diverse forms within and between all the different social groupings. It should be emphasized that both models of class can be used with considerable flexibility, a fact which is not sufficiently acknowledged. Nor are these two models as irreconcilable as some text-books suggest, the differences being ones of final orientation. We can say overall, however, that the logic of the Weberian model is to suggest the existence of a plurality of class groupings, while the logic of the Marxist model leads us inexorably to focus on the confrontation between the capitalist class and the working class.

Neo-Weberians have suggested that Marxist theory cannot successfully account for the complexity of contemporary class relations. In their view, the class structure has been subjected to increasing fragmentation so that class conflict as envisaged by Marx is no longer a feasible outcome. Weberians also criticize Marx's assertion that a collective consciousness of oppression will arise from work relationships and lead to class-based action, an argument described by David Lockwood (1981) as 'the weakest link in the chain' of Marx's logic. Lockwood's own work has emphasized that consciousness has many sources, arising from particular 'social milieux' or environments. Some environments have tended to foster individualized and privatized orientations to society, which militate against collective action by working people.

One of the most powerful proponents of the neo-Weberian critique of Marx has been Ralf Dahrendorf (1959), who argues that although Marx's analysis was apposite in the nineteenth century it has become outdated in the context of what he terms 'post-capitalist' society. The bourgeoisie and the proletariat have both fragmented, the former because of the separation of the ownership of capital (by shareholders) from its control (by managers), the latter because technological advance has not, as Marx predicted, led to homogenization of factory work, but has deepened divisions between the skilled, semi-skilled and unskilled labourers. The middle class has grown in size and in social significance. These developments, along with other important changes, such as increased social mobility and the consolidation of a democratic political system, have resulted in an increasingly fragmented and complex class structure and brought a diminution in hostility between the classes.

Marxists have responded to these criticisms by asserting that the changes can be accommodated within an elaborated version of the basic Marxist framework, which still retains the analysis of conflict and exploitation. Marx's term 'fraction' can be employed to cover splits within classes. A fraction is a sub-group within a class distinguished by its distinct economic situation (a difference in skill, for example, or in type of property owned) but which still shares the basic relation to the means of production of the class as a whole. Marxists argue that the competitive drive at the core of the capitalist dynamic fosters such splits in both the capitalist and the working class, and often deliberately exploits them in order to 'divide and rule'. The concept of 'fraction' has also been used as a way to incorporate the analysis of gender and race into class theory.

Neo-Marxists have given special attention to the problem of explaining the class position of the middle classes. Attempts to do so often utilize one of two strategies. Either the middle class is divided into groupings which are essentially part of either the bourgeoisie or the proletariat (managers and professionals linked to the former, clerks and low-level service workers to the latter); or it is suggested that relations of production place the middle groupings in a curious position in which they fulfil some of the productive functions of the proletariat (helping produce and realize surplus value) and some of the functions of the bourgeoisie (co-ordinating production and controlling the workers). This is the notion of 'structural ambiguity' or 'contradictory locations'.

The stress in neo-Marxism on fractions within classes may suggest, as in the Weberian model, that conflict is as likely within classes as between them. However, neo-Marxists wish to cling to the idea of a central and potentially transformative class struggle, while conceding that it is offset by many other factors, particularly the ideological control over society exercised by the dominant class. The means of information (especially the mass media) and the education system can be used to spread ideas which favour the status quo. This notion of the 'dominant ideology' has been used by Marxists to explain why the working classes have failed to develop a critical class consciousness.

Try to bear in mind the main points of these two perspectives (summarized in Table 1.1) as we look in detail at post-war changes in class relations.

Table 1.1   Neo-Marxist and neo-Weberian positions

Neo-Marxist	Neo-Weberian
Class divisions generated by relations of production especially by the mechanism of exploitation	Class divisions generated by the operation of the market
Unifying effect of exploitation emphasized	Classes seen as subject to growing processes of fragmentation
The existence of 'fractions' and conflicts within classes acknowledged but seen as less important than the conflicts between classes especially the central conflict between proletariat and bourgeoisie	Divisions and conflicts within classes seen as just as significant as conflicts between classes
Middle classes seen as linked to one of the two major classes or as 'structurally ambiguous'	Middle classes seen as an autonomous grouping and considered as socially significant as the propertied and working classes
Consciousness arises from relations of production	Consciousness has many different sources
Dominant ideology accounts for the failure of the working class to develop a critical class consciousness	Fragmentation, social mobility and growth of democratic political structures inhibit the growth of class consciousness
Revolutionary potential of the working class remains	Class revolution is improbable

1.2   THE UPPER CLASS

The very term 'upper class' shows the problems of defining classes accurately, as it is often used to connote the aristocracy. It would be more helpful to employ Weber's term, the propertied class. This consists of some elements from the old landed aristocracy and gentry and some elements from the bourgeoisie. A social fusion of these two social groupings was achieved in the course of the nineteenth century, with the new class of manufacturers aspiring to the lifestyle and status of the older privileged class; the public schools had an important role in bringing together these two groups and merging them into a new elite.

The socio-economic elite: Ascot

The major change in the composition of this class pre-dates the post-war developments listed earlier. Towards the end of the nineteenth century, capitalist enterprises were subject to a process of concentration and reorganization which has continued ever since. Privately owned family firms were displaced as the major capital form by joint-stock public companies. Small businesses were swallowed by large companies and conglomerates with multiple interests across the economy. Since the Second World War, this shift in ownership has been extended on an international as well as a national basis, with the multinational corporations dominating economic development and co-ordinating it across the globe. For Dahrendorf, these changes implied a *decomposition of capital.* Rather than a single capitalist group who owned and controlled industrial production, the class had split into two: on the one hand shareholders who owned but did not control companies and, on the other managers who did not own them; (in Dahrendorf's terms 'capitalists without function' and 'functionaries without capital').

It can be argued that the last couple of decades have witnessed a further fragmentation of capital, because of the diffusion of property ownership through the populace, encouraged in the 1980s by the policies of Margaret Thatcher's Conservative government. This diffusion has involved:

- an increase in home ownership so that approximately two thirds of households own their home.
- a further dispersal of share ownership across the nation; in 1989, twenty per cent of the adult population owned shares, a threefold increase on 1981.
- a major rise in the percentage of shares owned by insurance companies, pension funds and unit trusts, and a consequent massive increase in the numbers of wage-earners with stakes in these types of schemes (Central Statistical Office (1990) *Social Trends*, no.20).

These trends have led one author of a textbook on class to declare that the capitalist class has almost disappeared as a distinct stratum: 'Where is the capitalist class today? It has fragmented into millions of tiny pieces. To see these pieces, look around you' (Saunders, 1990, p.91).

This is a dramatic image! But most sociologists would reject this claim. One difficulty is that the upper class is hard to observe. It is not easy to discover who actually controls companies; moreover, top people are not keen to allow sociological researchers to sit in on their decision-making processes. The fragmentation process outlined above has contributed to making this class somewhat invisible. However, John Scott has carried out a series of studies of the propertied class and concluded that it definitely does still exist and 'derives its advantages from ownership of company shares *and* participation in strategic control. The "impersonal" structure of possession has not resulted in a loss of power by wealthy people...Wealthy families hold shares in a large number of companies and they form a group from which corporate managers are recruited' (Scott, 1979, p.175). He discerns three elements within the class: entrepreneurial capitalists, with large holdings in particular companies; internal capitalists, top executives who have risen to power within companies; and finance capitalists with interests across a range of companies. We could conceptualize these as either fragments or fractions of the capitalist class. He concludes, however, that 'the core of the class consists of those who are actively involved in the strategic control of the major units of capital of which the modern economy is formed' (Scott, 1982, p.114).

While it is true that many working- and middle-class people have, especially in the 1980s, acquired a few shares and have invested in a private pension scheme, this form of ownership is not just quantitively but qualitatively different from major capital ownership. Investment in shares may be the equivalent of a flutter on horses, a pension scheme an insurance against poverty-stricken old age. Possession of them makes little difference to people's working lives or lifestyles. Nor do they have any real say in the strategic decisions mentioned by Scott. By contrast ten per cent of the population still hold fifty per cent of the marketable wealth of the nation, if pension schemes are excepted.

Scott argues that this smallish upper class of wealthy families is linked together in a tight social network, which is strengthened by the 'Old Boy' network (based on attendance at public school and elite universities), and which also serves to deter women from participation in top political and economic decision making (Rogers, 1988). Male domination is marked within this class. Economic cohesion is also ensured by the system of interlocking directorships, whereby prominent members of the class have seats on the boards of a number of top companies. Although this elite is not closed (internal capitalists may have risen into it through company career lines) it is extremely exclusive. The greatest threat to it comes from the internationalization of capitalist production, which makes it harder for any national economy and its 'captains' to direct internal investment in the way they would prefer.

Major economic decisions are made by a few

We can, of course, identify individual members of this class who are prominent in the public eye. However, Scott suggests the class is better conceptualized as a structure, rather than as an identifiable group of people. The power of capital has taken a more impersonal form, embedded in a set of organizations and institutional practices. Neo-Marxists share this view, arguing that this class must be identified through its collective carrying out of the functions of capital (exploitation, accumulation and realization of profits, control of labour and production).

These developments have important consequences for the relationship of the propertied class with the working class. Victorian factory workers knew their bosses personally and could identify them as the 'exploiters'. This is not the case today, where many workers will know only their immediate superiors, not those on the directing boards. Moreover, many workers are now with companies where ultimate control is exercised from America, Germany and Japan. What we might call the 'depersonalization' of the capitalist class acts against workers developing the class awareness envisaged by Marx; indeed, those who work for the multinationals may be discouraged from industrial militancy by the knowledge that the company can close down production in their plant and move it to one of its sites in other countries. Rather than the disappearance of the capitalist class as suggested by Saunders, some would argue that the post-war period has seen the consolidation of a smaller, more integrated and internationalized capitalist class with heightened power. Others would argue that any such tendency is weakened by internal divisions such as the continuing rivalry between finance and manufacturing capital interests, and indeed by the fight for survival and growth inherent in the competitive process on a global scale.

ACTIVITY 1   Summarize the arguments *for* and *against* the continued existence of the capitalist class. (You may like to bear in mind the fact that you, your family and friends may well own shares and private pension and insurance schemes. What are the implications of this?)

1.3   THE WORKING CLASS

The working class has been the focus of particular attention, largely because of its role in Marx's class model as the 'historic class'; you will recall that in the *Communist Manifesto* he argued that it was the only class capable of the overthrow of the capitalist system. Weberians challenge this argument and furthermore point to tremendous changes affecting the working class in the post-war period.

One major issue is the effect of increased affluence on working-class culture and values. In the 1960s, sociologists developed the concept of *embourgeoisement*, the idea that the boundary between the working and middle classes was breaking down altogether. This was partly due to increased social mobility. Also, rising incomes enabled manual workers to adopt middle-class values and lifestyles, and encouraged a change in political allegiance from Labour to Conservative. The embourgeoisement thesis was effectively demolished by the *Affluent Worker* studies (Goldthorpe *et al.*, 1969). The research team concluded that their sample of well-paid manual workers in Luton had not adopted middle-class values nor was there any social mixing between them and white-collar workers. Rather, the researchers concluded that this must be seen as a 'new working class' with a new lifestyle different from that traditionally associated with the working class.

Lockwood (1966) had previously identified two types of 'traditional worker' and a newer 'privatized' working class segment. Traditional proletarian attitudes were associated with the old tightly integrated communities, based round industries like mining and shipbuilding, which fostered a collective 'them and us' spirit. The other type of traditional worker, associated with agricultural work, domestic service and small businesses such as shops, had a deferential attitude to society, accepting an inferior station as justified; close personal links with employers encouraged a forelock-tugging attitude like that of Walter Gabriel in *The Archers* (as opposed to the distinctly proletarian Grundys!). Both groups were in decline with the disappearance of traditional industries. In contrast, the growing number of workers in the new consumer industries had developed a much more individualistic consumerist outlook; detached from the old communities, they invested emotional energy in a family-based 'privatized' lifestyle. Economic self-interest promoted an 'instrumental' approach to politics and they joined trade unions for individualistic reasons, not because of class loyalties.

Lockwood's study, although written twenty-five years ago, remains the definitive study of working-class fragmentation. But a recent survey of class attitudes carried out by a team of researchers from Essex University makes the important point that the trends towards the private, and towards instrumentalism and self-interest among the working-classes are nothing new, but have been strands in working-class behaviour since industrialization. The Essex team suggests, moreover, that these tendencies may coexist with other contradictory tendencies to collectivism, solidarity and class identification. The specific economic and political context will affect the balance between these contradictory tendencies (Marshall *et al.*, 1988).

During the 1970s the focus in debates about the working class shifted from affluence to unemployment. The contraction of the manufacturing sector and the restructuring of the economy threatened traditional working-class jobs. Sociologists were drawn to the theories of post-industrialism and deindustrialization. Post-industrial theorists predict major upheavals in the class structure, affecting the working class in particular.

For example, André Gorz, in the dramatically titled *Farewell to the Working Class* (Gorz, 1982), suggested that new computer technology was, literally, making manual work redundant. So great was its productive potential that society would no longer need all its citizens to produce the necessary goods and services. Only a small technically advanced segment of the industrial proletariat would be needed to carry on production; the displaced industrial workers would become what Gorz called a 'neo-proletariat' consisting of the permanently unemployed, the semi-employed and casualized low-paid workers, effectively marginalized and with no stake in the economy. These developments would undermine the historic role of the working class. The employed minority would cooperate with capital interests because of fear of losing jobs. The neo-proletariat would be too distanced from work to be interested in the transformation of work relationships. Indeed, in strict Marxist terms this group is not a class at all as it has no relationship (other than exclusion) to the relations of production.

Gorz can be criticized for his assumption that unemployment rates would remain at the high levels of the early 1980s and for playing down the possibility that new types of jobs might evolve to replace those lost by automation; but other interpretations offered by sociologists also suggest that long-term unemployment will continue. Dahrendorf utilizes the concept of the *underclass*, a term developed in America in reference to the ghettoized black minorities. It refers to a group at the bottom of the class hierarchy, permanently trapped and unable to move upward because it faces multiple disadvantages.

Dahrendorf (1987) suggests that an underclass has emerged in Britain consisting of the unemployed and others who depend on benefits, such as one-parent families, and the sick, disabled and elderly. He argues that a culture of poverty develops among this group, making them fatalistic and apathetic, or else pushing them into crime or illegal participation in the 'black economy'. In this way the unemployed become unemployable. He also is concerned about the marginalization of this group suggesting that they are politically ignored and in danger of losing their citizen rights, as the state takes control of their life in return for benefits.

Critics of the underclass theory suggest that it overstates the extent to which this group is 'permanently trapped' by unemployment. A boom in the economy has often had the effect of drastically reducing the number of the supposed 'unemployable'. Unemployment and dependency on benefits can be seen as *cyclical* phenomena in two senses: first, they are linked to the fluctuations of the business cycle; secondly, people are more vulnerable to them at certain stages in the life-cycle, such as when they have small children, or in old age. Both Gorz and Dahrendorf might be criticized for extrapolating too much from short-term trends. By contrast many neo-Marxists view the future of the working class more flexibly. They suggest that processes of economic restructuring in Britain, along with a renegotiation of the international division of labour, have indeed brought increased unemployment, swelling the ranks of the 'reserve army of labour' or 'surplus population' which Marx saw as an integral part of the capitalist system. These changes imply not a disappearance but a *recomposition* of the working class. Capitalism is highly dynamic, ever engendering new markets, new processes and products, and its labour requirements also change. Wage labour in the coming decades may take the form of work in the newer service industries, for example leisure and retailing, which boomed in the later 1980s; or, if the international economy shifts again, there may be new forms of either 'high-tech' production work or low-wage assembly work provided by multinationals who decide it is profitable to invest in Britain.

Not all recent thinking puts unemployment and recession to the fore. A more optimistic version of post-industrial theory suggests that society is moving into a new phase based on information technology as the core of the production process, with a continued shift from manufacturing to service industries. Despite the short-term instability associated with the changes, the long-term outcome will be a more prosperous society, with increased leisure and greater democracy at work. Daniel Bell (1974), who exemplifies the optimistic strand in post-industrial theory, suggests an upgrading of the class structure and harmony between the classes as the end result: in effect, this amounts to a reassertion of the 'embourgeoisement' thesis.

We have, then, a number of possible interpretations of the future of the working class:

- increased affluence and upward mobility into the middle classes as a result of post-industrial change
- further decline of the traditional core of the industrial working class and development of a casualized 'neo-proletariat' as a result of automation
- recomposition of the working class into new forms dependent on the growth of the world economy
- the development of a marginalized 'underclass' underneath a relatively privileged working class which enjoys increased affluence.

1.4   THE MIDDLE CLASSES

'Between capital and labour' lies the middle class. Sociologists tend now to speak of 'the new middle classes', both to indicate the heterogeneity of this grouping and to distinguish it from the 'old' middle class, the Victorian bourgeoisie itself. The new middle classes include all the service groups thrown up by the spread of bureaucracy, the growth of the welfare state and recent rapid growth of service industries. This is now the largest class. Table 1.2 shows the rise in service employment and the decline in manufacturing in the past two decades.

Table 1.2   Employment in manufacturing and services 1971 to 1989, in thousands

	1971	1979	1981	1989
Manufacturing	8,065	7,253	6,222	5,234
Services	11,627	13,580	13,468	15,688

Source: Central Statistical Office (1991), *Social Trends,* no.21, Table 4.11, p.71

Sociologists have emphasized the diversity of the occupational groupings within the middle class. For example, we may distinguish a 'service class' (a high-level salaried group of managers, administrators and professionals who approach the privileged lifestyle of the propertied class) from the 'intermediate groupings' (a mass of lower-paid service workers, especially clerical workers, many with manual working-class backgrounds and connections). Another distinct and growing group are the self-employed, the petite bourgeoisie. Conservative ideology has supported the growth of small businesses. In 1989, $3\frac{1}{4}$ million people were self-employed, a 50 per cent increase since 1981.

The intermediate group have been the focus of a major debate between Marxists and Weberians. Neo-Marxists argue that clerical workers have been *proletarianized*, that is pulled down into the working class: like factory workers they are essentially powerless wage labourers. Although clerks have traditionally been seen by Marxists as not directly involved in producing surplus value since they do not produce goods, some neo-Marxists suggest that both groups could be conceived as part of the *collective worker,* that is the whole group involved in the cycle of surplus and profit: making goods, processing them, ensuring the goods can be sold and the profits realized.

In a classic study, the neo-Weberian Lockwood (1958) rejected the idea of proletarianization. Lockwood distinguished three dimensions of class: market situation (rewards, promotion chances, etc.), work situation (conditions, relations of control and workplace interaction) and status situation. He argued that clerks, despite declines in their pay, fared better than manual workers on each dimension.

Since Lockwood conducted his study, office life has been considerably altered by the implementation of computer technology. Braverman (1974), in a reassertion of the proletarianization thesis, argued that technology has been used to further erode the position of office workers. Braverman believed that there was a tendency towards task degradation (popularly known as 'deskilling') within capitalist industry which affected clerks as much as manual workers (see Book 2 (Allen *et al.*, 1992), Chapter 6). Braverman's account of the class position of American office workers makes a strong contrast to Lockwood.

Braverman also raised the issue of the feminization of clerical work, a factor ignored by Lockwood, who only studied male clerks. This is a major weakness in Lockwood's work: in Britain, too, clerical work has become a largely female occupation, as is shown in Table 1.3.

Table 1.3   Percentage of women in the clerical workforce England and Wales 1901–81

1901	1911	1921	1931	1951	1961	1971	1981
11	18	46	45	60	64	72	78

Source: Lewis, 1988, p.34

Crompton and Jones (1984) considered the gender issue more fully, arguing that clerical workers should be seen as a 'stratified hierarchy'.

Although male clerks have managed to retain some of their old privileges (such as promotion chances), they have done so at the expense of women. Jobs which have been degraded by new technology have been assigned to women. Rather than seeing women clerks as being proletarianized, however, the authors suggested that women were originally brought into clerical work under different conditions to men, forming a kind of proletarian layer in an occupational grouping regarded as having higher status than manual work. Status considerations may continue to prevent clerical workers, despite some growth in trade union membership, from developing an identification with manual workers.

It has been suggested that new technology could also be used to degrade the jobs of higher-level service workers, such as professionals and managers. Although these groups can use their expertise, prestige and professional organizational bodies as a defence, the potential of computers in terms of information-processing and monitoring may make some high-level skills redundant and lead to diminished autonomy for some occupational groups. However, the post-industrial framework suggests an alternative vision of the future of the middle classes. Bell envisages further expansion of all three main groupings (self-employed, service class and intermediate service workers), with jobs being upgraded rather than deskilled, and more and more people sharing the privileged employment conditions and lifestyles of the middle class.

Assessing the viability of these different accounts is complicated by the rapid pace of contemporary economic and technological change. These changes however, do seem likely to promote further class fragmentation, keeping the class structure in a state of flux. But it is worth re-emphasizing the need to take account of how gender interacts with class. As Figure 1 shows, 68 per cent of women workers are in non-manual jobs as opposed to 46 per cent of men. This casts doubt on the idea that a move into service jobs is necessarily a class upgrading; nor do we yet fully understand the effects of gender in terms of how people develop a class identification.

To summarize our discussion on the post-war growth of the middle classes:

- Weberians consider that the middle class groupings are becoming both numerically and socially more significant and that they are quite distinct from the working class.
- Marxists suggest that sections of the middle classes have been subject to processes of proletarianization; this applies in particular to the lower status service sector occupational groupings.
- Both Marxists and Weberians see the middle classes as fragmented internally into a number of subgroups, although they conceptualize these divisions in different ways. (Look back to Section 1.1 to remind yourself of the details of some of these ways.)

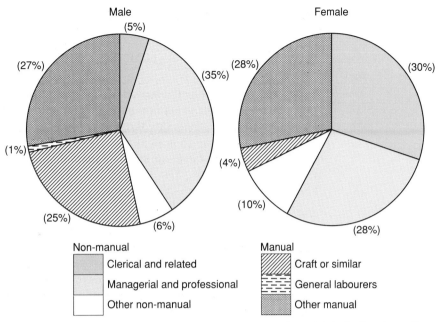

Figure 1.1   Sectoral employment of men and women in 1989, including the self-employed

Source: Central Statistical Office, *Social Trends,* no.21, 1991, Table 4.14, p.72

- Post-industrial theory suggests a continued expansion of the middle classes, embourgeoisement of the working classes and upgrading of jobs.
- Finally, no perspective has satisfactorily grappled with the conceptual difficulties associated with the fact that women predominate in many service-sector jobs.

ACTIVITY 2   You should now read **Reading A, 'Blackcoated worker'**, by David Lockwood and **Reading B, 'Labor and monopoly capital'**, by Harry Braverman, which you will find at the end of this chapter. These provide good examples of Weberian and Marxist approaches. Read each piece carefully and answer the following.

- How does Lockwood see the market, work and status situations of clerks differing from those of manual workers?
- What are the major points of disagreement between Lockwood and Braverman?

2 GENDER AND CHANGE

2.1 THEORIZING GENDER

Our study of class has led us to the study of gender. It has been argued that patriarchy did not disappear after industrialization but took new forms: Victorian society saw the elaboration of a new ideology of gender which promoted the idea of separate spheres and this was reflected in the employment sphere where the sexual division of labour became more rigid (see Book 1 (Hall and Gieben, 1992), Chapter 4). Has segregation now begun to disappear?

Since the Second World War there have been major changes in women's social roles. Women have pushed their way into many occupations from which they were excluded, and the proportion of women in the labour force has steadily increased, as shown in Table 1.4. The increase has been especially marked among married women, as the idea of mothers returning to employment has gained social acceptability.

Table 1.4   Women as a percentage of all employees

1931	1951	1961	1971	1981	1986
30	31	n.a.	38	43	45

Source: Derived from census data

Families have become more egalitarian with most of the legal backing for patriarchal domination now removed. Partly because of contraceptive improvements, women now have probably more sexual freedom than at any period in British history. These changes led in the 1950s and early 1960s to a widespread assumption that sex equality had been achieved in Britain. But the regenerated feminist movement of the late 1960s and 1970s challenged this assumption, demonstrating that gender inequalities were still marked in all spheres of life.

The theorists of this 'second wave' of feminism started to develop the concept of patriarchy as a way to understand gender relations. However, this key concept has been the subject of critical controversy. For example, Rowbotham (1981) argues that it is an imprecise and a historical term. Its use may encourage the unacceptable assumption that male dominance is universal, ruling out the possibility of the existence of societies characterized by sex equality or of matriarchal societies. Moreover, the term may imply a static view, whereas gender relations vary greatly between different historical periods and different societies. It has been suggested that a neutral term such as 'sex-gender system' or simply 'the sexual division of labour' would provide a more flexible analytic tool. More recently black feminists have criticized the use of the term. They argue it assumes a commonality between all women in their experience of male domination, which is not in fact the case. However, many feminist theorists have clung to the concept, perhaps because of the prominence it has come to enjoy within feminist literature. To overcome its shortcomings, they have attempted to define the term more precisely, to focus on the differential power positions of different groups and to develop historical typologies of its changing manifestations. We will turn shortly to Sylvia Walby's attempt to do this.

However, the analysis of patriarchy is not the only approach to understanding gender inequality. Many have tried to use the existing categories of class analysis to incorporate women into a class model. Neo-Marxists have suggested that women could be seen as a distinct fraction within each class or that their labour market role could be explained by the concept of the reserve army of labour. Neo-Weberians have considered women as a negatively-privileged status group and tried to explain their inferior work situation through the analysis of segmented labour markets. Such approaches, while not entirely satisfactory, are an improvement on the position taken by some mainstream stratification theorists. They argue that women are largely irrelevant to class analysis as they derive their class position from that of their father or husband, a claim tantamount to saying that sociology's most important category of analysis cannot be applied to half the population!

The major problem with adapting existing economic concepts to the analysis of gender is that gender is almost always reduced to a side effect of class. Such approaches imply that gender inequality is a direct product of the economic system in the same way as class differences. However, the insight of second-wave feminist theory was that gender divisions were rooted in every aspect of social life, including, in particular, the family, private life and sexuality. A convincing account of gender relations, therefore, has to be much more broadly based and comprehensive than any theory of class.

Traditional Marxism tended to link gender differentiation to class as an aspect of property relations, with the implication that when socialism brought an end to private property, gender divisions, like class divisions, would disappear. However, historical evidence shows quite clearly that gender divisions predate capitalism and persist after its overthrow. Thus, Marxist-feminist theorists came to accept the need for a separate theory of gender to be combined with Marxist class theory. Usually this has taken the form of an analysis of patriarchy. Some theorists have wished to conceptualize capitalism and patriarchy evolving jointly as a unified system, while others have suggested that they have to be seen as two analytically discrete systems. Two notable proponents of the latter *dual systems theory* have been Heidi Hartmann and Sylvia Walby.

Both have provided us with more precise definitions of patriarchy, either of which might serve as a useful 'working definition'. For Hartmann, patriarchy is 'a set of social relationships between men which have a material base, and which, though hierarchical, establish or create interdependence and solidarity among men that enable them to dominate women ... The material base upon which patriarchy rests lies most fundamentally in men's control over women's labour power' (Hartmann, 1981, pp.14–15). This definition enables us to link the two sites, the home and the workplace, where men can profit from women's contribution of labour provided either free or for an inferior economic reward. Thus it connects wage labour and domestic labour as a dual base for male exploitation of women. However, in its focus on *labour power* as the base of gender difference it reflects Hartmann's own adherence to Marxism. Indeed, Young (1981) argues that the notion of 'control of labour power' is so central to Marxist analysis that it would be more useful to redefine the concept of relations of production, working towards a unified theory of class and gender, rather than conceiving patriarchy as a separate system.

For other feminists, the ideas of both Hartmann and Young are too narrow and economistic. By contrast, Walby's approach appears to pull together a Marxist focus on production with strands from radical feminist thought which give primacy to personal relationships, sexuality, and power in a more general sense. For Walby, patriarchy is a 'a system of interrelated structures through which men exploit women. ...The key sets of patriarchal relations are to be found in domestic work, paid work, the state, male violence and sexuality; while other practices in civil society have a limited significance' (Walby, 1986, p.51). This definition is, admittedly, not as sharp as Hartmann's, but it has the merit of breadth, rightly suggesting that gender disparities are found in every sphere of social life and that these are mutually reinforcing. Moreover, Walby's schema can allow for the way that the particular focus of patriarchy can shift from one set of relationships to another at different times, so that, in the post-war period, paid work and the state have particular significance as the sites of patriarchy, with the family declining somewhat in importance. Walby conceptualizes this as a shift from private to public patriarchy; women are no longer subject to the same degree of domination by individual patriarchs as they were in pre-industrial or Victorian families. Instead, male control has become built into the structures of society, particularly the rules and procedures which regulate the public spheres of work and politics.

Not all Marxist feminists, however, are happy with the idea of patriarchy as a framework for analysing gender. Some wish to stay more firmly within the traditional Marxist framework. One possibility is to extend the idea of the production to include *reproduction*, that is the process whereby the human species reproduces itself. This concept can be used to cover all the activities such as childcare and housework that take place within the home and in which women's labour is central. Some, like Delphy (1977), see reproduction as a separate mode of production existing jointly with the capitalist wage labour system and having its own distinct relations of production whereby men exploit women's labour. A recent text by Glucksmann (1990) has suggested that it is better to see domestic labour and wage labour as two poles within one unified system, both being part of capitalist relations of production. Women's key role in the domestic relations of production means that they enter into wage labour relations of production at a particular disadvantage. This important idea of reproduction will be explored more fully in the next chapter.

Finally, in the last few years many feminists have been drawn to the theoretical framework of post-modernism, which challenges the validity of analysis of social systems and questions the value of overarching concepts such as capitalism and patriarchy. Post-modern feminists reject any idea of a universal pattern of male domination and female oppression and seek instead to trace out the many different variants of relations between the sexes. There is, they claim, no necessary logic of male domination; power relations between the sexes are flexible and often counter-balanced. Post-modern theory, however, is not very helpful in understanding patterns of inequality which have persisted over time, because its framework precludes the formulation of general statements or models of social structure. It is more useful as a critique of other approaches than as a way of understanding how societies work.

However, post-modernist feminism has one very useful insight in pointing to the differing experiences of women of different classes and ethnic groups. It is argued that, rather than making general statements which assume a common identity and experience among women, we must seek to unpack or 'deconstruct' the category of women. This involves exploring the specific situation of, for example, black women or homosexual women. The key concept here is *difference*. Michele Barrett (1987) has argued that this term is used in many diverse and rather confusing ways by post-modern theorists; but the sense in which it can help us towards an improved understanding of gender inequalities is that of 'experiential diversity', in Barrett's phrase. Black feminists have rightly criticized white feminists for assuming that the experience of white women was the norm.

As stated earlier, gender divisions permeate all social institutions from work to leisure, from the family to political organizations. Indeed, feminists argue that the very structure of language is itself 'man-made' (Spender, 1980) and reflects male control of cultural institutions and practices. This is crucial since it is only through language that we grasp the meanings of our social world and we are thus forced to apprehend it through categories derived from male experience. Within cultural discourses, male experiences are taken as the norm and women presented as 'the Other'. Women's experiences are unreported or marginalized and women's needs or desires obscured. The contemporary feminist project, then, must involve the re-examination of every aspect of social reality to uncover the experience of gender. This chapter, however, looks at just two aspects of the sexual division of labour, concentrating on the family and employment, as these were the prime areas in which the feminist re-examination commenced.

2.2   THE DOMESTIC DIVISION OF LABOUR

For many radical feminists, the family is the major locus of male power. For example, Firestone (1979) argues that what she calls 'sex classes' arose from family relationships, in which men took control of women's reproductive processes. The handicaps suffered by women during pregnancy and childbirth would inevitably lead to continued social inequality, she argued, unless women took control of new reproductive technologies and used them to free themselves from these biological constraints.

Yet conventional wisdom is that families are no longer patriarchal. The argument that industrial social development liberated women from control by fathers and husbands was picked up by post-war sociologists of the family. A classic example is the work of Young and Willmott (1973), who argued that the 'symmetrical family' had emerged as the dominant form in the post-war period. Although there was still some degree of specialization between husband and wife, their roles could be described as equal but different. Strict role segregation had broken down, with women more likely to be going out to work and husbands taking a share of the housework; improvements in contraception had shortened the period of childbearing for most women, labour-saving household appliances had eased the burden of housework, while changing social attitudes favoured women's return to the labour market.

However, more recent research challenges these findings and indicates that married women in paid work still bear a 'double burden' with major responsibility for housework. Ann Oakley's pioneering study (1974) suggested that housework was a major constraint on women's opportunities and that increased participation by husbands was, in the main, only 'help' with a limited range of tasks. Since Oakley carried out her research there has been a rise in male unemployment and a continued upward trend in married women's employment, but recent surveys indicate that changes to the domestic division of labour have still been slight. For example, the national 'Women and Employment Survey' (WES) findings on housework and childcare showed that women in the mid 1980s were still doing the bulk of the work, as shown in Table 1.5 (Martin and Roberts, 1984). Men help selectively, but prefer washing up and taking children to the park to ironing the shirts and changing dirty nappies! The WES data do, however, suggest that, where wives take on full-time employment, men's involvement in domestic labour is significantly increased.

It has been suggested that more equitable arrangements may be initiated in middle-class families where there is stress on women developing careers, but no clear pattern of class variation emerges from studies. In the more privileged 'dual-career' families studied by Rapaport and Rapaport (1971), the problem of housework was solved by the employment of paid helpers. But this solution only passes the problem on to the women who work as low-paid cleaners and childminders, very often working-class or black women with limited labour market

Table 1.5   Wives' and husbands' views about how housework and childcare are shared

| | Wife's work status | | | | | |
| Views about share of housework | Employed full-time | | Employed part-time | | Not in employment | |
	wife's view %	husband's view %	wife's view %	husband's view %	wife's view %	husband's view %
wife does all	13	9	26	15	32	22
wife does most	41	46	51	61	49	58
shared equally	44	43	23	24	17	19
husband does most	2	2	0	0	1	0
husband does all	0	0	0	0	1	1
Views about share of childcare						
wife does all	5	2	8	5	11	6
wife does most	24	24	36	44	48	64
shared equally	67	72	55	51	41	30
husband does most	4	2	1	0	0	0
husband does all	0	0	0	0	0	0
Feelings about husband's contribution to housework						
too much	4	4	2	3	3	2
about right	74	76	75	78	80	76
not enough	21	20	23	19	17	22

Source: adapted from Martin and Roberts, 1984, (based on a survey of 4000 women, 712 husbands), Tables 8.7, 8.8 and 8.9; pp.101 and 102

chances and domestic burdens of their own to shoulder. This does nothing to break the deeply-rooted association between women and domestic tasks.

The existing evidence suggests that, although there are many individual cases where the domestic division of labour is being renegotiated, housework and childcare are still seen as primarily 'women's work'. Psychological theories which stress the importance of the mother/child relationship in early childhood and posit the existence of the 'maternal instinct' have reinforced the idea that these tasks are naturally the duty of women and are best performed by them. Guilt often forces women to shoulder the double burden, which limits their ability to compete on equal terms in their jobs. Many women experience a 'career break' at a crucial time which blocks their promotion chances. Managers consider them less committed to their jobs and deny them training or promotion on the grounds that money will be wasted if they leave to have children. Women returning to work after childbearing have to take jobs at a lower level than when they left. They are forced into poorly rewarded part-time work and seek jobs close to home which are compatible with domestic responsibilities. All these factors combine to ensure that women's employment is still seen as subordinate to their primary household role.

ACTIVITY 3   Table 1.6 looks at social attitudes to housework. Study it carefully along with Table 1.5, and use the data to answer the following questions:

- What do you notice about the type of household tasks in which men participate more fully (Tables 1.5 and 1.6)?
- What can we learn from the disparity between the actual and ideal patterns of task allocation (Table 1.6)?
- How would you contrast the responses of married and non-married people (Table 1.6)?

Of course, women's domestic responsibility does not necessarily imply male dominance within the family. As Table 1.5 suggests, most women see existing arrangements as fair, so the prevalent division of labour could be seen as voluntarily chosen. Indeed, it can be argued that control over domestic labour gives women a power base in the home which they are reluctant to yield to men. Now that the legal backing for patriarchy is gone, we have insufficient information about exactly how power *does* operate in the family, both formally and informally. A survey by Morris (1990) of work on household budgeting suggests that, whereas women take most of the everyday household decisions, men are responsible for the more important decisions, while Edgell's study of middle-class couples (1980) revealed that husbands held the ultimate power, with both partners accepting this as desirable. Male violence, which may be more widespread in families than is generally acknowledged, can help men secure control. Male violence both within and outside the family has been seen as a defence against the weakened social legitimacy of patriarchal dominance (Wilson, 1983).

Further research is necessary to identify the power-holders in contemporary families. We also need more research on ethnic minority families, for, as Amos and Parmar (1984) have argued, most feminist discussion of family relationships is ethnocentric and generalizes from the experience of white women only. In many South Asian families a more traditional patriarchal structure still persists, favouring strict role segregation. Women from the Pakistani and Bangladeshi community have the lowest economic activity rate outside the home (21 per cent only). Many may be employed in family concerns or as low-paid home workers. By contrast, women of Afro-Caribbean origin are the most likely to be employed full-time and may have a more powerful role in the family. Although many British Afro-Caribbean families are of the nuclear type, there is a Caribbean tradition of woman-headed or 'matriarchal' families. The tendency for some Caribbean men to be

Table 1.6   The domestic division of labour

| | Married people[1] | | | | | | Never-married people[2] | | |
| | Actual allocation of tasks | | | Tasks should be allocated to | | | Task should be allocated to | | |
	Mainly man	Mainly woman	Shared equally	Mainly man	Mainly woman	Shared equally	Mainly man	Mainly woman	Shared equally
Household tasks (percentage[3] allocation)									
Washing and ironing	1	88	9	-	77	21	-	68	30
Preparation of evening meal	5	77	16	1	61	35	1	49	49
Household cleaning	3	72	23	-	51	45	1	42	56
Evening dishes	18	37	41	12	21	64	13	15	71
Organization of household money and bills	32	38	28	23	15	58	19	16	63
Repairs of household equipment	83	6	8	79	2	17	74	-	24
Child-rearing (percentage[3] allocation)									
Looks after the children when they are sick	1	63	35	-	49	47	-	48	50
Teaches the children discipline	10	12	77	12	5	80	16	4	80

[1] 1120 married respondents, except for the questions on actual allocation of childrearing tasks which were answered by 479 respondents with children under 16.

[2] 283 never-married respondents. The table excludes results of the formerly married (widowed, divorced, or separated) respondents.

[3] Don't knows and non-response to the question mean that some categories do not sum to 100 per cent.

Source: Central Statistical Office, *Social Trends*, no. 16, 1986, p.36.

loosely attached to the mothers of their children suggests that the burden of childcare may fall particularly heavily on women. Amos and Parmar, however, warn us against uncritical acceptance of stereotypes about black families and the assumption that black women are more oppressed in the family. Black families can be an important line of defence against white racism. Extended female kin networks prove a source of support for black women which is lacking to their white counterparts. The arguments of Amos and Parmar alert us to the ways in which racial divisions complicate patterns of gender differentiation, just as we have seen gender complicating class divisions. Their work exemplifies the challenge the issue of race poses to feminist analysis.

ACTIVITY 4   You should now read **Reading C, 'Challenging imperial feminism'**, by Valerie Amos and Pratibha Parmar.

2.3   THEORIZING THE DOMESTIC DIVISION OF LABOUR

The patterns described above have been explained in many ways. Here I will briefly outline four approaches which have been influential:

1   The functionalist perspective, dominant in the period when *The Symmetrical Family* (Young and Willmott, 1973) was written, sees the domestic division of labour as functionally effective for society. It enables the family to carry out its key tasks of socialization and stabilization of individual personalities by allowing the woman to specialize in caring, nurturing or *expressive* roles; these are seen as incompatible with the competitive *instrumental* role of the male breadwinner. Different personalities are required for these roles; Talcott Parsons, who is particularly associated with these ideas, suggested that biology predisposed women to develop expressive personalities (Parsons and Bales, 1956). This approach neglects the power relations within the family, implying that the arrangement is mutually satisfactory. It rests, anyway, on dubious empirical grounds, assuming that all married women are full-time housewives, since the theory of specialized personalities implies that housework and paid work cannot be successfully combined.

2   Traditional Marxism analysed the domestic division of labour in terms of the needs of capital. Women's unpaid domestic labour secures the physical reproduction of the labour force (caring for existing workers and producing the next generation). It also subsidizes the costs of subsistence of workers, which means that wages paid by capitalists are kept down and profits increased. In this way the unpaid work of women in the home is seen as contributing indirectly to capitalist accumulation. Domestic workers, therefore, are conceptualized as if they were *all* wives of wage labourers. (What about bourgeois wives? Or single women and for that matter single men!) This indicates the limitations of this approach. It is concerned only with the interests of

capitalism and overlooks what men gain from the system. Like the functionalist approach, it tends to assume that women work only as housewives overlooking the intersection of women's work in and out of the home.

3   Some Marxist feminists also see domestic labour in terms of reproduction, but suggest that this process jointly serves capitalist needs and maintains the power of men, both as individuals and as a class; women's unpaid labour is exploited by men as a way of controlling their womenfolk and keeping them in dependency, restricting their labour market chances. Although this approach brings male interests into the picture, it may lead to an overemphasis on women as mothers and an underplaying of woman's productive, as opposed to reproductive, role.

4   The theory of patriarchy sees the family as a site of male power, either the single most important one (Firestone), or one among many (Walby). The domestic division of labour reflects power disparities. It forces women into dependency and restricts their opportunities in the public sphere. In this approach the interests of men are strongly emphasised. A 'dual systems' theory linking the analysis of patriarchy to an analysis of capitalism will indicate how patriarchal interests interlock with the interests of capitalists, who are able to exploit women's weaker labour market situation, using them as cheap labour.

Both feminist positions are an advance on functionalism, in showing how class and gender interests interlock. Thus links can be made between women's work in and outside the home. I would argue that a dual systems approach is the most flexible; it can be utilized to show the pervasiveness of male dominance in contemporary societies. Although the concept of reproduction is an interesting one it pushes the focus onto childbearing as the central fact in women's lives; not all women are mothers. As the next section indicates, all women, whatever their marital status, face disadvantage in the employment sphere. Before we turn to this topic, however, it should be pointed out that none of these perspectives on the family deal with the issue of race.

2.4   GENDER DIVISIONS AT WORK

Since the war women have entered paid employment in increasing numbers. Table 1.7 shows the increasing proportion economically active since 1971. Note that the increase is particularly marked among women aged 25–44, the major childbearing group. The period which women spend out of the labour force for childrearing has become steadily shorter; not only are women having fewer children, they are also returning to work earlier.

However, much of this increase has been in part-time work. In 1986, over 4 million women worked part-time, as opposed to 800,000 men; this represents 44 per cent of all women in paid employment. Married women with small children are particularly likely to work part-time.

Table 1.7   Women's activity rates 1971 to 1989

	Age:16–19	20–24	25–44	45–54	55–59	60+	All age groups
1971	65.0	60.2	52.4	62.0	50.9	12.4	43.9
1976	68.2	64.8	60.0	66.5	54.3	10.3	46.8
1979	72.0	67.7	61.7	67.0	53.8	7.4	47.4
1981	70.4	68.8	61.7	68.0	53.4	8.3	47.6
1983	66.8	68.2	62.2	68.1	50.8	7.5	47.0
1984	69.4	70.2	65.9	69.5	51.8	7.8	49.0
1986	71.4	70.3	67.8	70.5	51.8	6.5	49.6
1988	72.2	71.3	70.9	70.6	52.7	6.6	51.0
1989	73.7	75.1	72.0	72.2	54.3	7.6	52.6

Source: Central Statistical Office, *Social Trends*, no.21, 1991, Table 4.6, p.68

Although part-time work may suit women with domestic responsibilities and be less exhausting than a full-time job, it has second-rate status. Generally part-time workers are lower paid, have few promotion chances and virtually no entitlement to paid holidays, redundancy pay or pension and maternity rights. Walby has argued that part-time work can be seen as a new increasingly significant form of gender segregation.

The more established form of gender segregation, however, persists as strongly as ever. In an influential paper, Hakim (1979) studied the pattern of segregation since 1900. She concluded that there had been no significant breakdown of segregation up to the late 1970s, although there was evidence of some improvement in the 1980s within the professional and managerial sectors. The majority of women and men are still likely to work only with their own sex. The clustering of men and women within different occupations is referred to as 'horizontal' segregation, in contrast to 'vertical' segregation which refers to differences within occupations (see Book 2 (Allen *et al.*, 1992), Chapter 6).

Figure 1.2 gives an indication of the clustering of women in certain occupations and also shows how part-time employment is concentrated in specific sectors.

Ethnic minority women often fare even worse than white women, at the bottom of the employment pyramid, where racial discrimination pushes them into unskilled and low-paid jobs. Black women are concentrated particularly in textiles, in the health service and in the hotel and catering industries. They are often left with backstage roles, in places such as kitchens and laundries, since racial prejudice can mean that white women obtain the more visible jobs (receptionists, bank cashiers) which exploit female glamour. The invisibility of black women, which serves to conceal the social benefits which the community gains from

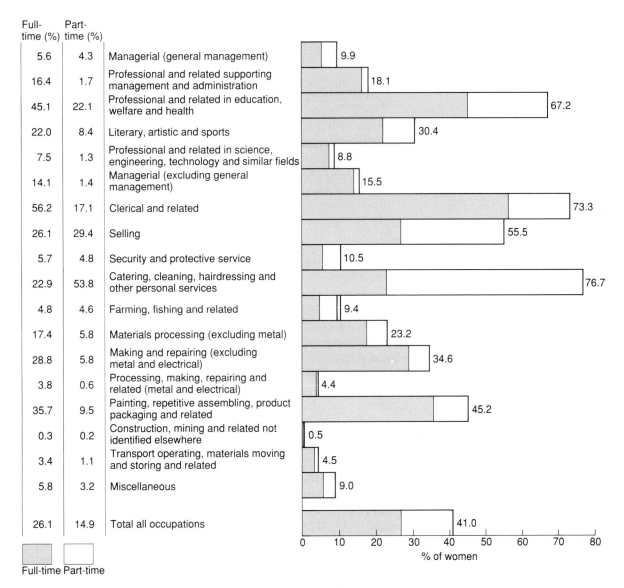

Full-time (%)	Part-time (%)		% of women
5.6	4.3	Managerial (general management)	9.9
16.4	1.7	Professional and related supporting management and administration	18.1
45.1	22.1	Professional and related in education, welfare and health	67.2
22.0	8.4	Literary, artistic and sports	30.4
7.5	1.3	Professional and related in science, engineering, technology and similar fields	8.8
14.1	1.4	Managerial (excluding general management)	15.5
56.2	17.1	Clerical and related	73.3
26.1	29.4	Selling	55.5
5.7	4.8	Security and protective service	10.5
22.9	53.8	Catering, cleaning, hairdressing and other personal services	76.7
4.8	4.6	Farming, fishing and related	9.4
17.4	5.8	Materials processing (excluding metal)	23.2
28.8	5.8	Making and repairing (excluding metal and electrical)	34.6
3.8	0.6	Processing, making, repairing and related (metal and electrical)	4.4
35.7	9.5	Painting, repetitive assembling, product packaging and related	45.2
0.3	0.2	Construction, mining and related not identified elsewhere	0.5
3.4	1.1	Transport operating, materials moving and storing and related	4.5
5.8	3.2	Miscellaneous	9.0
26.1	14.9	Total all occupations	41.0

Full-time   Part-time

Figure 1.2   Women as a percentage of occupational labour force, 1984
Source: Abercrombie *et al.*, 1988, p.219

their work, is epitomized by South Asian home workers. Cultural reasons may propel them into home working (their husbands' unwillingness for them to be exposed to contact with white men) but often no other work is available to them. In home work women may earn less than fifty pence an hour for unpleasant work in difficult conditions.

The increase in part-time work for women can be linked to the current stress on 'flexibility' (which was discussed in Book 2 (Allen *et al.*, 1992), Chapter 6). Using part-time women workers is one major strategy for employers seeking 'numerical flexibility'. Retailing provides a classic example. In supermarkets a small core of permanent staff can be supplemented by teams of part-timers employed to cater for peak periods of demand such as Friday evenings and Saturdays. Since part-timers can be paid lower wages and are ineligible for fringe benefits, this system of flexibility is highly beneficial to employers. But it has clear disadvantages for women, confirming their use as a secondary labour force. Historically, they have been especially vulnerable to casualized employment conditions. They are unlikely to benefit from other aspects such as 'functional' flexibility, since many employers' reluctance to provide training for women may well debar them from acquiring the range of skills associated with the 'polyvalent' or 'flexible worker'.

Gender divisions at work have been explained in many ways. Economists utilize the framework of supply and demand, in particular the idea of human capital, that is the assets (qualifications, training, skills, experience) accumulated by each individual. Jobs requiring workers to have invested more human capital in themselves through long periods of training are most highly rewarded. Women's domestic role means they characteristically possess less human capital and are forced to take the lowest-paid unskilled jobs. It then becomes economically rational for the wife to stay at home to care for children, because the husband's greater earning capacity makes him the more effective breadwinner.

These arguments seem reasonable, especially since women are less likely to gain access to training. However, research suggests that, even with equivalent training and qualifications, women do less well than men. A recent study found that women persistently received lower rewards for comparable skills (Rubery *et al.*, 1989). Single women with no domestic responsibilities are still found in stereotypical 'women's' jobs. While more women now possess graduate qualifications, the structure of segregation has been largely undented. The economic framework suggests reasons for some aspects of gender differentiation, but does not adequately acknowledge the sex-typing of jobs. Moreover, human capital theory has an uncritical approach to the notion of skill. Phillips and Taylor (1980) point out that skill is to a considerable extent socially constructed. Gender is a key factor in that construction: what men do is 'skilled' simply by virtue of being done by men, while what women do tends to be undervalued.

Other explanations consider the motives of employers. Marxists point to the way capitalists employ women as cheap labour. Beechey (1977) has suggested that women's labour power is actually of lower value than men's, in the sense that it costs less to supply a woman's subsistence needs (the value of labour for Marxists being determined by its costs of production as is the value of any commodity). Because women are subsidized by men within the family, employers can get away with paying them less than a subsistence wage (Beechey, 1977). Beechey also suggests that women's bodily needs are less than those of men. This idea is interesting, but does not explain why capitalist employers choose to employ cheaper female labour only in certain jobs, reserving others for men.

Marxists have also conceptualized women as a labour reserve, drawn into the economy at times of labour shortage and expelled back into the home in periods of recession. This idea fits well with the use made of women to cover jobs vacated by men during the two World Wars. But it does not explain why jobs are segregated. When women are drawn into the workforce, it is normally to fill 'women's jobs', not to substitute for men, and if jobs are 'feminized' (for example, clerical work), women subsequently retain them. Rather than being in the same market, in most cases men and women are in two separate non-competing markets.

According to the dual labour market thesis, discussed in Book 2 (Allen *et al.*, 1992), Chapter 6, women are seen as concentrated in the 'secondary' segment of the labour market, which is the segment characterized by low pay, poor conditions, insecurity and limited career prospects. Black workers and young people may be used as secondary labour, but women are especially suitable as they can resume their domestic role if made redundant. In other words, the construction of segmented labour markets helps employers achieve numerical flexibility.

Segmented labour market theory fits well with many of the facts about women's employment which we have reviewed and it takes on board the issue of segregation, but it does not altogether cope with all the complexities of the sexual division of labour. Not all 'women's work' is of the casualized secondary kind; there are some women's careers (nursing, teaching, textiles) and in these areas there have been persistent shortages of skilled women. There are also secondary-type jobs for men, in the construction industry for example, but even in these men habitually earn more than average female wages. Like the Marxist approaches, segmented labour market theory offers important insights into some of the ways in which employers exploit female labour, but does not sufficiently acknowledge the way in which gender segregation also benefits men. Some kind of dual systems theory is needed which would supplement an account of capitalist objectives with an understanding of how gender segregation at work is influenced by the domestic division of labour, and how it helps maintain male dominance.

Such a theory would take into account the disadvantages faced by married women because of the pressure of domestic duties. This pressure is compounded by the inadequate provision in Britain of childcare facilities and may be increased by the current policy of 'community care' which pushes more of the efforts and costs of social reproduction onto the shoulders of women. However, single and childless women also face disadvantage in the labour market. Gender inequality is more than simply a reflection of family relations. Paid work, as the preceding discussion has suggested, is a site of patriarchy, arranged on terms which favour male dominance.

The work of Cynthia Cockburn is particularly useful in demonstrating the centrality of gender at work. Cockburn's case studies of printing, tailoring, mail-order retailing and radiography revealed the importance of social attitudes about suitable work for each sex. Her study of the printing industry highlighted the longstanding efforts of male printers to keep women out of their jobs. She argues that jobs and workplaces must be understood as *gendered*. Jobs are characterized as male or female, on the base of particular assumptions about skill and technology. Men portray women as technologically incompetent, and ensure they are so by barring them from technological training. In Cockburn's words 'the appropriation of muscle, capability, tools and machinery by men is an important source of women's subordination, indeed it is part of the process by which females are constituted as women' (Cockburn, 1990, p.88). Technological competence is seen as a sign of superior male intellect and used to justify women's exclusion from top jobs.

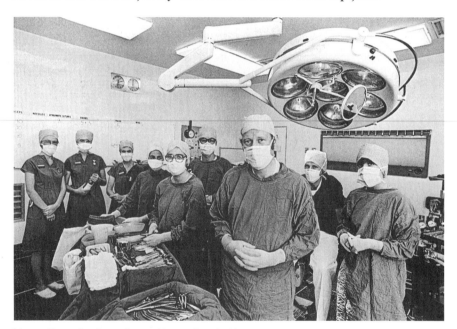

Men still predominate in positions of authority

Workplace groups are also often segregated, especially in manufacturing industry. Both men and women seem to prefer to work with their own sex. Workplace cultures develop from these segregated friendship groups, women's cultures focusing on domestic activities, families and romances, male cultures on sport and banter about drink and sex. Intruders of the opposite sex are often resented as they disturb the cosy atmosphere of the workgroups. Exclusionary tactics, sometimes quite vicious, may be adopted to freeze them out. In all these ways sexual divisions are actively developed within the workplace. Reading D from one of Cockburn's papers amplifies these points.

ACTIVITY 5   You should now read **Reading D, 'Women and technology'**, by Cynthia Cockburn. Then complete the following exercises.

List the various ways in which work is segregated by gender. Then list the other ways in which women's labour market position differs from men's.

How many of the features you have listed can be explained by

(a) human capital theory

(b) Marxist theory

(c) segmented labour market theory

(d) dual systems theory.

Use Table 1.8 to help you.

Table 1.8

Human capital theory	Neo-classical economics	Women's lower levels of training etc. confine them to lower-paid jobs	Rational choices made by couples on the basis of family needs and resources
Reserve army theory	Marxist	Women used as labour reserve	Serves capitalists' needs for cheap disposable labour
Segmented labour market theory	Weberian framework, also used by Marxists	Women clustered in secondary labour market sectors	Employers use labour market to 'divide and rule' and to secure flexibility
Dual systems theory	Marxist feminist	Gender segregation of jobs	Serves capitalists' interests (cheap labour) and helps secure continued male social dominance

This section has considered various explanations of gender inequality and looked at manifestations of inequality in the family and in paid work. I have argued that these inequalities combine to create a circle of disadvantage: domestic duties mean that women are liable to enter the labour market at a disadvantage; their weak labour market situation further holds them in domesticity and dependency. Both the family and the labour market, perhaps more markedly the latter in the post-war context, are sites of male control over women. I have suggested that I find a 'dual systems' theory of capitalism and patriarchy the most satisfactory approach to theorizing gender: But the term 'dual systems' might be viewed by black feminists as 'racist' in that it overlooks a third important 'system', that of racial hierarchies.

3 RACE AND CHANGE

3.1 THEORIZING RACE

Class and gender divisions have deep historical roots in Britain. A third dimension of inequality, race, has assumed increasing significance in the post-war period, with the entry into Britain of considerable numbers of immigrants from the West Indies, Africa and the Indian subcontinent. These groups, who have been officially categorized as 'of New Commonwealth ethnic origin', make up the core of what we might call the black British. In 1951 there were some 200,000 New Commonwealth (NC) born immigrants in Britain. By 1981 numbers had increased to over one and a quarter million born overseas, along with over a million children born in Britain into NC families.

Immigration into Britain is hardly new. There has been a black minority presence here since colonial development started, fostered particularly by the slave trade. Many Irish, Jewish and Polish immigrants, among others, entered Britain during the nineteenth and early twentieth centuries. Such groups have often been viewed with suspicion and hostility by the native-born population. However, in the post-war period race relations in Britain took a new orientation with colour in particular becoming the basis of hostility and conflict.

It is essential to see post-war immigration in a long-term context. In his notorious *Rivers of Blood* speech in 1968, Enoch Powell raised the spectre of black immigrants 'swamping' the country, draining economic resources from the indigenous population and diluting British culture, a theme which became central to the discourse of racism. But immigration only took place because the immigrants' home countries had at an earlier date been 'swamped' by thousands of white settlers who took political control, reconstructed the native economies and imposed aspects of British culture in countries where children still study Shakespeare and Dickens in schools and play cricket and football outside them.

Since the onset of colonialism, countries around the world have been intricately linked by chains of economic development. Wallerstein (1974) argues that colonialism brought into being an integrated world economy, in which the 'core' Western industrializing societies exploited the labour and resources of the 'peripheral' societies we now know as the Third World. Whether or not these processes fatally blocked Third World societies from developing is not an issue we have time to explore here, but economists like Barratt-Brown (1974) have suggested that British industrialization was founded upon the exploitation of slave labour in the West Indian and American colonies. Since then there has been a constant process of labour transference to and fro across the globe, with certain types of worker moving from the 'core' nations to the Third World, others moving from Third World nations to the industrialized West. The wholesale transportation of Africans to the West Indies and Americas is only the most dramatic example of this vast migrational network. Globally, race relations have developed on the basis of colonialism and labour mobility which set black populations in a disadvantaged and subordinate situation and emphasized the superiority of the more technologically advanced Western 'races'.

Race is in itself a problematic concept; as many have argued, it is doubtful whether it has any scientific base. In the discussion which follows I shall use the terminology suggested by Cashmore and Troyna (1983). They argue that race must be seen as real on the grounds that it has real effects on people's attitudes and behaviour. They distinguish between race as a label or stigmatized identity forced on one group by another and ethnicity as a self-defined and freely chosen cultural identity. Thus, in Britain, the assertion of ethnicity by black groups can be seen as a response to the experience of race. I use the term 'black', as they do, as the most acceptable term available to cover the various NC groups (South Asians, West Indians, Africans) and to distinguish them from other 'white' immigrant groups, such as Cypriots and Irish. The latter, while suffering some of the disadvantages of 'race', are not discriminated against to the same extent, as they are spared the visibility of 'colour'. We must remember, however, that black is a crude umbrella term covering numerous ethnic and regional groups, each of which has its own special position within the British social formation.

As in the case of gender, there is debate as to whether racial inequality can be explained within the framework of class or whether a separate framework, analogous to that of patriarchy, is necessary to understand the specificity of racial disadvantage. For Marxists, class is seen as primary, with race having secondary effects. They suggest that much racial disadvantage arises from the fact that most black British are members of the working class. A slightly different line is taken by Phizacklea and Miles (1980), who argue that black workers are a racialized fraction of the working class, whose economic position is significantly worse than that of white workers because of racist ideologies. The notion of fraction works better here (in the case of race) than in the case of gender. It is indeed true that black minority members are crowded into the lower occupational groupings. Recent research into 'black underachievement' at school suggests that the lower achievement of black students, previously explained as partly the result of cultural handicaps, more or less disappears when results are controlled for class (Asians do better than Afro-Caribbeans since they are more likely to have parents with educational qualifications). However, this approach underplays the role of racism among the white population, which makes the experience of minority groups different at *every* level of the class structure. Growing numbers of ethnic minority members have, as we shall see, moved out of manual jobs.

Something of the same objection can be raised to the application of the Weberian concept of the underclass to blacks in Britain. Black Britons cannot, in the main, be seen as permanently trapped in poverty in the same way as are the blacks in the ghettoes of many American cities, although this could happen in the future. At the moment, the position of racial minorities in the British class structure is rather more complex, and allows for considerable mobility.

Another concept used by Marxists has been that of migrant labour (see Book 2 (Allen *et al.*, 1992), Chapter 6). Castles and Kosack (1973) linked the black presence in Britain to international labour migration, conceiving migrant workers as part of a vast 'international reserve army of labour'. However, this works better for groups like the 'guestworkers' in Germany and Switzerland, whose stay in Europe is only temporary. It fits less well with British minorities who, despite the stress given by some commentators on the prevalence of the 'myth of return', are now widely accepted as being permanently settled. Indeed, in his later work (1984) Castles concedes that orthodox Marxist class theory is insufficient to explain the position of black people in Britain, which arises both from class situation and from ethnic minority status.

Here, Castles appears to be moving closer to a Weberian position, such as that of Rex, who conceptualizes race as a form of negative ascribed status. Rex also points to the importance of different consumption patterns, particularly with regard to housing (Rex and Tomlinson, 1979). For both Castles and Rex, economic and status divisions jointly lead to racial inequalities. Even more stress on status appears in the work of Parkin (1979), who adopts Weber's notion of social closure which refers to the strategies of exclusion used by specific groups against other rival groups. Parkin's explanation gives more weight than any previously discussed to the role of the white populace as a whole, rather than capitalists alone, in sustaining racial divisions.

Clearly, economic considerations, capitalist interests and the class positions in which black Britons are concentrated account for some of the disadvantages they face, but, in my opinion, racial differences cannot be reduced to class or to purely economic factors. We have to consider the important role of white racism in maintaining racial inequality and segregation. Racism is not itself a product of capitalist interests, although capitalists may well take advantage of racial divisions. The ideas of Castles and Parkin point the way towards examining race as a dimension of equality in its own right, although neither go far enough. As yet the idea of a separate racial dynamic is not as developed as the analysis of patriarchy. Such an analysis might proceed by showing how divisions backed by racist ideologies arose from the colonial process, slavery and white imperialism. Despite the decay of colonialism, racist ideas and power disparities between the ex-colonial Western nations and Third World nations have ensured that race divisions remain deep.

3.2 THE CHANGING PATTERNS OF RACIAL INEQUALITY

In the 1950s, NC immigrants were induced to come to Britain to offset the labour shortages which accompanied post-war economic reconstruction and expansion. Black immigrants took jobs that whites rejected, for example, in London Transport and the National Health Service. Such 'dirty jobs' were characterized by low pay, poor conditions and unsocial hours (black Britons are still concentrated in shiftwork). Decades later, black workers are still clustered in many of the same industries: textiles, transport, the NHS, hotels and catering. Although some black male workers gained access to better-paid skilled work in engineering and car factories, these are the areas of British manufacturing which have been particularly hit by recession, leading to high unemployment among black groups. Black women, as we saw in Section 2, often perform low-status service work.

When the first NC immigrants arrived, they found themselves openly excluded from access to better quality housing by estate agents and landlords. It was quite common to see notices displayed reading 'No coloureds here'. Rules and procedures governing council house allocation also discriminated against immigrants. This drove the newcomers to purchase cheap housing in decaying inner-city areas which had been vacated by affluent whites as they moved into the suburbs. Later immigrants moved into the same areas, either to be near relatives or friends, or to rent accommodation from their compatriots. Inexorably, black ghetto areas began to form. Not only was the housing in these areas of poor condition, but other resources and facilities, such as schools, were poor and rundown. Crime and unemployment made the ghettoes into 'problem areas', and problems were exacerbated when the remaining white residents vented their frustrations for their own deprivations in hostility towards their black neighbours.

Tension between blacks and whites exploded in the riots which took place in Notting Hill and Nottingham in 1958, and these events consolidated the view of race relations as a problem. The riots led to the passing of the 1962 Immigration Act, followed by several others enacted in the next two decades. The Acts limited rights of entry to black immigrants by various voucher, work permit and quota systems and by

Maisonette vandalized to prevent occupation by Asian family, Tower Hamlets, 1984

confining automatic rights to citizenship to 'patrials', that is those with British parents or grandparents. This latter move was seen as an attempt to cut down on black immigrants without restricting the movement of white ex-Commonwealth members such as Australians and Canadians.

Immigration controls were meant to reassure the white population that there would be no swamping, but arguably they only served to confirm the view that black immigrants were second-class citizens and a threat to the British nation. Race Relations Acts passed in 1965, 1968 and 1976 were designed to make discrimination illegal. They established a series of public bodies (the latest being the Commission for Racial Equality) which were supposed to work actively to promote good race relations. The race relations legislation did help to remove the blatantly discriminatory practices we noted when discussing housing, but did little to prevent the more subtle forms of discrimination, which are particularly widespread in employment.

Tests carried out as part of the Political and Economic Planning survey in the 1960s involved actors playing matched pairs of black and white applicants for jobs and revealed substantial discrimination in up to fifty per cent of cases. The tests have since been replicated a number of times and show that discrimination continues. It is particularly strong in manual work (Smith's report, published in 1977, found that white applicants were ten times more likely to be accepted). In the service sector black men are more likely to be rejected than black women. This kind of discrimination is hard to prove (except by these carefully staged sociological tests). Legislation appears fairly ineffective against it and also against 'institutional racism', that is, racist discrimination which is built into the practices and procedures of institutions such as schools and firms. One good example of institutional racism is exhibited through the widespread practice of obtaining jobs through personal recommendation, which becomes especially important in recession; it is said that 'who you know is more important than what you know' in getting a job. Wrench and Lee (1978) observed this happening in their study of Birmingham school leavers. White boys were more successful than black boys with similar qualifications in getting apprenticeships, and personal connections proved an important factor.

These processes of discrimination have led to the concentration of some minority groups in less skilled manual work, as shown in Table 1.9, which also shows the under-representation of black minority males in the professional and managerial sector. The table demonstrates that each group has its own distinctive labour market position. For example, West Indians fail to get into service jobs but dominate in skilled manual work. African Asians are the most successful in reaching top jobs, reflecting the fact that many were highly qualified professionals when they were forced to flee from Africa. The table indicates that the pattern of differentiation is less sharp between white and black females, although black women workers are more heavily concentrated in manual work. We should remember, though, that segregation is more marked at job level than sectoral level and this will be true for race as well as gender.

Table 1.9   Employment by ethnic group 1982 (percentages)

Men	White	West Indian	Asian	Indian	Pakistani	Bangladeshi	African Asian
Professional, employer, management	19	5	13	11	10	10	22
Other non-manual	23	10	13	13	8	7	21
Skilled manual and foreman	42	48	33	34	39	13	31
Semi-skilled manual	13	26	34	36	35	57	22
Unskilled manual	3	9	6	5	8	12	3

Women	White	West Indian	Asian	Indian	African Asian
Professional, employer, manager	7	1	6	5	7
Other non-manual	55	52	42	35	52
Skilled manual and foreman	5	4	6	8	3
Semi-skilled manual	21	36	44	50	36

Source: Brown, 1984, pp.197 and 198

Despite this picture of discrimination, small numbers of black Britons are moving into professional and managerial jobs. Another significant development is the rise in self-employment among some Asian communities. Self-employment, as we noted earlier, has been growing for all groups, but is especially marked among Asians. In 1985, 23.7 per cent of Indian males in the British workforce, and 21.4 per cent of Pakistani and Bangladeshi, were self-employed, as opposed to 17.7 per cent of whites (Afro-Caribbeans are least likely to be self-employed at 8 per cent). The figures are much lower for women, but even here Indian women lead at 9.4 per cent.

This trend has been linked to the growth of an Asian entrepreneurial culture and seen as a sign of successful adaptation to a new environment and evidence of a new prosperity among the Asian communities. It has also been linked to a tradition of successful business enterprise within Indian cultures, displayed earlier, for example, in East Africa. High value placed on hard work and self-sufficiency leads Asian families into this type of investment. However, reviewing the research on Asian businesses in Britain, Cashmore and Troyna conclude that entrepreneurialism may be forced on Asians because they face restricted opportunities elsewhere. Moreover, most of the businesses remain small and rely heavily on family labour, which can be experienced as highly self-exploitative. (One of the reasons for the failure of Afro-Caribbeans to develop a comparable community-centred enterprise sector may be the lack of tightly integrated family and kin networks to provide labour.) Some clothing businesses may be no more than a disguised form of homeworking. However, Asian

Asian business: a sign of increasing prosperity?

enterprises do provide a basis of independence and may be seen as part of the assertion of ethnicity as a response to white racism. In class terms, it means that around one fifth of the Asian minority are moving out of the working class into the petite bourgeoisie, which would provide a strong challenge to either the underclass theory or the Marxist contention that race disadvantage can be reduced to class. Rather it provides support for an approach showing how class and race interact together; Cashmore and Troyna suggest that Asian entrepreneurs have moved from a disadvantaged position as workers to a disadvantaged position as businessmen, on the basis of race.

Annie Phizacklea links the growth of Asian businesses to the recession of the 1970s (in 1971 only 6 per cent of Indian men were self-employed). Table 1.10 shows the vulnerability of minority groups to unemployment. This is especially marked for Afro-Caribbeans and for the younger age groups.

Table 1.10   Unemployment rates by ethnic origin 1986–88 (percentages)

	White	Afro-Caribbean	Indian	Pakistani/ Bangladeshi
Men	10	22	12	27
Women	10	16	16	na

Source: Central Statistical Office, *Social Trends,* no.20, 1990, Table 4.28, p.80

Stuart Hall in Hall *et al.* (1978) has argued that economic recession of the 1970s led to the scapegoating of black minorities by British governments wishing to draw attention away from the failures of their own economic policies. Recessions led to increased inner-city decline, with overburdened social services unable to provide funding for improvements. Unemployment among inner-city youths can be linked to rising problems of crime and vandalism. All this led to targeting of Afro-Caribbean youths as a problem group; increased intensity of policing in black areas helped exacerbate racial hostility and resentment. Racist attacks, particularly on Asian families, were on the increase throughout the 1980s (in 1987 there were 2,179 reported in the Metropolitan police area alone, including 47 cases of arson). In 1981, another wave of riots wracked inner-city ghettoized areas around the country. The recent Gifford Report on race relations in Liverpool (1989) exposed the extent to which race divisions had become rooted in the more highly depressed areas of the country, finding a systematic denial of jobs to black people, particularly in the city centre commercial and retailing enterprises, extensive black unemployment, and a failure of Liverpool City Council to implement its own equal opportunities policies: only 490 out of 30,410 council employees were black.

It is important to stress that racial disadvantage is not confined to the economic sphere. As is the case with gender, the experience of race and racism spreads itself across every area of life. For example, black groups are still concentrated in the least desirable sectors of the housing market. It was believed that young blacks 'underachieved' at school, although, as stated earlier, recent research has suggested that most of this could be accounted for in terms of class differences. However, research into patterns of interaction in schools has revealed that black students are subject to persistent racial harrassment from white pupils and that many teachers operate with racist stereotypes which make school an unhappy experience for many minority youngsters (Mac an Ghaill, 1988; Fleming, 1990).

There is some evidence that minority groups may experience higher infant mortality rates than the white population (perhaps indicative of poorer health care from doctors and clinics) and are more prone to certain types of fatal illness (Aggleton, 1990). Afro-Caribbeans are over-represented in the prison population (both male and female) and in mental hospitals. The state has an important role to play in these respects. Mama (1984) argues that agents of the state (social workers, doctors, police, magistrates) operate, if not always with overtly racist ideas, certainly with ethnocentric assumptions about normal behaviour which lead to the labelling of black people as deviant. For example, certain forms of expressive behaviour typical of Caribbean culture may be seen as eccentric and symptomatic of psychological disturbance. The smoking of 'ganga', considered socially respectable in the Caribbean, has been a persistent cause of tension between police and black youths. Black family structures and practices (the Caribbean woman-headed family, Asian arranged marriages) are seen as undesirable, as being social problems, by state agencies, which then attempt to normalize them. In this way, not only individuals from minority groups but minority cultures as a whole come under attack. (See Book 1 (Hall and Gieben, 1992), Chapter 6 for a discussion of the characteristic patterns of Western thought and discourse which underpin these attitudes.)

Minority groups have responded to these experiences in various ways. Some have tried to work for equal opportunities through existing bodies like the political parties or trade unions, though arguably white-dominated political organizations have done little to promote racial equality. Others have joined community groups or anti-racist campaigns. Young blacks seem to have responded to the discrimination they know they will face by putting more effort than white youngsters into education. Asian students out-perform whites at school and higher proportions of Asians and Afro-Caribbeans than of whites are currently in higher education. But perhaps most important has been the assertion of ethnicity. This takes differing forms. Afro-Caribbean youths have developed their own 'streetwise' culture and rastafarian creed. The consolidation of Asian community businesses can be read in this way; and the late 1980s have seen a more aggressive response from Muslim Asians with the growing popularity of militant Islamic fundamentalism. All these assertions of independent identity may do much to raise the self-esteem of minority groups (and incidentally add to the richness of cultural life in Britain). But an unfortunate side-effect is the consolidation of segregated lifestyles, which may heighten racial hostility.

This section has only begun to explore the many dimensions of racial segmentation in Britain, ignoring, for example, the differentiated experiences of many other ethnic groups (for example Cypriots, Jews and Irish), who also face discriminatory practices and prejudice. Racial diversity is an important feature of modern Britain.

This racial diversity adds to the difficulty of developing a theoretical understanding of race and ethnicity. In this section, I have argued that attempts to reduce race to class are insufficient. Racial disadvantage is not confined to economics, but is experienced in every area of life; in particular, notions of white supremacy and superiority are very deeply embedded in all the cultural discourses developed by 'Western' thought. Although the patterns of disadvantage experienced by some black groups are similar to those experienced by the working class as a whole (low educational achievement, poor health, poor housing), racism adds an extra dimension; and racism is not just experienced by working-class blacks. At all levels of the class structure, minority groups experience discrimination and exclusion. Although race is sharply linked to class and although capitalism has benefited from using minority workers as cheap labour (especially women), race, like gender, must be seen as an autonomous source of division.

ACTIVITY 6 Look again at Tables 1.9 and 1.10.

- What are the major patterns of difference they reveal between the different ethnic groups?
- What do these figures reveal about the way class and gender interact with racial divisions?

4   THE INTERACTING DYNAMICS OF CLASS, GENDER AND RACE

4.1   CLASS, RACE AND GENDER IN THE FASHION INDUSTRY: A CASE STUDY

So far, for the purposes of sociological analysis, I have considered class, gender and race as separate dimensions of stratification. But in the real world all three are found operating jointly. One recent study which has revealed this is Annie Phizacklea's *Unpacking the Fashion Industry*, (1990) which traces out the way dynamics of class, race and gender work together to produce work hierarchies in the garment-making industry.

Phizacklea shows how a particular division of labour is produced by class, race and gender factors in combination. In the latest phase of capitalist development, she argues that a dualistic structure has emerged in the garment industry, which is dominated by firms largely owned by multinational companies and run on a modernized capital-intensive basis. Linked to them are a multitude of small firms acting as subcontractors who carry out much of the assembly work for the large firms, often employing home workers at very low wages. In some European nations, large garment firms have chosen another course, farming out their labour-intensive processes to Third World countries (a practice known as 'outward processing') in order to cut labour costs. Phizacklea argues this has been unnecessary in Britain, because of the existence of reserves of cheap female minority labour, a kind of 'Third World at home'.

In class terms, she argues that this pattern of capitalist investment produces a highly exploited working-class sector. Race and class dynamics have also combined to bring into being a group of 'ethnic entrepreneurs' who run many of the small firms. The recession of the 1970s and 1980s brought unemployment to many male workers in manufacturing industry. Phizacklea argues that Asian workers, facing particular difficulties in becoming re-employed, were induced into starting small businesses as a defensive measure, subsequently employing women workers from their own families and communities. Here we can see how race and gender compound the disadvantages faced by these workers. Garment-making has traditionally been seen as 'women's work', drawing on stereotypes of 'natural attributes' and 'nimble fingers'; consequently the skills and effort involved are poorly rewarded. Asian women are particularly vulnerable to exploitation, because of immigration rules which force them into dependency on male relatives. Many need a sponsor if they are to gain entry and this imposes obligations upon them, heightened by their sense of loyalty to the family business as an ideal. On top of all this, racist discrimination limits their range of labour market options, pressurizing them into accepting this poorly-rewarded work.

Phizacklea's study is clearly specific to a particular industry and indeed to a particular region (the Midlands). We should not expect to find precisely the same pattern elsewhere. It does, however, indicate we might begin to investigate the way class, race and gender work together in industrial capitalist societies to produce social hierarchies. We need, now, to think a little more about how these three dimensions interact.

4.2   THE FRAGMENTED SOCIAL STRUCTURE: DIVISIONS AND DIVERSITIES

This chapter has indicated some of the ways in which class, race and gender impact upon one another. We have seen how the class structure has been subject to processes of fragmentation. This effect is heightened by the interaction of class with gender and ethnic divisions. This has been particularly significant in the case of the working class. Since industrialization, the movement of organized labour has been weakened by the splits between male and female workers, with male trade unionists operating policies of 'social closure' against women and minority workers. Although men and women, black and white, have united in industrial action, currents of racism and sexism have led to short-sighted policies which have made it more difficult to develop union solidarity. Women have always been under-represented in unions and only recently have unions seriously begun to develop policies aimed to increase female participation.

Many black workers have joined unions, but Cashmore and Troyna (1983) suggest this may be due to defensiveness and awareness of greater vulnerability, rather than commitment to the idea of class-based solidarity. By contrast, Phizacklea and Miles (1980) believed that the black workers they studied had a strong sense of working-class allegiance. But the experience of racism may erode that allegiance; many sociologists have suggested that race is a more potent form of identity than class, since class divisions are subtle and obscured and the experience of race is much more obviously oppressive.

Race and gender divisions will also add to the heterogeneity of the middle classes. The idea of embourgeoisement seems even less credible when we consider the market, class and status positions characteristic of women workers in many service sector jobs. The numerical dominance of women in lower-middle-class jobs may in the past have contributed to the lack of militancy in some of these occupational groupings; but if women's expectations continue to be raised, there may be less compliance among the 'white-collar proletariat'.

Race and gender divisions make the analysis of class much more complicated. A full understanding of class would, however, need to take these into account. Conversely, class and ethnicity serve to complicate the understanding of gender. Recently, feminist policies and theories have been criticized by black feminists as ethnocentric and class-biased, on the grounds that the feminist movement has been led by white middle-class women and its achievements have benefited them rather than black or working-class women. Moreover, white women in a colonial context have acted to exploit black women and still benefit today from the cheap labour of black and working-class women, either directly as servants, or indirectly through their situation of class privilege.

The experience of working-class and black women is obviously different from that of white middle-class women. Segregation is more marked in manual jobs and low-paid service work than in the professions. Family relations differ between class and ethnic groups. Black and working-class women suffer from the racist and patriarchal policies fostered by the state, while middle-class women may well be administering these policies to them. Post-modern feminist theory suggests that there may be little common ground for women to unite as a category, pointing to diversity in the interests and objectives of the different groups of women. Others, however, suggest this diversity might be used as a basis for enriching feminism, if differential aims and interests were taken into account to provide a much broader based account of the experience of gender and power.

Race and ethnicity are also sources of diversity in the social formation. Ethnicity is an important focus of identity and the late 1980s have witnessed a proliferation of ethnic movements around the globe. Here in Britain, too, there has been a strengthened assertion of ethnicity and cultural distinctiveness, partly as a response to the experience of racist hostility and of second-class citizenship. Race is itself fragmented, with a plurality of minority groups finding themselves particularly located within the social formation and developing their own community organizations. At present, the experience of race may be dominant, but Britain's minority population may come to be divided on the basis of class and gender as well as ethnicity. The development of a black bourgeoisie may split black communities, especially if the prosperity of black entrepreneurs is at the expense of black workers. While Britain's black communities have, in the past, been linked to the Labour Party, a growing number of successful Asians and Afro-Caribbeans are affiliating to the Conservative Party or the Liberal Democrats. Prevailing family arrangements create tensions between black women and men just as they do between white men and women.

All the splits and divisions of loyalty I have just been describing have particularly important consequences in terms of *social identity*. By social identity I mean the way that each of us as individuals locate ourselves within the society in which we live. Class, gender and race represent three forms of potential social identity which may well conflict with one another. I have already suggested that black people in Britain may experience their identity in racial rather than class terms, because of the greater visibility of racial differences and because the impact of racism is so strong and hurtful. The assertion of ethnicity as a defence against racism, as discussed in Section 3, has brought a heightened sense of racial and ethnic identities to late twentieth-century Britain.

In recent decades, feminist campaigns have brought a greater gender awareness to women, and to a lesser extent men, in the industrialized societies of the world. Women, in particular, may consciously identify themselves first and foremost as women, rather than members of a particular ethnic or class group, although this is more likely to be true of middle-class than working-class women. Some working-class women at present feel a hostility to the feminist movement which may actually serve to strengthen their class identification. For example, some activist women in trade unions reject feminist strategies, such as reserving special seats for women, because they see them as a distraction from the struggle to gain better conditions for working people. As for men, their gender identification is perhaps less consciously held because the male gender is still seen as the norm. This may change in the coming decades, as prevailing definitions of masculinity become challenged, a process which is already under way in the social sciences.

But it is class identity which has been most destabilized in the post-war period. Before the war, the relative lack of social mobility and the tendency for people to live in fairly stable geographical communities meant that many people developed a clear sense of class membership. This was particularly true of the 'traditional proletarian' communities identified by Lockwood, which we discussed in Section 1. By contrast, in the 1980s, class fragmentation and increased social mobility mean that there are a greater number of class identities available and that many individuals have a more confused sense of which class they belong to. Willis (1990) argues that this is particularly true of the younger generation. Today's young men and women have drifted away from the institutions which used to foster class identities (trade unions, community associations, churches, schools and so on). Willis argues their interests lie in commercialized culture which promotes individualized consumer identities rather than a sense of class membership. Widespread youth unemployment also deprives young people of work experience which is so central to class identification, as classically conceived by Marx. All this does not mean that the sense of class is lost; just that for some individuals it is weakened and that, for most of us, a wider range of identities is on offer than was the case in the 1930s.

5 CONCLUSION

This chapter has presented a picture of an increasingly complex social structure, generating a plurality of interests and conflicts, tensions and dilemmas. In recent decades, sociological attention has focused on these diversities and their divisive effects. However, it is important to remember that unifying tendencies remain, as Marshall and colleagues pointed out in their study of class. The experience of wage labour and powerlessness is still common for the majority of workers. All women, of whatever class or ethnic group, are constrained by their association with domesticity. The majority, even women in managerial and professional groupings, are subject to male authority in their jobs. Minority groups share the experience of white racist attitudes and the fight to establish their rights as British citizens and to assert the validity of their cultures and traditions.

The theme of fragmentation is often associated with the belief that class antagonisms are vanishing and social power is now more equally shared. But, as we saw, the fragmentation of propertied groups has *not* been matched by fragmentation of the propertyless class. Paradoxically, the economic control of the internationalized capitalist elite has been greatly consolidated as the class loyalties of the other groups fracture and weaken. In addition, this chapter has indicated that power disparities of gender and race are still very marked.

In the past, Marxists have claimed that race and gender divisions can be explained as part of capitalist development. Some have even argued, more crudely, that racial and gender inequalities are merely side-effects of class, which would vanish in a classless socialist society. In this chapter, I have suggested that a class analysis, whether neo-Marxist or neo-Weberian, is inadequate to explain gender and race. Gender, racial and ethnic divisions predate capitalism, although it is true that capitalism has incorporated them into its economic structures. But inequalities of race and gender are generated culturally as well as economically. Racism and sexism are not confined to a single type of economic structure. Class, race and gender need to be considered, I would argue, as three *separate but interacting dynamics.* Phizacklea's study suggests how these dynamics work in one particular context. In any given social structure, class, race and gender interact together in complex ways. The fragmentations produced by this interaction are the foundation of the social hierarchies and inequalities characteristic of contemporary social formations.

This chapter has suggested that some of the traditional and more rigid approaches to the study of stratification need to be modified, if not abandoned, because they fail to deal adequately with the dimensions of race and gender. A more flexible approach is needed to cope with the complexities of social divisions which have been outlined in this final section. This does not mean, as some post-modernists have suggested, that we should abandon the study of social structure, since, as I hope this chapter has shown, Britain is still a sharply stratified society; but it does imply a need to grapple with divisions and diversities and rethink some of the sociological dogmas of the past.

REFERENCES

Abercrombie, N., Warde, A. *et al.* (1988) *Contemporary British Society*, Cambridge, Polity Press.

Aggleton, P. (1990) *Health*, London, Routledge.

Allen, J., Braham, P. and Lewis, P. (1992), *Political and Economic Forms of Modernity*, Cambridge, Polity Press.

Amos, V. and Parmar, P. (1984) 'Challenging imperial feminism' *Feminist Review* 17, pp.3–18.

Barratt-Brown, M. (1974) *The Economics of Imperialism*, Harmondsworth, Penguin.

Barrett, M. (1987) 'The concept of difference', *Feminist Review* 26, pp.29–41.

Beechey, V. (1977) 'Some notes on female wage labour in capitalist production', *Capital and Class*, 3, pp.45–66.

Bell, D. (1974) *The Coming of Post-industrial Society*, Harmondsworth, Penguin.

Braverman, H. (1974) *Labor and Monopoly Capital*, New York, Monthly Review Press.

Brown, C. (1984) *Black and White Britain*, London, Heinemann.

Cashmore, E. and Troyna, B. (1983) *Introduction to Race Relations*, London, Routledge and Kegan Paul.

Castles, S. and Kosack, G. (1973) *Immigrant Workers and Class Structure in Western Europe*, Oxford, Oxford University Press.

Castles, S. (1984) *Here For Good*, London, Pluto.

Central Statistical Office (1986, 1990 and 1991) *Social Trends*, nos. 16, 20 and 21, London, HMSO.

Cockburn, C. (1990) 'The material of male power', in Lovell, T. (ed) *British Feminist Thought*, Oxford, Blackwell.

Cockburn, C. (1986) 'Women and technology: opportunity is not enough' in Purcell, K., Wood, S., Waton, A. and Allen, S. (eds) *The Changing Experience of Employment*, London, Macmillan.

Crompton, R. and Jones, G. (1984) *White-Collar Proletariat*, London, Macmillan.

Dahrendorf, R. (1959) *Class and Class Conflict in Industrial Societies*, London, Routledge.

Dahrendorf, R. (1987) 'The erosion of citizenship and its consequences for us all', *New Statesman*, 12 June, pp.12–15.

Delphy, C. (1977) *The Main Enemy*, London, Women's Research and Resources Centre.

Department of Employment (1984) *New Earnings Survey*, London, HMSO.

Edgell, S. (1980) *Middle-class Couples*, London, Allen and Unwin.

Firestone, S. (1979) *The Dialectic of Sex,* London, Women's Press.

Fleming, S. (1990) 'Sport and social divisions', presented at 1990 British Sociological Conference.

Gifford Report (1989) 'Loosen the shackles', Liverpool 8 Law Centre.

Glucksmann, M. (1990) *Women Assemble,* London, Routledge.

Goldthorpe, J., Lockwood, D., Bechhofer, F. and Platt, J. (1969) *The Affluent Worker in the Class Structure,* Cambridge, Cambridge University Press.

Gorz, A. (1982) *Farewell to the Working Class,* London, Pluto.

Hakim, C. (1979) 'Occupational segregation by sex', Department of Employment Research Paper No.9, London, Department of Employment.

Hall, S., Critcher, C., Jefferson, T., Clarke, J. and Roberts, B. (1978) *Policing the Crisis,* London, Macmillan.

Hall, S. and Gieben, B. (1992) *Formations of Modernity*, Cambridge, Polity Press.

Hartmann, H. (1981) 'The unhappy marriage of Marxism and Feminism: towards a more progressive union' in Sargent, L. (ed.).

Lewis, J. (1988) 'Women clerical workers in the late nineteenth and early twentieth centuries' in Anderson, G. (ed.) *The White Blouse Revolution*, Manchester, Manchester University Press.

Lockwood, D. (1958) *The Blackcoated Worker,* London, Unwin.

Lockwood, D. (1966) 'Sources of variation in working-class images of society' *Sociological Review* 14, 2, pp.249–67.

Lockwood, D. (1981) 'The weakest link in the chain? Some comments on the Marxist theory of action' *Research in the Sociology of Work* 1, pp.435–81.

Mac an Ghaill, M. (1988) *Young, Gifted and Black*, Milton Keynes, The Open University Press.

Mama, A. (1984) 'Black women, the economic crisis and the British State' *Feminist Review* 17, pp.21–33.

Martin, J. and Roberts, C. (1984) *Women and Employment: a Lifetime Perspective,* London, HMSO.

Marshall, G., Rose, D., Newby, H. and Vogler, C. (1988) *Social Class in Modern Britain,* London, Unwin Hyman.

Morris, L. (1990) *The Workings of the Household,* Cambridge, Polity Press.

Oakley, A. (1974) *Housewife,* Harmondsworth, Penguin.

Office of Population Censuses and Surveys, *Census* (various dates), London, HMSO.

Parkin, F. (1979) *Marxism and Class Theory,* London, Tavistock.

Parsons, T. and Bales, R. (1956) *Family, socialisation and interaction processes,* New York, Free Press.

Phillips, A. and Taylor, B. (1980) 'Sex and skill: notes towards a feminist economics', *Feminist Review*, 6, pp.70–83.

Phizacklea, A. and Miles, R. (1980) *Labour and Racism,* London, Routledge.

Phizacklea, A. (1990) *Unpacking the Fashion Industry: Gender, Racism and Class in Production,* London, Routledge.

Rapaport, R. and Rapaport, R. (1971) *Dual-Career Families,* Harmondsworth, Penguin.

Rex, J. and Tomlinson, S. (1979) *Colonial Immigrants in a British City,* London, Routledge.

Rogers, B. (1988) *Men Only,* London, Pandora.

Rowbotham, S. (1981) 'The trouble with "patriarchy"', in Feminist Anthology Collective (eds) *No Turning Back,* London, Women's Press.

Rubery, J., Horrell, S., and Burrell, B. (1989) 'Unequal jobs or unequal pay?' *Industrial Relations Journal,* 20,3, pp.176–91.

Sargent, L. (ed.) (1981) *Women in Revolution,* London, Pluto.

Saunders, P. (1990) *Social Class and Stratification,* London, Routledge.

Scott, J. (1979) *Corporations, Classes and Capitalism,* London, Hutchinson.

Scott, J. (1982) *The Upper Classes,* London, Macmillan.

Smith, D. (1977) *Racial Disadvantage in Britain,* Harmondsworth, Penguin.

Spender, D. (1980) *Man-made Language,* London, Routledge.

Walby, S. (1986) *Patriarchy at Work,* Cambridge, Polity Press.

Wallerstein, I. (1974) *The Modern World System,* New York, Academic Press.

Willis, P. (1990) *Common Culture,* Milton Keynes, The Open University Press.

Wilson, E. (1983) *What is to be Done about Violence against Women?* Harmondsworth, Penguin.

Wrench, J. and Lee, G. (1978) 'A subtle hammering — young black people and the labour market' in Troyna, B. and Smith, D. (eds) (1983) *Racism, School and the Labour Market,* Leicester, National Youth Bureau.

Young, I. (1981) 'Beyond the unhappy marriage: a critique of the dual systems theory' in Sargent, L. (ed.) (1981).

Young, M. and Willmott, P. (1973) *The Symmetrical Family,* London, Routledge and Kegan Paul.

READING A   BLACKCOATED WORKER

David Lockwood

... Any empirical study of class consciousness must begin by taking into account actual differences in the market situation of propertyless groups. Variations in class identification have to be related to actual variations in class situations and not attributed to some kind of ideological aberration or self-deception. ... Although he shares the propertyless status of the manual worker, the clerk has never been strictly 'proletarian' in terms of income, job security and occupational mobility. ... As a group blackcoated workers have enjoyed the following material advantages over the manual worker. In the first place, clerks have had a relatively high income throughout the greater part of the period with which we have been concerned. ... Secondly, and more important than sheer differences in income, blackcoated workers traditionally enjoyed a much greater degree of job-security than manual workers. ... Thirdly, clerks, and particularly male clerks, have had superior chances of rising to managerial and supervisory positions. Finally, in addition to the official and unofficial rights to pensions on retirement which many clerks have enjoyed, must be added the non-pecuniary advantages of office work — its cleanliness, comfort, tempo, hours, holidays. ...

Both in the factory and in the labour market, the outstanding features of the work situation of modern wage-labour are, on the one hand, the physical separation and social estrangement of management and workers, and, on the other, the physical concentration and social identification of the workers themselves. ... This type of work situation is one that clearly maximizes a sense of class separation and antagonism. Insofar as the work situation of the modern wage-earner approximated such a pattern of relationships, it took on the character of a 'proletarian' class situation. When, however, this type of 'proletarian' work situation is compared with that of the blackcoated worker, it is evident that in this respect, too, the behaviour of the clerk has been influenced by an administrative division of labour which, ... entailed radically different relationships ... The older, paternalistic work environment of the counting house was ... inimical to the development of any sense of common identity among clerks. At the same time, any feeling of class identification with the manual worker was absolutely precluded by the relations of production. Physically, clerks were scattered among a large number of small offices, working in close contact with employers, and divorced from the factory workmen. Their working relationships were largely determined by personal and particular ties, which meant that there was little uniformity in standards of work and remuneration, and that individualistic aspirations to advancement were strongly encouraged.

In the period of the modern office it is necessary to distinguish between those fields of clerical employment where paternalistic influences are still operative, and those where bureaucratic forms of administration have

Source: Lockwood, D. (1958) *The Blackcoated Worker*, London, Unwin, pp.203–8, 210–11.

been established. In the former, the relatively small size of the office, the internal social fragmentation of the office staff through occupational, departmental and informal status distinctions, and the absence of any institutionalized blockage of mobility, have continued to militate against the growth of collective action among clerks. ... In those bureaucracies, on the other hand, where larger office units, strict classification and grading, blocked upward mobility and unhindered horizontal mobility were the rule, there have been reproduced impersonal and standardized working relationships comparable with those created by the factory and labour market. It is here that the work situation of the clerk has been most favourable to the emergence of that feeling of collective interdependence among employees which is prerequisite to their concerted action. But even where working conditions have fostered group action by clerks, the continuing physical and social division between clerks and manual workers has generally remained a barrier to the mutual identification of the two groups. The sense of social distance between manual and non-manual worker may, in turn, be traced primarily to their relative proximity to administrative authority. Bound up as it is with the general organization of discipline and authority, the relationship between clerk and manual worker lends itself readily to hostility and resentment on both sides. ...

Having dealt with the two basic elements of the class situation, it is now necessary to specify how the factor of 'social status' enters into the pattern of class consciousness. Class focuses on the divisions which result from the brute facts of economic organization. Status relates to the more subtle distinctions which stem from the values that men set on each other's activities. ... Because the distinction between manual and non-manual work provided a clearly identifiable dividing line across which many other differences — in income, security, promotion possibilities, authority, education — could also be contrasted, it was readily seized on as a line of status demarcation. ... When differences in advantage are overlaid by differences in social worth, mutual identification is precluded; especially when superiority is asserted on the one side as vigorously as it is denied on the other. For the middle-class status of the clerk was not unequivocally recognized, particularly by the working man. ... The exaggerated status consciousness of the blackcoated worker was produced by his marginal social position, and by the vicious circle of clerical 'snobbishness' and working-class 'contempt' to which it gave rise. A self-perpetuating 'status' barrier between clerk and manual worker was thus brought into existence.

The lowered social status of blackcoated work at the present time is the outcome of a long and complex process of change whereby many of the former bases of the clerk's prestige have been undermined, making the line between the middle and working classes less distinct. As a group, clerical workers are now more heterogeneous and the sheer fact of 'brain work' is less and less the hallmark of middle-class status. Under these conditions the class consciousness of the blackcoated worker exhibits greater diversity. ... What does seem tolerably clear is that the traditional superiority of non-manual work has not been entirely eradicated by the changes of the last half-century, even though it has been more frequently questioned. This is best stated by saying that the loss of middle-class status by the clerk is not tantamount to the acquisition of working-class status, either from the point of view of the clerk or the manual worker. ... In short, differences in class situation, and especially in work situation, continue to incite status rivalry between clerk and manual worker, and status rivalry in turn weakens their consciousness of class identity.

READING B LABOR AND MONOPOLY CAPITAL

Harry Braverman

While the working class in production is the result of several centuries of capitalist development, clerical labor is largely the product of the period of monopoly capitalism. Thus the early post-Marx attempts to analyze this phenomenon were severely hampered by the fact that clerical work was as yet little developed as a capitalist labor process. ...

The general expectation of commentators, as a result, was the rapid increase of office functionaries of the then-dominant varieties. On this basis, the conclusion seemed inescapable: a very large new 'middle class' was coming into being. ...

In 1896, Charles Booth was able to write: 'The "average, undifferentiated human labour power" upon which Karl Marx bases his gigantic fallacy does not exist anywhere on this planet, but least of all, I think, is it to be found among clerks' (Booth, 1896). At the time there were few Marxists bold enough to try to counter this thrust. But within less than forty years the development of the capitalist office made it possible for some to comprehend all the essential elements of the process, although it was even then far from being well advanced. Thus Hans Speier, drawing chiefly on German experience, was able to write in 1934:

> *The social level of the salaried employee sinks with the increasing extent of the group.* This qualitative change, which has been termed "the proletarianization of the white collar worker", shows itself in a number of ways. It is most evident, perhaps, in the especially great increase in the women salaried workers, who mostly perform subordinate work ... it is the man who typically has the principal authority, the girl who is typically the subordinate. ... The great increase in salaried employees is especially traceable to a demand for subordinates, not for fully qualified responsible persons. As a result the average chance of advancing has declined. The majority of the subordinate employees in the large offices perform duties which are specialized and schematized down to the minutest detail. They no longer require general training; in part only a very limited and brief training is necessary, in part previous training has become quite

Source: Braverman, H. (1974) *Labor and Monopoly Capital,* New York, Monthly Review Press, pp.348–55.

unnecessary. ... One social result of this development is the rise of the unskilled and semi-skilled salaried workers, whose designation already indicates the assimilation of the processes of work in the office to that in the factory. In the case of the salaried workers who serve as subordinates on one of the many modern office machines, or, for example, who sell in a one-price store, the difference in the nature of the duties between such workers and manual workers is completely wiped out ... especially revealing with regard to the sinking of the social level of the white-collar workers is, finally, the change in the social antecedents. The growing tendency to employ salaried workers of "proletarian origin" indicates that the number of untrained and poorly paid positions is increasing faster than the number of middle and principal positions. In other words, the salaried employees as a whole are being subjected to a process of decreasing social esteem. (Speier, 1934.)

This was written before the mechanization of the office. Writing at about the same time, Lewis Corey was anticipating future events when he said: 'The mechanization of clerical labor becomes constantly greater; a typical large office is now nothing but a white-collar factory' (Corey, 1935)... But by 1951 ... C.Wright Mills was able to write, upon a solid basis of fact:

The introduction of office machinery and sales devices has been mechanizing the office and the salesroom, the two big locales of white-collar work. Since the twenties it has increased the division of white-collar labor, recomposed personnel, and lowered skill levels. Routine operations in minutely subdivided organizations have replaced the bustling interest of work in well-known groups. Even on managerial and professional levels, the growth of rational bureaucracies has made work more like factory production. ...

The alienating conditions of modern work now include the salaried employees as well as the wage-workers. There are few, if any, features of wage-work (except heavy toil — which is decreasingly a factor in wage-work) that do not also characterize at least some white-collar work (Wright Mills, 1951)....

At the same time, the labor market for the two chief varieties of workers, factory and office, begins to lose some of its distinctions of social stratification, education, family, and the like. Not only do clerical workers come increasingly from families of factory background, and vice-versa, but more and more they are merged within the same living family. The chief remaining distinction seems to be a division along the lines of sex. Here the distribution within the clerical and operative groups is strikingly congruent: in 1971, the category of operatives was made up of 9 million men and 4 million women, while that of clerical workers was made up of 10.1 million women and 3.3. million men. The sex barrier that assigns most office jobs to women, and that is enforced both by custom and hiring practice, has made it possible to lower wage rates in the clerical category, as we have seen, below those in any category of manual labor. The growing participation of women in employment has thus far been facilitated by the stronger demand for clerical employees and the relatively stagnating demand for operatives. The existence of two giant categories of labor, operatives and clerical workers, as the two largest major-occupational classifications, and the composition by sex of each of these categories, leads to the supposition that one of the most common United States occupational combinations within the family is that in which the husband is an operative and the wife a clerk. ...

The problem of the so-called employee or white-collar worker which so bothered early generations of Marxists, and which was hailed by anti-Marxists as a proof of the falsity of the 'proletarianization' thesis, has thus been unambiguously clarified by the polarization of office employment and the growth at one pole of an immense mass of *wage-workers*. The apparent trend to a large nonproletarian 'middle class' has resolved itself into the creation of a large proletariat in a new form. In its conditions of employment, this working population has lost all former superiorities over workers in industry, and in its scales of pay it has sunk almost to the very bottom.

References

Booth, C. (1896) 'Life and labour of the people' in *Labour*, Vol.II.

Corey, L. (1935) *The Crisis in the Middle Class*, New York.

Mills, C. W. (1951) *White Collar*, New York.

Speier, H. (1934) 'The salaried employee in modern society', *Social Research*, February, pp.116–18.

READING C CHALLENGING IMPERIAL FEMINISM

Valerie Amos and Pratibha Parmar

The family, rightly, has been the object of much debate in the women's movement and has been cited as one of the principle sites of women's oppression — women's role in reproducing the labour force, their supposed dependence on men and the construction of a female identity through notions of domesticity and motherhood have all been challenged. Indeed within that questioning there have been attempts to elevate domestic labour to the same level of analysis as the Marxist analysis of the mode of production and the relations between capital and labour. The family and its role in the construction of a consensual ideology remains central to discussions of feminism. We would question however the ways in which white academics, particularly sociologists and anthropologists, have sought to define the role of Black women in the family.

Much work has already been done which shows the ways in which sociology, especially the sociology of 'ethnicity', pathologizes and problema-

Source: Amos, V. and Parmar, P. (1984) 'Challenging imperial feminism', *Feminist Review 17*, pp.9–11.

tizes the Black communities in Britain. Our concern here is the impact the above analyses have had on Euro-American contemporary feminist thought, particularly socialist feminists. Although it is true to say that some of these feminists have distanced themselves from the crude stereotyping common in such analyses, some stereotypes do stick and they are invariably linked to colonial and historical interpretations of the Black woman's role. The image is of the passive Asian woman subject to oppressive practices within the Asian family with an emphasis on wanting to 'help' Asian women liberate themselves from their role. Or there is the strong, dominant Afro-Caribbean woman, the head of the household who despite her 'strength' is exploited by the 'sexism' which is seen as being a strong feature in relationships between Afro-Caribbean men and women. So although the crude translation of theories of ethnicity which have become part and parcel of the nation's common sense image of Black people ... may not be accepted by many white feminists, they are influenced by the ideas and nowhere is this more apparent than in debates about the family, where there has certainly been a failure to challenge particular pathological ideas about the Black family. There is little or no engagement by white feminists with the contradictions which constitute and shape our role as women in a family context, as sisters, aunts or daughters. ... It is Black women who have sought to look critically at the family, its strengths and weaknesses, its advantages and disadvantages, its importance for certain women in class and race terms and all this is in the broader context of state harassment and oppression of Black people. ...

There are further considerations which shape the socialist feminist view of the Black family in Britain and these relate strongly to the politics of the British left, and their perception of colonial, neo-colonial and imperialist relations. There has been much debate in the Left about the ability of Third World countries to successfully achieve socialism without first coming fully into capitalist relations ... Within this framework the Black family is seen as a problem in terms of its ability to adapt to advanced capitalist life — it is seen as a force prohibiting 'development' — and this view has been informed by the broader political and social analysis of our countries of origin as backward, needing to emerge into the full force of capitalist expansion before overcoming their economic, social, political and cultural 'underdevelopment'. ...

White feminists have fallen into the trap of measuring the Black female experience against their own, labelling it as in some way lacking, then looking for ways in which it might be possible to harness the Black women's experience to their own. Comparisons are made with our countries of origin which are said to fundamentally exploit Black women. The hysteria in the western women's movement surrounding issues like arranged marriages, purdah, female headed households, is often beyond the Black woman's comprehension — being tied to so called feminist notions of what constitutes good or bad practice in our communities in Britain or the Third World.

In rejecting such analyses we would hope to locate the Black family more firmly in the historical experiences of Black people — not in the romantic

idealized forms popular with some social anthropologists, and not merely
as a tool of analysis. There are serious questions about who has written
that history and in what form, questions which have to be addressed
before we as Black people use that history as an additional element of our
analysis. Black women cannot just throw away their experiences of living
in certain types of household organization; they want to use that experience to transform familial relationships. Stereotypes about the Black family have been used by the state to justify particular forms of oppression.
The issue of fostering and adoption of Black kids is current: Black families
are seen as being 'unfit' for fostering and adoption. Racist immigration
legislation has had the effect of separating family members, particularly of
the Asian community, but no longer is that legislation made legitimate just
by appeals to racist ideologies contained in notions of 'swamping'.
Attempts have actually been made by some feminists to justify such legislative practices on the basis of protecting Asian girls from the 'horrors' of
the arranged marriage system. White feminists beware — your unques-
tioning and racist assumptions about the Black family, your critical but
uninformed approach to 'Black culture' has found root and in fact informs
state practice.

READING D   WOMEN AND TECHNOLOGY

Cynthia Cockburn

The relations of technology and technological careers are profoundly gendered. In turn they gender the relations of work. A man takes on a manly
persona by grappling with machinery — and with the social 'machinery'
of the firm. A woman takes on a feminine one precisely by being technically incompetent. For a woman to aspire to technical competence is, in a
very real sense, to transgress the rules of gender. This is fully understood
by everyone, male and female. The social sanctions for flouting gender
rules may be informal but they are persistent and painful.

The overwhelming impression generated by the men in interview, from
the hands-on fitter/welder to the conceptual professional engineer, is one
of an energetic commitment to their occupation, to their own know-how
and competence and career. This is in part because the occupation is
intrinsically interesting, in contrast to much 'women's work'. And it is
partly because their freedom from childcare and housework sets them at
liberty to become absorbed in the relations of paid work. The effect is the
development of a masculine technological culture that sustains and
rewards men and constructs them as different from women and superior
to them. ...

Men in technical jobs are characteristically part of a team, a maintenance
workshop perhaps, or a design and development outfit. The team is a
social clique as well as a working group of colleagues. It involves

Source: Cockburn, C. (1986) 'Women and technology: opportunity is not enough',
in Purcell, K. *et al.* (eds) *The Changing Experience of Employment,* London, Macmillan, pp.184–7.

camaraderie, rivalry, humour and much talk about technology, technical problems and technical solutions. In some situations the competitive nature of capitalist business adds a zest and an overdrive to these masculine relationships. Some men don't survive in this environment, of course. Some go to the wall, some have coronaries. Skilled work is not free from worries about redundancy. But those who stay the pace have a relatively secure status in their own eyes and those of other men.

No ordinary woman with a ordinary woman's values and preoccupations can join this masculine club, fit in and survive there. It is only a woman who is prepared to sacrifice or greatly attenuate her female identity and those responsibilities normally designated as hers who can do so. For these jobs are not neutral, waiting innocently to be filled by either men or women. They are deeply into partitioned gendered terrain. ...

Most of the women interviewed in the course of the research were far lower down the scale of pay and 'skill' than the men. Many were, in the conventional way, self-deprecating about their technical abilities. But some expressed self-respect and an interest in 'machinery'. A few expressed irritation that they were prevented from doing and learning more, an appetite for technical competence that they felt they had been deprived of. Again, while some women, for obvious reasons, subordinated work to domestic responsibilities, there were plenty of others who were plainly committed to a life of work and achievement. On the other hand there was not one who deluded herself that the technological sphere could be entered by a woman without paying high costs.

Men's interactions with each other, the things they say about their jobs and about women, in women's hearing, make it clear that a woman is caught in a contradiction. If she is technically competent she may well feel herself empowered and be pleased by the power. But she will be considered unfeminine and unlovable, and that will hurt. She will be resented by men, and by some women. If she is technically incompetent, on the other hand, she will be personally handicapped as most women are. And though she will fit men's ideal for women she will also find herself scorned for it. 'Womendrivers!'.

It is not surprising then that the great majority of women, the absent thousands, do not set themselves on the technological course of training and work. What this research suggests is that women are not misguided, ill-informed or simply 'don't know what's good for them', as men so often propose. They may be consciously refusing a course of action that seems likely in present circumstances to waste their energies, prove a false start and finally fail to deliver what it promises. ... Women may be, in a sense, boycotting technology.

The concept of a 'sexual division of labour' is a relatively simple one. It refers to the bare fact that men and women tend to do different forms of work. To say that occupations are gendered is much more informative for it evokes the processes and relationships of power. It hints at how the sexual division of labour is reproduced over time. It is of interest to employers in keeping down the wage bill and in dividing the workforce against itself. But it is of interest also to men, who both secure, on average, better paid and more interesting jobs at the expense of women and also have the ability to build technical competence into one among the many superiorities they hold over women. If this is what keeps women in 'their place' and deprives them of equal earnings and equality of skills then it is the gendering of work and technology that have to be melted away. Perhaps even the cultural dichotomy of masculine and feminine has to be seen as impeding equality. ...

Equal opportunity to take up technological training and work will mean little more than the 'masculinizing' of a handful of women unless more profound changes occur at the same time. We have to uncouple gender from occupation. But more than that, we have to change the relationship between paid work and unpaid work, work and home. It is only bringing men more fully into responsibility for domestic life, making it an expectation that all workers of whatever sex give time and energy to both spheres, that will turn gendered terrain into common human ground.

CHAPTER 2 WOMEN AND THE DOMESTIC SPHERE

Helen Crowley

CONTENTS

1   INTRODUCTION

In the previous chapter Harriet Bradley analysed recent changes in gender and class relations. In terms of gender, these changes have been dramatic in many respects. Women now make up half the workforce and the span of their working lives contrasts with the greatly reduced time spent in caring for children in the home. Women with dependants are less reliant on the male wage and more directly supported by their own wages and state benefits. Marriage and the family have been transformed by changes in the law, by women's increased participation in the labour force, and by the extension of state welfare provision. Relations between women and men have been recast by these changes, particularly in so far as the balance of women's dependency on men has shifted. They have also been influenced by the emergence of the women's movement which challenged women's socially subordinate position within the domestic sphere, and demanded women's rights to independence and sexual equality.

Paradoxically, however, in spite of these changes, the position of women within the domestic sphere remains, in many respects, unaltered. Women continue to be responsible for the primary care of children and the private care of vulnerable adults such as the sick, the elderly, and the mentally and physically disabled. Women also continue to undertake the domestic servicing of able-bodied men, as well as the majority of tasks associated with the domestic maintenance of families and family life.

The aim of this chapter is to consider these continuities and discontinuities in the position of women, focusing in particular on the social and psychological processes that constitute women as primary carers. Within sociology, the place of women as primary carers is conventionally understood as an offshoot of the sexual division of labour, which is seen as naturally allocating nurturance and child care to women. The merits of this position, along with some closely aligned feminist conceptualizations of the sexual division of labour, will be considered in the latter part of this introductory section. Following this preliminary discussion, Section 2 will outline some of the changing patterns of family and household organization in the UK in the last fifty years, tracing the shifting balance between women's reproductive work in the domestic sphere and their economic activity in the labour force. The final section will consider some of the theoretical issues raised by conceptualizing the sexual division of labour as a social, and not biological, natural, or even patriarchal division.

1.1   THE SEXUAL DIVISION OF LABOUR

In the process of slow but profound social change traced by the emergence of the modern social formation out of the pre-industrial, agrarian society it replaced, the lines of demarcation between the work undertaken by women and the work undertaken by men were drawn and redrawn, and gradually emerged in a division of the social world into public and private spheres, with women's work being firmly positioned in the latter. One of the dominant explanations for the positioning of women in the private sphere of the family and men in the public sphere of work and polity was, and remains, that women are naturally suited to mothering and caring.

This idea of a natural sexual division of labour is a very powerful one, not least because we take the categories of women and men as self-evident. They are seen as biological categories, and biological difference is accepted as the guarantee of the naturalness of women and men. However, the idea that biology underwrites the unambiguous authenticity of womanliness and manliness is itself a historical one (and will be considered in more detail in Chapter 5). Far from being an absolute, biological difference is represented differently in different cultures, and in different historical periods within a culture.

The idea that women's reproductive biology casts them naturally and exclusively as mothers whose 'true sphere' is in a separate social domain is also historically specific. It might seem difficult to reconcile this idea of a natural sphere for women with 'modernity', since the idea of raising children as a purely natural activity sits uneasily with the grander Enlightenment claims of reason, progress, and the scientific domination of nature. However, historically, this dissonance was muted by the division of social life into 'public' and 'private', with all things intuitive and natural falling to women in the private sphere. Once these divisions were culturally consolidated, the link between gender (femininity) and sex (female) came to appear as both indissoluble and natural, thereby ultimately guaranteeing the social order as itself natural. Consequently, accepting sexual difference as natural and self-evident has led to acceptance of the social forms that sexual divisions take as themselves having a certain kind of inevitability.

Although mainstream sociology has directed attention to the historical and social circumstances of the divisions between men's tasks and spheres and those of women, it is presumed, rather than argued, that there is a natural association between women and mothering and caring. Sociology has analysed a wide range of institutional aspects of the family, including the organization of the household economy, the consumption, work and leisure activities of women and men, intersexual relations and intrafamily dynamics. However, woman's place in the family — a factor which links these different facets of the family together — has been assumed to be 'given' and not to require a sociological explanation. Thus Durkheim, for example, noted that while 'man is almost entirely the product of society', woman is 'to a far greater extent the product of nature' (Durkheim, 1952, p.385). Such an ideology not only makes women's labour in the private sphere appear to be natural, it also strips it of its status as *labour*, because women's work in the family is separated from the public domain of waged work. Consequently, a polarized view of the division between women and men has emerged as a division between non-work and work, and between the natural and the social.

Against such naturalistic conceptions of the sexual division of labour, some feminists have argued that the division between the public and private domains is a gendered structure in which women and men come to be identified with different social places, different values, and different activities and characteristics. This occurs through political and economic practices, as well as through those cultural and ideological systems which represent the social as naturally divided. These divisions between the public and private domains, and the work of women and men, are specific to modernity and mark the boundaries between historically specific forms of masculinity and femininity, and between different kinds of individuality. The public and the private have come to represent different values — rationalization, contract, and egalitarianism as counterposed to emotionality, bonding and difference; and different kinds of activities — productive work and rational calculation in the public sphere, and reproductive caring and intuitive empathy in the private sphere (Pateman, 1989).

However, this polarization of women's work in the home and men's in the workforce has obscured the more complex parameters of the modern socio-sexual, or gendered division of labour, in which women combine *two* kinds of labour which broadly can be defined as productive and reproductive labour. Both women and men undertake wage-earning activities, in addition to which women perform unwaged reproductive labour in the care of the young and dependent adults. In other words, the division between the work of women and men is asymmetrical, not symmetrical, and involves women combining productive and reproductive labour across the public/private divide.

The engendered separation of home and work, and the asymmetrical nature of the sexual division of labour, have constituted the position of women as economically subordinate and culturally inferior to that of men. Whilst traditional sociology was content to analyse this situation under the rubrics of the family, marriage and the *sexual* division of labour, feminist sociology has problematized it in the conceptual language of power, the *gendered* division of labour and patriarchy.

However, many feminist analyses which use patriarchy to explain the position of women tend not to question the fact that women *are* mothers and carers, and concentrate instead on the circumstances in which women perform these activities. Caroline Ramazanoglu, for example, argues that:

> Motherhood and childcare remain contradictory experiences for the majority of the world's women — an unparalleled experience of creativity, an area of limited control over their bodies for most, and a direct connection to economic and political subordination. Pregnancy and breastfeeding provide some restrictions on economic activity, but these natural functions cannot account for

the social mechanisms by which women are very generally
restricted to their roles as mothers, or potential mothers, or as
motherly people, in relation to dominant males.
(Ramazanoglu, 1989)

Here a distinction is made between women's natural functions and the
social mechanisms of male power. However, what is foregrounded in
this account are the natural functions of mothering ('pregnancy and
breastfeeding'); what is eclipsed are the social determinants of the
labour of mothering, what is entailed in this activity and how it is that
women come to mother. In this version of patriarchy, women's social
position is explained as the outcome of male power, so that, once again,
social and historical processes are reduced to the effects of biological
(i.e. natural) differences (female/male).

Sylvia Walby gives perhaps the most detailed social account of
patriarchy as an integrated system which socially subordinates women
(see Chapter 1, Section 2.1). Walby identifies women's position within
the family as a subjugated one involving the exploitation of women by
men. She argues, however, that the family no longer represents the
primary site of patriarchal domination which has shifted to the public
domains of the state and the economy. The patriarchal closure of the
labour market to women's equal participation as wage labourers is
identified by Walby as the most significant determinant of women's
continuing oppression within the family, and one which entraps women
within both public and private patriarchy. For Walby, patriarchy
operates in different sites — the family, economy, state, sexuality, male
violence, and cultural institutions which make up 'the system of social
structures and practices, in which men dominate, oppress and exploit
women' (Walby, 1990, p.20).

However, whilst Walby gives a detailed analysis of the social
mechanisms which restrict women, ultimately she understands these
mechanisms as the product of male power. There are two difficulties
with this. The notion of male power is an essentialist one; that is, it is
one which assumes that there is something in maleness as such which
determines this position of power. What this essence is, is unexplained;
nevertheless, patriarchy is characterized as a social system which is
controlled by men. However, not all men identify with this power, nor
are all men committed to ensuring that women's social subordination be
maintained. The other difficulty is that 'men' cannot be abstracted as a
homogeneous social group because of the intersections of gender, race,
class and sexuality which shape their identities differently. Social
systems *constitute* women and men as social subjects, as feminine and
masculine; these systems are not the *product* of individuals or a
particular group of individuals, i.e. men.

So the problem with the patriarchal explanation of women's position is
that it forecloses the question of how relations between women and
men are socially constituted. It does not fully address the issue of how
human reproduction is socially organized and controlled; for example,

how it affects and is affected by such factors as economic production. Women's fertility is constituted in part by forms of economic organization, as is the allocation of reproductive labour, and relations between women and men, women and women, and men and men. In other words human reproduction, intersexual relations and reproductive labour as well as productive labour are all social activities determined by historically specific forms of social organization. If women's reproductive labour is thus constituted, then the parameters of the issue go far beyond that of intersexual relations and male power (patriarchy). Most obviously it means that the position of women within the family casts women in a relationship to those *social* mechanisms and processes which give rise to particular forms of the family and gendered labour divisions. This is not first and foremost a relationship between women and men, but between women and 'society' or between women and the social, political and cultural institutions and processes which produce gendered labour divisions and construct intersexual relations.

Walby's account of patriarchy clearly shows how in modern societies these institutions are dominated by men and how women have politically engaged with that institutional power. But I am suggesting that the sociological parameters of engendered relations of reproduction are more important than those given by theories of patriarchy. They provide a wider framework in which to think about both the complex processes involved and the question of social change.

In this chapter we will consider the argument that gendered divisions of labour are neither natural, nor patriarchal, but *social.* They are a necessary and inevitable feature of all societies in much the same way as are production, politics and culture. By this I mean that all societies have to incorporate ways of caring for successive generations, and providing for vulnerable adults and children. Although these activities are qualitatively different from those involving material survival, they are no less necessary. Gendered labour divisions represent the way in which mothering and caring are allocated (historically but not inevitably) to women, and the way in which women combine this with economic activity. Relations of reproduction are very wide-ranging. They encompass relations between women and men, between wealth production and distribution, between cultural values and sexual identities, between the regulation of sexuality and generational renewal, between political power and individual rights, between parents and children, home and work, and even between life and death — things which make up much of the substance of social existence. These relations are not separate, as the ideology of the public/private division would have it. Rather, they are relations to which production and politics are integral. Nor are they subordinate; for how could it be that 'caring' is less important than 'work'? From this viewpoint, then, the social becomes integrated and continuous, and women belong as fully and centrally to it as men. In considering, in what follows, the modes of organization and changes that have occurred in gendered divisions of labour, it will, I hope, become even clearer just how *socially determined*

and *integrated* these relations are, and therefore how much more
encompassing our concept of 'society' must be.

2   CHANGES WITHIN THE FAMILY

Changes in the latter half of this century clearly illustrate the integrated
nature of women's work and the domestic dimensions of economic and
political life. During the Second World War, when women were
required to 'man' industry, the restraint that domestic responsibilities
placed on women's participation in the labour force became fully
apparent. Women needed to be mobilized as *the* workforce and the War
Ministry had to devise ways of releasing women from the family to
become 'free labourers', that is, to be able to sell their labour
unhindered by domestic responsibilities. Accordingly, during the war
years a comprehensive infrastructure of nursery provision was
developed to release women for war-time production. However, this
changed after the war, and in this section I want to look at the way in
which the gendered division of labour was *re-established* through the
policies of post-war welfarism. Then I will outline some of the changes
that developed out of the post-war settlement and their impact on
women and the family.

2.1   THE POST-WAR SETTLEMENT

At the end of the war, the gender division of labour both in the family
and the labour force broadly returned to the pre-war status quo. By
1947, there were as many women in the workforce, including married
women, as there would have been if pre-war trends had been
uninterrupted by the war. In that same year, however, the Ministry of
Labour launched a campaign to recruit more married women in an
attempt to alleviate post-war labour shortages. As part of this campaign,
a survey of married women was undertaken to establish women's
attitudes to returning to work. The report, *Women and Industry* (1947),
concluded that married women from lower income groups had already
been absorbed back into the workforce to a high degree and that, for
women from higher income groups, waged work remained an
unattractive proposition because of the lack of nursery provision, low
wages, and long hours (Riley, 1983, p.144).

Denise Riley has pointed out that the motives and reasons for women
surrendering their status as full-time workers were complex and varied.
The more conservative explanation — that women *wanted* to return to
their rightful place as mothers and homemakers — was, she has argued,
as unsatisfactory as the idea that they were forced back into the home
(Riley, 1983). In fact, the numbers of married women in the labour force
steadily increased in the post-war period. By 1951, 30 per cent of all
married women were in paid employment (Kiernan and Wicks, 1990),

signifying a shift in the balance between women's waged and unwaged work.

Paralleling women's increased participation in the labour force was the decrease in family size. Following the brief post-war baby boom, the average family size settled at 2.93 (Titmuss, 1963). The post-war economic boom and the change in life-style and consumption patterns gave the domestic sphere a new focus (see Chapter 3). In the immediate post-war period, however, the family was identified not in terms of changing patterns of domestic relations and leisure activity but in terms of the iconography of the mother and child. This represented a widespread social preoccupation with reconstituting the domestic domain as a place of nurture and security for children.

The backdrop to this preoccupation was the pronatalist concern about the falling birth-rate at the end of the depression in the 1930s. These worries proved to be unfounded — the birth-rate increased from 1941 — but much energy went into developing pronatalist policies during the 1940s and 1950s. Behind these policies lay a dramatic transformation in women's fertility. In the late 1890s, the average working-class woman experienced ten pregnancies and spent over fifteen years in nursing small children. A little over fifty years later, the time spent nursing was reduced to approximately four years.

The other significant development in the position of women was the mass exodus from domestic service and the absorption of women

A family in Greenwich, 1914

workers into the new light manufacturing sector. These changes in women's productive and reproductive labour provide the context of post-war welfarism. Although the social agenda of the post-war Labour government acknowledged the shifting pattern of women's family and economic activities, the execution of that agenda enshrined an ideal family form of dependent wife and mother and male wage-earner as both normative and unchanging.

In 1945, the long-standing tradition of the state rejecting the idea that it had any economic obligation towards women with children was broken with the introduction of the Family Allowance. Given to the mother on the birth of the second child, the allowance established a principle of direct benefit payment to women as mothers. Both Titmuss and Beveridge maintained that the allowance was not to encourage motherhood but to alleviate poverty. Indeed, many of the progressive advocates of pronatalism insisted that family planning was an important element in their social philosophy.

As Denise Riley noted in Chapter 4 of Book 2 (Allen *et al.*, 1992), Beveridge's 1942 Report dignified mothers with the status of worker. Mothers were not only 'promoted' by the Report, they were also identified as crucially necessary workers, whose mothering skills post-war welfarism was keen to support. Just how important this work was, was confirmed by the work of the psychoanalyst John Bowlby and his advocacy of early maternal bonding as the basis of individual and social well-being. Bowlby's 'maternal deprivation' arguments, which achieved great popularity, further underscored the importance of women's mothering.

This pronatalist policy-shift represented a commitment to improving the position of the family and the conditions of motherhood. Family planning, family allowance, public recognition of the work of mothers and of the importance of maternal love became the vehicles of this commitment. However these family policies were in effect concerned to support and secure women's role as mothers. As Elizabeth Wilson has argued, this attention to motherhood and the official definitions of femininity that accompanied it were 'central to the purposes of welfarism' and offered 'a unique demonstration of how the state can prescribe what woman's consciousness should be' (Wilson, 1977, p.7). The welfare state, in other words, was structuring not just the conditions of motherhood but women's identity as mothers. Motherhood was defined as a labour of love, private and unpaid, although socially supported and recognized.

Beveridge's acclaim of motherhood as the woman's 'job' sat uneasily with the dominant idea of the family as the private sanctuary from the travails of working life. However, Beveridge's commitment to this notion of mothers as workers did not extend to their inclusion in the insurance system as workers in their own right. The fact that many working-class women were workers as well as mothers had necessarily to be ignored by a pronatalist stance that was preoccupied with a conception of motherhood as an activity which excluded all others.

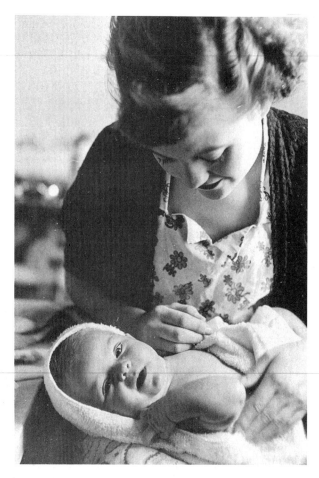

The iconography of
mother and child

Juliet Mitchell has noted that this ideology of 'the mother' and 'the
family' left most women in a difficult position:

> ... the decade and more following the war was above all the
> decade of the child. It is doubtful whether praise of the patriarchal
> family has ever, since its hey-day in the mid-nineteenth century,
> been as rampant as in the years of the cold war. ... in an effort to
> rebuild the family the equation went: delinquent=latch-key
> child=having been abandoned by its mother in infancy to creche or
> evacuation. From now onwards appeals to maternal guilt vied with
> the political exploitation of the economic situation to keep women
> at home. At least, at home in mind even if the mass of working-
> class mothers still in body had to go out to a job at half-pay.
> (Mitchell, 1974, p.228)

This illustrates the contradictory nature of social and economic policy
in respect of women and gendered labour divisions. Whereas the
Ministry of Labour attempted to recruit women, welfare legislation was
directed at securing women's position firmly in the family. The
contradiction faced by women themselves in combining productive and

reproductive labour was denied by post-war welfarism. Moreover, the dominant ideal of motherhood exacerbated the difficulties of this contradictory reality. The 'maternal deprivation' thesis was preoccupied with the needs of small children and it offered a version of motherhood which found the fulfilment of these needs entirely unproblematic. To again quote Elizabeth Wilson:

> Critics of Bowlby have never denied that babies — and children and adults — need warm, continuing relationships and that affection is essential in the context both of long term sexual and child-rearing relationships. What has caused disagreement is his picture of a stifling and possessive love, and the narrowly defined role of woman as mother.
> (Wilson, 1977, p.65)

The concern about maternal deprivation marked a significant shift in cultural perception in recognizing the emotional and psychological needs of children. However, these radical insights, which originally stressed the importance of affective bonding by a mother, *or* mother substitute, were deflected to fit with, and to rearticulate, the ideology of *natural* motherhood.

The policies implemented in the immediate post-war period mobilized the idea of the unitary family. The ideology of natural mothering directed attention away from the reality faced by women in the domestic sphere towards what Denise Riley has called 'the maternal function'. This failure to consider seriously the actual conditions constituting familial relations, the composition of households, the relation between the productive and reproductive labour of women, and the cast this gave to relations between women and men, had the immediate effect of reaffirming traditional conventions of the family and the private sphere.

This ideal family wanted for little in the way of strategic planning. However, developments undreamt of by the advocates of post-war pronatalism were to occur which radically restructured familial and intersexual relations and the public/private divide. The massive increase in married women entering the labour force, the changing status of marriage, the further reduction in family size, and the dramatic increase in lone-parent families were simply not entertained in the complacent, if well-meaning view, of 'the family' which informed the post-war settlement.

The agencies and policy makers of the post-war government had supported a family which was thought to be unchanging. In fact, different and conflicting demands were being made on the productive and reproductive labour of women. The changes which developed as a result of this will be considered in the next section. I aim to show how these changes can only be properly measured if the gendered division of labour is seen as a *social division* subject to the same forces as other dimensions of social life.

2.2   FAMILY DIVERSIFICATION: THE MYTH OF THE MALE BREADWINNER

In 1982 a major sociological study of families concluded that:

> Families in Britain today are in a transition from coping in a
> society in which there was a single overriding norm of what family
> life should be like to a society in which a plurality of norms are
> recognised as legitimate and, indeed, desirable.
> (Rapoport and Rapoport, 1982, p.476)

Notwithstanding attempts in the 1980s to reaffirm traditional family
values, it is now recognized that the male family wage no longer
accounts for the majority of household economies, and this has directed
attention to the vulnerability of women as productive and reproductive
labourers. The increase in married women's participation in the labour
force was initially trivialized as being motivated by the need for 'pin
money'. It is now clear, however, that the number of families in poverty
would increase by a third if women were not working (Lister, 1984). In
1990, more than half of all married couples with children were dual
worker families. These figures seriously challenge the idea that families
are provided for by the male family wage, and in fact 'a breadwinning
husband with a non-working wife at home with two dependent children
accounts for a mere eight per cent of all working men' (Henwood *et
al.*,1987). The 'normative family' is a statistical minority.

The influx of married women into the workforce has dramatically
expanded the numbers of part-time workers and altered the structure of
the labour market. Women's responsibility for children continues to
influence their ability to compete for full-time jobs (see Figure 2.1). The
logistics of juggling child care and work are an important determinant
of the working lives of mothers, often necessitating that women first
have to pay for child care before they themselves can work. State-
provided child care is minimal and Britain has one of the lowest levels
in Europe, accommodating only 2 per cent of the 0–2 age group. Most
working mothers rely on relatives or childminders to care for their
children. Registered childminders represent one of the lowest paid
sectors of the female workforce but, notwithstanding this, their numbers
increased by 60 per cent between 1975 and 1985. The UK Report on
Children for the European Commission found that it was predominantly
women who paid for child care and argued that: 'In the absence of
adequate public funding, women's low wages cannot sustain a
satisfactory structure of provision' (Cohen, 1988, p.4).

In an Equal Opportunities Commission Report published in 1986, Robin
Simpson estimated that the overall annual cost of child care provision
which would be necessary to enable women to compete equally with
men in the labour market was approximately two billion pounds. This
figure represented less than the then current married man's tax
allowance (approximately £2.6 billion), or an average increase of two

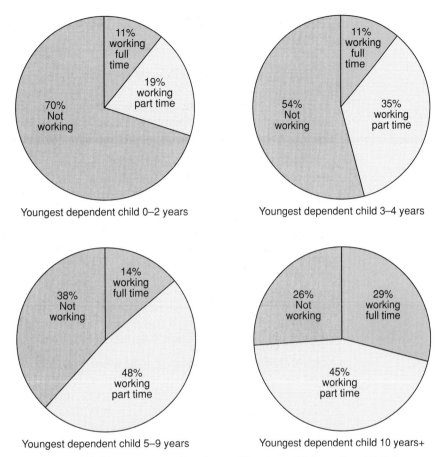

Figure 2.1   Working patterns of mothers with young children, Great Britain, 1987
Source: Kiernan and Wicks, 1990, based on Office of Population Censuses and Surveys, 1989

pence in the basic rate of taxation. This illustrates the politics of resource allocation entailed in fiscal expenditure, and the conflict of interests masked by ideas about 'the family'. It also illustrates how government policies structure the gender division of labour and women's position within the family.

The accepted definition of work is that it is waged labour in the formal economy. This renders women's work in the home as an economically marginal activity. It has been estimated, however, that working women with children work an average 77 hour week, and this, together with other caring responsibilities, would constitute a major drain on economic resources if these activities were carried out in the public sphere and paid from public funds. The ideological distinction between work and non-work derives its rationale not only from the power of the wage but also from the way in which 'women's work' is seen as being natural. This raises interesting conceptual issues, particularly around the question of how to theorize reproductive labour, to which we will return later in the chapter.

2.3   MARRIAGE AND DIVORCE: 'UNTIL DEATH US DO PART'

In 1969, the Divorce Reform Act went on to the statute books and initiated a process that not only altered the nature of families but also the relationship between marriage and the family. This coincided with changing demographic trends and together these brought about significant changes in household composition.

The Divorce Reform Act (1969) introduced irretrievable breakdown as grounds for legally ending a marriage. The initial effect of this legislation was dramatic and by the mid-1970s the number of divorces had increased, as compared with the mid-1950s, by 400 per cent. Initially, this sky-rocketing in the divorce rate led to an increase in the number of marriages. These 'reconstituted' families are often cited as evidence of the continuing popularity of marriage and family life. However, more recent statistics on the fate of these second marriages suggest that they are more likely to dissolve than first marriages. Figures also suggest that the rate of remarriage slowed down in the 1980s, although one explanation for this is that many families are re-formed through cohabitation rather than marriage.

This new flexibility within marriage has resulted in over a third of all marriages ending in divorce, with one in five children experiencing parental divorce by the age of 16. It is anticipated that this trend will grow, and that by the turn of the century only 50 per cent of children will experience 'conventional family life'. Most divorce cases are initiated by women and, for most women, divorce leads to relative impoverishment. Given the opportunity to live outside marriage, many women have found relative impoverishment preferable to remaining within marriage. In a survey of lone-parent families, Hilary Graham found that many women said they felt themselves to be economically better off because they were able to manage and control their own finances. Lone parenthood thus appears to represent greater poverty in the context of greater economic power; fewer resources but increased access to them. It is this complex equation that appears to lie behind mothers' assessment of themselves as 'better off poorer' (Graham, 1987, p.235).

As you can see from Figure 2.2, the largest category of lone mothers are such by virtue of divorce. It is worth remembering that many of the women in this category will remarry, but also the greatest increase in single mothers has been of unmarried mothers. This figure too has to be treated with caution because it in part reflects another trend towards cohabitation. Cohabitation before marriage has become 'virtually the norm', lasting for an average of three years (Rapoport and Rapoport, 1982). This 'norm' must be distinguished from a separate development, which is that more and more couples are having children outside marriage. In 1988, the 'extra marital birth ratio' was 25 per cent, although seven out of ten of all joint-registered births (that is, births registered by unmarried couples) give the parents as co-residents.

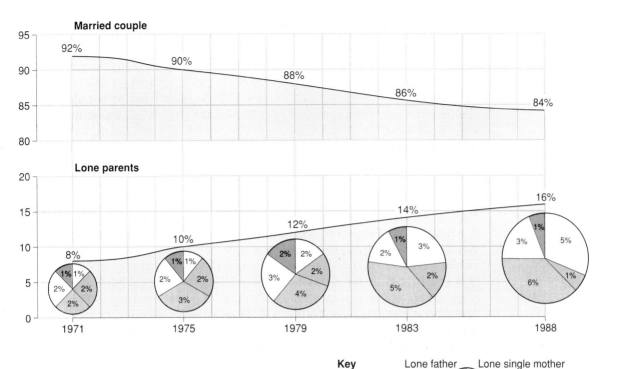

Figure 2.2   Families with dependent children, by type and, for lone mothers, by marital status, 1971-1988
Source: Kiernan and Wicks, 1990, based on Office of Population Censuses and Surveys, 1990

The number of lone-parent families now stands at one in seven of all families, and the majority of these are headed by women. Nearly two-thirds of lone-parent families live in poverty and most are dependent on social security benefits as their main source of income. In addition to their susceptibility to poverty, most of these families live in rented accommodation and are vulnerable to homelessness. Indeed, lone-parent families make up 40 per cent of the homeless accepted by local authorities, three times the proportion they represent in the community — 14 per cent (Greve, 1990).

These changes in forms of households have not altered women's responsibility for dependent members within families. However, the dimensions of that responsibility have changed because of alterations in demographic patterns, women's fertility patterns and the changing economic circumstances of young adulthood.

2.4   THE LIFE-CYCLE OF DEPENDENCE

Whilst there has been a steady reduction in family size, there has also been a parallel extension of children's dependence on families. State benefits for the 16–18 year-old age group have been restricted, thus reaffirming, particularly in times of high unemployment, the economic responsibility of families. However, the number of 18-year olds released on to the labour market has shown an unusual decline. This has been brought about by changes in women's fertility patterns. Many women now choose to establish their working career before having children and the effects of the new-found control over their fertility has produced a demographic downturn, and a distortion in anticipated labour supply. In turn, this labour shortage has created a greater demand for married women to re-enter the labour market. On the other hand, many of the married women potentially available for work are themselves facing new demands from another demographic development — the tendency for people to live longer.

Care of the elderly and the disabled is predominantly provided within the family. The General Household Survey of carers (Green, 1988) found that six million adults are engaged in what is somewhat euphemistically called 'community care'. Of these, the majority of whom are women, about half spend more than 50 hours a week providing for adult care. The over-65 age group has practically doubled since 1951, and in 1987 was over eleven million. The care of the elderly involves an immense amount of work for women and, for many, these additional demands on their labour prove impossible. In her study of family obligations, Janet Finch concluded that: 'Support between kin *is* important to many people in contemporary Britain, but it does not operate to the kind of fixed rules implied by the idea that caring is "naturally" part of family relationships' (Finch, 1989, p.240). If a growing number of women, for whatever reason, prove unable or unwilling to provide unwaged labour in the care of the elderly population, the economic consequences for state expenditure would be enormous. A recent Equal Opportunities Commission survey (1989) estimated that women's private care of vulnerable adults would cost approximately £24 billion pounds per year if provided in the public sector and out of public funds.

The combined effect of changes within marriage, cohabitation, divorce, family size, women's economic activity, types of family and demographic trends certainly seems to confirm the Rapoports' claim that Britain is in a period of transition from the normative family to a plurality of family forms. Change has occurred in the variety of families — nuclear, reconstituted, dual worker, single parent, cohabiting — and in the types of household (see Figure 2.3). By the year 2001, it is estimated that the number of one-person households will increase from 5.3 million to 7.1 million, and that the average household size will continue to decrease.

Change and diversification then cannot be denied, but the central axis of family life — the gender division of labour — remains in place. However, here too change has occurred in that women spend much less time caring for children and spend most of their working lives in wage labour, albeit part-time labour in the main. But, if the time spent caring for children has been reduced, the time spent caring for the elderly and infirm has increased, and will continue to do so. Thus the burden of care has shifted and women's waged labour continues to be influenced by the demands of their unwaged labour.

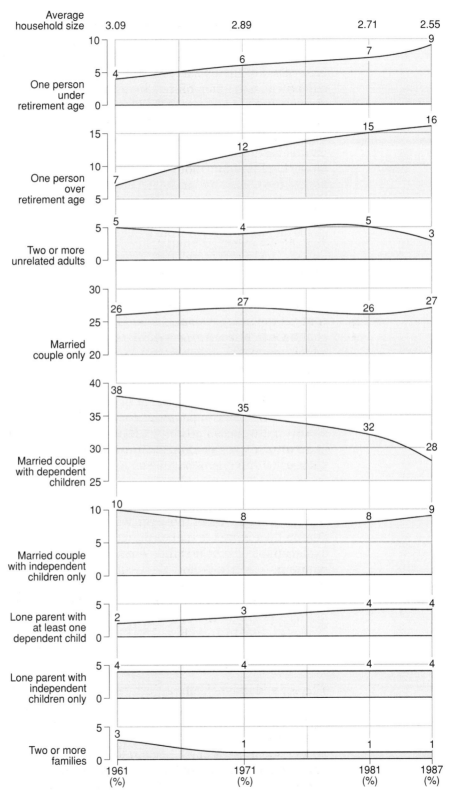

Figure 2.3   Households by type, shown as percentages, Great Britain 1961–1987
Source: Kiernan and Wicks, 1990, based on Central Statistical Office, 1989

One effect of these changes in family patterns, particularly the growth of lone-parent families, has been a massive increase in state expenditure on benefit provision. In the 1980s there was a major, but largely unsuccessful, attempt to reduce government spending on welfare. This attempted contraction of state involvement in family life was accompanied by appeals to the 'true' family values of economic independence and emotional autonomy. Ferdinand Mount, a neo-liberal theorist of the family, went so far as to suggest that 'the family' was a natural bastion of freedom and intrinsically opposed to state intervention of any kind (Mount, 1982). Contrary to Mount's conceptualization of the family, the history and changing character of the domestic sphere and women's position within it shows that it is constructed through a complex of economic, political and cultural processes which give it shape and meaning. Far from being the natural sphere of the free individual, the domestic domain is constituted through state regulation, economic practices, and cultural conventions which both structure and define gender divisions of labour, intersexual relations and women's relationship to reproductive and productive labour.

And yet the link between women, the domestic sphere and motherhood continues to be seen as a natural one, in spite of the political edifice which organizes mothering and caring and in spite of the variety of economic circumstances through which it supports these activities. This raises the question of the enormous durability of this ideology of naturalism as the cultural idiom or language in which these social processes continue to be understood. What is it about the domestic sphere and women's position within it, that so lends itself to such naturalistic explanations? And in what ways, if any, have the radical changes within domestic life come into conflict with such naturalist discourses?

These questions are taken up in the next section, which examines some theoretical accounts of these processes, starting with the state. The section then moves on to considerations of the domestic sphere and explanations of how it is that women occupy such a significant place within it.

3   WOMEN AND THE FAMILY: SOME THEORETICAL ISSUES

This section will consider several related theoretical issues which throw light on and help to explain both the changing patterns just identified and the persistence of the link between women, femininity and the family. First, we will attempt to explain the changes in state/family relations and in the shifting balance between reproductive labour and waged productive activity. Secondly, we will examine the different ways in which the link between women, the construction of femininity and the domestic sphere has been conceptualized. In discussing the

theoretical problems raised by these issues the central claim of this
chapter — that gendered labour divisions are produced through the
social organization of reproduction — will be developed further.

3.1   THE CHANGING STATE/FAMILY RELATION

What we saw in the previous section was the significant and clear
impact of welfare legislation on the family and women's place within it.
Uniquely of all the modern state forms, the welfare state concerns itself
with the private realm of domesticity. Social policy controls the level
and type of the redistribution of resources to families through the
provision of support services in health care, child welfare services,
social security benefits, and public housing. Taxation allows for the
reallocation of resources across the competing sectors of welfare,
industry, and defence, and provides a mechanism for differentially
subsidizing women's and men's labour. Labour legislation as well as
equal opportunities and community programmes mediate the
relationship between women's waged and unwaged labour. State
educational and nursery provision influence the balance between
women's reproductive and productive labour. Family law defines and
enforces legal obligations within the family, and the rights of individual
family members. In all these areas gender divisions of labour are both
assumed by the state and transformed according to the particular
conception of the family sustained by the policies of the respective state
agencies.

Yet notwithstanding these interventions of the state (which lies at the
heart of the *public* sphere) the domestic domain retains its status as the
private sphere of social existence. What are the consequences of the
family's ambiguous position in this public/private division? How,
theoretically, can we explain it? Before discussing this further I want
you to read the first article accompanying this chapter.

ACTIVITY 1   You should now read **Reading A, 'The family: private arena or adjunct
of the state?'**, by Faith Robertson Elliot, which you will find at the end
of this chapter.

Whilst reading the article you should bear the following questions in
mind:

1   Why is the relationship between the family and the state 'not
straightforward', according to Elliot?

2   What is distinctive about the 'multidimensional' or pluralist-
feminist approach to explaining family/state relations?

In her critical overview of the different theoretical positions on the
family/state relationship, Elliot rejects the idea that the family is private
and separate from the state. On the other hand, she rejects the

suggestion that it is politically determined by either capitalist or patriarchal interests exercised through state power. Advocates of the family as a discrete and naturally distinctive institution (the first position) completely underestimate the role and significance of political intervention in shaping familial relations. Conversely, those theorists who emphasize the importance of state policies in structuring the family in the interests of either capitalism or patriarchy (the second position), fail to account for the shifting legal and political balances between women and men within families, and between families and state regulation and support of those families. Even though state intervention into the family has increased, ultimately such intervention is limited in the degree to which it can influence people's behaviour. Institutions other than the state have a role to play in shaping desires and aspirations. State policies are mediated by other factors, such as class, ethnicity and religion. Women are not helpless victims but respond to, struggle against and deflect the strategies of the state.

Against the idea that the private family is determined by a natural sexual division of labour, or produced by the public power of capitalism or patriarchy which construct an ideological divide between the public and private realms, Elliot considers less deterministic accounts of the family/state relationship. She concludes that a less monolithic conception of the state is preferable. The state is a complex and diverse institution, not a single instrument. It is composed of different agencies with their own histories and internal power relations. So the state influences which shape the domestic sphere are complex. Its multidimensional political processes are formed through the attempts of various competing interest groups, all seeking to influence the public contours of domestic life. Thus, state policies on the family cannot be seen as monolithic precisely because they are mediated by the concerns and responses of different groups, including feminist groups.

This pluralist-feminist approach to the family/state relationship acknowledges that the differing interest groups competing to influence state policy are not equally powerful, and that the state is in no way a 'neutral arbiter' between them. The state arbitrates according to strategic interests. But this is not a form of state power which can be exercised unilaterally, either by a single group or without consideration of the balance of forces that make up the political process. The question of the family and the state is not, therefore, a question of centralized control but of negotiated and shifting relations of power; and within this process feminism has a long history of intervention in the political construction of women's position within the family, as well as, of course, within the public domain.

The questions this leaves unanswered are: What has necessitated the relationship between the welfare state and the family in the first place? What is the nature of the state's 'domestic' policies? Why should the state have strategic interests in family life? Clearly all states are concerned with the relationship between the population and the economic resource base, both in terms of whether the resource base is large enough to support the population, and in terms of whether demographic trends meet the requirements of the economy. However, far from being simple and monolithic, these politically mediated interests of the state are complex and contradictory. In China, for example, where it is feared that population growth will exceed, in the very immediate future, the economic capacity of the country to sustain it, the state has attempted to implement — largely unsuccessfully — a policy of one child per family. This population policy reflects the impact on family life of strategic political decisions about the pace of China's economic expansion. It is these decisions which affect the resource base and in turn lead to birth control policies (Hillier, 1988). In the Soviet Union, by contrast, where the concern was with a contracting (Russian) population, Russian women were awarded the Order of Lenin if they had six children (Molyneux, 1985). Here, population was privileged over production. In the Eastern Bloc countries during the post-war period of rapid industrialization, women's labour, both as full-time workers and as mothers, was required; a situation which produced a level of public child care provision necessary to 'free' women as workers equal to men. However, when these demands on women's labour produced a radical drop in the birth rate, some socialist states withdrew women's legal right to abortion (Scott, 1974). In each of these instances political decisions attempted to affect the balance between women's productive and reproductive labour but the motivations for these interventions were different. Moreover, as Elliot points out, these strategic interventions have had limited success, not least because countervailing forces sometimes deflect or reverse them.

There is however another reason for the state's strategic interest in the private sphere. This arises out of the separation of reproductive labour from production and the attendant economic vulnerability of those caring for the young and the old which we discussed earlier (Section 2.4). For example, the liberalization of divorce law has created additional pressure on governments in all advanced industrial societies to provide benefits adequate to support single parents. In the United Kingdom, the spectrum of possible political responses to this situation can be measured by comparing the Finer Report published in 1974, which made 130 recommendations for the support of lone-parent families, including equal pay for women, with the most recent Government White Paper, *Children Come First*, which concentrates instead on setting up an agency to extract financial support from the absent parent — usually the father (cf. Finer Joint Action Committee, 1975 and Department of Social Security, 1990). Other kinds of interventions have been made in this area. For example, in a recent ruling the court decided that genetic fingerprinting can be used to establish paternity for the purposes of the mother gaining some financial support for the upbringing of the child. Clearly, then, the state has very different ways, in different periods, of ensuring the economic viability of families and the caring role of women in the family.

State policies can also have contradictory effects for women. The political economy of the gendered division of labour necessitates that women be supported in some way if they are to sustain the social requirements of mothering and caring. The family wage was one solution. Its failure is measured by women's growing economic activity. Public provision in the form of welfare is another means of support which is also inadequate — a fact confirmed by the historically consistent, and currently increasing, levels of poverty sustained by women. This 'feminization of poverty' reflects the contradictory relation between women as carers and workers, and the welfare state. The state wants both to support women as carers and to keep public expenditure low. Social policy would be a far greater proportion of public expenditure if women's unpaid labour were to be adequately recompensed from the public purse. In this sense the position of women as reproductive labourers lies at the heart of the structurally and politically contested domain of the distribution of social wealth.

3.2   CONCEPTUALIZING REPRODUCTIVE LABOUR

How then should we conceptualize the unpaid labour of women caring for the young as well as vulnerable adults in the private domestic sphere? The term 'reproductive labour' which I have used in this chapter was chosen because it indicates a continuum between women's waged and unwaged work. This continuum is disrupted by the structural and ideological division between the public and the private but, notwithstanding this, reproductive labour represents socially necessary labour which constitutes an *integral* part of the social division of labour, and gives rise to a form of redistribution outside the wage form.

ACTIVITY 2   Before reading further, stop and make a list some of the features which you associate with the 'private' character of domestic life.

Perhaps you noted the private domestic sphere as the domain of personal relations, those affective ties that bind us to particular people in a unique way. It is this area of emotionality and love, of caring and nurturance, which is seen as both quintessential to family life and beyond the imperatives of rational social organization. Emotional and sexual relations within private life are experienced as not dictated by public policy or economic necessity, as embracing personal desires and needs which are neither public nor necessarily rational. It is the private satisfaction of these needs and desires which shapes our domestic relations.

Affective relations however are not free-floating. Even when confined to the private sphere, they are grounded in the social conventions and practices of caring for people and being cared for which prevail in a particular culture. As Barrett and McIntosh (1982) have noted in their critique of the claim that the domestic sphere is a 'haven in a heartless world', the haven, for women, is actually a place of *work*. This is not to deny its significance in the emotional lives of women as well as children and men. The family is privileged over all other institutions, by both men and women, as the place where emotional and sexual needs can be expressed and met. However, to conceptualize the family as an area of women's *work* raises questions about its 'private' character and the extent to which it is a separate, discrete domain, since women's work spans the family and the workplace. If we conceptualize women's caring role as *labour*, then its relationship to other kinds of work quickly becomes apparent. But certain aspects of reproductive labour have resisted incorporation into the arena of public work and the processes of economic rationalization. Reproductive labour has never been fully drawn into the process of refinement and the specialization of tasks that has transformed the sphere of public production. What is it about the primary labour process of 'people production' (Murgatroyd, 1985) that leads inevitably to locating it in the domestic sphere? What prevents us defining reproductive labour as a non-gendered labour process like any other?

There are two aspects of domestic life that largely continue to resist incorporation into the rationalistic world of calculation and contract. These are (a) child care and (b) emotionally intimate personal and sexual relations between adults. Of course, these relationships are not exclusive to the domestic sphere. Child care is sometimes organized as a public service. Equally, the sex industry is an economic complex which trades internationally in emotions and desires as well as people, bodies and services. What is distinctive about domestic relations is that they privilege the individual, emotionally and psychologically, in terms of the uniqueness of her/his emotional needs. In terms of the care of children, what is distinctive is the process of socially integrating the developing person through affective care, which actually brings a unique self into being. In terms of personal adult relationships, it is the sexual, emotional, and psychic needs of the individual which are satisfied in intimate interpersonal relationships. Thus, what we call reproductive labour — the 'work' of producing and caring for these subjective personal needs — is socially necessary labour, in the sense that it is necessary and inevitable and has to be done in every society irrespective of who takes responsibility for it. However, because it is necessarily interpersonal it is therefore outside the scope of collective labour practices, and tends to be separated off into a distinct sphere of social activity — the private. The private sphere, then, is the sphere of the individual subject, grounded in and defined by her/his own personal subjective needs, desires and history. What remains to be explained is how and why this domain of the private or domestic world came to be exclusively associated with the labour of women.

3.3   THE LOGIC OF THE PRIVATE SPHERE

The linkage between women and the private sphere is explored by
Anna Yeatman in Reading B. Yeatman suggests that the way sociological
theory has analysed the individual as socially constructed from within
society is limited by the conventional view of socialization advanced by
the leading American sociological theorist of the 1940s and 1950s,
Talcott Parsons.

ACTIVITY 3   You should now read **Reading B, 'Women, domestic life and sociology'**,
by Anna Yeatman.

As you read, think about the following questions:

1   Can the private domain be separated from the 'gender division of
labour' (i.e. from the way the tasks of this domain are currently
divided between men and women)?

2   What questions would be raised by separating the private sphere
from the reproductive labour of women?

Yeatman begins by making two sets of propositions in her argument.
The first is that the project within sociology to understand the
individual as *socially* constituted is potentially one which contains the
promise of an adequate sociological account of the domestic sphere.
The second, however, is that in order to extend and develop this
theoretical ground and deliver this promise, sociological explanation
has largely proceeded as if gender divisions play no part in this process.
What she is suggesting is that, unless we analytically separate the
elements involved in the constitution of the individual subject — that
is, the process of the personality development of the individual subject
through the taking on of cultural values — from the way this process is
currently divided between men and women, then we risk reducing
these elements to a mere description of what women and men do within
the family and interpersonal relations. Such a description fits with the
prevailing relations in the domestic sphere. But it does not, Yeatman
argues, allow the analysis to go beyond this division to consider *the
necessity of the domestic sphere irrespective of the particular gender
relations which currently sustain it*. The assumption that the domestic
sphere and gender divisions are one and the same thing displaces the
question of whether domestic tasks can be shared in ways which are not
gender-defined as they are now. Ignoring this possibility is, in effect, to
make the current gender division of labour in the family a natural and
inevitable one.

Yeatman has several criticisms of the Parsonian account of socialization
within the family. First, Parsons gives a behaviourist account of the
mother's role in primary child care. He did not analyse that role either
socially or in terms of its unconscious motivations (see Section 3.4

below). Secondly, Parsons argues that women as wives and mothers provide the necessary emotional work to satisfy the needs of men and children. This undermines the more general argument that, since the individuated personality must be able to gain satisfaction of its emotional needs, there is no necessity, as Parsons would have it, for one type of person (women) always to provide for the needs of other types of person (children and men). Finally, Parsons' account of domestic relations fails to develop the idea that the private sphere is necessary to the structure of *all* modern societies because private interpersonal relations are an inevitable part of the formation of the socialized individual subject whatever her/his gender. Parsons collapses this independent necessity of the private sphere into a theory of the *normative* family which in turn rests on the assumption that it is only women who can naturally mother.

If we accept Yeatman's argument that the domestic sphere is a necessary dimension of modern social life but that the nuclear family is only one of the many historic family forms in which its tasks have been performed, it follows that different kinds of relationships could potentially exist within the domestic sphere. The nuclear heterosexual family is currently the preferred form in the domestic sphere but it is not the only one and is certainly not *intrinsic* to it. What is intrinsic, or necessary, to the private sphere is simply that it provides support for these particularistic needs and relationships. How this is organized within different family and domestic arrangements varies widely from one culture to another and from one historical period to another. Indeed, as we saw earlier in the chapter, empirically in the contemporary post-war period, the domestic sphere is increasingly diversified by different types of relationships. Yeatman's argument therefore tallies with Barrett and McIntosh's analysis of what they call 'the anti-social family' in which they argue that the normative nuclear family seriously limits the kinds of intimate interpersonal relationship which are now potentially possible (Barrett and McIntosh, 1982).

3.4   WOMEN'S MOTHERING

If the exclusive feminization of the role of women in mothering is central to the current dominant form of the nuclear family, but is neither necessary nor intrinsic to the process of individuation and socialization as such, then it still remains a problem to try to explain the position of women as mothers within the domestic sphere. Why does the domestic remain so fixedly 'gendered'? One possible answer to this question is that there is, in addition to the social division of labour which organizes this sphere, an *unconscious logic* to women's identification with motherhood. In other words the identification of women with the domestic and familial may have both social and psychological foundations.

This is an argument put forward by Juliet Mitchell, the feminist theorist and psychoanalyst, who mobilizes psychoanalytic theory to explain the tenacity of gender identity and women's desire to mother. Mitchell's account of psychoanalytic theory is influenced by the work of the French psychoanalyst Jacques Lacan (1901–81), who emphasized the significance of language and the symbolic realm in bringing the individuated subject into being. According to Lacan, the child only gradually learns to live in a world that is differentiated. For Lacan, as for Freud, this takes place at the psychic level. It is related to those primary unconscious processes through which the infant comes to recognize and accept its separateness from others, enters the realm of language and resolves its intense early relationships to its parental figures. Lacan argues that the entry of the subject into language (which is a system of differences) is closely related to, occurs at the same time in early childhood as, and follows the same pathways as, the entry of the individual subject into the system of *sexual* difference (masculine/ feminine). For our purposes, what is interesting about Mitchell's account of the subject is the way in which she proposes that one of the consequences of the way that girls enter into the language and sexual systems of difference is an unconscious imperative which delivers women as mothers into, so to speak, the bosom of the family.

ACTIVITY 4   You should now read **Reading C, 'Psychoanalysis and feminism'**, by Juliet Mitchell.

This reading uses psychoanalytic language and concepts, which you may find unfamiliar. Read the passage carefully and slowly. To help you follow the main argument, try to keep the following points in mind as you read:

1   The child is not born with an already formed sexual identity.

2   The formation of sexuality in the child follows a long and complex unconscious path.

3   Sexual difference emerges through the child's unconscious identifications with, and the resolution of its relation to, its parental figures (what Freud called the 'Oedipus complex').

4   The child's relations to its 'self' and to its parental figures are 'imaginary' ones.

5   The Oedipus complex is resolved differently for 'girls' and 'boys'.

This is a dense and difficult reading, full of specialist psychoanalytic terms and concepts. Before discussing Mitchell's argument further, it might be helpful to take you briefly through the main relevant points of psychoanalysis on which her exposition depends. Freud argued that infantile sexuality was made up of several sources of pleasure and was both active and passive. In the beginning, the child occupies a sexually undifferentiated world. It is only after a long, complex and incomplete process that it learns to identify itself as 'male' or 'female'. Children of both sexes take the mother as their primary love object because it is she who provides most satisfaction, and their pleasure in the early stages of life is dependent on her presence. In the beginning the child does not differentiate itself from the mother, and only comes to do so through recognizing her absences (in the same way as, in language, we know what 'dark' is by what it isn't — it is the absence of 'light'). Having acknowledged both its dependence on the mother and her independence, the child wants to possess the mother, to retain her presence, and, therefore, its own pleasure. But this is a contradictory desire since the child also desires its own independence, and resents the power that the mother represents.

In the process of psychophysical development the child comes to recognize that one way of gaining the presence of the mother is to acquiesce to her desires. If only it can become what the mother wants, the child will be guaranteed her continued affections. Freud argued that this dovetails with the child's own narcissistic curiosity about where babies come from since this is one of the 'secrets' which the mother clearly possesses. Establishing that babies come from people, the child then wants to give the mother a baby, or to have the mother's baby. In the sexually undifferentiated world of the child, this is assumed to be a possibility by *both* little boys and little girls. The child takes this to be the ultimate gift it can give to or receive from the mother; that it will satisfy the mother's own desire and, therefore, sustain the child's wish for a possessive and exclusive relationship to the mother. Freud called this fantasy the 'Oedipus complex', after the Greek Myth of Oedipus, the hero who, by mistake, killed his father and married his mother. As Freud saw it, the child cannot take up a sexual identity until this complex relationship to the parental figures — the Oedipus complex — had been resolved.

Two things interrupt this unconscious infantile project. The child learns that only boys can give the mother a baby and that the father has greater powers to do this. He, therefore, has more privileged claims to the mother than the child. This recognition of the significance of sexual difference and the power of the father forces children to repress an aspect of their infantile sexuality. However, this repression is itself sexually differentiated. Boys have to surrender both their desire to have a baby and their expectation of claiming exclusive rights to the mother. Unable to dislodge the father, boys must renounce their Oedipal fantasy and instead become like their fathers. (In fact, the boy's renunciation of the Oedipal fantasy is often only a temporary surrendering which can be negated at a later stage in men's adult relationships with women, who symbolically represent the possibility of repossessing the mother of their unconscious desire.) For the little girl, on the other hand, the recognition that sexual relationships with women cannot produce that which women most desire, that is a baby, means that her only choice is to become like the mother. In this she transfers her affections to the father as the person who can give her a baby. These, according to Freud, are the unconscious origins of sexual difference.

The fact that the little girl has to surrender the mother as her primary love object means that her sense of self as powerful (or as Freud calls it, 'phallic') is massively undermined. The little girl is unable to do that which she originally most desires. So she becomes contemptuous of her own desires, and instead tries to satisfy the desires of her father. In this way, her sense of autonomy is radically diminished, in that her desires become predicated on *meeting the expectations of someone other than herself.* Juliet Mitchell sees this predicament as generating what she calls 'the inferiorized psychology of women'.

In acquiescing to the patriarchal law of the power of the father, women have to deny the universal unconscious desire for the primary love of the mother. This means that women are forever trapped within the family, for it is only there that their qualified unconscious desire, that is the desire for a child, can find expression. In short, Mitchell is suggesting that powerful unconscious motivations mean that both women and men will continue to hold women in disregard and that women will always be drawn to the family and motherhood. At the same time, however, women as mothers are also immensely powerful figures.

It also follows from Mitchell's argument that sexuality is necessarily structured heterosexually, through the logic of reproductive sexual difference. At the level of the unconscious this logic works itself out in symbolic terms. This 'desire for the mother' and the 'recognition' of the symbolic power of the father, are psychic processes which mean that both the boy and the girl have in different ways to give up the mother as primary love object. Unless they do so, they cannot leave the imaginary world of fantasy and accept their place in the social world of women and men, that is of *sexually differentiated people.* The pre-Oedipal child thinks it can be and do everything. It is omnipotent. But it learns that we only become someone by not being everyone. Femininity entails that women have to surrender this fantasy of infantile omnipotence. However, masculinity allows men to proceed as if that fantasy is still a possibility. When they grow up they will, symbolically, be able to assume the position of the powerful patriarchal 'father'. Hence, on one side of the equation we have the inferiorized psychology of women, and on the other, the over-valorized psychology of men. Or, as Mitchell puts it, we have women defined by nature and nurturance, and men by class and history. This is what Mitchell means by the 'logic of sexual difference'.

Since writing *Psychoanalysis and Feminism* (1974), Mitchell has qualified some of its arguments and rejected others. However, her account of the development of masculinity and femininity as outlined above remains largely intact. Mitchell is proposing a theory of psychosexual development to account for the way in which we come to accept our identities as heterosexual masculine and feminine subjects. In accepting this sexually differentiated structure the child is implicated in *both* a set of cultural, social meanings and in a set of unconscious motivations. Thereafter, gender differences are determined at both the cultural and psychic levels. You will recall, however, that these sexually differentiated unconscious structures emerge out of what Mitchell, following Freud, posited as a non-differentiated infantile sexuality. For both sexes therefore the possibility exists for resolving the Oedipus complex homosexually rather than heterosexually. Women could retain the mother as a love object and refuse to play the role accorded to them in the logic of reproductive sexuality. By implication then they would not become mothers, although, of course, their heterosexual desire would still remain part of their unconscious. This would be a 'homosexual' rather than a 'heterosexual' resolution to the Oedipus complex.

Mitchell gives no satisfactory account of why the heterosexual resolution of the Oedipus complex is the more commonplace one in our culture. She refers to motherhood as the most socially acceptable way for women to give expression to unconscious desire. But this is a sociological argument, not a psychoanalytic one. In Freud's account, heterosexuality is privileged over homosexuality because it encompasses more of the structure of desire. For women, to have a child satisfies the desire to be powerful (phallic) and whole, as well as to be like the mother. However, it could also be argued that women's homosexuality expresses a more 'pure' form of phallic desire — not just to be like but actually to possess the mother/woman. This does not satisfy the desire for a child; on the other hand, heterosexuality does not fully satisfy this homosexual desire to possess 'the mother'. For Freud there is another factor which comes into play. This is that sexuality is necessarily structured and subsumed by the logic of biological reproduction. In other words, in the end, Freud's argument resolves itself heterosexually because of the facts of biological reproduction and the anatomical differences between men and women with which even unconscious fantasies must come to terms. This is not an argument that sits well in Mitchell's account, however, not least because, once we accept that women's position is defined by the logic of reproduction, there is little else to be said about it. However, what Mitchell is concerned with is how we enter the realm of the social as masculine and feminine subjects, the significance of the realms of the symbolic and cultural in this process of sexual differentiation, and the unconscious processes involved in these, rather than with purely anatomical or biological differences.

Another difficulty with Freud's account of normative heterosexuality is that his psychoanalytic theory lays out the paths of psychosexual development but cannot say in advance which of these paths any particular individual will take. As Mitchell points out, Freud establishes the complex history of the unconscious by reading the history of the individual backwards. He starts with the adult patient and reconstructs the 'story' of how the patient's Oedipus complex was resolved. It was only by retracing the stories of his patients that Freud was able to understand retrospectively how their neuroses developed, and how and why they made the choices they did. However, if we can only 'know' how the Oedipal drama is resolved retrospectively, then psychoanalytic theory cannot be used as a theory of *normative* femininity and masculinity (i.e. it cannot predict in advance what will be the normal paths). If there is no one, necessary, predetermined and prescribed resolution, then more than one way of resolving the Oedipal dilemma must be 'normal'. We cannot account for this in advance. Clearly other factors must come into play to mobilize an individual's choice of normative heterosexuality and its resolution in the family.

Psychoanalysis tells the story of the differentiated personality as, within the limits of certain possibilities, a unique story. It is the story of how the individual subject enters culture and 'becomes' social, and, for modern industrial societies, this marks out as distinctive the context of the domestic sphere of private relations in which this 'becoming social' occurs. I have argued, however, that the gender division of labour cannot be exclusively derived from the psychoanalytic account of the process of social individuation. Although psychoanalytic theory can provide a *particularistic* explanation which is true for individual cases as to why some women want to mother, it cannot account for the *general* social fact of women's mothering. Clearly, the social construction of the gender division of labour is determined by social processes over and above those of the unconscious.

Masculinity and femininity exist not only as unconscious structures but also as cultural conventions which provide the socio-historical content and meanings of sexual identity. Moreover, unconscious desire is anarchic and diverse. It is not inevitably tied to the logic of reproduction and cannot easily be made to fit with, or give rise to, a system of gender relations organized around reproductive sexuality. The sexuality which Freud discovered in the unconscious is not necessarily geared to producing the neat package of gender differences that societies might require. How then do we explain the dominant resolution of sexuality in the normative familial relations typical of modern societies? We shall consider this question in the next part of this chapter.

3.5   THE SOCIAL CONSTRUCTION OF FEMININITY

One school of thought which has critically measured itself against the version of psychoanalytic theory outlined above is the post-structuralist tradition (so called because it was influenced by structuralism but abandoned some of its rigidities as a methodology). This approach has stressed that meanings are *always* socially produced and cannot be understood outside this process, and neither can they be fixed or frozen, even by the language of the unconscious. In contrast with the psychoanalytic story, this post-structuralist position suggests that a symbol, or referent, cannot structure or organize the unconscious because meaning is not intrinsic to the sign. The meaning of any sign is given by its relationship to other signs and the systems of difference which articulate it. In themselves, 'things' have no meaning because meaning is only produced *through* language.(You may remember the discussion of this theory of language and meaning from Chapters 5 and 6 of Book 1 (Hall and Gieben, 1992).) This standpoint therefore rejects the idea of sexual identity and desire being fixed and determined by the unconscious. Instead it stresses how cultural meanings change, shaping psychic life through the patterning and prescribing of particular structures of desire at different times and in different cultures. (This approach is discussed more fully with respect to sexuality in Chapter 5.)

One benefit of this perspective is that it emphasizes cultural values, how these may change, and their psychological significance in the formation of the individual subject. Its stress on social processes, rather than psychic determinants, alerts us to changes in the definitions and meanings of femininity and masculinity, arguing that it is these, rather than unconscious identifications and their 'resolution', which structure sexual identities and relations.

ACTIVITY 5   You should now read **Reading D, 'Female desire and sexual identity'**, by Rosalind Coward. What do you think is the main point of difference between the perspective of Coward and that of Mitchell?

The position taken by Coward is radically divergent from that of Mitchell. Mitchell argued that femininity and masculinity arises out of the resolution of the child's infantile relation to its parents. For her, there is a basic unconscious structure to femininity which is the desire for a child/phallus and this 'logic' determines women's dependent position in the family. However, Mitchell's framework tells us little of the changing patterns of gender relations and the shifts in meaning that occur in different periods and societies in definitions of masculinity and femininity and indeed of motherhood. These indices of historical change become negated, in Mitchell's account, by the overarching, predetermined power of the unconscious. In other words the domain of the social becomes subsumed by the ahistorical workings of the unconscious.

Coward, by contrast, is concerned to chart the way in which discourses and representations orchestrate desire not as a unitary structure but as a spectrum of pleasures. She rejects the idea that desire is psychically determined in the sense that it is possible to read off social relations directly from unconscious structures. Her argument is that desire is organized by cultural meanings which have the power to shape our deepest and innermost sense of selfhood. What it means to be a woman or man, a father or mother is, for her, socially produced and these changing cultural meanings alter the structures of desire. Coward also maintains that the discourses of femininity do not simply invoke motherhood as the exclusive source of identity and pleasure for women. Rather a range of activities centring on, for example, the body, the home, or food, are held up as offering women feminine gratification. Social relations are organized around specifying what kinds of activities can give us pleasure and those relations involve us at the deepest level of our subjectivity.

This approach allows us to see how the cultural meanings which structure desire can anchor particular forms of social relationship. For example, our desire to find solace, love and recognition within the confines of the family, structures an emotional commitment to ideas of the private, and to a narrow set of familial relations which in turn promise to meet some of the most fundamental needs surrounding our individuality. However, although this social constructionist perspective allows us to recognize the importance of sexuality in the organization of familial (and other) relations, it does have some weaknesses. It tends to assume that the structuring of desire is *exclusively* a social process. In this respect, the obverse of Mitchell's position prevails in Coward's version. Sexuality now comes to be seen, in Coward's account, as outside any form of psychic determination. But desire is not just a mechanism of social control. It is more complex than this. Our desires are invested with considerable power for which we cannot always rationally account. People also have a habit of resisting dominant cultural values, of parodying them, refusing them or simply carrying on in spite of them; cultural meanings do not have any guaranteed effect on our identities. In short, Coward's constructionist framework begs the question of why it is *sexual difference*, and not some other factor, which is the main vehicle of cultural patterns of desire.

The cultural construction of gender relations, outlined by Coward, invokes and consolidates a particular structuring of female desire. But it fails to account for the psychic mechanisms which predispose women to *identify* with the cultural representations of maternal desire. It seems, therefore, that *both* the unconscious formations of sexuality, and the social structuring of desire, are necessary for an analysis of women's mothering. In short, we need both Mitchell and Coward. The affective and physical labour of mothering is socially organized; but the effectiveness of women as mothers relies on the unconscious resonance of maternal desire.

4 CONCLUSION

At the heart of the construction of familial relations, and our private existence as social individuals, are ideas about women's *natural* identity as mothers. However, from our study of the changing ways in which families and the domestic sphere are organized, we can see that the domestic sphere, and the gender division of labour, are increasingly becoming spheres of political and social contestation in which ideas about 'the natural' and 'the family' are being increasingly questioned.

With the changing status of marriage, the state has come to accept the need to support lone mothers with children and this, in conjunction

with the increasing economic demand for women's labour, has meant
that women are now less economically dependent on the family and on
men, but more dependent on the state. However, this shift in the mode
of economic support of reproductive labour has made the question of
resource allocation a *public* issue, no longer simply a private one,
requiring collective social recognition of changing relations in the
domestic sphere. Women's growing ability to control their own fertility
also means that motherhood can now be a choice exercised by women,
and therefore that women have marginally greater control over the way
in which they combine their labour as mothers and workers, and define
their identity as women.

Increasingly, then, women's identities are formed outside the confines of
marriage and motherhood. Neither marriage nor cohabitation are any
longer cultural, or economic, prerequisites for women to have children.
Women have acquired a political voice which challenges, amongst other
things, the politics of redistribution and resource allocation. Indeed, the
family and the sexual division of labour can no longer easily be
explained as purely natural institutions. In many respects sociological
analysis of these processes lags behind these changes because of the
way in which the position of women in the domestic sphere has been
conceptualized as a fact of nature and thus marginalized within much of
sociology.

In spite of these changes women continue to mother. In this chapter, I
have argued that to understand this process fully, it is necessary to
include an analysis of *both* the unconscious structure of femininity and
the relation of this to the social definitions and cultural representations
of motherhood and domesticity.

The central argument of this chapter has been that modernity has
located relations of human reproduction at the heart of the *social,* but
continues to describe them in the *language* of the *natural.* The complex
interplay of political, economic and cultural forces which actually
sustain gendered divisions of labour is, however, increasingly entering
sociological discussion as a result of feminist theorizing. Once ideas
about 'the natural' are surrendered in analysing the position of women
within the family, the concepts of social structure and social process are
expanded. Questions are then raised — both politically and
theoretically — about sexuality, intersexual relations, mothering,
childhood, old age, wealth redistribution, individual freedom and social
control. These *social* questions are becoming a real testing ground of
modernity and of its original promise of liberty and equality for all —
women as well as men.

REFERENCES

Allen, J., Braham, P. and Lewis, P. (eds) (1992) *Political and Economic Forms of Modernity*, Cambridge, Polity Press.

Barrett, M. and McIntosh, M. (1982) *The Anti-Social Family*, London, Verso.

Central Statistical Office (1989) *Social Trends*, 19, London, HMSO.

Cohen, B. (1988) *Caring for Children: Report for the European Commission's Childcare Network*, London, Commission of the European Communities.

Coward, R. (1985) 'Female desire and sexual identity' in Diaz-Diocaretz, M. and Zavala, I. (eds) *Women, Feminist Identity and Society in the 1980s*, Amsterdam and Philadelphia, J. Benjamins.

Department of Social Security (1990) *Children Come First: The Government's Proposals on the Maintenance of Children*, London, HMSO.

Durkheim, E. (1952) *Suicide*, London, Routledge and Kegan Paul.

Elliot, F.R. (1989) 'The family: private arena or adjunct of the state?', *Journal of Law and Society,* vol.16, no.4, pp.443–63.

Equal Opportunities Commission (1989) *Annual Report*, London, EOC.

Finch, J. (1989) *Family Obligation and Social Change,* Cambridge, Polity Press.

Finer Joint Action Committee (1975) *A Guide to the Finer Report*, London.

Graham, H. (1987) 'Women's poverty and caring' in Glendinning, C. and Millar, J. (eds) *Women and Poverty in Britain*, Brighton, Wheatsheaf Books.

Green, H. (1988) *Informal Carers* (General Household Survey 1985, Supplement), London, HMSO.

Greve, J. (1990) *Homelessness in Britain,* London, Rowntree Foundation.

Hall, S. and Gieben, B. (eds) (1992) *Formations of Modernity*, Cambridge, Polity Press.

Henwood, M., Rimmer, L. and Wicks, M. (1987) *Inside the Family: Changing Roles of Women and Men,* London, Family Policy Study Centre.

Hillier, J. (1988) 'Women and population control in China: issues of sexuality power and control', *Feminist Review*, no.29.

Kiernan, K. and Wicks, M. (1990) *Family Change and Future Policy*, London, Family Policy Study Centre.

Lister, R. (1984) 'There is an alternative' in Walker, A. and Walker, C. (eds) *The Growing Divide*, London, CPAG.

Mitchell, J. (1974) *Psychoanalysis and Feminism*, Harmondsworth, Penguin.

Molyneux, M. (1985) 'Family reform in socialist states: the hidden agenda', *Feminist Review*, no.21.

Mount, F. (1982) *The Subversive Family: An Alternative History of Love and Marriage,* London, Jonathan Cape.

Murgatroyd, L. (1985) 'The production of people and domestic labour revisited' in Close, P. and Collins, R. (eds) *Family and Economy in Modern Society*, London, Macmillan.

Office of Population Censuses and Surveys (1989) *General Household Survey, 1987*, London, HMSO.

Office of Population Censuses and Surveys (1990) *General Household Survey, 1988*, London, HMSO.

Pateman, C. (1989) *The Disorder of Women*, London, Polity Press.

Ramazanoglu, C. (1989) *Feminism and the Contradictions of Oppression*, London, Routledge.

Rapoport, R. and Rapoport, R. (eds) (1982) *Families in Britain*, London, Routledge and Kegan Paul.

Riley, D. (1983) *War in the Nursery: Theories of the Child and Mother*, London, Virago.

Simpson, R. (1986) 'The cost of childcare services' in *Childcare and Equal Opportunities: Some Policy Perspectives*, London, EOC.

Scott, H. (1974) *Does Socialism Liberate Women?*, Boston, Beacon Press.

Titmuss, R. (1963) *Essays on the Welfare State,* London, Allen and Unwin.

Walby, S. (1990) *Theorizing Patriarchy*, Oxford, Basil Blackwell.

Wilson, E. (1977) *Women and the Welfare State*, London, Tavistock Women's Studies.

Yeatman, A. (1986) 'Women, domestic life and sociology' in Gross, E. and Pateman, C. (eds) *Feminist Challenges: Social and Political Theory*, Sydney, Allen and Unwin.

READING A   THE FAMILY: PRIVATE ARENA OR ADJUNCT OF THE STATE?

Faith Robertson Elliot

In the not so distant past, sociologists of all persuasions presented the family as a private arena, and thus implicitly or explicitly asserted its independence of the state. However, by the late 1970s this conception of the relationship between the state and family had given way to the feminist argument that state intervention in the family is extensive and pervasive, sustains a particular and oppressive family form, and takes place in terms of capitalist and/or patriarchal interests and ideologies. It was thus suggested that the family, far from being separate from the state, is sustained by, and is in some sense an adjunct of, the state. This argument has in turn been subjected to a far-reaching critique and to considerable revision. ...

1   Changing definitions of family relationships in the policies of the state

The history of family-relevant state activity is a history of substantial change in the definition of family and gender relationships. This is vividly demonstrated by the redefinition of marriage which is to be found in changes in divorce law.

For over a century marriage was defined in divorce law as a lifelong social contract that could be ended only where one partner was guilty of a fundamental moral offence. However the Divorce Reform Act 1969 has effectively redefined marriage. By making the irretrievable breakdown of marriage the basis of divorce, this Act defines marriage as a personal and terminable contract between a woman and a man, makes married persons potentially available to others as marital partners, and allows for the regular establishment of one-parent families and of serial monogamy. ...

These changes in family law point to a *substantial* redefinition of marriage and of the rights and responsibilities of men and women within marriage and the family. However, writers who see the state as sustaining a particular form of family organization tend to conceive of change in family policies as having *limited* significance. For example, ... Carol Smart (1984) views the institutionalization of divorce as the continuation of patriarchal modes of regulating sexual and reproductive relationships through the agency of marriage. She argues that, by freeing couples from dead marriages and facilitating remarriage, divorce 'reform' curbed sexual anarchy and kept couples within the legal framework of marriage. Moreover, Smart argues, we are pressured into marriage by material and ideological forces. Divorce reform, says Smart, did nothing to alter the institution of marriage and its structural effects. It offered only a spurious sense of liberalization and permissiveness.

Source: Elliot, F.R. (1989) 'The family: private arena or adjunct of the state?', *Journal of Law and Society*, vol. 16, no. 4, pp.443–63.

These arguments devalue the substantial redefinition of gender and family relationships that is to be found in the policies of the state. To say this is not to assert that state activity has either broken completely with the past or developed in a unilinearly progressive way for women. There are rigidities and inertias in state institutions; there are pressures by some groups of women to retain various aspects of the status quo; there are campaigns by men to recover what they perceive to be lost ground — as the debates over maintenance provisions and fathers' rights to child custody on divorce illustrate; there are inconsistencies and contradictions in state policies, and policies effecting change may be limited in focus, may represent only a change of emphasis and may be negated by rigidities elsewhere in the social system. ... Gains as well as set-backs, change as well as continuity must be given credence and *fully* incorporated into our model of the state–family relation.

2   The impact of state activity on family values and behaviour

A second set of problems concerns the impact of state activity on attitudes and behaviour.

Clearly the way in which the state orders the allocation of resources through its welfare and economic policies and through its regulation of the economic rights and obligations of marital and cohabiting partners privileges certain lifestyles and disadvantages others. So does the ideological approval or disapproval of particular lifestyles that state legislation implicitly or explicitly conveys. Nevertheless, to demonstrate that state activity advantages particular lifestyles *is not to tell us how people have responded.* This aspect of the relationship between state and family is not easily researched and has not been adequately documented. In most accounts of the family as an adjunct of a capitalist and/or patriarchal state, it is simply assumed that state action has coerced us into a particular form of family life. However, there are contrary arguments which suggest that it is unlikely that there is any straightforward relationship between state activity and patterns of family life.

First, a range of institutions other than the state — notably myths and folklore, religion, literature and the arts, and the media — have been shown to disseminate images of family life that privilege particular lifestyles and disadvantage others. Consequently, the impact of state action on the family must be discussed in the context of the activities of other institutions, and of their significance for the weakening or strengthening of particular family lifestyles.

Second, there is evidence that policies directed at the family do not affect all families in the same way, but are mediated by class, ethnic, religious, and generational divisions. ...

Third, it has been argued that assumptions of a straightforward relationship between state activity and patterns of family life slide into portraying women and men as helpless victims of an all powerful state. ...

Fourth, there is evidence that a privatized nuclear family and the sexual division of labour are not in fact being unproblematically reproduced. ...

3   The interests the state serves

Arguments which suggest that the state is reproducing a privatized nuclear family system in the interests of capitalism, or of patriarchy, or even of both run the the risk of functionalism and reductionism. This has been recognized and the whole question of the interests the state serves has been extensively debated. Four important sets of arguments are considered here.

First, it has been argued that neither capitalist nor patriarchal interests are unambiguously served by a privatized nuclear family system based on a sexual division of labour. ...

Second, the presentation of the state as capitalist or patriarchal tends to present the state as a homogeneous entity. This conception has been severely criticized by a number of writers. ...

Third, a conception of working-class struggle as ineffective is inherent in the logic of views of state power as monopolized by a ruling capitalist class. Theories of the patriarchal state face a similar problem and tend to slide into portraying women not only as dominated but also as helpless victims of patriarchal forms. ...

Fourth, interests and conflicts other than those of class and gender have been asserted. There are accounts of racial divisions and interests and of religious division and interests as influencing state policies. ...

4   The boundaries of state activity

I now turn to the fourth and final issue: the question of the boundaries of state activity.

Studies of family law and of social policies have convincingly shown that state intervention in family life is extensive and intrusive. It is extensive in that a wide range of family activities are subject to governmental regulation. It is intrusive in that it operates through the dissemination of family ideals as well as through formal legal and economic measures. But has the division between the public and the private been obliterated, as conceptions of the family as an adjunct of the state seem to presume? Or does some area of family privacy remain despite the extensiveness of state intervention? In other words are there limits to the state's surveillance of family relationships? ...

Alternative approaches

The pristine conception of the privatized nuclear family as sustained by, and as in some sense an adjunct of, the capitalist and/or patriarchal state has not survived the critiques that have been made of it. However, there have been attempts to qualify and revise the argument. I look at this revisionist project in this section. I also look at a radical alternative to the

feminist argument, Jacques Donzelot's elaboration of the Foucauldian perspective. Finally, I consider the idea of the multi-dimensional state which
may be drawn out of some recent feminist and other research and which, if
it were to be followed to its logical conclusion, would seem to lead to the
development of some kind of critical-pluralist-feminist perspective.

1 Revisionist Accounts

There are a range of revisionist approaches but in general terms they may
be characterized as retaining but qualifying the argument that the state
sustains and reproduces a particular form of gender and family relations
in the interests of capitalism and/or patriarchy. In revisionist accounts,
interests other than those of patriarchy and capital may be seen as
influencing state action, contradictions and inconsistency in state policies
may be recognized and reference may occasionally be made to the forces
that limit state power and that intervene between state action and ways of
behaving and acting. At the same time, the state remains capitalist and
patriarchal: it continues to be argued that although concessions may be
made to subordinate groups in the short run, state policies have neither
women's interests nor working-class interests as ends in themselves and
permit no real threat to the reproduction of either the capitalist system or
institutionalized male supremacy. ...

2 Donzelot

Donzelot's Foucauldian approach to the state–family relation is novel,
arresting, and radical. Donzelot (1980) rejects notions of the modern family as a creation of a capitalist and/or patriarchal state. He also rejects the
idea that the state is an overmighty source of authoritative regulation.
Following Foucault, Donzelot believes power to be diffuse, and delineates
a state that is part of a diffuse and multi-form apparatus of social control.
Moreover, he believes knowledge to be a source of power and depicts the
purveyors of knowledge as playing an important part in programmes for
the regulation of normal life. From these starting points, Donzelot argues
that the modern family was established within the context of a liberal
definition of the state through the diffusion of medical, educative, and
relational norms whose overall aim was the welfare of children and whose
end result was the commitment of family members to the values and
norms that control them. ...

Donzelot's account of the state–family relations denies the existence of a
hierarchy of determinate power relations and offers us a radical alternative to Marxist and feminist approaches. However, his analysis contains
important difficulties. First, class and gender interests receive scant attention. Donzelot depoliticizes academic discourses and in doing so obscures
the class and gender, race and age interests with which they are tainted,
even though they have their own logic and are not reducible to these
interests. Second, there is an important ambiguity in his argument. Donzelot seems to suggest that the commitment of most families to their own
betterment ensures their compliance with social norms and means that
they enjoy a loosely supervised autonomy. Yet, he also maintains that that

autonomy is conditional on conformity with social norms and that the cost of deviation is near total dispossession of private rights. This ambiguity renders his thesis puzzling. Third, the educative process that Donzelot describes seems to have a remarkable degree of coherence, even though it is mobilized by a wide range of groups. This raises questions as to what gives the regulation of family life the coherence it is presumed to have. Furthermore, its coherence and pervasiveness would seem to make it as coercive as the ideological indoctrination of much Marxist, Marxist-feminist and radical-feminist theorizing. ...

3   The multi-dimensional state

There are now a range of feminist commentators on state and family who appear to be neither Marxist-feminist nor radical-feminist and whose accounts of the state–family relation tend to be eclectic and descriptive rather than theoretical. However, considered as a whole, such accounts seem to suggest that the critical characteristic of the state is its diversity and multi-dimensionality. Diversity has been attributed to almost every aspect and level of the state. First, state institutions have been seen as having their own histories and logics, as complex, poorly articulated, and, in some measure, independent of each other. Second, it has been suggested that divergent interests — patriarchal and feminist, capitalistic and proletarian, racial and religious, local, national, and international — seek and hold state power and in varying degrees orchestrate state policies. There is recognition also of divergences in women's interests. Third, it has been argued that state policies reflect and disseminate ideologies that have arisen at different times, in relation to different concerns and interests, and on the basis of diverse criteria of evaluation. Fourth, the consequences of state policies have been shown to be ambiguous ... because a range of interests are represented, because women's interests change over time, and because any set of policies, including those fought for by women, can have unintended effects and can at one and the same time bring costs and benefits. ... Fifth, images of the state as multi-form and diversified have been linked ... with images of modern societies as comprised of shifting networks of associations, corporations, and domestic units, as having differentiated loci of decision-making, bodies of knowledge, and criteria of judgment, and as beset by cross-cutting conflicts of interest, volatile alliances and all-pervasive struggles for political ascendancy. Diversity is here taken to be a basic reality. ...

In this emergent 'pluralist-feminism', gender divisions remain a central feature of the social order and the primary object of study, and inequality, exploitation, conflict, and contradictions are pervasive concepts. However, diverse and competing interest groups with the power to shape state action are recognized, and multiple contradictions are presumed. It is thus implied that no one group is able to orchestrate a unified set of policies through which it systematically oppresses other groups and, conversely, that no one grouping is subject to a unified system of control. At the same time, this 'pluralist-feminism' differs from 'classical pluralism' in that it does not see interest groups as equal in political strength and it does not see the state as neutral arbiter between interest groups. It recognizes inequality and is concerned to show which interest groups make demands of the state and how they are differentially rewarded. ...

References

Donzelot, J. (1980) *The Policing of Families*, London, Hutchinson.

Smart, C. (1984) *The Ties that Bind: Law, Marriage and the Reproduction of Patriarchal Relations*, London, Routledge and Kegan Paul.

READING B   WOMEN, DOMESTIC LIFE AND SOCIOLOGY

Anna Yeatman

... The business of social scientists concerns 'gender' not biological sex difference, and the various ways, if at all, gender is socially structured to take the form of a division of labour, that is a division between men and women with regard to the social roles they assume. ... The condition of being a woman can be grasped now as a social condition, which means that women, no less than men, are social beings. With this, the central hindrance to drawing women within the ambit of social science has been overcome. This hindrance resided in the association of women with 'nature' rather than 'society', and in the correlative taking for granted that the proper object of social scientific interest was the activities and concerns of men. ...

Since there is an established history of the modern family within contemporary social history and a well-institutionalised sociology of the family within sociology, it may appear an odd claim to suggest that contemporary social science has some difficulty in accommodating the world of women. The point concerns the nature of this accommodation. Women in their distinctive domestic role and the domain of domestic or personal life are accommodated but at the expense of being located as the lesser part of a dual ordering of social life. The other part concerns the public aspects of our social existence, a world with which men are still more identified than are women.

Accordingly, 'the economy' is placed in the centre of the theoretical space which social science constructs, while 'love' is consigned to the margins if it receives a place at all. A moment's reflection is all it needs to indicate that these respective placements are arbitrary, for how are we to suppose that economic need is more primary than love to our lives? ...

In principle, sociology should be able to incorporate domestic and personal life as a particular and specialised branch of the division of labour in a modern, complex society. Since the idea of a division of labour emphasises the mutual *dependence* of specialised subsystems, sociology should be able to incorporate the domestic and personal aspects of social life in

Source: Yeatman, A. (1989) 'Domestic life and sociology' in Gross, E. and Pateman, C. (eds) *Feminist Challenges: Social and Political Theory*, London, Allen and Unwin, pp.158–172.

such a way as to bring to light the mutual dependence of public and domestic domains.

There is a further implication of this inclusiveness of the idea of society which is its universalism. Human beings are defined as social beings, and all that they do is located in aspects of their social existence. If we find differences between these social beings it is because they occupy different places in the social division of labour, and who goes where in this division of labour depends on what social skills they possess and where those skills belong. The skills are social because they are acquired through processes of learning in specific social interactional contexts. Hence, in principle, an individual actor can play any social role as long as s/he has had access to the right context of learning. This, of course, gives a fluidity to the distribution of actors between the branches of the social division of labour. There is no reason for one's role in life to be fixed, because in principle one can learn new roles if the opportunity to learn them exists. Since actors can change their roles, they have to be accorded an equality which recognizes this ability.

This is not all. It turns out to be a small step from the idea of a complex division of labour in society to the idea that a single personality may be internally differentiated. In other words, maturation of an individual personality as a social being is equated with the ability to play a number of different roles and still remain an integral whole. ...

That this kind of complexity of a single personality is possible deepens the idea of equality because it establishes credence for the idea of transferability and commensurability of skills. In other words, if the same actor can play a whole range of different skills, in large part this is because s/he is differentially applying the same general range of skills. ...

Despite such atavistic tendencies as may exist in individual sociologists to reduce gender difference to the simple assertion of biological sex difference, the *theoretical* tendency is to treat differences between men and women as social role differences and as, therefore, gender differences. If, to use a simplified representation of this role difference, men are workers and women are parents (mothers), in principle it is open to question why this is so, and whether each could play the other's role or would require new learning to do so. Equally, it is open to question whether the same individual could be sufficiently complex in their personality as to play both roles (that is, be both worker *and* parent).

As we know, it is the contemporary feminist agenda which is developing these questions and raising exciting new possibilities for a more flexible and equitable division of labour in society. My point is that the idea of a division of labour in society, which is a distinctively sociological idea, contained these possibilities. It requires only the setting of a feminist agenda to unravel them. ...

In making individuality subject to social determination, and thus abolishing a domain of private discretion, classical sociology in effect 'deprivatises' the individual. Now, in principle, all that an individual does and thinks and all to whom an individual relates are placed within the sphere of the social. There is, accordingly, no difficulty at all in locating women and domestic life within this sphere. Indeed, since the family is now accorded a central role in the social formation ('socialisation') of individuality, there is operating a strong theoretical permission for bringing women and domesticity within the theoretical object of sociology. That the classical sociologists so rarely do this in express terms may be attributed to masculinist bias, and the way in which this bias influences their conception of society. ...

The classical sociological project is caught by the inversion it has effected of the classical liberal starting point. In deprivatising the individual, it abolishes the field of social interaction that makes an individual a particular or unique individual. This makes it virtually impossible for classical sociology to recognise theoretically the sociological distinctiveness of the domestic domain — and of its feminine exponents — since it is in this domain that unique individuality is socially constituted and recognised. ...

The task of resituating individuality completely within social life, and of thereby ensuring reconciliation between the two terms of individuality and sociality, logically entails a particular proposition which is extremely promising from the point of view of bringing women and domestic life into sociological focus. The proposition is this: if individuality in all its aspects lies within social life, then society itself must be differentiated into those arenas of social interaction which speak to and express the unique or particularistic aspects of individuality and those which speak to and express the universalistic or public aspects of individuality. I refer to these as domestic and public aspects of social life respectively. ...

In his account of the modern family Parsons (1955) specifies it as a domain of social interaction for the constitution and expression of unique personality. For the first time we are offered in this a clearly *sociological conception* of the family: the family becomes that sphere of social interaction which functions on behalf of particular or unique personality. ...

What Parsons means by functioning on behalf of personality is quite clear. It means either the function of generating the particular personality — 'primary' socialisation — or the function, once the personality is produced, of its continuing maintenance through allowing the unique aspects of personality expression and recognition. Both these functions require a small-scale, intimate social-interactional context, where the orientation of the actors to each other is particularistic and committed. This orientation is a love relation. With Parsons, then, the sociological tradition achieves a theoretical discernment of domestic and personal life as an object for social science. ...

In Parsons' account of how the mother originally constitutes the infant as a personality within a system of interaction between mother and infant, there is no concrete theoretical specification of how it is the mother constitutes the infant as a particular or unique unit of agency. Instead, we have a sociologically sophisticated version of a behaviourist theory of conditioning whereby, through the use of sanctions, the mother harnesses the natural-behaviour drives of the infant to a symbolic structure of interaction. Here individual agency is taken for granted, as already residing in a natural given motivation of attraction to gratifications and avoidance of deprivations. Without an account of the social interactional determinations of individual agency, we do not have a sociological account of individual personality, and its place within social life is not theoretically secured. ...

To the extent that Parsons tends to identify the personality with its public expressions the necessity for the family as the social domain of mutual recognition of unique personality becomes lost. ...

The blind spot for feminists, which limits the power of their critique for social science, is their difficulty in analytically distinguishing the gender division of labour, on the one hand, from the differentiation of social life into public and domestic domains, on the other. It is true that these are historically conflated so that 'women' becomes a code name for the domestic domain, and 'men' a code name for the public domain. However, were the social categories of women and men to be deconstituted, that is, if the gender division of labour were to be abolished, the distinction between and mutual requirement of domestic and public aspects of social life would remain. Of course, if gender division is abolished, the differentiation of public and domestic domains must operate and appear very differently from when it is expressed as a gender division. In the former case, the differentiation and the mutual dependence of public and domestic aspects of society are expressed within the same personality, and not as two distinct types of personality. When public and domestic take the form of masculinity and femininity respectively, their expression as separate and opposed types of personality obscures their mutual dependence and the necessity for smoothly ensuring their continuing complementary relationship. In short, public and domestic, when expressed as a gender division of labour, necessarily assume a dualistic and dichotomous appearance, so that stress on one must marginalise and put into question the value of the other.

Feminists too often limit the theoretical promise of their critique by approaching the differentiation of public and domestic domains exclusively in terms of its expression as a gender division of labour. When this occurs the objects of inquiry too readily assume the respective forms of 'men' and 'women'. It cannot be clear what men and women denote in sociological terms if public and domestic are not separate categories of analysis. If men and women are the starting point, the likelihood is that analysis will be driven in the direction of constituting these categories as interest groups engaged in some form of competitive, albeit asymmetrical, power relation. There is nothing wrong with this as far as it goes, but it adds nothing to the extant theoretical agenda of sociology. ...

Reference

Parsons, T. (1955) Chapter 1 in Parsons, T. and Bales, R. (eds) *Family, Socialization and Interaction Process*, New York, The Free Press.

READING C PSYCHOANALYSIS AND FEMINISM

Juliet Mitchell

Psychoanalysis and the unconscious

No understanding of Freud's ideas on femininity and female sexuality is possible without some grasp of two fundamental theories: firstly, the nature of unconscious mental life and the particular laws that govern its behaviour, and secondly, the meaning of sexuality in human life. Only in the context of these two basic propositions do his suggestions on the psychological differences between men and women make sense. ...

The unconscious that Freud discovered is not a deep, mysterious place, whose presence, in mystical fashion, accounts for all the unknown; *it is knowable and it is normal.* What it contains is normal thought, utterly transformed by its own laws (which Freud called the primary process), but nevertheless only transformed and hence still recognizable if one can deduce the manner of the transformation, that is, decipher the laws of the primary process to which the thought is subjected. For instance, an unconscious wish originating in infancy becomes attached to the wish in the present time which has evoked it, but if it is unacceptable to consciousness, it is pushed down (repressed) into the unconscious where it is transformed and where it remains — until re-evoked, or until it breaks out (as a symptom), or until it is analysed. The point for our purpose here is that unconscious thoughts are repressed and thus transformed 'normal' ones, and that they are always there, speaking to us, in their way. ...

Sexuality

... Everyone knows that Freud 'discovered' what he admitted every nurse-maid already knew: the sexuality of children. What is far less popular, even today, is the implication of this. By implication, naturally, I do not mean that we won't acknowledge that every little three-year-old is a sex maniac but, simply the implications not for the child but for the nature of sexuality as such. Despite Freud's work, the temptation is still to see sexuality as interpersonal sexual relationships, and sexual phantasies or auto-eroticism as perverse. Thus in some ways it has been far easier for homosexuality to be accepted than, say, fetishism.

Instead of accepting the notion of sexuality as a complete, so to speak ready-made thing in itself which could then diverge, [Freud] found that 'normal' sexuality itself assumed its form only as it travelled over a long and tortuous path, maybe eventually, and even then only precariously, establishing itself. ... In other words, Freud put the stress entirely the other way round: instead of the pool which released itself in different ways, Freud asked from what sources was the pool formed. He realized that instead of a pool from which tributaries ran, the tributaries were needed in the first place to form the pool; these tributaries were diverse,

Source: Mitchell, J. (1974) *Psychoanalysis and Feminism*, Harmondsworth, Penguin, pp.5–7, 16–17, 42–3, 51 and 404–5.

could join each other, never reach their goal, find another goal, dry up, overflow and so get attached to something quite different. There is no nostalgic normality, nor (implicit in such a notion) any childhood bliss when all is as it should be. On the contrary in childhood all is diverse or perverse; unification and 'normality' are the effort we must make on our entry into human society. Freud had no temptation to idealize the origins with which he was concerned. ...

Masculinity, femininity and bisexuality

The baby ... possesses a sexual drive which is a complex structure of different component parts and which can have diverse aims and can be active or passive in its direction. Initially the baby satisfies his urges within himself — auto-erotically, or from his mother's body which seems to be experienced as an extension of his own. But the growing awareness of his incompleteness and of his separateness is forced on him by his acknowledgement that all satisfaction does not come from within, that, as a prime example, the breast that nourishes him comes and goes. ...

One of Freud's earliest hunches and lasting convictions was his notion of bisexuality. He was convinced that the human infant was at first bisexual ...

In 'Analysis Terminable and Interminable' Freud says that though the presence of two sexes is a fact of biology, the mental experience of this is a matter for psychology: it does not *cause* our mental life, but our mental life has to take it into account — indeed it is the most fundamental and difficult problem it has to face — on a par with only one other dilemma: where do we come from and how do we fit in? In taking into account the biological 'great antithesis' between the sexes, we are psychologically bisexual; each of our psychologies contains the antithesis. ...

At first both sexes want to take the place of both the mother and the father, but as they cannot take *both* places, each sex has to learn to repress the characteristics of the other sex. Both, as they learn to speak and live within society, want to take the father's place, [but] *only the boy will one day be allowed to do so.* Furthermore both sexes are born into the desire of the mother, and as, through cultural heritage, what the mother desires is the phallus-turned-baby, *both* children desire to be the phallus for the mother. Again, *only the boy can fully recognize himself in his mother's desire.* Thus *both* sexes repudiate the implications of femininity. Femininity is, therefore, in part a repressed condition that can only be secondarily acquired in a distorted form. It is because it is repressed that femininity is so hard to comprehend both within and without psychoanalytic investigation — it returns in symptoms, such as hysteria. In the body of the hysteric, male and female, lies the feminine protest against the law of the father. But what is repressed is both the representation of the desire and the prohibition against it: there is nothing 'pure' or 'original' about it.

The girl only acquires her secondary feminine identity within the law of patriarchy in her positive Oedipus complex when she is [or imagines she is] seduced/raped by, and/or [imagines she] seduces the father. As the boy becomes heir to the law with his acceptance of symbolic castration from the father, the girl learns her feminine destiny with this symbolic seduction. But it is less important than the boy's 'castration', because she has to some extent perceived her situation before it is thus confirmed by the father's intervention. She has already acquired the information that as she is not heir to the phallus [so] she does not need to accept symbolic castration (she is already 'castrated'). But without the father's role in her positive Oedipus complex she could remain locked in pre-Oedipal dilemmas (and hence would become psychotic), for the Oedipus complex is her entry into her human heritage of femininity. Freud always said that a woman was 'more bisexual' than a man. By this he seems to have been hinting at the fact that within patriarchy her desire to take the father's place and be the phallus for the mother is as strong as is the boy's ultimate right to do so. The bisexual disposition of her pre-Oedipal moment remains strong and her Oedipus complex is a poor, secondary affair. An affair in which she learns that her subjugation to the law of the father entails her becoming the representative of 'nature' and 'sexuality', a chaos of spontaneous, intuitive creativity. As she cannot receive the 'touch' of the law, her submission to it must be in establishing herself as its opposite — as all that is loving and irrational. Such is the condition of patriarchal human history.

With the ending of his Oedipus complex and the internalizing of the 'castrating' father as his authoritative superego, the boy enters into the prospect of his future manhood. The girl, on the contrary, has almost to build her Oedipus complex out of the impossibilities of her bisexual pre-Oedipal desires. Instead of internalizing the mark of the law in a superego to which she will live up, she can only develop her narcissistic ego-ideal. She must confirm her pre-Oedipal identification (as opposed to attachment) with the mother, and instead of taking on qualities of aggression and control she acquires the art of love and conciliation. Not being heir to the law of culture, her task is to see that mankind reproduces itself within the circularity of the supposedly natural family. The family is, of course, no more 'natural' than the woman, but its place within the law is to take on 'natural' functions. For sexuality, which supposedly unites the couple, disrupts the kingdom if uncontrolled; it, too, must be contained and organized. Woman becomes, in her nineteenth-century designation, 'the sex'. Hers is the sphere of reproduction. ...

READING D   FEMALE DESIRE AND SEXUAL IDENTITY

Rosalind Coward

Desire, the word, like the experience, tends to run off in all directions. Diffuse, difficult to pin down and give one meaning but it is always assumed to be inordinately important.

Source: Coward, R. (1985) 'Female desire and sexual identity', in Diaz-Diocaretz, M. and Zavala, I. (eds) *Women, Feminist Identity and Society in the 1980s*, Amsterdam and Philadelphia, J. Benjamins, pp.25–9.

In so far as sexuality is discussed and written about, it's the term desire which is currently in the foreground. Not the term desire ... implying a fundamental condition of the human being, separable from need and demand and forever unsatisfiable, but more broadly as a term implying our deepest needs within sexuality. More than sex or lust, definitely separable from love with all its ideological overtones, 'desire' is used to refer to what is most fundamental to our sense of selves in sex, what we really want and what we are driven by. ...

Female desire is crucial to our whole social structure. Our desire as women is one of the primary mechanisms by which consent for a particular way of living is constantly sought and frequently achieved. ...

I suggest female — or perhaps I should call it feminine — desire is to some extent the *lynch pin* of a consumerist society. Everywhere women are offered pleasure — pleasure for losing weight, pleasure for preparing beautiful meals, pleasure if we acquire something new — a new body, a new house, a new outfit, a new relationship, a new baby.

Pleasure is western society's permanent special offer for women. But some drive is required to take up that offer. And it is female desire which makes us respond and take up that offer. To be a woman is to be constantly addressed, to be constantly scrutinized, to have our desire constantly courted — in the kitchen, on the streets, in the world of fashion, in films and in fiction. Issuing forth from books and magazines, from films and television, from the radio, there are endless questions about what women desire, endless theories and opinions offered. Desire is stimulated and endlessly defined. Everywhere it seems female desire is sought, bought, packaged and consumed.

Female desire is courted with the promise of future perfection, by the lure of achieving ideals — ideal legs, ideal hair, ideal homes, ideal cream cakes, ideal relationships. Such ideas don't exist in reality, except as the end product of some elaborate photographic techniques or the work of complicated fantasies. But these ideals are held out to women everywhere, all the time. Things may be bad, life may be difficult, relationships may be unsatisfying, you may be feeling undervalued or unfulfilled at work, but there's always the promise of improvement. If only you could achieve these personal improvements, everything could be transformed, you'll almost certainly feel better. It's not the social structure or men that are seen as the problem but your own failure to come up to scratch. Female dissatisfaction is constantly recast in the discourses surrounding and dominating us, as desire. Constantly we are made to feel desire for something more, for a perfect reworking of what has gone before — dissatisfaction is displaced into desire for an ideal. ...

Take the issue of food photography, the pictures of sumptuous food and elaborate recipes with which women are regularly bombarded. Innocent enough, surely? But ... these pictures stimulate a desire, which reinforces women's position of subordination.

In many ways these pictures directed at women can be compared with pornography. This is food pornography. Like sexual porn, food pornography is a sex-specific mobilizing of desire or appetite which tends to leave the opposite sex stone cold. Like sexual porn, there's a hard-core and soft-core to food pornography. Sexual porn has the supposedly illicit hard-core, and soft-core version widely available in the daily newspapers and in the everyday representations of women in film. In food porn, there are the pictures aimed at slimmers, the forbidden fruits, the cream cakes and pancakes on which slimmers can feast their eyes only. Then there's the soft-core, the widely available images dominating women's magazines, recipe books and billboards.

These sex-specific representations reinforce the position of the sexes. Just as sexual porn directed at men feeds off women's subordination by representing women as endlessly desiring and available for men's pressing sexual needs, so food pictures give messages to women about their place in society. The primary message of these appetizing photos is that oral appetites are permissible for women. We don't as women have any representations which so blatantly encourage our sexual appetites, but around food we are presumed to be ever hungry voracious feeders. Sexual porn teaches that men's genital urges are perfectly alright and should be instantly satisfied. Food pornography seems to tell women that oral appetites are OK.

But of course it is not as simple as that. As in so many things for women, we are being encouraged in a desire which can't be satisfied unproblematically. Food is, after all, going to make us fat, and getting fat runs counter to the prevailing ideology about women's shape. We are tantalized with pictures of food but we daren't indulge in case we overspill the limits set for our body by the prevailing ideal — the fatless, firm, lean body much advertised by the likes of Jane Fonda. This ideal is of an almost adolescent body, and represents a disgust with mature flesh, a disgust with the idea of fat, as if it was some kind of advertisement for your lack of self-control, your greedy indulgence of the pleasures of appetite. So women's appetite and desire for food is stimulated so long as we don't really indulge it. And this is the other aspect of food pornography. It teaches us to pursue an interest in oral pleasures so long as they are directed primarily to the servicing of others, that is, usually men. For food is photographed in a very particular way; it's a regime of ideal imagery, the culinary equivalent of the removal of unsightly hairs on glamour models. The photographs, like those of models, are idealized, touched up, represent food at a perfect moment. And, what's more, any evidence of the labour women do to prepare food is totally suppressed. These pictures never show chaotic and steamy kitchens, the inevitable mess which cooking involves. They only ever show some imaginary perfect moment, the end-product of the labour when woman, the perfect hostess, lays her gift on the table for others to enjoy.

What is problematic about this is that women get trapped in a desire for perfection which is all about servicing others *and* about downgrading the value of women's labour. We are lured into a desire for preparing lovely food while hiding and devaluing the labour which women's domestic work inevitably involves.

The example may seem slight, but the point of this analysis is to show how even at the most everyday level, even in the most mundane moments of our existence, female desire is stimulated, mobilized, and tied to structures which ultimately oppress us. Here we are lured by pleasure but it's a pleasure which even if fulfilled can never bring us satisfaction as women, for we will be caught in those constructions of women which work against us.

It is important not to treat these practices of representation or discourses as something coming from outside women, as it were, and imposing false and limited stereotypes. The problem is deeper than that. Instead it [is] crucial to understand the desire presumed by various discourses, to understand the work undertaken around women to construct a constant lure of pleasure, a promise of satisfaction. The more I looked the more I became convinced that there was no one universal and timeless female desire arising from our feminine construction. Instead desire in discourses and representations was multiple and plural. And more important it is the representations and discourses around female pleasure themselves which were producing and sustaining feminine positions. Feminine positions are produced as responses to pleasures offered us; our subjectivity and identities are formed in the definitions of desire held out to us. And our responses to these can be to endorse them, sustain them or reject them. We can never fully escape them.

In short here is the knotty problem of female desire and identity. Women's deepest sense of ourselves is provided by our sense of what we want, what we desire, what we really yearn for. And this, our most crucial sense of ourselves, our desire and our pleasure, has been caught up and mobilized, has been made central in discourses which constantly sustain male power and privilege and female subordination. ...

CHAPTER 3 CONSUMPTION AND LIFESTYLES

Robert Bocock

CONTENTS

1 INTRODUCTION

> Years ago a person, he was unhappy, didn't know what to do with
> himself — he'd go to church, start a revolution — something.
> Today you're unhappy? Can't figure it out? What is the salvation?
> Go shopping!
> (Arthur Miller, *The Price*, 1985, Act 1)

It maybe somewhat surprising to find shopping prescribed as an
antidote to unhappiness in this quotation from Arthur Miller's play.
However, shopping has become a very popular activity in Britain and
the United States, in the last decades of the twentieth century, second
only to watching television as a favourite leisure time activity.
'Shopping' may not be quite the term to describe what many people do
when visiting shopping centres — they eat, drink, walk around,
purchase a few things, but they also look, or gaze, at the goods
displayed in the shops and at one another. Gazing, viewing, watching —
either on the small screen, or in shopping precincts or sports stadia —
has become a major social activity.

This looking at objects, places, events and other people can be seen as
part of a wider social process — the consumption of goods and services.
Literally 'consumption' means the use of commodities for the
satisfaction of needs and desires. It includes not only the purchase and
rise of a range of material goods, from cars to television sets, but the
consumption of services, such as travel and of a variety of social
experiences. Modern societies have developed the process of
consumption into a major social activity which uses large amounts of
time, money, energy, creativity and technological innovation to sustain
it. Everyone now consumes in modern societies — the old and the poor,
men and women, as well as the rich, the young and those in the middle,
though levels of consumption between these social groups differ.

The quality and degree of attention given by sociologists to
consumption changed considerably in the late 1980s and early 1990s. In
part, this reflects the growth of mass consumption in advanced
industrial societies since World War II. But it is also because the
concept 'consumption' marked an important theoretical move away
from seeing the mode of *production* as the major, even sole, determinant
of how modern societies have been shaped and of the ways in which
they have operated. The formation and composition of social classes in
capitalist societies has been seen by sociologists in the past as
fundamental to understanding the structure of such societies and the
ways in which they change. In some of the major sociological traditions
'class' was defined principally in terms of the relations of production
(Marxist theories) and work roles or occupations in productive industry
(stratification theories). However, in people's own subjective
perceptions of 'class', it has often been patterns of consumption, not
primarily occupation, which have been seen to be significant; and, as
we shall see, some sociologists have always highlighted consumption in

their analysis of modern industrial capitalism. It has recently acquired even greater importance in sociological analysis as mass consumption has spread, and the number of people employed in mass production has declined and those in the service sector and in marketing have expanded.

The model which saw the capitalist relations of production or occupations as being of foremost significance in social analysis has also been modified by the feminist intervention. Some feminists have pointed out, not only that the labour force contained many women, often employed in low paid, part-time work, but that women, whether employed in industry or not, played a key role in the *reproduction* of the labour force. This implied, not only that women bore and raised the next generation, but that they serviced the male labour force in the *unpaid* housework — cooking, cleaning and washing — which they provided, and also handed on cultural values, attitudes and gender roles. This made them key agents in family consumption.

The feminist intervention has had important effects in sociology. No longer does it seem so 'obvious' that work roles, or classes measured by the male householder's occupation (as it was in many traditional social surveys), are the fundamental, determining, features of modern social formations. Housework, food preparation, shopping and child-rearing, done so predominantly by women, can no longer be taken for granted as unimportant. Partly as a consequence, 'consumption' has become a significant area of analysis and theorizing.

I want to explore, in this chapter how the process of consumption has developed in western capitalist societies in the twentieth century. Consumption appears to be rooted in the satisfaction of purely natural, biological or physical needs. However, there is nothing *natural* about the ways in which millions of people now shop for and consume goods and services such as foods, cars, travel, or the media. The social processes of modern consumption have developed *historically*, the most significant expansion occurring in the twentieth century particularly. Patterns of consumption have changed and the scale and intensity of consumption in the developed societies seems to have reached a qualitatively new stage. The second section of this chapter explores some important aspects of this historical process through which consumption emerged in its modern form, and how this has been conceptualized by an earlier group of sociologists. Two key processes — (a) the relationship between patterns of consumption and major socio-economic groups ('classes') in early modern capitalist societies, and (b) the emergence of 'mass' consumption (as it has been called) in the middle of the twentieth century — are explored in the third section. The emergence of a *plurality* of patterns of consumption in the 1970s and 1980s is examined in the fourth section, a patterning which some claim is far removed from the earlier pattern of mass consumption. Finally, in Section 5, the implications of these developments for ways of conceptualizing modern capitalist societies are examined.

2   THE EMERGENCE OF MODERN CONSUMPTION

Weber's thesis about capitalism and the Protestant Ethic (Weber, 1976) emphasized how the asceticism of Calvinism aided the development of a specific type of capitalism — rational, bourgeois, non-violent or peaceable, capitalism (see Book 1 (Hall and Gieben, 1992) Chapter 5). This analysis is problematic, however. Even assuming that it does help to explain, and to make sense of, the rise of modern, rational capitalism by providing an explanation of how the early generations of capitalists were encouraged to work hard, invest and build up businesses, but *not to consume* the surplus profits they generated, a major gap in the argument remains. How can we understand and explain the subsequent breakdown of the asceticism of the first rational capitalists into an ethic which encouraged consumption? For not only did capitalists need customers for their products, but later on they and their families became consumers too. Why did the asceticism of the first rational capitalists break down? How did the spending ethos of modern consumerism emerge and develop from the asceticism of the early period?

One might posit the argument that people 'naturally' want to enjoy themselves, and that asceticism was a temporary aberration under exceptional, unique historical conditions. Once asceticism had encouraged and enabled a capitalist infra-structure to be built up, it disappeared in order that basic wants and needs could be satisfied through consumption. These wants and needs could be seen as 'natural' because they are given by human biology — food, liquids, medicines, warm clothing, safe housing, means of transport: all these seem to be requirements which are biologically determined. Consumption maybe seen as satisfying these basic, given needs.

The main difficulty with this type of argument (as we shall consider in more detail later on, in Section 5), is that such basic needs are not easy to specify in detail, and, in any case, they never arise outside a social, cultural, historical context. For example, the need for food seems basic, biologically given. Yet the kinds of food that groups eat vary enormously from one culture to another, from one historical period to another. People in Britain at the end of the twentieth century, do not eat snakes, for instance, even though some snakes are harmless and nutritious as sources of protein. On the other hand, many people do eat chocolates. Some of the British chocolate manufacturers were quakers, with roots in the protestant culture which Weber analysed as helping the development of early rational capitalist enterprises (Rowntree and Cadbury, for instance). So there is something of a puzzle here. Chocolate is not a necessary food for human beings to eat. It is a luxury item. Nor would it seem the most likely thing for Puritans to be involved in manufacturing. For that matter, the 'elegant' crockery, dining plates and tea sets that other protestant manufacturers produced (Wedgwood for example) would not seem to be essential items for satisfying the simple biological need to eat. Yet some early protestant manufacturers produced from the very beginning luxury consumption items, satisfying something beyond basic biological needs.

Who bought these items? Who consumed them? It may have been groups who were not so influenced by Puritanism as were the manufacturers. For there were other groups with values and philosophies of life other than puritanism in the seventeenth and eighteenth centuries. These included the landed gentry and aristocracy, who had retained a more pleasure-oriented lifestyle: a lifestyle which included dinner parties, hunting, theatre-going, dressing in 'elegant' clothes, and even eating chocolates! Putting the point in a more theoretical way, we can say that puritanism — protestant asceticism — was not hegemonic. That is to say, puritanism never became the basis of moral, philosophical leadership in the law, the Church of England, parliament, cultural institutions, universities and schools after the fall of Cromwell and the Restoration of the monarchy in 1660. A century later, in the mid 1700s, a group of families existed with enough surplus income to form the basis for patterns of consumption which went well beyond the basic necessities of simple food, shelter and clothing. This was initially restricted to 'the landed gentry', but then spread to middle class commercial farmers and their families in the eighteenth century and to a new urban bourgeoisie based, not only in the professions (the law, the church, medicine), but also in the new manufacturing and commercial enterprises in the nineteenth century. The new working class, in the industrial towns, also began to enter into consumerism when not totally poverty stricken.

Among such social groups, as it always had been for the aristocracy, 'consumption' became detached from the satisfaction of biological needs and entered into the processes surrounding the construction of social identities. This process of identity construction around patterns of consumption involved a 'symbolic' dimension, distinct from purely biological survival. Activities such as novel-reading developed in the early nineteenth century, for example. Ideas of romantic love began to be articulated in popular literature, in songs, and in poetry. Alongside these rather inner-life, social psychological developments, ideas of fashion in clothing became more widespread in the nineteenth century, particularly. Through such processes 'modern consumption' was born.

One sociologist, Colin Campbell, has articulated these processes in a text with a title which explicitly and deliberately plays upon the earlier text of Weber. In place of Weber's *The Protestant Ethic and the Spirit of Capitalism,* Campbell writes of *The Romantic Ethic and the Spirit of Modern Consumerism.* Campbell traces 'elective affinities' (social and psychological links) between the Romantic Movement in literature, painting, music and popular culture, and modern consumption. Campbell wrote, for example:

> ... it should be possible to see how that distinctive cultural complex which was associated with the consumer revolution in eighteenth century England, and which embraced the rise of the

> novel, romantic love and modern fashion, is related to the
> widespread adoption of the habit of covert day-dreaming. The
> central insight required is the realization that individuals do not so
> much seek satisfaction from products, as pleasure from the self-
> illusory experiences which they construct from their associated
> meanings. The essential activity of consumption is thus not the
> actual selection, purchase or use of products, but the imaginative
> pleasure-seeking to which the product image lends itself, 'real'
> consumption being largely a resultant of this 'mentalistic'
> hedonism.
> (Campbell, 1987, pp.88-9)

The important shift here from biologically-driven, or economistic,
'common-sense' notions of consumption, towards a more social,
symbolic and psychological concept of modern consumption is
controversial. Not all social scientists accept this move because, they
argue, it obscures and diverts attention from the study of physical
malnourishment, bad housing, the effects of poverty upon millions of
people, not only among the poorest sections of western societies, but
most importantly, among the poor in the 'Third World', and in what
was, until 1990, the Second World of Eastern Europe and the Soviet
Union. However, even in these societies, Western consumer goods, such
as jeans, radios, television sets, do take on a *symbolic* value for groups,
once they are in a position to take basic food supplies for granted.

In this chapter we shall be concerned with *modern consumption* in the
'first' world, i.e. industrial, capitalist societies. In these societies, and in
the rest of the world as the mass media penetrate into the lives of
people living there, even the poor who cannot afford to buy the goods,
or experiences, displayed in film and television, are invited to, and
probably do 'day-dream' about consumption. In this way, the poor, too,
can become hooked into the consumption process via the images,
symbols and representations which create, evoke and articulate *desire*.
Desires are shaped and evoked by the modern mass media. The mass
media helped to form the identities, the desires, of millions of people
who consume vicariously, psychically. To quote Campbell again:

> ... the spirit of modern consumerism is anything but materialistic.
> The idea that contemporary consumers have an insatiable desire to
> acquire objects represents a serious misunderstanding of the
> mechanism which impels people to want goods. Their basic
> motivation is the desire to experience in reality the pleasurable
> dramas which they have already enjoyed in imagination, and each
> 'new' product is seen as offering a possibility of realizing this
> ambition.
> (Campbell, 1987, pp.89–90)

As people the world over become caught up with compelling images
and 'pleasurable dramas' especially on television and in popular music,
so their imaginations become formed and shaped by 'modern
consumerism'.

We shall now turn to two major sociologists, writing at the turn of the nineteenth century and in the early twentieth century, who examined early forms of modern consumption in Europe (Simmel) and the United States (Veblen).

2.1 CONSPICUOUS CONSUMPTION

In the late nineteenth and early twentieth centuries new patterns of consumption began to develop among the urban middle and working classes. These patterns centred especially around the new department stores in city centres. The new department stores were sites for the purchase *and* display of a variety of commodities — groceries, furniture, clothing, crockery, kitchen utensils, and new electrical equipment as these were developed and mass produced in the course of the twentieth century — all under one roof. Such city centre shops offered more choice than local ones could do, although butchers, fishmongers, greengrocers and bakers remained in local high streets, and groceries in particular were obtainable in local corner shops. The city centre department stores developed as trams, trolley buses and railways emerged to carry people into the centre from the outlying suburban areas during the late nineteenth and early twentieth centuries.

Cities such as London, Paris, Glasgow, New York, Chicago, and Berlin expanded their transport networks and developed large city centre department stores from the 1890s up to the First World War in 1914. The sociologist George Simmel (1858-1918) observed Berlin during the late nineteenth century: a city bulging with new migrants, especially from eastern Europe, including Poland. In his essay *The Metropolis and Mental Life* (1903) Simmel argued that the modern city is 'not a spatial entity with sociological consequences, but a sociological entity that is

George Simmel (1858-1918)

Berlin in the early twentieth century — the city Simmel lived in

formed spatially' (quoted in Frisby, 1984, p.131). Cities grew around centres of government as well as around particular industries, from steel to lace-making. The shops and leisure facilities such as theatres, music halls and sports stadia, all grew up to satisfy the social and psychological desires of the new urban classes.

A new, distinctive urban culture, linked to consumption, thus emerged in these metropolises. The daily life of people who lived in a great metropolis, Simmel argued, is affected by the need to cultivate a 'blasé attitude' towards others, 'for it was only by screening out the complex stimuli that stemmed from the rush of modern life that we could tolerate its extremes. Our only outlet ... is to cultivate a sham individualism through the pursuit of signs of status, fashion, or marks of individual eccentricity' (quoted in Harvey, 1989, p.26).

Some became 'dedicated followers of fashion'; others walked around just looking — providing an urban audience for others to parade before. The stress was on the individual: everyone tried to remain socially detached from one another, or blasé as Simmel noted. One modern sociologist, D.Frisby, has written of Simmel's work on metropolitan life as follows:

> In the opening passage of his essay on the metropolis, Simmel asserts that 'the deepest problems of modern life derive from the claim of the individual to preserve the autonomy and individuality of his existence in the face of overwhelming social forces' and are concentrated in the metropolis. The individual must 'resist being levelled down and worn out by a social-technological mechanism' such as the metropolis. Extreme subjectivism is the response to the extreme objectification of culture that is found there. Hence the individual's struggle for self-assertion, when confronted with the pervasive indifference of much metropolitan social interaction, may take the form of stimulating a sense of distinctiveness, even in an excessive form of adopting 'the most tendentious eccentricities, the specifically metropolitan excesses of aloofness, caprice and fastidiousness, whose significance no longer lies in the content of such behaviour, but rather in its form of being different, of making oneself stand out and thus attracting attention'. In part, this arises out of 'the brevity and infrequency of meetings' which necessitates coming to the point as quickly as possible and making a striking impression in the briefest possible time.
> (Frisby, 1984, pp.131-2)

Modern consumerism, therefore, in part results from this new way of life in the metropolis, the city and its suburbs, for this gives rise to a new kind of individual who is anxious, as Simmel expressed it in the above quotation, 'to preserve the autonomy and individuality of his existence in the face of overwhelming social forces,' and thus to avoid 'being levelled down to and worn-out by a social-technological mechanism' — the metropolis (this argument is more fully developed in Chapter 9 of this book).

The processes involved in living in the city increased the awareness of style, the need to consume within a repertory or code which is both distinctive to a specific social group, and expressive of individual preference. The metropolitan individual is no longer the older type Max Weber had analysed in his work on Calvinism, who would not spend 'foolishly' on relatively trivial items of clothing or adornment. (This was discussed in Book 1 (Hall and Gieben, 1992, Chapter 5). Rather the person in the big city consumes in order to articulate a sense of identity, of who they wish to be taken to be.

The signs or symbols which a particular individual uses as a means of marking themselves from others have to be interpreted and understood by others. Someone can only mark themselves as being *different* from others if they also share some common cultural codes with others within which these signs of difference can be read and interpreted. This produces a ceaseless striving for the *distinctive*, with the higher social status groups continually having to change their patterns of consumption as the middle middle, lower middle and working class strata copy their habits. For example, drinking champagne or malt whisky, once the preserve of the aristocracy, has moved down the social status ladder in this century, so that the upper echelons either cease to drink these drinks, or consume more exclusive and expensive vintages.

This aspect of the consumption process was observed by the sociologist Thorstein Veblen in the United States during the late nineteenth century. He was concerned, particularly, with one specific social class, the *nouveaux riches* — the 'new rich' — of the late nineteenth century. These groups, whose wealth was recently acquired, aped the European aristocracy, or tried to do so in order to win social acceptance. The middle classes and the working classes, black and white, were not yet caught up in this process, which Veblen termed 'conspicuous *consumption*'.

ACTIVITY 1   Now read, **Reading A, 'The American leisure class',** by Thorstein Veblen, which you will find at the end of this chapter. Note down your own main response to the reading in one or two sentences at the end of your reading.

How did you respond to reading the extract from Veblen's *The Theory of the Leisure Class*? It is not a very theoretically conceived piece, so it may be easier to read than some other pieces which involve more theoretical concepts. Notice, however, that Veblen uses the concept of 'patriarchy' in the last paragraph of the extract. It is, he argues, as a consequence of our *patriarchal* past, that 'our social system makes it the woman's function in an especial degree to put in evidence her household's ability to pay'. Here is a specific example of what Veblen called *'conspicuous consumption':* that is social display, based upon a high surplus income, enabling people to indulge patterns of consumption which are designed to impress others in some way. The aim, Veblen argued, was to show that the family possessed 'good taste', a good background, and an ability to pay for consumption beyond what most other people can afford. The social values of patriarchy produce the feature Veblen commented on here, namely that husbands display their wealth and high income by keeping a wife at home, who wears good clothes and is able to be a leisured woman.

Veblen shared the widespread disdain for the *nouveaux riches.* For some, such disdain was based upon a secular version of Calvinism's moral disapproval of worldly pleasures and a life without work. For others, it was based upon European aristocratic disdain for those who had recently acquired wealth and who displayed it in a vulgar, open and too conspicuous a manner. However, we must be careful to avoid being preoccupied with making value-judgements about this group's lifestyle. The primary aim is to understand the role that consumption plays in human societies, in particular in twentieth-century western capitalism.

3   THE ANALYSIS OF PATTERNS OF CONSUMPTION

Both Simmel and Veblen provided some important and insightful ideas about this new social pattern: the metropolitan individual harnessing consumption to his or her drive for a distinctive individuality and blasé attitude, from Simmel's work; and the notion of a conspicuously consuming leisure class from Veblen. Simmel and Veblen were leading figures in developing the new discourse of sociology, which sought to provide analyses of social change focusing more on social factors and less on economic ones, such as those, for example, derived from classical Marxism.

3.1   ECONOMIC CLASS

Simmel and Veblen's work marked a shift of attention in sociology from economistic to social definitions of class. Classical Marxism operated within a broadly economistic set of assumptions, and emphasized the concepts of *economic class,* especially the bourgeoisie and proletariat. These were firmly located in terms of their respective relationship to the means of production, that is the factories, the mines, the machinery and energy sources, and (to a lesser extent) the means of distribution (the shops, department stores and transport systems) of modern capitalism. According to Marx, the bourgeoisie, which owned these means of production and distribution, had a set of economic interests which were directly opposed to those they employed, for they sought to maximize profits and to minimize costs, including wage and salary costs. This economistic model remained of great intellectual and political importance in the first half of the twentieth century; but it did present problems in understanding, explaining and conceptualizing the broader processes of social change taking place in the United States, Britain and Western Europe in this period. Quite apart from the great events — the First World War, the Depression, the Wall Street Crash, the rise of Nazism and Fascism, and the Second World War — there were other changes, which may not have seemed so important at the time because they were less dramatic, but which were, in one sense, underlying some of the major historical events. These included the changes in the class and status systems of such capitalist societies, which were, in turn, related to the process of consumption rather than to that of production. In peace time, the members of the proletariat were pre-occupied with building up and preserving, not only their wages and salaries, relative to others, but also their *social status*, that is their own sense of who they were, of how socially worthy they were: worthy, that is, of prestige or esteem from others.

3.2   SOCIAL STATUS

The concept of social status has its roots in the sociological perspective of the German sociologist, Max Weber (1864–1920) whose work is discussed in Book 1 (Hall and Gieben, 1992). Whilst Weber accepted the strengths and explanatory power of Marxism as an analytic model in the economic sphere, he held that it underestimated the crucial role of social status in capitalist societies. Far from being a left-over from an earlier, feudal epoch, as some Marxists argued, Weber articulated the view that social status had remained important, and that new bases of status had developed, in modern industrial capitalism. For our purposes in this chapter, with a focus upon consumption patterns, this notion of social status has considerable significance, so let us look at Weber's notion in more detail. Weber distinguished between 'class' and 'status', as follows:

> The term 'class' refers to any group of people [who have the same] typical chance for a supply of goods, external living conditions, and personal life experiences, insofar as this chance is determined by the ... power ... to dispose of goods or skills for the sake of income in a given economic order. ... 'Class situation' is, in this sense, ultimately 'market situation'.
> (Weber, 1970, pp.181–2)

For Weber, the basic condition of 'class' lay in the unequal distribution of economic power and hence the unequal distribution of opportunity. But this economic determination did not exhaust the conditions of group formation. He formulated the concept of status in such a way as to encompass the influence of ideas, beliefs and values upon the formation of groups without losing sight of economic conditions.

In contrast to the economically determined 'class situation' we wish to designate as *'status situation'* every typical component of the life fate of men that is determined by a specific, positive or negative, social estimation of *honor*. ... In content, status honor is normally expressed by the fact that a specific *style of life* can be expected from all those who wish to belong to the circle. Linked with this expectation are restrictions on 'social' intercourse (that is, intercourse which is not subservient to economic ... purposes). These restrictions may confine normal marriages within the status circle. ...

Stratification by status goes hand in hand with a monopolization of ideal and material goods or opportunities. ... Besides the specific status honor, which always rests upon distance and exclusiveness, we find all sorts of material monopolies. Such honorific preferences may consist of the privilege of wearing special costumes, of eating special dishes taboo to others, of carrying arms. ...

The decisive role of a 'style of life' in status 'honor' means that status groups are the specific bearers of all 'conventions'. (Weber, 1970, pp.186–8; 190–1)

When Weber turned his attention to economic class he used a somewhat different conception from that of classical Marxism, for he focused upon 'class situation': that is the access to goods and external living conditions which they can obtain by selling their skills in the labour market in return for wages and salaries. This economically based concept of class is contrasted with *status situation*, which is related to esteem, or honour given by others, and claimed by status group members from others. Some groups experience negative honour or esteem; they may be treated as outcasts, or marginal members of a society. Status is linked with a specific *style of life*, which involves consumption, that is the kinds of clothing, or house furnishings, foods and drinks, thought to be appropriate to a specific status group. Note also that carrying arms, in a European as distinct from North American context, is linked with high status groups. Marriage is important, Weber hints, in preserving property through a line of legitimate descent, and in maintaining the social cohesiveness of a given social status group. This was especially true in agricultural social formations where inheritance of land was central to social and economic order.

Status groups may aim at social closure by various techniques other than through marriage. The British sociologist Frank Parkin describes Weber's concept of social closure as follows (see also Book 2 (Allen *et al.*, 1992) Chapter 8):

The manner in which status groups seek to mobilize power in a similar way to class organizations is revealed most clearly in Weber's discussion of social closure. By social closure he means the process by which various groups attempt to improve their lot

> by restricting access to rewards and privileges to a limited circle.
> In order to do this they single out certain social or physical
> attributes that they themselves possess and define these as the
> criteria of eligibility. Weber says that almost any characteristic may
> be used ...

> Exclusionary social closure is thus action by a status group
> designed to secure for itself certain resources and advantages at the
> expense of other groups. Where the excluded themselves manage
> to close off access to remaining rewards to other groups, the
> number of strata or sub-strata multiplies ...
> (Parkin, 1982, p.100.)

Social status groups use patterns of consumption as a means of
establishing their rank or worth and demarcating themselves from
others. It is not only Veblen's *nouveaux riches*, or the metropolitan
individuals analyzed by Simmel, but *all* status groups, which use some
markers to differentiate themselves from others, in the Weberian view.
The markers they use to do this include group values about
consumption, although as Parkin points out any social or physical
attribute may be used to effect social closure, to mark who belongs to a
particular social group and who is excluded. The types of housing,
furnishings and decorations; the types of music enjoyed; the kinds of
clothing which are worn; the type of transport used; all these aspects of
the process of consumption may be used as markers of difference
between social status groups.

The existence, persistence and increasing growth of social status groups
in the twentieth century has helped to generate a plethora of patterns of
consumption. The growth of consumption in modern capitalist societies
now affects, not only the upper and middle class, but the two-thirds of
the population which made up what most sociologists called the
'working classes', i.e. those earning a wage for manual work of some
kind. In other words, the twentieth century has witnessed the increasing
growth of consumerism among most, if not all, major social status
groups, including those who have the lowest incomes, from the state or
from paid employment. As was pointed out by Campbell, in Section 2
above, everyone can desire, or dream, about consuming, even if they
cannot afford to purchase the objects or experiences.

In North America the Depression of the 1930s and in Europe, the two
World Wars (1914–18 and 1939–45) delayed the development of 'mass
consumerism', as the process of the incorporation of the broad working
class into consumerism came to be called in the 1950s and 1960s. Since
the end of the 1940s, however, the capitalist societies of North America,
Western Europe, Britain, Japan and Australia, have experienced a
massive development of 'mass consumption'. This phrase encapsulates
the processes whereby the majority of the working classes in these
societies became 'consumers', not only, or even primarily, 'workers' in
the production process.

3.3   THE AFFLUENT WORKER

The changes associated with the mass consumption which developed in the years after the end of the Second World War in Britain were summed up in the phrase 'the affluent worker'. During the economic expansion of the 1950s, unemployment was comparatively low, and manufacturing industry enjoyed boom conditions. Wage levels rose, especially where skilled labour was in short supply. The phrase 'the affluent worker' was used in both political science and in sociology to describe the new, well-paid worker who emerged in this period. The ideal-typical affluent worker seemed to be the car-worker, for car manufacturing was one of the leading, new, mass consumer-oriented, industries of the period. A major study was carried out by a team of sociologists into the lifestyle, voting habits and intentions, of this new type of worker (see Goldthorpe *et al.*, 1968–9). The affluent worker was contrasted with the traditional workers who worked in heavy, basic industries such as coal-mining, iron and steel-making, and ship-building.

This study suggested that the affluent workers, who emerged in the 1950s and 1960s, epitomized by the car worker in the Midlands and the South East, were more privatized, home-centred, spent more time at home with wife, or husband, and children. They watched television, first in black and white, later in colour, in their well-furnished homes. They spent time and money on do-it-yourself decorating and re-designing their houses. They had at least one car in the family, which was used for pleasure trips at weekends, increasingly for shopping trips. The workers in heavier industries, on the other hand, were not home-centred; the men spent more time with other males in pubs or going to football matches and were less interested in home decorating, child-care, or even spending time in the home, than the newer style affluent male workers. Thus, there were said to be at least two distinct patterns of consumption and lifestyle in the 1950s and 1960s among industrial workers: the post-war, affluent worker in new industries such as car production, and the traditional worker in heavy industries.

Whether or not this distinction was ever as clear-cut as some sociologists suggested it had been in the 1960s in Britain, it did soon change. As the older, heavy industries declined, in the 1970s and 1980s, so the older patterns of life based on men doing heavy manual work in large groups and women doing part-time lighter jobs in factories, or in cleaning offices and other large organizations such as schools, universities or hospitals, began to decline. Male unemployment rose in those towns and areas dependent on one of the traditional 'heavy' industries, such as coal-mining, ship-building and steel, thereby increasing the pressures on women to work, especially when there were young children to be fed and clothed. Consumption patterns were, of course, altered by the rise in male unemployment in such areas: basic items becoming more important than conspicuous consumption of clothes, cars, holidays, home furniture or exotic foods.

However, those employed in occupations which continued to provide well-paid employment could consume more conspicuously, spending more on what were considered to be less essential items in the household budget. Among the relatively well-paid sections of the manual workers, and among the clerical and service industries' workers, a concern with earning to provide enough income to support a relatively affluent lifestyle developed. This marked a move from the primary source of identity being based upon the paid work role a person performed to identities being constructed around lifestyles and patterns of consumption.

As the majority (between two-thirds and three-quarters) of the populations of western capitalist societies became more affluent, the mode of consumption changed from one concerned primarily with basic material provision (which many people still lack in the major capitalist societies as well as in the world as a whole) to a mode concerned more with the status value and symbolic meaning of the commodity purchased. Even so, we should remember the point made above, in the second section of this chapter, that as consumerism spreads and becomes a 'global' phenomenon, those in most societies in the world who live above subsistence level may find themselves caught up emotionally in desiring consumer goods and experiences (such as travel) which they cannot afford to buy for themselves. In this way 'consumerism' may influence even the symbolic life of the poor. More traditional religious, ethnic and political symbols still hold tremendous appeal to many groups in the world, but the symbols surrounding western consumption often co-exist with these other forms of symbolism. Indeed, in some situations wearing blue jeans, drinking Cola, eating a Big Mac burger, playing or listening to rock, jazz, reggae and other forms of popular music, can be used as symbolic ways of representing disaffection with a political-economic regime, as happened in the Soviet Union in the last decades of the twentieth century.

The next section will focus upon new processes which some see occurring in the area of consumption, processes which generate groups with identities independent of economic class, or more well established status groups. Before doing this, we shall examine how consumers have been categorized in the decades since the end of the Second World War.

4 THE NEW CONSUMERS

The emerging affluent working class in western societies from 1950 onwards was seen as a new relatively undifferentiated 'mass' market by producers, department stores, advertisers and distributors of all types of what were termed 'consumer durables', such as televisions, washing machines, cars, transistor radios and record players. However, by the end of the 1980s, many market researchers and advertisers were becoming dissatisfied with the older, social class, or social status group, categories, which had been in use for thirty years or more. New categories of consumer began to be developed. This section will examine this shift from a social class/status group method of categorising consumption patterns to new conceptualizations of patterns of consumption.

The early 1960s saw affluence develop among the workers in consumer-oriented industries, such as the Luton car workers

During the 1950s, 1960s and 1970s, the patterns of consumption, in Britain particularly, but in other western societies too, tended to follow well established social status group and economic class categories. Until the 1980s, most marketing researchers conducting research into which groups would buy what kinds of consumer goods, and advertisers in designing advertising campaigns for selling products, saw the population as divided into several categories of social class, distinguished by a combination of income level, occupation, and an associated pattern of expenditure.

The standard version of the stratification system used by many market researchers from the 1950s to the early 1980s was as in Table 3.1.

On the whole, occupational categories correlated highly with income levels, with social class A having higher disposable income than social class B, and so on.

In 1987, for example, the proportion of the British population in each of these categories was as in Table 3.2.

Table 3.1   Social classes

Social Class A	Higher managerial, administrative, or professional
Social Class B	Intermediate managerial, administrative, or professional
Social Class C1	Supervisory or clerical, and junior managerial, administrative, or professional
Social Class C2	Skilled manual workers
Social Class D	Semi and unskilled manual workers
Social Class E	State pensioners or widows (no other earners), casual or lowest grade workers, or long-term unemployed

Source: The Institute of Practitioners of Advertising

Table 3.2 Percentage of U.K. population by social class, 1987

Class A	3%
Class B	15%
Class C1	23%
Class C2	28%
Class D	18%
Class E	13%

Source: based on O'Brien and Ford, 1988, p.306

The percentages of the population in these various categories can change over time for two different reasons. First, certain occupations may be re-categorized for some reason. A job in nursing, for example, may be in C2 one year, but be re-graded into C1 another year, if some supervision and administration element has been added. Secondly, real changes may occur, such as higher levels of unemployment, or more retired people living longer, which would push up the proportion of the population in Class E. These categories also fail to show the owners of wealth, as distinct from income: that is, the ownership of significant shares in companies, family businesses, or large amounts of land.

The patterns of consumption, recorded by the Central Statistical Office for 1988–89, the latest available when this chapter was written, show that 18.5% of total weekly household expenditure went on food, for example. 6.5% of total expenditure was spent on alcohol and tobacco, in the United Kingdom as a whole. Table 3.3 (overleaf) shows the figures for other items of consumption expenditure for the UK as a whole (the top line) and regions and nations (in other lines).

ACTIVITY 2   Pick out from the table and note down which regions/nations spent most on 'leisure goods and services'; which spent most on 'alcohol and tobacco'; which spent least on 'housing' and on 'motoring and fares'.

The Central Statistical Office also provides data on which groups purchase a list of specific consumer durables. (The categories of the 'economically active' include, broadly, Social Classes A, B, C1, C2, D, and the seventh column in Table 3.4 (overleaf) shows the figures for Social Class E.)

Table 3.3   Household expenditure as a percentage of total: by commodity and service and region, United Kingdom 1988–9[1]

	Housing	Fuel, light and power	Food	Alcohol and tobacco	Clothing and footwear	Household goods and services	Motoring and fares	Leisure goods and services	Miscellaneous and personal goods and services
				Average weekly household expenditure as a percentage of total					
United Kingdom	17.2	4.9	18.5	6.5	6.9	13.2	15.3	13.4	4.2
North	15.7	5.4	19.5	7.7	7.0	12.7	15.9	12.4	3.6
Yorkshire and Humberside	15.0	5.5	19.5	7.4	7.7	12.5	15.8	12.5	4.3
East Midlands	17.2	5.2	18.8	6.8	6.2	12.7	16.1	12.6	4.5
East Anglia	17.6	4.7	18.2	5.4	6.2	13.0	15.1	15.6	4.2
South East	18.6	4.1	17.7	5.5	6.8	13.8	14.8	14.3	4.5
South West	17.0	4.9	18.1	5.9	6.0	13.9	15.8	14.5	3.9
West Midlands	17.9	5.1	19.1	6.6	6.8	13.0	16.2	11.4	4.0
North West	16.8	5.1	18.3	7.7	6.7	12.2	14.6	14.2	4.4
England	17.5	4.7	18.3	6.3	6.7	13.2	15.3	13.6	4.3
Wales	15.4	5.7	19.2	7.0	7.6	13.1	15.8	11.8	4.2
Scotland	16.3	5.4	19.6	7.9	8.1	12.4	14.2	12.1	4.0
Northern Ireland	11.9	7.4	21.0	5.7	9.2	13.9	17.6	9.7	3.7

[1] Averages for the two calendar years taken together.

Source: Central Statistical Office (1991) *Social Trends* no.21, Table 6.5, p.102.

Table 3.4 Households with durable goods: by socio-economic group of head, Great Britain 1988

	Professional	Employers and managers	Other non-manual	Skilled manual[1]	Unskilled manual	All economically active heads of households	Economically inactive heads of households	All heads of households
Percentage of households with:								
Deep-freezers[2]	88	91	84	85	75	86	61	77
Washing machine	93	95	89	91	83	91	72	84
Tumble drier	60	62	45	50	36	52	25	42
Microwave oven	51	60	50	48	32	51	21	39
Dishwasher	32	27	19	6	1	14	4	10
Telephone	98	97	92	83	63	88	80	85
Television	98	98	98	98	98	98	97	98
Colour	96	96	92	93	90	94	87	91
Black & White only	3	2	6	5	8	4	10	7
Video	67	76	65	72	60	71	25	53
Home Computer	44	33	23	22	14	26	4	18
Sample size (number)	*473*	*1485*	*1199*	*2844*	*224*	*6225*	*3840*	*10065*

[1] Includes semi-skilled manual
[2] Includes fridge-freezers

Source: Central Statistical Office (1991) *Social Trends* no.21, Table 6.4, p.101.

ACTIVITY 3   Examine Table 3.4 and note down:

Which consumer items are found in almost every household?

Which consumer durable goods are found more in the 'Professional'
and 'Employers and managers' categories than in other categories?

The social class categories in Tables 3.1 and 3.2 have been used, and
found to 'work' by market researchers when trying to predict *patterns of
consumption.* Such categories might be used to analyse alcohol
consumption for both men and women, in each social class, for
example. Wine drinking was found to be greater among A and B groups
than other groups in Britain. Expensive drinks such as whisky, gin, or
brandy were also more likely to be purchased by A and B groups. C2
and D groups would consume beers and lagers more than other kinds of
alcohol.

These categorizations of the population according to consumption
pattern seemed to work well enough in the eyes of the clients of
advertisers and market researchers for many years. However, some
market researchers, advertisers and companies designing new products
such as clothing for men and women, began to detect significant
changes in consumer patterns in the 1980s. The old social class
categories seemed less good at predicting who would consume what,
whereas age-grades — young adult, middle-aged, or older people —
became increasingly significant. The notion of 'lifestyle' emerged as part
of the attempt to capture this set of changes in consumers' patterns of
purchasing. 'Lifestyles' may differ, not only between social classes, as in
the past, but also *within* social classes. Mike Featherstone has defined
'lifestyle' as follows:

> The term 'lifestyle' is currently in vogue. While the term has a more
> restricted sociological meaning in reference to the distinctive style of
> life of specific status groups, within contemporary consumer culture
> it connotes individuality, self-expression, and a stylistic
> selfconsciousness. One's body, clothes, speech, leisure pastimes,
> eating and drinking preferences, home, car, choice of holidays, etc.
> are to be regarded as indicators of the individuality of taste and sense
> of style of the owner/consumer. In contrast to the designation of the
> 1950s as an era of grey conformism, a time of *mass* consumption,
> changes in production techniques, market segmentation and
> consumer demand for a wider range of products, are often regarded
> as making possible greater choice (the management of which itself
> becomes an art form) not only for youth of the post 1960s generation,
> but increasingly for the middle aged and the elderly. ... We are
> moving towards a society without fixed status groups in which the
> adoption of styles of life (manifest in choice of clothes, leisure

activities, consumer goods, bodily dispositions) which are fixed to
specific groups have been surpassed.
(Featherstone, 1987, p.55)

One example of changing patterns of consumption is the emergence of a
distinctive youth culture in the 1950s. The young emerged as a new
major market in the 1950s in Europe, a little earlier in the United States.
Some young people found relatively well paid jobs in the new
industries manufacturing and selling consumer goods. The increase in
disposable income enabled them to buy consumer goods such as
motorbikes, scooters, clothes, records, radios, television sets, and non-
alcoholic drinks in coffee bars — commodities closely associated with a
distinctive youth lifestyle. This new market was at first differentiated by
social class: a small but very rich group; about one third from homes in
which the father was in a 'middle class' occupation; and about two
thirds from working class homes in which fathers had a skilled, or
unskilled, manual occupation. However, by the 1980s, market
researchers began to change their categories. A sociologist, Paul Willis,
has characterized this change in emphasis as follows:

> No consumer meanings are written on blank slates. No marketeer
> or advertiser can determine, though they may certainly seek to
> influence, the 'message-making' of our consumption. ...
>
> The early history of marketing was precisely about separating
> consumer groups into socio-economic categories so that products
> could be aimed at them more exactly. Modern marketing, however,
> has moved on from delineating socio-economic groupings to
> exploring 'new' categories of life style, life stage, and shared
> denominations of interest and aspiration. This is a crucial move
> since it attempts to describe market segments not from an
> 'objective' point of view, but from the point of view of the
> consumer. Far from being the passive victim of commercialism's
> juggernaut, the consumer has progressively been recognized as
> having substantial and unpredictable decision-making power in
> the selection and use of cultural commodities. In the case of young
> people, marketeers have moved on from defining them as a social
> group with certain material interests (reflecting their place in the
> labour/family/education structures), expressed, however opaquely,
> in consumer tastes and habits, to 'youth' defined as a market
> category. Such a change has registered most clearly in youth
> magazines. For instance the traditional concern in teenage girls'
> magazines with romance/boy friends is being replaced by a new
> emphasis on consumption for its own sake. Adulthood is now
> achieved, it seems, by spending money in a certain way rather
> than 'settling down' to a life of wedded bliss.
> (Willis, 1990, pp.137-8)

Since the 1950s, contemporary youth culture has been divided into a
number of distinctive 'sub-cultures', each distinguished by the objects

and insignia of a particular consumer style. The first of these was the 'Teddy Boys', whose identity was constructed in large part around the consumption of certain types of clothes (based on copying what they believed to be 'Edwardian' styles), hair cuts and music. The film, *Rock around the clock,* featuring Bill Haley, was both popular and notorious. Teddy Boys identified with the lifestyle and music represented in the film and there were riots in many cinemas where it was first screened.

In the 1960s, a major social differentiation was perceived between two different 'styles' within working class and lower middle class youth, and, again, this differentiation was based on consumer patterns. Journalists, the media, the advertisers and marketing men drew on these labels and thus helped to strengthen the distinctions. 'Mods' rode on scooters, 'rockers' on motor bikes. Mods wore 'Italian-style' ties and suits, rockers wore black leather. Hair styles also differed for both males and females in the two groups. Again, the identifications were fierce and ritual fighting between the groups at seaside resorts on Bank Holiday weekends was reported by, if not actually staged for, the TV cameras and newspaper photographers (Cohen, 1972). This pattern continued, with the 'Hippie' or 'flower-power' styles of flowing dress and psychedelic music and the aggressive hard-rock music of the 'Punks' in the 70s.

The argument made by those who analysed this phenomenon is that it was only when young people earned enough discretionary income to be able to spend money on consuming the clothes, music and objects symbolic of a distinctive lifestyle that this phenomenon could arise. Table 3.5 includes some of the broad patterns of consumption which differentiated the 'youth market' in the 1980s.

Table 3.5   The Youth Market: some statistics from the 1980s

5% of the UK population attend the theatre, opera or ballet.
4% of the UK population attend museums or art galleries.
2% of the UK working class attend any of the above.
2% of all young people (excluding students) attend the theatre (the most popular traditional arts venue).
0% of the young unemployed attend the theatre.
98% of the population watch TV on average for over 25 hours a week.
92% of 20–24-year-olds listen to the radio.
87% of 20–24-year-olds listen to records/tapes.
75% of 16–24-year-olds go to pubs on average about four times a week.
40% of 16–24-year-olds go to the cinema at least once in three months.
38% of 11–25-year-olds go to discos.
26% of 11–25-year-olds go to nightclubs.

Whilst cultural statistics are notoriously patchy and difficult to compare, the above is a fair reflection of what is available. Unless otherwise stated, statistics refer to visits or activities undertaken with a four week period. Sources: *General Household Survey,* 1983 and 1986; *Cultural Trends* (PSI), 1989; *The Youth Review* (Willis *et al.,* 1988, Avebury); The *Smash Hits* Youth Survey, 1985.
Source: Willis 1990, p.ix

'Mods' and 'Rockers' — two youth groups still loosely tied to social classes in the 1960s

Another 'lifestyle' group related to distinctive consumer patterns can be identified at the other end of the age scale. The population of Britain, like that of most other western societies, excluding Japan and Australia, is growing older, unlike third world societies where young people predominate. Consumption patterns among the older segments of the population have become important since the explosion of youth culture(s) and the associated patterns of consumption during the 1950s, 1960s and 1970s. Market researchers have devised new categorizations of the population, based upon what they call *life-stages*. An example is given in Table 3.6 (notice that 'head of the household' is assumed to be male).

Table 3.6   Life-stages

Granny Power:	People aged 55–70, living in households where neither the head of the household nor the housewife works full time. They have no children and no young dependent adults, i.e. no non-working 16–24s live with them (14%).
Grey Power:	People aged 45–60, living in households where either the head of the household or the housewife is working full-time. They have no children and no young dependent adults (12%).
Older Silver Power:	Married people with older children (5–15 years) but *no* under-fives (18%).
Young Silver Power:	People who are married, with children aged 0–4 years (16%).
Platinum Power:	Married people aged 40 or under, but with no children (7%).
Golden Power:	Single people, with no children, aged 40 or under (15%).

This categorization covers 82 per cent of the adult population, each group being described as a 'power' group — *power reflecting their spending power in terms of disposable income*

Source: O'Brien and Ford, 1988, pp.293–4

So far disposable income and stage in life have been mentioned as affecting consumption patterns. Gender has also been an important factor influencing consumption in the period 1950–90, and will continue to be so. Girls and women have been targetted as major consumers of perfume, jewellery, clothing, baby products, furniture, holidays, and foodstuffs for instance. In general, women do most of the household shopping in supermarkets and shopping centres and are thus thought of as the 'ideal consumers'. A great deal of advertising on television and in women's magazines is aimed at developing, eliciting, articulating and shaping the desires of women which will lead them to purchase particular products and to live according to a distinctive lifestyle. As a result debt, credit and bank borrowing have grown in these decades, as households seek to create a lifestyle they have come to desire but cannot easily afford.

In the 1980s yet another growing consumer market from manufacturers' and commercial sellers' points of view has emerged: that of men. Young men with reasonably well paid jobs, or with a disposable income as a result of living with parents, were the first major target group in the youth market in the 1960s. However, as patterns of consumption and relative affluence have spread in the 1980s, older groups of men have become targets for consumption by advertisers. It is important here not to conceptualize either women or men as *target* groups only, however. They are not only the passive targets of the advertisers. They desire to articulate and express their own sense of identity, their own sense of who they are, through what they wear, buy and consume. Such an articulation of identity is done through clothing, hair-styles, body decoration (from perfume to ear-rings), as well as through house-style, cars, travel, music and sport, hi-fi's, video cassette recorders, personal stereos, and other electronic consumer goods.

ACTIVITY 4   Now read **Reading B, 'Boy's Own? Masculinity, style and popular culture'**, by Frank Mort. Try to identify how the main changes in conceptions of masculinity between the 1950s and the 1980s, discussed by Frank Mort, are signalled by the use of different consumer styles.

The famous 'Laundrette' ad. featuring Nick Kamen

Frank Mort identified an increase in individuality between the 1950s and 1980s, articulated through clothes, hair, body decoration, and body movements among young men in the U.K. This has been *followed* rather than simply *created* by advertisers and marketing people. The advertisements, together with photographs attached to fashion spreads and feature articles in the new men's style magazines, have contributed to a *sexualization* of the male body in ways which would have been unthinkable in the 1950s. The male imagery used is no longer the old macho image but has become more openly erotic, even narcissistic. Men no longer simply consume, but must be *seen* to consume: consumption is a badge of social and sexual identification. Street culture is a matter of glances, looks, making a quick impression: it is a highly *visual* culture. (Note the echo here of the analysis that Simmel made of the city of Berlin and its blasé attitude before 1910, mentioned in Section 2 of this chapter.)

Young men, Mort argues, have become as much a part of consumerism as women. Their construction of a sense of who they are is as much through style, clothing, body image and the right look as is that of women. This type of consumption is not so much a trivial extra on top of 'real life' as a means of establishing and perhaps reworking social identities. Consumption built around the human body — its attractiveness to the self as much as to others; its sexual, erotic appeal; its use as a means of expressing a sense of identity — has become a process in which *desire* is embedded, in which major meanings are located. We shall look at this linkage between *desire* and consumption in a more theoretical way in the next section.

5   CONCEPTUALIZING CONSUMPTION

Traditionally, consumption has been seen as either a *material* process, rooted in human biological *needs*, or as an *ideal* practice, rooted in symbols, signs, codes. (The word 'ideal' in this context is being used to mean something which is related to the realm of *ideas*, of symbolic signs, *not* the realm of moral values, or moral worth.) For example, the influential social theorist Herbert Marcuse (1898–1979) used the notion of 'needs', based in human biology, in his critical theoretical analysis of modern capitalism. In *One Dimensional Man* (1964) Marcuse wrote:

> We may distinguish both true and false needs. 'False' are those which are superimposed upon the individual by particular social interests in his repression: the needs which perpetuate toil, aggressiveness, misery and injustice. ... Most of the prevailing needs to relax, to have fun, to behave and consume in accordance with the advertisements, to love and hate what others love and hate, belong to this category of false needs.

> The people recognize themselves in their commodities; they find their soul in their automobile, hi-fi set, split-level home, kitchen equipment. The very mechanism which ties the individual to his society has changed; and social control is anchored in the new needs which it has produced.
> (Marcuse, 1964, pp.5 and 9)

Marcuse distinguished between 'true' needs and 'false' needs. 'True' needs are seen as based in human and social interaction, uninfluenced by modern consumer capitalism. 'False' needs are induced, or produced, by modern capitalism, by advertising and marketing strategies; they have no basis in genuine human social interaction.

This distinction between 'true' and 'false' needs has proved difficult to sustain. Even Marcuse accepted that 'needs' were shaped by social, economic and cultural conditions and that, therefore, they varied from one historical period to another. 'True' needs are difficult to establish outside any particular social and economic system.

Look after your bodywork.

Simply for men. A straightforward solution to bodycare. Developed for easy, everyday use. To suit normal or sensitive skin. Everything you need from unperfumed shaving gel to lightly fragranced anti-perspirant. Practical, masculine. Simply for Men. Only from Boots.

Available in most stores. Prices range from 99p – £1.95.

A better buy at

Men became more fashion-conscious, especially in the 1980s

In recent years, the approach Marcuse took has been subject to an even more fundamental critique. For example Roland Barthes, a French social theorist writing in the 1970s, developed an approach to consumption which became significant in later decades (Barthes, 1973). He argued that there was always a dual aspect to consumption — that it fulfilled a need, as with food or clothing, but also conveyed, and was embedded within, social, cultural symbols and structures. A sweater, for example, could both keep you warm and signify an image, like a romantic walk in the woods. The function of consumer goods in satisfying material human needs could not be separated from the symbolic meaning of commodities, or what Barthes call their 'significations'. Consumption is embedded within systems of signification, of making and maintaining distinctions, always establishing boundaries between groups.

This approach was further developed by Pierre Bourdieu, a French social anthropologist and sociologist.

5.1 BOURDIEU ON 'DISTINCTION'

We have been arguing that, in western societies, consumer items of clothing, eating and drinking, music, furniture, cars, motor-cycles, paintings, and home entertainments — from television, video-games, computer-games to home decorating — can be used by groups to demarcate a lifestyle, to mark out their way of life from those of others. Pierre Bourdieu has conceptualized these processes in a study of France, carried out in the 1970s, published in English as *Distinction: A Social Critique of the Judgement of Taste* (Bourdieu, 1984). Bourdieu analysed the ways in which status and class groups differentiate themselves one from another by patterns of consumption which help to *distinguish* one status group's way of life from another. Hence the focus on 'distinction' and the analysis of how matters of taste may be used in this complex social process.

Bourdieu examined distinctions between groups, especially in the top sectors of French society: similar processes, he argued, operate in Britain, West Germany and in some ways in the United States too. A major distinction Bourdieu made, was that between groups with access to two different types of *capital*. The business, entrepreneurial, management, commercial and financial groups emphasize *economic capital*. Such groups seek to amass money capital, real estate, factories, shops, shares and bonds. Their way of life is akin in some ways to the conspicuous consumption Veblen analysed in his analysis of the American *nouveaux riches* in the late nineteenth century. However, post-Second-World-War France was not as dominated by aristocratic lifestyles as the America Veblen analysed. 'Old money' families tend to be less flashy, to consume less conspicuously, than the *nouveaux riches* in western societies. They may use appreciation of well-established art forms and other aspects of culture, as a key means of distinguishing themselves from the self-made businessman, from those who have become newly wealthy through some successful deal or business venture. The *nouveaux riches* have what the older rich families regard as uncultivated tastes — in the field of the fine arts (which they do not appreciate), in food and drink (the *nouveaux riches* tend to eat large amounts of red meats, sweet tasting desserts, and to drink 'too much', even mixing beer, or lager, and wine), in being over-dressed and over-elaborate in home furnishings and decorations.

The second meaning Bourdieu gives to the concept of 'capital' extends it into the realm of culture and education. He argued that there are forms of *intellectual capital* which are distinct from economic forms. The educational systems in modern capitalist societies generate another *structure* of capital, based upon being able to talk about, or to create new cultural products, from major philosophical or social scientific texts, to novels, paintings, buildings, films, television programmes, clothes, furniture and interior décor. In the universities the highest social prestige continues to be attached to non-utilitarian studies, especially in Europe, but also in the United States (in spite of the high prestige of institutions like the Harvard Business School, for example). In the period during which Bourdieu was writing, philosophy and literary studies held the highest status in western universities, in the eyes of many elite groups, followed by pure, rather than applied, mathematics and natural sciences.

Bourdieu's approach is *structuralist* in the sense that he continues to emphasize the positions which individuals or groups occupy in a structure of access to *both* economic and symbolic forms of capital. However, he does not think that social, cultural and economic distinctions only exist in the symbolic sphere. He wrote: 'By structuralism or structuralist, I mean that there exist, within the social world itself and not only within symbolic systems (language, myths, etc.), objective structures independent of the consciousness and will of agents, which are capable of guiding and constraining their practices or their representations' (Bourdieu, 1989, p.14).

This approach is a powerful one, which does not abandon the fundamental notion of there being structures (class structures, status group structures, structures affecting ethnicity and gender) which have real *effects* on people, independently of their own subjective consciousness. On the other hand, these structures may constrain but do not *determine* agents' actions, beliefs, values or desires. Poor people may desire to be rich, but remain poor because of their structural position, to take the most obvious example. However, the desires of the poor, their belief and value systems, are not produced, nor directly determined, by their structural position in the economic system. In this sense, Bourdieu's approach differs from more economistic versions of Marxism. Such desires, beliefs and values, he argues, have a high degree of autonomy from a group's position in the structure of capital, without being completely detached from it.

Bourdieu is anxious to emphasize that the positions in a structure do not produce unified groups who will act politically in a concerted way together in order to preserve or protect their way of life. (This was another false assumption of economistic Marxism.) They may do so; but if, and when this occurs, it is a result of a separate activity, such as political mobilization, through which they become constituted as agents of social action. The structural position is just that: a position which may be occupied by any specific individual as a result of upward or downward social mobility. Such positions in a structure do not generate ways of life, or symbolic meanings, of themselves. Symbolic activity, including consumption, is a relatively autonomous practice. It is not directly produced or determined by a position in the social structure of a social formation.

Consumption is an example of this kind of 'relatively autonomous' symbolic activity. It becomes a way of *establishing* differences between social groups, not merely *expressing* differences which are already in place as a result of a determining set of factors. There are major differences, for example, with respect to the consumption of food, drink, consumer durables, home furnishings and decoration between different sections of the working class. Some aim at respectability, picking up cues from 'higher' middle class groups about how and what to consume, others are more interested in 'having a good time', in direct pleasures.

You can gain a more detailed understanding of Bourdieu's argument by reading an extract from a social anthropologist, Daniel Miller, who offers an outline of Bourdieu's book *Distinction*. There are a number of new concepts which Bourdieu introduced, which you will encounter in the extract. These include:

habitus: that is the relatively stable set of classificatory principles and dispositions which mark out the 'taste' of one group from that of another.

aesthetic: that is a contrast between tastes in the arts and decoration. 'Kantian' refers to the approach of some groups to the arts as one in which the form or *mode of representation* is important; 'anti-Kantian' refers to an approach in which *subject-matter*, or content, is more significant.

capital: this refers not only to economic, or financial capital, or wealth, but also to *cultural capital*, as discussed above: that is, higher education, ownership and appreciation of works of art, and the capacity to produce culture, and make cultural distinctions.

social reproduction: the processes by which a fraction of a socio-economic class group tries to ensure that the next generation can maintain the same lifestyle as that of their parents, by inheritance of wealth or by education, or both.

structuralist: the approach Bourdieu uses which emphasizes positions within the social structure which constrain and limit the actions of an individual agent.

ACTIVITY 5   Now read **Reading C, 'Material culture and mass consumption'**, by Daniel Miller. The terms mentioned above are important in the extract. Refer back to them as you meet them in your reading.

Bourdieu, as you can see from this extract, sought to combine the importance that Veblen, and Weber gave to social status and to patterns of consumption as a way of marking one way of life from another, with the idea that consumption involves signs, symbols, ideas, not only the satisfaction of a biologically rooted set of needs. In this, Bourdieu may be seen as having attempted to combine the well-established approach to consumption through notions of social status groups, (especially the upper, middle and working classes), with the newer analytical approach to signs, symbols, ideas and the cultural.

Bourdieu's analysis of the role of education in these processes is especially important: the sons and daughters of the wealthy industrial and commercial groups who consumed material objects, as in Veblen's leisured class, enter universities. They thus add cultural capital to their economic capital: if they are successful in absorbing the right kind of cultural capital at university: not business studies but philosophy or art criticism; not engineering but pure physics. 'Cultural capital' is not defined by the industrial and commercial classes but by intellectuals and artists whose tastes and definitions of what matters in culture typically differ from those of the industrial classes, both bourgeois, petit bourgeois and working class. The social sciences, incidentally, hover uneasily in this schema: they are neither 'pure' enough for some people, unlike philosophy or art criticism, nor practical enough for others.

5.2 BAUDRILLARD ON CONSUMPTION

An important critique both of the earlier conception of biologically ordered 'need' as a basis for an approach to consumption and of an approach such as that of Bourdieu which used a notion of social *structure*, may be found in the work of the French sociologist, Jean Baudrillard. He argued that we cannot operate within a theoretical framework based upon 'needs', nor one based upon economic class or social status groups. This is so because there is no way of fixing the categories of 'fundamental needs' versus 'media induced consumption' or of distinguishing between Marcuse's 'true' and 'false' needs.

All consumption is always in part the consumption of symbolic signs in Baudrillard's view. These signs, or symbols, do not express an already pre-existing set of meanings for a person or a group such as a social class. The meanings are generated *within* the system of signs/symbols which engage the attention of a consumer. So, far from consumption being conceptualized as a process in which a purchaser of an item is either trying to satisfy a basic, pre-given human need, a need rooted in biology, or responding to a prompt, or a message they have received from advertising media, the consumer, as we have seen in Section 4, is always actively creating a sense of identity. 'Consumption' for Baudrillard is no longer seen as an action induced by advertising upon a passive audience which belongs to a specific social class or life-stage, but as an active process involving the symbolic construction of a sense of both collective and individual identity. Because this sense of identity is no longer seen as given to us by our membership of a specific economic class or social status group, consumption becomes an absolutely necessary process to the construction or articulation of a sense of identity. Baudrillard suggests that we do not purchase items of clothing, food, body decoration, furniture or entertainment to express a pre-given sense of who we are. Rather, we become that which what we

Style affects the ways in which food is served: *Nouvelle Cuisine* became one such innovation

buy makes us. In other words, he argues, the sphere of the symbolic has become primary in modern capitalism; the 'image' is more important than the satisfaction of material needs. In the words of a famous contemporary poster, 'I shop, therefore I am'.

The important element in this shift is the role of desire. We are not already constituted as an attractive woman, or handsome man. Rather, we try to become the beings we desire to be, by purchasing the clothes, foods, perfumes, cars, and experiences which will *signify* that we are x or y to ourselves and to others who share the same code of signifiers, the same system of signs/symbols and their socially produced meanings.

ACTIVITY 6   Now read **Reading D, 'Towards a definition of "consumption"'**, by Jean Baudrillard.

This is not an easy piece to read, so do not panic if you wondered what it was about — read it again if you think you would benefit from so doing. It is difficult in part because Baudrillard is trying to develop an innovative approach to consumption, one which breaks with earlier approaches such as Veblen's and those based on 'needs', as was discussed above. For Baudrillard, 'consumption' is *not* a material process, such as consuming food or drink. It is, as he says, rather provocatively, a *'total idealist practice'*. The reason Baudrillard can make this claim, which runs counter to commonsense notions that when we eat, we eat something which is obviously material, is that he wants to emphasize *relations* between signs — consumption as 'a systematic act of the manipulation of signs' (see Reading D, paragraph 4).

Baudrillard argues that 'in order to become object of consumption, the object must become sign' (see opening of paragraph 5). It is the relation between signs which enables *difference* to be established. It is difference from others, which at the level of everyday experience, we can see is frequently one of the main 'uses' of consumption. People seek to establish that they have more 'taste' than others; that they support a better team, *their* team, by wearing special clothing to football matches; that they are English or French; well educated or 'all right as I am, take it or leave it'. The point Baudrillard is concerned to make here is that it is through being caught up in systems of signs that difference can be established, and the essence of the modern consumer society is this construction of difference.

Furthermore, there is no limit or end to consumption. Because it is an idealist practice, there can be no final, physical satisfaction. We are fated to continue to desire, 'a frustrated desire for totality' (first sentence, final paragraph). Consumption, in modern social formations, is founded on a lack or the absence of satiation. Therefore, consumers will never be satisfied. The more they consume, the more they will desire to consume.

This 'they', the groups who are caught up in consumption for consumption's sake, can be seen not so much as an amorphous mass, according to the 'mass consumerism' perspective which was popular in the writings of social scientists in the 1950s and 1960s, but rather as differentiated groups. The bases of the differentiation between groups are not only to be found in people's class position, in the Marxist sense of a group's position in relation to the capitalist means of production, but in other dimensions including gender, status, age, ethnicity, education and religious affiliations. Once populations of modern social formations are broken down in these ways, patterns of consumption will vary from one group to another, including some groups who purport precisely to be *not* caught up in modern consumerism. Certain groups in the working classes, for instance, may be less consumer orientated, in the sense of aiming to buy new consumer goods or experiences as often as possible, and this is so not just because they cannot afford to do so. Members of puritanical religious sects, for example, may have moral objections to expenditure on alcoholic drinks, rich food, 'fashionable' clothing, or even on modern entertainments, including television. Leading a simple life may be given a positive moral value in such sects. Some communes were established in the 1960s with similar objectives — to avoid consumerism.

Baudrillard has tried to develop an innovative approach to the analysis of modern consumption. He emphasizes the symbolic, the *idealist*, aspects of consumption. The emergence of new groups of consumers, new ways of life, not dependent upon the old class, or status groups, of earlier forms of capitalism is also an important component of Baudrillard's approach. However, we have taken this as far as we can without breaking into new ways of theorizing.

6   CONCLUSION

Consumption has emerged in the course of the twentieth century as a core social process in western societies. From the work of Simmel, Veblen and Weber, there has emerged the notion of social status groups using consumption patterns as a major means of marking out and symbolizing or signifying their group identity, their lifestyle, from that of others, and this idea has been developed by sociologists writing after the 1950s period. The emphasis some feminists gave to the process of *reproduction* of the labour force, played an important role in effecting a move away from the analysis of modern societies in terms of the mode of *production* alone, towards an awareness of the importance of *consumption*. Later theorists have extended this shift to the sphere of the symbolic.

Los Angeles epitomized the autonomy of *ways of life* from older social classes of the European variety

Sociologists continue to take different views about the significance of economic factors, such as income levels, in the analysis of patterns of consumption. Some argue that these are still of major importance in affecting who buys what. Others would argue that in recent decades, since the 1950s or 1960s, income levels are only one part of the explanation of the new patterns of consumption which emerged in the 1970s and 1980s. On this second view, consumer items from clothing to motor-cycles or cars, from food and drinks to tourism, have become involved in processes which have a *high degree of autonomy* from economic class or even traditional social status groups (such social status groups are somewhat confusingly called *'social class'* groups in some texts and in market research). Young men and women from different social status groups, as measured by the occupations of their fathers, or the male head of household, consume in ways which articulate to themselves and others a sense of identity which may be autonomous from such traditional social status groups. (Remember here the quotation from P. Willis and the reading from F. Mort used in this chapter.)

Quite how to conceptualize and to theorize these kinds of changes in consumption was discussed in relation to Marcuse's approach, based on a notion of 'true' and 'false' needs, and in relation to the work of Bourdieu who emphasized the *symbolic* aspects of consumption. In Bourdieu's work, consumption was linked to the making of distinctions and the marking of difference between groups whose position was established both by their socio-economic position in the system of relations of economic capital, and by their position in the systems which transmit and reproduce cultural capital. These two systems were, however, regarded as linked but relatively independent of each other. This linkage is dropped in the analysis of consumption provided by Baudrillard. In Baudrillard's approach, the *signs* or *symbols*, of consumption become more significant than the material objects of consumption. Signs and symbols are not linked in any necessary, or even contingent, way with economic class or social status groups. Identities can be constructed through the *desire* for consumer goods as much as through actually purchasing them. Indeed, for many people, consumption is now their major means of establishing, and creating, who they wish to be. As Arthur Miller observed in the opening quotation, shopping has taken over from politics and religion as a means of warding off unhappiness — unhappiness produced by a loss of a sense of self, of identity.

REFERENCES

Allen, J., Braham, P. and Lewis, P. (1992) *Political and economic forms of modernity*, Cambridge, Polity.

Barthes, R. (1973) *Mythologies*, London, Paladin.

Baudrillard, J. (1988) *Selected Writings*, Poster, M. (ed.) Cambridge, Polity/Oxford, Blackwell.

Bourdieu, P. (1984) *Distinction: A Social Critique of the Judgement of Taste*, translated by R. Nice, London, Routledge.

Bourdieu, P. (1989) 'Social space and symbolic power,' *Sociological Theory*, vol.7, pp.14-25.

Campbell, C. (1987) *The Romantic Ethic and the Spirit of Modern Consumerism*, Oxford, Blackwell.

Central Statistical Office (1991) *Social Trends* no.21, London, HMSO.

Cohen, S. (1972, 1980) *Folk Devils and Moral Panics: the Creation of Mods and Rockers*, London, MacCribbon and Kee.

Featherstone, M. (1987) 'Lifestyle and consumer culture', *Theory, Culture and Society*, vol.4. no.1, pp.55–70.

Frisby, D. (1984) *George Simmel*, London, Tavistock/Routledge.

Goldthorpe, J. *et al.* (1968–9) *The Affluent Worker in the Class Structure*, 3 vols., Cambridge, Cambridge University Press.

Hall, S. and Gieben, B. (1992) *Formations of Modernity*, Cambridge, Polity.

Harvey, D. (1989) *The Condition of Postmodernity*, Oxford, Blackwell.

Marcuse, H. (1964) *One Dimensional Man*, London, Routledge.

Miller, D. (1987) *Material Culture and Mass Consumption*, Oxford, Blackwell.

Mort, F. (1988) 'Boy's Own? Masculinity, style and popular culture', in Chapman, R. and Rutherford, J. (eds) *Male Order: Unwrapping Masculinity,* London, Lawrence and Wishart.

O'Brien, S. and Ford, R. (1988) 'Can we at last say goodbye to social class?', *Journal of the Market Research Society,* vol.30, No.3, pp.289–332.

Parkin, F. (1982) *Max Weber*, London, Tavistock/Routledge.

Simmel, G. (1903) 'The metropolis and mental life' in Levine, D. (ed.) (1971) *On Individuality and Social Form*, Chicago, Illinois.

Veblen, T. (1953) *The Theory of the Leisure Class*, New York, Mentor; first published in 1899 by Macmillan, New York.

Weber, M. (1970) *From Max Weber*, Gerth, H. and Mills, C.W. (eds), London, Routledge.

Weber, M. (1976) *The Protestant Ethic and the Spirit of Capitalism*, London, George Allen and Unwin.

Willis, P. (1990) *Common Culture*, Milton Keynes, Open University Press.

READING A   THE AMERICAN LEISURE CLASS

Thorstein Veblen

During the earlier stages of economic development, consumption of goods without stint, especially consumption of the better grades of goods — ideally all consumption in excess of the subsistence minimum — pertains normally to the leisure class. This restriction tends to disappear, at least formally, after the later peaceable stage has been reached with private ownership of goods and an industrial system based on wage labour or on the petty household economy. ...

The quasi-peaceable gentleman of leisure ... consumes freely and of the best, in food, drink, narcotics, shelter, services, ornaments, apparel, weapons and accoutrements, amusements, amulets, and idols or divinities.

This growth of punctilious discrimination as to qualitative excellence in eating, drinking, etc., presently affects not only the manner of life, but also the training and intellectual activity of the gentleman of leisure. He is no longer simply the successful, aggressive male — the man of strength, resource, and intrepidity. In order to avoid stultification he must also cultivate his tastes, for it now becomes incumbent on him to discriminate with some nicety between the noble and the ignoble in consumable goods. He becomes a connoisseur in creditable viands of various degrees of merit, in manly beverages and trinkets, in seemly apparel and architecture, in weapons, games, dances and the narcotics. This cultivation of the aesthetic faculty requires time and application, and the demands made upon the gentleman in this direction therefore tend to change his life of leisure into a more or less arduous application to the business of learning how to live a life of ostensible leisure in a becoming way. Closely related to the requirement that the gentleman must consume freely and of the right kind of goods, there is the requirement that he must know how to consume them in a seemly manner. His life of leisure must be conducted in due form. Hence arise good manners. ... High-bred manners and ways of living are items of conformity to the norm of conspicuous leisure and conspicuous consumption.

This blending and confusion of the elements of expensiveness and of beauty is, perhaps, best exemplified in articles of dress and of household furniture. The code of reputability in matters of dress decides what shapes, colors, materials, and general effects in human apparel are for the time to be accepted as suitable; and departures from the code are offensive to our taste, supposedly as being departures from aesthetic truth. The approval with which we look upon fashionable attire is by no means to be accounted pure make-believe. We readily, and for the most part with utter sincerity, find those things pleasing that are in vogue. Shaggy dress-stuffs and pronounced color effects, for instance, offend us at times when the vogue is goods of a high, glossy finish and neutral colors. A fancy bonnet of

Source: Veblen, T. (1953) *The Theory of the Leisure Class*, New York, Mentor, pp.64-5, 97 and 126. First published by Macmillan in 1899 and 1912.

this year's model unquestionably appeals to our sensibilities today much more forcibly than an equally fancy bonnet of the model of last year; although when viewed in the perspective of a quarter of a century, it would, I apprehend, be a matter of the utmost difficulty to award the palm for intrinsic beauty to the one rather than to the other of these structures.

... It has in the course of economic development become the office of the woman to consume vicariously for the head of the household; and her apparel is contrived with this object in view. It has come about that obviously productive labor is in a peculiar degree derogatory to respectable women, and therefore special pains should be taken in the construction of women's dress to impress upon the beholder the fact (often indeed a fiction) that the wearer does not and can not habitually engage in useful work. Propriety requires respectable women to abstain more consistently from useful effort and to make more of a show of leisure than the men of the same social classes. It grates painfully on our nerves to contemplate the necessity of any well-bred woman's earning a livelihood by useful work. It is not 'women's sphere'. Her sphere is within the household, which she should 'beautify', and of which she should be the 'chief ornament'. The male head of the household is not currently spoken of as its ornament. This feature taken in conjunction with the other fact that propriety requires more unremitting attention to expensive display in the dress and other paraphernalia of women, goes to enforce the view already implied in what has gone before. By virtue of its descent from a patriarchal past, our social system makes it the woman's function in an especial degree to put in evidence her household's ability to pay. According to the modern civilized scheme of life, the good name of the household to which she belongs should be the special care of the woman; and the system of honorific expenditure and conspicuous leisure by which this good name is chiefly sustained is therefore the woman's sphere. ...

READING B   BOY'S OWN? MASCULINITY, STYLE AND POPULAR CULTURE

Frank Mort

Imagine yourself on Tottenham High Road on a winter Saturday afternoon. The pavements are blocked, but not with Christmas shoppers. A continuous stream of male youth are making for the Spurs ground. Look once and it might be the rituals of the class played out unchanged since the 50s. Look again. It *is* 1987, not 1957. What has changed are the surfaces of the lads themselves, the way they carry their masculinity. Individuality is on offer, incited through commodities and consumer display. From jeans: red tabs, designer labels, distressed denim. To hair: wedges, spiked with gel, or pretty hard boys who wear it long, set off with a large earring. And the snatches of boy's talk I pick up are about 'looking wicked' as well as the game. Which is not to say the violence is designer label! ...

Source: Mort, F. (1988) 'Boy's Own? Masculinity, style and popular culture', in Chapman, R. and Rutherford J. (eds.) *Male Order: Unwrapping Masculinity*, London, Lawrence and Wishart, pp.143-209.

Something is happening to 'menswear'; something is happening to young men.

The rise and rise of advertising and marketing aimed at young men is part and parcel of the current enterprise boom in the service sector and media industries. But what is going on here is more subtle than advertising hype and the profit motive. Young men are being sold images which rupture traditional icons of masculinity. They are stimulated to look at themselves — and other men — as objects of consumer desire. They are getting pleasures previously branded taboo or feminine. A new bricollage of masculinity is the noise coming from the fashion house, the marketplace and the street.

Masculinity and Old Youth

... Over the last fifteen years men have been asked some awkward questions about the power they hold, their identities, sexuality and desire. One of the biggest questions the women's movement has put to men is this: how can we negotiate a new settlement around sexual relations, a settlement which problematises men's identities and lays the ground for a different version of masculinity?

... Along with theories of patriarchy and a discourse of rights, moral languages have been crucial to the political vocabulary of the present-day women's movement. Especially around the issues of sexuality, pornography and male violence, languages of morality have given women a public voice to raise consciousness *and* make demands of men. But moral discourses can often turn out to be double-edged. While empowering they can degenerate into *moralism*, a politics of 'thou shalt not's' and 'do's and don't's' which preaches only to the converted. More to the point, when moralism has been tied to certain forms of revolutionary feminism the upshot has been a total pessimism on the question of men. Men are thus cast as the monolithic oppressors of women. This comes close to an innate but unexplained essentialism, implying that men are incapable of changing *because they are men.*

Against this we need a more sophisticated account of masculinity — but not one so sophisticated as to let men off the hook! Point one is that we are not dealing with masculinity, but with a series of *masculinities.* Differences of class, race and sexual orientation may be some of the big structures at work here, though we should also be aware of how specifically — and at times contradictorily — masculinity is represented in particular discourses or social practices: work as opposed to the media, education as against popular culture, and so on. This makes visible the very uneven access specific groups of men have to the structures of sexual power. But it should not be a recipe for simple forms of constituency politics, where black men are produced as a category distinct from gay men, working-class men and so on. Neat distinctions like these are blind to the cultural cross-overs, the smudging of boundaries between identities.

The fact is that individuals do not live out their masculinity in quite that neat way. As men (and as women) we carry a bewildering range of different and often contradictory identities around with us in our heads at the same time. One of the biggest problems of constituency politics is that it wants to nail them down to 'real', quasi-biological entities. Blacks, gays and the rest are partly symbolic categories, though with real effects on the way people live out their lives. What is the upshot of all this for a politics of masculinity? Anybody working on popular culture knows how awkwardly notions of fixed identity sit with the fluidity of sexual images represented in fashion, music, nightlife. There is a continual smudging, as well as policing, of personas and lifestyles. So point two is the need for a different set of languages to speak about masculinity — languages which grasp masculinity as process rather than as static and unchanging. Such languages do not just drop from the sky. They have to be worked at, forged out of what is currently available, however unpromising.

… it is here that the noises coming from the spaces and places of popular culture become important — from the marketplace, the fashion house and the street. If we are looking for a different vocabulary of masculinity, which speaks of some potentially progressive renegotiations of maleness, then we should at least pay attention to the ways young men are representing themselves and being represented in the culture of popular consumerism.

Wolf in Sheep's Clothing? The Rise and Rise of the New Man

Summer holiday 1987. Wandering down the main street of a small town in Crete. Window shopping. Suddenly I caught Nick Kamen staring out at me from a cardboard cut out. Frozen images of the by now famous 'bath' and 'launderette' ads. And behind them, rows and rows of the real thing: stonewashed, blue originals and black denims. It was a blisteringly hot day but the shop was full. International marketing had made red tabs as 'def' for Greek youth as they were for Soho fashion victims or the lads of Manchester's Arndale Centre.

Opening up young men's markets has been a real feature of consumer trends in the 80s. Whether it's products like 501s or Brylcream, outlets from Top Man to Next, or magazines like *The Face* and *Arena,* advertisers and marketers are hot on the trail of the 16–24 year old male. The so-called new man isn't simply a marketing creation, very few successful trends ever are. But he did become publicly visible through the recent bout of media campaigns for key product ranges. Looking at the images of masculinity on offer and listening to the marketing talk about young men gives us a shorthand way into the sexual politics of the marketplace.

… The modern cityscape was where our Levis hero was launched. The James Dean type loner; vulnerable and arrogant, soft yet muscular, tough but tender. Nick Kamen played out a real life success story through his role in 'launderette'. Here was the Essex lad, ex-Freeman's mail order model, who got a date with Madonna by selling his looks and his body. But the story lines were really much less interesting than the visual messages coming over about the male body. This is where new man advertising breaks the rules, fracturing traditional codes of masculinity. In other words, it's where marketing imagery enters the realm of sexual politics.

Two features are especially worth noting. First, the fracturing and sexuali-
sation of the male body, condensed around the display of the commodity
— the jeans. Cut close-up focus on bum, torso, crutch and thighs follows
standard techniques of the sexual display of women in advertising over
the last forty years. But now the target is men. More to the point, male
sexuality is conjured up *through the commodity*, whether jeans, hair-gel,
aftershave or whatever. Though Kamen stripped to his boxer shorts and
white socks and 'bath' began with a naked torso, it was the display of the
body *through the product* that was sexy. Belt, button-flies, jeaned thighs,
bottoms sliding into baths was what made the ads erotic, less the flesh
beneath. And so the sexual meanings in play are less to do with macho
images of strength and virility (though these are certainly still present)
than with the fetished and narcissistic display — a visual erotica. These
are bodies to be looked at (by oneself and other men?) through fashion
codes and the culture of style.

Something uncomfortable, transgressive even, is going on in these images.

... So the new man is circulating up and down market, as much part of
mainstream fashion as the avant-garde, there in the dole queue and on the
cat-walk. Current menswear is about blurring some of the divisions which
have always dogged the fashion industry, perpetuating caste-like hierarchies between style and the mass market. Gaultier titillates haut couture
by quoting from street style and gay subculture. Halpern's success story
comes out of a similar sort of smudging. The store has picked up on both
designer-led and subcultural trends, offering them to working-class youth.
It may not quite be Boy George's idea of gender-bending, but the visual
reassembly of masculinity through popular fashion has been a hallmark of
the last few years. What is common to different ends of the market is the
desire to play about with masculinity, to rearrange traditional icons of
maleness. Mix 'n' match has got itself a new meaning.

... So much of what is going on here is part of a visual culture, put together
in fashion spreads and ads, street looks and glances. Haircuts, the cut of
jeans, ways of walking and being are points of comparison between young
men, not now just as aggressive competitors, but as stylists in the same
club. They encourage men to look at themselves and other men, visually
and as possible objects of consumer desire, and to experience pleasures
around the body hitherto branded as taboo or only for women. The effect
of all this is to open up a space for some new visual codes of masculinity.
...

By Christmas 1986 it had all got too much for the tabloids. Lumping these
disparate male markets together, they came up with 'the toyboy'. Pics and
tales of young, stylish lads snapped in their boxer shorts; the supposed
playthings of older women. As usual the *Sun* led the field, treating 'lady'
readers to its 'Good Toyboy Guide' — a list of haunts where these youngsters could be picked up. Clubs, wine bars, trendy clothes and record
shops, we were told, all had potential. After all, if 48 year old 'rock granny'
Tina Turner could 'boogie the night away' with her 'German hunk', so
could any ordinary woman. ...

Ever since the teenager first became visible in the sales-talk of marketers and advertisers in the 1950s, young men and women have rarely been out of sight of the consumer economy. At various points over the last thirty years young men have been high profile in the fashion industry. Carnaby Street in the 60s and unisex slightly later led to the growth of male boutiques not just in 'swinging London' but across the country. As a teenager in Manchester in the late 60s I well remember how important these places were. They provided me with an alternative version of masculinity from the images on the football terraces and in pub culture. So I am not arguing that the 80s new man is totally new. But nor am I saying that nothing has changed. The current syndrome does throw up different *types* of male imagery which are the visual endpoint of rapid shifts in our patterns of buying and selling. For we are not just talking images here: images are underscored by the economics and cultures of consumption. Opening up new markets, more sophisticated design and marketing technologies, above all changing lifestyles — taken together, these have been branded the retail revolution.

... Spending on the never-never has never been so acceptable (and so necessary!), rising three times faster than incomes since 1980 and producing its own growth industries — debt-collectors and re-possession merchants. Young men's clothing chains like Burton and Next offer easy instant credit. Students, the unemployed, as well as those of us in work are tempted to buy now and pay later — at high rates of interest.

... Two basic concepts ring the changes. One points up the move towards market segmentation and diverse lifestyle profiles. The other underlines the design input, and especially the emphasis on visuals, in the marketing brief. The argument runs like this. The cultural as well as economic splintering of what in the 60s and 70s were solid market blocs — the working class, youth, the housewife, etc — calls for a rethink. The market has filled up with segmented consumer profiles both up and down the scale: C1s, C2s, yuppies, sloanes, the working woman, gay men, the young elderly. A changed situation demands a different type of campaign. This is where the design input comes in. Lifestyle advertising, where the message is more 'emotional' than rational and informational, feeds off design and visual imagery. The idea is to create a mood where consumers experience their quintessential individuality in the product. *Campaign* makes the point that: 'Lifestyle advertising is about differentiating oneself from the Jones', not as in previous decades, keeping up with them. Levis jeans, Dr. White's, Saga holidays all work with this brief. Put that simply, it sounds as if the advertising profession had just discovered individualism as a way of selling commodities. Of course, the special, unique *you* has been the staple diet of so many campaigns over the last thirty years, from coffee to cosmetics, from cars to chocolates. What we can say is that the 80s has seen an intensification of that process and proliferation of individualities — of the number of 'you's' on offer. ...

READING C   MATERIAL CULTURE AND MASS
CONSUMPTION

Daniel Miller

Consumption as Social Differentiation

... one particular perspective demands more substantial resumé and
analysis. This perspective is here distilled out of the similarities between
two major studies of consumption, one of which may almost be credited
with initiating such studies, while the other provides the most extensive
contemporary survey. These are Bourdieu's recent book *Distinction* (1984)
and Veblen's *The Theory of the Leisure Class* (1899, here 1970). Although
the former makes no mention of the latter, and despite a number of differences, the two share certain central assumptions.

One of the distinctions between these two works is that Veblen's goal is
more limited; he is not concerned with consumption in general so much as
a specific type of consumption which was of particular importance in the
period during which he was writing, a period which may be seen as marking the transition to the age of mass consumption. Veblen, like Simmel,
had the advantage of seeing as new and shocking many phenomena of
mass consumption which today are regarded as commonplace and natural. Veblen's particular interest in the leisure class determined the direction of his argument. Leisure is to be understood as the ability to absent
oneself from work. ...

The tradition which links Veblen and Bourdieu is evident in their mutual
emphasis on the area of taste as the key dimension controlling the significance of ordinary goods, and their common location of the source of taste
in distance from work. Bourdieu, though less witty and stylish, achieves a
large number of advances over Veblen's account in terms of the sophistication of his analysis and his ability to move this critique away from the
characterization of a particular segment of the population to the analysis
of French society as a whole, and from simple emulation and display to
complex forces of strategy and social reproduction. These moves are
necessary, given both the democratization of mass consumption and the
growth in sophistication and subtlety of the ideological practices of dominant groups in the intervening period.

Bourdieu's first task is to rescue taste as preference from essentialist doctrines of aesthetics, and thereby free it as a potential tool for the contingent
historical analysis of society. He achieves this by taking a central pillar in
this tradition, Kant's concept of the aesthetic as distanced contemplation
which transcends the immediacy of experience, and demonstrating that
this is only a single perspective, that of the dominant class. The Kantian
aesthetic is one of refusal, a forgoing of the immediate pleasure of the
sensual and the evident in favour of a cultivated and abstracted appropriation through an achieved understanding. It therefore tends towards a

Source: Miller, D., (1987) *Material Culture and Mass Consumption*, Oxford,
Blackwell, pp.147–54.

rejection of representation of the signified or naturalistic, in favour of the principles of convention, the esoteric and formal. The overt display of wealth and consumption by Veblen's leisure class is challenged by a more subtle, detached and inconspicuous form to be appreciated only by those sufficiently cultivated or civilized. It is an aesthetic clearly expressed in the cool, detached and 'difficult' forms of modern art.

The Kantian aesthetic achieves its meaning only by contrast to what Bourdieu terms an anti-Kantian aesthetic. This is the aesthetic of popular culture, a preference for immediate entertainment, pleasure, the gut feeling, a regard for the sensual and the representational. Here, it is the substance and the signified which are of importance. A telling illustration resulted from questions concerning suitable subjects for photography. The Kantian perspective prefers cabbages and a car crash, the anti-Kantian favours sunset and first communion (Bourdieu, 1984, pp.34–41). For the former, beauty is created through the mode of representation; for the latter, it is inherent in the subject. These differences in taste, which are equally evident in a wide range of media — for example, a preference for 'difficult' as opposed to popular music — provide the basis for unearthing a deep classificatory device which Bourdieu identifies as an example of ... 'habitus'. ...

As habitus, this distinction between the Kantian and anti-Kantian aesthetic is both derived from material conditions, and in turn provides an insight into a classificatory scheme which may be applied to an infinite number of actual material and consumption domains. The term 'taste' provides a clue to its deep rooted nature. When faced with what we regard as consummately bad taste, or people who seem to revel in exactly the behaviour we abhor, we often feel revolted, nauseous or acutely embarrassed. ...

When mapping these differences in taste, the sociological criterion used by Bourdieu tends to be either occupation or educational level, but both are related to the common conception of class, as upper, middle and working. Taste is then seen principally as the cause of 'classism', which can be defined as the kind of distaste the middle and upper classes feel for the vulgar in fun fairs, cheap commodities, artificial copies, or lack of style, and the contempt working people feel for the pretentious, cold and degenerate middle and upper classes.

The source for the basic difference in taste is traced by Bourdieu to the different experiences of these classes in modern society. The immediacy of working people's tastes derives from the immediacy of their work experience, and the pressure imposed by their needs. A person who provides manual labour, and whose access to the basics of sustenance and comfort is not guaranteed, has a respect and desire for the sensual, physical and immediate. An individual who has been brought up in the abstractions of education and capital, and who is certain of obtaining daily necessities, cultivates a distance from these needs, and affects a taste based in the respect and desire for the abstract, distanced and formal. These objective conditions are interiorized through habitus as desire expressed in taste. Habitus thereby mediates between material conditions including, but not entirely reduced to, productive relations, and the observable practices of the social group.

Although in Veblen's time dominant groups could flaunt their birth or wealth, these were already undergoing the crises of legitimacy indicated in the venom of Veblen's writings. Much of Bourdieu's work in *Distinction* and other books is concerned with how these legitimatory principles have been replaced by others based on the education system. Education is used to support current social differences, since it claims to generate distinctions based on merit rather than birth or wealth, being itself the means by which differential ability is identified. Along with other sociologists (e.g. Goldthorpe *et al.*, 1980; Halsey, Heath and Ridge, 1980) who have used statistical analyses of education and occupation over several generations to question assumptions concerning increased social mobility, Bourdieu is able to demonstrate the largely illusory nature of this claim (1984, pp.135–68). The rise of mass education saw a decline in social mobility and merely an inflation in employers' demands for qualifications.

The basis for education's ability to bring about this process of social reproduction lies in what Bourdieu terms cultural capital. Cultural capital is based on time invested in obtaining certain kinds of knowledge. Learning Classics or memorizing the year by year achievements of a football club will enhance the individual's reputation in certain environments, but will prove a poor investment if used in the wrong circumstances. Bourdieu's main original contribution to analyses of education is to distinguish between that which is directly inculcated in the education process and that which is indirectly absorbed.

Some capital may be obtained through direct transference, as when an acquired skill for keeping in touch with the latest developments and information in a given academic field is then applied to the world of fashion. Less obvious is Bourdieu's evidence that education fosters a general tendency towards the use of high culture. His surveys indicate that the likelihood of visiting the theatre, art galleries or museums will depend not upon subjects studied or grades of qualification achieved, but simply upon the length of time spent in a higher academic institution.

One possible reason for this relationship between education and culture is brought out especially clearly in an earlier article by Bourdieu (1968). The increasing abstraction of modern art has tended to extend this distance from the immediacy of forms, and to make such art increasingly difficult to interpret for those not familiar with the conventions and history of the field. This is true for abstract modern theatre, painting, avant-garde music, literature and so forth. In a sense, if cultural products are regarded as a code which must be interpreted, this code has become increasingly difficult to decipher without access to some key. Education, on the other hand, has become increasingly important as a discriminating variable, that is, in terms of the level of education achieved. It also provides the key to the translation of high culture by emphasizing the importance of attaining knowledge about abstract and esoteric subjects. Thus, the difficulty of deciphering the cultural code has been compounded by the difficulty of gaining access to the devices for its decoding. These two factors act together to create and reproduce social hierarchy. At the top of the scale there is a close relationship with high avant-garde arts and esoteric social theories, the best current example of which is the relationship between post-modernism and post-structuralism (e.g. Foster (ed), 1983).

The relationship between the two kinds of capital — cultural and economic — is uneasy. On the one hand, education provides a means by which business capital may reproduce its social order. The children of the rich may work in health food shops or other faddish and esoteric pursuits which utilize their educational experience and may provide a more acceptable form of class reproduction than simple inheritance. There is, however, also an antagonism between the two orders, as the holders of cultural capital deride money capital as mere wealth and its conspicuous expressions as high vulgarity, while the holders of money capital regard the pretensions and esoteric forms of high cultural capital as parasitic and irrelevant. In modern British society, this often takes the form of a left-right political division between fractions of the upper classes. Bourdieu's own analysis of politics, however, stresses rather the division between the 'knows' and the 'don't knows', in relation to the pressure put on the general public to have an informed opinion on often very distant issues (1984, pp.397–465).

Society, then, is not to be understood in terms of a simple hierarchy, but as a continual struggle over the hierarchy of hierarchies; that is, whether, in this case, that of wealth should prevail over that of knowledge. In a sense, this is the modern version of ancient struggles between church, state, military and trading concerns, and the continuance of the French court traditions studied by Elias (1978). Each group attempts to project its interests, its 'capital', as the proper source for social reputation and status. In the main, the holders of cultural capital can be regarded as the dominated fraction of the dominant class.

Although the examples above relate to the arts, the importance of using the concept of taste is that it applies equally to the world of mass consumption. Bourdieu provides a fascinating array of domains divided according to the criteria of taste. An obvious case is that of food, which may be graded according to the social position of the consumer. Working people are found to prefer the immediacy of abundance, a plentiful table proclaiming its sustenance, strong red meats, solid breads and cheeses, an unfussy array of quantity wherever possible. Middle class food becomes cuisine. Taste is here based on knowledge of the proper methods of preparing and presenting foods, and there is a moral interest in food as wholesome, healthy and sustaining. Food for higher classes is increasingly split between the two fractions of the dominant class. The food associated with economic capital is characterized by rich sauces and desserts, and rare and luxurious items such as truffles. The ultimate food for the display of cultural capital today is the *nouvelle cuisine*, which refuses any suggestion that food might be for sustenance, a minimalist food which emphasizes the aesthetic of presentation, an austere but cultivated pleasure.

A similar set of divisions can be identified in a vast range of goods. The middle-class children's toy is never intended for mere amusement or pleasure; its prime interest is its educational value, the child must absorb the toy as a challenge, something from which it will learn in order to improve itself. Similarly, there is an array of products for producing the body beautiful, a tall elegant figure disdainful of practical or even biological constraint. In every consumer domain, fashion provides opportunities for differentiation, in terms of speed of access to knowledge. Through such examples, it becomes clear how the habitus acts both to generate the diversity of forms and, in turn, to classify these same diverse fields. It provides a set of dispositions promoting self-recognition and the creation of relationships such as friendships and marriages with others who share that set of prejudices concerning the correct nature of things; but the individuals concerned rarely possess any awareness of the social origins of these tastes.

It is this structuralist mode, through which the particularities of the object world at a given time may help generate the objectifications by which a set of social relationships comes to know itself through an array of everyday taxonomies which makes Bourdieu's work such an advance on previous analyses of consumption. It accounts for the way in which goods not merely reflect distinction, but are an instrument of it. It indicates the power and importance of consumption trivia, both in everyday social encounters and at the level of meta-social alignments. Bourdieu's habitus is as deeply rooted in material culture as in cognitive orders and social divisions, and it provides the means for combining an approach to all three. It also accounts for the extraordinary ability of shoppers to select from a huge array those goods most appropriate to themselves and their close friends or relatives.

As a modern social analyst, Bourdieu is exemplary in his refusal to reduce his model of society to any single social attribute. Although he often uses occupation and length of time in educational institutions as the axes for his displays and charts, in the text he attempts to encompass a far greater range of differences based on gender, age and expectation. He clearly regards these as always interconnected; the meaning of gender depends upon one's class, and vice versa. He provides a polythetic perspective on social position, exhibiting the structuralist preference for relationships over entities, so that all social attributes are understood primarily in terms of their co-variant properties. This relational approach is opposed to Marx's theory of class, conflating a theoretically constructed concept with a given body of people defined largely by economic position; although Bourdieu recognized that such has been the impact of Marx and Marxism that class as representation has by now been realized, through sheer symbolic efficacy, to an extraordinary degree (Bourdieu, 1985).

Bourdieu also attempts a balance between relativism and moral judgement. One of the work's main strengths is that it covers all social positions. A radical lesbian whose main concerns are CND and South Africa is as likely to be placed in terms of education and occupation (e.g. teaching or social work), as the home-loving, conservative, television absorbed, do-it-yourself enthusiast might represent the aspiring white collar working class. The work is, however, clearly intended to expose the pretensions to a superior rationality of middle and upper-class taste.

References

Bourdieu, P. (1968) 'Outline of a sociological theory of art perception', *International Social Science Journal*, 20.4, 589–612.

Bourdieu, P. (1984) *Distinction: A Social Critique of the Judgement of Taste*, London, Routledge and Kegan Paul.

Bourdieu, P. (1985) 'The social space and the genesis of groups', in *Theory and Society* 14, 723-44.

Elias, N. (1978) *The Civilizing Process*, Oxford, Basil Blackwell.

Foster, H. (1983) *The Anti-Aesthetic*, Port Townsend, Bay Press

Goldthorpe, J.H., with Llewellyn, C. and Payne, C. (1980) *Social Mobility and Class Structure,* Oxford, Clarendon Press.

Halsey, A.H., Heath A. and Ridge J. (1980) *Origins and Destinations* Oxford, Clarendon Press.

Veblen, J. (1970) *The Theory of the Leisure Class,* London, George Allen and Unwin.

READING D TOWARDS A DEFINITION OF 'CONSUMPTION'

Jean Baudrillard

I would like to conclude the analysis of our relation to objects as a systematic process, which was developed on different levels, with a definition of 'consumption', since it is here that all the elements of an actual practice in this domain converge.

In fact we can conceive of consumption as a characteristic mode of industrial civilization on the condition that we separate it fundamentally from its current meaning as a process of satisfaction of needs. Consumption is not a passive mode of assimilation (*absorption*) and appropriation which we can oppose to an active mode of production, in order to bring to bear naive concepts of action (and alienation). From the outset, we must clearly state that consumption is an active mode of relations (not only to objects, but to the collectivity and to the world), a systematic mode of activity and a global response on which our whole cultural system is founded.

We must clearly state that material goods are not the objects of consumption: they are merely the objects of need and satisfaction. We have all at times purchased, possessed, enjoyed, and spent, and yet not 'consumed'. 'Primitive' festivities, the prodigality of the feudal lord, or the luxury of the nineteenth-century bourgeois — these are not acts of consumption. And if we are justified in using this term for contemporary society, it is not because we are better fed, or that we assimilate more images and messages, or that we have more appliances and gadgets at our disposal. Neither the

Source: Baudrillard, J., (1988) *Selected Writings* (Poster, M. ed.) Cambridge, Polity Press/Oxford, Blackwell, pp.21–5.

quantity of goods, nor the satisfaction of needs is sufficient to define the concept of consumption: they are merely its preconditions.

Consumption is neither a material practice, nor a phenomenology of 'affluence'. It is not defined by the food we eat, the clothes we wear, the car we drive, nor by the visual and oral substance of images and messages, but in the organization of all this as signifying substance. Consumption is *the virtual totality of all objects and messages presently constituted in a more or less coherent discourse*. Consumption, in so far as it is meaningful, is *a systematic act of the manipulation of signs.*

... *In order to become object of consumption, the object must become sign;* ... yet obtaining its coherence, and consequently its meaning, from an abstract and systematic relation to all other object-signs. It is in this way that it becomes 'personalized', and enters in the series, etc.: it is never consumed in its materiality, but in its difference.

... Leather couch, phonograph, bric-à-brac, jade ashtrays: it is the *idea of a relation* that is signified in these objects, 'consumed' in them, and consequently annulled as a lived relation.

This defines consumption as a systematic and *total idealist practice*, which far exceeds our relations to objects and relations among individuals, one that extends to all manifestations (*registers)* of history, communication and culture. Thus, the need for culture is alive: but in the collector's book or in the dining room lithograph only the *idea* is *consumed.*

... This suggests that *there are no limits to consumption*. If it was that which it is naively taken to be, an absorption, a devouring, then we should achieve saturation. If it was a function of the order of needs, we should achieve satisfaction. But we know that this is not the case: we want to consume more and more. This compulsion to consume is not the consequence of some psychological determinant etc., nor is it simply the power of emulation. If consumption appears to be irrepressible, this is precisely because it is a total idealist practice which has no longer anything to do (beyond a certain point) with the satisfaction of needs, nor with the reality principle; it becomes energized in the project that is always dissatisfied [*deçu*] and implicit in the object. The project, made immediate in the sign, transfers its essential dynamics onto the systematic and indefinite possession of object-signs of consumption. Consequently, it must transcend itself, or continuously reiterate itself in order to remain what it is: a reason for living. The very project of life, segmented, dissatisfied, and signified, is reclaimed and annulled in successive objects. Hence, the desire to 'moderate' consumption or to establish a normalizing network of needs is naive and absurd moralism.

At the heart of the project from which emerges the systematic and indefinite process of consumption is a frustrated desire for totality. Object-signs are equivalent to each other in their ideality and can proliferate indefinitely: and *they must* do so in order continuously to fulfill the absence of reality. It is ultimately because consumption is founded on a *lack* that it is irrepressible.

CHAPTER 4   HEALTH, THE SELF AND SOCIAL INTERACTION

David Boswell

CONTENTS

1   INTRODUCTION

This series of volumes is concerned with the passage of time, with history, and the means by which social events are perceived, explained and manipulated. Enlightened *philosophes*, no less than subsequent history builders, Marxian revolutionaries and conservative functionalists, were primarily concerned with societies as wholes. Although individual independence might be analysed and evaluated variously, people were identified with some larger collectivity within which they acted and from which they took their characteristics. Although these writers were all concerned to compare and contrast their conception of their own society with those of other periods, other continents, or other forms of political economy, it was this broad level of analysis that held their attention.

However, there are other significant levels of analysis which warrant attention. Some social historians have challenged and augmented the work of political historians by writing from another frame of reference — the experience of 'ordinary' working men and women. Another group, the 'Chicago School' of urban sociologists, who started publishing in the 1920s and the 1930s, examined the lives of migrants and marginal men like street-corner gangsters, drug users and jazz musicians. And a third category of sociologists, of prime interest here, focused upon inter-personal relations, grass-root patterns of social interaction, and the ways in which people give meaning to their behaviour and act on it.

Although commonly done, it is unhelpful to categorize one form of analysis as 'Sociology' and another as 'Social Psychology' because each of these disciplines carries its own conceptual assumptions which impede other viewpoints. In any case, social interaction forms so vast a part of people's conscious and unconscious activity that by ignoring it one risks abandoning the hope of any wider sociological understanding of that behaviour. We are not concerned with exploring the byways of behaviour or the particularities of individuals but the patterns and regularities in those interactions.

To focus our analysis of social interaction, we shall consider it in the context of health and illness, and also give consideration to some significant related issues. We need some way of capturing individual behaviour in a social context in order to analyse social interaction. The concept of a *social role* — that is, a regular pattern of expected behaviour in social interaction — provides this.

This chapter will introduce the work of two North American sociologists on social role and social interaction. The first, Talcott Parsons (1902–79) highlighted the operation of social roles by analysing the reciprocal relationship between sick people and medical practitioners. Parson's general work formed one of the pillars of sociology in the first twenty years after the Second World War and many of his concepts remain in other writers' work.

The second, Erving Goffman (1922–82), a Canadian who undertook anthropological fieldwork in Scotland, spent most of his working life in the USA. Noting Durkheim's interest in social rituals, he investigated those of social interaction and the regular patterns of behaviour to be found in all sorts of social encounters. Some of his most influential writing followed participant observation in highly structured and hierarchical mental hospitals and, perhaps unwittingly, influenced the development of powerful arguments for organizational change, as we shall see.

Much sociological work has been concerned with chronically sick and behaviourally deviant people. Of particular relevance is the philosophical and sociological work of the French writer, Michel Foucault (1926–84). His conception of the power of ideas, as knowledge in the hands of dominant social groups, has influenced a line of enquiry into psychiatric and penal institutions, as well as sexuality.

The critical significance of the *interactionist perspective*, which uses the concept of social role, lies in its place within more general theories of deviance and labelling. In this context, Goffman's general analysis of stigma in human society is of great interest. In his analysis of total institutions, and of the moral career of the mental patient, Goffman used the particular situation to construct a general analysis of human social behaviour with regard to stigma. Its relevance is immediately apparent in the penetrating reflections of Susan Sontag, an American literary and social critic, on the ways in which illness has been, and is still being, used as a metaphor for other social judgements by which the sick are stigmatized. From her own experience of cancer, and her observation of TB and AIDS, she presents an historical analysis of the conceptualization of disease which shows how relevant are many of the sociological ideas in this chapter to a critical understanding of the human condition. An enthusiastic rationalist, Sontag carries the Enlightenment forward to our own day.

2   THE CONCEPT OF SOCIAL ROLES WITHIN A SOCIAL SYSTEM

Although the concept of social role obviously originates in a dramaturgical analogy of actors playing parts in a play, it was developed sociologically within the conception of society as a social system. Social roles, as formulated by Linton (1936), were seen as independent from the particular performances of individuals and formed the building blocks of the whole social order. But they were complex. Any individual is likely to hold a variety of positions in society. Men may be fathers, husbands, employees, workmates, voters and football spectators at almost one and the same time. Children may be daughters, pupils, playmates, delinquents etc. The permutations are numerous. The observation is simple.

Having admitted these combinations into the analysis one can see the complexity of any social situation because expectations of behaviour are associated with these roles, which may conflict with one another rather than coincide. Individuals are expected to act in relation to others within a set of reference points. The many roles an individual may be expected to play, however, are only one complication. Robert Merton took this a step further by demonstrating that:

> A particular social status involves, not a single associated role, but an array of associated roles. This is a basic characteristic of social structure. This fact can be registered by a distinctive term *role-set*, by which I mean that *complement of role relationships which persons have by virtue of occupying a particular social status.* As one example: the single status of medical student entails not only the role of a student in relation to his teachers, but also an array of other roles relating the occupant of that status to other students, nurses, physicians, social workers, medical technicians, etc. (Merton, 1968, p.423)

So, not only do people fill several different social positions simultaneously, they also have to deal with a whole set of others, even when behaving appropriately in any one social position.

2.1   TALCOTT PARSONS: THE CASE OF MODERN MEDICAL PRACTICE

We must study how such complex patterns of behavioural expectations have been analysed by sociologists, starting with the work of Talcott Parsons. He was one of many who viewed society as an organic structure, held together by the homoeostatic — that is, mutually supportive — functions of social institutions. By conforming to social roles people effectively worked to integrate and maintain the whole social system. Conflict and deviance, on the other hand, were seen as aberrations that had to be accommodated and resolved.

Parsons' theoretical formulation of structural functionalism has been criticized for providing no adequate *theory of conflict* due to his concern with social equilibrium; for being unable to offer a valid theory of *social change*; and for not addressing the general problem of *power* in an analytically satisfying and empirically sensitive manner. However, it would be quite false to think he was protecting the *status quo,* although he was not concerned with social reform or critical journalism (see Robertson and Turner, 1989, p.546). Within a clear conservative framework, Parsons was actually seeking to combat two powerful contemporary ways of looking at the world — which he perceived to consist of complex social relations. The first was the individualistic utilitarian economism built into American capitalism. The second was the prevailing scientistic medical model in which 'sickness' was considered specifically biological without a social dimension. Parsons (1978) accepted the direct association between illness and environmental factors that lead to infection, and effects of internal pathological processes. But he was particularly interested in the breakdown of people's capacity to perform in social interaction and some people's incapacity to 'pull themselves together'.

In the context of contemporary American society, which had just experienced the great Wall Street crash of 1929 and the ensuing slump, he had witnessed the impact of failure on a society ideologically geared to success. He observed that societies differed in how they considered illness was caused and how they responded to sickness and sick people. Parsons argued that sickness was a form of deviance from accepted social norms, which presumed that being healthy was *normal* both in the sense of being valued and of being the common condition. In this he followed Merton's analysis of sickness as social: 'By their very nature, societies constantly reproduce sickness and, so to speak, invent new categories of sickness to correspond to new strains in the structure of social relations' (quoted in Turner, 1986, p.142). Sickness was therefore normalized deviance, or, in Parsons' words, 'motivated deviance'. The essence of healing (that is restoration to healthy social functioning) lay in the social relationship of doctors with their patients. There was more to this process than biology. And there was also more to it than the fact that American patients paid their doctors. Parsons saw the medical profession as exemplary of a sort of social institution that diverged from that of a profit-motivated businessman because it had different goals and a different mode of operating. In this, the medical profession indicated that there was more to human relations than the cash-nexus. The case of modern medical practice was therefore a crucial example for his general theory of social action within a social system — a theory which aimed to move away from the over-economic focus to be found in both free-market capitalist theories and in some forms of Marxism.

ACTIVITY 1

You should now read **Reading A, 'Social structure and dynamic process'**, by Talcott Parsons, which you will find at the end of this chapter.

While reading you may find it useful to make notes on Parsons' treatment of the following:

• The sick role; i.e. what is expected of patients.

• The professional role; i.e. what is expected of medical practitioners.

• What constitutes sickness and treatment, with particular reference to the place of what he terms 'psychotherapy'.

Consider, furthermore, what breaches of normally expected behaviour are permitted to physicians, and what the terms or conditions are for permitting them.

We may see the roles of both patient and physician as constituting two rights, or exemptions from normal expectations of behaviour, and two obligations, or positive requirements of their related behaviour. Being sick exempts one from the usual duties to one's family, work etc., and one is not held responsible and liable to punishment but to support and, in some countries, even to an income. The patient is also obliged to leave the sick role speedily, i.e. to strive to get well, and to submit to the regime of those with the technical expertise to effect that, i.e. doctors, in order to return to health and the usual obligations of family life and work. Patients are treated by doctors impersonally; that is, as cases. Patients are expected to make use of a doctor's technical competence and he is expected to provide this to the best of his ability (NB: to Parsons, doctors were always 'he'). Finally, patients are expected to cooperate with their doctors in trying to get well and doctors, as professionals, work to a code of honour dedicated to their calling as distinct from commercial men seeking the highest monetary return for their services (Gerhardt, 1987, pp.114–20).

From Parsons' analysis we can see that there are all sorts of normal, or everyday, expectations of behaviour that are set aside or revised and reinterpreted when healthy people become sick patients and doctors are admitted into a professional relationship with them. Their interaction has to be unexploitative, therapeutic, and reintegrative, because patients are licensed deviants, who should strive to get better just as physicians are detached, professional healers.

Critics argued that such analysis presented, not only an idealization of role-relationships, but one that defined patients in terms convenient to doctors. Furthermore, the medical profession, far from being as Parsons portrayed it, was a self-selecting and privileged corporation enhancing and protecting its position of dominant power in the field of medicine, in effect what George Bernard Shaw had called 'a conspiracy against the public'. Others argued that Parsons had only acute and curable illness in mind and left little scope in his model for people unable to get better, and who, therefore, remain deviant, or may be regarded as sick when they have simply reached a particular stage in their life cycle. The model did not apply to the chronically sick or to disabled people; nor to women in menstruation or pregnancy, nor elderly people. Even in the case of people with mental disorders, whom he did consider, Parsons was primarily concerned with what broke down in their domestic social relations or at work, and with the explicit or more generally unconscious use of psychotherapy. He was not interested in the organizational side of health service delivery or the inequalities of experience of morbidity and mortality in society. All of these form part of the sociology of medicine (see Turner, 1987 and Gerhardt, 1989), but most of them can only be referred to in passing here because we are primarily concerned with the analysis of patterns of social interaction, that is, the level of interpersonal relations.

In this context, it was argued that the sort of role analysis one finds in Parsons' work left little scope for the variety of role performances and

outcomes likely to occur in such interaction situations as a hospital
ward or a general practitioner's clinic (see e.g. Strauss, *et al.*, 1964).

3   THE RITUAL OF SOCIAL INTERACTION

One of the most influential analysts of social interaction was Erving
Goffman. As a social ethnographer often focusing on the underlife of
social organizations, he has been coupled with other theorists of
deviance and labelling, for example by Gerhardt (1989). Parsons was
concerned with how those who have become unwell can be restored to
health; so, *deviance* was a temporary and even avoidable state.
Deviance theorists have been concerned with how people afflicted in
some way became *labelled* 'ill', 'criminal' or whatever. From this
perspective, illness is seen as being constructed by professionals. This
does not arise from their attitudes but is a product of social interaction.
One deviance theorist, Howard Becker, summarized the position thus:
'The deviant is one to whom the label has successfully been applied;
deviance is behaviour that people so label' (1963, p.9). It is this process
of labelling that effectively socializes someone into the role of deviant.

But Goffman's aim was more extensive than the analysis of how people
become or remain social deviants. He argued that the label 'deviant' was
simply an important category through which it was possible to explore
the underlying patterns, or regularities, in human social behaviour as
expressed through social interaction. Without denying the significance
of broader theoretical questions concerning social structure and
empirical enquiry at a macro-level of analysis, Goffman provided a
multi-faceted series of commentaries on face-to-face interaction as such.
This was not just to *illustrate* social structure in practice as Parsons had
done. Nor was interaction seen as a product of behavioural role-
performance with stress laid on the meaning and motivation underlying
the actions (see Williams, 1988). Goffman's dramaturgical approach to
the analysis of social interaction was not merely an analogy but a new
line of analysis to add to technical, political, structural and cultural
perspectives (Strong, 1988, p.228). As Goffman himself said, 'My
concern over the years has been to promote acceptance of this face-to-
face domain as an analytically viable one' (1983, p.2). Following
Durkheim's approach, if some kind of regular, or ritual, order was to be
found in social relations, it had both to have moral properties and to
take a standardized form in human interaction. This 'ritual order' was
what linked the micro-world of social interaction with the macro-world
of societies as such.

Goffman's style of argument was essentially literary, using surprising
paradoxes and colourfully juxtaposed examples from his carefully
compiled card index of exotic cases drawn from both fact and fiction.
One critical response to his work has, therefore, been that it was great
fun but really rather trivial, concerned with what is here today but gone

tomorrow. But Goffman had a different perspective, seeing patterns of everyday life as enduring and, in certain respects, universal because it was through such interaction that people developed and presented themselves. In this sense he was concerned with individuals but not the values of individualism.

This is well demonstrated in his analysis of deference and demeanour (Goffman, 1967a). Goffman used the comparison of patients' behaviour on different sorts of mental hospital wards, and their interaction with each other as well as with staff, to extend previous sociological discussion of different types of social rules, for example, by Durkheim and Parsons. He did so by focusing on the ceremonial rules, as distinct from substantive injunctions, which have primary importance 'as a conventionalized means of communication by which the individual expresses his character or conveys his appreciation of other participants in the situation' (Goffman, 1967a, p.54). Goffman made use of his mental hospital data, 'on the assumption that a logical place to learn about personal proprieties is among persons who have been locked up for spectacularly failing to maintain them. Their infractions of propriety occur in the confines of a ward, but the rules broken are quite general ones, leading us outward from the ward to a general study of Anglo-American Society' (Goffman, 1967a, p.48). Some rules are substantive, like injunctions against stealing, but others are ceremonial, such as rules of good manners, for interaction between those of different gender or status. Many roles are symmetrical, in that much the same behaviour is expected of each party to an encounter, but others are not. Asymmetrical rules of interaction generally pertain to social relationships between people of significantly different social status.

Deference is a ceremonial activity, a symbolic means of conveying appreciation and interpreted as such. The two main types of deference are 'presentational rituals through which the actor concretely depicts his appreciation of the recipient; and avoidance rituals, taking the form of proscriptions, interdictions and taboos, which imply acts the actor must refrain from doing lest he violate the right of the recipient to keep him at a distance' (Goffman, 1967a, p.73). On the wards, doctor/patient relationships were notably asymmetrical. Mental patients were not even expected to question the doctors about their own cases and were subject to a wide range of violations of privacy: e.g. searches, surveillance, being talked about in public, sleeping in dormitories, and being expected to perform normally private acts in unlockable and therefore potentially public rooms. Patients responded by overreaching the bounds of polite interaction in paying contextually inappropriate compliments or through excessively physical conveyance of appreciation. At the same time the presentation rituals of daily encounters enjoined them to provide appropriate positive responses, e.g. in asking about the health and well-being of those staff or patients encountered. Clearly, when to intervene and when to avoid doing so requires judgement and the application of the rules is uncertain. 'The human personality is a sacred thing; one does not violate it nor infringe its bounds, while at the same time the greatest good is in communion with others.' (Durkheim, 1953, p.37.)

By *demeanour*, Goffman referred to the ways in which people present themselves as desirable or undesirable through outward signs of deportment, dress and bearing: i.e. the presentation of character through behaviour. Meanings are pieced together based upon one person's image of another. Between social equals such presentations tend to be symmetrical and those who break the relevant rules are usually of higher status: e.g. doctors sitting on the desks in the nursing station. Patients on wards for the least and most severe cases presented themselves quite differently; those in the former category appearing and acting much as they would in a public place, while more severely disturbed patients behaved in all sorts of ways that broke the conventions of, for example, behaviour at table or in dress. Goffman concludes:

> Each individual is responsible for the demeanor image of himself and the deference image of others, so that for a complete man to be expressed, individuals must hold hands in a chain of ceremony, each giving deferentially with proper demeanor to the one on the right what will be received deferentially from the one on the left. While it may be true that the individual has a unique self of his own, evidence of this position is thoroughly a product of joint ceremonial labour, the part expressed through the individual's demeanor being no more significant than the part conveyed by others through their deferential behaviour towards him. (Goffman, 1967a, pp.84–5)

Just as Parsons conceived the sick and professional medical roles as interdependent, and health as something to be worked for, so Goffman uses the image of 'ceremonial labour' in the context of the ways in which meaning is conveyed in social relations.

Clive's encounter group

4   THE CEREMONIAL ORDER OF THE CLINIC

One indication of the power or relevance of a writer's work is the extent to which it is used by others working in the field. An example of this is the way Goffman's concepts were used by Philip Strong in *The Ceremonial Order of the Clinic* (1979), a comparative study of British and American paediatric clinics. Strong observed the actual encounters between staff, usually doctors, and the parents or foster parents of the child patients in a wide range of Scottish clinics.

Strong used the term *ceremony* to describe the overt (public) and covert (private) interaction which occurred as a form of celebration (or mutually respectful role-playing) by doctors and patients. This interaction was associated with a shared inattention on the part of the participants to anything that might disrupt their shared maintenance of this overt order. Significantly, the nature of this order became clearer when the regularity or pattern of behaviour in Scottish NHS clinics was both compared and contrasted with some similar and some very different forms of clinic encounter that Strong observed in the USA. The sociological significance of his observations lies in his concept of a *ritual order* that links the apparently particular micro-world of face-to-face interaction with the macro-world of social organization, i.e. the dynamic association between these apparently discrete levels of analysis.

A description of what Strong analysed, and some illustration of the sorts of encounter and interchange that he and his research assistant witnessed, will indicate the manner in which the wider society impinged on these brief encounters. It will illustrate also the morally charged assumptions which formed the constraints upon this type of relationship between doctors and parental clients (for the children who were the actual patients seldom figured as active participants).

Strong aims 'to set the business of diagnosis, treatment and their discussion within an organizational framework. ... All social life has an artificial, rule-governed and ceremonial aspect (and may thus be seen as artfully constructed), though many of our calculations are so routine that they pass unnoticed by ourselves' (Strong, 1979, p.6).

Social interaction between doctors and patients is strongly constrained. The common National Health Service *format*, or pattern of interaction, in the Scottish clinics that Strong studied, may be characterized as *bureaucratic*, in the Weberian sense of being rational, regular, and impersonal. Strong found that this was based on the assumption of professional — in this case, medical — dominance and competence, to such an extent that, even where second opinions were sought from other consultants (a little-used right under the NHS), these transactions were negotiated as between colleagues rather than as a challenge to the competence of the first consultant. The consultations were conducted in a form that also assumed a model of natural parenthood which included the parents, and especially the mothers, of child patients. Mothers were assumed to be careful, loving, competent and able to cope with what could well be increasingly demanding burdens. An indication of these assumptions was that mothers were not praised for their performance whereas fathers, who sometimes came instead, were praised and foster parents were treated as professionals, on a par, one suspects, with the paramedical or auxiliary staff. Mothers were expected to be good mothers and even if, in the context of the consultation, they were delinquents, they were addressed as if they were good mothers, or at any rate could be if they followed the instructions they had ignored. The following extract is an example from Strong's research report:

> Here ... is a quotation from a Scottish local authority clinic in which a mother was interviewed by a female paediatrician about her grossly overweight baby, who at six months was covered in rolls of fat and weighed twenty pounds:

> DR B   And you feed him on Farex?
>
> MOTHER In the morning and evening.
>
> DR B   And porridge?
>
> MOTHER Aye.
>
> DR B   Does he get anything for elevenses?
>
> MOTHER Just biscuits.
>
> DR B   How much porridge does he get?
>
> MOTHER Oh, not much.
>
> DR B   How much does he get at lunch time?
>
> MOTHER Oh, just mince and tatties.
>
> DR B   Do you give him anything in mid-afternoon?
>
> MOTHER No.
>
> DR B   And what does he get for his tea?
>
> MOTHER Oh, a boiled egg or a scrambled egg.
>
> DR B   And this is as well as milk?
>
> MOTHER Aye.
>
> DR B   Does he get anything else?
>
> MOTHER Aye ... [rest inaudible].
>
> DR B   Well, I think he's putting on a bit too much weight. Is he fatter than your other children?
>
> MOTHER Aye.
>
> DR B   If I were you I'd miss out the Farex and the porridge at breakfast and the biscuits as well. It's best to do this now because if children get fat now often they tend to be fatter later in life. He's supposed to be twice his birthweight now and he's a good bit more than that, isn't he? This is very important. He's putting on a bit too much weight.

(Strong, 1979, pp.46–8)

The focus was on the facts of the case and, although specific advice was given, this was within a neutral frame of reference. The assessment and advice given in the encounter were not demeaning to the mother. It took the form of 'face-work', as Goffman (1967b) called it, in which, notwithstanding an attempt to change the mother's child-care practices, the identity and moral status ascribed to her as a mother were treated as the real situation and any discrepancies between that and her actual behaviour were glossed over. Strong concludes by observing that this form of socialized medicine has adapted a bourgeois pattern, generally concerned with organic disorders, in which mutual respect between professionals and patients is expected.

Of course this may be patronizing, or evade discussion of severe problems of various kinds, but here we are primarily concerned with the pattern, or ceremonial, of the encounter and its basis, not its functionality for a wide range of purposes. Of considerable interest are the contrasts that Strong found in other modes of health service provision in the USA. Private practice followed a similar pattern to that found in the British National Health Service with two important distinctions. First, it was only available to those who could pay, either directly or through insurance. This meant that the consultation was actually 'bourgeois' in character, a fee-for-service encounter initiated by the patient's family. In the case of the British NHS, the form of the consultation was bureaucratically cast, as a means of treating all patients alike. All mothers were treated as good mothers seeking to follow professionally approved modes of child care etc., whereas they were actually drawn from all walks of life with potentially very different ways of life, economic means, and varying patterns of family life and child care. Secondly, the American private consultants not only personalized the encounters with a high degree of politesse, they also prominently displayed their skills and qualifications, just as the private health services they used advertised their own facilities on the clinic walls. In Britain, the rooms were usually bare and certainly provided no information on the consultants' technical expertise, which was taken for granted as an NHS provision.

However, what Strong terms *the charity format* — that is, public assistance by private or public agencies — was based in the USA on a frame of reference quite different from that of the NHS in Britain (although the American form does occur in other British welfare agencies which are required to means-test their potential beneficiaries). Rather than attempt to save the face of patients, the American charity doctor's approach took the active form of 'character-work', attempting either to ameliorate the situation by criticism and exhortation or to reconstitute it by directly challenging the propriety and rectitude of parents' behaviour. As Strong observes:

> Whereas face-work was the staple diet of the bureaucratic format, character-work was the standard fare in the charity mode. The doctor who used it, a doctor in a clinic run by an American city,

distinguished three types of moral character in mothers. First, there were the penitent and eager to learn. Second, there were those who might seem overtly penitent but whose capacity or willingness to make amends was in some doubt. Finally, there were the impenitent or those of revealed bad character. In the fifteen consultations all but two mothers were identified as being of the second, rather dubious type, for the standards set to enter the first category were those of the doctor herself. To count as moral and competent and to be treated as such, mothers had to do exactly what she would have done; and she was middle-class, white and medically trained, whereas the mothers were poor and mostly black or Puerto Rican. The only mother with whom the doctor enjoyed an easy relationship was a young white woman of a serious demeanour who engaged in self-criticism. She described how she fed the child, mentioned what she had read about feeding and asked for the doctor's advice in this matter. In all, she enacted the role of a humble but keen medical student. In return the doctor provided her with reassurance and a mass of technical information. But other mothers did not formally ask her advice, nor did they mention any books or articles they had read and thus demonstrate their concern. They were therefore subjected to forceful interrogation, which undercut any of their claims to competence as a mother. Here, for example, is an excerpt from a case in which the presenting problem was nappy rash. All the doctor's remarks were made in a most aggressive fashion:

DR S   What do you wash her nappies in?

MOTHER   Ivory Snow.

DR S   Why do you use Ivory Snow?

MOTHER   Well, it's supposed to make the nappies softer than washing powders.

DR S   How do you know Ivory Snow makes nappies softer?

MOTHER   [shrugs awkwardly] Well, um ... [she mumbles something about her mother and advertisements].

DR S   You don't want to believe everything you see in the adverts. It's a business. That's *their* business. *Your* business is your baby.

The doctor then explained that nappy rash was due to ammonia in the urine and that Ivory Snow was too weak. The mother should therefore use an ordinary washing powder.

MOTHER   I do put vinegar in it.

DR S   [in amazed tone] Why do you do that?

MOTHER   Well, I was told.

DR S   Who told you?

MOTHER   Well my mother did.

DR S   What difference does it make?

MOTHER   Well, she said … I thought it …

DR S   It doesn't do any good at all.

The doctor then gave an explanation of the chemistry involved.

Since the doctor held that the only rational criteria for behaviour were her own, those who behave in a different fashion were deemed irrational, and ignorance was seen as lack of love towards the child and even, on some occasions, as proof of hatred: feeding a two-and-a-half month baby on solid food was characterized as a 'hostile' action.
(Strong, 1979, pp.43–4)

ACTIVITY 2   From your reading of Sections 3 and 4, make notes on the following:

• What did Goffman mean by the terms *deference* and *demeanour*?

• Give some examples of how Strong has used these terms in analysing the differences between different types of clinic interaction formats.

From Strong's analysis of clinical-practice patterns, based upon the everyday experience of these encounters, one can see that the use of interactional analysis is no less theoretical and of no less significance in understanding the wider society than Parsons' approach considered in Section 2. But the aims and constituent variables are different and situationally much more specific in Strong's research than in Parsons'.

5   PROCESSING PEOPLE AND THE CONCEPT OF A MORAL CAREER

We have seen that encounters in social situations follow regular patterns that may be formally structured although they usually involve only small numbers of people at a time. But Strong's comparative clinic example has introduced several new aspects because one can see that behaviour is not simply ascribed to certain social positions, but learnt or taught, and given a moral evaluation. This process may be generally termed 'socialization'. It will be useful to explore this further within the health service context. Goffman does just this in his inimitable paradoxical way in 'The moral career of the mental patient' (1961a), thereby linking personal matters such as self-image and felt identity with the public position of a mental patient in an institutional complex.

In an earlier paper entitled 'On the characteristics of total institutions' (first published in 1957; see Goffman, 1961b), Goffman had already staked out much of the ground that he was to explore in greater detail here, by outlining the common features of that apparently disparate category of establishments that were based on rigidly routinized

behaviour within residential establishments. In these institutions the
inmates slept, lived, ate and took their recreation together in one
bounded space. They were *total* in the sense that whole lives were
played out in them. They exhibited a great social distance between
hierarchical grades of staff and inmates, and a pattern of social relations
in which the inmates were depersonalized and treated as common, even
interchangeable, elements in the organization, as well as in ways that
often expected them to behave in a common manner. Examples of such
total institutions are boarding schools and barracks, prisons,
monasteries and mental hospitals. They were analysed by Goffman as a
single social type with the mental hospital as their archetype — i.e. a
public institution in which people could be compulsorily confined and
in which they had to live out their lives in a context which both
combined and confused discipline and treatment because its
authoritarian setting was pre-eminent.

ACTIVITY 3   You should now read **Reading B, 'The moral career of the mental
patient'**, by Erving Goffman.

While you are reading, make a note of your answers or reactions to the
following questions and observations:

- We keep encountering the use of occupational analogies in these
  analyses of social interaction. Why does Goffman use the term
  'career', and what is he implying by using it in this setting?

- How may a patient's social construction of his or her past be related
  to subsequent experiences as an inmate, and what threatens even this
  self-image?

6 ANTI-PSYCHIATRY: A DISPARATE MOVEMENT IN IDEAS

After reading some of Goffman's writing it will come as no surprise that
his analysis of total institutions proved highly influential in fields of
social interaction in which he was neither particularly interested nor
involved: those of protest and social reform. To the generations familiar
with the ultimate lengths to which total institutionalization could be
taken (the Nazi concentration camps), and convinced of the ill effects of
social stereotyping, the ameliorative and socially therapeutic goals of
such establishments as mental hospitals seemed to have been exposed
as bogus and reprehensible. Busfield writes of this period as one in
which there was a 'diversity of ideas and assumptions about the nature
and causes of mental illness, about the efficiency and values of
therapeutic techniques, about the power of professionals, and about the

structure and organization of society and the distribution of power within it' (Busfield, 1986, p.15).

In Britain, movement for reform had for a long time been contained within the psychiatric establishment. Russell Barton (1959) had argued that long-stay mental patients suffered an *institutional neurosis* brought on by the limitations of their environment, and Maxwell Jones (1952) had implemented a discursive, communitarian and less hierarchical regime in some hospital wards. Coupled with a general policy of discharging and not detaining patients, and the use of chemotherapy to modify patients' disturbed and/or disturbing behaviour, the momentum of public policy swung against the mental hospitals.

In retrospect, one can see the strands that made up the intellectual and socio-political rejection of psychiatry as very disparate. They included psychiatrists like Laing (1960), Laing and Esterson (1964), and Cooper (1971) whose arguments took up Gregory Bateson's (1956) thesis that forms of schizophrenia were generated by the social and psychological impact of inescapable, but conflicting and therefore unattainable, demands by other family members. Laing and Cooper ultimately took the thesis to its logical conclusion that, in an insane world, only the mad were sane because their response to it was the only honest and possible one. Goffman had argued that there were rational and socially regular ways of behaving in a madhouse and that it was not a world of meaningless irrationality. Laing and Cooper argued that madness was a reasonable reaction and response to unrealizable demands. Busfield (1986) usefully contrasts the conventional scientific–medical model of illness with that effectively put forward by critics of the concept of mental illness (see Table 4.1).

Table 4.1   Contrasting conceptions of physical illness and functional mental illness

Characteristic of the conception	Physical illness	Functional mental illness
Appropriate label	Illness	Problem in living/deviance
Refers to	Bodily functioning	Human action
Type of norms	Norms of bodily functioning	Social, ethical and legal rules
Nature of judgement	Objective, value-free scientific	Subjective, value-laden, ideological
The individual's relation to the deviation	Passive, victim	Active agent
Type of explanatory factors	Organic	Social and psychological
Type of explanation	Causal	Non-causal, rule-following, understanding
Role of medicine	Care and cure	Social control

Source: Busfield, 1986, p.93.

We have seen how, from Parsons onwards, sickness may be viewed as a form of social deviance leading to the intervention of others to deal with it. Deviance and labelling theorists have taken the patients' perspective, as we have seen in the case of Goffman. In all these cases, even implicitly in Parsons, it is quite clear where power lies — medicine is seen as an agent of social control. Goffman, like most social anthropologists, had little concern with history, seeing a similarity in certain social institutions irrespective of time and place, and seeing the patterns as formed by social interaction. But other sociologists have taken a more historical approach, seeking to explain the origin of current institutional models.

6.1 MICHEL FOUCAULT: CONFINEMENT AND THE ROLE OF THE DOCTOR

One highly influential philosophical historian and sociologist is Michel Foucault, who introduced the important concept of *discourse* (see *Penguin Dictionary of Sociology:* DISCOURSE). Foucault sought to give meaning to ideas that arose at particular periods by exploring their association with the dominant pattern of social relations at the time and therefore the ways in which general ideas were socially grounded. Unlike Goffman's intellectual basis in Durkheim's perspective and terminology, Foucault's post-Marxian concept of discourse is based on the view that pre-eminent ideas are generated by the social forces predominant in and characteristic of their epoch. A discourse is therefore the historically and logically apposite frame of reference within which something may be discussed, considered and acted upon within a given period in the social development of such ideas. A key to power is knowledge, and the development of the medical profession with control of entry to, training for, and regulation of its members as well as their working establishments, in hospitals and clinics, exemplified this association.

Goffman sought to analyse the social characteristics of total institutions. Foucault sought a logical reason for their emergence as the socially preferred mode of treating particular categories of people at a particular point in history. In *Madness and Civilization* (1967), his study of insanity during the Age of Reason, Foucault presented the case as a Europe-wide one, but largely drew on the model of historical developments in France, with additional exemplification from other countries. The period of social legislation, which in England is characterized by the Elizabethan Poor Law and dependence on local government, is in France characterized by a later and more specifically classical age in culture and centralizing state-craft. This phase of French history coincided with the Civil War in England, which France had experienced in the context of religious wars a generation earlier. Foucault therefore saw the ideas of mental treatment which coincided with the French Revolution as a distinct development, whereas in England the conception of 'moral treatment' is less obviously distinct from the economistic ideas that preceded it. (See also Book 1 (Hall and Gieben, 1992), Chapter 3.)

In this study, Foucault was attempting to refute the liberal-scientific, conventional historical interpretation of psychiatric development. This view of progress is well represented in English by the work of Kathleen Jones (1955 and 1960). Jones presented the trend in mental health services as a sequence of humanitarian medical advances, from the barbarism of physical constraints to a liberal, restorative application of new treatments, with some setbacks in the nineteenth century when doctors did not control access to mental hospitals and these were expanded far beyond their potential therapeutic uses.

Seeing the seventeenth century in France as an era in which institutional confinement was officially promulgated and generalized, Foucault argued that there was a form of positional succession, with one set of deviants, or pariahs, succeeded by another (a viewpoint we shall consider later with reference to AIDS).

> To inhabit the reaches long since abandoned by the lepers, they chose a group that to our eyes is strangely mixed and confused. But what is for us an undifferentiated sensibility must have been, for those living in the classical age, a clearly articulated perception. It is this mode of perception which we must investigate in order to discover the form of sensibility to madness in an epoch we are accustomed to define by the privileges of reason. ... What made it [confinement] necessary was an imperative of labour. Our philanthropy prefers to recognize the signs of a benevolence towards sickness where there is only a condemnation of idleness. ... In fact, the relation between the practice of confinement and the insistence on work is not defined by economic conditions, far from it. A moral perception sustains and animates it.
>
> (Foucault, 1967, pp.46–8).

The workhouse of that period was, in other words, not defined by utilitarian arguments of self-sufficiency, but as a means of combating sloth.

Foucault rejected the anachronistic gloss that has been placed on the innovations specifically associated with Philippe Pinel (1745–1826) and William Tuke (1732–1822) in the late eighteenth century. The former had removed the chains from some of his Parisian hospital patients in 1793, and the latter had founded the Retreat at York in 1796, initially to provide Quaker patients with a structured, domestic regime that called for appropriate behaviour. Praised as liberators and enlightened in their respectful treatment of patients as potentially socially responsible people, they were seen as founding fathers of good psychiatry, despite the abandonment of their concept of 'moral treatment' in later psychiatry and hospital organization. Foucault's approach was to situate such institutional models in their particular historical contexts. He was less judgemental in his analysis of the development of mental hospitals and psychiatry. The alternative proposition that he formulated is set out in 'The birth of the asylum' (Reading C), which concludes his study of insanity.

The Rake in Bedlam. Originally painted in 1735, this represents the final stage in Hogarth's *Rake's Progress* and depicts both the unreformed use of the hospital as a fashionable peep-show and most of the classic types of insanity. In front is the melancholic madness of the rake and, in a cell behind, the raving madness of a religious fanatic. Other inmates suffer from delusions of royal or papal grandeur, etc. For Pinel's 'synthetic' treatment of these disorders, as well as Tuke's moral regime at the Retreat, see Reading C.

Philippe Pinel, Médecin en chef de la Saltpêtrière, delivering his patients from their chains. Painted by Tony Robert Fleury (1837–1912), this large picture hangs in the hospital's main staircase to commemorate and promulgate the myth to which Foucault refers in Reading C.

ACTIVITY 4   You should now read **Reading C, 'The birth of the asylum'**, by Michel
Foucault. While you are reading it make a note of particular points
which may help you answer the following questions:

* What do you understand Foucault to be getting at when he asserts
  that '… Tuke created an asylum where he substituted for the free
  terror of madness the stifling anguish of responsibility; fear no longer
  reigned on the other side of the prison gates, it now raged under the
  seals of conscience'?

* What were the principal means by which Pinel tried to instil moral
  syntheses in his asylum?

* What was the significance of the medical officer (or *medical
  personage*) in all this? Why does Foucault see the role of the doctor
  as so important for the future?

Goffman, Strong and now Foucault have all used the term 'moral' in
describing and analysing patterns of behaviour and expectation in
mental hospitals and other clinical settings — that is to say, the exercise
of judgement and correction through regimes conducive to the practice
of approved modes of behaviour. Nothing could seem further from the
notion of scientific medical practice in the cure of diseases. Foucault
did not see the knowledge exercised by Tuke and Pinel as particularly
significant or lasting. What was enduring was their creation of the
medical officer and the asylum. Foucault wrote subsequently (1973) of
the birth of the clinic, or hospital, as the site of control, by doctors,
through the means of the specialized knowledge that was developed
through the nineteenth century. 'There is no power relation without the
correlative constitution of a field of knowledge, nor any knowledge that
does not presuppose and constitute at the same time power relations.'
(Foucault, 1977, p.27.)

In her critical review of research into the ideas and practice of managing
madness, Busfield (1986) provides some useful qualifications to the
sorts of historical interpretations of history offered by Foucault and
others. In England, the eighteenth century was a period of private
madhouse development and one in which even mania, hitherto
considered most bestial and least manageable at home, was opened to
these new behavioural treatment approaches. In the nineteenth century,
lunatic asylums were required to perform general public functions as
part of the regulatory apparatus of the Poor Law. This, as Scull (1984)
and Porter (1987) pointed out, was an era of such substantial increases
in the quantity of incarcerating institutions, and the numbers of people
put away in them, as to make Foucault's 'Great Confinement' of
previous centuries seem more formal and legalistic than actually
practised.

What Foucault certainly contributed to, along with the variety of other
analyses of institutional psychiatry, was the discourse of his own time,

i.e. the 1960s and '70s. Stimulated by Foucault's work to explore the
ways in which insane people have provided their own stories, Roy
Porter observes that:

> ... psychiatry has itself formed part of a common consciousness.
> The mad and the mad-doctors are often saying intriguingly
> comparable things about agency and action, rights and
> responsibility, reason and nonsense, though applying them in
> fundamentally reversed ways. Indeed, in this century, as
> psychiatry has become part of the common cultural image, it is
> often hard to tell when the psychiatrist is speaking and when the
> patient. ... The delusions of the mad, the myths of psychiatry and
> the ideologies of society at large all form part of a common
> ideological fabric.
> (Porter, 1987, p.4)

Whether or not their authors intended to make an impact on the ways
in which the mentally ill were treated, the writings of Foucault,
Goffman and others helped to create a climate of opinion which led to
the changes. Of course these changes were not independent of other
strong economic and political pressures. Mental illness came to be seen
more and more as socially constructed. Through the theories of
deviance and labelling, such ideas were already current with reference
to young offenders, pensioners and others.

Peter Sedgwick, a sociologist with personal experience of psychiatric
treatment, who was actively seeking mental health service reforms,
wrote his own critique of these writers. Contrasting this sociological
perspective with that common in epidemiology, which accepts medical
definitions, Sedgwick wrote:

> We have a contrast, in brief, between what might be called an
> *exterior* sociology of mental illness and an *immanent* (or in-
> dwelling) sociology of 'mental-illness-as-a-social-construct'. The
> same contrast, as a matter of fact, is visible in the sociological
> treatment of several social problem areas outside the aetiology of
> madness: prostitution, homosexuality, drug addiction and criminal
> delinquency are all topics which can be discussed in the literature
> either via an external sociology analysing pathological 'givens' or
> from an immanent, critical perspective which sees the official
> comments and categories of deviancy as more projections of
> society's formal or informal control process, and performs an
> imaginative entry into the deviant's own actions, viewing these as
> an attempt to manufacture significance for his or her life within
> and against a rejecting, 'labelling' world.
> (Sedgwick, 1982, pp.16–17)

It is useful to follow Sedgwick's line of argument because it indicates
both the radical and practical, as distinct from the negative and
dismissive, response to sociological analysis. Sedgwick was prepared to

propose developments in social practices which would offer more positive social situations for severely ill and troubled people. That is to say, he accepted the idea of the social construction of mental illness in some cases but not all. He struggled against the manipulation of the mentally ill in battles which used them as surrogates for much larger underclasses in the general population.

Sedgwick regarded the stress that Foucault laid on confinement of insane people in the Age of Reason as out of proportion, because its scale was slight compared with the colossal increase in confinement which followed the New Poor Law of 1843. This act exemplified the expansion of social control in the nineteenth century and Sedgwick, like Scull (1984), associated changes in social policy with the current states of the national economy. He was particularly sceptical of there being any radical message in Goffman's work. Sedgwick put forward his own communitarian support programme because he considered that those conventionally lumped together as anti-psychiatrists failed, or even did not wish, to present any relevant programme of action (Sedgwick, 1982).

"I have an alternative psychiatrist – he slaps you around and tells you to pull yourself together."

Sedgwick confused the intentions of those writers he criticized with the impact of their ideas and observations, coming as they did in the wake of other profound economic and socio-political changes. Irrespective of Goffman's own intentions or theoretical grounding, it is wrong to assume that his work could have no significant practical application because several action-based research programmes have demonstrated that it could. One example is the work of King, Raynes, and Tizard (1971), which compared the characteristics of different sorts of children's residential and hospital care and was associated with the radical transformation of the Wessex Hospital Region's system of care for mentally handicapped people in the British National Health Service. Large, isolated hospitals were replaced by other forms of residential care which were also more personalized and developmental.

Using Goffman's characterization of total institutions, Raynes and King (1974) isolated key features of social practices that could be seen as either primarily institutionally *or* inmate (i.e. child) orientated. These included: the extent to which routines were rigidly followed or left flexible to suit individuals or day-to-day events; the treatment of inmates as a 'block' in getting up, toileting, feeding etc.; the level to which inmates were depersonalized with reference to clothing, toys etc.; and the extent to which social distance was maintained between the staff and the children.

Although there were great differences between the highly institutionalized hospital regimes and those of the local authority and voluntary homes and hostels, this did not turn out to be simply the result of the size of the wards or child-care units within them. Even the number of staff available made no generally significant difference. What did make a difference were the roles assumed by the staff heading these child-care units. Those who played a direct part in the social and physical care of the children, and in supervising other staff in these activities, had low institutionalization scores, whereas those who spent their time on administration and domestic work scored more highly. Parallel differences were observed in the extent to which staff interacted directly with individual children or not.

What emerged clearly was the degree of association between these scores and the child-care *or* nursing training and work-experience background of the staff in charge of the hostels or hospital wards (see Figure 4.1). Among those who were trained in child care, 'a model of care for retarded patients has been taken over from traditional care of deprived children. ... Hospitals for subnormals, on the other hand, have taken over a model of care based partly on that for acute cases and partly on the tradition of care of the chronic sick' (Raynes and King, 1974, p.304). Nurses in charge of smaller-scale hostels, as opposed to impersonal hospital wards, performed partway between the two forms of care. Subsequent research contrasted the extent to which the children themselves developed in various ways under the two regimes. Those in hospital did not flourish.

I think this is enough to indicate that the concepts resulting from Goffman's approach to institutional analysis are capable of being operationalized in the context of research using quite different, quantitative, methods from those he adopted. We have thus seen

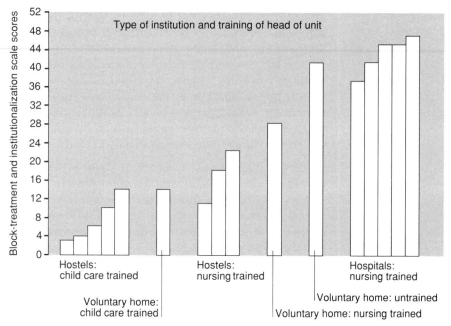

Figure 4.1   Block-treatment and institutionalization scale scores by training of head of unit and type of institution*

* Each column represents a single institution
Source: Raynes and King, 1974, p.305

Goffman's concepts and approach fruitfully adopted by Strong and by Raynes and King in two different types of research in different settings, in both of which the passage of information, or the developmental prospects for patients, may actually be based on the form of the encounter. Situational analysis is therefore neither trivial nor irrelevant to understanding the real world and changing aspects of it.

7   SELF-IDENTITY AND STIGMATIZATION

We started this chapter with the rather abstract concepts of social role and social structure and their use in formulating specific constellations of related roles, such as those of a sick person and a medical practitioner. We proceeded to explore patterns of social interaction, such as may be found in various kinds of health service and, in particular, the formation of different social and other analyses into a discourse — in this case anti-psychiatry — which had its own impact on society in the form of social policy. In this final section we shall shift the focus of attention from patterns of interaction and institutional forms to the issue of self-identity, again with special reference to illness.

Goffman's analysis, *Stigma: Notes on the Management of Spoiled Identity* (1963), sets out the ground. He distinguishes the plight of those known to be discredited by some known or observable blemish (e.g. some physical deformity) and those who are potentially discreditable: i.e. fearful of secrets being divulged (e.g. those who have been imprisoned, or been in a mental hospital). Goffman noted the social consequences of being discreditably different from other people — of being stigmatized. We are therefore considering the stigmatized person's self-conception, his or her estimate of him/herself as a person with a spoiled identity.

Some of Goffman's concepts already introduced in this chapter are applied to this situation as well: for example, the idea that social relationships have to be worked at, or managed; that a stigmatized person may encounter particular categories of people in his or her role-set who may be wise to his/her condition; or someone with particularly close inside knowledge and attachment by kinship or some other close bond.

Of course, one response to this characterization of stigma is like the reassessment of mental illness considered in Section 6. Having been shown to be a social construct, it can be treated as an artificial fabrication, as something which one can ignore because 'it is not really there'. If so, the chances are that society will remain the same, and some material benefits which stigmatized people might expect could be removed on the grounds that what is not real needs no compensation. One has only to think of homeless or imprisoned ex-mental patients to understand this. Alternatively, compensatory measures and positive discrimination may be adopted in order to enable at least certain categories of people (for example, those who are disabled) to share opportunities for interaction which most people (in this case, those who are able-bodied) consider normal.

We now need to consider the relation of self and self-identity to the wider world of daily experiences. The context in which we stigmatize others or feel defiled, occurs from day to day in ordinary encounters with people. But it is defined by a variety of judgements and assumptions of what is right and proper, good and bad, fruitful and harmful, etc. These form sets of beliefs and practices associated with concepts of pollution and taboo, which can only be superficially explained and rationalized by forms of natural materialism, e.g. by reducing food or washing rituals to climatic and germicidal explanations.

Mary Douglas analyses the concepts of hygiene and pollution (see Book 1 (Hall and Gieben, 1992), Chapter 5). In *Purity and Danger* she argued:

> Dirt is matter out of place. ... It implies two conditions; a set of ordered relations and a contravention of that order. ... Where there is dirt there is a system. ... In short, our pollution behaviour is the reaction which condemns any object or idea likely to confuse or contradict cherished classifications.
> (Douglas, 1966, pp.34–6)

This introduces a new dimension into relationships which may be governed by external referents and meanings imbued with especial moral evaluations and injunctions. Central to them is the concept of a whole and wholesome body:

> The body ... provides a basic scheme for all symbolism. There is hardly any pollution which does not have some primary physiological reference. As life is in the body it cannot be rejected outright. And as life must be affirmed, the complete philosophies ... must find some ultimate way of affirming that which has been rejected.
> (Douglas, 1966, pp.163–4)

This is the terrain over which the American writer and critic Susan Sontag is effectively ranging in her perceptive and reflexive analysis of the meanings given to illness through the centuries and, in particular, the somewhat parallel roles and status given to a succession of severe diseases. *Illness as Metaphor* (1983) provided a vehicle for her to consider her own experiences as a cancer patient expected to die, but who failed to do so and therefore lived to reflect on her traumatic socio-psychological experiences. In *Aids and its Metaphors* (1989), Sontag reflected upon the emergence of yet another incurable disease which cut down some of her closest friends and colleagues.

Sontag's own position is quite clear:

> My subject is not physical illness itself but the uses of illness as a figure of metaphor. My point is that illness is *not* a metaphor, and that the most truthful way of regarding illness — and the healthiest way of being ill — is one most resistant of, most resistant to, metaphorical thinking. Yet it is hardly possible to take up one's residence in the kingdom of the ill unprejudiced by the lurid metaphors with which it has been landscaped.
> (Sontag, 1983, p.7)

She takes a rationalist and materialist stance that disease is organic and in due course, one hopes, curable, and that its other meanings — as a scourge, a punishment or in some way related to the temperament and psychology of those sickened with it (what we might term its social construction) — are things that can be exposed and jettisoned. But she is equally aware of the deep-seated attractions of such judgemental metaphors.

> The age-old, seemingly inexorable process whereby diseases acquire meaning (by coming to stand for the deepest fears) and inflict stigma is always worth challenging, and it does seem to have more limited credibility in the modern world, among people willing to be modern — the process under surveillance now. With this illness [AIDS], one that elicits so much guilt and shame, the

effort to detach it from these meanings, these metaphors, seems
particularly liberating, even consoling. But the metaphors cannot
be distanced just by abstaining from them. They have to be
exposed, criticized, used up.
(Sontag, 1989, pp.94–5)

One could not seek a clearer expression of the Enlightenment project
with which Book 1 of this series began (see Hall and Gieben (1992),
Chapter 1).

Susan Sontag by David Levine

In her consideration of cancer, Sontag emphasized the unique horror
that the disease holds; for in the United States of America, the 1966
Freedom of Information law specifically exempts cancer on the grounds
that its disclosure 'would be an unwarranted invasion of personal
privacy'. Sontag compares cancer with tuberculosis, its predecessor as
an object of metaphor, and brings together such general social reactions
as those that characterize these diseases as 'morally, if not literally,
contagious' and too awful to name, as well as the cultured literary
metaphors with which both diseases have been cloaked (Sontag, 1983,
p.10). 'As cancer is now imagined to be the wages of repression, so TB
was once explained as the ravages of frustration. ... The Romantics
invented invalidism as a pretext for leisure and for discussing bourgeois
obligations in order to live only for one's art. It was a way of retiring
from the world without having to take responsibility for the decision'
(Sontag, 1983, pp.26, 37–8). (The myth of invalidism survived until

cures for TB were found in the 1940s.) Cancer has not taken on this role, but she opines: 'In the twentieth century, the repellant, harrowing disease that is made the index of superior sensitivity, the vehicle of "spiritual" feelings and "critical" discontent, is insanity' (ibid, p.39). The socio-psychological attributes of TB have been split between romanticizing insanity and agonizing cancer.

Although Sontag's argument is different, I think one can see the same type of historical argument at work here as in Foucault's analysis of the succession of social pariahs and the development of institutionalization. The difference is that Sontag sees much the same forces at work, and even most of the same metaphors, time after time as each new disease takes the limelight. And, as already mentioned, Sontag objects to the use of what she terms 'psychology' in this process: 'A large part of the popularity and persuasiveness of psychology comes from its being a sublimated spiritualism: a secular, ostensibly scientific way of affirming the primacy of "spirit" over matter. That ineluctably material reality, disease, can be given a psychological explanation. Death itself can be considered, ultimately, a psychological phenomenon' (Sontag, 1983, p.59).

She argues further that, 'Psychological theories of illness are a powerful means of placing the blame on the ill. Patients who are instructed that they have, unwittingly, caused their disease are also being made to feel that they have deserved it' (ibid, p.61). In the case of AIDS there is nothing indirect about the metaphor. As in the earlier case of syphilis, those afflicted can be blamed for their behaviour only too easily.

> In recent years some of the onus of cancer has been lifted by the emergence of a disease whose charge of stigmatization, whose capacity to create spoiled identity, is far greater. It seems that societies need to have an illness which becomes identified with evil, and attaches blame to its "victims", but it is hard to be obsessed with more than one at once. ... For several generations now, the generic idea of death has been a death from cancer, and a cancer death is experienced as a generic defeat. Now the generic rebuke to life and hope is AIDS.
> (Sontag, 1989, pp.16, 24)

What could be called the primitive question in relation to disease causation, 'Why me?', was always something of an open question in relation to cancer. It can be associated with unsafe dietary habits and lifestyles. But with AIDS the question seems answered in the most dramatic of apocalyptic ways: *The Wages of Sin is Death!* 'The illness flushes out an identity that might have remained hidden from neighbors, job-mates, family and friends. It also confirms an identity and, among the risk groups in the US most severely affected in the beginning, homosexual men, has been a creator of community as well as an experience that isolates the ill and exposes them to harassment and persecution.' (Sontag, 1989, p.25.) Sontag argues that AIDS is a disease:

> ... in which people are understood as ill before they are ill; which produces a seemingly innumerable array of symptom illnesses; for which there are only palliatives; and which brings to many a social death that precedes the physical one — AIDS reinstates something like a premodern experience of illness, as described in [John] Donne's *Devotions,* in which "everything that disorders a faculty and the function of that is a sickness".
>
> (Sontag, 1989, p.34)

One can think of the impact, fear and stigmatization of the leper, or the victim of plague or syphilis, each suffering from 'a disease that was not only repulsive and retributive but collectively invasive' (ibid, p.46).

Sontag has a clear perception of the impact of AIDS in at least two significant respects. First, 'hardly an invention of the male homosexual subculture, recreational risk-free sexuality is an inevitable reinvention of the culture of capitalism, and was guaranteed by medicine as well. The advent of AIDS seems to have changed all that irrevocably' (ibid, p.77). Freedom has been replaced by limits, caution and constraints. Nowhere was this change more dramatically apparent than the abandonment of organized religious objection to advertising contraceptives and the regular advocacy on British television in the 1980s of barrier methods of birth control for prophylactic purposes. Secondly, Sontag argues that, 'Future-mindedness is as much the distinctive mental habit, and intellectual conception, of the [twentieth] century as the history-mindedness that ... transformed thinking in the nineteenth century. A vision of linear progress has given way to one of a disaster already upon us that may be incapable of rejection' (ibid, p.89). (For further discussion of these ideas, see also Chapter 5, by Jeffrey Weeks.)

8 CONCLUSION

We have explored a set of common and important social concepts in the context of *social interaction*, a level of human behaviour that not only reflects, but contributes to, the form taken by the wider social structure. We have sought to maintain, again at this interactional level, the debate with history about the Enlightenment era. This has been done in the example of the health services and in the analysis of various kinds of social encounter. We have also taken the opportunity to explore some of the social characteristics of the *self*, the *social identity* of individuals, and to relate this to the experience of some socially significant diseases — mental and physical — in our own and preceding periods of history.

At the beginning of this chapter, I suggested that the study of social interaction was not some fascinating byway, but a crucial means of understanding everyday life and the operation of societal forces and patterns at the level of ordinary people. In conclusion, it may be useful to make explicit the association between social interaction patterns and the wider societies within which they lie embedded.

In Parsons' case, this association is quite explicit. The case of modern medical practice, and the related social roles of patient and physician, exemplify the functional interconnections of the social system. They illustrate the sorts of social mechanism by which deviance — in this case sickness — is accommodated, and the situation of 'disorder' resolved by working back to health. Goffman used a different model, drawing on Durkheim's conception of ritual. He developed a ceremonial and dramaturgical model of modern society. Goffman was concerned with regular patterns in social behaviour which offered a common means of understanding institutional and organizational structures. From Strong's comparison of different types of clinical formats, one can see that these may be related to the economic and social policies and interests under which they become established. Particular forms of professional interaction, perceptions of patients and how to treat them are intelligible in terms of dominant values in the societies that give rise to them. The micro- and the macro-worlds are seen to be socially linked.

In the formulations of what became known as the 'anti-psychiatry' approach, this link is made even more explicitly. The concatenation of events leading to someone being labelled as mentally-ill, and to hospital incarceration, is seen as essentially 'political' because of an association between social values, social structure, power and interpersonal relations. Foucault sought to establish the origins of the dominant professional and institutional forms of power of which current practices are the legacy. The ideas of the time, he argued, were specifically expressed in the psychiatric ideologies of earlier historical periods and formed the basis of specialized knowledge, without which the medical profession would have been unable to act and around which it structured its *raison d'être*.

In addition to the interest of some sociologists in power, and in forms of exploitation, one can see a continuing concern with morality and with the notion of social relations and social interaction as being analogous to work. Social encounters and social interaction convey meaning. They enhance or belittle reputations. They are played out against expectations of behaviour which are understood even if they are not accepted. Social behaviour is taught and learnt and evaluated. Social goals have to be worked at, or worked for. Parsons saw health as a goal one should work for. Goffman analysed socialization into the role of a mental patient as a 'career'. Raynes and King came to the conclusion that the characteristics of child-care regimes were related to the past ways in which senior staff had been trained for their occupational roles, rather than the differences between the types of children in their care. Even a stigma is not as final as it seems because people may work to conceal or explain it, or rely on a protective penumbra of people wise to it or closely allied to them. In a contemporary expression of the Enlightenment project, Sontag argues the case for revising accepted metaphors by which sick people are stigmatized. Social interaction is not just exemplary of big issues on a little stage. It is the means by which the social relations of a society are manifested in an observable way.

REFERENCES

Abercrombie, N., Hill, S. and Turner, B.S. (eds) (1988) *The Penguin Dictionary of Sociology*, 2nd edn, Harmondsworth, Penguin.

Barton, R. (1959) *Institutional Neurosis,* Bristol, John Wright.

Bateson, G. *et al.* (1956) 'Toward a theory of schizophrenia', in *Behavioural Science,* vol. 1, pp.251–64.

Becker, H. (1963) *Outsiders*, New York, Free Press.

Busfield, J. (1986) *Managing Madness: Changing Ideas and Practice,* London, Hutchinson.

Cooper, D.G. (1971) *The Death of the Family,* New York, Pantheon.

Douglas, M. (1966) *Purity and Danger: An Analysis of Concepts of Pollution and Taboo,* London, Routledge.

Durkheim, E. (1953) 'The determination of moral facts', in *Sociology and Philosophy,* Glencoe, Free Press.

Foucault, M. (1967) *Madness and Civilization: A History of Insanity in the Age of Reason,* London, Tavistock.

Foucault, M. (1973) *The Birth of the Clinic: An Archaeology of Medical Practice,* London, Tavistock.

Foucault, M. (1977) *Discipline and Punish: The Birth of the Prison,* London, Allen Lane.

Gerhardt, U. (1987) 'Parsons, role theory and health interaction', in Scambler, G. (ed.) *Sociological Theory and Medical Sociology,* London, Tavistock.

Gerhardt, U. (1989) *Ideas about Illness: An Intellectual and Political History of Medical Sociology,* London, Macmillan.

Goffman, E. (1961a) 'The moral career of the mental patient', in *Asylums: Essays on the Social Situation of Mental Patients and Other Inmates,* New York, Doubleday.

Goffman, E. (1961b) 'On the characteristics of total institutions', in *Asylums: Essays on the Social Situations of Mental Patients and Other Inmates,* New York, Doubleday.

Goffman, E. (1963) *Stigma: Notes on the Management of Spoiled Identity,* Englewood Cliffs, Prentice Hall.

Goffman, E. (1967a) 'The nature of deference and demeanour', in *Interaction Ritual: Essays on Face-to-Face Behaviour,* Chicago, Aldine.

Goffman, E. (1967b) 'On face-work', in *Interaction Ritual: Essays on Face-to-Face Behaviour*, Chicago, Aldine.

Goffman, E. (1983) 'The interaction order', in *American Sociological Review*, vol. 48, pp.1–17.

Hall, S. and Gieben, B. (eds) (1992) *Formations of Modernity*, Cambridge, Polity Press.

Jones, K. (1955) *Lunacy, Law and Conscience, 1744–1845*, London, Routledge.

Jones, K. (1960) *Mental Health and Social Policy, 1845–1959*, London, Routledge.

Jones, M. (1952) *Social Psychiatry: A Study of Therapeutic Communities*, London, Tavistock.

King, R.D., Raynes, N.V. and Tizard, J. (1971) *Patterns of Residential Care: Sociological Studies in Institutions for Handicapped Children*, London, Routledge.

Laing, R.D. (1960) *The Divided Self: An Existential Study in Sanity and Madness*, London, Tavistock.

Laing, R.D. and Esterson, A. (1964) *Sanity, Madness and the Family, Vol. 1: Families of Schizophrenics*, London, Tavistock.

Linton, R. (1936) *The Study of Man*, New York, Appleton-Century.

Merton, R. K. (1968) *Social Theory and Social Structure* (enlarged edition), Glencoe, The Free Press.

Parsons, T. (1951) *The Social System*, London, Routledge.

Parsons, T. (1978) 'Health and disease: a sociological perspective', in *Action Theory and the Human Condition*, New York, Free Press.

Penguin Dictionary of Sociology: see Abercrombie *et al.* (1988).

Porter, R. (1987) *A Social History of Madness: Stories of the Insane*, London, Weidenfeld and Nicolson.

Raynes, N.V. and King, R.D. (1974) 'Residential care for the mentally retarded', in Boswell, D.M. and Wingrove J.M. (eds) *The Handicapped Person in the Community: A Reader and Sourcebook*, London, Tavistock.

Robertson, R. and Turner, B.S. (1989) 'Talcott Parsons and modern social theory: an appreciation', in *Theory, Culture and Society*, vol. 6.4, pp.539–58.

Scull, A. T. (1984) *Decarceration: Community Treatment and the Deviant: A Radical View*, Cambridge, Polity Press.

Sedgwick, P. (1982) *Psycho Politics*, London, Pluto Press.

Sontag, S. (1983) *Illness as Metaphor*, Harmondsworth, Penguin.

Sontag, S. (1989) *AIDS and its Metaphors*, London, Allen Lane.

Strauss, A. *et al.* (1964) *Psychiatric Ideologies and Institutions*, London, Collier-Macmillan.

Strong, P.M. (1979) *The Ceremonial Order of the Clinic: Parents, Doctors and Medical Bureaucracies*, London, Routledge.

Strong, P.M. (1988) 'Minor courtesies and macro-structure', in Drew, P. and Wootton, A. (eds) *Erving Goffman: Exploring the Interaction Order*, Cambridge, Polity Press.

Turner, B.S. (1986) 'Sickness and social structure: Parsons' contribution to medical sociology', in Holton, R. J. and Turner, B. S. (eds) *Talcott Parsons on Economy and Society*, London, Routledge.

Turner, B.S. (1987) *Medical Power and Social Knowledge*, London, Sage.

Williams, R. (1988) 'Understanding Goffman's methods', in Drew, P. and Wootton, A. (eds) *Erving Goffman: Exploring the Interaction Order*, Cambridge, Polity Press.

READING A   SOCIAL STRUCTURE AND DYNAMIC PROCESS

Talcott Parsons

We may say that illness is a state of disturbance in the 'normal' functioning of the total human individual, including both the state of the organism as a biological system and of his personal and social adjustments. It is thus partly biologically and partly socially defined. Participation in the social system is always potentially relevant to the state of illness, to its etiology and to the conditions of successful therapy, as well as to other things. ...

The Situation of Medical Practice

The Situation of the Patient

The first step is to go more in detail into the analysis of relevant aspects of the situation in which the doctor and the patient find themselves. This will provide the setting in which the importance of the broad patterning of both physician's and patient's role can be interpreted, and will enable us to identify a series of mechanisms which, in addition to the physician's deliberate application of his technical knowledge, operate to facilitate his manifest functions in the control of disease, and to promote other, latent functions which are important to the social system. ...

It will be convenient first to take up the salient features of the situation of the patient and his 'lay' associates, particularly members of his family. These may be classified under the three headings of helplessness and need of help, technical incompetence, and emotional involvement.

By institutional definition of the sick role the sick person is helpless and therefore in need of help. If being sick is to be regarded as 'deviant' as certainly in important respects it must, it is ... distinguished from other deviant roles precisely by the fact that the sick person is not regarded as 'responsible' for his condition, 'he can't help it'. He may, of course, have carelessly exposed himself to danger of accident, but then once injured he cannot, for instance, mend a fractured leg by 'will power'. ...

By the same institutional definition the sick person is not, of course, competent to help himself, or what he can do is, except for trivial illness, not adequate. But in our culture there is a special definition of the kind of help he needs, namely, professional, technically competent help. The nature of this help imposes a further disability or handicap upon him. He is not only generally not in a position to do what needs to be done, but he does not 'know' what needs to be done or how to do it. ...

Only a technically trained person has that qualification. And one of the most serious disabilities of the layman is that he is not qualified to judge technical qualifications, in general or in detail. Two physicians may very well give conflicting diagnoses of the same case, indeed often do. In gen-

Source: Parsons, T. (1951) 'Social structure and dynamic process: the case of modern medical practice', in *The Social System*, London, Routledge, pp.431–53.

eral the layman is not qualified to choose between them. Nor is he qualified to choose the 'best' physician among a panel. If he were fully rational he would have to rely on professional authority, on the advice of the professionally qualified or on institutional validation. ...

Finally, third, the situation of illness very generally presents the patient and those close to him with complex problems of emotional adjustment. It is, that is to say, a situation of strain. Even if there is no question of a 'physic' factor in his condition, suffering, helplessness, disablement and the risk of death, or sometimes its certainty, constitute fundamental disturbances of the expectations by which men live. They cannot in general be emotionally 'accepted' without the accompaniments of strain with which we are familiar and hence without difficult adjustments unless the patient happens to find positive satisfactions in them, in which case there is also a social problem. ...

The range of possible complexities in this sphere is very great. The problems are, however, structured by the nature of the situation in certain relatively definite ways. Perhaps the most definite point is that for the 'normal' person illness, the more so the greater its severity, constitutes a frustration of expectancies of his normal life pattern. He is cut off from his normal spheres of activity, and many of his normal enjoyments. He is often humiliated by his incapacity to function normally. His social relationships are disrupted to a greater or a lesser degree. He may have to bear discomfort or pain which is hard to bear, and he may have to face serious alterations of his prospects for the future, in the extreme but by no means uncommon case the termination of his life. ...

To come back to the main theme. There are two particularly important broad consequences of the features of the situation of the sick person for the problem of the institutional structuring of medical practice. One is that the combination of helplessness, lack of technical competence, and emotional disturbance make him a peculiarly vulnerable object for exploitation. It may be said that the exploitation of the helpless sick is 'unthinkable'. That happens to be a very strong sentiment in our society, but for the sociologist the existence of this sentiment or that of other mechanisms for the prevention of exploitation must not be taken for granted. There is in fact a very real problem of how, in such a situation, the very possible exploitation is at least minimized.

The other general point is the related one that the situation of the patient is such as to make a high level of rationality of judgement peculiarly difficult. ... The world over the rational approach to help through applied science is ... the exception rather than the rule, and in our society there is, even today, a very large volume of 'superstition' and other non- or irrational beliefs and practices in the health field. This is not to say that the medical profession either has a monopoly of rational knowledge and techniques, or is free of the other type of elements, but the volume of such phenomena outside the framework of regular medical practice is a rough measure of this factor. ...

The Situation of the Physician

... The primary definition of the physician's responsibility is to 'do every-thing possible' to forward the complete, early and painless recovery of his patients. ...

But the function of 'doing everything possible' is institutionalized in terms of expectations, and these expectations are most vividly and immediately embodied, besides in the physician's own attitude system, in the attitudes of [his patients and their intimates]. But compared to most such groups their involvement is ... peculiarly intensive, immediate, and likely to contain elements of emotional disturbance which are by defi-nition tendencies to deviant behaviour. Hence the elements of strain on the physician. ...

There are, however, certain other features of the situation of the physician which are not common to many other fields which share those so far discussed. The engineer, for example, deals primarily with non-human impersonal materials which do not have 'emotional' reactions to what he does with them. But the physician deals with human beings, and does so in situations which often involve 'intimacies', that is, in contexts which are strongly charged with emotional and expressively symbolic signifi-cance, and which are often considered peculiarly 'private' to the individ-ual himself, or to especially intimate relations with others.

One whole class of these concerns the body. For reasons which undoubt-edly go very deep psychologically, certain of the sentiments relative to what [Vilfredo] Pareto [1848–1923] called the 'integrity of the individual' are focused on the 'inviolability' of the body. Their structuring will vary greatly according to the society and culture. But the amounts and occasions of bodily exposure and of bodily contact are carefully regulated in all societies, and very much so in ours. To see a person naked in a context where this is not usual, and to touch and manipulate their body, is a 'privilege' which calls for explanation in view of these considerations. ... It is clear ... that both the parts of the body themselves, and acts of exposure and of bodily contact are expressive symbols of highly strategic significance.

It is essential for the physician to have access to the body of his patient in order to perform his function. Indeed, some of his contacts, as in the case of a rectal or a vaginal examination, would not be permitted to any other person by most normal individuals, even to a sexual partner. Various others would be permitted only to special intimates.

Along with all this goes the problem of sentiments toward 'injury' of the body. Certainly many complex anxieties centre about this in many respects. It is, for example, noteworthy how many people have really severe anxieties about the insertion of a hypodermic needle even when this has become such a commonplace in our society. Obviously the prob-lem of securing consent to surgical procedures and many types of diagnos-tic procedures — such as the use of a gastroscope or a bronchoscope — is not to be too easily taken for granted. The essential point in all this is that these are no simple matters of weighing a rationally understood 'need' against an equally rationally assessed 'cost' in the form of discomfort or inconvenience, but very complex non- and irrational reactions are inevitably involved with the typical, not only the 'abnormal' patient. The fact that these elements are organized and controlled does not make them unproblematical. On the contrary, in the light of the *potentialities* of disturbance, the fact of successful control presents peculiarly important sociological problems.

Similar considerations apply to the physician's need of access to confidential information about his patient's private life. For reasons among which their place in the system of expressive symbolism is prominent, many facts which are relevant to people's problems of health fall into the realm of the private or confidential about which people are unwilling to talk to the ordinary friend or acquaintance. Some of these concern only 'reticences' about himself which are not specially bound up with intimate relations to others. A man will often, for example, hesitate to tell even his wife — even if he is on excellent terms with her — about many things which might well be of symptomatic significance to a physician. Others concern the privacies of intimate personal relationships, not only, but perhaps particularly those with sexual partners. Such information, however, is often essential to the performance of the physician's function. His access to it presents the same order of problems as does access to the body.

Modern developments in psychology, particularly psycho-analysis, have made us aware that in addition to resistances to access to the body, and to confidential information, anyone taking a role like that of the physician toward his patients is exposed to another sort of situational adjustment problem. That is, through processes which are mostly unconscious the physician tends to acquire various types of projective significance as a person which may not be directly relevant to his specifically technical functions, though they may become of the first importance in connection with psychotherapy. The generally accepted name for this phenomenon in psychiatric circles is 'transference', the attribution to the physician of significances [by] the patient which are not 'appropriate' in the realistic situation, but which derive from the psychological needs of the patient. ...

If all these factors be taken together it becomes clear that, in ways which are not true of most other professional functions, the situation of medical practice is such as inevitably to 'involve' the physician in the psychologically significant 'private' affairs of his patients. Some of these may not otherwise be accessible to others in any ordinary situation, others only in the context of specifically intimate and personal relationships. What the relation of the physician's role to these other relationships is to be, is one of the principal functional problems which underlie the structuring of his professional role. ...

READING B   THE MORAL CAREER OF THE MENTAL PATIENT

Erving Goffman

Traditionally the term *career* has been reserved for those who expect to enjoy the rises laid out within a respectable profession. The term is coming to be used, however, in a broadened sense to refer to any social strand of any person's course through life. ... Such a career is not a thing that can be brilliant or disappointing; it can no more be a success than a failure. In this light, I want to consider the mental patient.

One value of the concept of career is its two-sidedness. One side is linked to internal matters held dearly and closely, such as image of self and felt identity; the other side concerns official position, jural relations, and style of life, and is part of a publicly accessible institutional complex. The concept of career, then, allows one to move back and forth between the personal and the public, between the self and its significant society, without having to rely overly for data upon what the person says he thinks he imagines himself to be.

This paper, then, is an exercise in the institutional approach to the study of self. The main concern will be with the *moral* aspects of career — that is, the regular sequence of changes that career entails in the person's self and in his framework of imagery for judging himself and others.

The category 'mental patient' itself will be understood in one strictly sociological sense. In this perspective, the psychiatric view of a person becomes significant only in so far as this view itself alters his social fate — an alteration which seems to become fundamental in our society when, and only when, the person is put through the process of hospitalization. ... And I include anyone, however robust in temperament, who somehow gets caught up in the heavy machinery of mental-hospital servicing. ...

This general sociological perspective is heavily reinforced by one key finding of sociologically oriented students in mental-hospital research. As has been repeatedly shown in the study of non-literate societies, the awesomeness, distastefulness, and barbarity of a foreign culture can decrease to the degree that the student becomes familiar with the point of view to life that is taken by his subjects. Similarly, the student of mental hospitals can discover that the craziness or 'sick behaviour' claimed for the mental patient is by and large a product of the claimant's social distance from the situation that the patient is in, and is not primarily a product of mental illness. Whatever the refinements of the various patients' psychiatric diagnoses, and whatever the special ways in which social life on the 'inside' is unique, the researcher can find that he is participating in a community not significantly different from any other he has studied. Of course, while restricting himself to the off-ward grounds community of paroled patients, he may feel, as some patients do, that life in the locked wards is bizarre;

Source: Goffman, E. (1961) *Asylums: Essays on the Social Situation of Mental Patients and Other Inmates*, New York, Doubleday, pp.127–31, 146–51, 161–2, 168–9.

and while on a locked admissions or convalescent ward, he may feel that chronic 'back' wards are socially crazy places. But he need only move his sphere of sympathetic participation to the 'worst' ward in the hospital, and this, too, can come into social focus as a place with a livable and continuously meaningful social world. This in no way denies that he will find a minority in any ward or patient group that continues to seem quite beyond the capacity to follow rules of social organization, or that the orderly fulfillment of normative expectations in patient society is partly made possible by strategic measures that have somehow come to be institutionalized in mental hospitals.

The career of the mental patient falls popularly and naturalistically into three main phases: the period prior to entering the hospital, which I shall call the prepatient phase; the period in the hospital, the inpatient phase; the period after discharge from the hospital, should this occur, namely, the ex-patient phase. ...

The inpatient phase

Once the prepatient begins to settle down, the main outlines of his fate tend to follow those of a whole class of segregated establishments —jails, concentration camps, monasteries, work camps, and so on — in which the inmate spends the whole round of life on the grounds, and marches through his regimented day in the immediate company of a group of persons of his own institutional status.

Like the neophyte in many of these total institutions, the new inpatient finds himself cleanly stripped of many of his accustomed affirmations, satisfactions, and defenses, and is subjected to a rather full set of mortifying experiences: restriction of free movement, communal living, diffuse authority of a whole echelon of people, and so on. Here one begins to learn about the limited extent to which a conception of oneself can be sustained when the usual setting of supports for it are suddenly removed.

While undergoing these humbling moral experiences, the inpatient learns to orient himself in terms of the 'ward system'. In public mental hospitals this usually consists of a series of graded living arrangements built around wards, administrative units called services, and parole statuses. The 'worst' level often involves nothing but wooden benches to sit on, some quite indifferent food, and a small piece of room to sleep in. The 'best' level may involve a room of one's own, ground and town privileges, contacts with staff that are relatively undamaging, and what is seen as good food and ample recreational facilities. For disobeying the pervasive house rules, the inmate will receive stringent punishments expressed in terms of loss of privileges; for obedience he will eventually be allowed to reacquire some of the minor satisfactions he took for granted on the outside.

The institutionalization of these radically different levels of living throws light on the implications for self of social settings. And this in turn affirms that the self arises not merely out of its possessor's interactions with significant others, but also out of the arrangements that are evolved in an organization for its members.

... In short, assignment to a given ward is presented not as a reward or punishment, but as an expression of his general level of social functioning, his status as a person. Given the fact that the worst ward levels provide a round of life that inpatients with organic brain damage can easily manage, and that these quite limited human beings are present to prove it, one can appreciate some of the mirroring effects of the hospital.

The ward system, then, is an extreme instance of how the physical facts of an establishment can be explicitly employed to frame the conception a person takes of himself. In addition, the official psychiatric mandate of mental hospitals gives rise to even more direct, even more blatant, attacks upon the inmate's view of himself. The more 'medical' and the more progressive a mental hospital is — the more it attempts to be therapeutic and not merely custodial — the more he may be confronted by high-ranking staff arguing that his past has been a failure, that the cause of this has been within himself, that his attitude to life is wrong, and that if he wants to be a person he will have to change his way of dealing with people and his conceptions of himself. Often the moral value of these verbal assaults will be brought home to him by requiring him to practice taking this psychiatric view of himself in arranged confessional periods, whether in private sessions or group psychotherapy.

Now a general point may be made about the moral career of inpatients which has bearing on many moral careers. Given the stage that any person has reached in a career, one typically finds that he constructs an image of his life course — past, present, and future — which selects, abstracts, and distorts in such a way as to provide him with a view of himself that he can usefully expound in current situations. Quite generally, the person's line concerning self defensively brings him into appropriate alignment with the basic values of his society, and so may be called an apologia. If the person can manage to present a view of his current situation which shows the operation of favourable personal qualities in the past and a favourable destiny awaiting him, it may be called a success story. If the facts of a person's past and present are extremely dismal, then about the best he can do is to show that he is not responsible for what has become of him, and the term 'sad tale' is appropriate. Interestingly enough, the more the person's past forces him out of apparent alignment with central moral values, the more often he seems compelled to tell his sad tale in any company in which he finds himself. Perhaps he partly responds to the need he feels in others of not having their sense of proper life courses affronted. In any case, it is among convicts, 'winos', and prostitutes that one seems to obtain sad tales the most readily. It is the vicissitudes of the mental patient's sad tale that I want to consider now. ...

In general, ... mental hospitals systematically provide for circulation about each patient the kind of information that the patient is likely to try to hide. And in various degrees of detail this information is used daily to puncture his claims. At the admission and diagnostic conferences, he will be asked questions to which he must give wrong answers in order to maintain his self-respect, and then the true answer may be shot back at him. An attendant whom he tells a version of his past and his reason for being in the hospital may smile disbelievingly, or say, 'That's not the way I heard it', in line with the practical psychiatry of bringing the patient down to reality. When he accosts a physician or nurse on the ward and presents his claims for more privileges or for discharge, this may be countered by a question which he cannot answer truthfully without calling up a time in his past when he acted disgracefully. When he gives his view of his situation during group psychotherapy, the therapist, taking the role of interrogator, may attempt to disabuse him of his face-saving interpretations and encourage an interpretation suggesting that it is he himself who is to blame and who must change. When he claims to staff or fellow patients that he is well and has never been really sick, someone may give him graphic details of how, only one month ago, he was prancing around like a girl, or claiming that he was God, or declining to talk or eat, or putting gum in his hair.

Each time the staff deflates the patient's claims, his sense of what a person ought to be and the rules of peer-group social intercourse press him to reconstruct his stories; and each time he does this, the custodial and psychiatric interests of the staff may lead them to discredit these tales again. …

Each moral career, and behind this, each self, occurs within the confines of an institutional system, whether a social establishment such as a mental hospital or a complex of personal and professional relationships. The self, then, can be seen as something that resides in the arrangements prevailing in a social system for its members. The self in this sense is not a property of the person to whom it is attributed, but dwells rather in the pattern of social control that is exerted in connection with the person by himself and those around him. This special kind of institutional arrangement does not so much support the self as constitute it. …

In the usual cycle of adult socialization one expects to find alienation and mortification followed by a new set of beliefs about the world and a new way of conceiving of selves. In the case of the mental-hospital patient, this rebirth does sometimes occur, taking the form of a strong belief in the psychiatric perspective, or, briefly at least, a devotion to the social cause of better treatment for mental patients. The moral career of the mental patient has unique interest, however; it can illustrate the possibility that in casting off the raiments of the old self — or in having this cover torn away — the person need not seek a new robe and a new audience before which to cower. Instead he can learn, at least for a time, to practise before all groups the amoral arts of shamelessness.

READING C THE BIRTH OF THE ASYLUM
Michel Foucault

We know the images. They are familiar in all histories of psychiatry, where their function is to illustrate that happy age when madness was finally recognized and treated according to a truth to which we had too long remained blind.

Source: Foucault, M. (1967) *Madness and Civilization: A History of Insanity in the Age of Reason*, London, Tavistock, pp.241–78.

> The worthy Society of Friends [Quakers] ... sought to assure those of its members who might have the misfortune to lose their reason without a sufficient fortune to resort to expensive establishments all the resources of medicine and all the comforts of life compatible with their state; a voluntary subscription furnished the funds, and for the last two years, an establishment that seems to unite many advantages with all possible economy has been founded near the city of York. If the soul momentarily quails at the sight of that dread disease which seems created to humiliate human reason, it subsequently experiences gentler emotions when it considers all that an ingenious benevolence has been able to invent for its care and cure. ... This house is situated a mile from York, in the midst of a fertile and smiling countryside; it is not at all the idea of a prison that it suggests, but rather that of a large farm; it is surrounded by a great, walled garden. No bars, no grilles on the windows.
> (de la Rive, 1798)

As for the liberation of the insane at Bicêtre [a Parisian asylum], the story is famous: the decision to remove the chains from the prisoners in the dungeons; Couthon[1] visiting the hospital to find out whether any suspects were being hidden; Pinel[2] courageously going to meet him, while everyone trembled at the sight of the 'invalid carried in men's arms'. The confrontation of the wise, firm philanthropist and the paralytic monster. 'Pinel immediately led him to the section for the deranged, where the sight of the cells made a painful impression on him. He asked to interrogate all the patients. From most, he received only insults and obscene apostrophes. It was useless to prolong the interview. Turning to Pinel: "Now, citizen, are you mad yourself to seek to unchain such beasts?" Pinel replied calmly: "Citizen, I am convinced that these madmen are so intractable only because they have been deprived of air and liberty."

'"Well, do as you like with them, but I fear you may become the victim of your own presumption". Whereupon, Couthon was taken to his carriage. His departure was a relief; everyone breathed again; the great philanthropist immediately set to work.' (Pinel, 1836, p.56.)

These are images, at least insofar as each of the stories derives the essence of its power from imaginary forms: the patriarchal calm of Tuke's home, where the heart's passions and the mind's disorders slowly subside; the lucid firmness of Pinel, who masters in a word and a gesture the two animal frenzies that roar against him as they hunt him down; and the wisdom that could distinguish, between the raving madman and the bloodthirsty member of the Convention, which was the true danger: images that will carry far — to our own day — their weight of legend.

The legends of Pinel and Tuke transmit mythical values, which nineteenth-century psychiatry would accept as obvious in nature. But beneath

---

[1]Georges Couthon (1756–94), a crippled member of the French Convention's Committee of Public Safety, and a leading *terroriste*, was executed with Robespierre and Saint-Just.

[2]Philippe Pinel (1745–1826) was physician at two Parisian asylums: La Bicêtre from 1793, and later also La Saltpêtrière.

the myths themselves, there was an operation, or rather a series of operations, which silently organized the world of the asylum, the methods of cure, and at the same time the concrete experience of madness.

Tuke's gesture, first of all. Because it is contemporary with Pinel's, because he is known to have been borne along by a whole current of 'philanthropy', this gesture is regarded as an act of 'liberation'. The truth was quite different:

> ... there has also been particular occasion to observe the great loss, which individuals of our society have sustained, by being put under the care of those who are not only strangers to our principles, but by whom they are frequently mixed with other patients, who may indulge themselves in ill language, and other exceptionable practices. This often seems to leave an unprofitable effect upon the patients' minds after they are restored to the use of their reason, alienating them from those religious attachments which they had before experienced; and sometimes, even corrupting them with vicious habits to which they had been strangers.
> (Tuke, 1813, p.50)

The Retreat would serve as an instrument of segregation: a moral and religious segregation which sought to reconstruct around madness a milieu as much as possible like that of the Community of Quakers. And this for two reasons: first, the sight of evil is for every sensitive soul the cause of suffering, the origin of all those strong and untoward passions such as horror, hate, and disgust which engender or perpetuate madness. ... But the principal reason lies elsewhere: it is that religion can play the double role of nature and of rule, since it has assumed the depth of nature in ancestral habit, in education, in everyday exercise, and since it is at the same time a constant principle of coercion. ... Religion safeguards the old secret of reason in the presence of madness, thus making closer, more immediate, the constraint that was already rampant in classical confinement. There, the religious and moral milieu was imposed from without, in such a way that madness was controlled, not cured. At the Retreat, religion was part of the movement which indicated in spite of everything the presence of reason in madness, and which led from insanity to health. Religious segregation has a very precise meaning: it does not attempt to preserve the sufferers from the profane presence of non-Quakers, but to place the insane individual within a moral element where he will be in debate with himself and his surroundings: to constitute for him a milieu where, far from being protected, he will be kept in a perpetual anxiety, ceaselessly threatened by Law and Transgression. ...

Samuel Tuke[3] tells how he received at the Retreat a maniac, young and prodigiously strong, whose seizures caused panic in those around him and even among his guards. When he entered the Retreat he was loaded

[3]Samuel Tuke (1784–1857), like his grandfather William Tuke (1732–1822) who founded the Retreat in 1796, maintained the dual role of a tea and coffee merchant and advocate of moral methods of mental treatment.

with chains; he wore handcuffs; his clothes were attached by ropes. He had no sooner arrived than all his shackles were removed, and he was permitted to dine with the keepers; his agitation immediately ceased; 'his attention appeared to be arrested by his new situation'. He was taken to his room; the keeper explained that the entire house was organized in terms of the greatest liberty and the greatest comfort for all, and that he would not be subject to any constraint so long as he did nothing against the rules of the house or the general principles of human morality. For his part, the keeper declared he had no desire to use the means of coercion at his disposal. 'The maniac was sensible of the kindness of his treatment. *He promised to restrain himself.*' He sometimes still raged, shouted, and frightened his companions. The keeper reminded him of the threats and promises of the first day; if he did not control himself, it would be necessary to go back to the old ways. The patient's agitation would then increase for a while, and then rapidly decline. 'He would listen with attention to the persuasions and arguments of his friendly visitor. After such conversations, the patient was generally better for some days or a week.' At the end of four months, he left the Retreat, entirely cured. Here fear is addressed to the invalid directly, not by instruments but in speech; there is no question of limiting a liberty that rages beyond its bounds, but of marking out and glorifying a region of simple responsibility where any manifestation of madness will be linked to punishment. ...

We must therefore re-evaluate the meanings assigned to Tuke's work: liberation of the insane, abolition of constraint, constitution of a human milieu — these are only justifications. The real operations were different. In fact Tuke created an asylum where he substituted for the free terror of madness the stifling anguish of responsibility; fear no longer reigned on the other side of the prison gates, it now raged under the seals of conscience. ...

Let us not forget that we are in a Quaker world where God blesses men in the signs of their prosperity. Work comes first in 'moral treatment' as practiced at the Retreat. ... Through work, man returns to the order of God's commandments; he submits his liberty to laws that are those of both morality and reality. ... In the asylum, work is deprived of any productive value; it is imposed only as a moral rule; a limitation of liberty, a submission to order, an engagement of responsibility, with the single aim of disalienating the mind lost in the excess of a liberty which physical constraint limits only in appearance.

Even more efficacious than work, than the observation of others, is what Tuke calls 'the need for esteem'. ... In classical confinement, the madman was also vulnerable to observation, but such observation did not, basically, involve him; it involved only his monstrous surface, his visible animality; and it included at least one form of reciprocity, since the sane man could read in the madman, as in a mirror, the imminent movement of his downfall. The observation Tuke now instituted as one of the great elements of asylum existence was both deeper and less reciprocal. ... Tuke organized an entire ceremonial around these observations. There were social occasions in the English manner, where everyone was obliged to imitate all the formal requirements of social existence; nothing else circulated except the observation that would spy out any incongruity, any disorder, any awkwardness where madness might betray itself. The directors and staff of the Retreat thus regularly invited several patients to 'tea-parties'; the guests 'dress in their best clothes, and vie with each other in politeness and propriety. The best fare is provided, and the visitors are treated with all the attention of strangers. The evening generally passes with the greatest harmony and enjoyment. It rarely happens that any unpleasant circumstance occurs; the patients control, to a wonderful degree, their different propensities; and the scene is at once curious and affectingly gratifying.' Curiously, this rite is not one of intimacy, of dialogue, of mutual acquaintance; it is the organization around the madman of a world where everything would be like and near him, but in which he himself would remain a stranger, the Stranger *par excellence* who is judged not only by appearances but by all that they may betray and reveal in spite of themselves. ...

We see that at the Retreat the partial suppression of physical constraint was part of a system whose essential element was the constitution of a 'self-restraint' in which the patient's freedom, engaged by work and the observation of others, was ceaselessly threatened by the recognition of guilt. Instead of submitting to a simple negative operation that loosened bonds and delivered one's deepest nature from madness, it must be recognized that one was in the grip of a positive operation that confined madness in a system of rewards and punishments, and included it in the movement of moral consciousness. ... The science of mental disease, as it would develop in the asylum, would always be only of the order of observation and classification. It would not be a dialogue. It could not be that until psychoanalysis had exorcised this phenomenon of observation, essential to the nineteenth-century asylum, and substituted for its silent magic the powers of language. ...

Surveillance and Judgments: already the outline appears of a new personage who will be essential in the nineteenth-century asylum. ... Tuke himself suggests this personage [the keeper] when he tells the story of a maniac subject to seizures of irrepressible violence. ... The keeper intervenes, without weapons, without instruments of constraint, with observation and language only. ... The absence of constraint in the ... asylum is not unreason liberated, but madness long since mastered. ...

Madness is childhood. Everything at the Retreat is organized so that the insane are transformed into minors. ... The entire existence of madness, in the world now being prepared for it, was enveloped in what we may call, in anticipation, a 'parental complex'. The prestige of patriarchy is revived around madness in the bourgeois family. It is this historical sedimentation which psychoanalysis would later bring to light, according it through a new myth the meaning of a destiny that supposedly marked all of Western culture and perhaps all civilization. ... In the modern world, what had been the great, irreparable confrontation of reason and unreason became the secret thrust of instincts against the solidity of the family institution and against its most archaic symbols.

There is an astonishing convergence of the movement of fundamental institutions and this evolution of madness in the world of confinement. The liberal economy ... tended to entrust the care of the poor and the sick to the family rather than to the State: the family thus became the site of social responsibility. But if the patient can be entrusted to the family, he is nonetheless mad, which is too strange and inhuman. Tuke, precisely, reconstitutes around madness a simulated family, which is an institutional parody but a real psychological situation. ... The asylum would keep the insane in the imperative fiction of the family; the madman remains a minor, and for a long time reason will retain for him the aspect of the Father.

Closed upon these fictitious values, the asylum was protected from history and from social evolution. In Tuke's mind, the problem was to constitute a milieu which would imitate the oldest, the purest, the most natural forms of coexistence: the most human milieu possible, while being the least social one possible. In fact, he isolated the social structure of the bourgeois family, reconstituted it symbolically in the asylum, and set it adrift in history. ...

Pinel advocates no religious segregation. Or rather, a segregation that functions in the opposite direction from that practiced by Tuke. The benefits of the renovated asylum were offered to all, or almost all, except the fanatics 'who believe themselves inspired and seek to make converts'. Bicêtre and La Salpêtrière, according to Pinel's intention, form a complementary figure to the Retreat.

Religion must not be the moral substratum of life in the asylum, but purely and simply a medical object:

> Religious opinions in a hospital for the insane must be considered only in a strictly medical relation, that is, one must set aside all other considerations of public worship and political belief, and investigate only whether it is necessary to oppose the exaltation of ideas and feelings that may originate in this source, in order to effect the cure of certain alienated minds. ...
> (Pinel, 1801, p.265)

Nothing takes us further from Tuke and his dreams of a religious community that would at the same time be a privileged site of mental cures, than this notion of a neutralized asylum, purified of those images and passions to which Christianity gave birth and which made the mind wander toward illusion, toward error, and soon toward delirium and hallucinations.

But Pinel's problem was to reduce the iconographic forms, not the moral content of religion. Once 'filtered', religion possesses a disalienating power that dissipates the images, calms the passions, and restores man to what is most immediate and essential: it can bring him closer to his moral truth. And it is here that religion is often capable of effecting cures. ... [The asylum] must resume the moral enterprise of religion, exclusive of its fantastic text, exclusively on the level of virtue, labour, and social life. ...

In one and the same movement, the asylum becomes, in Pinel's hands, an instrument of moral uniformity and of social denunciation. The problem is to impose, in a universal form, a morality that will prevail from within upon those who are strangers to it and in whom insanity is already present before it has made itself manifest. In the first case, the asylum must act as an awakening and a reminder, invoking a forgotten nature; in the second, it must act by means of a social shift in order to snatch the individual from his condition. The operation as practiced at the Retreat was still simple: religious segregation for purposes of moral purification. The operation as practiced by Pinel was relatively complex: to effect moral syntheses, assuring an ethical continuity between the world of madness and the world of reason, but by practicing a social segregation that would guarantee bourgeois morality a universality of fact and permit it to be imposed as a law upon all forms of insanity.

In the classical period, indigence, laziness, vice, and madness mingled in an equal guilt within unreason; madmen were caught in the great confinement of poverty and unemployment, but all had been promoted, in the proximity of transgression, to the essence of a Fall. Now madness belonged to social failure, which appeared without distinction as its cause, model, and limit. Half a century later, mental disease would become degeneracy. Henceforth, the essential madness, and the really dangerous one, was that which rose from the lower depths of society.

Pinel's asylum would never be, as a retreat from the world, a space of nature and immediate truth like Tuke's, but a uniform domain of legislation, a site of moral syntheses where insanities born on the outer limits of society were eliminated. The entire life of the inmates, the entire conduct of their keepers and doctors, was organized by Pinel so that these moral syntheses would function. And this by three principal means:

1. *Silence* ... [Pinel released from his chains a former ecclesiastic who believed he was Christ, and instructed that he should not be spoken to. Deprived of such attention] '... he returned to more sensible and true ideas' (Pinel, 1836, p.63). Deliverance here has a paradoxical meaning. The dungeon, the chains, the continual spectacle, the sarcasms were, to the sufferer in his delirium, the very element of his liberty. ... Delivered from his chains, he is now chained, by silence, to transgression and to shame. He feels himself punished, and he sees the sign of his innocence in that fact; free from all physical punishment, he must prove himself guilty.
...

  The absence of language, as a fundamental structure of asylum life, has its correlative in the exposure of confession. When Freud, in psychoanalysis, cautiously reinstitutes exchange, or rather begins once again to listen to this language, henceforth eroded into monologue, should we be astonished that the formulations he hears are always those of transgression? In this inveterate silence, transgression has taken over the very sources of speech.

2. *Recognition by Mirror.* At the Retreat, the madman was observed, and knew he was observed; but except for that direct observation which per-

mitted only an indirect apprehension of itself, madness had no immediate grasp of its own character. With Pinel, on the contrary, observation operated only within the space defined by madness, without surface or exterior limits. Madness would see itself, would be seen by itself — pure spectacle and absolute subject. ...[Pinel's keepers encouraged those with delusions of royal grandeur to reflect upon the anomalies of their actual asylum situation.] 'At first the maniac felt shaken, soon he cast doubts upon his title as sovereign, and finally he came to realise his chimerical vagaries ... and after several months of tests ... was restored to his family.' (Pinel, 1801, p.256.)

This, then, is the phase of abasement: presumptuously identified with the object of his delirium, the madman recognizes himself as in a mirror in this madness whose absurd pretensions he has denounced; his solid sovereignty as a subject dissolves in this object he has demystified by accepting it. He is now pitilessly observed by himself. And in the silence of those who represent reason, and who have done nothing but hold up the perilous mirror, he recognizes himself as objectively mad. ...

3. *Perpetual Judgment.* By this play of mirrors, as by silence, madness is ceaselessly called upon to judge itself. But beyond this, it is at every moment judged from without; judged not by moral or scientific conscience, but by a sort of invisible tribunal in permanent session. ...

The justice that reigned in Pinel's asylum did not borrow its modes of repression from the other justice, but invented its own. Or rather, it used the therapeutic methods that had become known in the eighteenth century, but used them as chastisements. ... With Pinel, the use of the shower became frankly juridical; the shower was the habitual punishment of the ordinary police tribunal that sat permanently at the asylum: 'Considered as a means of repression, it often suffices to subject to the general law of manual labor a madman who is susceptible to it, in order to conquer an obstinate refusal to take nourishment, and to subjugate insane persons carried away by a sort of turbulent and reasoned humor'. (Pinel, 1801.) ...

There were, however, madmen who escaped from this movement and resisted the moral synthesis it brought about. These latter would be set apart in the heart of the asylum, forming a new confined population, which could not even relate to justice. When we speak of Pinel and his work of liberation, we too often omit this second reclusion. ... Disobedience by religious fanaticism, resistance to work, and theft, the three great transgressions against bourgeois society, the three major offenses against its essential values, are not excusable, even by madness; they deserve imprisonment pure and simple, exclusion in the most rigourous sense of the term, since they all manifest the same resistance to the moral and social uniformity that forms the *raison d'être* of Pinel's asylum. ...

The asylum of the age of positivism, which it is Pinel's glory to have founded, is not a free realm of observation, diagnosis, and therapeutics; it is a juridical space where one is accused, judged, and condemned, and from which one is never released except ... by remorse. Madness will be punished in the asylum, even if it is innocent outside of it. For a long time to come, and until our own day at least, it is imprisoned in a moral world.

To silence, to recognition in the mirror, to perpetual judgment, we must add a fourth structure peculiar to the world of the asylum as it was constituted at the end of the eighteenth century: this is the apotheosis of the *medical personage.* Of them all, it is doubtless the most important, since it would authorize not only new contacts between doctor and patient, but a new relation between insanity and medical thought, and ultimately command the whole modern experience of madness. Hitherto, we find the asylums only the same structures of confinement, but displaced and deformed. With the new status of the medical personage, the deepest meaning of confinement is abolished: mental disease, with the meanings we now give it, is made possible.

The work of Tuke and Pinel, whose spirit and values are so different, meet in this transformation of the medical personage. The physician ... played no part in the life of confinement. Now he becomes the essential figure of the asylum. He is in charge of entry. ...

It is thought that Tuke and Pinel opened the asylum to medical knowledge. They did not introduce science, but a personality, whose powers borrowed from science only their disguise, or at most their justification. ...

> It is a very important object to win the confidence of these sufferers, and to arouse in them feelings of respect and obedience, which can only be the fruit of superior discernment, distinguished education, and dignity of tone and manner. Stupidity, ignorance, and the lack of principles, sustained by a tyrannical harshness, may incite fear, but always inspire distrust. The keeper of madmen who has obtained domination over them directs and rules their conduct as he pleases; he must be endowed with a firm character, and on occasion display an imposing strength. He must threaten little but carry out his threats, and if he is disobeyed, punishment must immediately ensue. (Haslam, 1798; cited in Pinel, 1801, pp.253–4)

The physician could exercise his absolute authority in the world of the asylum only insofar as, from the beginning, he was Father and Judge, Family and Law — his medical practice being for a long time no more than a complement to the old rites of Order, Authority, and Punishment. And Pinel was well aware that the doctor cures when, exclusive of modern therapeutics, he brings into play these immemorial figures. ...

What we call psychiatric practice is a certain moral tactic contemporary with the end of the eighteenth century, preserved in the rites of asylum life, and overlaid by the myths of positivism. ...

There remains, beyond the empty forms of positivist thought, only a single concrete reality: the doctor–patient couple in which all alienations are summarized, linked, and loosened. And it is to this degree that all nineteenth-century psychiatry really converges on Freud, the first man to accept in all its seriousness the reality of the physician–patient couple, the first to consent not to look away nor to investigate elsewhere, the first not to attempt to hide it in a psychiatric theory that more or less harmonized with the rest of medical knowledge; the first to follow its consequences with absolute rigour. Freud demystified all the other asylum structures: he abolished silence and observation, he eliminated madness's recognition of itself in the mirror of its own spectacle, he silenced the instances of the condemnation. But on the other hand he exploited the structure that enveloped the medical personage. ...

To the doctor, Freud transferred all the structures Pinel and Tuke had set up within confinement. He did deliver the patient from the existence of the asylum within which his 'liberators' had alienated him; but he did not deliver him from what was essential in this existence; he regrouped its powers, extended them to the maximum by uniting them in the doctor's hands; he created the psychoanalytical situation where, by an inspired short-circuit, alienation becomes disalienating because, in the doctor it becomes a subject.

References

de la Rive, C.-G. (1798) Letter to the editors of the *Bibliothèque britannique* about his visit to the Retreat.

Haslam, J. (1798) *Observations on Insanity with Practical Remarks on this Disease,* London.

Pinel, P. (1801) *Traité medico-philosophique sur l'aliénation mentale,* Paris.

Pinel, S. (1836) *Traité complet du régime sanitaire des aliénés,* Paris.

Tuke, S. (1813) *Description of the Retreat, an institution near York for Insane Persons of the Society of Friends,* York.

CHAPTER 5　THE BODY AND SEXUALITY

Jeffrey Weeks

CONTENTS

1   WHAT DO WE MEAN WHEN WE TALK ABOUT THE BODY AND SEXUALITY?

1.1   INTRODUCTION

Let's start with an image that has haunted our imagination in the past decade: the sunken eyes, the emaciated bodies, the apparently doomed courage of people with AIDS.

In a period which as never before saw the celebration of healthy, perfectly-tuned bodies (thousands of people running the London Marathon provides an apt memorial of this new fetish for fitness), a new syndrome emerged which ravaged the body. It was intimately connected with sex — with acts through which the HIV virus could be transmitted. Many people, not least in the tabloid press, presented AIDS as a necessary effect of sexual excess, as if the limits of the body have been tested, and found wanting by 'sexual perversity'. This, according to the more brazen propagandists, was nature's revenge on those who transgressed its boundaries.

The assumption seemed to be that the body expresses a fundamental truth about sexuality. But what can this truth be? We now know that the HIV virus, which causes the breakdown of the body's immunities and so in turn gives rise to AIDS, is not selective in its impact. It affects heterosexuals and homosexuals, women and men, young and old. Yet at the same time it does not affect everyone in these categories, nor even necessarily the partners of people infected with HIV. Who gets HIV is partly a matter of chance, even for those who engage in what we now call 'high-risk activities'.

Of course, any life threatening illness should arouse anxiety, and I am not seeking in any way to minimize the terrible effects of the syndrome. But AIDS has become more than a set of diseases: it has become a potent metaphor for our sexual culture. The response to it has been seen as a sign of our growing confusion and anxieties about our bodies and their sexual activities (Sontag, 1989). It has been presented as a dire warning concerning the effects of sexual change. In the process the experiences of people living with HIV and AIDS, stories of courage and resilience in the face of illness, have often been ignored.

What is the relationship between the body as a collection of organs, feelings, needs, impulses, biological possibilities and limits, on the one hand, and our sexual desires, behaviours and identities, on the other? What is it about these topics that make them so culturally significant and morally and politically fraught? These, and others like them, have become key questions in recent sociological and historical debates. In attempting to respond to them I will argue that though the biological body is the site for, and sets the limits on, what is sexually possible, sexuality is more than simply about the body. In fact, with Carole Vance (1984) I am going to suggest that the most important organ in humans is that between the ears. Sexuality is as much about our beliefs, ideologies and imaginations as it is about the physical body.

This chapter is concerned, then, with the ways in which bodies and sexuality have been endowed with importance and rich meanings in modern societies. The remainder of this section, starting with a closer look at the literature on sexuality, will explore the significance of seeing sexuality as a social and historical phenomenon. It will argue that bodies have no intrinsic meaning, and that the best way of understanding sexuality is as an 'historical construct'.

Section 2 will then go on to discuss the ways in which the dominant definitions of sexuality have emerged in modernity. Section 3 will be concerned with how power relations, particularly with regard to gender, class and race (that is, socially differentiated bodies) become meaningful in defining sexual behaviour. Section 4 will be primarily concerned with the problem of defining sexualized identities, especially as they have been made and remade over the past 100 years or so, in an effort to understand the forces at work in shaping sexuality. It will explore the institutionalization of heterosexuality and the 'invention' of homosexuality, and then look at ways of rethinking sexual identity.

Finally, Section 5 will look in more detail at the social regulation of bodies and sexuality, concentrating on the implications of the public/ private division — a division we take for granted as natural, but which also has a history, in fact, many histories. The chapter will conclude by posing the question: What is the future of sexuality and the body? — a vital issue in the wake of the crisis generated by HIV and AIDS.

1.2 THE SUBJECT OF SEX

Although there is a strong case for arguing that issues relating to bodies and sexual behaviour have been at the heart of western preoccupations for a very long time, until the nineteenth century they were largely the concern of religion and moral philosophy. Since then they have largely been the concern of specialists, whether in medicine, the professions, or amongst moral reformers. Since the late nineteenth century the subject has even produced its own discipline, sexology, drawing on psychology, biology and anthropology as well as history and sociology. This has been enormously influential in establishing the terms of the debate about sexual behaviour. Yet sexuality is clearly a critical social and political issue as well as an individual concern, and it therefore deserves a sustained historical and sociological investigation and analysis.

Sexology has been an important factor in codifying the way we think of the body and sexuality. In his famous study *Psychopathia Sexualis* (first translated into English in 1892), Richard von Krafft-Ebing, the pioneering sexologist of the late nineteenth century, described sex as a 'natural instinct' which 'with all conquering force and might demands fulfilment' (1931, p.1). What can we deduce from this? First, there is the emphasis on sex as an 'instinct', expressing the fundamental needs of the body. This reflects a post-Darwinian preoccupation in the late nineteenth century to explain all human phenomena in terms of identifiable, inbuilt, biological forces. Today we are more likely to talk about the importance of hormones and genes in shaping our behaviour, but the assumption that biology is at the root of all things persists, and nowhere more strongly than in relation to sexuality. We talk all the time about the 'sex instinct' or 'impulse', and see it as the most natural thing about us. But is it? There is now a great deal of writing which suggests, on the contrary, that sexuality is in fact a 'social construction', a historical invention, which of course draws on the possibilities of the body, but whose meanings and the weight we attribute to them are shaped in concrete social situations. This has profound implications for our understanding of the body, sex and sexuality, which we will need to explore.

Take the second part of the Krafft-Ebing quote: sex is an 'all-conquering force', demanding fulfilment. Here we can see at work the central metaphor which guides our thoughts about sexuality. Sex is seen as a volcanic energy, engulfing the body, as urgent and incessant in pressing on our conscious selves. Few people, Krafft-Ebing wrote, 'are conscious of the deep influence exerted by sexual life upon the sentiment, thought and action of man in his social relations to others'. I don't think we could make such a confident statement of ignorance today. We now take for granted, in part because of the sexologists, that sexuality is indeed at the centre of our existence.

The following quotation from the English sexologist, Havelock Ellis, who was very influential in the first third of this century, illustrates the ways in which sexuality has been seen as offering a special insight into the nature of the self: 'Sex penetrates the whole person; a man's sexual constitution is a part of his general constitution. There is considerable truth in the dictum: "a man is what his sex is".' (Ellis, 1946, p.3.)

Not only is sex seen here as an all-conquering force, but it is also apparently an essential element in a person's bodily make-up ('constitution'), the determinant of our personalities and identities — at least, if we take the language at its surface value, if we are men. This poses the question of *why* we see sexuality in this way. What is it about sexuality that makes us so convinced that it is at the heart of our being? Is it equally true for men and women?

This leads us to the third point that we can draw from the original Krafft-Ebing quotation. The language of sexuality appears to be overwhelmingly male. The metaphors used to describe sexuality as a relentless force seem to be derived from assumptions about male sexual experience. Havelock Ellis appears to be going beyond the conventional use of the male pronoun to denote universal experience. Even his use of metaphors ('penetrates') suggest a sublimely unconscious devotion to male models of sexuality. On one level this may seem an unfair criticism, given that the sexologists did attempt to recognize the legitimacy of female sexual experience. In fact, sexologists often

Havelock Ellis:
pioneer sexologist

followed a long tradition which saw women as '*the* sex', as if their
bodies were so suffused with sexuality that there was no need even to
conceptualize it. But it is difficult to avoid the sense that the dominant
model of sexuality in their writings, and perhaps also in our social
consciousness, is the male one. Men were the active sexual agents;
women, despite or because of their highly sexualized bodies, were seen
as merely responsive, 'kissed into life', in Havelock Ellis's significant
phrase, by the man.

I am not attempting to suggest that definitions such as Krafft-Ebing's are
the only ones, or even the dominant ones today. I have chosen this
starting point to illustrate the major theme of this chapter — that our
concept of sexuality has a history. The development of the language we
use is one valuable index of that: it is in constant evolution. The term
'sex', for example, originally meant 'the results of the division of
humanity into male or female *sections*'. It referred, of course, to the
differences between men and women, but also to how they were related.
As we shall see below, this relationship was significantly different from
the one our culture now understands as given — that men and women
are fundamentally different. In the past two centuries or so, 'sex' has
taken on a more precise meaning: it refers to the anatomical differences
between men and women, to sharply differentiated bodies, and to what
divides us rather than unites us.

Such changes are not accidental. They indicate a complicated history in
which sexual difference (whether we are male or female, heterosexual
or homosexual) and sexual activity have come to be seen as of prime
social importance. Can we therefore, with justice, describe sexual

behaviour as either 'natural' or 'un-natural' in any unproblematical sense? I believe not.

The second major theme of this chapter is closely related to this. Our sexual definitions, conventions, beliefs, identities and behaviours have not simply evolved, as if propelled by an incoming tide. They have been shaped within defined power relationships. The most obvious one has already been signalled in the quotation from Krafft-Ebing: the relations between men and women, in which female sexuality has been historically defined in relationship to the male. But sexuality has been a peculiarly sensitive marker of other power relations. Church and state have shown a continuous interest in how we behave or think. We can see the intervention over the past two centuries or so of medicine, psychology, social work, schools and the like, all seeking to spell out the appropriate ways for us to regulate our bodily activities. Racial and class differences have further complicated the picture. But alongside these have appeared other forces, above all feminism and the sex reform movements of various types, which have resisted the prescriptions and definitions. The sexual codes and identities we take for granted as inevitable, and indeed 'natural', have often been forged in this complex process of definition and self-definition that have made modern sexuality central to the way power operates in modern society.

In the discussion that follows we shall be very concerned with the use and meanings of terms, so to close this part of the argument I want to clarify the basic term we are going to use. 'Sex' will be used in the sense mentioned above: as a descriptive term for the basic anatomical differences, internal and external to the body, that we see as differentiating men and women. Although these anatomical distinctions are generally given at birth, the meanings attached to them are highly historical and social. To describe the *social* differentiation between men and women, I shall use the term 'gender'. I shall use the term 'sexuality' as a general description for the series of historically shaped and socially constructed beliefs, behaviours, relationships and identities that relate to what Michel Foucault has called 'the body and its pleasures' (Foucault, 1979).

The phrase 'social constructionism' will be used as a shorthand term to describe the historically oriented approach towards bodies and sexuality that we shall be adopting. The phrase has perhaps a harsh and mechanistic ring to it, but all it basically sets out to do is argue that we can understand attitudes to the body and sexuality only in their specific historical context, by exploring the historically variable conditions that give rise to the importance assigned to sexuality at any particular time, and by grasping the various power relations that shape what comes to be seen as normal and abnormal, acceptable and unacceptable behaviour. Social constructionism is counterposed to sexual 'essentialism', the position expressed in the Krafft-Ebing definition, and dominant in most discussions of sexuality until recently. Essentialism is a viewpoint that attempts to explain the properties of a complex whole by reference to a supposed inner truth or essence. Such an approach reduces the complexity of the world to the imagined simplicities of its constituent parts, and seeks to explain individuals as automatic products of inner propulsions.

Against such assumptions I shall argue that the meanings we give to sexuality and the body are socially organized and sustained by a variety of languages which seek to tell us what sex is, what it ought to be, and what it could be.

ACTIVITY 1   Pause at this point to think about the range of meanings of sexuality that we regularly encounter.

- Write down the different meanings you can think of for 'sex' and 'sexuality'.
- Think about the ways in which your own use of these terms have changed over your lifetime, and ask yourself whether this is the result of personal experience or of changing social meanings.

1.3   HISTORICIZING THE BODY

The study by Michel Foucault (1926–84) of the 'history of sexuality' has been central to recent discussions about the body and sexuality amongst historians and social scientists. Consider this quotation: 'Sexuality must not be thought of as a kind of natural given which power tries to hold in check, or as an obscure domain which knowledge gradually tries to uncover. It is the name that can be given to a historical construct.' (Foucault, 1979, p.152.) Who and what is he challenging here?

Michel Foucault: sexuality is a 'historical construct'

Most clearly it is a challenge to the essentialist views we have already surveyed. He is quite firmly stating that sexuality is not a 'dark continent' (in Freud's famous phrase relating to female sexuality) that needs its specialist explorers. Sexologists, the would-be scientists of sex and the body, are the targets here, with a strong hint that they have, in part, helped to 'construct' sexuality as a privileged domain of knowledge. By establishing a special sphere of knowledge, by seeking the 'laws of nature' which supposedly govern the sexual world, by arguing that sexuality has a particular influence on all aspects of life and that the body speaks an ultimate truth, sexologists have, in a sense, helped to 'invent' the importance we assign to sexual behaviour.

There is also another target, however, and that is that particular tradition of sexual theorizing which has seen sexuality as itself a force which provides a form of resistance to power. Writers like Wilhelm Reich in the 1930s and 1940s argued that capitalist society survived and reproduced itself by repressing our natural and healthy sexuality (Weeks, 1985): if the body could be freed from the constraints of enforced labour, if its basically healthy instincts could have free play, then the ills of society would fade away. 'Sexual liberation', therefore, offered the possibility of challenging the oppressive social order, and was a key element in the struggle for social change.

Foucault, on the other hand, rejected what he termed the 'repressive hypothesis': the belief that society is all the time attempting to control an unruly natural energy emanating from the body. This was not because he did not want a more liberal sexual order; on the contrary. But he believed essentialist arguments ignored the central fact about modern society: that sexuality was a 'historical apparatus' which had developed as part of a complex web of social regulation which organized and shaped ('policed') individual bodies and behaviour. Sexuality could not act as a resistance to power because it was so bound up in the ways in which power operated in modern society.

Foucault has been the most influential of the theorists of the 'social constructionist' approach to the history and sociology of sexuality. Foucault's own work can best be understood, however, if we appreciate that he was building on a sustained critique of sexual essentialism that had a number of discrete sources. I want to look briefly at some of the streams that have fed the historical approach. (For a fuller discussion, see Weeks, 1985.)

1   From social anthropology, sociology and the work of sex researchers has come a growing awareness of the vast range of sexual patterns that exist both in other cultures *and* within our own culture. An awareness that the way we do things is not the only way of doing things can provide a salutary jolt to our own ethnocentricity. It should force us to ask searching questions about why things are as they are today. Other cultures and subcultures are a mirror to our own transitoriness.

What does this imply for our thinking about modern sexuality? The American sociologists John Gagnon and William Simon, in their book

Sexual Conduct (1973), have argued that sexuality is subject to socio-cultural moulding to a degree surpassed by few other forms of human behaviour. This is quite contrary to our normal belief that sexuality tells us the ultimate truth about ourselves and our bodies; rather, it might tell us something more of the truth of our culture.

2   The legacy of Sigmund Freud and his theory of the dynamic unconscious provides another source for the new approach to sexuality. What psychoanalysis, at least in its original form, sought to establish was that what goes on in the unconscious mind often contradicts the apparent certainties of conscious life. It has been argued that we can detect, in neurotic symptoms, or through the analysis of dreams and the accidents of daily life, traces of repressed wishes or desires — repressed because the desires are of a 'perverse' kind. Such arguments unsettle the apparent solidities of gender, of sexual need and of identity because they suggest that these are precarious achievements, shaped in the process of the 'human animal' acquiring the rules of culture through a complex psycho-social development.

3   Alongside these theoretical developments, the 'new social history' of the past two decades has explored areas hitherto ignored by historians, of which the history of gender and the body (e.g. Turner, 1984, Laqueur, 1990) as well as sexuality are of central interest to our concerns. Various studies have questioned the fixity of the prevailing ideas of what constitutes masculinity and femininity, have explored the changing nature of domesticity and work (see Chapter 2), and have thrown new light on the development of social categorizations (for example, those of childhood, of prostitution and homosexuality) and on the development of individual sexual identities (Weeks, 1989).

4   Finally, the emergence of a new politics around sexuality — such as feminism, lesbian and gay politics, and other radical sexual movements — have challenged many of the certainties of our sexual traditions, and have offered new insights into the intricate forms of power and domination that shape our sexual lives. Why is male dominance so endemic in culture? Why is female sexuality so often seen as subsidiary to that of men? Why does our culture celebrate heterosexuality and discriminate against homosexuality?

All these streams force us to confront questions which are fundamentally social and historical; to ask: what are the cultural forces that shape our sexual meanings?

ACTIVITY 2   You should now read **Reading A, 'Social construction theory'**, by Carole Vance, which you will find at the end of this chapter. As you read, consider the following questions:

- Does constructionism go too far in denying the body?
- If 'sexuality' is an historical 'apparatus' is there anything fixed in sexual life?

Vance quite rightly asks us to recognize that we cannot forget the body. It is through the body that we experience both pleasure and pain. Moreover, there are male bodies and female bodies, and these give rise to quite different experiences, for example childbirth. Another powerful point is that we do not experience our sexual needs and desires as accidental, or as the product of society. They are deeply ingrained in us as individuals.

This does not mean that they cannot be explained socially: one of the attractions of psychoanalysis, for example, is that it does challenge us to ask about the relationship between psychic processes, social dynamics and historical change. The meanings which we give to our bodies and their sexual possibilities do become a vital part of our individual make-up, whatever the social explanations.

This does not, nevertheless, invalidate the main lesson of social constructionist arguments, whose main purpose is not to offer dogmatic explanations about how *individual* sexual meanings are acquired. Constructionism is, in a sense, agnostic about this question. We are not concerned with the question of what causes heterosexuality or homosexuality in individuals, but rather with the problem of why and how our culture privileges the one and marginalizes — where it does not discriminate against — the other. Social constructionism also poses another central question: Why does our culture assign such an importance to sexuality, and how has this come about?

All these are legitimately questions for social investigation, and in the next section we shall begin to look at them in more detail.

2   SEXUALITY AND SEXUAL NORMS

2.1   ESTABLISHING 'THE NORMAL' AND 'THE ABNORMAL'

One of the more intriguing of Michel Foucault's works is his 'dossier' on the memoirs of a nineteenth-century French hermaphrodite, Herculine Barbin. He sums up the tragic story in the following terms:

> Brought up as a poor and deserving girl in a milieu that was almost exclusively feminine and strongly religious, Herculine Barbin, who was called Alexina by her familiars, was finally recognized as being 'truly' a young man. Obliged to make a legal change of sex after judicial proceedings and a modification of his civil status, he was incapable of adapting himself to a new identity and ultimately committed suicide. I would be tempted to call the story banal were it not for two or three things that give it a particular intensity.
> (Foucault, 1980, p.xi)

Alexina/Herculine was born of indeterminate sex — that is, with bodily characteristics which made it difficult to determine clearly whether the child was a boy or a girl. This was an anomaly not particularly common then or now, but certainly not unknown. In this case the body was ambiguous; it did not reveal an unproblematical truth. Foucault's point is that, while awkward and graceless as a 'normal' girl, nevertheless during her early life she was able to be accepted within a particular milieu without especial stigmatization. She lived the 'happy limbo of a non-identity' (Foucault, 1980, p.xiii).

Eventually, however, those 'two or three things' mentioned by Foucault forced a choice about identity. It became necessary to insist on a 'true sex', whatever the consequences. Chief amongst these factors, Foucault suggests, during the 1860s when the tragedy occurred, was the new concern amongst doctors, lawyers and the like with classifying and fixing the different sexual types and characteristics. Because Alexina had certain evidence of a masculine body, that is a small penis, 'she' had to become 'he'.

We can leave aside for present purposes the question of whether the dossier gives a full picture of the processes at work, or how representative Herculine Barbin's experience was of a new classifying zeal. Rather, this case should be seen as symbolic of a wider process: a complexly intertwined process by which the sharpening definition of 'true' male and female characteristics is allied to a new zeal in defining what is 'normal' or 'abnormal' in judicial, medical and political discourses. Indeed, by defining what is abnormal (a girl with bodily evidence of masculinity in this case), it became fully possible to attempt to define what is truly normal (a full correspondence between the body and socially acceptable gender identity).

As we have already seen, one characteristic way of perceiving this is as a process of discovery of the true facts about human sexuality by a new objective science. Foucault, like others who have been exploring the sexuality of modernity, is saying something much more: that this process is the result of a new configuration of power which requires us to place a person by defining his or her true identity, an identity that fully expresses the real truth of the body.

The history of sexuality is, for Foucault, a history of our discourses about sexuality: discourses through which sexuality is constructed as a body of knowledge which shapes the ways we think and know the body. The western experience of sexuality, he suggests, is not the inhibition of discourse. It cannot be characterized as a 'regime of silence', but is, on the contrary, a constant and historically changing incitement to discourse about sex. This ever-expanding discursive explosion is part of a complex growth of control over individuals, control not through denial or prohibition, but through production: by the imposition of a grid of definition on the possibilities of the body through the apparatus of sexuality.

> The deployment of sexuality has its reasons for being, not in reproducing itself, but in proliferating, innovating, annexing, creating and penetrating bodies in an increasingly detailed way, and in controlling populations in an increasingly comprehensive way.
> (Foucault, 1979, p.107)

Foucault's study of the sexual apparatus is closely related to his analysis of the development of what he sees as the 'disciplinary society' characteristic of modern forms of social regulation — a society of surveillance and control that he sketches in his book *Discipline and Punish* (1977). He argues here that in the modern period we should see power, not as a negative force operating on the basis of prohibition ('thou shalt not'), but as a positive force concerned with administering and fostering life ('you must do this or that'). This is what he terms 'bio-power', and here sexuality has a crucial role. For sex is the pivot along which the whole technology of life developed: sex was a means of access both to the life of the body and the life of the species; that is, it offered a way of regulating both individual bodies and the behaviour of the population (the 'body politic') as a whole (Foucault, 1979).

Foucault pinpoints four strategic unities which link together a variety of social practices and techniques of power since the eighteenth century. Together they form specific mechanics of knowledge and power centring on sex. These are concerned with the sexuality of women; the sexuality of children; the control of procreative behaviour; and the pinpointing of sexual perversions as problems of individual pathology. In the course of the nineteenth century these strategies produced four figures for social observation and control, invented within the regulative discourses: the hysterical women, the masturbating child, the married couple using artificial birth control, and 'the pervert', especially the homosexual.

The significance of this argument is that it fundamentally challenges the idea that social regulation sets out to control pre-existing types of being. What is actually happening is that a generalized social concern with controlling the population gives rise to a specification of particular types of people, who are simultaneously evoked and controlled within the complex of power–knowledge. This does not mean that female sexuality, masturbation, birth control or homosexuality did not exist before. What it does mean is that the specification of people by these characteristics, the creation of 'subject positions' around these activities, was a historical phenomenon.

2.2   THE SOCIAL DIMENSIONS OF SEXUALITY

Sexuality, we are suggesting, is shaped at the juncture of two major concerns: with our subjectivity (who and what we are); and with society (with the health, prosperity, growth and well-being of the population as a whole). The two are intimately connected because at the heart of both is the body and its potentialities. As society has become more and more concerned with the lives of its members — for the sake of moral uniformity, economic prosperity, national security, or hygiene and health — so it has become increasingly preoccupied with disciplining bodies and with the sex lives of its individuals. This has given rise to intricate methods of administration and management, to a flowering of moral anxieties, medical, hygienic, legal and welfarist interventions, or scientific delving, all designed to understand the self by understanding, and regulating, sexual behaviour.

The Victorian period is a key one in understanding the process in all its complexity. Traditionally, historians have commented on the repressiveness of the period, and in many ways this is an accurate picture. There was indeed a great deal of moral hypocrisy, as individuals (especially men) and society avowed respectability but did something else. Women's sexuality was severely regulated to ensure 'purity' at the same time as prostitution was rife. Venereal disease posed a major health threat, but was met by attempts to control and regulate female sexuality rather than male. The famous Contagious Diseases Acts of the 1860s, which enforced compulsory examination in a number of garrison towns of women suspected of prostitution and carrying VD, was widely seen by feminists and working class people as an attack on individual freedom (Walkowitz, 1980). And the new, more secular legal order that gradually developed during the century, marking the decisive shift from ecclesiastical to state regulation of sexual behaviour, was often much more effective in controlling even minor misdemeanors than previously. For example, though the death penalty for sodomy ended in 1861, in practice the regime of control of male homosexuality tightened after the passing of the Criminal Law Amendment Act of 1885, which effectively made all forms of homosexual activity between men illegal, whether in private or public (Weeks, 1990).

But these developments, with all the anxiety and delicacy about the body they imply, should not lead us to believe that the Victorians were averse to discussing sex. On the contrary, it is possible to argue that they, like their successors, were very nearly obsessed with it.

If we look at the key moments in British history since the beginning of the nineteenth century we see that, in one way or another, a preoccupation with sexual behaviour has been central to them. During the crisis of the French Revolutionary Wars early in the century, we see a concern with moral decline which, it was believed, was integral to the collapse of the *ancien regime*. Middle class ideologies sought a new bourgeois morality to challenge the immorality of the aristocracy and the amorality of the labouring masses. In the 1830s and 1840s, with the first crisis of the new industrial order, there was a near obsessive interest in the sexuality of working women, and of children working in the mines and factories. The great series of Royal Commissions of the period reported in detail on the sexual licence of the new manufacturing centres.

By the mid-nineteenth century, fuelled by the spread of epidemics such as cholera and typhoid in the overcrowded towns and cities, attempts to reform society concentrated on questions of health and personal morality. From the 1860s to the 1890s, prostitution, venereal disease, public immorality and private vice were at the heart of debate, many choosing to see in moral decay a symbol of imperial decay.

Such preoccupations were not unique to the nineteenth century. If anything, sexuality became more and more a public obsession, particularly in relation to the integrity of the British population (Weeks, 1989). In the years before the First World War, there was a vogue for eugenics, the planned breeding of the best. Though never dominant, it had a significant influence in shaping welfare policies and the attempt to reorder national priorities in the face of international competition. It also fed into a burgeoning racism in the inter-war years as politicians feared a declining population which would give dominance to 'inferior races'. In the 1940s, the key period for the establishment of the Welfare State, there was an urgent concern with the merits of birth control ('family planning') in ensuring that the right sort of people built families, and with the appropriate roles of men and women (especially women) in the family in the brave new world of social democracy.

Linked with this, by the 1950s, in the depth of the Cold War, there was a new searching out of sexual degenerates, especially homosexuals, who not only lived outside families but were also, apparently, peculiarly susceptible to treason. By the 1960s, a new liberalism ('permissiveness') seemed torn between relaxing the old authoritarian social codes and finding new modes of social regulation, based on the latest in social psychology, and a redefinition of the public/private divide. During the 1970s and 1980s there was, in effect, the beginning of a backlash against what were seen as the excesses of the earlier decade, and perhaps for the first time sexuality became a real front-line political issue as the emergence of the New Right identified the 'decline of the family', feminism and the new homosexual militancy as potent symbols of national decline.

What is at stake in these recurrent debates about morality and sexual behaviour? Clearly a number of different but related concerns are present: the relations between men and women, the problem of sexual deviance, the question of family and other relationships, the relations between adults and children, and the issue of difference, whether of class, gender or race. Each of these has a long history, but in the past couple of hundred years they have become central concerns, often centring around sexual issues. They illustrate the power of the belief that debates about sexuality are debates about the nature of society: as sex goes, so goes society.

So far we have concentrated on the symbolic importance attributed to sexuality, and some of the reasons for this. But it is important to recognize that sexuality is not a unified domain. In the next section we shall look at some of the forces that shape sexual beliefs and behaviour, complicating sexual identities.

The assumption here is that power does not operate through single mechanisms of control. In fact, it operates through complex and overlapping — and often contradictory — mechanisms which produce domination and oppositions, subordination and resistances. There are many structures of domination and subordination in the world of sexuality, but three interdependent elements or axes have been seen as particularly important today: those of class, gender and race. We shall look at each of these in turn.

3   SEXUALITY AND POWER

3.1   CLASS AND SEXUALITY

Class differences in sexual regulation are not unique to the modern world, but they have become more sharply apparent over the past 200 years. Foucault has argued that the very idea of 'sexuality' as a unified domain is essentially a bourgeois one, developed as part of the self-assertion of a class anxious to differentiate itself from the immorality of the aristocracy and the supposedly rampant promiscuity of the lower classes. It was basically a colonizing endeavour, seeking to remould both the polity and sexual behaviour in its own image. The respectable standards of family life developed in the nineteenth century ('Victorian values'), with the increased demarcation between male and female roles, a new emphasis on the need to bring public behaviour up to the best standards of private life, and a sharpened interest in the public policing of non-marital, non-heterosexual sexuality, became increasingly the norm by which all behaviour was judged.

This does not mean, of course, that all or even most behaviour conformed to the norm. Historians have provided plentiful evidence that the working class remained extremely resistant to middle-class manners. Patterns of behaviour inherited from their rural predecessors continued to structure the sexual culture of working-class people well into the twentieth century. The fact that such patterns were different from those of the bourgeoisie does not mean that they were in themselves worse. Nevertheless, it is true that the patterns of sexual life of the present century are the results of a social struggle in which class and sexuality were inextricably linked. This is even reflected at the level of fantasy, particularly in the belief, evident in both heterosexual and homosexual upper class male culture, that the working class woman or man was somehow more spontaneous, closer to nature, than other people.

A somewhat idealized version of 19th-century working-class life

The result has been the existence of quite distinct class patterns of sexuality at various times. For example, attitudes to birth control varied considerably, with the professional classes leading the way in the adoption of artificial contraception from the 1860s, and working class families on the whole having larger families until after the Second World War (McLaren, 1978, Weeks, 1989). But it is also unwise to generalize about class patterns. Textile workers from early in the nineteenth century tended to have smaller families. In the inter-war years there were marked differences between the contraceptive activities of female factory workers, who had access to cultures of knowledge about birth control, and domestic workers, who often did not. As in the Third World today, to have large families was often economically rational in many social situations, and inappropriate in others. Geographical, religious, employment and other factors inevitably came into play.

The same is true in relation to many other aspects of sexual behaviour, for example in attitudes to masturbation, acceptance of casual prostitution, attitudes to homosexuality, and the like (Kinsey *et al.*, 1948, and 1953). Class, in other words, was a key factor, but not always a decisive one in shaping choices about sexual activity.

3.2   GENDER AND SEXUALITY

This leads us to the question of gender itself. Classes consist of men and women, and class and status differences may not have the same significance for women as for men. Gender is a crucial divide.

Gender is not a simple analytical category; it is, as feminist scholarship has increasingly documented, a relationship of power. So, patterns of female sexuality are inescapably a product of the historically rooted power of men to define what is necessary and desirable.

The nineteenth century was a key point in the definition of female sexuality in terms which have greatly influenced our own concepts, and not least our assumptions about the importance of bodily differences. We have already looked at one example of the processes at work — that of Herculine Barbin, discussed in Section 2.1. Let us now look at the issue again, in a wider historical framework. Thomas Laqueur (1990) has argued that the political, economic, and cultural transformations of the eighteenth century created the context in which the articulation of radical differences between the sexes became culturally imperative.

In a long and subtle examination of the evolution of concepts of the body and gender from the Greeks to the twentieth century, Laqueur suggests that there have been fundamental shifts in the ways we see the relationship between male and female bodies. He argues that, until the eighteenth century, the dominant discourse 'construed the male and female bodies as hierarchically, vertically, ordered versions of one sex' (Laqueur, 1990, p.10). The hierarchical but single-sex model certainly interpreted the female body as an inferior and inverted version of the male, but stressed nevertheless the important role of female sexual pleasure, especially in the process of reproduction. Female orgasm and pleasure were seen as necessary to successful impregnation. The breakdown of this model, in political as well as medical debates, led to its replacement in the nineteenth century by a reproductive model which emphasized the existence of two, sharply different bodies, the radical opposition of male and female sexualities, the woman's automatic reproductive cycle, and her lack of sexual feeling. This was a critical moment in the reshaping of gender relations, because it suggested the absolute difference of men and women: no longer a single, partially differentiated body, but two singular bodies, the male and the female.

Laqueur argues that the shift he traces did not arise straightforwardly from scientific advance, nor was it the simple product of a singular effort at social control of women by men. The emergent discourse about sexual difference allowed a range of different, and often contradictory, social and political responses to emerge. But at the heart of the emerging definitions were new cultural and political relations, the product of shifts in the balance of power between men and women. The new perception of female sexuality and reproductive biology has been absolutely central to modern social and political discourse because it stressed difference and division rather than similarity and complementarity.

ACTIVITY 3
You should now read **Reading B, 'Class and gender'**, by Leonore Davidoff.

This is a case study of a specific relationship between a man and a woman in the late nineteenth century. What does this tell us about male assumptions concerning female sexuality? Have these changed since the last century? What does this study suggest about the interaction of class and gender?

Perhaps the most dramatic feature of this extract is Arthur Munby's preoccupation with the bodily characteristics of Hannah Cullwick: her hands, her general physical appearance (her lowliness, her wearing of heavy boots), her submissiveness as a servant, and, implicitly, her closeness to the dirty and dumb world of animals. Note too how he ignored her efficiency in managing his household, and the exhaustion it produced. The sheer 'animality' of Cullwick as perceived by Munby is what shocks us today, and perhaps we are also startled by Hannah

Hannah Cullwick: servant and wife

Cullwick's apparent acceptance of the terms of the relationship. Two issues come out clearly: the vast gap between the classes, which prevented Cullwick's entry into respectability and status, and the imprisoning effects of the idea of separate spheres for men and women, which itself was one of the results of the changing perceptions of gender difference that Laqueur has traced. Both Cullwick and Munby battled with these divisions but their efforts were shaped by the powerful imaginative impact of those divisions themselves.

At the same time, it is important to remember that women have been active participants in shaping their own definition of need. Not only feminism, but the practices of everyday life have offered spaces for women to plot out their own lives. Since the nineteenth century, the acceptable spaces have expanded to include, not only pleasure in marriage, but also relatively respectable forms of non-procreative behaviour. The patterns of male sexual privilege have not been broken, but there is now plentiful evidence that such privilege is neither inevitable nor immutable.

3.3   RACE AND SEXUALITY

Class and gender are not the only differences that shape sexuality. Categorizations by class or gender intersect with those of ethnicity and race. This aspect of sexuality has generally been ignored by historians and social scientists until recently, but it is a vital element of the history of sexuality nonetheless.

The sexual ideologies of the latter part of the nineteenth century presented the black person — 'the wild savage' — as lower down the evolutionary scale than the white: closer to the origins of the human race, closer that is to nature. Such views survived even among the culturally relativist anthropologists who displaced many of the evolutionary theorists after the turn of the century (Coward, 1983). One of the attractions of portrayals of non-industrial cultures was precisely the subliminal feeling that the people there were indefinably freer of the constraints of civilization. Whether non-European peoples represented the childhood of the race, or the promise of a spontaneity free of the effects of a corrupting civilization, the common thread was the symbolic difference represented by the non-white body.

The awareness of other cultures, and of other sexual mores, therefore offered a challenge and a threat. For sexologists like Havelock Ellis the evidence from non-industrial societies provided a justification for their reformist critiques of western sexual norms. At the same time, Ellis, like many others of his generation, supported eugenicist policies, which were based on the belief that it was possible to improve the 'racial stock' by the planned breeding of the best in society. The assumption that the racial stock could (and should) be improved was based on two related assumptions: first, that the labouring poor, whose bodies were enfeebled by ill-health and the effects of industrial society, were disqualified from the hope of social progress; and, secondly, that the world's 'inferior races' posed a threat (particularly because of their fertility) to the future of the imperial races of Europe. The aim of people like Ellis was ostensibly to improve the human race rather than any particular race, but inevitably assumptions of what was socially desirable were filtered through beliefs of the time.

Black and British

It can be argued that the very definitions of masculinity and femininity, and of the appropriate sexual behaviour for either sex, during the past two centuries have to a high degree been shaped in response to the 'Other' represented by alien cultures. Think, for example, of the myths of black men's hyper-sexuality and of the threat to female purity represented by them, common in many colonial situations as well as in the Deep South of the USA. Consider the importance in South African apartheid of the banning of sexual relations between members of different racial groups. Or of the fascination with the exotic sexuality of women in other cultures as represented in art and literature. Western sexuality, with its norms of sexual differentiation, monogamy, heterosexuality and (in some periods at least) respectability, has been both challenged and undermined, as well as triumphantly reasserted, by knowledge of other cultures, other bodies, and other sexualities. The following extract (a larger version of which appears as Reading C in Chapter 1 of this book), by Valerie Amos and Pratibha Parmar, two contemporary black feminists, suggest that we have not yet escaped this history:

> White feminists have fallen into the trap of measuring the Black female experience against their own, labelling it as in some way lacking, then looking for ways in which it might be possible to harness the Black women's experience to their own. Comparisons are made with our countries of origin which are said to fundamentally exploit Black women. The hysteria in the western women's movement surrounding issues like arranged marriages, purdah, female-headed households, is often beyond the Black woman's comprehension — being tied to so-called feminist notions of what constitutes good or bad practice in our communities in Britain or the Third World.
>
> In rejecting such analyses we would hope to locate the Black family more firmly in the historical experiences of Black people — not in the romantic idealized forms popular with some social anthropologists, and not merely as a tool of analysis. There are serious questions about who has written that history and in what form, questions which have to be addressed before we as Black people use that history as an additional element of our analysis. Black women cannot just throw away their experiences of living in certain types of household organization; they want to use that experience to transform familial relationships. Stereotypes about the Black family have been used by the state to justify particular forms of oppression. The issue of fostering and adoption of Black kids is current: Black families are seen as being 'unfit' for fostering and adoption. Racist immigration legislation has had the effect of separating family members, particularly of the Asian community, but no longer is that legislation made legitimate just by appeals to racist ideologies contained in notions of 'swamping'. Attempts have actually been made by some feminists to justify such legislative practices on the basis of protecting Asian girls from the 'horrors' of the arranged marriage system. White feminists beware — your unquestioning and racist assumptions about the Black family, your critical but uninformed approach to 'Black culture' has found root and in fact informs state practice.
> (Amos and Parmar, 1984, p.11)

The examination of the relations of power concerning class, gender and race demonstrates the complexity of the forces that shape sexual attitudes and behaviour. These forces in turn open the way to the development of differentiated sexual identities. In the next section, we are going to look at the whole question of identity in more detail, to show the main factors that have shaped the divisions that we assume to be natural, but that are actually historically constructed.

4   SEXUAL IDENTITIES

4.1   THE INSTITUTIONALIZATION OF HETEROSEXUALITY

Let's look again at words — at the language used to describe sexuality. In particular I want to look at the history of two principal terms we now take for granted to such an extent that we assume they have a universal application: 'heterosexuality' and 'homosexuality'. In fact, these terms are of relatively recent origin, and I am going to suggest that their invention — for that is what it was — is an important marker of wider changes. To be more precise, the emergence of the two terms mark a crucial stage in the modern delimitation and definition of sexuality. No doubt it will surprise many that it was the attempt to define 'homosexuality', the 'abnormal' form of sexuality, which forced a sharper definition of 'heterosexuality' as the norm, but the evidence now available suggests that this was the case.

The two terms were, it seems, coined by the same person, Karl Kertbeny, an Austro-Hungarian writer, and were first used publicly by him in 1869. The context in which these neologisms emerged is critical: they were deployed in relation to an early attempt to put on the political agenda in the soon-to-be unified Germany the question of sex reform, in particular the repeal of the anti-sodomy laws. They were part of an embryonic campaign, subsequently taken up by the developing discipline of sexology, to define *homosexuality* as a distinctive form of sexuality: a benign variant in the eyes of reformers of the potent but unspoken and ill-defined notion of 'normal sexuality' (apparently another concept first used by Kertbeny). Hitherto, sexual activity between people of the same biological sex had been dealt with under the catch-all category of sodomy, which was generally seen, not as the activity of a particular type of person, but as a potential in all sinful nature. Early campaigners who aimed to change attitudes to same-sex relations were anxious to suggest that homosexuality was a mark of a distinctive sort of person. As Michel Foucault has noted, the sodomite was seen as a temporary aberrant, whereas the homosexual belonged to a species (Foucault, 1979).

The deployment of these terms must be seen, therefore, as part of a major effort at the end of the nineteenth and beginning of the twentieth centuries to define more closely the types and forms of sexual behaviour and identity; and it is in this effort that homosexuality and heterosexuality became key oppositional terms. In the process, however, the implications of the words subtly changed. Homosexuality, instead of describing a benign variant of normality, as Kertbeny originally intended, became a medico-moral description in the hands of pioneering sexologists such as Krafft-Ebing. Heterosexuality, on the other hand, as a term to describe the hitherto untheorized norm, slowly came into use in the course of the twentieth century — more slowly, it should be noted, than its partner word. A norm, perhaps, does not need an explicit descriptor; it becomes the taken-for-granted framework for the way we think, part of the air we breathe.

What are the implications of this new language, and the new realities they signal? Our present day commonsense takes for granted that these terms demarcate a real division between people: there are 'heterosexuals' and there are 'homosexuals', with another term for those who do not quite fit into this neat divide, 'bisexuals'. But the real world is never as tidy as this, and recent historical work has demonstrated that, not only do other cultures not have this way of seeing human sexuality, neither did western cultures until relatively recently.

We are not arguing of course that what we know today as heterosexual or homosexual activity did not take place before the nineteenth century. The real point is more subtle: that the way sexual activity is conceptualized, and consequently divided, has a history, and a history that matters. The argument over terms at the end of the nineteenth century signals a new effort at redefining the norm. A central part of this was the definition of abnormalities. The two efforts are inextricably linked.

The attempt to define more rigorously the characteristics of 'the pervert' (descriptive terms such as 'kleptomania', 'sado-masochism', 'transvestism' for sex-related activities emerged at the end of the nineteenth century alongside 'homosexuality' and 'heterosexuality') was an important element in what I am calling the institutionalization of heterosexuality in the course of the nineteenth and twentieth centuries. In part this was a sexological endeavour. Sexology took upon itself two distinct tasks at the end of the nineteenth century. First, it attempted to define the basic characteristics of what constitutes normal masculinity and femininity, seen as distinct characteristics of biological men and women. Secondly, by cataloguing the infinite variety of sexual practices, it produced a hierarchy in which the abnormal and the normal could be distinguished. For most of the pioneers, the two endeavours were closely linked: heterosexual object-choice was closely linked to genital intercourse. Other sexual activities were either accepted as fore-pleasures, or condemned as aberrations.

Sexology, however, only set the terms of the debate. The social history of heterosexuality in the twentieth century is much more complex than a simple sexological reflex. It is tempting to see this social history as the sum total of all the developments in relation to sexuality in the century, because even the changing ideas about sexual diversity make sense only in relation to an apparently nature-given norm. We can, however, point to some key elements which suggest that heterosexuality as an institution is itself a historically changing phenomenon. For example, consider:

- Changes in family life, and the recognition of diversity in patterns of domestic life, which suggest that the family itself is a historically changing form.

- The changing patterns of employment, and women's fuller integration into the paid workforce, which have inevitably shifted the balance between men and women, even if major inequalities survive and remain deeply entrenched.

- Changes in the patterns of fertility, the widespread use of birth control techniques, abortion etc., that have opened new potentials in the sexual relations of men and women.

- A new emphasis in the twentieth century on sex as pleasure, reflected in the explosion of literature on how to attain sexual pleasure, how to avoid frigidity, premature ejaculation etc., which has served to put an overwhelming emphasis on sexual relations in binding couples together.

Some feminist writers have suggested that what has happened is that heterosexuality has been institutionalized as 'compulsory', in a way which binds women ever more tightly to men (Rich, 1984; Jackson, 1987). The interesting point to note here is that very little attention has been paid by historians and social scientists to this process of institutionalization.

ACTIVITY 4   Look again at Carole Vance's comments on this (Reading A). Consider what the implications are of seeing heterosexuality, like homosexuality, as a historical phenomenon.

4.2   INVENTING HOMOSEXUALITY

Let us now turn to the history of homosexuality, about which a great deal has been written in the past 20 years. It may seem strange to look in detail at what will seem to many to be a minority activity. But I believe that in understanding the history of homosexuality we can gain new insights into the social construction of heterosexuality and of sexuality as a whole.

I shall begin with a bald assertion: before the nineteenth century 'homosexuality' existed, but 'the homosexual' did not.

Put simply, this suggests that while homosexuality has existed in all types of societies, at all times, and has been variously accepted or rejected as part of the customs and social mores of these societies, only since the nineteenth century, and in the industrializing societies of the West, has a distinctive homosexual category and associated identity developed. The emergence in Germany, and other Central and West European countries such as Britain, in the 1870s and 1880s of writings about, and crucially by, homosexuals was a critical stage in this shift. By defining the 'contrary sexual feeling', or the existence of a 'third' or 'intermediate' gender, Richard von Krafft-Ebing, Magnus Hirschfeld, Havelock Ellis and others were attempting to signal the discovery or recognition of a distinct type of person, whose sexual essence was significantly different from that of the 'heterosexual' — another category invented, as we have seen, at about the same time.

Now, I am not arguing that these newly defined homosexuals were figments of the imaginations of these distinguished writers. On the contrary, these writers were attempting to describe, and explain, individuals they were encountering through the law courts, their medical practices, their friends, or in their personal lives (Ulrichs and Hirschfeld, for example, were themselves homosexual; Havelock Ellis was married to a self-defined lesbian). What I do assert, however, is that this new categorizing and defining zeal towards the end of the nineteenth century was as significant a shift in the public and private definition of homosexuality as the emergence of an open and defiant lesbian and gay politics in American cities in the late 1960s and early 1970s. Both represented a critical transformation of what it meant to be sexual. They symbolized crucial breakthroughs in the meanings given to sexual difference.

So what existed before the nineteenth century? The American historian Randolph Trumbach (1989) has detected two major patterns of homosexual interaction in the West since the twelfth century, which in turn echo the two great patterns of the organization of homosexuality on a world scale, as revealed by the evidence of anthropologists. Around the year 1100, he argues, a distinctive western cultural pattern begins to emerge. Marriage was late and monogamous. Sexual relations outside marriage were forbidden, but licensed in the form of regulated prostitution. However, all forms of sexual activity which were not procreative were regarded as sinful, whether they were solitary, between men and women, men and men, men and beasts (relations between women, though sometimes noted, did not achieve the same ignominy).

Nevertheless, homosexual activities between men did occur. When they did, they were usually between an active adult and a passive adolescent. Usually, the adult male also had sexual relations with women. The boy, provided he adopted an active role in adulthood, did not suffer a loss of status or of manhood. On the contrary, as long as the role was active, homosexual activity could be seen as a sign of manhood. But the same was not true of those who retained a passive role in adulthood: they were stigmatized, and often abused.

This pattern is very common in various parts of the world. It is essentially the ancient Greek model, but has survived well into the twentieth century, particularly in Mediterranean countries, and also in some subcultures of western societies. Nevertheless, from the early eighteenth century it was gradually superseded by a second model, which increasingly associated any male homosexual behaviour, whether active or passive, with effeminacy, with breaching the accepted or expected gender behaviour. The emergence in the early eighteenth century of male transvestite subcultures in London and other major western cities marks the shift. Here 'mollies', as they were called in

England, could meet others like themselves, and begin to define some sort of sense of difference and identity. By the mid-nineteenth century, this sort of subculture was well-developed in cities such as London, Paris and Berlin.

Basically, what seems to have happened is that the transformation in family life from the eighteenth century, and the sharpening distinctions of male and female social and sexual roles associated with it, had the effect of increasing the stigmatization of men who did not readily conform to their expected sexual and social roles. Those who breached the social expectations of what it was to be a man were categorized as being not real men, what Marcel Proust in the early twentieth century called the *homme-femme* ('man-woman'). Attitudes to women were significantly different, reflecting the social and sexual subordination of women, and the expectation that they could not be autonomously sexual (something I'll come back to in a moment).

If this overview is accurate, it suggests that what was taking place in the late nineteenth century in countries such as Germany and Britain grew out of subcultural developments which were already a couple of hundred years advanced. In Britain, the flurry of scandals and court cases, culminating in the most famous of all, Oscar Wilde's trials in 1895, revealed to an amazed public the existence of an already-complex sexual underground alongside the now hegemonic sexual respectability. The theorizing about 'the urning' or 'third sex' by writers such as Ulrichs, Hirschfeld or Edward Carpenter can then be seen as a description of a type of person who had already differentiated himself from the norm. Simultaneously, the construction of the sexological and psychological category of 'the homosexual' by the new sexual scientists of the late nineteenth century was an attempt to define the natural laws which explained what was usually seen as a pathology. Similarly, the legal changes, for example in Germany and Britain, which sharpened the penalties against male homosexuality, marked an attempt to regulate and control sexual perversity.

But while in one sense these developments represented a rationalization of long-term developments, and would not have been possible without them, this is not the whole story. Just as the explosive appearance of gay liberation in the USA in 1969 grew out of well-established community networks, but then began something distinctly new, so the changes of the late nineteenth century put the discourse of homosexuality on a new footing. Homosexuality became a scientific and sociological category, classifying sexual perversity in a new way, and this inevitably had its effects in legal and medical practice from then on. It constructed the idea of a distinctive, and perhaps exclusively homosexual, nature. And, possibly even more importantly, it initiated a new phase of homosexual self-definition in the face of the defining work of the new medical and psychological norms.

From the nineteenth century a new model of 'the homosexual' emerged from the scientific literature, though there were all sorts of disputes

Gay male couple: identity and desire

about the explanations for this strange phenomenon: biological, hormonal, environmental, psychological (Plummer, 1981a). This model provided, in a sense, the norm around which the people so defined were constrained to live their lives until very recently. But their lives were of course differentiated by many other factors. Class differences in gay lifestyles have been apparent since at least the nineteenth century, since before Oscar Wilde 'feasted with panthers', as he described his dalliances with working-class boys. More recently, we have been forcefully reminded in the West that there are also sharp racial and ethnic differences in attitudes towards, and responses to homosexuality (see below). But the best documented differences are between men and women.

The model of the homosexual that emerged in the nineteenth century attempted to explain homosexual women and men in the same terms, as if they had a common cause and common characteristics. In fact, the model was overwhelmingly based on male homosexuality, and was never straightforwardly applicable to women. Lesbian scholars have documented the ways in which intimate relations between women formed part of a continuum of close relationships, with no distinctive lesbian identity clearly developing until this century (Faderman, 1980). Men and women might be classified by the same psychological labelling, but their histories are different (Vicinus, 1989).

It should be apparent from what I have said that the new history of homosexuality is a history of identities: their emergence, complexities, and transformations. This does not, of course, exhaust the subject of homosexuality. Much same-sex activity goes on that is never defined as 'homosexual', and does not radically affect someone's sense of self: in closed institutions such as prisons, in casual encounters, and in one-to-one relations which are seen as special, but not defining. For distinctive identities to emerge, and set themselves against the heterosexual norms of our culture, something more than sexual activity, or even homosexual desire, is needed: the possibility of some sort of social space, and social support or network which gives meaning to individual needs.

The growth from the eighteenth century onwards of urban spaces, making possible both social interaction and anonymity, was a crucial factor in the development of a homosexual subculture. The increasing complexity and social differentiation of a modern industrialized society in Europe and North America from the end of the last century provided the critical opportunity for the evolution of the male homosexual and lesbian identities of this century. More recently, gay historians have shown the essential role played by the development of highly organized gay communities in cities such as San Francisco, New York and Sydney in providing the numbers necessary for the mass organization of gay politics.

As civil society in western countries becomes more complex, more differentiated, more self-reliant, so the lesbian and gay community has become an important part of that society. Increasingly, homosexuality becomes an option, or choice, which individuals can follow in a way which was impossible in a more hierarchical and monolithic society. The existence of a gay way of life provides the opportunity for people to explore their needs and desires in ways which were sometimes literally unimaginable at an earlier period. This is, of course, why homosexuality is still often seen as a threat to those wedded to the moral status quo, whether from the left or right of the political spectrum. The existence of positive lesbian and gay identities symbolizes the ever-increasing pluralization of social life, and the expansion of individual choice that this offers.

4.3   RETHINKING SEXUAL IDENTITIES

Let us now look at the issue of sexual identities in a wider context. The idea of a *sexual* identity is an ambiguous one. For many in the modern world it is an absolutely fundamental concept, offering a sense of personal unity, social location and even a political commitment. Not many people may say 'I am a heterosexual', because it is the great taken-for-granted. But to say 'I am gay' or 'I am lesbian' is to make a statement about belonging, and to take a specific stance in relation to the dominant sexual codes.

Yet at the same time the evidence looked at above suggests that such identities are historically and culturally specific, that they are selected from a host of possible social identities, that they are not necessary attributes of particular sexual drives or desires, and that they are not *essential* parts of our personality. We are increasingly aware that sexuality is as much a product of language and culture as of nature. Yet we constantly strive to fix it, stabilize it, and say who we are by telling of our sex.

How important, then, is sexual identity, and what does it tell us about the question of identity in the modern and post-modern world? Several different emphases on identity can be traced.

1   **Identity as destiny**. This is the assumption behind the essentialist tradition as we have traced it. It underpins such phrases as 'biology is destiny'. It assumes that the body expresses some fundamental truth. But, as we have seen, such assumptions themselves have a history. Everything we now know about sexuality undermines the idea that there is a predetermined sexual destiny based on the morphology of the body. We must find the justification for identity elsewhere.

2   **Identity as resistance**. For the social theorists of the 1950s and 1960s, who first brought the question of identity explicitly onto the agenda by speaking of 'identity crises' — psychologists and sociologists such as Erik Erikson (1968) and Erving Goffman (see especially Goffman's *Stigma*, 1968) — personal identity roughly equalled individuality, a strong sense of the self, which was attained by struggling against the weight of social conventionality. For the 'sexual minorities' coming to a new sense of their separateness and individuality during the same period — especially male homosexuals and lesbians — the finding of identity was like discovering a map to explore a new country. As Plummer put it, the processes of categorization and self-categorization (that is, the process of identity formation) may control, restrict and inhibit, but simultaneously they offer comfort, security and assuredness (Plummer, 1981a).

  So, the preoccupation with identity among the sexually marginal cannot be explained as an effect of a peculiar personal obsession with sex. It can be seen, more accurately, as a powerful resistance to the organizing principle of traditional sexual attitudes. It has been sexual radicals who have most insistently politicized the question of sexual identity. But the agenda has largely been shaped by the importance assigned by our culture to 'correct' sexual behaviour.

3   **Identity as choice**. This leads us to the question of the degree to which sexual identities, especially those stigmatized by the wider society, are in the end freely made choices. Many people, it has been argued, 'drift' into identity, battered by contingency rather than guided by will. Four characteristic stages in the construction of a 'stigmatized personal identity' have been identified:

  (i)   *sensitization:* the individual becomes aware through a series of encounters of his or her difference from the norm, e.g. through being labelled by peers as a 'sissy' or 'tomboy';

  (ii) *signification:* the individual begins to assign meaning to these differences, as she or he becomes aware of the range of possibilities in the social world;

(iii) *subculturization:* the stage of recognizing oneself through involvement with others, e.g. through first sexual contacts;

(iv) *stabilization:* the stage of full acceptance of one's feelings and way of life, such as through involvement in a supportive subculture of similarly inclined people.

There is no automatic progression through these stages. Each transition is as dependent on chance as on decision. There is no necessary acceptance of a final destiny, an explicit socio-sexual identity, for example as gay or lesbian. Some individuals have choices forced on them, through stigmatization and public obloquy — for example, through arrest and trial for sexual offences. Others adopt open identities for political reasons.

ACTIVITY 5   You should now read **Reading C, 'Going gay'**, an extract from an article by Kenneth Plummer about gay identity.

Although focusing on homosexuality, this piece throws considerable light on the whole process of sexual identity formation. Consider how changing social circumstances shape the choices that can be made about sexual identity.

The implication of arguments such as Plummer's is that sexual feelings and desires are one thing, while acceptance of a particular social position and organizing sense of self — that is, an identity — is another. There is no necessary connection between sexual behaviour and sexual identity.

Take, for example, Alfred Kinsey's best known statistic: some 37 per cent of his male sample had had homosexual experiences leading to orgasm. But less than 4 per cent were exclusively homosexual, and even they did not necessarily express a homosexual identity (Kinsey, *et al.*, 1948). So the apparent paradox is that there are some people who identify themselves as gay and participate in the gay community, but may not have any homosexual sexual activity. And others may be homosexually active (for example, in prison) but refuse the label of 'homosexual'.

The conclusion is inescapable. Feelings and desires may be deeply embedded, and may structure individual possibilities. *Identities*, however, can be chosen, and in the modern world, with its preoccupation with 'true' sexuality, the choice is often highly political.

Take an example of this. During the 1980s, questions of race and ethnicity assumed a new prominence, and often these challenged many of the assumptions about the unitary nature of the newly openly-expressed lesbian and gay identities. The result was to highlight the different implications of homosexuality in different communities, and therefore the different meanings it might have. Here, for example, are the comments of an Asian gay man:

> Our community [i.e. the Asian community] provides a nurturing space. ... [Families] are often bulwarks against the institutional and individual racism that we encounter daily. ... And then we discover our sexuality. This sets us apart from family and community, even more so than for a white person. ... More often than not, we live two lives, hiding our sexuality from family and friends in order to maintain our relationships within our community, whilst expressing our sexuality away from the community.
> (quoted in Weeks, 1990, p.236)

The conflicting loyalties posed by 'identity' are real. But again, they suggest the importance of choice in adopting an identity that can help an individual negotiate the hazards of everyday life.

5   SEXUALITY AND POLITICS

5.1   CURRENT DEBATES

Concern with sexuality has been at the heart of western preoccupations since before the rise of Christianity. And it has been a key element of political debate for most of the past two centuries. More recently, it has become a major factor in the redefinition of political battle lines associated with the rise of the New Right in the USA and Britain. It seems that for many people the struggle for the future of society must be fought on the terrain of contemporary sexuality.

It has been argued that this intense preoccupation with the erotic grows out of, and simultaneously contributes to, a growing sense of crisis about sexuality. At its centre is a crisis in the relations between the sexes, relations which have been profoundly unsettled by rapid social change and by the impact of feminism, with its wide-ranging critiques of the patterns of male domination and female subordination. This in turn feeds into a crisis over the meaning of sexuality in our culture, about the place we give sex in our lives and relationships, about identity and pleasure, obligation and responsibility, and about the freedom to choose. Many of the fixed points by which our sexual lives were organized have been radically challenged during the past century. But we do not seem quite certain what to put in their place. A growing willingness to recognize the huge diversity of sexual beliefs and behaviours has only sharpened the debate about how to cope with these in social policy and personal practice.

A crisis about the meaning(s) of sexuality has, then, accentuated the problem of how we are to regulate and control it. What we believe sex is, or ought to be, structures our response to it. It is difficult to separate the particular meanings we give to sexuality from the forms of control we advocate. If we regard sex as dangerous, disruptive and fundamentally anti-social, then we are more likely to adopt moral positions which propose tight, authoritarian regulation. This I shall call the *absolutist* approach. If, on the other hand, we believe that sexual desire is fundamentally benign, life-enhancing and liberating, we are likely to adopt a relaxed, and perhaps radical set of values, to support a *libertarian* position. Somewhere between these two approaches we can find a third, which may be less certain as to whether sex is good or bad. It is convinced, however, of the disadvantages both of moral authoritarianism and of excess. This is the *liberal* position. These three strategies of regulation have been present in our culture a long time. They still provide, I suggest, the framework for most current debates about sexual morality.

Historically, we are heirs of the absolutist tradition. This has assumed that the disruptive powers of sex can only be controlled by a clear-cut morality that is embedded in social institutions: marriage, heterosexuality, family life, and monogamy. Though it has its roots in the Judeao-Christian religious tradition, absolutism is now grounded much more widely. The major set of legal changes in Britain in the nineteenth and the early twentieth centuries on obscenity, prostitution, the age of consent, homosexuality, and incest were promoted by absolutist social morality movements, propelled in many cases by an evangelical moral fervour. In practice, of course, this fervour was tempered by political pragmatism and by selective enforcement. Female prostitution, for example, the frequent target of moralizing fervour and of legislative intervention, was in practice tacitly accepted. Nevertheless, it is basically the case that an essentially authoritarian moral code dominated the regulation of sexuality until the 1960s.

The libertarian position can best be seen as an oppositional tendency, whose task has been to expose the hypocrisies of the dominant order in the name of a greater sexual freedom. Its politics have been an important part of various radical political movements over the past 150 years. From the point of view of the analysis we have been following, however, perhaps the most interesting feature of libertarianism is its structural affinity with the absolutist approach: both assume the power of sexuality, and take for granted its disruptive effect. They draw, however, fundamentally divergent conclusions from this.

In practice, the regulation of sexuality for the past generation has been dominated by various forms of the liberal tradition. In Britain this approach was most clearly articulated in the Wolfenden report on male homosexuality and prostitution, published in 1957 (Home Office, 1957). The report made a classic distinction between what should be allowed in public, and what could be tolerated in private. The duty of the law, it suggested, was to regulate the public sphere and, in particular, to maintain public decency. There were limits, however, to the law's obligation to control the private sphere, the traditional arena of personal morality. Churches might strive to tell people what to do in private; it was not the task of the state to attempt to do the same. The state, therefore, had little place in the enforcement of private standards, except (a major qualification) when harm was threatened to others. By such an approach there was an implicit assumption that society was no longer governed — if indeed it ever had been — by a moral consensus. The law should therefore limit itself to maintaining common standards of public decency.

The Wolfenden report provided the theoretical framework for the series of reforms concerning sexuality that were enacted in Britain in the 1960s: reforms of the laws concerning obscenity, homosexuality, abortion and family planning, theatre censorship and divorce. Their starting point was the assumption that absolutist approaches were inadequate for regulating sexuality because there was no agreed, common morality to underpin them (Weeks, 1989).

It is important to note, however, that the argument that the law should be cautious about intervening in private life, to impose a single moral standard, did not lead to the belief that no control of sexuality was necessary. The law was indeed tightened in relation to public manifestations of sex, with regard both to prostitution and male homosexuality. Furthermore, although the Wolfenden report recommended the decriminalizing of homosexuality, it nevertheless urged further research into the possibility of a 'cure'. This underlines an important point about the liberal reforms of this period: they did not involve a positive endorsement of either homosexuality, abortion, divorce or explicit sexual representations in literature, film, or theatre. Just as the liberal approach was uncertain about the merits of legal enforcement in a complex society, so it was undecided about the merits of the activities to which it directed its attention. The main purpose of the reforms was to relieve the burden of increasingly unworkable laws, whilst maintaining the possibility of a more acceptable form of social regulation: what Stuart Hall (1980) has called the 'double taxonomy' of freedom *and* control.

I am arguing that the liberal reforms of the 1960s were attempts to come to terms with social change, and to establish a more effective form of social regulation. That is not, however, how they have been seen. Here, for example, are the views of a conservative commentator, Ronald Butt, concerning what became known as 'permissiveness'. Its essence, he suggested, was:

> ... permissiveness in one strictly limited social area (i.e. sex) coupled with the exaction of strict obedience to new norms prescribed by the liberal orthodoxy in another. In some matters, a charter of individual licence was granted which unleashed an unprecedented attack on old commonly held standards of personal behaviour and responsibility. ...
> (Butt, 1985)

The attack on permissiveness as an attempt to establish a new norm has been central to conservative mobilization around sexual issues in the 1970s and 1980s. It has focused in particular on what it sees as several significant changes:

- the threat to the family;
- the challenge to sexual roles, particularly that posed by feminism;
- the undermining of heterosexual normality particularly through the attempts of the lesbian and gay movement to advance the full equality of homosexuality;
- the threat to values posed by a more liberal sex education, which was seen as inducting children into the acceptance of hitherto unacceptable sexual behaviour;
- all these fears were compounded by, and thought to be symbolized in, the emergence of a major health crisis associated with HIV and AIDS.

It can be seen that all these concerns are related to a number of central questions that have existed throughout the modern history of sexuality: questions concerning family, the relative positions of men and women, sexual diversity, children. These remain the issues on which the history of sexuality still revolves.

There is, in fact, growing evidence that the distinctions codified by the Wolfenden report between public and private life are perhaps not subtle enough to deal with some of the sexual issues which are now to the fore. If we take an issue like child sex abuse, it becomes clear that intervention to stop abuse may be regarded as transcending any respect for the inviolability of private life. What we think should be legitimately allowed in private is always controlled by wider values about the sort of society we want to see. These values, I would argue, are at the moment in a period of great flux and change. This is why issues such as pornography, which turn on the public impact of private taste and fantasy, become so controversial.

5.2   THE FUTURE OF SEXUALITY

Despite the counter attack against 'permissiveness' there are clear signs that less authoritarian attitudes towards sexuality continue to grow. The framework for this is a profound change in family relationships, which has two main aspects. The first is a critical shift in attitudes towards marriage and the family. Most people still get married, and this key feature of institutionalized heterosexuality does not appear to be threatened. But, to an important extent, the idea that marriage is for life does seem to have been undermined. A third of marriages now end in divorce, as do a high percentage of second marriages. The fact that people remarry so enthusiastically underlines the importance given to formal legal bonds. But even more importantly, there seems to be a will to try to get it right, by trying again.

This can be related to the belief that domestic intimacy is of fundamental importance as the basis for social life. 'Modern society is to be distinguished from older social formations', Niklas Luhmann has argued, 'by the fact that it has become more elaborate in two ways: it affords more opportunities both for impersonal and for more intensive personal relationships' (1986, p.12). Marriage remains the dominant focus for the latter, as is suggested both by the continuing public disapproval of extra-marital relations, and the acceptance of pre-marital sexual relations if they are seen to be stable, marriage-like relations. But this is accompanied by a strong sense that modern marriage has to be worked at, and if it goes wrong it should be tried again.

The second feature about attitudes to the family that deserves attention is the growing perception that there are many different types of families. Families change over the life-cycles of their members. More importantly, however, for historical and cultural reasons different forms of family life have evolved, and the term 'family' is now often used to describe domestic arrangements that are quite different from what was once 'the norm'. The best examples of this are provided by the phrase 'one-parent families', and the gradual disappearance of the stigma of illegitimacy.

Alongside these changes there exists the widespread acceptance of birth control and support for liberal abortion laws, both of which underline a general belief that sexual activity should involve a degree of choice, especially for women.

There has been, however, one major exception to this gradual liberalization, and that is in attitudes towards homosexuality. There now seems to be a general acceptance that homosexual relations should not be subject to punitive laws, but their legality is still subject to tight limits. (Following the Wolfenden report, the law reforms of 1967 decriminalized male homosexual acts for two men over the age of 21, as long as these acts are carried out in private, which is narrowly defined.) But, as the debates over 'Section 28' of the Local Government Act of 1988 have made clear, there is no general acceptance of homosexual relations as being on a par with heterosexual ones (Weeks, 1989). The key clause sought to ban the promotion of homosexuality as a 'pretended family relationship'. The phrase was new, and like all innovations in the language of sexuality was an attempt to deal with an emergent reality: this time, the claims of lesbians and gay men that their sexual choices were on a par with those of heterosexuals.

Clearly, the background to this, as well as to the public's hesitant attitudes towards homosexuality generally, was the crisis caused by the emergence of HIV and AIDS as a major health threat. The fact that the first people in the West identified as having AIDS were gay men has profoundly shaped responses to the health crisis, leading to a general stigmatization of people with the syndrome. AIDS served to crystallize a range of anxieties about shifts in sexual behaviour that focused on the growth of a self-assertive gay consciousness since the 1960s. These

'Pretended families': parents on Clause 28 protest march, London, 1988

anxieties seem, in turn, to have been part of the social anxiety generated by wider shifts in the culture of western societies caused by a growing social diversity. Alongside gay men, especially in the USA, black people were seen as a potent source of 'pollution' — they too were strongly linked to the new virus. Both sexual and racial diversity were seen as portending a threat to the hegemonic values of modernized societies.

What we are seeing is a growing recognition of the *facts* of social and sexual diversity, but only to a limited degree so far has this recognition been turned into a positive acceptance of diversity and moral pluralism. On the contrary, as we have seen, diversity, and the ever-growing social complexity which gives rise to it, arouses acute anxieties, which provide the basis of a constituency for the revival of more absolutist values. A more pluralist position, however, would seem to be more in line with the complexity and variety that can be observed in the history of sexuality as we have traced it. It seems likely that in the years ahead the challenge of sexual diversity will grow rather than diminish.

But will the question of sexuality remain central to social and moral debates? Rosalind Coward (1989) has suggested that, as we approach the end of the twentieth century, 'the body', its fitness, health and well-being, particularly in the wake of the AIDS crisis, is displacing a concern with 'sex' in the traditional sense as focus for social concern. A final question we might ask ourselves is whether we are beginning to see the end of what Foucault called the 'regime of sexuality'? Is the throne of 'King Sex' beginning to totter? And if so what would this mean?

Everything we have learnt about the history of sexuality tells us that the social organization of sexuality is never fixed or stable. It is shaped in complex historical circumstances. As we enter the period known as 'post-modernity' we are likely to see a new and radical shift in the ways we relate to our bodies and their sexual needs. The challenge will be to understand the processes at work in a more effective way than was apparent in the period of modernity.

REFERENCES

Amos, V. and Parmar, P. (1984) 'Challenging imperial feminism', in *Feminist Review,* no.17, pp.3–19.

Butt, R. (1985) 'Lloyd George knew his followers', *The Times,* 19 September.

Coward, R. (1983) *Patriarchal Precedents: Sexuality and Social Relations*, London, Routledge & Kegan Paul.

Coward, R. (1989) *The Whole Truth: The Myth of Alternative Medicine.* London, Faber.

Davidoff, L. (1983) 'Class and gender in Victorian England', in Newton, J. L. *et al.* (eds) *Sex and Class in Women's History*, London, Routledge.

Ellis, H. (1946) *The Psychology of Sex*, London, William Heinemann.

Erikson, E. (1968) *Identity: Youth and Crisis,* London, Faber and Faber.

Faderman, L. (1980) *Surpassing the Love of Men*, London, Junction Books.

Foucault, M. (1977) *Discipline and Punish: The Birth of the Prison*, London, Allen Lane.

Foucault, M. (1979) *The History of Sexuality: Volume 1, An Introduction*, London, Allen Lane.

Foucault, M. (1980) *Herculine Barbin, Being the Recently Discovered Memoirs of a Nineteenth Century French Hermaphrodite,* Brighton, Harvester.

Gagnon, J. and Simon, W. (1973) *Sexual Conduct*, London, Hutchinson.

Goffman, E. (1968) *Stigma. Notes on the Management of Spoiled Identity,* Harmondsworth, Penguin Books.

Hall, S. (1980) 'Reformism and the legislation of consent', in Clarke, J. *et al.* (eds) *Permissiveness and Control: The Fate of the Sixties Legislation*, London, Macmillan.

Home Office (1957) *Report of the Committee on Homosexual Offences and Prostitution*, Command 247, London, HMSO.

Jackson, M. (1987), '"Facts of life" or the eroticisation of women's oppression? Sexology and the social construction of heterosexuality', in Caplan, P. (ed.) *The Cultural Construction of Sexuality*, London, Tavistock.

Krafft-Ebing, Richard von (1931) *Psychopathia Sexualis,* New York, Physicians and Surgeons Book Company.

Kinsey, A. *et al.* (1948) *Sexual Behaviour in the Human Male,* Philadelphia and London, W.B. Saunders.

Kinsey, A. *et al.* (1953) *Sexual Behaviour in the Human Female,* Philadelphia and London, W.B. Saunders.

Laqueur, T. (1990) *Making Sex: Body and Gender from the Greeks to Freud,* London, Harvard University Press.

Luhmann, N. (1986) *Love as Passion,* Cambridge, Polity Press.

McLaren, A. (1978) *Birth Control in Nineteenth Century England,* London, Croom Helm.

Plummer, K. (ed.) (1981a) *The Making of the Modern Homosexual,* London, Hutchinson.

Plummer, K. (1981b) 'Going gay: identities, life cycles, and lifestyles in the male gay world', in Hart, J. and Richardson, D. (eds) *The Theory and Practice of Homosexuality,* London, Routledge.

Rich, A. (1984) 'Compulsory heterosexuality and lesbian existence', in Snitow, A. *et al.* (eds.) *Desire: The Politics of Sexuality,* London, Virago.

Sontag, S. (1989) *AIDS and its Metaphors,* London, Allen Lane.

Turner, B.S. (1984) *The Body and Society,* Oxford, Basil Blackwell.

Trumbach, R. (1989) 'Gender and homosexual roles in modern western culture: the 18th and 19th centuries compared', in van Kooten Niekerk, A. and van der Meer, T. (eds) *Homosexuality, which Homosexuality?,* London, GMP Publishers.

Vance, C. (1984) 'Pleasure and danger: towards a politics of sexuality', in Vance, C. (ed.), *Pleasure and Danger: Exploring Female Sexuality,* London, Routledge & Kegan Paul.

Vance, C. S. (1989) 'Social construction theory: problems in the history of sexuality', in van Kooten Niekerk, A. and van der Meer, T. (eds) *Homosexuality, which Homosexuality?,* London, Routledge.

Vicinus, M. (1989) 'They wonder to which sex I belong: The historical roots of the modern lesbian identity', in van Kooten Niekerk, A. and van der Meer, T. (eds) *Homosexuality, which Homosexuality?,* London, GMP Publishers.

Walkowitz, J.R. (1980) *Prostitution and Victorian Society: Women, Class and the State,* Cambridge, Cambridge University Press.

Weeks, J. (1985) *Sexuality and its Discontents: Meanings, Myths and Modern Sexualities,* London, Routledge & Kegan Paul.

Weeks, J. (1989) *Sex, Politics and Society: The Regulation of Sexuality since 1800,* 2nd edn, Harlow, Longman.

Weeks, J. (1990) *Coming Out: Homosexual Politics in Britain from the Nineteenth Century to the Present,* 2nd edn, London, Quartet.

SOCIAL CONSTRUCTION THEORY

Carole S. Vance

Different degrees of social construction

The widespread use of social construction as a term and as a paradigm obscures the fact that constructionist writers have used this term in diverse ways. It is true that all reject transhistorical and transcultural definitions of sexuality and suggest instead that sexuality is mediated by historical and cultural factors. But a close reading of constructionist texts shows that social construction spans a theoretical field of what might be constructed, ranging from sexual acts, sexual identities, sexual communities, the direction of sexual desire (object choice) to sexual impulse or sexuality itself.

At minimum, all social construction approaches adopt the view that physically identical sexual acts may have varying social significance and subjective meaning depending on how they are defined and understood in different cultures and historical periods. Because a sexual act does not carry with it a universal social meaning, it follows that the relationship between sexual acts and sexual identities is not a fixed one, and it is projected from the observer's time and place to others at great peril. Cultures provide widely different categories, schemata, and labels for framing sexual and affective experiences. The relationship of sexual act and identity to sexual community is equally variable and complex. These distinctions, then, between sexual acts, identities, and communities are widely employed by constructionist writers.

A further step in social construction theory posits that even the direction [of] sexual desire itself, for example, object choice or hetero/homosexuality, is not intrinsic or inherent in the individual but is constructed. Not all constructionists take this step; for some, the direction of desire and erotic interest are fixed, although the behavioural *form* this interest takes will be constructed by prevailing cultural frames, as will the subjective experience of the individual and the social significance attached to it by others.

The most radical form of constructionist theory is willing to entertain the idea that there is no essential, undifferentiated sexual impulse, 'sex drive' or 'lust', which resides in the body due to physiological functioning and sensation. Sexual impulse itself is constructed by culture and history. In this case, an important constructionist question concerns the origins of these impulses, since they are no longer assumed to be intrinsic or, perhaps, even necessary. This position, of course, contrasts sharply with more middle-ground constructionist theory which implicitly accepts an inherent sexual impulse which is then constructed in terms of acts, identity, community, and object choice. The contrast between middle-ground

Source: Vance, C.S. (1989) 'Social construction theory: problems in the history of sexuality', in van Kooten Niekerk, A. and van der Meer, T. (eds) *Homosexuality, which Homosexuality?*, London, GMP Publishers pp.18–19, 21–4.

and radical positions make it evident that constructionists may well have arguments with each other, as well as with essentialists. Each degree of social construction points to different questions and assumptions, possibly to different methods, and perhaps to different answers. ...

The instability of sexuality as a category

Because they were tied to essentialist assumptions which posited biological and physiological factors as influential in determining the contours of sexuality, sexological and biomedical paradigms of sexuality nevertheless offered one advantage: sexuality enjoyed the status of a stable, ongoing, and cohesive entity. The constructionist paradigm more flexibly admits variability in behaviour and motive over time and place. But to the extent that social construction theory grants that sexual acts, identities and even desire are mediated by cultural and historical factors, the object of study — sexuality — becomes evanescent and threatens to disappear. If sexuality is constructed differently at each time and place, can we use the term in a comparatively meaningful way? ...

Some social constructionists explicitly encourage the total deconstruction of the category of the sexual, for example, Foucault. Others have not taken this theoretical position, though it remains implicit in their work. For, if sexuality is constituted differently in different times and places, it follows that behaviors and relations seen as sexual by us (contemporary Euro-Americans) may not be by others, and vice versa. ...

The role of the body

Social construction's greatest strength lies in its violation of our folk knowledge and scientific ideologies that would frame sexuality as 'natural', determined by biology and the body. This violation makes it possible, indeed compels us to raise questions that a naturalizing discourse would obscure and hide. Social constructionists have been even-handed in this endeavor, dethroning the body in all fields — in heterosexual history as well as in lesbian and gay history. At first, we greeted this development with good cheer, happy to be rid of the historical legacy of 19th-century spermatic and ovarian economies, women's innate sexual passivity, and the endless quest to find the hormonal cause of homosexuality. Yet the virtue of social construction may also be its vice.

Has social construction theory, particularly variants which see 'sexual impulse', 'sex drive', or 'lust' as created, made no room for the body, its functions, and physiology? As sexual subjects, how do we reconcile constructionist theory with the body's visceral reality and our own experience of it? If our theory of sexuality becomes increasingly disembodied, does it reach the point of implausibility, even for us? And if we wish to incorporate the body within social construction theory, can we do so without returning to essentialism and biological determinism?

Let me discuss these points more concretely by giving an example from my own work on female circumcision. ... [This topic] illuminates the difficulty of thinking about the relationship of sexuality to the body and has much to offer for other body issues.

Briefly, female circumcision is an umbrella term for traditional customs carried out in various Middle Eastern and African countries. These customs involve the surgical alteration and removal of female genital tissue, usually performed by midwives and female kin. The procedures vary in severity and range from removing part or all of the clitoris (simple circumcision) to removing the labia (excision). In infibulation, the most radical form of surgery, the clitoris and labia are excised, and the vaginal opening is sutured to reduce its circumference, making heterosexual penetration impossible and thus guaranteeing virginity. These operations are done at different ages and for different reasons — to promote hygiene and fertility, to render women aesthetically more feminine and thus marriageable, and to promote virginity. It is important to understand that these procedures are widespread and in local terms thought to be required by religion or custom.

In the past ten years, an intense conversation has developed between Western and Third-World feminists over these practices. It is not my goal here to thoroughly describe this debate, or to suggest, by examining Western views, that we enjoy a privileged vantage point or right to intervene. What interests me here is how we think about these practices and the body in less guarded moments. ... We tend to think about the effects of these customs, particularly on sexual functioning. We draw on a physiological model of Masters and Johnson, which places the clitoris at the center of female sexual response and orgasm. We reason that removal of part or all of the clitoris interferes with orgasm, perhaps making it impossible. That is, we are universalizing a physiological finding made on American subjects without much thought. Could Sudanese women's responses be different?

READING B   CLASS AND GENDER

Leonore Davidoff

Images, Games and Transformations

In 1854, when A.J. Munby was twenty-five he met Hannah Cullwick, aged twenty-one, on a London street. In his usual manner he struck up a conversation with her. She combined all the qualities he prized most highly: she was from a country background; strong and robust but good-looking; a maid-of-all-work, but exceptually [sic] intelligent and lively. From then on she was the center of his emotional life as he was for hers. For nineteen years until their marriage they were involved with each other, although during all that time he remained a nominal bachelor living at 6 Fig Tree Court, the Temple, and she living in various residential servant situations. It is not clear from the sources we have whether theirs was, in conven-

Source: Davidoff, L. (1983) 'Class and gender in Victorian England', in Newton, J.L. *et al.* (eds) *Sex and Class in Women's History,* London, Routledge.

tional terms, a sexual relationship and there are some indications that Munby may have been impotent. In any case, there were no children nor indications that Hannah ever thought she was pregnant, a situation which might have totally altered their relationship. Munby and Hannah finally married in 1873 when he was forty-four and she was thirty-nine. She lived with him for just over four years as his servant, not openly as his wife. After a period of increasing tension in their relationship, she returned to her people in Shropshire and lived for the rest of her life in a cottage provided for her by Munby where he visited her regularly. Her relatives and friends accepted him; while his middle-class circle, with the exception of two of his closest friends, never knew of her existence.

Soon after their relationship began, they started a series of games and playacting in which they used the differences between them to emphasize their love and devotion. They were intensely aware of the impression that they made on other people. In public, Hannah would act the perfect servant, demurely walking behind Munby, carrying his heavy luggage, calling him Sir and meekly obeying his orders. He would act especially 'masterful', give her ostentatious tips, and send her off to do his bidding. Later they would meet in his rooms and giggle like children over the incident revelling in the 'if they only knew' aspect of their situation. ...

The point about Hannah and Munby's 'scripts' is that they were written around the theme of class and gender differences played out through games of mastery and submission. ...

Most of the themes which preoccupied Munby, and to a lesser extent Hannah, clustered around the questions of dominance and subordination, strength and weakness, autonomy and dependence. The dichotomies and contrasts allied to these subjects are characteristic of much Victorian culture: respectable/not respectable, lady/woman, pure/impure, clean/dirty (and by extension white/black), indoor/outdoor, fairness/suntanned or ruddy (blushing was thought to be a sign of sexual arousal in middle-class women), clothed/uncovered skin, and above all, of course, feminine/masculine. Many of these themes are related either directly or indirectly to the major Victorian preoccupation with *work:* what was it, who did it, where did they do it. This produced another set of contrasts: work/leisure, work/home, manual work/brain work.

Connected to both sets of contrasts ... *hands* take on a special significance and play a central role in both class and gender imagery, e.g., 'the language of gloves'. They also carry an explicitly sexual connotation for Munby, and one would guess, for many other Victorians as well. White, dainty hands indicated gentility as well as femininity. They were symbolic of inner breeding but also of life-style. ...

When Munby tried to persuade Hannah to dress as a gentlewoman he wanted her to wear gloves, but she resisted saying 'they baffle my hands so'. He quotes this statement approvingly, however, for contrary to what had usually been considered attractive, Munby is fascinated by, even addicted to looking at, touching (at times cutting the skin from) large, rough, red, work-hardened hands of working girls. With monotonous repetition Munby's diary entries and poems dwell on the motif of hands, their color, shape and texture:

> For she is still a working wench
> and sits with hands still bare
> (Munby, 1891)

Hannah deliberately rubbed the bars of grates and cleaned knives with her bare hands, despite the unpleasant feeling, in order to harden them in a paean of love for Munby, expressed through work.

A similar, although slightly less compelling preoccupation of Munby's was with women who either had large masculine-looking feet or who wore heavy boots; in fact Hannah often wore his old boots. He writes approvingly of a colliery girl: 'Her ponderous boots with iron on the sole, shod like a horse's hoofs.' Here Munby connects this image with one of his favorite animal analogies. Small, dainty feet and hands, of course, were the pride of middle-class Victorian women and figure widely in descriptions of feminine attractiveness, a physical characteristic evoked in characters from Dora, the wife in [Charles Dickens'] *David Copperfield,* to Meg in [Louisa Alcott's] *Little Women*, or Rosamund in [George Eliot's] *Middlemarch. ...*

The animal/human analogy which Munby used for his colliery girl pervades his diary. It indicates lowliness and degradation, but also a brute strength and dumb loyalty expressed through love and service. In his poetry, girls and women are compared to cows, horses, dogs, and in the case of the 'ebony slave girl' (who eats on all fours out of a bowl on the ground), even an elephant. Note that all these are examples of domesticated animals [that] have been 'trained' and 'broken in' by man. ...

For Munby, ... one of the most important transformations was the crossing of sex lines. The more sharply that gender was differentiated in dress, looks, voice, walk, coloring, and size, the more intriguing and exciting passing through or reversing these boundaries could be. Victorian writing, costume, and visual imagery constantly emphasizes the largeness, hardness, and muscularity of men as opposed to the small fragility and roundness of middle-class women. The Victorians took every opportunity to emphasize and create differences between the sexes just as they did between the working-class woman and middle-class lady. Or in Munby's phrase the shoulders of the girl farm servant, whom he compares to a young guardsman, are three foot broad and 'square, massive, muscular, made for work, just as those sloping white ones of a drawing room were made for show.' ...

Contradictions

It seems evident that Hannah tried, and to an extent, succeeded in accepting and believing in Munby's equation of dirt, lowliness, even degradation with love and inner worth. On the other hand, she admits that most servants, herself included before her 'training', would have wanted to rise above scullery work or a maid-of-all-work position if they could. She too had internalized conceptions of respectability, order, and cleanliness. It was, after all, partly her task to create that order. After [an] incident where she rubbed her face in the dirt and kissed the mat on the pavement in front of Munby, she records her feelings [in her diary]: 'i was glad i'd done it, but i felt so overcome somehow with the feeling of love and degradation — been in the street like that — so low and so dirty — yet liking the work so and especially for Massa's ['Master's' i.e. Munby's] sake that it was some time afore i could feel calm.' ...

Hannah was in many ways a more independent agent than Munby as she had supported herself from the age of eight while he was financially and in many ways still emotionally and socially dependent on his parents. Yet for all her strength and independence, Hannah's position forced her into a childish dependency on Munby. Both referred to her moods and outbursts as 'being naughty'. When she is put in an intolerable situation by her employer, Munby gives her a double message; backing up the authority of the employer yet obviously enjoying her show of spirit especially as he knew that he had ultimate loyalty over her life through love. ...

Hannah's relationship to Munby in his persona as *gentleman* was extremely important to her. She claimed several times that she had 'seen his face in the tea-cups' before she met him; in other words that she was psychologically attuned to finding someone of higher status as proof of her own self-worth. She muses in her diary at various points about whether she could have ever fallen in love with a man of her own rank and comes to the conclusion that it is doubtful. Yet, as with women of any class, without marriage, the final mark of her dependent status was the lack of a home of her own. Unmarried female servants no matter what their age, were always considered 'girls'. The mythology of the middle class maintained that these women would be taken care of as Munby took care of his old nurse, Hannah Carter, by giving her a pension in her old age. ...

Munby too was torn by the contradictions implicit in his relationship with Hannah. He resented what he felt to be her under-estimation of what he had sacrificed in remaining loyal to her. Most importantly, he didn't see, as most employers of servants didn't see, the physical and mental burden of the work load a servant such as Hannah was expected to carry. Despite the vivid, detailed description of her daily work that Hannah provided in her diary, and his own observations of working women, Munby, who had never worked with anything heavier than a pen in his life, romanticized manual work. He delighted in the fact that Hannah spent her Sunday afternoons off with him doing his housework, getting his tea, washing his feet. She also took his laundry, mending, and sewing away to do in her spare time. ...

Conclusions

A detailed study of such a source as the Munby collection brings alive the connection between social structure and personality. The pervasiveness of both class and gender categories, which it illustrates, stems from the effect of often unconscious, highly charged, emotional expectations laid down in childhood, which in many cases appear in the form of subliminal images. The mutual preoccupations of Munby and Hannah with boundaries and their experience of crossing these boundaries in both fantasy and reality can tell us a great deal about the way the fabric of Victorian society was created and maintained.

References

Munby, A. J. (1891) *Vulgar Verses* (by 'Jones Brown'), London, Reeves & Turner.

READING C   GOING GAY

Kenneth Plummer

Each person's life ... has a history: of growth, crisis and change. Until recently, accounts of this history were notorious for focusing upon the earliest years of life to the relative neglect of patterns of adult development. Life seemed to end at five. More recently there has been a growing interest in lifespan development through which the predictable crises in adult life are charted. Through intensive studies of individual lives, portraits are becoming established of critical turning points that most people will encounter. Levinson (1978, p.58), for example, suggests there may be an 'age thirty transition' which provides an 'opportunity to work on the flaws and limitations of the first adult life structure, and to create the basis for a more satisfactory structure with which to complete the era of early adulthood.' With only a few exceptions, however, this work has been dominated by the heterosexual assumption. Erikson's (1977, p.239) celebrated account, for example, highlights a sixth stage — of intimacy versus isolation — where 'a mutuality of orgasm *with a loved partner of the other sex*' (my emphasis) becomes essential. Homosexuality is here defined out of the model.

To avoid such devaluation, we need to analyse the specific 'turning points' — or crises — entailed in gay life cycles. Only when we are clear about these should they be related to a broader conception of development from womb to tomb. For the time being, I would like to suggest two such crises: 'coming out' and 'opting for a lifestyle'.

Coming out

The first, and usually most momentous, moments in any gay life cycle are those involved in coming out. Given both the heterosexual assumption and the homosexual taboo, those who may later in life 'go gay' will initially be socialized to believe that they are heterosexual; nagging feelings of being different may emerge very early in childhood or adolescence,

Source: Plummer, K. (1981b) 'Going gay: identities, life cycles, and lifestyles in the male gay world', in Hart, J. and Richardson, D. (eds) *The Theory and Practice of Homosexuality*, London, Routledge.

but a clear sense of being gay will only unfold later. Coming out refers to this complex process of moving from a heterosexual (and confused) identity, given to one in childhood, to a strong, positive and accepting sense of one's identity as gay being given to one through awareness of the gay community. It is a momentous, frequently painful, experience in any gay person's life — comparable in impact perhaps to the birth of one's first child in the heterosexual cycle. Experiencing it will dramatically reshape one's life-route: life will never be the same again. Quite when 'coming out' will occur in any particular life is — as yet — unpredictable; many will find it occurring during their first heterosexual marriage, some may find it taking place in mid-adolescence, and others can move through it during their retirement. Most typically, though — in America during the 1970s — it seems to occur somewhere between the late teens and early thirties. ...

Coming out is a complex business involving at least three intertwined stages, which probably most people can never quite complete. They are:

1   coming out to oneself — starting to see oneself as homosexual;
2   coming out in the gay world — starting to meet other gay people;
3   coming out in the straight world — starting to be open to non-gays about one's gayness.

The first step is often the hardest, since it usually has to be taken alone without support from others: the whole weight of cultural indoctrination has to be broken down. This, to engage in understatement, is not easy. At home, at school, with one's peers or confronting the media, the message has insidiously been the same: the only path is the heterosexual one, and 'queers' are few and sick. How can you — in spite of your vague feelings and fantasies — be one of that sick few? You can't — and even if by some freak chance you were, it must be kept as a dark and hidden secret to be carried quietly to your grave. Yet to even start to have such ponderings is to set in motion the spiral of signification by which the idea that you could indeed be homosexual slowly becomes more and more central to your life. At what point it breaks through — 'I am like that, I must do something about it' — is largely unpredictable; but that this breakthrough does happen — against all odds — is unmistakable. ... An open mind, a liberal peer group, access to gay books, articles and films, sight of a Gay Switchboard sticker, knowledge of a homosexual person, etc. may all play their contributory roles in facilitating this self awareness; but in the end it is only the individual himself who can make the decision that he is gay and act upon it.

These first tortured stages of coming out can usually be circumvented speedily once the second stage — of meeting other homosexuals — is reached. This involves gaining access to homosexual role models that openly counterbalance the heterosexual role models of the preceding years. ... The earlier doubts — the guilt, identity confusions, secrecy and sexual frustrations — can begin to fade once homosexuals are met who, curiously enough, are 'glad to be gay', living reasonably contented and productive lives. The gay bar is extremely important in this 'meeting' process, and more recently the development of smaller, more intimate groups of gays have strengthened this supportive process in coming out.

The final stage in the coming out process centres around relationships with the non-gay world: to tell others, and thereby establish a continuity of identity between self and the world at large; or to keep it a secret, and thereby live a marginally dishonest, slightly dissonant existence. A whole range of people could be told of one's gayness — family, neighbours, work-mates, spouse, children, community — and whom to tell and when to tell can become significant issues for the gay person.

In general, not coming out in this third sense does seem to be linked to a less positive gay adjustment. ... On the other hand, more and more gays do seem to be telling others; and although there are often initial traumas (it is obviously hard for many non-gays to understand what homosexuality is all about — they may never have thought about it before), acceptance usually follows. Often, indeed, it can be positively beneficial to all parties — and in the long run it can only serve to break down further the hostility and mythology which surround the whole subject. Coming out to the straight world is often the first sign that the homosexual person has suc-cessfully navigated his own problems and has moved on to those of others. From an inward-looking perspective to the gay world which has helped him find himself, he can now look outward to the community which pre-viously rejected him.

Opting for a lifestyle

The first set of turning points, then, are all concerned with establishing a sense of who one really is — an identity which ideally exists not just for oneself alone, but which is also at home in the wider world. To summarize from Rainwater (1970, p.375): 'A valid identity is one in which the indi-vidual finds congruence between who he feels he is, who he announces himself to be, and where he feels his society places him.'

In coming out to himself, to the gay community and to the wider environ-ment, the homosexual man can develop a consistent, integrated sense of a self; a sense of self as gay which studies suggest is most compatible with a reasonably well-adjusted life. ...

Knowing who one is, however, does not necessarily tell one what to do or where to go. And here the second set of gay turning points enter, which can be referred to as 'opting for a lifestyle'. Although, arguably, the issue of choosing a life-style is increasingly an option for all people in capitalist cultures — gay and straight alike — it is still true that for most heterosex-uals there is little perceived choice: round about their late teens and early twenties they are likely to be dragooned into the 'rating-dating-going steady-engagement-marriage-raising children' syndrome. Many people who become gay later will initially move, more or less unthinkingly, into this pattern. But this is most unlikely for those who have fully come out — indeed it would usually be a contradiction of their gay identity.

For many homosexual men, then, there is no obvious and immediate lifestyle available: however dimly, it has to be reflected upon, and this can be a painful and prolonged search. Confusion arises not from being gay — for that is clear and accepted — but from not knowing how to incorporate gayness into an overall life pattern. A host of questions will be pondered upon, but three can be pulled out as particularly significant.

First, the person will have to decide how far he wants to become involved in the organized gay world: he may decide to totally immerse himself in it and to sever contacts with non-gay people, or he may decide to keep a great distance from all organized gays. Second, the person will have to decide on the kinds of gay relationships he wants: he may decide to imitate the heterosexual world and establish a kind of psuedo-marriage situation, he may decide to experiment with more diffuse, couple relationships or he made decide to remain firmly single. Third, the person will have to decide on the pattern and type of sexual involvement he wants: he may decide to have a lot of sex partners and to experiment with different activities, he may opt for a monogamous partner, or he may decide to forgo sex and remain celibate. These and many other questions may crowd into the homosexual man's mind, and whether by default or conscious choice, some outcome will have to be established. ...

References

Erikson, E. (1977) *Childhood and Society*, St. Albans, Paladin.

Levinson, D. J. (1978) *The Seasons of a Man's Life*, New York, Knopf.

Rainwater, L. (1970) *Behind Ghetto Walls*, Chicago, Aldine Publishing Co.

CHAPTER 6 EDUCATION, ECONOMY AND NATIONAL CULTURE

Geoff Whitty

CONTENTS

1   INTRODUCTION

The complex nature of what has come to be termed the 'Enlightenment project' has been explored earlier in this series (see Book 1 (Hall and Gieben, 1992), Chapter 1). It is hardly surprising that education has often been seen to be at the centre of such a project, associated as it is with ideas about the development of mind, the triumph of reason, scientific progress, and the rational ordering of society. You will therefore not be surprised that the study of modern education systems picks up on a number of themes that have already appeared in this series. Not only does it relate to the theme of economic 'modernization', it also entails consideration of the ways in which classed and gendered human subjects are constituted within modern nation-states.

Education has been seen to have a vital role both in producing and distributing the knowledge upon which a modern rational social order might be founded. Such a view is evident in this idealized account of the development of the system of public education in the USA during the early part of this century:

> The traditional explanation for what happened is one of inevitable progress. Reformers and educational leaders, dedicated to the goal of effective education and possessed of the best scientific knowledge about how to achieve it, succeeded in building a rational system of schools for the nation as a whole, triumphing over the parochialism, fragmentation, and party machines of an unenlightened past. The system they created was bureaucratic and professional, designed to ensure, so the story goes, that education would be taken out of politics and placed in the hands of impartial experts devoted to the public interest. It was the 'one best system'. (Chubb and Moe, 1990, p.4)

Chubb and Moe go on to point out that this 'rosy account' was somewhat misleading:

> The new educational institutions imposed on the nation were neither inevitable nor uniformly progressive. They were the result of a haphazard series of political victories, slowly realised over a period of many years, in which social groups that benefited from and supported institutional reform gradually won out over those that were disadvantaged by it ... The winners were elements of business, the middle class, the educational professionals — especially the latter, for they would be running the new bureaucratic system. The losers included ... a sizable portion of the less powerful segments of the American population: the lower classes, ethnic and religious minorities, and citizens of rural communities. Their traditional control over local schools was now largely transferred to the new system's political and administrative authorities — who, according to what soon became official

doctrine, knew best what kind of education people needed and how it could be provided most effectively.
(ibid., p.4)

These two accounts neatly encapsulate, on the one hand, a view of the growth of public education as embodying positive aspects of modernity and, on the other, some of what have increasingly come to be seen as its negative features. You will find, as you work through this chapter, that a similar tension is evident in recent debates about education policy in England.

Nevertheless, education in one form or another has usually been seen as an important element in the creation of a healthy society as well as in the development of individual minds. In 'conservative' versions of the role of education, the emphasis has often been on preserving elements of traditional culture in the face of modernization. A distinction was often made between the education of an élite, who would ensure that society was ordered upon rational principles, and that of the masses, whose 'irrationality' might pose a threat to it. Indeed, the schooling of the masses in nineteenth-century England was explicitly justified as 'gentling the masses'. It was not envisaged that their education would go beyond what was necessary to their position in the labour market or to the preservation of social order. In 'progressive' versions of education's role, education for all was seen as producing enlightened citizens who would accept both the rights and obligations of the emerging social order. It was regarded as a major 'modernizing' force in society, not only in relation to the new skills required in the changing labour market, but also in gaining commitment to changing modes of social solidarity. Socialists often saw education as an essential component of the emancipation, not only of individuals, but of the whole working class, while some regarded it as a key element in social revolution.

Sociologists, whose own discipline can itself be seen as an integral part of the Enlightenment project, have tended to see education in terms of its relationship to other elements of society. Émile Durkheim (1956) pointed out, in challenging widespread assumptions about education, that 'far from having as its unique or principal object the individual and his interests, [it] is above all the means by which society perpetually recreates the conditions of its very existence'. The key role of education in positioning human subjects in relation to the prevailing social order makes it an important site of cultural struggle and contestation. Some sociologists have explored its essentially conservative role in reproducing culture and the social division of labour, while others have assigned it a major role in building a new social order, via notions of progress, perfectability, and empowerment. Education has thus tended to be conceived by sociologists as a massive exercise in social control, social engineering or social emancipation — though some recognize major tensions between education as a conservative force, its role in modernization, and its revolutionary potential.

In this chapter, we shall explore some of the more influential sociological theories of the role of education in modern society and then try to make sense of contemporary developments in terms of these theories. The chapter will concentrate on the development of state education systems and, within that, its focus will be on schools rather than on further and higher education. Although many of the examples are drawn from education policies that were introduced in the 1980s, the central aim of the chapter is to provide you with insights into ways of looking at education sociologically, so that you can utilize them to explore any policies that may emerge in the future.

2   THE SOCIAL ANALYSIS OF EDUCATION

2.1   THE EMERGENCE OF MODERN EDUCATION SYSTEMS

Education in its broadest sense is not, of course, a phenomenon associated only with modern societies. Nor does all education take place in formal institutions devoted to that purpose. What is a peculiar feature of modern societies is the growth of public systems of mass schooling. These systems are often called 'state educational systems', which Margaret Archer defines in the following terms: 'a nation-wide and differentiated collection of institutions devoted to formal education, whose overall control and supervision is at least partly governmental, and whose component parts and processes are related to one another' (Archer, 1984, p.19).

Archer points out that such a definition can embrace very dissimilar types of education, depending upon the structural and cultural factors at work in different contexts.

The fact that such systems of schooling appear to have developed in many countries at about the same time as industrialization has led many people to assume a causal relationship between the two developments. Indeed, many developing countries have regarded the provision of a public education system as a prerequisite of economic modernization. Publicly provided, regulated, or financed systems of mass schooling are certainly a feature of all modern societies. However, the nature of the relationship between schooling and industrialization is a complex one and the assumption of a straightforward causal relationship is difficult to sustain. In some parts of Europe, systems of state-provided schooling were in place well before the industrialization took hold, while the so-called 'First Industrial Revolution' in Britain was underway before mass, let alone state, schooling developed on a widespread scale. This suggests that it would be simplistic to suppose either that a formal education system was a necessary prerequisite of industrial take-off or that industrializationism was the key stimulus for mass schooling.

Historians and sociologists have offered a number of different explanations of the rise of public education systems. Some of these are derived from grand theories about the nature of society, others from detailed historical study of the emergence of education systems in particular societies. The most interesting are those that seek to develop theory from a comparative study of the growth of education systems in different societies. In Reading A, Andy Green outlines the conclusions from his own comparative study of the rise of education systems in England, France and the USA.

ACTIVITY 1   You should now read **Reading A, 'Education and state formation'**, by Andy Green, which you will find at the end of this chapter. While reading it, make a note of Green's view of each of the following explanations of educational change:

(a)   the development of Enlightenment values;

(b)   the influence of Protestantism;

(c)   the skill requirements of industrialization;

(d)   the effects of urbanization.

Then identify what Green himself sees as the key factor influencing the nature of modern education systems and summarize the ways in which this seems to have influenced the development of education in England.

Green regards the possible explanations for the rise of public education systems that can be found in each of the existing theories to be of limited explanatory value. He claims that his own research, and that of others, shows that there were cases in which education systems developed in the absence of the conditions which each of those theories posits as implicated in the process. While, in particular cases, education systems were no doubt partly a response to these other factors, the key factor for Green in explaining the timing and form of the development of education systems is 'the nature of the state and the process of state formation'. He traces this argument through different examples, showing the crucial role of education systems in training state administrators and forging political and cultural unity in developing nation-states. Like Archer (1984), he explores differences in the education systems of centralized and decentralized states, and he relates them explicitly to differences in the process of state formation. He argues that, in England, the nature of the state has militated against the development of a genuinely modern education system. Nevertheless, even if the state played a less directive role in the development of education in nineteenth-century England, the system's characteristics can themselves be related to the peculiar nature of the British state. While this summary cannot do justice to the detail of Green's argument, his thesis is certainly one which calls into question both lay and sociological theories about the role of education in society. We shall return to Green's argument at various points in this chapter.

Green's thesis raises major questions about the centrality of economic considerations to the rise of modern education systems. However, differences in the genesis of public education systems in different contexts do not preclude the possibility that, over time, the education system and the economy have come to enter into a different relationship and one which is common to most modern societies.

2.2   EDUCATION AND THE ECONOMY

You will find that questions about the relationship between schooling and the economy figure prominently in the extensive literature on schooling and society. Thus, for example, the concern of many sociologists in post-war Britain to explain and overcome what was seen as a wastage of working-class talent derived, not only from a democratic concern to foster equality of opportunity, but was also a response to a growing demand for skilled labour to fuel a booming economy. Particularly influential in the growth of public education systems, not only in western societies but also in many post-colonial nations in the Third World, has been 'human capital theory', which seemed to indicate that a better educated workforce could make a major contribution to economic growth (Karabel and Halsey, 1977).

At the present time, considerable political and media attention is devoted to concerns about how far education systems in western societies are adequate for the needs of the late twentieth-century world economy. International league tables of pupil performance in mathematics and science are causing considerable alarm, particularly in Britain and the USA, as pupils in countries such as Germany, Japan and South Korea consistently appear to out-perform their own. In Britain, there is additional concern about the percentage of young people in education and training after the age of 16, compared with much higher proportions in most other advanced industrial societies (see Table 6.1).

Table 6.1   Participation in education and training of 16–18 year olds by age and mode, in 1986

| | Percentage of age group 16–18 year olds | | |
	Full-time	Part-time	All
Canada	75	–	75
France	66	8	74
Germany	47	43	90
Japan	77	3	79
USA	79	1	80
UK (1988)	35	34	69

Source: DES, 1990a, *Statistical Bulletin*, no.1, January

There are major difficulties in making these sorts of comparisons and you can no doubt think of some of these. However, what we are concerned with here is not so much whether these comparisons are statistically valid or educationally meaningful, but with the widespread assumption that they are important. Many of the press commentaries on such statistics point to the fact that those higher up in the league tables are 'our economic competitors' or 'our European partners'. There is usually a clear implication that these apparent differences in educational participation and performance are not merely disturbing in their own right, but also have implications for the wider health of society and, in particular, its economic prosperity.

Although these particular examples are recent, this way of thinking about education is not new. Indeed, it can be found throughout the history of state education in Britain (Reeder, 1979; Roderick and Stephens, 1982). However, the extent to which it has dominated policy discourse has varied. Furthermore, the extent to which governments have responded with detailed regulation of educational practice has differed. In particular, in Britain, direct government intervention was limited during the period of so-called 'social democratic consensus' that followed the 1944 Education Act (CCCS, 1981; Whitty, 1985). Central government provided broad policies, which were then administered and interpreted by county or district councils acting as local education authorities which, in turn, entrusted curriculum decision making largely to professionals in the schools (Kogan, 1975). That approach worked best during the 1950s and 1960s, when the contradictions between the various functions ascribed to education, and the different aspirations of the parties involved, could be broadly reconciled in an expanding system.

However, a growing economic crisis during the 1970s provided the occasion for calls for a reduction in the rate of growth of state spending and the specification of clearer priorities for the education service. At the same time, deficiencies in the education service were themselves looked to as a possible cause of economic decline. A speech by the Labour Prime Minister James Callaghan at Ruskin College Oxford in October 1976, which launched a 'Great Debate' on education (Callaghan, 1976), reflected an acceptance by the Labour leadership that the sort of progressive education which had developed in a period of relative professional autonomy in the 1950s and 1960s was out of step with both the needs of British industry and the wishes of parents. Amongst the solutions canvassed were the development of a core curriculum for all schools and new mechanisms of accountability.

Labour's Great Debate served to legitimate a number of themes which were taken up with greater vigour by the first two Conservative administrations of Margaret Thatcher. The 1980 Education Act sought to make schools more accountable by extending parental choice and began to erode the power of local education authorities, while a Technical and Vocational Education Initiative (TVEI) sought to modernize the school curriculum and make it more relevant to the needs of industry.

This coupling between education and the economy has not only been constituted in recent official policy discourse about education: even those writers critical of an economic and social system based upon capital accumulation have often stressed the centrality of a link between education and the economy. In particular, it has been central to the work of many neo-Marxist sociologists of education. Although their attempt to explain the rise of mass schooling in the nineteenth and twentieth centuries in terms of its relationship to industrial capitalism would be susceptible to the sorts of criticisms made by Green in Reading A, their analysis of the way in which education now interacts with the world of work gained considerable currency within the sociology of education during the late 1970s. Particularly influential was the so-called 'correspondence theory' of Samuel Bowles and Herbert Gintis (1976), developed in a book entitled *Schooling in Capitalist America.*

ACTIVITY 2

You should now read **Reading B, 'The correspondence principle'**, Samuel Bowles and Herbert Gintis's account of their correspondence theory. How do they see the relationship between education and what they call the social relations of production? What do you think they mean by this term? Make a list of aspects of education that they claim can be related to:

(a) work tasks;

(b) the division and organization of labour in the workplace; and

(c) work discipline.

How convincing do you find their argument? To what extent might their theory help us to understand Labour's 'Great Debate', described above?

While Bowles and Gintis argue that there is an intimate link between education and the capitalist economy, the nature of that linkage is represented rather differently from the way it is constituted within official discourse. For instance, Bowles and Gintis recognize that formal education systems often have only a limited role in the transmission of practical skills. Much more central to their own analysis is what is learned in school about social relationships or what is sometimes termed the 'hidden curriculum'. A similar point is made by the French social theorist, Louis Althusser in his claim that education is centrally concerned with the 'reproduction of submission to the ruling ideology for workers, and a reproduction of the ability to manipulate the ruling ideology correctly for the agents of exploitation and repression' (Althusser, 1971, p.128). In Bowles and Gintis's view, particular forms of schooling are linked to particular positions in a hierarchical division of labour under capitalism and this serves to reproduce the workforce in relation to the needs of capital. Their correspondence theory of mass schooling is perhaps particularly plausible in relation to the 'Fordist' system of production (discussed in Book 2 (Allen *et al.*, 1992), Chapter 5). Rather like a production line, schools can be seen as 'mass-producing common educational experiences [and] marked by authoritarian relations and centralized planning and rigid organization' (Ball, 1990a, p.182).

Although they were writing specifically about the USA, Bowles and Gintis's work stimulated considerable debate amongst sociologists about the relationship between education and the economy in Britain. At first sight, though, the very need for Labour's 'Great Debate' would seem to raise some major problems for the correspondence thesis in the British context. The fact that the education system appeared to be out of step with the imperatives of the economy in the post-war period, and that it was characterized as contributing to Britain's economic decline, would seem to contradict the theory. However, Bowles and Gintis's theory actually grants the education system a limited degree of autonomy, in that there can be a time-lag before the education system adapts to changes in the system of production. If the mode of regulation within the system of production changes, then one would ultimately expect similar changes to take place in the mode of regulation of schooling. The considerable degree of variation in the nature of education systems from one society to another can also be accommodated, to some extent, in the correspondence theory by pointing to the 'uneven' development of capitalism.

Nevertheless, both the detail of Bowles and Gintis's substantive arguments and what their theory leaves out have been the subject of much criticism. Some critics argue that they define the economy too narrowly and that they see the division of labour largely in class terms, rather than recognizing the full significance of divisions of race and gender. Others argue that they employ too passive a model of socialization and pay insufficient attention to the role of contradiction and resistance (Giroux, 1983). Although there have been many severe criticisms, there have also been numerous attempts to 'rescue' the theory by making it more complex (Cole, 1988).

The notion that the 'logic' of production carries over into education in the straightforward manner implied by Bowles and Gintis is particularly problematic. Furthermore, Bowles and Gintis's original theory conflates the social relations of production (or the relation between capital and labour) and the social relationships within the process of immediate production (or the occupational system). Robert Moore (1988) argues that both the occupational system and the educational system need to be seen 'as distinctive sites of production (under the social relations of production) with their own intrinsic principles and possibilities'. They can each take various forms and relate to each other in a variety of ways, so that the nature of social relationships within one does not necessarily determine that within the other. Moore expresses this diagrammatically, as shown in Figure 6.1 overleaf.

In different circumstances, education can enter into different sorts of relationships with the occupational system — that of 'correspondence' being merely one possibility. While the social relations of production may set limits to the range of possibilities, the reproduction of the social relations of production, even under capitalism, can be achieved in a variety of ways. Such a view clearly helps us to understand how there

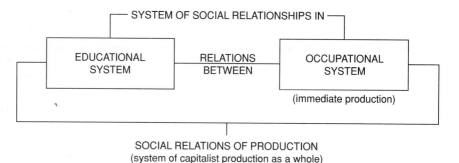

Figure 6.1   Moore's model of the relationship between the educational and the occupational systems within the system of capitalist production
Source: Moore, 1988, p.74

can be differences in the nature of education systems in different modern societies, even in terms of a theory that places a major emphasis on the relationship between education and the economy. Thus, some of the differences between, say, Britain, the USA, and Japan might be attributed to differences in the nature of their economies, but others might be better understood in terms of the degree of autonomy granted to the education system in those societies.

Yet, despite his attempt to move beyond the Bowles and Gintis thesis by exploring the way in which the autonomy of education systems is regulated, Moore accepts that, empirically, there has been a recent tendency in Britain for modes of regulation associated with the industrial and commercial world of 'immediate production' to be applied to the education system. He particularly identifies the notion of 'the discipline of the market' in this context, and the impact of this on contemporary education systems will be explored in some detail later in the chapter. This idea of the transportation of modes of regulation between relatively autonomous parts of the social system is, to some extent, compatible with Bowles and Gintis's own reworking of their correspondence thesis into a more complex theory (Gintis and Bowles, 1981).

2.3   EDUCATION AND THE STATE

However, there are those who would argue that the whole debate about the Bowles and Gintis thesis reflects an undue obsession within the sociology of education with the relationship between schooling and the economy. Schooling is as much about the education of citizens as it is about the training of workers, while the knowledge that is produced and reproduced within the education system is by no means confined to technical knowledge or knowledge required in the context of immediate production. Some of the major contributions to the sociology of education have been concerned with the role of state apparatuses, including education, in the reproduction of ideology (Althusser, 1971).

We have already seen how Green claims that the development of education can only be understood as part of the wider process of state formation that has led to the emergence of the modern capitalist nation-state. Note that he is not denying that the states he discusses are capitalist states. He would, however, presumably argue that the state, even the advanced capitalist state that has come to dominate the western world, operates in a relatively autonomous manner and that its imperatives are not merely those of industrial capitalism. Yet, in Bowles and Gintis's *Schooling in Capitalist America*, the state is largely invisible, even though the book is mainly about developments that led to the creation of what, in terms of Archer's definition cited at the beginning of Section 2.1, is clearly a 'state educational system'. As in many accounts of education which start with the economy, the state seems to act as a direct relay between the 'needs' of the economy and the system of schooling. Even in their early work, Bowles and Gintis recognized a time-lag that permitted some slackness in the relay, but assumed that the economy had the capacity to pull the education system back into line with its requirements. Leaving aside the question of how any such 'requirements' are identified and articulated, we now need to consider the extent to which the state's role in education is a more active and distinctive one than implied in the early work of Bowles and Gintis.

Dale (1989) argues that the role of the capitalist state is a complex one. However, while accepting that not all state activity derives from its role in the maintenance and reproduction of the capitalist mode of production, he argues that the state faces three core problems, namely:

- support of the capital accumulation process

- guaranteeing a context for its continuing expansion

- the legitimation of the capitalist mode of production, including the state's own part in it.

Eschewing correspondence theory, Dale argues that the modern state's need to confront these problems does not determine the detailed specification of the nature of any particular state education system. The state has to respond to a variety of influences and its role in the preservation of the process, context and legitimacy of capital accumulation is based on an 'exclusionary' principle of selection. It will act to exclude anything that appears to threaten the long-term progress of the capital accumulation process, but many different styles of education are (more or less) compatible with that end. In other words, even analysing education as a function of the capitalist state does not entail arguing that the nature of education has to correspond in any detailed way to the nature of the capitalist economy.

Dale further argues that the dynamics generated by contradictions entailed in trying to tackle the three core problems shape the nature of the system in unpredictable ways. In particular, the problem of legitimation, or securing consent to the maintenance of the system as a whole, may require taxation and public expenditure policies that conflict with the imperatives of capital accumulation. Non-instrumental aspects of education (i.e. those that are not directly relevant to needs of immediate production) might be seen as making the system more acceptable. They come under particular pressure when there is a capital accumulation crisis, but their abandonment poses problems of legitimation which the state then has to manage.

2.4   THE NATURE OF EDUCATIONAL KNOWLEDGE

Understanding modern education systems also entails understanding the nature of educational knowledge, since 'knowledge functions as a form of power and disseminates the effects of power' (Foucault, 1980, p.69). As you will know from Chapter 5, Foucault had a particular interest in the ways in which the knowledge claims and practices of the social sciences are used in the surveillance and regulation of the populations of modern societies. Clearly this is relevant to our understanding of the ways in which the knowledge claims of educational experts, such as educational psychologists, operate within bureaucratic education systems. However, while there have been a few attempts to explore education in terms of Foucault's ideas (Walkerdine, 1984; Donald, 1985; Ball, 1990b), most of the work within the sociology of education that discusses the relationship between knowledge and power has hitherto focused on the ideological role of the form and content of the school curriculum. Indeed, the nature of the school curriculum, and its role in social and cultural reproduction and transformation, has been a major interest of sociologists of education since the early 1970s (Young, 1971; Bernstein, 1977; Bourdieu and Passeron, 1990). Bernstein put it this way:

> How a society selects, classifies, distributes, transmits and evaluates the educational knowledge it considers to be public, reflects both the distribution of power and the principles of social control. From this point of view, differences within and change in the organization, transmission and evaluation of educational knowledge should be a major area of sociological interest. (Bernstein, 1977, p.85)

He suggests that the organization of educational knowledge in England has traditionally been based on what he terms a 'collection code', where there are strong boundaries between academic subjects, between what may be taught and what may not be taught, and between school knowledge and non-school knowledge. He hypothesizes that, for a variety of reasons ranging from changes in the division of labour and the rise of the new middle classes to an underlying crisis in society's structures of power and principles of control, the 1960s and 1970s may have been witnessing a shift towards 'integrated codes', in which some of these boundaries become weakened.

For Bernstein, the main interest is in 'how' knowledge is selected, organized and distributed, but other scholars have taken an interest in 'what' knowledge is selected and distributed in school. Particularly useful here is Raymond Williams's notion of a 'selective tradition'. This he defines as:

> that which, within the terms of an effective dominant culture, is always passed off as 'the tradition', *the* significant past. But always the selectivity is the point; the way in which from a whole possible area of past and present, certain meanings and practices are chosen for emphasis, certain other meanings and practices are neglected and excluded. Even more crucially, some of these meanings are reinterpreted, diluted, or put into forms which support or at least do not contradict other elements within the effective dominant culture.
> (Williams, 1976, p.205)

Michael Apple draws upon these ideas to ask:

- Why and how are particular aspects of the collective culture presented in school as objective, factual knowledge?
- How, *concretely*, may official knowledge represent ideological configurations of the dominant interests in society?
- How do schools legitimate these limited and partial standards of knowing as unquestioned truths?

(Apple, 1990, p.14)

The exercise of the sociological imagination involves using the answers to such questions to relate the principles of selection and organization that underlie the overt and hidden curicula of schooling to their institutional and interactional setting in schools and classrooms and to the wider social structure (Young, 1971). One attempt to do this can be found within the work of the leading French sociologist, Pierre Bourdieu, whose ideas you have encountered in Chapter 3. In a paper entitled 'The school as a conservative force' (1974), Bourdieu states:

> ... each family transmits to its children, indirectly rather than directly, a certain *cultural capital* and a certain *ethos*. The latter is a system of implicit and deeply interiorized values which, among other things, helps to define attitudes towards the cultural capital and educational institutions. The cultural heritage, which differs from both points of view according to social class, is the cause of the initial inequality of children when faced with examinations and tests, and hence of unequal achievement. ...

> In fact, to penalize the underprivileged and favour the most privileged, the school has only to neglect, in its teaching methods and techniques and its criteria when making academic judgements, to take into account the cultural inequalities between children of different social classes. In other words, by treating all pupils,

however unequal they may be in reality, as equal in rights and duties, the educational system is led to give its *de facto* sanction to initial cultural inequalities. The formal equality which governs pedagogical practice is in fact a cloak for and justification of indifference to the real inequalities with regard to the body of knowledge taught or rather demanded. Thus, for example, the 'pedagogy' used in secondary or higher education is, objectively, an 'arousing pedagogy', in Weber's words, aimed at stimulating the 'gifts' hidden in certain exceptional individuals by means of certain incantatory techniques, such as the verbal skills and powers of the teacher. As opposed to a rational and really universal pedagogy, which would take nothing for granted initially, would not count as acquired what some, and only some, of the pupils in question had inherited, would do all things for all and would be organized with the explicit aim of providing all with the means of *acquiring* that which, although apparently a natural gift, is only *given* to the children of the educated classes, our own pedagogical tradition is in fact, despite external appearances of irreproachable equality and universality, only there for the benefit of pupils who are in the *particular position* of possessing a cultural heritage conforming to that demanded by the school. ... (Bourdieu, 1974, pp.32–3; 37–8)

Bourdieu's analysis not only illustrates the 'selective tradition' at work, but also the way in which it can serve to legitimate the success of those who possess the appropriate 'cultural capital' and the failure of those who do not. Bourdieu thus claims that the cultural attributes that are valued by the school provide part of the clue as to why education systems so often seem to reproduce existing patterns of inequality. Aristocratic language and 'manners' are more highly valued in education than those of the working class; consequently privileged students have a distinct advantage. Bourdieu has looked at the issue largely in terms of social class, but similar analyses have subsequently been developed to explore the role of the school in the reproduction of race and gender inequalities (MacDonald, 1981). MacDonald suggests, for example, that Bourdieu's work could be developed to explore the ways in which the relationships between the sexual division of labour, the social division of labour, and particular forms of language, culture and education serve to constitute classed and gendered subjects through a complex and sometimes contradictory process of social and cultural reproduction (MacDonald, 1979/80).

2.5   EDUCATION, CULTURE AND POWER

The relationship of the cultural capital valued by the school to class relations in the wider society is not, however, necessarily a straightforward one. As we have seen, Althusser and Bowles and Gintis tended to see the ideological content of schooling as related to workers' positions in the division of labour within immediate production.

Randall Collins (1977), a neo-Weberian writer on education, agrees that 'the interaction of cultural organization with the material economy is the key to all structures of domination' (for discussion of the neo-Weberian position, see Chapter 1). However, Collins goes on to point out that:

> Three lines of societal division — economic, organizational-political, and cultural (or in Weber's terms, 'class', 'party' and 'status') — mesh, so that economic classes or organizational politicians are stronger if they possess the unity that comes from common cultural resources. But the three types of resources may be differentially distributed; strong ethnic, national, religious, or other cultural divisions can shape struggles for economic or political domination into patterns very different from those emerging along [economic] class lines.
> (Collins, 1977, p.3)

Since these resources may also be brought to bear in struggles over the nature of schooling, we can begin to see another explanation of how the form and content of schooling comes to vary between different nation-states. Collins's paper goes on to explore how the differential disposition of economic, political and cultural resources in different societies has produced these different emphases within their educational systems.

ACTIVITY 3   You should now read **Reading C, 'Some comparative principles of educational stratification'**, which is taken from the paper by Randall Collins. Consider how far it succeeds in bringing together, within an overall explanatory framework, the various aspects of the relationship between schooling and society considered in this chapter so far. You might also consider what groups are currently involved in struggles over the nature of the education system in England.

Collins's paper, while clearly not overcoming all the difficulties of other theories, points to things that most modern educational systems have in common, such as a degree of bureaucratization, while offering a theory of cultural markets to show how other features of particular education systems are highly contingent upon the social and cultural characteristics of different nation-states. Different styles of education have attained influence in different contexts as a result of compromises between groups holding different economic, political and cultural resources and struggling to attain influence in education systems. Amongst the significant groups often identified as contributing to the English compromise in the past are 'old humanists', 'industrial trainers', 'public educators' and 'state bureaucrats' (Williams, 1965; Salter and Tapper, 1981), though Ball has suggested that this typology may now need refining (Ball, 1990a).

The extent to which a technocratic ideology has replaced a concern with the culture of traditional élites has certainly differed between England and the USA and this may be attributed to the enduring influence of the 'old humanists' in England. It is often claimed that the apparent lack of competitiveness of British industry stems partly from the embeddedness of inappropriate cultural values within various institutions including education (Wiener, 1981; Barnett, 1986). We have already seen this argument at work in the Great Debate of the 1970s and we will return to it later in the chapter when we discuss the significance of the National Curriculum.

While Collins's paper helps us to understand something of the complexity of the relationship between schooling and society, macro-sociological accounts of the role of education in social and cultural reproduction and transformation, by their very nature, offer us only very limited insights into what actually goes on in schools. As Apple (1990) says:

> What schools do ideologically, culturally, and economically is very complicated and cannot be fully understood by the application of any simple formula. There *are* very strong connections between the formal and informal knowledge within the school and the larger society with all its inequalities. But since the pressures and demands of dominant groups are highly mediated by the internal histories of educational institutions and by the needs and ideologies of people who actually work in them, the aims and results will often be contradictory as well.
> (Apple, 1990, pp.x–xi)

Although it is beyond the scope of this chapter, a great deal of work by sociologists of education concerns itself with the ethnographic study of life in educational institutions. While some of this work is primarily concerned with studying the world of classrooms and staffrooms largely for its own sake (Hammersley, 1990), many people working on the ethnography of the school do not see that enterprise as separate from a concern with the relationship between school and society (Willis, 1977). By exploring the interface between biography and social structure (Mills, 1965), they draw our attention to complexities and resistances that are often missing from broader accounts. Another potential advantage of this work is that it can make us very aware of the importance of history and culture in structuring the experience of schooling, even in societies with apparently similar economies. Foucault's work, too, reminds us that 'power in its exercise goes much further [than the state apparatus], passes through much finer channels and is much more ambiguous' (Foucault, 1980, p.72), and demonstrates the importance of undertaking studies of the micro-politics of the school (Ball, 1987).

3   CONTEMPORARY DEVELOPMENTS IN ENGLISH EDUCATION

3.1   FROM COMMON SCHOOL TO DIVERSITY OF PROVISION

You will recall that, in Green's analysis, the English educational system had not completed the process of modernization that he argued had taken place in other societies. He suggested that, in particular, England had always shown 'a relatively weak commitment to collective or public provision'. Later in his book, Green goes on to claim that:

> The system as a whole has remained multiply fragmented and unsystematic. It has stubbornly resisted modernization and measures to increase standardization and rationality which on the Continent have long been considered essential for the promotion of equality ... Permissive legislation on comprehensive reform in the 1960s allowed the development of many different models of secondary schooling, encouraging considerable regional disparities ... Most notably, we have delayed instituting a national curriculum years after other European countries with the consequence that, in the absence of those normative expectations which encourage achievement amongst all children, many are not reaching their potential.
> (Green, 1990, p.314)

Green's view of other education systems, certainly when summarized this baldly, is perhaps rather idealized and does not seem too far away from the picture of the 'one best system' described by Chubb and Moe in the introduction to this chapter. It is also worth remarking that the system in some other countries is at least as fragmented as that in England. For Green, though, modernization clearly entails standardization. In support of this argument he cites the view of French sociologist Raymond Boudon, who argues that:

> ... in societies structured by class and other inequalities, the greater the variety of different routes through the education system, the more the 'branching-off' points, the greater the likelihood that differential class expectation, engendered from outside the education system, will structure student choices, even in a situation of ostensible equality of access, so that educational opportunities will be structured along class, race and gender lines.
> (Green, 1990, p.315)

In passing, you might like to reflect how far Boudon's compatriot Bourdieu would agree with this analysis. He would presumably argue that the problems would not be overcome by standardized provision if the criteria of success within it traded on the cultural capital of dominant groups, such as the cultural advantages resulting from a pupil's gender or family background. We shall return to this issue when we discuss the National Curriculum.

Nevertheless, in the English case, Green looks to increasing standardization as a way of modernizing the system and enhancing equality of opportunity. He would presumably see this route as fostering economic growth and contributing to political and cultural unity. Interestingly, he makes the case at the very time when, in his own words, 'the country which was the last to create a national education system, and which never quite completed the job' looks set to become the first to dismantle it in the name of 'market liberalism' (Green, 1990, p.316). In this section of the chapter, we shall try to make sense of these recent moves away from the very concept of the common or comprehensive school back towards a plurality of types of educational provision.

In England, to a much greater extent than in the USA, a much clearer and more explicit distinction has traditionally been made between the types of education available to different social classes. Although the notion of a common school, attended by all pupils from a locality, was an aspiration rather than a reality even in the USA, it has often been attributed a powerful symbolic role in the creation of that country's national identity over the past century (Glenn, 1988). In England, comprehensive schooling is a relatively recent phenomenon at secondary level, but was partly designed to ameliorate some of the effects of traditional social class divisions in English society. It thus fits Green's notion of a modern education system. Many of the arguments put in its favour drew upon the work of sociologists of education in the 1950s and 1960s, which had demonstrated a huge disparity in the average educational achievements of children from middle-class and working-class backgrounds.

Comprehensive education was arguably an exercise in social engineering, predicated upon a view of social class as the most significant dimension of cleavage in English society. Partly, the intention was to remedy a loss of working-class talent from the economy, but it was also argued that comprehensive schools were an important means of breaking down cultural barriers between social classes and even contributing to the development of a common culture. Initially, the reform movement paid relatively little attention to forms of social division other than class. Indeed, in so far as it was often associated with a move towards coeducation, comprehensive education has sometimes been seen as exacerbating gender differentials in educational achievement rather than reducing them. More recently, though, efforts have been made to take account of the significance of gender and ethnic divisions within the context of comprehensive education.

However, comprehensive schools had only just become established as the predominant type of school at secondary level when they fell victim to concerns about falling educational standards and to broader attacks on universalistic and bureaucratically planned approaches to welfare provision. This has resulted in the recent shift towards the alternative pluralistic, targeted, and market-oriented modes of educational provision, identified by Green. While stopping short of the introduction of a market in education via vouchers, many of the policies introduced in England during the 1980s reflected the influence of neo-liberal thinkers, whose ideas were promulgated through the publications of New Right think-tanks such as the Institute of Economic Affairs and the Adam Smith Institute. Such publications revealed, not only a confidence in the power of market forces to raise educational standards, but a belief in 'the superior rationality of unfettered, unregulated markets' over the cumbersome interventions of the state (Joseph, 1976, p.57), and in 'the general principle of consumer sovereignty' (Ashworth *et al.*, 1988, p.11).

Leaving aside the National Curriculum, to which we shall return in Section 3.3, many of the features of the 1988 Education Reform Act were intended to make state schools more responsive to market forces. Amongst its key elements were:

1   Open enrolment of pupils to schools in accordance with parental preference was permitted, removing the powers of local education authorities to impose artificial limits on particular schools to maintain the viability of others.

2   All larger LEA schools and colleges were freed from the detailed bureaucratic control of LEAs by a system of devolved budgets and local management, which effectively only delivered resources to institutions in proportion to their capacity to attract clients.

3   Some parents were given the opportunity to vote to take their schools out of LEA control in order to become free-standing Grant Maintained Schools. (An initial ruling that they could not change their character or admissions policies within five years was subsequently removed.)

4   City Technology Colleges, centrally funded independent schools with industrial sponsors, announced at the 1986 Conservative Party Conference, were given a statutory basis by the Act.

5   The Inner London Education Authority was abolished and its powers devolved to the individual inner-London boroughs.

Many of these items could be seen as a direct response to New Right criticisms, on the one hand, of teacher autonomy and, on the other hand, of LEA (especially left-wing LEA) bureaucracy and interference. Producer interests, especially those of teachers and LEA officers, were to be downgraded, while the system's consumers, seen here as parents and industry, were to be given a greater voice in its operation.

One declared aim of this approach is to encourage the growth of different types of school, responsive to the needs of their local communities. In the vision of one former government minister, it will produce 'more and more specialized and differentiated schools ... without any one being regarded as inferior to the others' (Dunn, quoted in *Education*, 8 July 1988). Many of these would be schools which, like City Technology Colleges, specialize in particular subjects or activities, but some people have also seen this as a way of meeting the aspirations of some Moslem parents to have their own schools (Dooley, 1991). At the time the Reform Bill was going through parliament, the New Right Hillgate Group (1987) argued that the government should encourage 'new and autonomous schools ... including Church schools of all denominations, Jewish schools, Islamic schools and such other schools as parents desire'. While the Moslem argument was resisted by government, there is continuing pressure on all political parties to find ways of allowing more schools to develop a religious or cultural distinctiveness (Cumper, 1990).

There has been, then, a considerable shift within official discourse on education from an espousal of commonality towards an espousal of differences along a number of dimensions — though, as we shall see, the National Curriculum somewhat complicates the issue. How, in sociological terms, might we understand some of the developments outlined so far? Is Green right to see this as an essentially anti-modernist movement, reflecting a nostalgia for the '*laissez-faire*' traditions of the last century? Or do these shifts reflect a recognition that bureaucratized state education systems have failed to fulfil their promise and are inappropriate to the needs of the late twentieth century?

ACTIVITY 4   Consider some of the ways in which the shift away from a bureaucratically planned system of schooling to one consisting of individual units competing for clients in the market might be understood in sociological terms. You might find it helpful to consider possible explanations in terms of (a) political, (b) economic and (c) cultural changes in modern society.

At one level, the changes in Britain might be attributed merely to the short-term ascendancy of market liberal ideas within the Conservative Party under Margaret Thatcher's leadership. Some of the specific policies outlined here may even have been abandoned by the time you read this chapter. However, it is unlikely that the general trends will have been entirely reversed. The Labour Party is proposing to accommodate Moslem schools within a broad comprehensive education system, and some of its leaders have flirted with the idea of specialist or magnet schools. The idea of a social market has gained widespread acceptance within British politics and no major party is likely to enter an election advocating a return to a system dominated by 'producer interests'. Similarly, although school choice policies in the USA received particular encouragement from Republican presidents Reagan and Bush, the growth in site-based management policies, magnet schools, and other schools of choice has received broader support. A market approach to education has now entered mainstream social thinking in the USA, and is by no means narrowly associated with the New Right (Chubb and Moe, 1990). Furthermore, similar policies have been pursued by social democratic as well as conservative governments in Australia and New Zealand while, in parts of Eastern Europe, the centrally planned education systems of the Communist regimes are also being replaced with experiments in educational markets. Even Japan, where standardization of educational provision is often seen as having contributed to the nation's modernization and its extraordinary economic success, has recently been considering policies to enhance choice and diversification, 'so as to secure such education as will be compatible with the social changes and cultural developments of our country' (Stephens, 1991, p.148).

Thus, while there is no doubt that such policies are particularly closely associated with neo-liberal political ideology, they may also reflect a broader shift in the role of the state in modern societies, or at least a change in the way it regulates major areas of social activity. In so far as market-oriented policies are also being pursued in other areas of welfare provision, they may well represent a new way of resolving the core problems and contradictions which, as we saw in Section 2.3, Dale (1989) identified as confronting the state. Or, in Green's terms, perhaps the changing approaches to the provision of education represent a new phase of state formation.

Another interpretation of current school reforms sees them (Ball, 1990a) partly as a response to changes in the sphere of immediate production, reflecting a shift from the 'Fordist' school of the era of mass production to the 'post-Fordist school'. Thus, if there has been a shift away from a system of mass production towards a 'post-Fordist' mode of accumulation (see Book 2 (Allen *et al.*, 1992), Chapter 5), then a correspondence theory might lead one to expect similar changes in schools. As Jessop *et al.* (1988, p.142) point out: 'The post-Fordist mode of accumulation places a lower value on mass individual and collective consumption and creates pressure for a more differentiated production and distribution of health, education, transport and housing.'

In other words, newly differentiated forms of schooling could be seen as the educational equivalent of the rise of what is sometimes termed 'disorganized capitalism', or of 'flexible specialization in place of the old assembly-line world of mass production' (Hall and Jacques, 1989). In terms of the refined version of the correspondence thesis, the changing logic of the mode of regulation within production can be seen to be 'transported' into schooling in the manner we discussed earlier. The physical appearance of some of the new City Technology Colleges might seem to support this more sophisticated version of a 'correspondence thesis'.

Djanogly City Technology College: modern school buildings resemble business park architecture. Does this support the 'correspondence thesis'?

Following the argument through, you might also expect changes in the patterns of authority within schools and in the forms of knowledge and modes of transmission that are valued within the education system. The concurrent shift away from a national industrial base towards a multinational and finance-based world economy might also lead one to expect such changes to happen on a global scale, and there is certainly evidence that they are by no means limited to England.

A less economy-centred attempt to understand current changes in schooling might look to broader changes in modes of social solidarity, and thus see the changes in schooling as a response to the complex patterns of political, economic and cultural differentiation in contemporary society which have replaced the traditional class divisions upon which comprehensive education was predicated. Such an interpretation could take account of the influence of the different dimensions of stratification and cleavage discussed in Chapter 1, and drawn on in Reading C by Collins. If, as is sometimes argued, these have brought about a qualitatively new mode of social solidarity, new approaches to the organization of schooling might then be seen as responding to some of the characteristics associated with post-modernity and thus as creating an appropriate education system for a post-modern society.

Certainly, the fact that there is a shift away from large-scale social engineering through bureaucratically administered common schools, not just in Britain but in many societies with different histories and different ruling parties, could be seen as supporting such an interpretation. The encouragement of local control and local initiatives can be seen as challenging the totalizing tendencies of liberal, social democratic or (in the case of Eastern European states) communist master-narratives in the interest of individual or community empowerment.

The emergence of comprehensive education in England was, as we have seen, linked to a politics that assumed social class was the most significant dimension of social differentiation. Feminists have often seen attractions in the shift towards pluralist models of society associated with post-modernism and post-modernity. Furthermore, Phillips (1988) has argued that ethnic minorities supported the Thatcher government's educational reforms; and support for policies of local control, and for the development of school choice, is certainly strong amongst black communities in many US cities. In Chicago, reforms which sought to dismantle the vast bureaucracy under which the Chicago School District was perceived to be failing the majority of its pupils, even when controlled by black politicians, were only enacted as a result of an alliance between New Right advocates of school choice, black groups seeking to establish community control of their local schools, disillusioned white liberals, and some former student radicals of the 1960s (Moore, 1990). Policies which seem to emphasize heterogeneity, fragmentation and difference certainly seem to represent more than a passing fashion amongst New Right politicians.

If, in a post-modern society, social development is perceived as 'a pragmatic matter of inventing new rules whose validity will reside in their effectivity rather than in their compatibility with some legitimating discourse [or] their role in the fulfilment of some grand historical narrative' (Boyne and Rattansi, 1990, p.18), then one might expect more alliances of the type that emerged in Chicago. The conventional notion that these are 'unprincipled alliances' is associated with a politics based on more traditional patterns of social division and the meta-narratives of grand social theories. Furthermore, if major attempts at social engineering through education have been perceived as failing in the past, less ambitious aspirations may now seem in order.

However, some of the groups which may benefit from the devolved and pluralistic patterns of education which such thinking encourages themselves espouse philosophies that are as totalizing in their aspirations as those which have dominated educational politics in the past. This is one argument that has been used against state funding of new religious schools in Britain, particularly Moslem schools with their assumed stance on the role of women (Walkling and Brannigan, 1986). However, you may feel that this criticism itself reflects a prevailing stereotype of eastern culture which serves to maintain the West's sense of its own cultural superiority (Said, 1978; Parmar, 1981; Halstead, 1986; see also the discussion of orientalism as a discourse in Book 1 (Hall and Gieben, 1992), Chapter 6). You will be able to reflect on this further when we discuss the National Curriculum in Sections 3.3 and 3.4.

3.2   RHETORIC AND REALITY

Although we have tried to make sense of recent reforms in sociological terms, we have so far been analysing them largely on the basis of the rhetoric of their sponsors. From this, it appears that the encouragement of choice and diversity will open up genuinely equal opportunities for all those individuals who wish to benefit from them. The reforms are also presented as appropriate to the changing character of late twentieth-century society, while some of the support for them derives from an expectation that they will challenge traditional hierarchies and interrupt existing patterns of social and cultural reproduction. We now need to look behind these positive images of the reforms and consider what they conceal.

Furthermore, in considering whether the new policies can be related to a qualitatively new mode of social solidarity, loosely described as post-modernity, we need to bear in mind that the political implications of post-modernism are notoriously difficult to 'read' (Giroux, 1990). Many critics have pointed to the essentially conservative nature of the discourse of post-modernism, which is often associated with the concept of post-modernity (Habermas, 1981; see also Book 4 (Hall *et al.*, 1992)). Analyses that celebrate fragmentation and the atomization of decision-making at the expense of social planning and government intervention may merely be replacing one oppressive master-narrative with another, that of the market.

Indeed, the espousal of heterogeneity, pluralism and local narratives as the basis of new social order is seen by many sociologists as mistaking phenomenal forms for structural relations. Harvey (1989) sees post-modernist cultural forms and more flexible modes of capital accumulation more as shifts in surface appearance rather than as signs of the emergence of some entirely new post-capitalist or even post-industrial society. The sociological project of digging beneath the surface to reveal deep structures has by no means been abandoned and, to many, the emergent global capitalist economic order and its associated structural inequalities remains the most significant feature of modern societies.

Green has suggested that, in England, the market-oriented approach to education will actually exacerbate traditional class divisions and that 'in the new educational market "freedom" and "choice" will be for those who can afford them and "diversity" will be a polite word for multiple educational apartheid' (Green, 1991, p.30). Early research on the effects of the reforms suggests that they may already be producing greater differentiation between schools on a linear scale of quality and esteem rather than the positive diversity that some of their supporters hoped for (Coulby and Bash, 1991). Walford and Miller (1991) claim that 'City Technology Colleges have played a major part in re-legitimizing inequality of provision for different pupils' and that the 'inevitable result' of the concept of CTCs, especially when coupled with Grant Maintained Schools and Local Management of Schools, is 'a

hierarchy of schools with the private sector at the head, the C'
GMSs next, and the various locally managed LEA schools foll
This argument certainly resonates with Green's view that the eiiect oi
implementing neo-liberal policies would be 'to create a new hierarchy
of élite schools and thus greatly to increase educational inequality'
(Green, 1990, p.315).

The recent reforms may thus represent a continuity with a long history
within English education of class-related forms of educational provision
(Banks, 1955; Halsey *et al.*, 1980). Rather than producing a genuinely
open and pluralist system, the reforms may be providing a legitimating
gloss for the perpetuation of long-standing forms of structural
inequality. If the early indications about their effects are borne out over
time, the reforms could disadvantage those unable or unwilling to
compete in the market they are intended to foster. For those members of
disadvantaged groups who are not sponsored out of schools at the
bottom of the status hierarchy, either on grounds of exceptional
academic ability or alternative definitions of merit, provision could
even deteriorate. This would have serious consequences for the
predominantly working-class and black populations who inhabit the
inner cities, and there is a possibility that an educational underclass
would then emerge in such areas.

Green (1991) argues that current policies are 'atavistic and backward-
looking', while Walford and Miller (1991) contrast them with
comprehensivization which, they suggest, constituted a serious attempt
to overcome the historic links between diversity of provision and
inequalities of class and — more questionably — gender. Advocates of
the new policies would claim, though, that such social democratic
policies have failed (amongst other things) to interrupt traditional
patterns of social and cultural reproduction and that a new approach is
needed. While there is some evidence that comprehensive education in
Scotland has begun to narrow social class differentials in educational
achievement (McPherson and Willms, 1987), it is certainly the case that
there is no firm evidence that this has happened in England. Indeed,
Heath (1987) suggests that the traditional differentials have remained
stubbornly consistent throughout a century of reform, from which he
deduces that the impact of the new policies can be expected to be
equally minimal.

It may be that the new arrangements will prove to be just another way
of reproducing deeply entrenched class divisions. In terms of its
outcomes, the reformed system might then not look so very different
from that described by Bowles and Gintis. This would seem to justify
considerable sociological scepticism about the notion that we are
witnessing a shift towards a qualitatively different relationship between
education and society. Even if there has been a shift away from
traditional patterns of social solidarity, the reforms we have considered
here would, at most, seem to relate to a version of post-modernity that
emphasizes 'distinction' and 'hierarchy' within a fragmented social

order, rather than one that actually celebrates 'difference' and 'heterogeneity' (Lash, 1990).

There are some sociologists who argue that current modes of theorizing that focus on difference and heterogeneity themselves contribute to a failure to recognize the enduring relationship between education and the structural inequalities of capitalist societies. Jennifer Ozga (1990) sees recent studies of education policy as providing rich descriptive data, but smuggling in a pluralist orthodoxy which dominates the ways in which we now read education policy. She insists that we need to locate studies of the apparent fragmentation and atomization of the education service in the aftermath of the Education Reform Act within an attempt to understand what she calls the creation of the 'bigger picture', involving the theorization of the role of the state in education (Dale, 1989). We shall return to that 'bigger picture' after trying to understand a further element of current education policy in England, the so-called National Curriculum.

3.3 THE NATIONAL CURRICULUM AND 'THE NATIONAL CULTURE'

Much of what has been said here about the increasing heterogeneity of the school system in England appears to be belied by the recent imposition of a National Curriculum on all state schools. Green (1990, pp.315–16) argues that a national curriculum is a genuinely 'modernizing measure', which breaks with past traditions of autonomy, but one which, in Conservative policy, 'co-exists in contradiction with other measures … designed to create a "market" education system … making planning and rationalization difficult, and undercutting any otherwise beneficial effects from the national curriculum'. Presumably, it is the idea of a national curriculum to complete the creation of a national education system in a country that 'never quite completed the job' that appeals to Green, rather than its detail.

The particular National Curriculum introduced by the Thatcher government consists of core and foundation subjects (English, mathematics, science, technology, history, geography, art, music, PE, and a modern foreign language), and an associated system of attainment testing for all children in state schools at ages 7, 11, 14 and 16. Attainment targets and programmes of study for the core foundation subjects have been developed by curriculum working groups. This work has formed the basis of advice from the National Curriculum Council to the Secretary of State, who has enshrined curriculum requirements in statutory orders which are binding on state schools.

It can be argued that the government's original conception of the National Curriculum was consistent with Green's view that such a device could help to overcome long-standing inequalities in education, by ensuring that all pupils are entitled to the same curriculum and making explicit what is required of them. Insisting that all girls should

study science up to the age of 16 might, for example, help to c
long-standing under-representation of women in the physical
However, you will recall Bourdieu's view that merely to make ... ...g..
status curriculum available to all pupils, without reference to the
cultural resources they bring to it, is likely to favour the already
privileged. Alison Kelly (1989) has argued that the 'masculine'
characteristics of conventional approaches to the physical sciences give
boys a gender-based advantage in science. The effects of the National
Curriculum will thus very much depend on what is defined as
legitimate knowledge and the style in which it is presented. In any case,
the government has decided that some pupils will be permitted to
follow a restricted curriculum in science in the later years, thus limiting
the likelihood that the National Curriculum will significantly alter
gender inequalities in science education. Another government proposal,
allowing some pupils to follow vocational courses at school, might seem
to suggest that the content of school knowledge is being changed in
ways that will favour the least privileged. Yet, if the curriculum for the
most privileged remains unchanged, this too could actually reinforce
rather than challenge existing inequalities.

Clearly the National Curriculum embodies contradictory tendencies,
though the issue is further complicated by divisions amongst the New
Right about whether there should be a National Curriculum at all. It was
dismissed by advocates of neo-liberal policies as incompatible with the
espousal of market forces, and a retreat from the Thatcher government's
own commitment to an eventual free market in education (Sexton,
1988). Such commentators regard the National Curriculum as an
unnecessarily bureaucratic 'nationalized' curriculum and fear that the
'educational establishment' could still subvert the government's reforms
from within. Indeed, they see some of the National Curriculum working
group reports (DES, 1989a, 1989b) as vindicating this view. Far better
than anything prescribed by such groups, or even by ministers and civil
servants, would be a 'free enterprise curriculum' — or that mixture of
contents and styles that a 'free citizenry' plumps for. As O'Keeffe puts it,
'if you do not like the groceries at one supermarket, try another. The
system which has utterly outperformed all others in history in the
production of a wide range of goods and services needs trying out in the
field of education too' (O'Keeffe, 1988, p.19). This is a classic example
of the transportation of a particular mode of regulation, the 'discipline
of the market', from one discursive field to another.

It should also prompt us to reflect on Green's assumption that
modernization involves some form of central planning. Part of the
debate between those who favour a corporatist approach to planning
education and training and those who advocate a market-oriented
approach is about what constitute the 'needs' of a modern economy as
well as the best ways of serving them. Of course, the notion that it is
meaningful to talk of the needs of the economy outside the manner in
which they are represented in discourse is clearly a problematic one for
many theories. But it is clear that the sub-texts of many of the debates

about choice in education and about curriculum prescription concern the creation of the most appropriate context in which capital accumulation can take place.

There is an unresolved debate in and around government about the extent to which the National Curriculum, whether in its prescribed version or one that might emerge from a neo-liberal market approach, can provide an appropriate curriculum model for the late twentieth century. Some of the concerns about the appropriateness of what is taught in schools in relation to the requirements of industry and the labour market, as reflected in Callaghan's Great Debate and the early policies of the Thatcher government, appear to have been somewhat marginalized in more recent policies. The Confederation of British Industry has argued that the National Curriculum, which seems to re-emphasize strong boundaries between subjects, is giving 'too much importance to narrow academic knowledge and too little to the fostering of transferable skills' (Jackson, 1989). Some people on the Right have attacked the very notion of 'relevance' (North, 1987) and seem to support a return to that traditional view of the school curriculum that has often been seen as partly, or even largely, to blame for the decline of British industry (Callaghan, 1976; Wiener, 1981; Barnett, 1986). There are many who claim that the curriculum provisions of the Education Reform Act will spell the end of the shift towards 'integrated codes' represented by the Technical and Vocational Education Initiative and that, in curricular terms, the traditionally oriented Hillgate Group rather than the advocates of the enterprise culture eventually won the battle for the high policy ground under the Thatcher government (Jamieson and Watts, 1987). The attempt to combine what, in Randall Collins' terms, might be considered 'theoretically incompatible' types of education clearly creates some unresolved tensions.

However, Andrew Gamble, amongst others, has argued that what is distinctive about Thatcherism as a force within British conservatism is its capacity to link the neo-conservative emphasis on tradition, authority and national identity/security with an espousal of neo-liberal free market economics and the extension of its principles into whole new areas of social activity, including the provision of welfare (Gamble, 1983). In many ways, the National Curriculum created by the Education Reform Act reflects nostalgia for a national 'past' as much as it does a concern with modernization. While many of the other reforms had the support of neo-liberal members of the New Right, the National Curriculum was partly a response to the concerns of other members of that grouping — this time its neo-conservative elements, or what Ball (1990a) terms the 'cultural restorationists'.

Thus, alongside the advocacy of the beneficial effects of market forces on educational standards and productivity, a concern with tradition and national identity was clearly evident in the official discourse which justified the Education Reform Act. Neo-conservative rhetorics of legitimation are evident in the very emphasis on 'National' in the National Curriculum, and both the content and the form of the National

Curriculum are interesting in sociological terms. Its apparent view of the curriculum as a collection of individual school subjects is a version of Bernstein's 'collection code', a form of organization of school knowledge reminiscent of the nineteenth-century public school curriculum. At least implicitly, it seems to reject that move towards 'integrated codes' which had seemed to be associated with the demands of more flexible modes of economic and cultural production. With regard to the content of the National Curriculum, it is possible to discern 'the selective tradition' at work in the constitution of the programmes of study for some of the school subjects.

You will recall that Williams defined the selective tradition as 'that which, within the terms of an effective dominant culture, is always passed off as "the tradition", *the* significant past' (Williams, 1976, p.205). In launching the working group on history, Kenneth Baker, the then Secretary of State, stated that 'the programmes of study should have at the core the history of Britain, the record of its past and, in particular, its political, constitutional and cultural heritage' (quoted in *The Times,* 14 January 1989). Attempts to construct a particular sense of national identity, together with a prescribed epistemology to secure adherence to one particular way of reading history, were evident in the debate surrounding the work of the history curriculum working group. Despite recent trends in school history, there were concerted efforts to deny the multiplicity and provisionality of perspectives in favour of an authoritative (or authoritarian) emphasis on 'the facts'.

ACTIVITY 5

Look at the collage of extracts from press coverage of the debate about the nature of school history that accompanied the deliberations of the history working group (see pages 296–8).

1   To what extent does it suggest that what counts as school history is a highly contested issue?

2   How far does the government's contribution to the debate seek to construct and represent a sense of national identity via an authoritarian reading of history?

3   Do the critical responses offer alternative authoritarian readings or do they see history as offering pupils a range of perspectives on the same issues?

Clearly some critics felt that Margaret Thatcher (though not necessarily all ministers or the history working group itself) was trying to embody a version of the nation's past within school history that would construct subjectivities in pupils appropriate to the New Right's political project. Dawn Gill (1990) has pointed out that, even in the working group's final report (DES, 1990b), of the thirty-one named individuals who were suggested for compulsory study, only two were women and all were Europeans. The proposed curriculum could thus be seen as embodying

History and Thatcher

The Historical Association has written to the Prime Minister asking her to outline what she considers to be her appropriate constitutional role in relation to influencing the details of school history courses.

For its part The Historical Association is concerned about recent reports that Mrs Thatcher and her colleagues discussed the Interim Report of the History Working Group and that Mr MacGregor's commentary on the report was influenced by those discussions.

A dangerous precedent may have been set. If Labour win the next election presumably Mr Kinnock will feel entitled to have school history syllabuses amended according to the predilections of himself and his Cabinet colleagues.

And the association stretches it further in saying that "if the Greens were to triumph in 1997 will the whole National Curriculum be revised to an appropriate 'greenness'?"

The Historical Association says it awaits the Prime Minister's reply with interest and concern. It believe that the British tradition of political non-interference in history syllabuses should be preserved and that the final form of history in the National Curriculum should be decided, without excessive political interference, by the History Working Group and the National Curriculum Council (NCC), which includes former teacher and broadcaster Beverley Anderson.

This challenge will give the NCC a timely opportunity to prove that it is genuinely independent and influenced neither overtly nor covertly by the Department of Education and Science.

(*Caribbean Times*, 8 September 1989)

Thatcher changes course of history

by JUDITH JUDD

In a new tussle with education Ministers and officials over what children should learn, Mrs Thatcher is pressing for a more traditional approach to the curriculum.

She has made a dramatic intervention and overridden the wishes of former Education Secretary Kenneth Baker by demanding changes in an interim report on history. The report had already been accepted by Mr Baker and his department.

She has told the new Education Secretary, Mr John MacGregor, to take a tougher line than Mr Baker and to insist on more British and less world history, a more chronological approach and greater emphasis on facts rather than on skills and understanding.

Mr Baker, in the last of a series of disagreements with the Prime Minister over education, argued that the Government should not dictate recommendations to its own working party before its deliberations were complete.

Mrs Thatcher's refusal to endorse the report prepared by Commander Michael Saunders Watson, a former naval commander, came on the eve of its publication in mid-July — at the time when she was enlarging on French shortcomings in the management of revolutions.

Mr Baker is thought to have delayed publication of the report because he did not wish to be involved in a row with the Prime Minister just before moving to his new job as Tory Chairman.

His successor, Mr MacGregor, was called in and told by Mrs Thatcher that the Government's response must be critical. The report was published 10 days ago and Mr MacGregor asked the working party to reconsider its decision to exclude 'historical knowledge' from the five attainment targets which set out the objectives for the study of history under the national curriculum.

He also said he wanted 50 per cent of the time devoted to British history in secondary schools, compared with just over a third envisaged by the group for students aged 14–16.

The group has to produce its final report by Christmas and the signs are that it will stick to its guns.

Mr Jim Hendy, Stockport's director of education and a member of the committee, thought that when Ministers looked closely at the proposals they would see that much more British history was involved than might at first be apparent. For example, pupils studying the American Revolution or India would inevitably learn a lot about British history. Themes such as 'sport in society' which were suggested for study were much more likely to be about sport in Britain than sport in, say, Japan.

On the question of knowledge, he said the group would need to spell out more clearly how understanding was impossible without a sound grasp of dates and events. 'You can't argue whether Stalin was good or bad without knowing about the collectivisation of farms, pogroms and massacres.'

The National Curriculum Council is due to make its final recommendations on the English report to Mr MacGregor on 10 November.

(*The Observer*, 20 August 1989)

Dangers of changing the course of history

Government plans to change the way history is taught could threaten the identities of black children, a parents group has warned.

An education department report says that history lessons should be weighted in favour of the British experience. But Michael La Rose of the Black Parent's Movement has protested that this could only make it "more difficult" for children to establish a cultural identity.

"There is a danger of a very racist history being taught. I would like to see the emphasis on a global history so that children have a fuller understanding.

"The question of colonialism, for example, should not be told from a narrow British view, with racist assertions. I think both parents and teachers will resist this proposal."

But Beverly Anderson, a lecturer and member of the National Curriculum Council, said: "Black people are British — I don't see that this is necessarily a cause for concern. The history of this island is intrinsically linked with Africa anyway."

And a spokeswoman from the Department of Education and Science commented: "The working group are not talking about British history to mean white history. Part of British history does include people of ethnic minorities."

(*The Voice*, 19 September 1989)

Chewing over history's core

IF THERE is any subject which justifies the concept of a national core curriculum it is, for three main reasons, history. The importance attached to the subject fluctuates wildly from age group to age group and school to school. Without a planned element of chronological continuity, schoolchildren may be obliged to flit from, say, the Middle Ages to the nineteenth century. Finally, the subject lends itself to ideological, religious and nationalist tampering. Of its importance there is no doubt. Learning history may not yield the immediate practical advantages of basic literacy and numeracy. But no subject can do more to give a child a sense of identity, a rewarding curiosity, an understanding of other nations and cultures, and skills in marshalling and analysing facts.

Yet, as the interim report published yesterday by the history working group states, more than half of today's school pupils drop history after the age of 14; and in the quality and quantity of what is taught to the rest, too much is left to chance. The eventual core curriculum will establish a framework of subjects and themes, specifying what should be taught and when, while — notionally at least, should time enough remain — leaving some freedom to teachers. The working group's intention is that the curriculum should be broad, balanced and coherent, and make history challenging, relevant and interesting to schoolchildren. They have set a good example: their document is sane, well-written and broad-minded. It is concerned that children should not be taught to see England as the centre of the world, should understand the rich range of possible interpretations of history, and should study China or Africa as well as Europe and the Americas.

John MacGregor, the new Secretary of State for Education, suggests in his appended comments that they have gone too far by providing for less than half the available time to be given to British history in the 11–16 age-groups. He is anxious too that due importance should be attached, in the final recommendations, to the acquisition and testing of factual knowledge. Mr MacGregor's points are both reasonable and compatible with the report's approach. A sound knowledge of Britain's history and peoples is the natural priority for British children, and cannot properly be divorced from the study of Europe, whose peoples and cultures have variously invaded and enriched these islands. The working group will, similarly, have no quibble with Mr MacGregor's belief that a firm grasp of key dates and facts is the best foundation on which to build new knowledge. The challenge is to devise ways in which such globules of fact can be imparted without making history seem dry and tedious.

In no subject is the inspiration of good teaching more vital. The core curriculum can do much to bring coherence and breadth to history lessons throughout a child's schooling. But without the right teachers there is no hope of putting the material across convincingly. The present crisis of morale and numbers in the teaching profession will have to be overcome if history is to be taught at all in some schools, let alone well.

(*The Independent*, 11 August 1989)

Why should black history be taught in schools?

By Debbie Plentie

If a fairy godmother had been present at my christening, the most precious gift that she could have bestowed upon me would not have been beauty, wealth or happiness, but knowledge of my history.

But life is not a fairytale and there was no fairy godmother at hand to help me contend with the harsh reality of living in a racist society that has sought to hide the dirty deeds perpetuated in its colonial past. And the cover-up does not stop there.

In addition to concealing or justifying the oppression and exploitation of black people, this society has also attempted to obliterate the many achievements of black people throughout history.

Cover-up

The cover-up worked most effectively during my school years. My hard-working parents were anxious that their children should have access to all the opportunities denied to them and believed that a good education was the key that opened many doors.

They scrimped and saved to send me to a private school at which there was only one other black pupil. Isolated from my former black friends, and at an impressionable age, I turned to my new white environment for role models.

Needless to say, no black history was taught at the school I attended. There were few occasions when black people were mentioned at all. I can recall the odd geography lesson where black people were alluded to as backward people who were sometimes fortunate enough to be rescued from their primitive lifestyles by philanthropic white do-gooders.

And, of course, there were the history lessons where details of the slave trade were given and I was left with the impression that black people were either too passive or too stupid to resist the atrocities committed against them.

Everything I saw and heard in the classroom reinforced the message that pervaded society in general: If you want to succeed, you have to be white.

(*The Voice*, 14 February 1989)

Succeed

I desperately wanted to succeed and, without making a conscious decision to do so, I was assimilated totally into the mainstream white culture. I could not alter my black skin, but in every other way I took on the characteristics of my white peers.

It was years later before I realised that I had been duped, and set about the painful process of rediscovering my heritage and reclaiming my black identity.

Now I know something of the diverse accomplishments of the black races around the globe. I know that for every white inventor, writer or leader of note, there has been a black equivalent, even if their achievements have not been documented in the white annals of history. I know that one of the main reasons for the abolition of slavery was the ceaseless resistance of slaves.

I now know that there is a legacy of an indomitable spirit that has enabled black people to endure and overcome even the bleakest moments in our history.

Since the heady days of civil rights and black power campaigning, there has been a growth in positive black consciousness. But a recent visit to my local chemist showed me that that is not sufficient cause for complacency.

The black cosmetics shelves were packed with skin lighteners and hair-straighteners. We do not have to look far to see proof of the use of such products amongst black people, demonstrating that whatever we may say, in their hearts some black people still believe that the whiter we are, the better we are.

In the past, well-meaning but inept attempts at putting multi-cultural education on the syllabus in British schools have probably reinforced as many stereotypes as they have demolished.

But we must not be deterred by this. It is crucial that black history is taught in schools, not only to foster confidence, pride and self-awareness in black pupils, but to make their white contemporaries aware of the significant contributions black people have made to their lives, and those of their ancestors.

Black people cannot make sense of the present and look to the future without fear until they understand their past. The teaching of black history in schools is a powerful means of ensuring that future generations are enabled to do just that.

the culture of 'dead white males', limiting the 'subject' positions or role models open to girls and black pupils and thereby confirming existing patterns of domination. However, we should be sceptical about the simplistic conception of the way ideology works displayed by contributors on all sides of the debate about school history. As Williams puts it, 'if what we learn were merely an imposed ideology, or it were only the isolable meanings of the ruling class ... occupying merely the top of our minds, it would be ... a very much easier thing to overthrow' (Williams, 1976, p.205).

In reading curriculum prescriptions sociologically, as in analysing school textbooks, we need to avoid seeing them as 'instruments for socializing passive individuals into the dominant values', and recognize them as 'offering solutions and making places available for ... contradictory and problematic ... subjects' (Ahier, 1988, p.6). However, even though the debate about National Curriculum history ended with a degree of compromise, critics still argue that any apparent broadening of the content conforms to Williams's claim that alternative meanings are often 'reinterpreted, diluted or put into forms which support or at least do not contradict other elements within the effective dominant culture' (Williams, 1976, p.205).

Neo-conservative concerns are also revealed in other aspects of the debate about the National Curriculum. Particularly interesting are the representations in the debate of the 'others' of western culture. The Hillgate Group, for example, expressed a concern about the pressure for a multicultural curriculum that 'has been felt throughout the western world, and most notably in France, Germany, and the United States, as well as in Britain'. They joined with those 'who defend the traditional values of western societies, and in particular who recognize that the very universalism and openness of European culture is our best justification for imparting it, even to those who come to it from other roots' (Hillgate Group, 1987, p.3). While, as we have seen, the Hillgate Group were happy to see the emergence of new and autonomous schools, including Moslem schools, this commitment to market forces was in the context of an insistence that all children 'be provided with the knowledge and understanding that are necessary for the full enjoyment and enhancement of British society'. Nothing, they said, was more important than to 'reconcile our minorities, to integrate them into our national culture, and to ensure a common political loyalty, independent of race, creed or colour'. 'Our' culture, being part of the universalistic culture of Europe, 'must not be sacrificed for the sake of a misguided relativism, or out of a misplaced concern for those who might not yet be aware of its strengths and weaknesses' (Hillgate Group, 1987, p.4).

I have quoted at length from a pamphlet by the influential Hillgate Group because it is a text which bears careful deconstruction. It works both to acknowledge difference and to defuse its potential challenge to the prevailing social order. Given its influence on government policies at the time when the Education Reform Act was being finalized, the reading of those policies with which we flirted in Section 3.1, seeing them as a reflection of the sort of post-modern society which positively celebrates heterogeneity and difference, becomes even more questionable. Within the discourse of the Hillgate Group there is clearly a master-narrative that differentiates cultures on a hierarchical basis. Indeed, alongside nostalgia for a supposedly lost past, a conservative version of the Enlightenment project is evident in their characterization of European culture, whereby social progress is seen in terms of assimilation into that culture. A member of the Hillgate Group was also responsible for introducing a successful House of Lords' amendment to the Education Reform Bill which required agreed syllabuses for education in state schools to 'reflect the fact that the religious traditions in Great Britain are in the main Christian whilst taking account of the teaching and practices of the other principal religions represented in Great Britain', and, with certain qualifications, their daily act of collective worship to be 'wholly or mainly of a broadly Christian character'.

Ironically, some Islamic groups are as critical as the Hillgate Group of multiculturalism. They argue that it claims to be founded on a notion of 'shared values', but this means that 'the multicultural curriculum ... will reflect the cultural heritage of the selector, and lead to cultural domination in disguise by the selector's group'. The 'national values' envisaged even by the Swann Report (DES, 1985) 'are derived basically from pseudo Judaeo-Christian and mainly secularist stances, which do not take account of values upheld by the Muslim, Hindu, Sikhs, Buddhist and other faith communities' (Islamic Academy/Islamic Cultural Centre, 1985). Jones (1986), in discussing this debate, argues that Swann's notion of 'rationally justifiable shared values' is problematic in a pluralist context because:

> ... rationality involves more than agreement on the valid forms of argument. It also involves agreement on basic prejudgements which are problematic in that they are assumptions basic to various culturally 'vouched for' ways of looking/modes or reasoning, but are themselves intractable to any known verification procedure ... In an important sense, foundational prejudgements are 'articles of faith'.
> (Jones, 1986, pp.108–9)

This might be taken as evidence that the assumptions of liberal pluralism have run their course and that we now have to face up to the incommensurability of cultures and values in a post-modern society in which the Enlightenment project no longer seems realizable. Nevertheless, at least outside the realms of post-modern philosophy, the curriculum debate remains structured by a widespread attachment to Enlightenment values and the quest for a common culture.

3.4 CONTRADICTORY OR COMPLEMENTARY?

We saw that Green argued that the National Curriculum exists in contradiction with the reforms designed to stimulate a market in education. We should, perhaps, not be surprised that there are some apparent tensions and contradictions within any set of policies. Any government is subject to a range of influences, and even the political philosophy of the New Right is based on a blend of moral, economic, and philosophical doctrines. These are sometimes complementary, but sometimes in tension, particularly in the mediated political versions of such doctrines (Edwards *et al.*, 1984; Whitty and Menter, 1989). Greater consumer power over choice and management of schools (a neo-liberal response to criticisms of LEA bureaucracies), *and* a national curriculum (a neo-conservative response to charges that trendy teachers are subverting traditional moral values and selling the nation short) may *both* resonate with popular experience and be electorally attractive, even if the whole package does *not* add up in logical terms. We should certainly not assume that the *effects* of government policies will all point in the same direction.

However, it is also possible to read a degree of coherence into these various policies and to see them as all addressing the core problems facing the modern state. Gamble has suggested that the seeming paradox of, at one and the same time building a strong state through increased expenditure on the military and the apparatuses of law and order, while also using state power to roll back state intervention from whole areas of social activity, does have a degree of consistency. This is because the state needs to protect the market from vested interests and restrictive practices and prevent the conditions in which it can flourish being subverted either from without or within (Gamble, 1983).

On this basis, the Thatcher government's curriculum policies may not necessarily have been as much at variance with its policies on the structure of the education system as is sometimes suggested, even at the level of principle. The contrast between apparent centralization in one sphere and apparent decentralization in the other may not be the paradox it first appears. Schools which are responsive to choices made by parents in the market are believed by the government to be more likely than those administered by state bureaucrats to produce high levels of scholastic achievement, to the benefit of both individuals and the nation. The strength of the state therefore has to be used to remove anything that interferes with this process or with the development of an appropriate sense of self and nation on the part of citizens who will be making their choices in the market.

Thus, not only is government's traditional partnership with LEAs and teachers' trade unions abandoned in favour of the discipline of the market, it also becomes imperative (at least in the short term) for central government to police the curriculum to ensure that the pervasive collectivist and universalistic welfare ideology of the post-war era is restrained. In this way, support for the market, self-help, enterprise, and concepts of the 'responsible' family and a common 'national identity' can be constructed. Thus, whether or not a former government minister's intriguing suggestion that there should be compulsory teaching of free market economics in all schools was offered tongue in cheek, it may merely be an extreme example of a more general approach to the problem confronting the political project of Thatcherism within education. In other words, the overt ideology of the curriculum needs to be addressed directly before the 'hidden curriculum' of the new structure is sufficiently developed to do its work.

The two central strands of New Right thinking come together particularly clearly in the writings of the Hillgate Group (1987). This group seems to accept that market forces should ultimately be seen as the most effective way of determining a school's curriculum, but argues that central government intervention is necessary as an interim strategy to undermine the power of vested interests that threaten educational standards and traditional values. The Thatcher government's own long-term preference for market forces was reflected in the fact that it did not feel it appropriate to impose the National Curriculum and the associated attainment targets and testing arrangements on independent schools, and imposed them only in broad terms on the new City Technology Colleges.

However, it remains the case that, while current policies look forward to a time when a market ideology pervades whole new areas of social life, they also embody a nostalgia for the imagined community of the nation's past, as we saw in the debate about school history. This phenomenon was a major element in the appeal of Thatcherism as a political ideology. Dale (1989/90) argues that a policy of 'conservative modernization', which entails 'freeing individuals for economic purposes while controlling them for social purposes', was a key feature of the Thatcher government's education policy. It was perhaps most evident in the concept of City Technology Colleges, which Ball sees as going some way towards resolving the tensions between the 'cultural restorationists' and those who argue that education should be more closely geared to the needs of industry (Ball, 1990a, p.129). In a recent paper, Green too adopts the term 'conservative modernization programme' to characterize the 'backward-looking' policies of the Thatcher government, though he still does not appear to regard them as constituting a policy of genuine 'modernization' (Green, 1991, p.30).

Overall, while current education policies do seem to be a response to changing economic, political and cultural priorities, it would be difficult to argue that they should be read as indicating that we have entered into a qualitatively new phase of social development. To date, the market-oriented elements of current reforms still conform to Archer's definition of a state education system cited at the beginning of Section 2.1, even if Green (1991) and other commentators regard them as a first stage towards privatization. The new modes of regulation being employed by the state, particularly as they are evident in some countries which do not display what Green terms 'the peculiarities of

English education', may indicate a move towards a new phase of state formation linked to new forms of capital accumulation. They may also be partly a response to new cultural forms associated with complex patterns of social differentiation, but the continuities in the nature of what is being reproduced are equally striking. Whether the reforms are indicative of a move beyond modernity is thus highly questionable. The continuities suggest that, at most, we have been looking at the education system of post-modern capitalism, and I prefer to see this as a development of modernity rather than something distinctly post-modern.

In policy terms, 'conservative modernization' remains in evidence, still counterposed to the 'progressive' alternative championed by commentators such as Green. The alternative strategy favoured by Green has not yet produced the degree of progress that its advocates originally envisaged, even in societies where it has been adopted with more vigour than in Britain. In many societies, for whatever reason, existing state education systems no longer appear to resonate with the demands of consumers. They are seen as unduly bureaucratic, and as not serving the needs of disadvantaged groups in the community. To that extent, whatever its eventual effects, the conservative approach may have been more responsive to those subtle social and cultural shifts that have been taking place in modern societies. Social democratic approaches to education which favour the idea of a common school and, indeed, usually some version of a common curriculum (Lawton, 1975) are themselves now faced with the need to respond to the social diversity of contemporary societies. Just as current discussions on the Left about citizenship are seeking ways of 'creating unity without denying specificity' (Mouffe quoted in Giroux, 1990), so will responding to social diversity be a challenge for future education policies. Donald (1989/90) calls for approaches which are based on 'participation and distributive justice rather than simple egalitarianism and on cultural heterogeneity rather than a shared humanity' — a project which he argues puts a question mark against the idea of comprehensive education. My own view, for what it is worth, is that the social and cultural developments in modern societies point to the need for a redefinition of comprehensive education rather than its abandonment.

4   CONCLUSIONS

Finally, let us return to Ozga's demand that we should not lose sight of the 'bigger picture'. Given that we have detected in current developments in education underlying continuities with the class-based patterns of social reproduction that have dominated English educational history, it would perhaps be premature to abandon the meta-narratives of the traditional sociological theories that have helped us to make sense of them. Certainly, many sociologists of education are still seeking to develop all-embracing (or what their critics would call 'totalizing') theories which try to understand schooling in terms of the complex relationship between economic, political and cultural practices. Stephen Ball's recent attempt to explore contemporary education policy in England probably strikes the right balance (Ball, 1990a).

Ball draws on Althusser's overall schema of the social totality, although he argues that the economic, political and ideological dimensions of education, being relatively autonomous of each other, each need to be understood using different sets of theoretical and methodological tools. His own account of education policy seems to give some causal precedence to the economic, but in a considerably more sophisticated way than was implied in Bowles and Gintis's original 'correspondence thesis'. He recognizes that any process of restructuring in response to changes in the economy is a complex and messy one and highly contingent on the historical and cultural specificities of particular nation-states. His account also recognizes that there is conflict 'within the state and within and across the various sites which make up the state' (ibid., p.21). In rejecting any simple model of economic determination, he points out that 'the processes of restructuring and repositioning education in relation to the economy are multi-faceted, in some respects dislocated, and sometimes incoherent'.

Partly for this reason, Ball is currently engaged in ethnographic studies of the implementation of recent reforms at school level. Ball takes the view that any sociological account of the nature of contemporary education policy must encompass complexity, since it is infused with economic, political and ideological contradictions. Nor, in looking at the detail of what happens within education, should we forget that not everything 'can be reduced to the requirements of production, nor to the play of political ideologies' (Ball, 1990a, p.211). Conflicts and struggles in and around education 'may very well be based on or organized around all kinds of non-economic considerations — those of race, gender, religion, for instance' (Ball, 1990a, p.15).

Ball is far from alone in this view. Indeed, there now tends to be broad agreement between sociologists from a wide range of theoretical perspectives that a sociological understanding of schooling in modern societies requires careful exploration of its specificities rather than seeing it as a mere adjunct to or relay for the supposed needs of the economy, while recognizing that (as we saw earlier) it is sometimes represented as such in policy discourse about education. But in deconstructing that discourse, it is by no means clear that sociologists need entirely abandon the project of 'making sense' of what Ozga (1990) called the 'bigger picture'.

REFERENCES

Ahier, J. (1988) *Industry, Children and the Nation,* Lewes, Falmer Press.

Allen, J., Braham, P., and Lewis, P. (eds) (1992) *Political and Economic Forms of Modernity*, Cambridge, Polity Press.

Althusser, L. (1971) *Lenin and Philosophy and other Essays*, London, New Left Books.

Apple, M.W. (1990) *Ideology and Curriculum*, London, Routledge.

Archer, M. (1984) *Social Origins of Educational Systems*, London, Sage.

Ashworth, J., Papps, I., and Thomas, B. (1988) *Increased Parental Choice*, Warlingham, Institute of Economic Affairs Education Unit.

Ball, S. (1987) *The Micro-politics of the School,* London, Methuen.

Ball, S. (1990a) *Politics and Policy-making in Education*, London, Routledge.

Ball, S. (ed.) (1990b) *Foucault and Education: Disciplines and Knowledge,* London, Routledge.

Banks, O. (1955) *Parity and Prestige in English Secondary Education*, London, Routledge.

Barnett, C. (1986) *The Audit of War*, London, Macmillan.

Bernstein, B. (1977) *Class, Codes and Control*, vol.3, London, Routledge.

Bourdieu, P. (1974) 'The school as a conservative force', in Eggleston, J. (ed.) *Contemporary Research in the Sociology of Education*, London, Methuen.

Bourdieu, P. and Passeron, J. (1990) *Reproduction in Education, Culture and Society,* London, Sage.

Bowles, S. and Gintis, H. (1976) *Schooling in Capitalist America*, London, Routledge and Kegan Paul.

Boyne, R. and Rattansi, A. (eds) (1990) *Postmodernism and Society,* London, Macmillan.

Callaghan, J. (1976) 'Towards a national debate', *Education*, vol.148, no.17.

CCCS (1981) *Unpopular Education*, London, Hutchinson.

Chubb, J.E. and Moe, T.M. (1990) *Politics, Markets and America's Schools,* Washington DC, Brookings Institution.

Cole, M. (ed.) (1988) *Bowles and Gintis Revisited*, Lewes, Falmer Press.

Collins, R. (1977) 'Some comparative principles of educational stratification', *Harvard Educational Review,* vol.47 no.1, pp.1–27.

Coulby, D. and Bash, L. (eds) (1991) *Contradiction and Conflict in Education,* London, Cassell.

Cumper, P. (1990) 'Muslim schools: the implications of the Education Reform Act 1988', *New Community*, vol.16, no.3, pp.379–89.

Dale, R. (1989) *The State and Education Policy*, Milton Keynes, Open University Press.

Dale, R. (1989/90) 'The Thatcherite project in education', *Critical Social Policy*, vol.9, no.3, pp.4–19.

DES (1985) *Education for All*, Report of the Committee of Inquiry into the Education of Children from Ethnic Minority Groups (Chairman: Baron Swann), Cmnd 9453, London, HMSO.

DES (1989a) *Mathematics in the National Curriculum*, London, HMSO.

DES (1989b) *Science in the National Curriculum*, London, HMSO.

DES (1990a) *Statistical Bulletin*, no.1, January, London, HMSO.

DES (1990b) *History in the National Curriculum*, London, HMSO.

Donald, J. (1985) 'Beacons of the Future', in Beechey, V. and Donald, J. (eds) *Subjectivity and Social Relations,* Milton Keynes, Open University Press.

Donald, J. (1989/90) 'Interesting times', *Critical Social Policy*, vol. 9, no. 3, pp.39–55.

Dooley, P. (1991) 'Muslim private schools', in Walford, G. (ed.) *Private Schooling: Tradition, Change and Diversity*, London, Paul Chapman.

Durkheim, E. (1956) *Education and Sociology*, New York, Free Press.

Edwards, A. D., Fulbrook, M., and Whitty, G. (1984) 'The state and the independent sector', in Barton, L. and Walker, S. (eds) *Social Crisis and Educational Research,* London, Croom Helm.

Foucault, M. (1980) *Power/Knowledge: Selected Interviews and Other Writings 1972–77*, Brighton, Harvester Press.

Gamble, A. (1983) 'Thatcherism and Conservative politics', in Hall, S. and Jacques, M. (eds) *The Politics of Thatcherism*, London, Lawrence and Wishart.

Gill, D. (1990) 'A response on behalf of Hackney teachers to the National Curriculum History Working Group Final Report', paper presented to the Annual Conference of the British Educational Research Association.

Gintis, H. and Bowles, S. (1981) 'Contradiction and reproduction in educational theory', in Dale, R. *et al.* (eds) *Education and the State*, vol.1: *Schooling and the National Interest,* Lewes, Falmer Press.

Giroux, H. (1983) *Theory and Resistance in Education*, London, Heinemann.

Giroux, H. (ed.) (1990) *Postmodernism, Feminism, and Cultural Politics*, New York, SUNY Press.

Glenn, C.L. (1988) *The Myth of the Common School,* Amherst, University of Massachusetts Press.

Green, A. (1990) *Education and State Formation*, London, Macmillan.

Green, A. (1991) 'The peculiarities of English education', in Education Group II, *Education Limited: Schooling and Training and the New Right since 1979,* London, Unwin Hyman.

Habermas, J. (1981) 'Modernity versus postmodernity', *New German Critique,* no.22, pp.3–14.

Hall, S. and Gieben, B. (eds) (1992) *Formations of Modernity*, Cambridge, Polity Press.

Hall, S., Held, D. and McGrew, A. (eds) (1992) *Modernity and Its Futures*, Cambridge, Polity Press.

Hall, S. and Jacques, M. (eds) (1989) *New Times: The Changing Face of Politics in the 1990s*, London, Lawrence and Wishart.

Halsey, A., Heath, A., and Ridge, J. (1980) *Origins and Destinations*, Oxford, Clarendon Press.

Halstead, J. M. (1986) *The Case for Muslim Voluntary-Aided Schools*, Cambridge, The Islamic Academy.

Hammersley, M. (1990) *Classroom Ethnography*, Milton Keynes, Open University Press.

Harvey, D. (1989) *The Condition of Postmodernity*, Oxford, Basil Blackwell.

Heath, A. (1987) 'Class in the classroom', *New Society,* 17 July, pp.13–15.

Hillgate Group (1987) *The Reform of British Education*, London, Claridge Press.

Islamic Academy/ Islamic Cultural Centre (1985) *Swann Committee Report: An Evaluation from the Muslim Point of View*, Cambridge, Islamic Academy.

Jackson, M. (1989) 'CBI struggles to "save" curriculum from Baker', *Times Educational Supplement*, 24 March.

Jamieson, I. and Watts, T. (1987) 'Squeezing out enterprise', *Times Educational Supplement,* 18 December.

Jessop, B. *et al.* (1988) *Thatcherism: A Tale of Two Nations*, Oxford, Basil Blackwell.

Jones, M. (1986) 'The Swann Report on "Education for All": a critique', *Journal of Philosophy of Education*, vol.20, no.1, pp.107–12.

Joseph, K. (1976) *Stranded on the Middle Ground*, London, Centre for Policy Studies.

Karabel, J. and Halsey, A.H. (eds) (1977) *Power and Ideology in Education,* New York, Oxford University Press.

Kelly, A. (1989) 'The construction of masculine science', in Arnot, M. and Weiner, C. (eds) *Gender and the Politics of Schooling*, London, Hutchinson.

Kogan, M. (1975) *Educational Policy-making*, London, Allen and Unwin.

Lash, S. (1990) *Sociology of Postmodernism*, London, Routledge.

Lawton, D. (1975) *Class, Culture and the Curriculum*, London, Routledge.

MacDonald, M. (1979/80) 'Cultural reproduction: the pedagogy of sexuality', *Screen Education,* nos 32/33, pp.141–53.

MacDonald, M. (1981) 'Schooling and the reproduction of class and gender in relations', in Dale, R. *et al.* (eds) *Education and the State*, vol.2: *Politics, Patriarchy and Practice*, Lewes, Falmer Press.

McPherson, A. and Willms, J.D. (1987) 'Equalisation and improvement: some effects of comprehensive reorganisation in Scotland', *Sociology*, vol.21, no.4, pp.509–39.

Mills, C.W. (1965) *The Sociological Imagination*, Harmondsworth, Penguin.

Moore, D. (1990) 'Voice and choice in Chicago', in Clune, W. and Witte, J. (eds) *Choice and Control in American Education,* vol.1, Lewes, Falmer Press.

Moore, R. (1988) 'The correspondence principle and the Marxist sociology of education', in Cole, M. (ed.) (1988).

North, J. (ed.) (1987) *The GCSE: An Examination*, London, Claridge Press.

O'Keeffe, D. (1988) 'A critical look at a national curriculum and testing: a libertarian view', paper presented to American Educational Research Association, New Orleans, April.

Ozga, J. (1990) 'Policy research and policy theory', *Journal of Education Policy,* vol.5, pp.359–62.

Parmar, P. (1981) 'Young Asian women: a critique of the pathological approach', *Multi-racial Education*, vol.9, no.5, pp.19–29.

Phillips, M. (1988) 'Why black people are backing Baker', *The Guardian,* 9 September.

Reeder, D. (1979) 'A recurring debate: education and industry', in Bernbaum, G. (ed.) *Schooling in Decline*, London, Macmillan.

Roderick, G. and Stephens, M. (eds) (1982) *Where Did We Go Wrong?*, Lewes, Falmer Press.

Said, E. (1978) *Orientalism,* London, Routledge.

Salter, B. and Tapper, F. (1981) *Education, Politics and the State,* London, Grant McIntyre.

Sexton, S. (1988) 'No nationalized curriculum', *The Times,* 9 May.

Stephens, M. (1991) *Japan and Education*, London, Macmillan.

Walford, G. and Miller, H. (1991) *City Technology College*, Open University Press.

Walkerdine, V. (1984) 'Developmental psychology and the child-centred pedagogy', in Henriques, J. *et al.*, *Changing the Subject*, London, Methuen.

Walkling, P. and Brannigan, C. (1986) 'Anti-sexist/anti-racist education: a possible dilemma', *Journal of Moral Education*, vol.15, no.1, pp.16–25.

Whitty, G.(1985) *Sociology and School Knowledge,* London, Methuen.

Whitty, G. and Menter, I. (1989) 'Lessons of Thatcherism: education policy in England and Wales 1979–88', *Journal of Law and Society,* vol.16, no.1, pp.42–64.

Wiener, M. (1981) *English Culture and the Decline of the Industrial Spirit 1850–1980*, Cambridge, Cambridge University Press.

Williams, R. (1965) *The Long Revolution*, Harmondsworth, Penguin.

Williams, R. (1976) 'Base and superstructure in Marxist cultural theory', in Dale, R. *et al.* (eds) *Schooling and Capitalism*, London, Routledge.

Willis, P. (1977) *Learning to Labour*, Farnborough, Saxon House.

Young, M.F.D. (ed.) (1971) *Knowledge and Control*, London, Collier-Macmillan.

READING A EDUCATION AND STATE FORMATION

Andy Green

The aim of [my] book [was] to analyse the social origins of certain histori-cally specific forms of education known as national education systems. These were defined as systems of formal schooling at least partly funded and supervised by the state which provided universal education for all children of school age in a given nation. A set of educational institutions constituted a national system when it supplied the majority of the nation's needs in formal education and did so through an integrated and co-ordi-nated network of institutions. For the most part such systems were con-solidated in the nineteenth century and they represented the precursors of modern state schooling.

... Such systems arose unevenly in the major nations of Europe and North America. Countries developed their school systems at different times and according to different organizational models. Some of these differences are historically quite significant. A gap of nearly a century, for instance, separated the formation of an integrated administrative apparatus of state schooling in France and Prussia from England. Similarly almost a century separated the creation of state secondary schools in France and Prussia from those in England. Whilst Prussia legislated for compulsory attend-ance at school until 14 years in 1826, similar provisions were not applied in England until 1921.

The speed with which countries adopted education systems also appears to correlate with the extent of their education provisions as measured in enrolment, access and literacy rates. This would seem to be hardly sur-prising since the extent of popular participation in schooling depended to a large degree on the availability of finance for schools and the determi-nation or otherwise of governments and dominant social groups to encourage attendance. Mass schooling did not arise spontaneously from popular demand or from the action of market forces alone. It was to a large degree organized from above by the state. This conclusion clearly contra-dicts the neo-liberal argument that education developed in response to the market and that in a liberal England the market provided quite adequate schooling through voluntary initiatives. In comparison with other states English education was most inadequate and this appears to be related to the slow development of state intervention in education.

... It was found that none of [the existing theories of educational change] can adequately explain the social origins of national education systems nor their different chronologies of development. Traditional 'Whig' expla-nations have stressed the role of Enlightenment philosophy, Protestant religion and institutional democratization. However, this perspective can-not explain why education should have developed fast in an undemo-cratic state like Prussia and relatively slowly in a supposedly more

Source: Green, A. (1990) *Education and State Formation*, London, Macmillan, pp.308–14.

'democratic' state like England. Nor can Protestantism offer an adequate explanation of differential educational advance since some Catholic countries like Austria were pioneers in national education and since several Protestant areas like England and the southern US states do not fit the pattern of Protestant educational ascendancy. Functionalist theories which have linked education with economic skill requirements fare no better as general theories since the international pattern of educational development bears no close correlation with the process of industrialization at all. The first industrial country, England, was not the pioneer in educational change, whereas many of the less industrialized nations in Europe reacted much more speedily to bring education in line with the needs of developing economies. Lastly, theories which have attempted to link educational change with urbanization, proletarianization and the changing structures of family life, whilst suggesting many significant connections between the development of schooling and these social variables, are unable to explain significant degrees of educational development in regions which were predominantly rural and pre-proletarian.

The key social factor in explaining the timing and form of the development of education systems is rather ... the nature of the state and the process of state formation. The major impetus for the creation of national education systems lay in the need to provide the state with trained administrators, engineers and military personnel; to spread dominant national cultures and inculcate popular ideologies of nationhood; and so to forge the political and cultural unity of burgeoning nation states and cement the ideological hegemony of their dominant classes. This inevitably entailed at different times using education to perform some of the functions suggested by existing theories. In societies undergoing the proletarianization of labour, education could be a useful tool in acclimating workers to waged employment whether in workshops, factories or on the land. Equally, in regions undergoing rapid urbanization, numerous social conflicts were thrown up which it fell to schools to attempt to control and ameliorate. The break-up of traditional pre-proletarian family forms caused particular problems for youth socialization in the context of antagonistic class societies and education was frequently seen as a substitute mechanism to achieve this in ways which were acceptable to the dominant classes. However, it was specifically the intervention of the state which effected the formation of national education systems, and it is therefore the nature of the state in different countries which must carry the largest burden of explanation for the particular national forms and periodizations of the development of school systems.

The formation of national systems occurred first and fastest in countries where the process of state formation was most intensive. Three historical factors have been particularly associated with this accelerated and compacted process of state formation or 'nation-building'. One has been the existence of external military threats, or territorial conflicts, which have often propelled the victim nations into vehemently nationalistic responses and deliberate actions to strengthen their state machines. Another has been the occurrence of major internal transformations resulting either from revolution, as in France, or from a successful struggle for national independence, as in America. In each case the country concerned has emerged from major conflagrations with an urgent task of national reconstruction, not only to repair the ruins of war but also to establish a new social order which will reflect the principles for which the struggle was originally undertaken. Lastly, there have been the situations where nations have been prompted into state-led programmes of reform to escape from relative economic underdevelopment. Where one country is significantly behind other competitor countries economically it has generally not been possible to catch up simply by the spontaneous initiatives of individual entrepreneurs. Liberal politics have not been much use to underdeveloped countries, since they favour the already powerful, and nations which have successfully reversed histories of underdevelopment have generally done so either under the wing of other more powerful states or through concerted, centrally directed programmes of reform.

The development of national education systems has been historically closely connected with these phenomena, not only during our period here but also in the modern day where education has been a major priority of countries undergoing national reconstruction after war or successful struggles for independence. In the eighteenth and nineteenth centuries it was those nations which underwent this kind of state formation which were prone to develop national education and generally they did this at the precise period when the process was at its highest pitch. Militaristic state-building first propelled the eighteenth-century Prussian state into educational development and the pressures of economic advance kept the process on the boil in the next century, as absolutism gave way to constitutional bourgeois rule. Absolutism played a similar if lesser role in France. But here it was principally revolution and bourgeois social and economic reconstruction under Napoleon and after that fuelled a similar educational drive. In the United States, another leading country for educational reform, it was the need to consolidate a new American state after the break with England that did most to galvanize educational reform. Unlike in continental countries this was achieved less through the work of the central state and more through the initiative of individual reformers and the local state and county administrations with which they were closely allied. If the process here appears to have been based on broader democratic foundations and owed less to the etatist spirit that characterized continental development, it was still clearly understood as a means of developing the national culture and securing the political system and was no less a process of organized state formation.

Not only the timing, but also the forms of national systems reflected the nature of the state which created them. Most obviously centralized states created centralized educational bureaucracies whilst more liberal states, like the USA, created more decentralized systems. This had effects on the nature of the schooling provided ... . A centralized bureaucracy was better placed to engineer education systems where the various parts were more systematically linked with the whole. This tended to promote national systems of examinations, organized teacher training and policies on the

curriculum that dovetailed between the various parts. Decentralized public systems, on the other hand, typically involved less draconian controls
over the practice of education making it more difficult for the state to use
schooling as a means of securing uniform ideological beliefs. The voluntary system, as in England, was neither genuinely public nor really a system and had less co-ordination or integration than any other arrangement.

However, it was not only the degree of central control which effected the
forms and content of education. Schooling was a product not only of the
state but also of civil society and it was the nature of class relations there
which finally determined the purposes of schooling. It was the different
forms of hegemony operating between the dominant and subordinate
classes which was ultimately responsible for what schools did, for who
they allowed to go to what type of school and for what they taught them
when they were there. The modernizing but still hierarchical and militaristic junker state of Prussia produced an education system that was universal but authoritarian and multiply segmented. The working class received
what was for the time an ample and ruthlessly efficient education in the
public *Volksschule* system, but its object was most clearly not only to train
them to be skilled and productive workers but also to be loyal servants of
the state. For the middle and upper classes the secondary education was as
extensive as anywhere in Europe at the time, but it was clearly divided
between the traditional classical education received by the upper strata in
the *Gymnasien* and the more utilitarian education received by the mainly
middle-class clientele in the *Realschulen*. The more thoroughly 'bourgeois' state of Napoleonic and Restoration France, achieved a less comprehensive and efficient elementary school system but its secondary
education was arguably more modern than any, imbued with a circumscribed but potent meritocractic ideology and reflecting a notably cohesive and unified bourgeois culture. American education, as befitted a state
which had gone furthest down the road of political democracy, had a less
authoritarian system of education and one that undoubtedly offered more
in the way of egalitarian access to post elementary education than any
other nation. However, for all the populist rhetoric of America's
'democratic' capitalism, this was still severely circumscribed along class
and ethnic lines; if what the schools taught was not so tightly controlled
by the central state and owed something to an exceptionally broad social
consensus, it still reflected in the main the ideology and political purposes
of the dominant, white, Anglo-Saxon middle class.

England represents the most exceptional case of educational development. Of all the countries considered it had the greatest accumulation of
unsolved educational problems and was probably further behind in
reform than any area except the southern US states. Although religious
divisions and the continuing sway of a conservative gentry culture had
some part in this, it was the nature of the state which was most responsible. During this period Britain never experienced the kind of deliberate
and concerted process of state formation that occurred in the other countries and which was the driving force behind their educational reforms.
Absolutism was cut short by early seventeenth-century revolution and in

the eighteenth and nineteenth centuries there were neither external military threats, social revolutions nor problems of economic backwardness of the sort to engender intensive programmes of nation building. National identity, strong institutions and a relatively stable ruling-class hegemony had already been established by earlier revolutions. Economic ascendancy was achieved on the back of this without concerted state direction. Instead it was the liberal market order and the doctrine of the minimal government which shaped the relations between society and state. Such an order served the capitalist economy well, at least for the first half of the nineteenth century, but it was inimical to systematic educational development. The result was the distinctive Victorian voluntary system of schooling which dominated education throughout the century and has left a strong imprint ever since.

The decisive feature of English education was the relative weakness of state or public forms. This not only limited the overall extent of educational provision, since there were clear limits to what voluntary initiative could achieve, but it also gave distinctive forms to the system as a whole. Lacking whole-hearted state encouragement and with no effective central authority to co-ordinate it, education developed in an unsystematic and almost haphazard fashion. Teacher training and inspection were weak, curriculum and examination reform was exceptionally slow and guided by no comprehensive or rational plan, and the various parts of the system were not methodically articulated one with another. Overall the system reflected the contradictory nature of mid-Victorian bourgeois hegemony. Its main purpose in popular schooling was to promote acquiescence in middle-class morality and the nostrums of liberal political economy and it did this in a typically partisan and doctrinaire fashion. However, the system also reflected the individualist and fissiparous character of the liberal order. Different parts of the school system were dominated by powerful interest groups which maintained exceptional levels of autonomy.

The result in secondary education was the survival of an antiquated system of gentry education in the public schools and the absence of any normatively middle-class schooling such as had been achieved with the continental *lycée* and *Realschule,* and the American high school. The result in working-class education was faction and conflict and thus the long delay of reforms which were necessary to improve the system. These factors alone well justified England's poor reputation in education. When to these problems were added the very partial development of technical and scientific education and the rather limited extent of higher education generally, an overall picture emerged of pervasive neglect of an essential national and public resource. Such was the record of nineteenth-century liberalism in education.

The legacy of Victorian policies on education have had a profound influence on the development of education in the twentieth century. Many of the typical features established then have continued to characterize English education even during the era of the interventionist welfare state, and in many respects our system still suffers from the pattern of relative underdevelopment first inscribed in those years. Technical education has remained rooted in the apprentice model of practical, on-the-job training, marginalized from mainstream education, anti-theoretical and low in status. Attitudes towards mass education have been marked by that Victorian blend of ruling-class paternalism and working-class deference and defensiveness which have contributed much towards the alienation felt by pupils and parents to state schools and the widespread preference for early school leaving. Our public schools continue to represent a uniquely independent, influential and elitist private sector which has no real foreign equivalents and which contributes to our well deserved reputation for class division in education. ... The corollary of this entrenchment of private interests has been a relatively weak commitment to collective or public provision ...

READING B   THE CORRESPONDENCE PRINCIPLE

Samuel Bowles and Herbert Gintis

> In the social production which men carry on they enter into definite relations which are indispensible and independent of their will; ... The sum total of these relations of production constitutes ... the real foundation on which rise legal and political superstructures, and to which correspond definite forms of social consciousness.
> (Karl Marx, *Contribution to a Critique of Political Economy*, 1857)

... The initiation of youth into the economic system is facilitated by a series of institutions, including the family and the educational system, that are immediately related to the formation of personality and consciousness. Education works primarily through the institutional relations to which students are subjected. ...

To reproduce the social relations of production, the educational system must try to teach people to be properly subordinate and render them sufficiently fragmented in consciousness to preclude their getting together to shape their own material existence. The forms of consciousness and behaviour fostered by the educational system must themselves be alienated, in the sense that they conform neither to the dictates of technology in the struggle with nature, nor to the inherent developmental capacities of individuals, but rather to the needs of the capitalist class. It is the prerogatives of capital and the imperatives of profit, not human capacities and technical realities, which render US schooling what it is. ...

The educational system helps integrate youth into the economic system, we believe, through a structural correspondence between its social relations and those of production. The structure of social relations in education not only inures the student to the discipline of the work place, but develops the types of personal demeanour, modes of self-presentation, self-image, and social-class identifications which are the crucial ingredi-

Source: Bowles, S. and Gintis H. (1976) *Schooling in Capitalist America*, London, Routledge and Kegan Paul, pp.129–33.

ents of job adequacy. Specifically, the social relationships of education — the relationships between administrators and teachers, teachers and students, students and students, and students and their work — replicate the hierarchical division of labor. Hierarchical relations are reflected in the vertical authority lines from administrators to teachers to students. Alienated labor is reflected in the student's lack of control over his or her education, the alienation of the student from the curriculum content, and the motivation of school work through a system of grades and other external rewards rather than the student's integration with either the process (learning) or the outcome (knowledge) of the educational 'production process'. Fragmentation in work is reflected in the institutionalized and often destructive competition among students through continual and ostensibly meritocratic ranking and evaluation. By attuning young people to a set of social relationships similar to those of the work place, schooling attempts to gear the development of personal needs to its requirements.

But the correspondence of schooling with the social relations of production goes beyond this aggregate level. Different levels of education feed workers into different levels within the occupational structure and, correspondingly, tend toward an internal organization comparable to levels in the hierarchical division of labor. The lowest levels in the hierarchy of the enterprise emphasize rule-following, middle levels, dependability, and the capacity to operate without direct and continuous supervision while the higher levels stress the internalization of the norms of the enterprise. Similarly, in education, lower levels (junior and senior high school) tend to severely limit and channel the activities of students. Somewhat higher up the educational ladder, teacher and community colleges allow for more independent activity and less overall supervision. At the top, the elite four-year colleges emphasize social relationships conformable with the higher levels in the production hierarchy. Thus schools continually maintain their hold on students. As they 'master' one type of behavioural regulation, they are either allowed to progress to the next or are channeled into the corresponding level in the hierarchy of production. Even within a single school, the social relationships of different tracks tend to conform to different behavioral norms. Thus in high school, vocational and general tracks emphasize rule-following and close supervision, while the college track tends toward a more open atmosphere emphasizing the internalization of norms.

These differences in the social relationships among and within schools, in part, reflect both the social backgrounds of the student body and their likely future economic positions. Thus blacks and other minorities are concentrated in schools whose repressive, arbitrary, generally chaotic internal order, coercive authority structures, and minimal possibilities for advancement mirror the characteristics of inferior job situations. Similarly, predominantly working-class schools tend to emphasize behavioral control and rule-following, while schools in well-to-do suburbs employ relatively open systems that favor greater student participation, less direct supervision, more student electives, and, in general, a value system stressing internalized standards of control.

The differential socialization patterns of schools attended by students of different social classes do not arise by accident. Rather, they reflect the fact that the educational objectives and expectations of administrators, teachers, and parents (as well as the responsiveness of students to various patterns of teaching and control) differ for students of different social classes. At crucial turning points in the history of US education, changes in the social relations of schooling have been dictated in the interests of a more harmonious reproduction of the class structure. But in the day-to-day operation of the schools, the consciousness of different occupational strata, derived from their cultural milieu and work experience, is crucial to the maintenance of the correspondences we have described. That working-class parents seem to favor stricter educational methods is a reflection of their own work experiences, which have demonstrated that submission to authority is an essential ingredient in one's ability to get and hold a steady, well-paid job. That professional and self-employed parents prefer a more open atmosphere and a greater emphasis on motivational control is similarly a reflection of their position in the social division of labor. When given the opportunity, higher-status parents are far more likely than their lower-status neighbors to choose 'open classrooms' for their children.

Differences in the social relationships of schooling are further reinforced by inequalities in financial resources. The paucity of financial support for the education of children from minority groups and low-income families leaves more resources to be devoted to the children of those with more commanding roles in the economy; it also forces upon the teachers and school administrators in the working-class schools a type of social relationship that fairly closely mirrors that of the factory. Financial considerations in poorly supported schools militate against small intimate classes, multiple elective courses, and specialized teachers (except for disciplinary personnel). They preclude the amounts of free time for teachers and free space required for a more open, flexible educational environment. The well-financed schools attended by the children of the rich can offer much greater opportunities for the development of the capacity for sustained independent work and all the other characteristics required for adequate job performance in the upper levels of the occupational hierarchy.

READING C   SOME COMPARATIVE PRINCIPLES OF EDUCATIONAL STRATIFICATION

Randall Collins

… I shall deal with the historical evidence under three main headings, each of which is associated with different demands for education — practical skills, status-group membership, and bureaucracy. … The three categories may be thought of as corresponding in spirit with Weber's three bases of stratification — class, status and party. …

Source: Collins, R. (1977) 'Some comparative principles of educational stratification', *Harvard Educational Review*, vol.47, no.1, pp.5, 6, 9, 12–13, 20–3, 26.

Practical skills

The most common modern interpretation of the role of education is that it meets the demand for technical skills. Most contemporary evidence, however, contradicts this interpretation. The content of most modern education is not very practical: educational attainment and grades are not much related to work performance, and most technical skills are learned on the job. Although work skills are more complex in *some* modern jobs than in most pre-industrial jobs, in many modern jobs they are not. Similar patterns appear in an overview of societies throughout history. ...

Status-group membership

... In historical perspective education has been used more often for organizing status groups than for other purposes. Since the defining locus of status-group activity is leisure and consumption, status-group education has been sharply distinguished from practical education by the exclusion of materially productive skills. Because status groups have used a common culture as a mark of group membership, status-group education has taken the form of a club and has included much ceremony to demonstrate group solidarity and to publicly distinguish members from non-members. ...

The contents of status-group education ... vary predictably with the class situations of the groups that espouse them. We find aesthetic education, often combined with games and a reverence for tradition, in the status cultures of privileged upper classes. Moral respectability, usually in the form of religious doctrine, has been the cultural ideal of moderately aspiring middle classes or upper working classes. Rising classes in revolutionary periods have often taken practical and scientific education as their cultural ideal. Perhaps, though, we are generalizing about rebellious groups from a set of cases that is too historically limited; the more universal principle might be that revolutionary groups draw on whatever cultural form can be claimed to be both progressive and sharply distinct from traditional status claims.

Bureaucracy

Bureaucracy is a style of organization based on rules and regulations, written reports, and files of records. The use of such written materials tends to make control appear abstract and generalized; bureaucracy makes possible the separation of the individual officeholder from the powers of the position. ... The multiplication of ranks and the setting of regular career sequences with limited periods in each office keep officials concerned with their organizational futures and motivated toward higher offices. Formal examinations maximize the impersonality and competitiveness of the system when they are the basis for entrance into the bureaucracy or promotion within it. ...

Historical evidence indicates that mass, compulsory education was first created not for industrial, but for military and political, discipline. ... Capitalists' interest in using education to ensure labor discipline may have been a force behind the development of mass, compulsory education in some of these countries, but it was not the central motive ... The safer generalization is that bureaucratic states impose compulsory education on populations which are seen as potential threats to state control, and that [those] economic classes which are influential in the state will help define the nature of the 'threat'.

Finally, it seems clear that the initial impetus behind the development of bureaucratized schooling did not come from the bureaucratization of business enterprises. ... Most nineteenth-century British or German clerks were trained through work 'apprenticeship' after elementary schooling in literacy. Even in the twentieth century, managers in Britain and Germany have tended to have had little formal education, because the higher schools have been connected with careers in government and the élite professions. ...

Towards a theory of cultural markets

... We have examined three types of education. Training in practical skills exists in any economy but is usually built informally into the work process. The practical skills of literacy and numeracy have been especially demanded, and sometimes provided by special teachers, wherever there has been literate administration or the development of commerce. Education in the leisure culture of a status group has prospered in relatively peaceful periods during which there is decentralized competition within a wealthy aristocracy, within a prosperous bourgeoisie, or within a rising working class; the nature of the status culture has varied with the groups involved. Highly formal educational systems with specified time sequences, examinations, and elements of compulsion have developed as bureaucratic devices are used, especially by centralized states, to control officials, feudal aristocracies, or, in modern periods of mass political mobilization, the general population.

Historically, these types of education have sometimes combined. To be sure, some of them are theoretically incompatible; for example, aristocratic status education has emphasized aesthetic and leisure themes that are explicitly intended to oppose both practical training and the narrower specializations of thoroughly bureaucratic education. But in practice, these seemingly incompatible types of education have appeared in combination. For example, familiarity with the status culture of the aristocracy has often been used as a criterion for selection of government officials in bureaucratic systems. The Chinese examination system tested the genteel skills of poetic composition and use of literary allusions, just as the British civil-service examinations tested knowledge of the literary classics. In modern times, bureaucratic and compulsory mass education has incorporated elements of practical education by training students in literacy and arithmetic. Similarly, secondary schooling, which developed in post-Renaissance Europe as a support of the status cultures of the prosperous classes, has been incorporated into a standard sequence of educational levels leading up to the university.

Bureaucratization has been the principal means for combining different types of education. The essence of bureaucratic controls is a stress on the keeping of formal regulations and records; any content, whether it be originally aesthetic, religious, legal, scientific, or practical, may be fitted into this system. ... What [modern] educational programs have in common is structural formality: grades, examinations, required sequences, and set time periods for instruction that are absent from the pure forms of practical and status-group education. ...

The various kinds of demand for education — practical, status-group, and bureaucratic — may be viewed more broadly as part of a *cultural market* in which social actors simultaneously attempt to attain certain goals. The interest of government in bureaucratic control over particular classes may mesh with the interest of these very classes in improving their cultural attainments for the sake of status. Thus, we find a symbiosis between the control interest of the Chinese emperors and the status interest of the gentry and, more ironically, between government concern for compulsory educational indoctrination of the modern masses and some interest in status mobility on the part of those masses. The interest of capitalists in ensuring labor discipline adds yet another demand to this market, as does the interest of a particular ethnic group in maintaining its opportunities *vis-à-vis* other ethnic groups ...

The parties that enter the cultural marketplace usually are involved in social conflicts of some sort — whether struggles by economic classes for domination, revolution, or self-improvement, or the more complex conflicts that result when class struggle meshes with the prestige struggle of ethnic or other status groups. The differences among the main types of educational structures in the modern world can be explained by differences among lineups of contending interests. ...

CHAPTER 7 RELIGION, VALUES AND IDEOLOGY

Kenneth Thompson

CONTENTS

1   INTRODUCTION

How important is a shared culture in binding people together in a modern society? Is it necessary for a society's existence that people should share certain values and beliefs in order for them to engage in social cooperation, or it is enough that they seek to maximize their individual interests or that they submit to the dull compulsion of routine and necessity? Finally, does culture affect how people perceive their interests and, even, their sense of themselves as individuals with an identity derived from membership of some larger community or grouping? In the previous chapter, Geoff Whitty dealt with educational processes that contribute to the construction and reproduction of national cultures. (See also Book 1 (Hall and Gieben, 1992), where Chapter 5 deals with cultural formations in the emergence of modern society, and Chapter 6 discusses the links between discourses and power in the construction of a new sense of cultural identity in Western Europe.)

These questions about the part played by culture in modern society have been central to sociology since its emergence in the nineteenth century, and religion has figured prominently in the debates. This is not surprising in view of the derivations of the two terms 'religion' and 'sociology':

> The term 'religion' is derived from *religio*, the bond of social relations between individuals; the term 'sociology' is derived from *socius*, the bond of companionship that constitutes societies. Following Durkheim (1961), we may define religion as a set of beliefs and practices, relating to the sacred, which create social bonds between individuals. We may define sociology, naively, as the 'science of community' (MacIver, 1917, p.45). Sociology in general and the sociology of religion in particular, are thus concerned with the processes which unite and disunite, bind and unbind social relationships in space and time.
> (Turner, 1983, p.8)

However, modern industrial societies are often referred to as 'secular societies', meaning that religious, or other absolute moral values, no longer play a central role as cultural bonds uniting and disuniting social relationships (as Robert Bocock explained in Book 1 (Hall and Gieben, 1992), Chapter 5 on 'Culture and the transition to modernity'). Is this the case? Or might there be another side to the story in which there could still be some such cultural bonds operating as a kind of cultural 'cement' to varying degrees in modern society? This is the main issue we will be addressing in this chapter. It seems to be a topical question if we are to judge from some of the most heated public controversies of recent years. The political movements of the New Right that came to prominence during the 1980s in Britain, America, and some other western countries, were also moral reform movements, supported by the so-called 'Moral Majority' and various pressure groups campaigning over moral issues concerning the family, sex, abortion, education, broadcasting, etc. Above all, however, these were struggles to define or redefine national culture and identity. On some issues, such as government social policies, some of the most prominent critics of the New Right were to be found among bishops of the Church of England and the American Catholic Bishops Conference (both churches produced official reports that criticized government social and economic policies on moral grounds). Whatever the merits of the arguments coming from different sides of these controversies, the amount of attention devoted to them by the mass media suggested that questions concerning the cultural and moral bases of society were still regarded as vitally important.

The discussion of the issues in this chapter will be structured as follows:

1   We will begin by considering what social thinkers in the wake of the Enlightenment had to say about the dilemma which the development of modernity had produced: namely how to reconcile the critique, even the overthrow, of traditional social bonds with the need for some new basis of moral community. Some of the heirs of the Enlightenment, whether in the social sciences or in liberal, reformist and socialist political movements, believed that science, and the reorganization of society along more rational lines, would supply adequate foundations for the new social order. At the same time, there were occasional suggestions that some elements of the sacred basis of social order might still persist, even though the process of secularization in the *public* sphere would mean that religion and other 'pre-modern' or 'irrational' philosophies would be increasingly confined to the *private* sphere.

2   We will examine some of the theories and evidence about the process of secularization in order to determine to what extent these predictions have been borne out. Some attention will be given to the suggestion by a recent social philosopher, Alasdair MacIntyre, that bonds of community based on shared moral values of an absolute sort have declined, leaving only appeals to people's feelings as the ground for moral judgment. However, we will see that surveys of beliefs and values show that some values are quite widely shared in modern societies.

3   These considerations lead on to a critique of that aspect of the secularization thesis which maintains that there is a separation between the public and private spheres, and that religion is increasingly confined to the private sphere. Foucault's account of the ways in which social integration is ensured on the basis of power mediated through dominant discourses will be used to raise questions about the separation of the public and private spheres. It also raises questions about the authority of such discourses and whether they are purely secular, or whether they still have traces of a religious, or sacred/ absolute element, which produce feelings of moral obligation and guilt.

4   Finally, we will combine insights drawn from a number of theorists, including Gramsci, Althusser and Durkheim, who have analysed those cultural processes that have the effect of creating ideological communities and identities. Here the emphasis is on the symbolic and ritual aspects of discourses. Our aim is to examine the claim that, although there may not be a single dominant ideology based on shared values in a modern society, there are cultural processes that reproduce some social integration. For example, there is a certain degree of cultural integration to the extent that people are won over by the symbolic appeal of a combination of discourses, as in the appeal of the 'imagined community' of the nation.

To summarize: It will be argued that the transition to modernity has not been marked by total eradication of the sacred and the triumph of the secular-profane. As Durkheim predicted, there will always be some sacred cultural elements in even the most modern, secularized society. On a day-to-day basis, these are likely to be less prominent than the rationalities and routines of mundane activities. However, there are traces of such sacred elements on three levels of culture that we will examine: belief in God and certain traditional moral values; discourses and discursive practices that regulate behaviour; and ideological or 'imagined' communities such as the nation. In this chapter, therefore, we will look for the traces which may reveal elements of culture that have a sacred character, or can take on such a character when activated by emotional appeals or threats. Gramsci described this search for traces as making an inventory of the 'stratified deposits' of all the previous ways of thinking that make up a culture. This can be a way of knowing oneself 'as a product of the historical process to date which has deposited in you an infinity of traces, without leaving an inventory' (Gramsci, 1971, p.324). You might like to think of the sections of this chapter as suggesting ways in which you could draw up your own inventory of such traces in yourself.

ACTIVITY 1   Ask yourself the question: What, if anything, do I hold sacred?

Can you make a list, or inventory, of the key ideas and beliefs that have influenced your 'philosophy'? In your opinion, how widely held are these beliefs and where do they come from?

2   ENLIGHTENMENT: THE DILEMMAS OF MODERNITY

The critical thought of the Enlightenment challenged the dominance of religion in the realms of ideas, including social and political thought, and the French Revolution seemed to deal a fatal blow to traditional institutions that embodied those ideas. Both in the realm of thought and the institutional sphere, modern societies were loosening their religious ties: they were described as undergoing a process of 'secularization'. The question for an emerging sociology was: What, if anything, will take the place of these ties? Could there be, or need there be, new ties that would serve the same social functions as religion?

Sociology was born in the nineteenth century in the aftermath of the French Revolution and in the midst of the socially disruptive developments of industrialization and urbanization. Old community ties were being broken and the new social relations were largely contractual, as between individual buyers and sellers, including individuals who sold their labour and those who bought it. According to Karl Marx, this kind of relationship was bound to produce alienation and conflict. In the short term, the conflict might be kept down if the real nature of the exploitative relations could be masked by 'ideology' — ways of thinking that distract or distort perception — and so produce a 'false consciousness'. He explained the persistence and apparent revivals of religion by arguing that these served the interests of the dominant class, whilst recognizing that it answered some real needs for believers, even if the causes of those needs were socially derived. Marx's radical diagnosis was that religion, or ideologies serving similar functions, would not finally disappear, despite the intellectual critiques of the Enlightenment, until there was a revolutionary change in social relations. The political revolutions in France had not gone far enough because they had not produced a revolutionary change in economic relations. For this reason, Marx and Engels did not expect to see an automatic process of secularization in which religion would wither away, particularly in its adaptable modern form. Marx explained that, as far as western capitalist society was concerned, Christianity, especially Protestantism, was an ideally suitable belief system:

> The religious world is but the reflex of the real world. And for a society based upon the production of commodities, in which the producers in general enter into social relations with one another by treating their products as commodities and values, whereby they reduce their individual private labour to the standard of homogeneous human labour — for such a society, Christianity with its *cultus* of abstract man, more especially in its bourgeois developments, protestantism, Deism, etc., is the most fitting form of religion.
> (Marx, 1974, vol. 1, p.83, and in Marx and Engels, 1955, p.135)

Engels maintained that such modern forms of monotheistic religion would prove extremely durable: 'In this convenient, handy, and universally adaptable form, religion can continue to exist as the immediate, that is, the sentimental form of men's relation to the alien natural and social forces which dominate them, so long as men remain under the control of these forces' (Engels in Marx and Engels, 1955, p.148).

Less radical social theorists feared that society would indeed disintegrate if there was not religion, or an equivalent belief system to bind it together. In France, Alexis de Tocqueville (1805–59) warned of the socially disintegrative effects of the decline in shared 'public virtues' and the increasing individualism, which involved the apathetic withdrawal of individuals from public life into a private sphere, absorbed in pure egoism, with a dangerous weakening of social bonds. He pinned his hopes on the development of voluntary associations between the State and the individual. Later in the century, this theme was developed by Émile Durkheim, who made causal connections between high rates of suicide resulting from conditions of egoism (an exaggerated emphasis on the self) and 'anomie' (that is the absence of shared values and norms of behaviour). Durkheim found lower rates of suicide among Catholics and Jews compared with Protestants. He thought that the excessive individualism of Protestantism was a major cause of this, compared to the stronger communal ties among Catholics and Jews. Similarly, there were lower rates in wartime, when even Protestants felt their social ties more strongly and had a sense of common national identity (a finding borne out in Britain during the Falklands War). He noted that the French Revolution had given rise to attempts to establish a religion of reason, in order to create a new sacred basis for society. He thought that such efforts to create such a basis for a nation-state would recur in one form or another.

Victory parade after the Falklands War, 1982

According to Max Weber, with the disappearance of the ethical
foundations of economic activity, such as those provided by the
Protestant Ethic, cooperation would rest on the narrow basis of
individuals' rational calculation of how far they could pursue their
interests without breaking the law. The ideas of pursuing a vocation and
of altruistic service, which provided a religious foundation for the ethic
of the professions, would wither in this climate. With the decline in
traditional bases of authority, the only alternatives were rational-legal
authority (such as rule-following in a bureaucracy) or charismatic
authority, based on irrational attraction to a leader, in a devotion and
identification akin to that of love. Whilst Durkheim believed that there
would inevitably be periodic revivals of sacred social ties, Weber was
more sceptical and simply expressed the hope that 'entirely new
prophets', or charismatic leaders, would emerge to give a new moral
basis to modern societies.

The issue, of whether modern societies are exhausting their 'cultural
capital' of shared values and are likely to face increasing social
problems as a result, was given a topical expression in the 1990 BBC
Reith Lectures on 'The Persistence of Faith'. In his first lecture, the
Chief Rabbi-elect (as he then was), Jonathan Sachs, claimed that the
crumbling of Communism in Eastern Europe during 1989 had been as
significant a turning point in history as 1789, the year of the French
Revolution and the birth of the secular state. In the middle of it all, the
American historian Francis Fukuyama wrote an article, 'The end of
history?' stating that the struggle between competing ideologies, or sets
of social values and ideals, was virtually dead. (This article (Fukuyama,
1989) is discussed more fully by David Held in Book 4 (Hall *et al.*,
1992), Chapter 1.) Instead, we would increasingly see societies based on
nothing but 'economic calculation, the endless solving of technical
problems, environmental concerns, and the satisfaction of sophisticated
consumer demands'. Sachs responded by arguing that: 'The human
being as consumer neither is, nor can be, all we are, and a social system
built on that premise will fail'. He set out the dilemmas posed by the
transition from traditional communities, where identities, beliefs and
life chances were narrowly circumscribed, to a modern situation in
which careers, relationships and lifestyles have become things to be
chosen from a superstore of alternatives:

> Modernity is the transition from fate to choice. At the same time it
> dissolves the commitments and loyalties that once lay behind our
> choices. Technical reason has made us masters of matching means
> to ends. But it has left us inarticulate as to why we should choose
> one end rather than another. The values that once led us to regard
> one as intrinsically better than another — and which gave such
> weight to words like good and bad — have disintegrated, along
> with the communities and religious traditions in which we learned
> them. Now we choose because we choose. Because it is what we
> want; or it works for us; or it feels right to me. Once we have
> dismantled a world in which larger virtues held sway, what is left

are success and self-expression, the key values of an individualistic culture.

But can a society survive on so slender a moral base? It is a question that was already raised in the nineteenth century by figures like Alexis de Tocqueville and Max Weber, who saw most clearly the connection between modern liberal democracies and Judaeo-Christian tradition. It was de Tocqueville who saw that religion tempered individualism and gave those engaged in the competitive economy a capacity for benevolence and self-sacrifice. And it was he who saw that this was endangered by the very pursuit of affluence that was the key to economic growth.

Max Weber delivered the famous prophetic warning that the cloak of material prosperity might eventually become an iron cage. It was already becoming an end in itself, and other values were left, in his words, 'like the ghost of dead religious beliefs'. Once capitalism consumed its religious foundations, both men feared the consequences.

The stresses of a culture without shared meanings are already mounting, and we have yet to count the human costs. We see them in the move from a morality of self-imposed restraint to one in which we increasingly rely on law to protect us from ourselves. In the past, disadvantaged groups could find in religion what Karl Marx called 'the feeling of a heartless world'. A purely economic order offers no such consolations. A culture of success places little value on the unsuccessful.

The erosion of those bonds of loyalty and love which religion undergirded has left us increasingly alone in an impersonal economic and social system. Emile Durkheim was the first to give this condition a name. He called it anomie: the situation in which individuals have lost their moorings in a collective order. It is the heavy price we pay for our loss of communities of faith.
(Sachs, 1990, p.6)

Although advanced from a religious point of view, this statement of the dilemmas faced by modern societies corresponds in many respects to those identified by social theorists in the post-Enlightenment period, as the references to figures such as Marx, de Tocqueville, Durkheim and Weber make clear. According to these theorists, the long historical processes which formed modern industrial society included fundamental cultural developments. (Some examples of these are discussed by Robert Bocock in Book 1 (Hall and Gieben, 1992), Chapter 5.) They included such tendencies as increased differentiation of institutions, thereby increasing cultural variations between social spheres, progressive rationalization of more and more areas of life, demystification of the world, and the civilizing of patterns of behaviour in everyday life. An underlying theme was that of 'secularization': the reduction of the space occupied by religion in social life. This theme of

secularization has remained central to sociological theories of
modernity. However, as mentioned above, from the beginning of
sociology there has been a debate about whether modern societies could
exist without some balancing tendency to that of progressive
secularization: that is, what might be termed 'sacralization' tendencies.
Even Max Weber, who emphasized the role of processes of
demystification and progressive rationalization giving rise to
secularization of the modern world, nevertheless talked about periodic
explosions of 'charisma' and charismatic leadership; he also
emphasized the part played by religion in the formation of modern
notions of the individual and in the development of capitalism.
Similarly, his French contemporary, Émile Durkheim, whilst
emphasizing increasing specialization of the division of labour and the
rights of the individual, also wrote about periodic revivals of sacred
elements in society:

> Also, in the present day just as much as in the past, we see society
> constantly creating sacred things out of ordinary ones. If it
> happens to fall in love with a man and if it thinks it has found in
> him the principal aspirations that move it, as well as the means of
> satisfying them, this man will be raised above the others and, as it
> were, deified. ...This aptitude of society for setting itself up as a
> god or for creating gods was never more apparent than during the
> first years of the French Revolution. At this time, in fact, under the
> influence of the general enthusiasm, things purely laical by nature
> were transformed by public opinion into sacred things: these were
> the Fatherland, Liberty, Reason.
> (Durkheim, 1961, pp.243–5)

During the First World War, Durkheim noted that the communal
experience of warfare had created a moral consensus in France and an
involvement in public ceremonies, which had served to accentuate the
sense of being part of a sacred community.

It seems to be the case, therefore, that for the early sociologists, both
tendencies co-exist in the cultures of modern societies — secularization
and sacralization. Societies do become more differentiated into
specialized institutional spheres of activity, with each institution
enjoying a degree of relative autonomy, and so there is less scope for
tight social integration by an overarching belief system, particularly one
that prescribes standard norms for behaviour in all public and private
spheres. However, this does not rule out the possibility that some
inherited values, symbols and discourses may persist and be drawn on
in recurring efforts to create cultural or ideological unity. These efforts
may take various forms, such as moral crusades, revivals of nationalism,
or religious revivals. We will concentrate on just two questions. The
first is to ask whether there is an inevitable tendency in modern society
for secularization to result in a loss of moral consensus and so of any
shared cultural basis for social solidarity or community? The second
question asks whether there are contrary tendencies, such as tendencies

that make the 'imagined community' of the nation into a sacred collectivity? The latter tendency occurs where there is an appeal to some collective identity derived from membership of an 'imagined community' (Anderson, 1983), which can involve combinations of the discourses of nationalism, ethnicity and religion. We will examine some of the cultural processes involved in these trends, in the next section.

3   SECULARIZATION AND COMMUNITY

Rabbi Sachs' concern about the loss of moral community in modern society bears a strong resemblance to the theme of 'secularization' that has been a major strand in the theoretical legacy of Enlightenment social theory. At one level, secularization refers to a process of institutional differentiation, commencing in the Middle Ages and linked to the processes of industrialization, urbanization and the rise of science. According to the secularization thesis, the bonds of community are subject to irreversible decline, and relationships between persons are reduced to the instrumental/technical level outside close family and friendship networks (Wilson, 1982; Dobbelaere, 1981). This historical process of secularization is said to be paralleled by a rejection of philosophical notions of an essential human nature and purpose, such as those of Aristotle which informed medieval thinking. According to the social theorist, Alistair MacIntyre, the coherence of the medieval moral scheme was destroyed and the Enlightenment project of discovering rational secular foundations for morality collapsed in failure (MacIntyre, 1981). In his view, the result is a decline into 'emotivism' in the twentieth century, where the only ground for making moral judgements is that which appeals to feelings. Although some claim that this represents an increase in individual choice and freedom from moral constraints, it runs the danger of leaving individuals open to manipulation. The commercial appeal is to individual rather than collective satisfaction, which makes it difficult to appeal for restraint (e.g. appeals for wage restraint to curb inflation) or to encourage community care on a moral basis. According to Wilson, the collapse of community means that 'the large-scale social system...seeks not to rely on a moral order, but rather ...on a technical order ... Where morality must persist, then it can be politicized, and subject to the direct coercive power of the state': for example in the case of sexual or racial discrimination (Wilson, 1982, p.161).

Is it the case that there is now no moral community in modern society? And are the main cultural processes that reproduce social order to be found in various institutional discourses, or in the manipulation of emotions, such as those evoked in nationalism? If there are still significant traces of religion in these different cultural processes then it could be that modern societies have not yet used up that part of their 'cultural capital'.

ACTIVITY 2 Now read **Reading A, 'The population: religious disposition, belief and practice at a glance'**, by David Gerard, which you will find at the end of this chapter.

The findings reported here are from the British section of the European Value Systems Study Group survey carried out in the early 1980s, which compared beliefs in several European countries.

How far do the findings on beliefs and values in Britain substantiate the contention that there are now no absolute grounds for moral values and so there can be no moral consensus in modern society?

The findings of the European Value System Survey (Abrams *et al.*, 1985) show that in Britain, which is supposedly one of the most secularized societies, there is still a very high level of generalized commitment to belief in the existence of God, however vague, and also a high degree of consensus on moral issues and continuing commitment in principle to the Old Testament commandments. There is less explicit commitment to absolute, as opposed to relative, guidelines concerning good and evil. Clearly, therefore, in view of these findings about the persistence of a shared core of values, it would be difficult to substantiate the most extreme version of the secularization thesis.

In contrast to the stark version of the secularization thesis, there are a number of alternative perspectives. One perspective, whilst accepting that aspect of the secularization thesis concerning institutional differentiation and loss of the overarching social significance of religion, argues that religion does not necessarily decline, but rather evolves and changes its form. It adapts in response to wider social and cultural forces. The adaptation will vary between societies, groups and periods. One obvious contrast is between the high level of religious activity in America and the relatively low levels in Western Europe (Eastern European countries have varied, with high involvement in Poland and lower levels in some other countries such as Hungary.) There are also variations in terms of strategies of resistance or accommodation to wider cultural trends, and in terms of what is 'sacred'. (Although we will focus on Western societies, it is in non-western societies that one might find some of the most striking examples of varied strategies of resistance or accommodation to global trends such as modernization and secularization. It would be instructive to compare Islamic and Buddhist cultures in this respect.)

ACTIVITY 3 Now read **Reading B, 'Religious change and institutional involvement'**, by David Gerard.

What are some of the main adaptations of religion in modern societies?

What explanations are offered for different patterns of people's involvement in religion?

The main adaptations of religion in modern Western societies are divided into two sorts. The first sort concerns formal religious groups (churches, denominations and sects) and the extent to which they accommodate themselves to mainstream social trends. American religious organizations appear to have been particularly successful in fitting in with the demands of the wider society and meeting the needs of their constituents. European churches have been less successful at adaptation, although the prominence of religion in the recent changes in some East European countries suggests that religion can still be a powerful force when combined with other discourses, such as nationalism. The second sort of adaptation is concerned with informal or 'invisible' religion, which would seem to be infinitely variable as it leaves individuals free to construct their own meaning systems and versions of the sacred. However, there are problems in pinning down such beliefs and in discovering how much commitment people have to them.

Religious involvement is clearly not uniform throughout society, but is related to key socio-demographic indicators, such as age, sex, class, occupation and education. Other important determining factors that have been suggested include experiences of deprivation of various kinds (e.g. loss of health, loss of close relatives or friends, loss of status, etc.), involvement in certain types of industry, and the decline or persistence of local community. Forecasts of future trends on the basis of the present religious involvements of different age groups have sometimes produced contradictory conclusions.

Strategies of religious adaptation in modern society range from accommodation — going along with cultural trends (sometimes referred to disparagingly as 'internal secularization') — to various strategies of resistance. Weber, and his colleague Tönnies, drew a sharp contrast between the church type of religious organization, which represented the response of accommodation to society, and the sect type, which was oppositional. However, Bryan Wilson points out that the picture is more complicated and he has sub-divided sects into seven types of response to the world:

1   The *conversionist* sect: typical of evangelical, fundamentalist Christianity, which aims to change a corrupt world by changing individuals, as in the case of the Salvation Army in its early days. This response may also take the form of a cult of those who follow a charismatic leader, as in the case of followers of certain 'televangelists' in America.

2   The *revolutionary* sect: these groups look forward to the passing of the present social order, as in the case of Jehovah's Witnesses, and the Fifth Monarchy Men of seventeenth-century England.

3   The *introversionist* sect: here the response to the world is not to try to convert it or to overturn it, but to retire from it and seek the security of personal holiness as with certain 'holiness movements'.

4   The *manipulationist* sect: examples of this type are Christian Scientists, Rosacrucians and Scientologists, who claim some special

knowledge and techniques for attaining goals generally accepted by society.

5   The *thaumaturgical* sect: this is composed of people who come together more as an audience than a fellowship, in order to make contact with the supernatural for personal purposes, as with Spiritualists who seek contact with dead relatives.

6   The *reformist* sect: this is often a later stage, rather than the original orientation, of a sect (such as the Quakers), and the sect remains separate and apart in order to provide a critique and an ethic for the society to which it is no longer hostile or indifferent.

7   The *utopian* sect: here the response to the world is mainly that of withdrawal into a perfectionist community life, as with the Tolstoyan communities and some 'hippie' communes in the 1960s.

It is worth noting that at the time when Wilson developed this typology of sectarian responses (Wilson,1963), its relevance seemed to be confined to relatively small groups in marginal organizations. Such groups were on the fringes of society and had little impact on mainstream political and cultural life. The subsequent 'cultural revolutions' of the late 1960s and the conservative reactions of the late-1970s and 1980s have shown that such sectarian responses to the world can be much more widespread in their impact and have an effect on mainstream culture. The rise of the New Christian Right or Moral Majority in support of Reaganism in America, and the controversies over religion and Thatcherism in Britain in the 1980s, testify to the capacity for religious discourses to enter into potent combinations with others, such as political, economic and nationalist discourses. It is clear that the contrast between accommodation and resistance does not necessarily equate with different types of religious organization, such as the church-sect typology. The political ideology of Thatcherism was supported by many fundamentalist sect members and opposed by a number of bishops of the Church of England. Meanwhile in Latin America and Eastern Europe the Roman Catholic Church provided some of the strongest resistance to the dominant political forces.

The extent to which religion continues to play an important role in the public life of modern societies depends on a combination of factors. For example, Wallis and Bruce (1986) compared the relationship between a particular form of religion — conservative Protestantism — and politics in several societies, and found that there was a limited range of patterns. These were placed on a continuum between two types of society. The first type of society was that in which conservative Protestantism had a high degree of impact on politics (e.g. Ulster and South Africa). At the other end were societies where conservative Protestantism had little continuous significant impact on politics, but in which it might be periodically mobilized for issue specific campaigns to amend some unacceptable feature of society (e.g. Canada, Australia, New Zealand, England and Scotland). Occupying an intermediate position were societies in which conservative Protestants were able to exercise some continuing influence on the political process over a broad

Parade of Orangemen in Northern Ireland

range of concerns and possessed established institutional machinery for articulating their political views, but did not dominate the social and cultural basis of politics, having to compete with other organized blocks of opinion (e.g. the USA, Netherlands and Scandinavia). Wallis and Bruce suggested that these patterns can be explained in terms of certain specifiable factors:

1   the circumstances of formation of the socio-religious culture;

2   the changes which have occurred affecting the socio-religious culture, especially patterns of migration, secularization and church accommodation;

3   the structure of politics and communications in the surrounding society (Wallis and Bruce, 1986, p.231).

In summary, their argument is that a high level of political involvement on the part of conservative Protestants results from:

1   a socio-religious culture formed by sectarianism, rather than more tolerant denominations or a state church;

2   a situation where subsequent social changes continue to threaten the dominance of the ethnic group, but its own identity is not diluted by subsequent waves of immigrants of heterogeneous cultural character;

3   a structure of politics and communication which inhibits a cohesive two party system along class lines.

Perhaps the most interesting examples are the intermediate cases, such as the United States and the Netherlands, because they illustrate how a minority religious group can maintain a strong base within an advanced industrial society and exert considerable influence at times. In the American case, conservative Protestantism has been able to benefit from the high degree of regionalism in American politics, the susceptibility of national politicians to pressure groups (e.g. 'political action committees'), and from the fact that groups can buy time on radio or television or purchase their own station. Although there is some debate about how important 'new Christian right' organizations such as the Moral Majority were in American politics during the 1980s, there is no doubt that they had considerable influence, especially in local politics. In the Netherlands there is a different structure. The Calvinists created a series of institutions to oppose the influence of secular liberalism and Catholicism, including separate trades unions, schools and a political party, the Anti-Revolutionary Party. These divisions were carried into almost every sphere of Dutch life, producing three integrated 'pillars' (*zuilen*) containing all the institutions essential to modern life, within which individuals could conduct their activities and form their own *weltanschauung* (world view). This situation is known as *verzuiling*: 'columnization' or 'pillarization' (Wallis and Bruce, 1986, p.231).

Such examples of the public role of religion also call into question the assumption in the secularization thesis that religion retreats into the private sphere. However, there is some truth in Luckmann's contention that the secularization thesis ignores the extent to which 'invisible' religion thrives in the private sphere, even if it appears to decline in the public sphere (Luckmann, 1967). Luckmann shares his colleague Peter Berger's phenomenological perspective in which individuals are seen as creating their own private meaning systems, which provide them with an interpretative framework and chosen identity. This view is contradicted by Foucault's work on discourses, which insists that prevailing notions of individuality tend to be moulded to suit the interests of the dominant powers. As Beckford puts it,

> Indeed, the most provocative and disturbing aspect of Foucault's thought is the implication that the very idea of privatized religion, far from being marginal to the operation of modern society, might actually be a pre-condition for the latter's success. It would be thoroughly in keeping with his philosophical position for Foucault to have regarded the belief that private thoughts and feelings were marginal to the reproduction of societal domination as evidence that exactly the opposite was true, namely, that effective control and surveillance was conditional upon the belief that the individual could be considered as an autonomous monad.
> (Beckford, 1989, p.127)

Foucault's ideas are explored further in the next section of this chapter.

4 FOUCAULT: INTEGRATION THROUGH DISCOURSES

Foucault calls into question the usefulness of examining cultural integration on the basis of a single dominant ideology. In particular, he questions the assumption that societies have ever been integrated on the basis of anything other than power, mediated through the dominant discourses of the period. The religious input to these discourses has always been considerable: discourses and discursive practices concerning the self, the body, sexuality, death, illness, health and spiritual well-being, as well as discourses of human rights, justice and peace. (Foucault's work on power and mental illness and on sexuality was discussed earlier, in Chapters 4 and 5 of this book, for example.) As Beckford points out, one of the effects of Foucault's approach is to show that the very distinction between private and public spheres is itself a cultural product; similarly, the meaning attributed to the 'individual' and to the individual's rights and beliefs derive from particular cultural-historical contexts. Foucault would have been reluctant to accept the idea that personal meanings, or values, have been cut adrift from systems of public regulation in modern societies.

ACTIVITY 4   Now read **Reading C, 'Confession'**, by Michel Foucault, and then **Reading D, 'Domination and its discontents: Michel Foucault'**, by James Beckford.

In what ways does Foucault's work on discourses bring into question the distinction between private and public, especially as made by those sociologists of religion who locate religion in the private, as distinct from the public, sphere of modern societies?

Foucault's work on discourses and discursive practices, such as sex and confession, helps us to understand some of the ways in which modern societies cohere at the cultural level by constructing and regulating individuals and their subjectivity. One of the social functions of discourses is that they close off alternative ways of speaking and thinking, often in ways that reflect the distribution of power in society. In this respect discourses have an effect similar to that of ideology as portrayed by Marx, for whom 'the ideas of the ruling class are, in every age, the ruling ideas: i.e. the class which is the dominant material force in society is at the same time its dominant *intellectual* force' (Marx and Engels, 1972, p.172). However, although Foucault showed that there may be similarities (or articulations) between discourses of different topics at any one time, which strengthen their power, it is important to stress that they may also conflict. At various moments in the history of western societies, for example, different and contradictory discourses of the individual have co-existed, some of which stressed a freedom to act, whilst others emphasized the individual's duty to society. (See the *Penguin Dictionary of Sociology:* DISCOURSE.)

Confession at Gdansk:
Polish shipyard strikers

5 GRAMSCI: THE STRUGGLE FOR IDEOLOGICAL HEGEMONY

Marx's ideas on ideology have also been developed by Gramsci in directions that emphasize the fact that there may be conflict and struggle over ideologies in modern society. (See the *Penguin Dictionary of Sociology:* GRAMSCI; DISCOURSE; and HEGEMONY.) The *Selections from Prison Notebooks* (Gramsci, 1971) written between 1929 and 1935, have been important in this respect. Gramsci insisted on the relative independence of politics and ideology from economic determinants and emphasized the ways in which people can change their circumstances by struggle. The capitalist class could not secure domination by economic factors alone, and it might have to resort to political coercion through the state, but increasingly it sought to attain domination through the ideological apparatuses of civil society — the churches, the family, education and even trades unions. (If he were alive today, he would probably give a prominent place in that list to the media of mass communication.) He suggested that this ideological domination (hegemony) was seldom complete because the working class had a dual consciousness, one part of which reflected the ideas of the capitalist class and its intellectuals, whilst the other part was a common sense knowledge derived from the workers' everyday experience of the world.

Gramsci's ideas have been particularly influential in the study of ideologies in relation to the culture of everyday life and popular culture. Gramsci maintained that moral and philosophical intellectual leadership (hegemony) could only be achieved by connecting up with the common-sense, or popular culture, of the subordinate classes. There are many layers of different cultural elements within such cultures: residues of old philosophies and practices, folklore, superstitions, popular religion (as distinct from intellectually formulated, official religion), local and family customs. In modern society this popular culture is frequently penetrated by elements of mass media culture, which become lodged in the common consciousness: hence the popularity of 'golden-oldies' programmes, particularly at times of nostalgic remembrance, such as Christmas and New Year's Eve. It is not surprising, therefore, that an Open University course on 'Popular Culture' began with a case study of Christmas. It was pointed out that discourses focusing on the family were accorded a pivotal significance in the Christmas editions of the popular press and television programmes. A number of other ideological themes or discourses were articulated with, or grafted on to this concern with the family, especially discourses of community and of the nation, through which real social divisions were transcended and an idealized past was symbolically recaptured. Raymond Williams, in his *The Country and the City* (1975) provided a detailed historical study of this ideology, showing how the series of contrasts it draws — between the past and present, the country and the city, the simple and the complex, the individual and the mass, the naive and the corrupted — have been strongly present in English literature since the sixteenth century, and especially since the development of industrial capitalism in the early nineteenth century. It is probably not fortuitous that a nostalgic idealization of the past has been a core element in the inherited repertoire of ideological themes handed down to us from the Victorian period. In his *Leisure in the Industrial Revolution* (1980), Hugh Cunningham argues that the development of the provision of Christmas parties for members of the working class by philanthropic organizations such as the Mechanics Institutes during the 1830s and 1840s, a period of acute class conflict, was conceived very much as an enterprise in class amelioration. He suggests that the symbols of 'Olde England', with which such parties were festooned, formed part of 'a romantic attempt to re-create a socially-harmonious medieval past' (p.101), to transport the members of different classes from the real antagonism of the present into an imaginary universe of class-concord founded on tradition. These symbols are still at work in Christmas card scenes of snow-covered villages and families of all classes flocking into the village church or singing carols with neighbours round the Christmas tree. Many of the customs and rituals that regulate our practice of Christmas — rituals of neighbourliness and charity, family and local traditions — can be seen as binding us at the level of our behaviour to an imaginatively reconstructed past, a golden age of warm community. Such Christmas themes, with their idealized solutions to social difficulties, cannot be separated, in western societies, from their Christian basis:

> It is by virtue of this sedimented substratum of Christian belief that, no matter how much Christmas may have been secularized, Christmas is the period of the year *par excellence* in which we are constituted as subjects of the 'as if'; that is, induced to live our relations to the world *as if* certain conditions that we know do not obtain did exist, *as if* imaginary ways of posing and resolving real difficulties were practicable.
> (The Open University, 1981, p.63)

Of course, there is another side to Christmas, as we all know. The idealized picture of harmony in family, community and nation, is

Christmas tree in Trafalgar Square: given by the people of Oslo as a mark of Britain's help during the Second World War

constantly in danger of being shattered. Christmas is often a time of tension and strain for families. Local communities, and the nation at large, may be shocked by the realities of homelessness, drunken behaviour and violence. Even the Church has had to struggle to safeguard this Christian festival against complete take-over by popular culture, whether carnivalesque revelry or commercialization.

Gramsci insisted that there was nothing automatic about the working of ideology — the different discourses and cultures were not articulated together without constant effort and even contestation. He frequently illustrated this problem by reference to religion and the efforts of the Catholic Church to cement different classes and their cultures into a single social bloc:

> The problem is that of preserving the ideological unity of the entire social bloc which that ideology serves to cement and unify. The strength of religions, and of the Catholic Church in particular, has lain, and still lies, in the fact that they feel very strongly the need for the doctrinal unity of the whole mass of the faithful and strive to ensure that the higher intellectual stratum does not get separated from the lower. The Roman church has always been the most vigorous in the struggle to prevent the 'official' formation of two religions, one for the 'intellectuals' and the other for the 'simple souls'.
> (Gramsci, 1971, p.328)

In so far as ideological unity is achieved in a culturally complex and class-divided society, it is secured by an articulating principle which ties together the various cultural elements or discourses. Ideological struggle is concerned with efforts to put such an articulating principle into effect, which can entail 'disarticulation' and 'rearticulation' of cultural layers or discourses. Gramsci gave some indication as to what would determine the victory of one hegemonic principle over another when he declared that a hegemonic principle did not prevail by virtue of its intrinsic logic but rather when it manages to become a 'popular religion'. He explained what this means by stating that a class which wishes to become hegemonic has to 'nationalize itself', and that:

> the particular form in which the hegemonic ethico-political element presents itself in the life of the state and the country is 'patriotism' and 'nationalism', which is 'popular religion', that is to say it is the link by means of which the unity of leaders and led is effected.
> (Gramsci, 1975, vol.2, p.1084, and in Mouffe, 1981, p.232)

In the next section on 'Ideological community' we will examine some of the ways in which different discourses are articulated together (combined in new ways) to construct particular versions of the nation as an imagined community. The analysis will draw on Durkheim's sociology of religion and Althusser's theory of ideology in addition to the ideas that we have already covered. Althusser's contribution is significant because it marked another step forward in the reformulation of Marx's theory of ideology, moving away from economic determinism and the idea that ideology is merely an illusion, and also developing Gramsci's ideas on hegemony through the concept of ideological state apparatuses. (See the *Penguin Dictionary of Sociology:* ALTHUSSER and IDEOLOGICAL STATE APPARATUSES.)

6 IDEOLOGICAL COMMUNITY

Durkheim's theory of religion was based on the study of totemism in the aboriginal, classless, societies of Australia and North America, but it was intended to have a wider applicability to modern societies. Although he did not use the word 'ideology' in this connection, it can be argued that his theory has some similarities to theories of ideology as developed by Marxists such as Althusser. Both Durkheim and Althusser described the socially binding functions of ideologies, and emphasized the ways in which they gave individuals a sense of identity. According to Durkheim, religious beliefs and practices are collective representations that carry and bestow authority because they seem to emanate from a transcendent source: they transcend the individual, sectional interests, utilitarian or mundane considerations. They have a 'halo of disinterestedness', as Benedict Anderson says of the ties that bind us to the nation as an 'imagined community' (Anderson, 1983). Durkheim also provides examples of the symbolic codes through which these systems of representation are constructed in the form of discursive chains that articulate differences and unity. (Durkheim's structuralist approach was discussed by Bocock in Book 1 (Hall and Gieben, 1992), Chapter 5.) For example, in the case of the totemic religion of the clan-based societies of the Australian aborigines, sometimes the collective representations are arranged in terms of differences that accord with a binary logic of opposition, such as sacred versus profane; others are unitary like the clan totem. These categories are socially constraining; they set rules of thought and behaviour which have the power to elicit obedience. However, the social conditions or relations that gave rise to them are no longer evident, they seem to have taken on a life of their own. In other words, these symbolic codes, or discursive chains, have become relatively autonomous, although they may still bear the imprint of the conditions that gave rise to them.

Marx had suggested that there was an affinity or fit between religion and economic relations, which he described in terms of a fairly direct (although distorted) reflection. He gave the example of the fit between capitalist relations, where labour was reduced to standard units whose value depended on commodity prices, and a corresponding Christian doctrine, especially in Protestantism, which talked in terms of abstract individuals (Marx, 1974, vol. 1, p.83). Althusser attempted to move away from this economic determinism in which superstructural elements like religion are seen as simply 'reflections' of the economic base. He developed the concept of Ideological State Apparatuses — institutions such as religion, the media and education — which helped to reproduce the conditions which made it possible for the relations of production to continue.

Althusser says that Ideological State Apparatuses (ISAs), which appear as 'private' institutions, such as the Church, law, media, trades unions, schools, political parties, are really part of the public state because they function for the state in reproducing ruling class power, and they are called ideological because they function primarily through ideology (Althusser, 1971). They function by incorporating all classes in society within a dominant ideology, securing the hegemony of the dominant classes. Through the process of what Althusser called 'interpellation', people are made into agents, or carriers, of social structure. Interpellation is analogous to hailing a person in the street: ideologies 'address' people and give them a particular identity or subjectivity and a position in society.

A number of criticisms have been made of Althusser's theory. One criticism is that it is still too deterministic and ignores the fact that, throughout history, subordinate groups have developed their own interpretations of beliefs and symbols and frequently opposed those of dominant classes (Abercrombie *et al.*, 1990). It also ties ideology too closely to serving the function of reproduction of the relations of production. One consequence of this is that he downgrades the contemporary importance of religion and says that the crucial ideological institution is now education. Clearly, there is some reason for this downgrading if the comparison is being made between the role of the Church in reproducing the relations of production in feudalism and the situation in contemporary capitalism. However, it offers no insights for comparing different capitalist societies, or different ideological tendencies between groups within the same society. For this purpose it is more fruitful to adopt a sociological approach that is sensitive to cultural differences, concentrating on the actual articulation of various discourses or institutions in concrete social formations (e.g. Britain compared with America, in particular periods). Furthermore, although education may be found to contribute more directly to the reproduction of relations of production in all capitalist societies, religion may still be a potent factor in combination with other discourses in the construction of ideological communities, such as the imagined community of the nation.

Benedict Anderson defines the nation as 'an imagined political community — imagined as both inherently limited and sovereign' (outside it are 'alien Others', inside there is a demand for total allegiance). He adds that 'It is *imagined* because the members of even the smallest nation will never know most of their fellow members, meet them, or even hear of them, yet in the minds of each lives the image of their communion' (Anderson, 1983, p.15). The fraternity of nationalism is so deeply established that people are prepared to kill or die for it. With the pluralization of religions and the break-up of dynastic empires, which had preceded nation states, the nation emerged as the ultimate ideological community for most people, and the one with the strongest imagined sense of timelessness, disinterestedness and naturalness. These are the same characteristics that Durkheim said gave a society its god-like power and its binding sacredness.

Despite the assumption of theories of secularization stemming from the Enlightenment that religion would steadily decline in significance, it continues to play a prominent role in the ideological construction of national communities. Islamic Iran and Catholic Poland are obvious examples. In Britain, a variety of discourses, and sets of differences, have been rearticulated to construct the imagined community of the British nation at different times. Some of the most interesting are those in which religious and political discourses were combined in attempts to produce an ideologically unifying nationalism. In the period of internal upheaval and class conflict that accompanied the Industrial Revolution, such a combination occurred in response to the perceived threat posed by revolutionary France. New politically conservative theories of the nation were developed by Burke, Coleridge and others, drawing on religious as well as political discourses. Public opinion was mobilized against the alien threat and British national characteristics were rediscovered or invented. Religious discourse was one of the key sites where there was a struggle to produce the required ideological effect of cementing national unity and rooting out any divisive tendencies. Nowhere was this more evident than in the remarkable change that took place in Methodism, which at one stage was regarded as something akin to a revolutionary fifth column, but which after the French Revolution became a pillar of support for King and country, and during the French wars passed resolutions to that effect at its annual conferences (Andrews, 1970; Thompson, 1986).

The great theorist of English Conservatism, Edmund Burke, in his *Reflections on the Revolution in France* (1790), emphasized cultural practices which instilled social and moral discipline, and an essential part of that discipline derived from the established Church, which consecrated the state and provided powerful incentives to obedience and order. Similarly, William Coleridge argued against religious individualism, such as that featured in the ideas leading to American independence. He said that the French wars had made the nation more serious, moral and unified, and in 1834 he suggested that another threat of invasion might be good for morale (Stafford, 1982). This yearning for a return to wartime unity has sometimes been heard again in the post-Second World War period and appears to be a recurring feature in the construction of the imagined community of the British nation: a closing of ranks against the external threat of an alien Other, variously represented by Revolutionary France, Napoleonic France, Fascist Germany, Communist Russia in the cold war, Galtieri's Argentina in the

Falklands War of 1982 and the Iraq of Saddam Hussein in 1991. Although there were economic and political conflicts involving national interests in each case, they were also efforts at ideological self-definition of the national community, contrasting Britain's virtuous characteristics with the dangerous and even insane vices of the alien Other.

It is not difficult to understand why periods of social tension or crisis should give rise to more pronounced efforts to articulate a dominant discourse defining the sacred character of the imagined community by contrasting it with an alien opponent. Most people would agree that in such periods of social tension public discourse becomes more like that of an intense social drama and that there is a shift away from the mundane concerns with means and ends that characterize the discourses of everyday life. What is more controversial is whether modern societies *need* to incorporate members into a dominant ideology with shared values. The authors of *The Dominant Ideology Thesis* (Abercrombie *et al.*, 1980) are critical of Althusserian and Durkheimian theories for suggesting that ideology, or shared values, have to fulfil such a need in order for capitalist societies to go on reproducing themselves. They are particularly critical of the neo-Durkheimian argument put forward after the Coronation of Queen Elizabeth II by Edward Shils and Michael Young in their famous article 'The meaning of the coronation' (1953). The critics interpret this neo-Durkheimian argument as being to the effect that modern capitalist societies require a powerful set of rituals in order to sustain a core of common values, into which the British working class had supposedly been incorporated at that time. This interpretation appeared to be borne out by Shils's subsequent statement that 'the coronation of Elizabeth II was the ceremonial occasion for the affirmation of the moral values by which the society lives. It was an act of national communion' (Shils, 1975, p.139). This was certainly a common view shared by many sociologists, such as Talcott Parsons in America, who had developed Durkheim's ideas in a functionalist direction. It was attacked at the time by the Marxist sociologist Norman Birnbaum, who criticized Shils and Young for providing no evidence for the supposed value consensus in Britain and for underestimating the extent to which there existed conflicting values and even outright political opposition on the part of the working class (Birnbaum, 1955). The critique was extended by Abercrombie and his colleagues to cover studies such as that by Blumler of the investiture of the Prince of Wales, where the ceremony was said to serve the social function of reaffirming values associated with family solidarity and national pride (Blumler *et al.*, 1971).

However, there is a difference between a functionalist Durkheimian theory which assumes that modern capitalist societies need rituals in order to incorporate the working class into a core of common values, and a more structuralist Durkheimian theory of ideology. The latter does not assume that a capitalist society is held together by incorporating the working class into a common culture including a set of core values held by all members. Durkheim himself did not believe that existing modern

The Coronation of Queen Elizabeth II, 1953

The Investiture of the
Prince of Wales, 1971

societies were very successful in integrating their members through shared values, even though he hoped that some day they might develop such a moral unity. He charted their failure by reference to their high suicide rates and other indicators of lack of social integration. Although he left unspecified the degree to which civic rituals and ceremonies might continue to have some solidifying effects, he believed that certain national symbols, such as the flag, and ceremonies like those of Bastille Day in France, clearly had some effect. They re-presented significant events as portrayed in discourses concerning the nation's history and they generated in people a sense of common identity.

The lesson to be drawn from this debate is not that civic symbols and ceremonies testify to an existing unity, or that these are essential to the very existence and functioning of a capitalist society. The implication of Durkheim's sociology is that modern society contains a variety of 'collective representations' — discourses and practices that are economic, political, religious, etc. — and that sociological analysis is concerned with showing how they 'articulate' with each other to promote or hinder different sorts and levels of social solidarity. Some social pressures towards cooperation will be based on routine and custom, including customary working practices; or on 'disciplinary regimes' mediated by institutions such as education and the law. Other sources of cooperation rest on complementarity of functions and exchange of services, as in many market transactions. At the most general cultural level of moral values the secularization thesis suggests that there is a weakening of consensual ties in modern society, although the European Value Systems Study and other research reveals a surprisingly high level of general agreement. Finally, Durkheim seems to have been proved right in coming to the conclusion that there would continue to be some solidarity ties that resulted from the awe and reverence inspired by symbols and ceremonies expressive of the experience of the transcendence and power of the collectivity itself. Viewed from this perspective, it does seem plausible to suggest that, in Britain for example, discourses concerning royalty and religion can articulate together to produce a sense of awe and reverence for the imagined political community of the nation. International sporting contests may both heighten the sense of national bonding and emphasize national differences. None of these can be taken as representing a core set of values that are essential for the reproduction of capitalist relations of production. But they are none the less important in constructing ideological communities and interpellating individuals as subjects within such communities. However, individuals and groups are not passive receivers of such discourses; they are actively involved, in varying degrees, in interpreting and sometimes even contesting them, as illustrated by the different sectarian subcultural responses described by Bryan Wilson. The question of exactly how, and to what extent, people are integrated into ideological communities, can only be answered by following up the theoretical analysis with empirical investigations of the creation of ideologies, their transmission, and responses to them.

In the case of civic symbolic events and rituals, such as those which involve royalty, analysis shows that they have some success in combining several discourses to produce dramatizations of the nation as a symbolic or imagined community. The Queen is spoken of as the head of the great family of the nation (and head of a family of nations — the Commonwealth), she is also Head of State and Head of the Church. Familial discourse features prominently in combination with political and religious discourses. Many civic rituals celebrate points in the life cycle of members of the royal family, such as the marriage of Prince Charles and Lady Diana in 1981 and the annual celebrations of the Queen's birthday. They frequently involve and cement a link with other institutions, as when the Queen as Head of State takes part in the State Opening of Parliament, or engages in the military ritual of the Trooping of the Colour on the monarch's official birthday. Not the least important function is the link forged with the nation's past by ceremonies such as that on Remembrance Day, when members of the royal family lay wreaths on the Cenotaph, and veterans of past wars join in the parade.

Remembrance Day at the Cenotaph

All these events contain 'manufactured' or 'invented' traditions, many of them of quite recent origin, which are broadcast to the nation, and members of the vast audience are drawn to identify with the imagined community and its past: in this way they are constituted and addressed ('interpellated') as subjects. The development of the 1953 coronation ceremony in Britain as a televised event is a good illustration of the invention of tradition, and of the manufactured nature of the process of creating a sense of community. The ceremony was adapted to the needs of television, whilst the BBC took upon itself the responsibility for deciding what kind of tone and impression should be created and transmitted, even down to the specification of what sorts of scenes and objects should be given prominence. The decision to go for a 'reverential' approach, with one-third of the total footage taken up with symbolic shots (focused on inanimate features of Westminster Abbey — altar cross, Coronation Plate, stonework, etc.), was aimed at eliciting a sense of respectful awe and reverence, which was further communicated by the invention of an appropriate style of hushed-voice commentary by Richard Dimbleby (Chaney, 1983). These are all aspects of the process of communalization and interpellation of subjects through which discourses can have ideological effects. To the extent that millions of viewers and listeners are won over by the discourse, with all its attractive pageantry, nostalgia and familiar symbols, they recognize themselves as the subjects addressed, and willingly consent to their 'subjection' to the sovereign power that it represents: that of the transcendent or 'sacred' collectivity, the imagined community.

What is being suggested here is not a defence of the 'dominant ideology thesis', which was effectively criticized by Abercrombie *et al.* (1980; 1990). There is no question of there being any functional necessity for, or economistic determination of, these ideological discourses. It cannot be established that they are essential to the reproduction of capitalist relations of production or that they are determined in the last instance by the economy. What is being argued is that various forms of culture — Durkheim's 'collective representations', Foucault's 'discourses', or what are more generally referred to as symbols, beliefs, values, rituals and socially meaningful practices — can all have ideological effects. That is to say, they are ideologically effective if they persuade people that their society is a particular kind of unitary entity in which they have a particular kind of identity.

Modern societies are complex entities and it is not surprising that they are often described as 'multicultural'. In Britain there are minority groups whose religions are not Christian — e.g. Jews, Moslems, Hindus, Buddhists and others. However, even if there is seldom a single dominant ideology that unites all social classes and sub-cultural groups together, there is evidence of ideological processes at work in binding many of them together to varying degrees. We have mentioned some of these, including the rituals surrounding the Royal Family, various inherited religious beliefs and values, ceremonies and popular culture. Individuals, groups, and institutions that wish to influence people or exercise power, will struggle to control this cultural 'capital'. Politicians, preachers, advertisers, managers and other professional 'cultural persuaders' are adept at manipulating symbols and constructing discourses that have an emotional appeal. The more deeply sedimented the layers of culture that they appeal to, the greater will be their persuasiveness. Much of the debate about the relative success or failure of the New Right movement for ideological renewal in the 1980s, particularly the British version labelled 'Thatcherism', has been concerned with identifying the key elements in its cultural appeal and assessing their impact on different groups. It is worth taking note of these assessments, but the main purpose in considering them here is to illustrate the ways in which cultural processes do have ideological effects without there being a unitary dominant ideology.

As Gill Seidel pointed out, in an article comparing the British and French New Right, their ideology combined a neo-liberal emphasis on individual enterprise and free markets with more conservative ideas of national culture and identity (Seidel, 1986). In Gramsci's terms, its proponents were engaged in a cultural struggle to create a counter-hegemonic ideology to replace what they saw as the dominant ideology of the post-war era — the liberal and social democratic consensus. The French New Right group GRECE *(Groupement de Recherche d'Etude pour une Civilisation Europèenne)* referred to this strategy quite explicitly as 'right-wing Gramscism' (Seidel, 1986, p.108). The British conservative philosopher, Roger Scruton, editor of *The Salisbury Review* and author of a weekly column in *The Times*, expressed this in terms of rhetoric:

> The main tasks for conservative rhetoric are to establish in the public mind the inseparability of market freedom and economic leadership, and to integrate the philosophy of the market into the underlying principle of order which both motivates conservative politics, and attracts the votes of a conservative electorate ... Such a rhetoric ... must ... be taken from the broader realms of political ideology ... Conservative rhetoric is, or ought to be ... a rhetoric of order.
> (Scruton, 1982, p.38)

This rhetoric constitutes what Foucault called a 'discursive ensemble' — a network of interlinked words and meanings with its own internal coherence. Scruton argued that the most important social forces are 'language, religion, custom, associations and traditions of political order — in short, all those forces that generate nations' (Scruton, 1982, p.14). For Scruton and the strand of the British New Right grouped around *The Salisbury Review*, the cultural construction or imagining of the 'nation' was central to their ideological project. The first issue in 1982 included an article with the revealing title: 'One nation: the politics of race' (Casey, 1982). It began with two quotations from Burke, reflecting his traditional and organicist view of society, followed by a quotation from T.S. Eliot on culture:

> ... the term *culture* ... includes all the characteristic activities and interest of a people: Derby Day, Henley Regatta, Cowes, the twelfth of August, a cup final, the dog races, the pin table, the dart board, Wensleydale cheese, boiled cabbage cut into sections, beetroot in vinegar, nineteenth-century Gothic churches and the music of Elgar.
> (Eliot quoted in Seidel, 1986, p.110)

As Seidel points out, these quotations 'symbolize the shared political and white (Christian) culture, the "us"'; in the rest of Casey's article, as the title suggests, the nation is discussed in terms of race. Seidel notes that, by January 1985, after eight issues of *The Salisbury Review,* there had been six articles which specifically addressed the question of nation and race, or racism, all within an implicit or explicit vision of national culture (1986, p.110). In addition, a number of articles explicitly concerned with Christian theology and liturgy, reinforced the same discourse. Whilst rejecting the accusation that their views might be considered racist, the authors insisted that a nation is defined by a traditional culture, and they condemned ideas of 'multiculturalism', 'mother-tongue' teaching for different ethnic groups (even though this was endorsed by an EEC directive), and 'comparative religion' teaching if it weakened the pre-eminence of Christianity.

How successful the New Right was in winning the ideological struggle is a subject of much debate. Unemployment and economic recession may have done more to change economic attitudes than the writings of New Right intellectuals and politicians. With regard to neo-liberal values, evidence from surveys of attitudes and values in the 1980s suggests that most people continued to subscribe to collectivist values such as those of the welfare state and the caring community (the evidence is summarized in Abercrombie *et al.*, 1990, pp.19–24). Similarly, with respect to conservative views of national culture and identity, although certain sections of the Press gave a great deal of publicity to New Right views and their claims to represent traditional British values, which they contrasted to the 'alien' views of 'multiculturalists' and the 'race relations industry', there is no clear evidence of a change in values in Britain. Where there may have been some success was where government policies and legislation had an effect on the discourses and disciplinary regimes in key institutions, such as education, trades unions, local government, housing, and through structural changes which gave greater prominence to managerial culture in fiercely contested institutions such as health care.

In the field of education, as pointed out by Geoff Whitty in Chapter 6 of this book, conservative attempts to construct a particular sense of national identity were not limited to writing pamphlets and articles in the press; they also sought institutional changes. Whitty discussed the examples of the reform of the history curriculum and the requirement in the Education Reform Act of 1988 that education in state schools should 'reflect the fact that the religious traditions in Great Britain are in the main Christian whilst taking account of the teaching and practices of the other principal religions represented in Great Britain' and that, with certain qualifications, their daily act of collective worship should be 'wholly or mainly of a broadly Christian character'. Clearly, there were contradictory tendencies within the New Right ideology which limited its potential dominance. As Whitty notes, for example, the ideas of free choice and a free market in education, which might be thought to include the emergence of Moslem and other ethnically divided schools, were in tension with a concern to integrate minorities into a national culture based on shared values. Some conservatives were happy to see the emergence of Moslem schools, provided the pupils were integrated into 'our' national culture; but, equally, some Moslems were suspicious that the 'national values' envisaged by the Department of Education and Science would simply reflect the cultural heritage of the group that selected what would be taught, and lead to cultural domination in disguise.

The other cultural level where Thatcherism enjoyed some success was in articulating nationalist sentiments during the Falklands War, which some commentators saw as a major explanation for the sudden and dramatic revival of the political fortunes of the Conservative Party during 1982, culminating in electoral victory in 1983 (subsequent studies have produced different estimates of the importance of this factor). Whether a political ideology such as Thatcherism (or Reaganism, the New Right, etc.) represents a good example of the ways in which different discourses have ideological effects, is open to debate. It might be more realistic to regard such political ideologies as merely the most overt and explicit examples of cultural processes that have ideological effects: changing or sustaining relations of domination in a society. Such relatively short-lived movements for ideological change or renewal as Thatcherism and the New Right are interesting mainly for what they reveal about these underlying and continuing cultural processes.

In this chapter we have chosen to focus not so much on the many sources of social and cultural division within an advanced industrial society, but on cultural processes which may have the ideological effect of sustaining the existing social order. We have noted the persistence of certain traditional beliefs and moral values, which suggest that Britain is a relatively conservative society compared with some of its European neighbours. There is also some evidence of the continuing attachment of a large proportion of Britons to shared national symbols, particularly those associated with the monarchy. The level of such attachment is probably much less than Walter Bagehot suggested in the nineteenth century, or even Shils and Young in the 1950s. However, the *British Social Attitudes: Special International Report* of 1989 (Topf *et al.*, 1989), reporting on a comparative survey of national pride in Britain and Germany (West Germany as it was then), found that the monarchy was chosen as a source of pride by 65 per cent of British respondents and rated higher than any other single factor. Interestingly, second choice was 'scientific achievements' (61 per cent), which over half of the British felt the government did not fund sufficiently, followed by 'welfare state' (52 per cent). Bottom of the list was occupied in Britain by 'economic achievements' (16 per cent), compared with Germany where it ranked joint first with the 'Basic Law' or constitution (51 per cent). However, attachment to the monarchy varied considerably between social groups — more so than to other objects of national pride. It appealed more to women, older age groups, members of the Church of

England, the less educated, routine non-manual workers, people in England. It was relatively less popular among men, the young, people of no religion, graduates, salaried workers, people in Scotland and Wales. Despite these variations, it should be noted that the monarchy still featured as a source of national pride for the majority of the British population and that only 7 per cent of respondents said they felt no national pride in terms of what was put to them (Topf *et al.*, 1989).

7 CONCLUSION

It is not difficult to see why the study of culture should occupy an important place in sociological analysis. If it has such ideological effects — persuading people to see their society as a particular kind of unitary entity in which they themselves have a certain identity and so sustaining or changing relations of domination — then it is indeed powerful. The very legitimacy of the state's claim to exercise power over individuals rests on its success in convincing people that it acts in their interests. In circumstances of international economic competition and periodic crises, the state depends on its success in harnessing the solidary feelings of national community in support of its power. It is in such circumstances that we are likely to witness the sorts of upsurges of nationalist symbolism, including civil religion involving royalty and civic rituals, that we have discussed.

However, there is nothing mechanical or inevitably determined in the working of such ideologies. Whether culture has particular ideological effects depends on processes of social construction and transmission of meanings and their reception. The sense of being part of a unitary entity such as a national community may well be rooted in real elements of shared characteristics and common history, but these are frequently matters of dispute and contestation, linked to different interests and power struggles. Territory, language, religion, race, etc., are all sources of dispute and have to be ideologically constructed, or interpreted, in order to produce a sense of belonging to a national community, as a glance at the history of the peoples living in the British Isles instantly makes clear. Some people would express a preference for Welsh or Scottish nationality over British nationality if allowed a choice. Whilst, in Northern Ireland, according to a recent survey, although 66 per cent of Protestants thought of themselves as British, 60 per cent of Catholics saw themselves as Irish. (Significantly, 54 per cent of the people in Northern Ireland said they attended church at least once a week, compared with only 13 per cent in mainland Britain (Jowell *et al.*, 1990).)

The imagined community of the nation is the site of ideological contestation and power struggles as we have seen in the case of Britain and as is evident in the resurgence of ethnic-religious nationalisms throughout the world. In this chapter we have tried to show how ideological community is produced, or imagined, and individual identity constructed. We have also shown that older symbols and values, such as those deriving from religious sources, do not necessarily disappear from modern society as the inevitable result of a unilinear process of secularization. There are strong traces of them in various layers of culture and they are capable of being adapted, or articulated with non-religious elements in new combinations. The extent to which these have an ideological impact depends on a range of factors, as we have seen.

REFERENCES

Abercrombie, N., Hill, S. and Turner B.S. (eds) (1988) *The Penguin Dictionary of Sociology*, 2nd edn, Harmondsworth, Penguin.

Abercrombie, N., Hill, S. and Turner, B.S. (eds) (1980) *The Dominant Ideology Thesis*, London, Unwin Hyman.

Abercrombie, N., Hill, S. and Turner, B.S. (eds) (1990) *Dominant Ideologies*, London, Unwin Hyman.

Abrams, M., Gerard, D. and Timms, N. (eds) (1985) *Values and Social Change in Britain*, London, Macmillan.

Althusser, L. (1971) *Lenin and Other Essays*, London, New Left Books.

Anderson, B. (1983) *Imagined Communities*, London, Verso.

Andrews, S. (1970) *Methodism and Society*, London, Longman.

Beckford, J.A. (1989) *Religion and Advanced Industrial Society*, London, Unwin Hyman.

Birnbaum, N. (1955) 'Monarchs and sociologists: a reply to Professor Shils and Mr Young', *Sociological Review*, vol. 3, 1, pp.5–23.

Blumler, J.G. *et al.*, (1971) 'Attitudes to the monarchy: their structure and development during a ceremonial occasion', *Political Studies*, vol.19, pp.149–71.

Casey, J. (1982) 'One nation: the politics of race', *The Salisbury Review*, 1 (Autumn), pp.23–8.

Chaney, D. (1983) 'A symbolic mirror of ourselves: civic ritual in mass society', *Media Culture and Society*, vol.5, 2, pp.119–35.

Cunningham, H. (1980) *Leisure in the Industrial Revolution*, London, Croom Helm.

Dobbelaere, K. (1981) 'Secularization: a multi-dimensional concept', *Current Sociology*, 29, London, Sage.

Durkheim, E. (1961) *The Elementary Forms of the Religious Life*, New York, Free Press. Original published in French, 1912.

Foucault, M. (1980) *The History of Sexuality* vol.1, New York, Vintage Books. Original published in French, 1976.

Fukuyama, F. (1989) 'The end of history?', *The National Interest*, no.16 (Summer), pp.3–18.

Gerard, D. (1985) 'Religious attitudes and values' in Abrams, M. *et al.* (1985).

Gramsci, A. (1971) *Selections from Prison Notebooks,* London, Lawrence and Wishart.

Gramsci, A. (1975) *Quaderni dal Carcere,* vol.2, ed. V. Gerratana, Turin, Einaudi.

Hall, S. and Gieben, B. (eds) (1992) *Formations of Modernity,* Cambridge, Polity Press.

Hall, S., Held, D. and McGrew, A. (eds) (1992) *Modernity and its Futures*, Cambridge, Polity Press.

Jowell, R. *et al.* (1990) *British Social Attitudes 1990–91*, Aldershot, Gower.

Luckmann, T. (1967) *The Invisible Religion*, London, Macmillan.

MacIntyre, A. (1981) *After Virtue,* London, Duckworth.

MacIver, R.M. (1917) *Community, a Sociological Study,* London, Heinemann.

Marx, K. (1974) *Capital*, London, Penguin.

Marx, K. and Engels. F. (1955) *On Religion*, Moscow, Foreign Languages Publishing House.

Marx, K. and Engels, F. (1972) 'The German Ideology' in Tucker, R.C. (ed.) *The Marx-Engels Reader*, New York, W.W. Norton. First published in 1845–6.

Mouffe, C. (1981), 'Hegemony and ideology in Gramsci' in Bennett, T. *et al.*, (eds) *Culture, Ideology and Social Process*, London, Batsford.

Penguin Dictionary of Sociology: see Abercrombie *et al.* (1988).

Sachs, J. (1990) 'The persistence of faith', the Reith Lectures, Lecture 1 'The environment of faith', *The Listener,* November 15, pp.4–6.

Scruton, R. (1982) *The Salisbury Review*, 1 (Autumn).

Seidel, G. (1986) 'Culture, nation and "race" in the British and French new right' in Levitas, R. (ed.) *The Ideology of the New Right*, Cambridge, Polity Press.

Shils, E. (1975) *Centre and Periphery: Essays in Macrosociology*, Chicago, University of Chicago Press.

Shils, E. and Young, M. (1953) 'The meaning of the coronation', *Sociological Review*, vol.1, pp.63–82.

Stafford, W. (1982) 'Religion and the doctrine of nationalism in England at the time of the French Revolution and Napoleonic Wars' in Mews, S. (ed.) *Religion and National Identity*, Oxford, Blackwell.

The Open University (1981) U203 *Popular Culture*, Units 1-2, Milton Keynes, The Open University.

Thompson, K. (1986) *Beliefs and Ideology,* London, Tavistock.

Topf, R., Mohler, P. and Heath, A. (1989) 'Pride in one's country: Britain and West Germany' in Jowell, R., Witherspoon, S. and Brook, L. (eds) *British Social Attitudes: Special International Report*, Aldershot, Gower Publishing.

Turner, B.S. (1983) *Religion and Social Theory,* London, Sage.

Wallis, R. and Bruce, S. (1986) *Sociological Theory, Religion and Collective Action*, Belfast, The Queen's University.

Williams, R. (1975) *The Country and the City*, London, Paladin.

Wilson, B.R. (1963) 'A typology of sects in a dynamic and comparative perspective', *Archives des Sciences Social des Religions*, vol.16, pp.49–53.

Wilson, B.R. (1982) *Religion in Sociological Perspective*, Oxford, Oxford University Press.

READING A   THE POPULATION: RELIGIOUS DISPOSITION, BELIEF AND PRACTICE AT A GLANCE

David Gerard

It was earlier suggested that Christianity possesses both an integrated system of beliefs and a means of expressing commitment through ritual participation; these two dimensions were referred to as 'meaning' and 'belonging'. Whilst they reinforced each other, the former was held to be prior. In discussing both emotivism and secularisation, it was also noted that a number of sociologists have argued in favour of the existence of a fundamental religious disposition, independent of any explicit attachment to the beliefs and rituals of the major religious traditions. Rooted in man's capacity for reflection on his circumstances, and his search for meaning and identity, such a disposition may find contemporary expression only in subjective, private realities. Although the EVSSG questionnaire was not designed for the purpose and the indicators available within it are not necessarily those best suited for the task, the values data do provide the opportunity to explore all three dimensions and to assess the degree to which they are related to each other. Table 1 provides selected indicators of religious disposition, orthodox belief and institutional attachment for Great Britain compared with the overall European population. Many of these items are later combined to form a scale to measure the intensity of overall religious commitment.

Three-quarters of the British sample reported a belief in God (Q.163). As far as evidence of an underlying religious disposition is concerned, three-fifths identified themselves as 'religious persons' (Q.158), half regularly felt the need for prayer, meditation or contemplation (Q.169), half scored above the mid-point on the 'importance of God' scale (Q.167) and a little under half indicated that they drew comfort and strength from religion. Those who identified themselves as convinced atheists (Q.158) comprised only 4 per cent of the population. Indeed, an examination of the responses of the 45 self-confessed atheists reveals that twenty of them claimed some form of denominational attachment, ten believed in the existence of some sort of spirit or life force, ten believed in life after death, one actually believed in a personal God, eight asserted a belief in God (Q.163) and seven were agnostic. The true figure for convinced atheists is therefore nearer 2 per cent.

On the other hand, evidence of a reflective disposition and widespread 'spiritual experience' is limited. Only one-third of the population reported frequent reflection about the meaning and purpose of life; one-in-five reported having a profound spiritual experience; one-in-seven frequently contemplated death. Further, two-fifths of the sample were of the opinion that religion would become less important in future (Q.162) — twice the proportion who believed it would become more important — and the proportion who believed that religious faith was an important value to be encouraged at home among children (Q.262) was low.

Gerard, D. (1985) 'Religious attitudes and values', in Abrams, M. *et al.* (eds) *Values and Social Change in Britain*, London, Macmillan, pp.58–64.

Table 1

Indicators of moral values:	Great Britain	European average	Indicators of Institutional Attachment:	Great Britain	European average
Absolute guidelines exist about good & evil	28	26	Great confidence in Church	19	21
			Church answers moral problems	30	35
Personally fully accept Commandments prohibiting:			Church answers family problems	32	33
			Church answers spiritual needs	42	44
Killing	90	87	Attend church monthly	23	35
Adultery	78	63	Denomination:		
Stealing	87	82	Roman Catholic	11	54
False Witness	78	73	Protestant (Established	68	29
Agree with unrestricted sex	23	23	Free Church/Non-conformist)	6	2
Terrorism may be justified	12	14	Believe religion will become:		
Following acts never justified:			More important in future	21	19
Claiming unentitled benefit	78		Less important in future	40	34
Accepting a bribe	79		Believe in one true religion	21	25
Taking marijuana	81		Religious faith an important value to develop in children	14	16
Homosexuality	47				
Euthanasia	30				
Political assassination	77				
Greater respect for authority:					
good	73	59			
Willing to sacrifice life	34	33			

The evidence suggests that such general expressions of religious commitment vary both with the degree of orthodox belief and practice and with important socio-demographic characteristics such as age, sex and occupational status. ... Subjective perception of the importance of God (Q.167) — the single most useful summary indicator of religiosity emerging from multi variate analysis of the data — varies with the intensity of church attendance (Q.157), the conception people have of god (Q.166) and the degree of comprehensiveness of the orthodox beliefs held (Q.163). Thus, whilst there is widespread evidence of some form of religious commitment, it remains doubtful whether this is indicative of the existence of a dimension of religiosity which is *independent* of attachment to orthodox Christian teaching. Rather, it appears consistent with previously reported American evidence (Nelson *et al.*, 1976; Roof *et al.*, 1977) which suggests that non-doctrinal commitment varies *directly* with traditional beliefs.

Examination of people's conception of God and attitudes to orthodox belief help to throw some further light on the question. Two-fifths of the population conceive of God as some sort of spirit or life force; a little under one-third believe in a personal God; one-fifth are unsure what to think, and a further ten per cent profess no belief in either.

Given the centrality of the notion of a personal God to the Christian tradition, the data support the view that belief in, and attachment to, a deity persist but that only a minority inhabit the Christian tradition in the full sense. However, as Kerkhofs (1983) has noted, lack of endorsement of the 'personal God' item in the questionnaire may be indicative not so much of outright rejection of the notion itself as rejection of an exclusively anthropomorphic image of God. On the other hand, it is clear that little more than a quarter of the population accept absolute, as opposed to relative, guidelines concerning good and evil (Q.154) and only a quarter accept the full range of Christian beliefs (Q.163) when these are taken to include both Hell and the Devil. These results could be taken to imply widespread rejection of the traditional Christian paradigm which may be manifest in a search for a new paradigm.

The percentage accepting absolute guidelines (28 per cent of the total population) is higher among those who believe in a personal God (45 per cent) than among those who conceive of God as a spirit or life force (37 per cent). More pronounced differences are apparent between these two groups when the full range of Christian beliefs is considered.

More than two-fifths of those who believe in a personal God accept the comprehensive range of beliefs (Q.163). Yet, these results are in themselves indicative of a degree of selectivity in belief among more orthodox Christians. However, the proportion who do so among those who adopt the alternative conception of God is no higher than the population average, less than a quarter accepting the full range of beliefs. These differences are reflected in differing attitudes to personal and sexual morality, and in the need to pray — the former group being stricter.

The most startling contrasts however, are in the attitudes of the two groups to the importance of developing religious faith in children and in church attendance. Seven out of ten of those who believe religious faith is an important value to develop in children, accept a personal God; only a quarter adopt the alternative immanentist conception. Nine-tenths of those who attend church weekly are drawn from the former group, less than one-in-ten from the latter.

The acceptance of a personal God is correlated with age, the contrast being most marked between the very young (less than one-fifth of those under 25 years adopting such a conception) and the very old (half of those aged over 75 years holding the belief). The notion of God as a spirit or life force is less influenced by age, though it is a belief more prevalent among the middle-aged than among either young or old. Whatever the particular conception of God, however, belief in God is clearly related to age, the proportion increasing from about three-fifths among the 18-24 year olds to about nine-tenths among those aged 75 years or over. Whether this variation is an enduring generational effect or a function of age itself it is not possible to establish on the basis of these data alone.

The widespread rejection of absolute guidelines in favour of a more relativist moral position, tends to bear out one element in MacIntyre's (1981) thesis. Yet, as can be seen from Table 1, there remains a very high degree of consensus on moral issues and continuing commitment to the moral commandments of the decalogue. This contradicts another important element in his argument and suggests that his assertion that contemporary moral arguments are interminable and unsettleable is an overstatement. Whether generalised commitment to the existence of God but apparently weak assent to the detail and range of Christian belief will be sufficient to sustain the existing moral consensus is, nevertheless, open to doubt, given MacIntyre's view that in the absence of a teleological framework there is no rational basis for such values.

References

Kerkhofs, J. (1983) 'God in West Europe', *Streven,* November.

MacIntyre, A. (1981) *After Virtue,* London, Duckworth.

Nelson, H.H. and Everett, R.F. (1976) 'A test of Yinger's measure of non-doctrinal religion: implications for invisible religion as a belief system,' *Journal for the Scientific Study of Religion,* 15, pp.263–7.

Roof. W.C. *et al.* (1977) 'Yinger's measure of non-doctrinal religion: a north eastern test', *Journal for the Scientific Study of Religion*, 16, pp.403–8.

READING B   RELIGIOUS CHANGE AND INSTITUTIONAL INVOLVEMENT

David Gerard

The form and content of religious beliefs and rituals, the structure and organization of religious authorities, undergo evolution and change in response to wider social and cultural forces. New religious communities emerge and decline. *Religious change* (Yinger, 1962), therefore, varies over time and from place to place but fundamentally involves either strategies of resistance or strategies of accommodation (Berger, 1967). Such strategies will differ both in the extent to which they emphasise the need for personal values and beliefs to be closely integrated with those of the wider society, and in the definitions they offer of what is 'sacred' — and thus the scope for conflict with other social institutions (Fenn, 1978). Berger suggests that in America the churches have maintained a position of central symbolic importance because they have accommodated themselves to, and support, the American Way of Life, have 'modernised' and marketed their product, adapting it to meet the needs of their constituents. Consequently church involvement has remained much higher than in Europe where 'internal' secularisation and the process of adjusting to the demands of the wider society have proceeded much slower. Both strategies require theoretical legitimation and pose theological problems (Berger, 1961; 1967). The accommodation strategy may reduce conflict and tension between denominations, each being regarded as a different form of expressing a common national identity and common faith (Herberg, 1967).

Apart from hypotheses about adaptations of formal religious groups to the process of social change, other sociologists identify evolutionary developments towards individuation, autonomy and purely subjective 'invisible' religion which undermine institutional forms (Bellah, 1964; Luckmann, 1967). Luckmann argues that society no longer requires religious legitima-

Source: Gerard, D.(1985) 'Religious attitudes and values', in Abrams M., *et al.* (eds) *Values and Social Change in Britain*, London, Macmillan, pp.54–8.

tion and that religion has become transformed into a subjective, private, reality. This reality is, he suggests, characterised by autonomy, choice and personal preference and an emphasis on self-realisation; mobility; self-expression; sexuality and familism. It does not conform to the demands of the specialised institutional form of religion with its defined doctrine, specialised ministry and ecclesiastical organization. The latter is consequently undermined. Such a private religious reality depends on restricted kin and friendship networks to support it and enables the individual to 'manage' his own relationship to God and to choose with whom he will worship (Parsons, 1967). There is a danger, however, that defining as religious all privately created meaning systems, whether God centred or not, which provide some form of interpretive framework and confer identity, empties the term of content. Such definitions, for example, may encompass — as the Greeley/Geertz formulation (Greeley, 1972) suggests — evolutionism, Marxism and scientism, inhibiting empirical studies of comparative religiosity and rendering the notion of secularisation redundant if every solution to problems of ultimate concern is regarded by definition as 'religious'.

Attempts empirically to validate the existence of some form of privatised religion independent of any institutional framework or doctrinal system of beliefs have been made using student samples. Accepting Geertz's (1968) thesis that man's ultimate values and beliefs are rooted in his reflections about the inevitability of his own death, and the consequent need to determine whether any transcendent reality is benign or malicious, Yinger (1977) developed a religious 'scale' based on experiences of meaninglessness, suffering and injustice. He reported that a religious disposition was as evident among those without any formal religious identity as among adherents to the major religions. Other studies indicate that Yinger's scale lacks internal consistency, being composed of two or three separate dimensions. Further, whilst indicative of some form of non-doctrinal religious commitment, it is clear that the extent of such commitment varies *directly* with traditional forms of religious attachment (Nelson *et al.*, 1976; Roof *et al.*, 1977).

Religious involvement is clearly influenced by the processes of secularisation and change. The evident decline in belief, practice and religious vocations in the post-war period is not uniform throughout all sections of society, but related both to key socio-demographic indicators (age, sex, class, occupation, education) and to moral values.

Some social scientists see religious involvement as primarily a function of social class or as a response to different forms of deprivation (material, social, psychological) — providing consolation, comfort, or substitute rewards in a situation of powerlessness or distorted perception of the cause of disadvantage (Glock and Stark, 1965; Glock *et al.*, 1967). Empirical studies, however, indicate that social class differences contribute little by way of explanation of patterns of church involvement (McCready and Greeley, 1976). Similarly, empirical verification of Glock's theory is lacking (Stark, 1972; Roof, 1978).

Luckmann emphasises the degree of involvement in the work process and the spread of functional differentiation and urban culture into rural localities via the media (Luckmann, 1967). Martin (1978) goes so far as to identify specific occupational categories at risk in particular cultural contexts — for example process workers in impersonal, large scale, highly mechanised heavy industrial sectors and employees in large scale farming projects subject to economic uncertainty. Others have stressed the seeming irrelevance, indeed apparent opposition, of the values promoted by the churches to many contemporary concerns (Schmidtchen, 1972).

The importance of value change is often regarded as stimulating a rapid short term deterioration in involvement (Hoge and Roozen, 1979), particularly following the emergence of a 'counterculture' among the younger generation during the 1960s, which emphasised rights, protest, change and the rejection of traditional moral values and constraints on 'permissive' social behaviour (Wuthnow, 1976, (i)). The defence of traditional values was defined in fact by some sociologists as a response of a threatened group to potential loss of social status (Zurcher and Kirkpatrick, 1976).

Wilson focuses on the displacement of symbolism and religious ritual formerly used to celebrate and legitimise social life: to initiate the young; celebrate the harvest; heal the sick; revere the old; and sustain the bereaved. The modern, mobile, large-scale society has little communal life to sustain, legitimise or celebrate. The system relies, he suggests, less on people being good, more on their actions being calculable. The conception of the supernatural as a meaningful reality is remote from everyday life (Berger, 1969). Yet where people's life and work continue to be lived 'in contexts which are familiar and on a human scale, they are more likely to practise Christianity and be sensitive to it' (Martin, 1978, p.160).

The quality of relationships in the parental home — between mother and father, parent and child — has also been shown to contribute significantly to explanations of religious self-definition and church attendance (McCready and Greeley, 1976). In addition to the family, ethnic-group attachment and local community orientation, as opposed to a wider 'cosmopolitan' perspective, appear to underpin both belief and practice — particularly among 'liberal' protestants and catholics (Roof, 1978; Roof and Hoge, 1980). Dobbelaere, commenting on Roof's research, suggests that 'declining community attachment, more than erosion of traditional beliefs *per se*, is the critical factor in accounting for the decline in church attendance and church support' (Dobbelaere, 1981, p.141), and that whilst the influence of parental religiosity and social status on church attendance are stronger among 'locals', it is the 'localism' itself which is the 'primary plausibility structure'. Roof further speculates that the increasingly 'cosmopolitan-modernist' sub-culture of the young and better educated and the identification of institutional church membership with the local-tradition sub-culture is a cause of declining church commitment. The result, he suggests, is likely to be a widening cleavage between older traditionalists, holding conventional moral values and involved in the church and the young cosmopolitan embracing the new morality (Roof and Hoge, 1980). Others see the potential for a return to the church in the middle life — particularly among those whose parents were religious, or for religious values to re-assert themselves in later generations not exposed to the counterculture of the sixties (Wuthnow, 1976, (i) and (ii); McCready, 1981).

References

Bellah, R.N. (1964) 'Religious evolution', *American Sociological Review*, 29, pp.358–74.

Berger, P. (1961) *The Noise of Solemn Assemblies*, New York, Doubleday.

Berger, P. (1967) *The Sacred Canopy*, New York, Doubleday.

Berger, P. (1969) *The Social Reality of Religion*, London, Faber and Faber.

Dobbelaere, K. (1981) 'Secularization: a multi-dimensional concept', *Current Sociology* 29, London Sage.

Fenn, R.K. (1978) *Towards a Theory of Secularization,* Storrs, Connecticutt, Society for the Scientific Study of Religion.

Geertz, C. (1968) 'Religion as a cultural system' in Banton, M. (ed.) *Anthropological Approaches to the Study of Religion*, London, Tavistock.

Glock, C.Y. and Stark, R. (1965) *Religion and Society in Tension,* Chicago, Rand McNally.

Glock, C.Y., Ringer, B.B. and Bobbie, E.R. (1967) *To Comfort and to Challenge: A Dilemma of the Contemporary Church*, Berkeley, University of California Press.

Greeley, A. M. (1972) *Unsecular Man: The Persistence of Religion*, New York, Schocken.

Herberg, W. (1967) 'Religion in a secularized society: the new shape of religion in America' in Knudten, R. (ed.) *The Sociology of Religion*, New York, Appleton Century Crofts.

Hoge, D.R. and Roozen, D.A. (1979) *Understanding Church Growth and Doctrine 1950–1978,* Derby, Pilgrim Press.

Luckmann, T. (1967) *The Invisible Religion,* London, Macmillan.

Martin, D. (1978) *A General Theory of Secularization,* Oxford, Blackwell.

McCready, W.C. and Greeley, A.M. (1976) *The Ultimate Values of the American Population*, vol.23, Sage Library of Social Research, Beverley Hills, Sage.

McCready, W.C. (1981) 'A researcher's view' in *Towards More Effective Research in the Church: A National Catholic Symposium*, FADICA.

Nelson, H.H. and Everett, R.F. (1976) 'A test of Yinger's measure of non-doctrinal religion: implications for invisible religion as a belief system', *Journal for the Scientific Study of Religion,* 15, pp.263–7.

Parsons, T. (1967) 'Christianity and modern industrial society' in Tiryakian, E.A. (ed.) *Sociological Theory, Values and Sociocultural Change,* London, Harper and Row.

Roof, W.C. *et al.* (1977) 'Yinger's measure of non-doctrinal religion: a north eastern test', *Journal for the Scientific Study of Religion*, 16, pp. 403–8.

Roof, W.C. (1978) 'Social correlates of religious involvement: review of recent research in the United States', *The Annual Review of the Social Sciences of Religion*, p.2.

Roof, W.C. and Hoge, D.R. (1980) 'Church involvement in America: social factors affecting membership and participation', *Review of Religious Research* 21, pp.405–26.

Schmidtchen, G. (1972) *Zwischen Kirche und Gesellschaft. Forschungsbericht uber die Umfragen zur Gemeinsamen Synode der Bistumer in der Bundesrepublik Deutschland,* Herder.

Stark, R. (1972) 'The economics of piety: religious commitment and social class' in Thielbar, C. and Feldman, A. (eds) *Issues in Social Inequality*, Harpers Ferry, Little Brown.

Wuthnow, R. (1976(i)) 'Recent patterns of secularization: a problem of generations?' *American Sociological Review,* 41, 5, pp.850–67.

Wuthnow, R. (1976(ii)) *The Consciousness Reformation,* Berkeley, University of California Press.

Yinger, J.M. (1962) *Sociology Looks at Religion*, London, Macmillan.

Yinger, J.M. (1977) 'A comparative study of the substructures of religion', *Journal for the Scientific Study of Religion,* 16, pp.68–86.

Zurcher, L. and Kirkpatrick, G. (1976) *Citizens for Decency: Anti-Pornography Campaign and Status Defence*, Austin, University of Texas Press.

READING C   CONFESSION

Michel Foucault

Since the Middle Ages at least, western societies have established the confession as one of the main rituals we rely on for the production of truth.

… For a long time, the individual was vouched for by the reference of others and the demonstration of his ties to the commonweal (family, allegiance, protection); then he was authenticated by the discourse of truth he was able or obliged to pronounce concerning himself. The truthful confession was inscribed at the heart of the procedures of individualization by power.

In any case, next to the testing rituals, next to the testimony of witnesses, and the learned methods of observation and demonstration, the confession became one of the West's most highly valued techniques for producing truth. We have since become a singularly confessing society. The confession has spread its effects far and wide. It plays a part in justice, medicine, education, family relations, and love relations, in the most ordinary affairs of everyday life, and in the most solemn rites; one confesses

Source: Foucault, M. (1980) *The History of Sexuality*, vol.1, New York, Vintage Books, pp.58–63.

one's crimes, one's sins, one's thoughts and desires, one's illnesses and troubles; one goes about telling, with the greatest precision, whatever is most difficult to tell. One confesses in public and in private, to one's parents, one's educators, one's doctor, to those one loves; one admits to oneself, in pleasure and in pain, things it would be impossible to tell to anyone else, the things people write books about. One confesses — or is forced to confess. When it is not spontaneous or dictated by some internal imperative, the confession is wrung from a person by violence or threat; it is driven from its hiding place in the soul, or extracted from the body. Since the Middle Ages, torture has accompanied it like a shadow, and supported it when it could go no further: the dark twins. The most defenseless tenderness and the bloodiest of powers have a similar need of confession. Western man has become a confessing animal.

… The confession is a ritual of discourse in which the speaking subject is also the subject of the statement; it is also a ritual that unfolds within a power relationship, for one does not confess without the presence (or virtual presence) of a partner who is not simply the interlocutor but the authority who requires the confession, prescribes and appreciates it, and intervenes in order to judge, punish, forgive, console, and reconcile; a ritual in which the truth is corroborated by the obstacles and resistances it has had to surmount in order to be formulated; and finally, a ritual in which expression alone, independently of its external consequences, produces intrinsic modifications in the person who articulates it: it exonerates, redeems, and purifies him; it unburdens him of his wrongs, liberates him, and promises him salvation. For centuries, the truth of sex was, at least for the most part, caught up in this discursive form.

… The confession was, and still remains, the general standard governing the production of the true discourse on sex. It has undergone a considerable transformation, however. For a long time, it remained firmly entrenched in the practice of penance. But with the rise of Protestantism, the Counter Reformation, eighteenth-century pedagogy, and nineteenth-century medicine, it gradually lost its ritualistic and exclusive localization; it spread; it has been employed in a whole series of relationships: children and parents, students and educators, patients and psychiatrists, delinquents and experts. The motivations and effects it is expected to produce have varied, as have the forms it has taken: interrogations, consultations, autobiographical narratives, letters; they have been recorded, transcribed, assembled into dossiers, published, and commented on. But more important, the confession lends itself, if not to other domains, at least to new ways of exploring the existing ones. It is no longer a question simply of saying what was done — the sexual act — and how it was done; but of reconstructing, in and around the act, the thoughts that recapitulated it, the obsessions that accompanied it, the images, desires, modulations, and quality of the pleasure that animated it. For the first time no doubt, a society has taken upon itself to solicit and hear the imparting of individual pleasures.

READING D   DOMINATION AND ITS DISCONTENTS: MICHEL FOUCAULT

James Beckford

Foucault was prepared to find constellations of power relations in such specific social settings as the professions, the police, churches and social welfare agencies. He associated the growing power of these agencies with the production of ever more specialized knowledge which, in turn, has served to control more and more areas of so-called private life. The control is supposedly exercised by imposing categorizations and classifications which have the effect of inducing progressively sharper distinctions between acceptable and unacceptable notions of what a normal human individual is like.

The use of the sacrament of confession in the Roman Catholic Church, for example, was cited by Foucault (1978) as a practice which became adapted to the modern discourse of sexuality. It did not consign sex to the shadows but it compelled professionals and experts in many specialisms to speak about sex endlessly whilst, at the same time, insisting that it be kept a secret. Euphemisms, metaphors and sanitized analogies therefore cloaked the compulsory topic in mystery. Foucault believed that this combination of a compelling discourse with a secret subject-matter generated more and more opportunities and methods for the control of human beings. According to Foucault, this is a good example of the way in which people have learned to regard themselves as 'subjects' in the light of modern knowledge. In other words, the discourse of sexuality has transformed people into objects by individualizing them in particular ways.

Religion, as an institution and in the form of concrete groups and professional roles, interested Foucault mainly for the techniques that it allegedly supplied to the overall 'economy of power relations' — partly from the point of view of domination and partly from the point of view of struggle and resistance against domination. Thus, the Reformation represented

> a great crisis of the Western experience of subjectivity and a revolt against the kind of religious and moral power which gave form, during the Middle Ages, to this subjectivity. The need to take a direct part in spiritual life, in the work of salvation, in the truth which lies in the Book — all that was a struggle for a new subjectivity.
> (Foucault, 1982, p.213)

The ironic importance of this kind of struggle, for Foucault, was that it led to the eventual rise of the nation state as a novel complex of power relations. For the kind of 'pastoral power' that had previously been fostered by the major Christian churches was apparently assimilated by the post-Reformation states in such a way that religious techniques of individualization were combined with the political technique of totaliza-

Source: Beckford, J. (1989) *Religion and Advanced Industrial Society*, London, Unwin Hyman, pp.123–7.

tion. The result, as Foucault argued in a thoroughly functionalist vein, was that the declining vitality of church organizations was accompanied by the diffusion of individualizing pastoral power throughout modern societies:

> Power of a pastoral type, which over centuries — for more than a millenium — had been linked to a defined religious institution, suddenly spread out into the whole social body; it found support in a multitude of institutions. And, instead of pastoral power and a political power, more or less linked to each other, more or less rival, there was an individualizing 'tactic' which characterized a series of powers: those of the family, medicine, psychiatry, education, and employers.
> (Foucault, 1982, p.215)

... In some respects, Foucault's work seems to stand Weber's account of modernity on its head. Instead of positing rational individuals as the originators of a rationalized world, Foucault seems to posit structures of power as the originators of modern individuality. ... A further effect of Foucault's approach to the key problem of modernity is to call in question the assumption that human societies have ever been integrated on the basis of anything other than power. This means that communally based societies were never based primarily on normative consensus and that the prevailing notions of individuality tended to be moulded to suit the interests of the dominant powers. For Foucault, then, the main problem of modernity was not social differentiation, the decline of community, or the separation between public and private spheres. On the contrary, it was what he considered to be the dehumanizing power of the many institutions which elicited from individuals a pervasive sense of being subjects and of thereby being duped into conformity with ruling interests. The problem is therefore one of excessive integration or control.

... Although Foucault may have correctly described the diffusion of 'pastoral power' across many non-religious institutions, it does not follow that religion has been deprived of all power. It is ironic that Foucault's project for a history of the present remained stalled at the medieval and Reformation periods as far as religion is concerned. But it would be well worthwhile to examine the interrelatedness of contemporary discourses about the self, the body, birth, death, illness, health and spiritual well-being. The religious input to these discourses is considerable, as it is to the discourses of human rights, justice and peace as well. Moreover, the practices of confession and testimony, in addition to being diffused throughout modern society, according to Foucault, are still central to the activities of many religious organizations.

References

Foucault, M. (1978) *The History of Sexuality*, vol.1, *An Introduction*, New York, Random House.

Foucault, M. (1982) 'The subject and power', in Dreyfus, H.L. and Rabinow, P. *Michel Foucault: Beyond Structuralism and Hermeneutics*, Chicago, University of Chicago Press.

CHAPTER 8   POPULAR CULTURE AND THE MASS MEDIA

Celia Lury

CONTENTS

1   INTRODUCTION

It is only relatively recently that social scientists have begun to devote serious attention to the study of culture in its own right. There are various definitions of culture, but for a long time sociologists and anthropologists were mainly interested in culture in the broad sense of the meanings, values and ways of life of particular nations, groups, classes and periods (see Book 1 (Hall and Gieben, 1992), Chapter 5). In recent years there has been a shift of emphasis from this broad interest in the content of culture (e.g. religious beliefs) to a focus on culture as a set of practices which produce meaning — 'signifying practices'. This shift has been described as a movement from 'what' to 'how'. In other words, whereas the earlier focus was on the content of culture viewed as a whole way of life, the contemporary approach concentrates on the interrelationships between the components that make up a particular cultural practice which produces meanings. One result of this development has been a growth in studies of the media of mass communication and the practices involved in the production, transmission and reception of meanings.

Despite the prominence of the mass media in modern society, analysis of them, and of culture, have traditionally presented a problem for social scientists. Culture has often been seen as something intangible: too fluid, imprecise and subjective to be amenable to rigourous analysis. Alternatively, culture may be argued to be little more than a reflection or legitimation of dominant social relations, dependent upon the social structure, and thus unworthy of independent study. The paradox that has frustrated social scientists is the way in which culture is both always tied to power relations and, at the same time, only recognizable as culture by its apparent distance from those same relations.

This chapter will introduce an approach to the study of culture which may help explain this paradox. It will do this by looking at the historical conditions in which the cultural sphere emerged as a relatively distinct set of activities, with its own internal criteria of quality. The chapter will focus on this socially achieved *differentiation* of the cultural sphere — that is, its separation from other kinds of activity. It will look at arguments which suggest that this differentiation was the historical result of the interaction of a number of processes. These include the development of the cultural technologies or means of production commonly known as the media, the specialization of cultural production, and, perhaps most importantly, the attempted *autonomization* of cultural objects. This term (*autonomization*) refers to the ways in which cultural activity or work is separated off, more or less successfully, from other kinds of work. This is most clear in relation to artistic activities, which are often evaluated in terms of their purposelessness, or their practically useless imaginative element. However, the term can also be applied more generally to any cultural activities where these tend to be evaluated in terms of an autonomy or distance from any externally defined purpose or end: that is, in opposition to any utilitarian function.

One consequence of the emergence of the cultural sphere as a distinct set of activities was that it became possible to define culture in terms of all those practices whose principal or specialized function is making meaning, the institutions that organize such practices, and the agents that initiate and receive them (a definition adapted from that given by Mulhern, 1980). Robert Bocock argues (see Book 1 (Hall and Gieben, 1992), Chapter 5) that the separation of culture as a distinct sphere was not as complete as in the cases of the political, economic and social spheres. However, the existence of a distinction between practices whose *sole* or *primary* significance is the making of meaning and those in which this is subordinated to some other purpose, while never absolute, is a defining characteristic of modern societies. It is important to recognize that, in focusing on this notion of culture as a specialized set of practices, this chapter will be primarily discussing only the second and fifth of the five definitions of culture given by Bocock (Book 1 (Hall and Gieben, 1992), Chapter 5): culture as 'the arts', extended to include 'popular culture', and as 'signifying practices'. However, as we shall see, the changing relation between culture as a distinct set of practices and broader definitions of culture as a whole way of life is a central concern in debates about the status of contemporary culture.

A further question to be considered in this chapter is the nature of the relationship between production and reception within this newly emergent sphere. For example, is the interchange between producers and audiences characterized by cooperation, mutual support and reciprocal influence? Or are there divisions of interest and differences of judgement between the two groups? If there are such divisions or asymmetries, which group has the greater power? — that is, who has the power to define the meanings of cultural goods? How has this relationship changed over time? And, in particular, how has the development of the media transformed this relationship?

In order to explore these issues, this chapter will make use of the idea of a circuit or cycle of cultural production and reception, in which production and reception are related activities but not necessarily determined by each other. We might call this a *mode of appropriation,* using that term to refer to all the social relations within which cultural goods are produced, distributed and received. A mode of appropriation also isolates certain moments in the circuit as particularly significant for the fixing of meanings. For example, we often take it for granted that the most authentic meaning of an artwork can be found by relating it to the producer as a creative individual — to his or her intentions, other work, life history and so on. However, this is only one of a number of possible techniques of interpretation that can be applied to artworks. Instead of simply applying this technique, this chapter will investigate the social and political conditions in which 'the author' or creator of an artwork came to function as a category of interpretation in this way. It will also explore the implications of this technique for the kinds of meanings that can be attributed to cultural goods — that is, for the nature of cultural experience — within the overall mode of appropriation.

This chapter will also investigate the emergence of distinctions *within* the cultural sphere, in particular that between high culture and popular culture. It will look at the argument that the emergence of this distinction can be understood in relation to the different ways in which the relationship between cultural production and cultural reception has been organized historically. Indeed, it will suggest that this use of 'the author' as a means for interpretation has been one of the principal mechanisms by which high culture has not simply been distinguished from, but also privileged above, popular culture. However, it will also argue that popular culture needs to be analysed in terms of its own intrinsic character and relations, and not simply in terms of what it has been opposed to — i.e. high culture. In general, then, this chapter will consider the ways in which cycles of cultural production and reception have been organized historically, and will seek to avoid making judgements about the cultural value of any one particular organization of those processes.

The chapter is organized as follows. In Section 2 we consider the emergence of print technology as a form of cultural mass reproduction and the various possibilities which this opened up for different groups to use its products in different ways ('modes of appropriation'). In Section 3 we examine the struggles that this gave rise to over who should be taught to read and to what level, struggles that had effects on social divisions. Section 4 then considers one of the most enduring conflicts in the history of the mass media: that between the interests of the state and of the market in regulating the production and circulation of cultural goods such as newspapers and books. Section 5 proceeds to analyse some of the processes by which culture became hierarchical, as reflected in the distinction between high culture and popular culture; one such process involves the ways in which importance is attributed to the status and intentions of the author of cultural goods such as novels (the 'author function'). In Section 6, we examine the development of rival models of broadcasting organization — public and commercial — and the different sorts of audiences that these produce. In Section 7, the examination of different audiences leads on to a consideration of how audiences receive broadcast programmes: whether they are relatively passive or active, and how their viewing practices fit in with their domestic circumstances. This is related to the issue of whether the technologies of mass reproduction of cultural goods result in the automatic reproduction of culture and society itself, or whether popular culture is the site of negotiation, transformation and creativity with regard to meanings. In conclusion (Section 8), we return to the issue that threads its way through most of this chapter (including Section 7): namely, the extent to which culture is determined by factors in other spheres — the economy, politics and social relations such as class — or whether it has its own logic and hierarchies.

2 PRINT TECHNOLOGY AS A MEANS OF CULTURAL PRODUCTION

The emergence of modern society has often been conceptualized in terms of a differentiation of the social, economic, political and cultural spheres of activity. However, the special or distinctive character of the cultural sphere is often taken for granted in today's society. This may be, in part, because of the public visibility of the institutions of the mass media which act as specialized systems for the production and distribution of cultural goods, such as television programmes, films, books, records, tapes, compact discs, newspapers and magazines. It may be helpful, then, in considering the distinctive features of the cultural sphere to contrast the modern understanding of what is cultural or artistic with that of traditional or pre-modern societies.

A number of writers have argued that such pre-modern societies were characterized by cultural integration: that is, what we would now recognize as 'art' or 'culture' were then seen as more or less inseparable aspects of some other social practice. Let us take the example of totemism, a term that refers to the symbolic association of plants, animals or objects with individuals or groups of people within what is called a totemic system. Association is a characteristic feature of many traditional societies. In one of the most well-known analyses of totemism, the anthropologist Claude Levi-Strauss (1908–) argues that totemism is a common process in which the natural world is divided into different groups of species or things in ways which reflect and construct social differences (Levi-Strauss, 1969). In this way, an object stands for, or is the symbolic representation of a clan or social group that, in turn, is recognized by its use of the object and its members' shared appreciation of what the object stands for. The object is thus a cultural object, and its meaning is closely tied to the ways in which it acts as a marker for the social hierarchies of the group for whom it has cultural significance. It is in this sense that totemism is an example of culturally integrated practice: the meanings of the objects involved form an integral aspect of the social relations of which they are a part.

Modern societies also display forms of 'totemism' but, in addition, are more commonly characterized by sets of practices which have no other purpose than to be artistic. Under what conditions, then, has there been this separation of the cultural from other spheres of activity? In his book *Culture* (1981), Raymond Williams develops a sociological framework for the analysis of the emergence of this sphere. He argues that the process of cultural differentiation was linked to the development of certain kinds of cultural technology or means of communication. He suggests that 'means of production' as a general category includes both those means which depend on inherent, human resources — such as the body — and those which depend on the use of non-human material objects and forces. Although he notes the continuing importance of the first group of means of production (or 'technologies') in contemporary

society, he argues that the development and implementation of the
second group has been particularly important for the processes of
cultural differentiation.

ACTIVITY 1

You should now read **Reading A, 'Means of cultural production'**, by
Raymond Williams, which you will find at the end of this chapter. What
role does Williams suggest that the second type of means of production
played in the differentiation of the cultural sphere?

Williams suggests that the second type of means of production
facilitated the large-scale production of identical cultural goods. Most
importantly, these mass-produced objects could be, and were, separated
from their context of production: their distribution to an extended but
indeterminate audience led to a profound shift in the *mode of
appropriation* which determined their use and meaning. Print, the
major form of technology which makes possible the reproduction of
writing, is identified by Williams as a key example of this second type
of means of cultural production.

Death among the printers: the earliest known illustration of a printing press, from
Danse Macabre, Lyons, 1499

Other writers too have argued that the introduction of print was an
epoch-making event. Elizabeth Eisenstein (1979), among others, suggests
that it played an important part in the shift from a predominantly oral
to a largely literate culture. It provided a new technological means of

recording, codifying, retrieving, and transmitting information and ideas. It made possible the production and distribution of large quantities of cultural objects (books) that were easily distributed, carried on one's person or posted, and that gave images and texts a more substantial presence and a more familiar reality in more people's everyday lives. Printing extended people's reach through time and space, Eisenstein notes, by making possible new kinds of continuity and access to writing and the ideas it contained.

One important example of the implications of this shift is discussed by the German cultural critic, Walter Benjamin in his article 'The storyteller' (Benjamin,1970a). Benjamin argues that the validity of the kind of experiential knowledge which was passed on in oral cultures from storyteller to audience through the traditional narrative form of the shared story was undermined by the introduction of print. The oral way of knowing was replaced by a modern understanding of knowledge as information: that is, a form of knowledge which holds true independent of its meaning for any particular individual. For Benjamin, this represented a loss; it contributed to the erasure of perspective in ways of knowing and a flattening out of the depths of experience, and was one factor in the break-down of traditional forms of community. Benjamin suggests that information is a form of knowledge which lacks what he calls 'the epic side of truth [that is] wisdom'. However, other writers — and, indeed, Benjamin on other occasions — have been less confident about describing such changes simply as loss, and point to the emergence of new kinds of cultural experience facilitated by the development of print. For example, it has been suggested that the written word came to provide a novel way of linking generations by contributing to novel understandings of the self and its relations to others through the development of such new cultural forms as the biography, the autobiography and the diary.

However, neither of these examples is intended to imply that there is a direct relationship — negative or positive — between technologies or means of communication and the particular cultural forms they come to be associated with. As easily identifiable forces, technologies are often singled out as the prime causes of change: for example, in the work of Marshall McLuhan (McLuhan,1962; McLuhan and Fiore,1967). From McLuhan comes the famous aphorism, 'the medium is the message', which still provides a useful insight into the role of technological form in shaping the message it transmits. However, McLuhan's explanatory framework, which construes more or less everything that has happened as the effect — either direct or indirect — of changes in communications technologies, has been widely criticized. Both Eisenstein (1979) and Williams (1974) argue that this kind of approach is misleading. In contrast to McLuhan's technological determinism, they stress the importance of locating technologies within the social contexts of their development. It is not enough, they argue, to present the technology concerned as the outcome of a purely autonomous history of technical development. Instead, it must be understood as the outcome of a complex series of related technical developments, each of which needs to be understood, not only in relation to an internal technical history, but also in relation to other, external determinations and considerations, including changes in the potential audience.

In the case of the technology of print, Eisenstein and Williams suggest that its emergence in the late Middle Ages must be understood in relation to a growing demand for books, and the market opportunities this presented for the development of a more efficient mode of production. The demand for books can itself be related to urbanization and the growth in merchant trade, which created a need for information to be available to new social groups in new kinds of ways. For these reasons, the technology of print can be seen as a response to changes in the social conditions of cultural need, and not as a purely internal step in the history of the technology of cultural production. In this respect, it is also interesting to note that 'silent' reading — the now common way of reading — had begun to replace the practice of oral reading well before the development of print, and was not simply its consequence.

ACTIVITY 2   Consider the following question:

What according to Williams was the relationship between producers and audiences in this newly differentiated cultural sphere?

Williams points out that the advantages which the technology of print offered, including the possibility of an enormous increase in the output of books, were limited by the disadvantage of the need for special training to make use of its potential. This training was necessary, not only for producers, as had become common in other cultural practices such as dance or song, but also for receivers. Nevertheless, given access to this training, the potential of the new means of communication was never wholly controllable: 'There was no way to teach a man to read the Bible — a predominant intention in much early education in literacy — which did not also enable him to read the radical press' (Williams, 1981, p.101).

And it was precisely the new reach of print, across space, time and occasion, which provided the conditions for its highly variable reception, and contributed to the many uses of literacy. The new mass accessibility of written materials meant that audiences were less constrained in their use and understanding of these materials.

What Williams is suggesting is that the differences between the producers and the audiences for cultural goods — differences already present in oral cultures — were exacerbated by the new means of communication and took on a new social significance in literate culture. To use his terms, an *asymmetry* or division of interests began to emerge between producers and audience. He points out that while the development of print increased the potential power of cultural producers relative to that of the audience, the cultural significance of print was never limited to the intentions of its developers. The audience were able to make use of the skills of reading in ways which were not only unintended by producers, but were also sometimes in conflict with such intentions.

3   STRUGGLES OVER LITERACY

Williams's view is supported by recent work on the growth of literacy which focuses on struggles over its extension and uses. As the quotation from Williams in the previous section implies, it has sometimes been argued that the increase in literacy during the period of industrialization can be explained by the growing demand for an educated and God-fearing workforce. According to this view, mass literacy was a functional response to the needs of social reproduction of the time. However, in his study, 'The cultural origins of literacy in England 1500–1850', Thomas Laqueur argues that the fact that a surprisingly large number of people could read and write in seventeenth- and eighteenth-century England cannot adequately be understood in these terms. He writes:

> Neither economic necessity imposed by commercial or industrial developments nor schools founded by the higher orders to convert, control, or in some way mould the working classes can explain how literacy became so widespread. The adoption and use of a technology, like writing, by large numbers of people is not explicable by institutional or material forces.
> (Laqueur, 1976, p.255)

Laqueur prefers to explain the growth of literacy and the spread of literate forms of culture into all aspects of people's lives in terms of a desire to read which was prompted by increasingly diversified needs. These included the wish to participate in the formal processes of dominant economic and political activity which were increasingly coming to require the skills of literacy; the desire to join in radical political protest and popular forms of protestant religion; and, not least, the wish to enjoy recreational forms of literature.

Moreover, personalized reading in private, although increasingly common, was not the sole use of print objects: they were also used collectively in festive, ritual, civic and pedagogic practices. Such uses invested the handling of the chapbook, the tract, the broadsheet and the reproduced image with values and intentions which had little to do with those of solitary book reading. Laqueur provides further evidence to show that the skills of reading, and to a lesser extent writing, were not only acquired in schools, but were often picked up from literate parents, relatives or friends as part of the general processes of socialization. His research thus suggests that the growth of literacy was linked to the early stages of the development of a specifically modern organization of the audience as public (or, more accurately, a variety of publics). That is, the spread of literacy was not simply a passive response to the new availability of print, nor was its use confined by the intentions of those who provided formal training in the skills of reading in response to the needs of the economy; rather, the spread of literacy was a consequence (in part, at least) of the growth of an audience with its own, pre-existing desires and demands for information and entertainment.

ACTIVITY 3   In the light of the above discussion, consider why it is, then, that Williams links the need for special training with the emergence of a new kind of stratification?

Williams points out that literacy gradually came to be understood, not simply as the ability to read, but also as the ability to read in certain ways: as the ability to display a particular kind of sensitivity and discrimination. That this was so is indicated by the dual meaning of the word 'literate', which has both a categorical and a social meaning: in the first case referring to the ability to read, and in the second case to the state of being well-read. Williams suggests that the development of this distinction of levels in literacy should be understood as the result of an attempt to set up a kind of internal hierarchy within the reading public. He argues that access to the second, or higher, level of literacy was determined by access to the skills and conventions of reading and that this was initially tied to more general social hierarchies. This implies that the acquisition of the specialized skills of reading and writing were directly determined by an individual's position within the social order. Although Laqueur suggests (as we have seen) that training was not entirely limited in this way, Williams maintains that the earliest forms of specialized training were developed by, and confined to, very limited groups.

In general, however, while there is some debate about the conditions under which ordinary people learned to read, it is clear that the implications of unequal access became more and more significant in social terms as the skills of reading and writing came to be required for participation in a wider and wider range of everyday activities. As a result, the technical innovation of printing had the effect of contributing to a new kind of stratification, in which the power and public presence of the oral majority was diminished. As Williams goes on to argue, this stratification, while still loosely related to existing forms of inequality, gradually came to be ordered in terms of status and knowledge organized through the specialized institutions of publishing, criticism, and, perhaps most importantly, education. As a result, in some respects at least, this new type of hierarchy did not directly support traditional forms of stratification, although, as we shall see, it did draw on the already existing social divisions between social groups, particularly those of class and gender. Nevertheless, it was not simply a replication of an existing pattern of inequality, but one that established new relations of authority between social groups. Using Williams's framework, it is thus possible to see the growth of this new type of stratification and the emergence of these specialized institutions as further stages in the differentiation of the cultural sphere from the social. These developments structured a new field of forces in which individuals and groups of individuals struggled over the meanings and uses of the new means of communication.

4   MARKET RELATIONS AND THE DEVELOPMENT OF THE PRESS

The discussion of literacy so far suggests that the emerging sphere of culture was an area of exchange or negotiation in which different groups struggled over the implications of the new means of cultural production. This is particularly clear from the way in which literacy became an issue in public political debate during the eighteenth and nineteenth centuries. During this period, the state, which was increasingly dependent on the use of literate forms of culture itself, implemented new methods of control, including, for example, new forms of censorship and new legislation defining the terms of criminal libel. However, the state's control was initially exerted primarily through its use of the right to license printing. This enabled it to restrict use of the new means of cultural production to those bodies of whom it approved.

However, this system of regulation collapsed under pressure from market forces in the late seventeenth century, as the commercial opportunities presented by the new technology of printing became more and more obvious. This event marks the initial stages of what Williams suggests is one of the most enduring conflicts in the history of the mass media: that is, the conflict between the interests of the state and those of the market in regulating the production and circulation of cultural goods. This conflict arises from the differences of interest between different groups of producers and/or those in a position to regulate use of the new means of production. In observing this conflict, Williams makes an important point about the need to recognize differences between different groups of producers, and directs attention to the conflicting interests of the state and commercial groups in the exploitation of the new media.

This victory for commercial interests did not mean the end of the state's attempts to contain the politically disruptive potential of print, in particular the press, which grew rapidly in circulation during this period. For example, press taxation — taxes on newspapers, pamphlets, press advertisements and paper — was implemented in the early nineteenth century in an attempt to restrict both ownership and readership of the press to the 'respectable' sections of society by pricing participation out of the reach of many in the lower classes. In addition, some of the traditional legal sanctions were retained, including the laws of treason and seditious libel, while financial subsidies, bribes and the management of news were also developed as new methods of controlling the press.

Nevertheless, although press taxation undoubtedly slowed down the continued growth of the commercial press, it did not halt its expansion altogether, and the late eighteenth and early nineteenth centuries saw a growth in both the regional and the metropolitan press as part of a significant increase in total newspaper consumption. The increasing vitality of the press was closely linked with the growth of the urban bourgeoisie, but the new reading public also included working people, small shopkeepers, skilled journeymen, independent tradesmen and the artisan classes. A further feature of the general expansion of this period was the emergence of a radical press. Directed particularly towards the lower income groups in the country, radical newspapers were produced on cheap iron-frame presses and overall production costs were extremely low. This development produced an important channel through which radical political ideas were distributed to an increasingly politically conscious working class.

Indeed, the commercial press as a whole became progressively more independent of the landed political elite in the late eighteenth and early nineteenth centuries as divisions between different factions within the ruling group became more visible. Press independence was supported by two Acts of Parliament in particular. Fox's Libel Act of 1792 blunted the ability of governments to harass the commercial press with libel suits by making juries the judges of guilt in seditious libel prosecutions. Lord Campbell's Libel Act of 1843 made the statement of truth in the public interest a legitimate defence against the charge of criminal libel. Both these Acts, as well as the piecemeal abolition of the press taxes in the mid-nineteenth century, emerged as part of the political compromise which was forged between the interests of the commercial sector of the middle classes and those of the bourgeois philanthropists as old forms of aristocratic power were eroded. The terms of this compromise acknowledged the importance of the newly emerging public sphere: a forum for public discussion made possible by the emergence of mass communications that were relatively independent of the state.

The political implications of this shift in the mode of regulation of the press, from a predominantly statist to a commercial form, have been much debated. Some people see this as the period in which the press, acting as a check or 'fourth estate' in relation to the power of the state, achieved a degree of independence from dominant political interests. They point to the emergence of a new professional ethos in journalism as an indication of the growing autonomy of the cultural producer. Certainly the unrestricted growth of advertising patronage and sales revenue allowed the commercial press to become yet more detached from the political elite. However, others have suggested that while the measures discussed above, particularly the abolition of press taxes, significantly altered the character of all newspapers, the period did not see the emergence of an independent press, but rather the replacement of state constraints with new forms of commercial regulation. They suggest that commercial pressures provided their own particular set of conditions for the production and distribution of information.

James Curran (1986), for example, argues that the advertising dependence of all competitively priced newspapers in the mass market meant that the radical press was forced to move up-market in order to attract the audiences which advertisers wanted to reach, and in doing so modified their radical political stances. *Reynold News* is a good example of a paper which faced such a dilemma. Founded in 1848 as a radical Chartist paper, it was gradually forced to go up-market in order to maintain its competitiveness and sales, and as a consequence its radicalism disappeared. In a similar vein, Stuart Hall (1986) suggests that, when a popular commercial press did emerge, it addressed the reading audience not as a public but as a cultural market. What he means by this is that, while the commercial press came increasingly to depend on the popular classes for its survival, they regarded the press, not as something which championed their cause or mobilized them as a popular force, but as just another commodity and an avenue through which the advertisers could display their goods.

REYNOLDS'S NEWSPAPER.

A Weekly Journal of Politics, History, Literature, and General Intelligence.

No. 39.   LONDON: SUNDAY, MAY 11, 1851.   Price Threepence.

JOHN BULL'S BOASTS.

John Bull has got the reputation on the Continent of being, in certain matters, the most frothy braggart and vapouring blusterer that ever provoked ridicule or excited disgust. He vaunts the excellence of the British constitution, but if asked to produce it, he is thrown quite aback. Should he attempt to prove that there is really such a thing in existence, he speedily finds himself floundering in a bog of difficulties; or else he is compelled to slink out of the argument in shame and confusion, and experience the contempt so deservedly bestowed upon every ignorant, besotted, and prejudiced master who fails to make good his vaunt. But generally speaking, John Bull is a thorough bully in his boasts; and whatever impudent and preposterous assertions he who may question his accuracy. He seldom has recourse to argument, because in making his vaunts he only retailing the traditionary prejudices with which he is saturated, and to which he gives utterance as methodically as a school-boy repeats a lesson with which he is well crammed. Thus John Bull's prejudices are not his opinions formed after a careful consideration of the subject; but they are the ideas which he has received cut and dried from his ancestors, and which he regards as gospel because they have descended to him from that source. The consequence is that he is seldom prepared with argument to enforce the truth of his assertions; and his mind is too dull, opaque, and clumsily constituted, to have recourse to the refinements of sophistry. Thus John Bull's vaunts are the vulgarest, coarsest, and most brutal of all the shades and degrees of braggadocia: they are arrogant assertions impudently advanced, pompously maintained, and set forth with a pigheaded defiance of all argument that can possibly be brought against them.

interest consists in excluding that man from those rights; and therefore at the very outset they are predisposed to punish him for even thinking of claiming them. The Jury List is made up of names belonging to the middle and upper classes, whose interests are totally opposed to the interests of the working classes; and therefore the whole of the working-class population, in all matters that have to be decided, are actually and positively at the mercy of their natural enemies.

But this is not all that can be said against our boasted system of trial by jury. An admirable principle has been so scandalously perverted that it really serves the purpose of destroying what it pretends to secure namely, the liberty of the individual. Government can use it at any time as an engine of tyranny and oppression. Opinions which are unpalatable to the upper classes, may be referred to a jury with the certainty of being punished in the person of him who enunciates them. Thus juries are used to try opinions, and to pass an opinion upon opinions; as if this process could be conclusive in respect to any controversy! The nameness, rascality, and infamy of the system become patent enough when we reflect that in such matters nothing can be really proven after all except that the twelve men in the box representing a dominant class, think one way, while the defendant echoing the opinions of a crushed and enslaved class, thinks another way. The Constitution of which John Bull boasts, should, if it at any time assert the right of freedom of opinion, and thus at the very outset proclaim that government has nothing to do with opinions themselves.

The Aristocracy, through the medium of juries, has been merciless, pitiless, and bloodthirsty to a degree, in punishing the opinions of democracy. Suppose now, that democracy became dominant in the land to-

FOREIGN INTELLIGENCE.

FRANCE.

The 4th of May passed off without any disturbance or demonstration. The proclamations of the different republican organs and that of the Mountain, urging the democratic work-people of the capital to refrain from any manifestation on Sunday, had the desired effect. The democratic "sections" were in readiness for any emergency, and only waited, it is said, a word from their chiefs to have acted with energy and resolution. The signal was not given. At six o'clock on Sunday morning the cannon of the Invalides announced the opening of the *fete*. The morning was bright and cloudless, but soon the rain began to fall, though not in abundance The character of the decorations on this occasions were different from that of last year, particularly as respects the Place de la Concorde and the Champs Elysees. Along the grand avenue of the latter were placed opposite each other, and raised on pedestals of more than six feet high, the colossal statues of Pupin the mechanist, who is said to have first applied steam to machines in the reign of Louis XIV. and of Jacquart, the inventor of a new kind of loom in the reign of Napoleon; of Pierre Corneille and Moliere; of Nicholas Poussin, and Jean Goujon, the sculptor in the reign of Charles IX; of Mathew Mole and Cardinal Richelieu; of Jean Bart and Duguay Trouin, both naval commanders of distinction under Louis XIV; of Joan Hachette, the heroine of Beauvais under Louis XI; and of Joan of Arc; of the great Conde, the conqueror of Rocroy, under Louis XIV, and the no less great Turenne, the conqueror of Mulhaused; of Marshal Ney, "the bravest of the brave;" and General Kleber, the conqueror of Heliopolis. The church of the Madeleine had its beautiful *facade* ornamented with tapestry of alternate crimson and gold, and garlands of lamps suspended from its columns facing the Place de la Concorde. At the angles of the *facade* were placed two colossal statues, one representing Faith the other Hope. Along the Rue de la Concorde were extended rows of lamps suspended from pillars placed at short distances from each other. On the middle arch of the Pont de la Concorde, and in front of the

SPAIN.

A Carlist conspiracy on a small scale has been discovered, and seven members of it, having been secured, and attempting to escape, were shot by the troops. A disturbance of a serious nature took place at the Circo Theatre lately. A song containing some democratic sentiments was *encored* by the audience, whereupon some of the municipal authorities instantly left the house and summoned two companies of artillery soldiers to clear the theatre with fixed bayonets. This was accomplished, and owing to the good-natured manner in which the soldiers evidently reluctantly obeyed their orders, more serious consequences were avoided. It is said that the Queen and her mother were both anxious that an armed intervention on the part of Spain, in the affairs of Portugal, should be immediately effected; but remonstrances made by several foreign diplomatists have served to convince them that such a step would be highly injudicious. The *Espana* publishes the manifesto of the electoral committee of the democratic progressist party. It demands universal suffrage and the exercise of national sovereignty, the right of public meeting, the abolition of all monopolies, entire freedom of the press, an elective council of state, the independence of municipalities, trial by jury in all cases, civil and criminal, the gratuitous administration of justice, gratuitous public education, reduction of the budget, and the abolition of the military conscription, and the consideration of the social condition of the people with a view to its amelioration. The 27th being the anniversary of the birth of the Queen, there was a grand reception at court. It was again rumoured in Madrid, that the Queen is in "an interesting situation." It is not stated who is, this time, the father of this coming bantling.

PORTUGAL.

The Queen, yielding to circumstances, has dismissed the count de Thomar from his post, which, she says, he exercised "much to her content;" thus again offending the nation. Saldanha was received in Coimbra enthusiastically, and complimented by an infinite number of people. The king, on the contrary, entered Coimbra, and while he was passing through the various streets, the most sullen silence prevailed; he was received only by those officials

Reynolds News started as a radical newspaper

What I have suggested so far, then, is that the introduction and implementation of a new means of communication — print — helped provide the basis for the social differentiation between cultural and other kinds of activities. I have further suggested that the effectiveness of this distinction was determined by the regulation of the uses of this new technology, and by the social and political conditions which determined access to the techniques of both production and reception. However, I also argued that the spread of literacy into more and more aspects of everyday life was not simply achieved by a process of imposition, but was, in part, struggled for by subordinate groups. This is evident in the struggles, not only over the uses of literacy, but also over its very definition. These struggles were a consequence of the attempt to contain the variety of interpretations opened up by the new mobility of texts. Literacy was thus a site of cultural struggle, and as such it was an independent mechanism which structured the relations between social groups: it provided the basis for a new form of stratification.

5   THE NOVEL AND THE DISTINCTION BETWEEN HIGH CULTURE AND POPULAR CULTURE

At the same time that the readership for newspapers was growing, the audience for a wide range of fictional genres of writing was also increasing. Although the state restricted production in this area, through legislation relating to issues such as obscenity and blasphemy, its influence was more indirect than in the area of political information or news. Other institutions — associated with education, publishing, and the elite circles of the public sphere — were more directly involved in the regulation of fictional written material, through their roles in training, and the setting of criteria by which certain kinds of writing and reading came to be valued more highly than others. This was, in part, related to the emergence of the hierarchy in levels of literacy which has already been noted; but a further means by which this distinction was made was through the selective application of the *author-function*. The meaning of this term needs some explanation.

It has often been pointed out that our modern notions of authorship and creativity began to develop in the second half of the sixteenth century in contradistinction to the earlier notion of craftsmanship. According to Graham Murdock (1980), at that time craftsmanship was characterized by two essential features: a command over technical knowledge and skills which were acquired by a process of training and apprenticeship; and the deployment of those skills to make products demanded by somebody else — usually a patron. In contrast, creative activity came to be defined precisely by its relative freedom from the demands of either patrons or audiences, and was associated with the opportunity to sell work through the market. Indeed, the modern notion of the cultural producer as an author — that is, an independent agent — can be seen to derive from the opportunity to sell artistic work on the market.

However, this was a double-edged development: on the one hand, artists or writers no longer needed to be directly dependent on any of the various forms of patronage; yet, on the other hand, the commercial logic of the market required that artists should become 'artistic proletarians', producing whatever would sell. To some extent the latter tendency predominated, but it was mediated by a romantic discourse of authorship and creativity which cut across the emerging market relations. Within this discourse the author was conceived as an individual producer, an autonomous creative source, unfettered by obligation to patron, client or audience, and free to express his (or, less commonly, her) self. It is this *conception* of the author, rather than the actual writer or artist, which is described by the term 'author-function'. It is a specialized term which refers to the way in which the author is seen to be manifest in the text.

ACTIVITY 4   Now read **Reading B, 'What is an author?'**, by Michel Foucault. Foucault suggests that the author-function came to act as a principle of 'hermeneutic' or interpretative unity. What does he mean by this?

Foucault is highly suspicious of the view that understanding a text in terms of its author is the key to unlocking its true meaning. Indeed, he starts from the assumption that texts have no inherent meaning, but rather are attributed meaning through certain techniques of interpretation which are socially maintained. He further suggests that, within the discourse of authorship and creativity, the author is not to be confused with the real individual who produced or 'authored' the work. Rather, 'the author' should be thought of in terms of what function this construct performs in relation to the work. Its function, Foucault argues, is to provide an explanation for the work's existence, a framework for its interpretation and a method for considering it as a coherent whole. For example, there is still some debate in scholarly circles as to whether a real person called Shakespeare did write the plays attributed to him. But, whether he did or not, scholarship and criticism needs such a figure: the author, 'Shakespeare'. That allows critics and scholars to clarify questions of interpretation in the plays by referring to the experience, biography or intentions of 'Shakespeare'; and to explain discrepancies between one play and another in terms of the vision and 'genius' of the author who wrote them all. Thus, when a number of texts are assumed to be the work of a particular author, relationships of homogeneity and reciprocal explanation are expected to obtain between them. We commonly understand the early and late works of an individual author, such as, for example, the novelist, Virginia Woolf, both in relation to each other, and in relation to what is known of the author's life. Indeed, interpretations of the ending of her life — whether her suicide was the result of mental instability, a consequence of her

fears about the ways in which her husband might respond to her mental
instability, or despair brought on by her recognition of the seriousness
of the political situation which faced Europe — have dominated many
readings of her work.

Virginia Woolf: How far
does knowledge of her
life influence your
appreciation of her
works?

ACTIVITY 5   What are some of the ways in which the operation of the author-
function is maintained today? You might like to consider the ways in
which biographies of authors have influenced your appreciation of their
works.

More generally, the widespread use of the author-function by critics and
reviewers established a special way of defining the link between the
social relations in which culture was produced and the cultural product
itself. This link was defined in terms of 'creative autonomy'. The
artwork was seen as entirely the product of the author's artistic
intentions, and thus came to be interpreted solely in relation to the
author's aesthetic purpose. In this way, the author-function came to be a
key mechanism by which the artwork could be separated from other
kinds of work, and creative activity was distinguished from and
privileged above other, less aesthetic, more instrumental kinds of
activity. The application of the author-function can thus be seen as an
important process in the differentiation of the cultural sphere through
its autonomization of the cultural object.

One example of the institutionalized support for the existence of an author-function is the laws of copyright which give an author sole rights over his or her own work. One consequence of this was the degree of independence which it allowed to artistic producers. It has therefore played an important part in the development of a relatively independent sphere of cultural activities. The artist or writer could, by occupying the position of the author within the discourse of creative autonomy, resist commercial or political pressures. In this context, many artists and writers explicitly denied performing any service role towards the state and its ruling groups, asserting instead that they produced work which was critical of the established social order, as is evident in the often-noted tendency of the English novel towards anti-capitalist sentiments.

However, while Foucault points to the use of the author-function as a means of creating meanings, he also suggests that the fixing of meaning in this way is a limitation on what he calls the 'polysemous' (i.e.'with multiple meanings') nature of fiction. This limitation operates in a number of ways. For example, research indicates that access to the position of authorial autonomy, and the independence which it allowed, was limited in such a way as to either systematically exclude certain groups from cultural production altogether, or deny their work the status of true art. Both Terry Lovell (1987) and Gaye Tuchman (in Tuchman and Fortin, 1989) point to the existence of a critical double standard in the literary culture of the mid-nineteenth century, which resulted in the differential publication and reception of novels by men and women. In her study of the Macmillan publishing company, Tuchman also shows that women writers were offered less financially remunerative contracts as part of what she sees as a form of occupational segregation amongst novelists.

What such research suggests, then, is that the social organization of the author-function provided a means, not only of distinguishing between artistic activity and other kinds of activity, but also of making distinctions between different kinds of artwork. As Tuchman points out, one of the most important distinctions in the literary field during the nineteenth century was that between the realist novel — a form or *genre* which critics now associate more with a masculine point of view and with male writers like George Meredith and Thomas Hardy — and the romantic and gothic novels, more associated by literary critics with feminine experience and female writers like Mrs Oliphant and Charlotte Yonge. She also suggests that this hierarchy in genres was enforced by literary middlemen or cultural brokers and that they did so, in part, by their selective use of the author-function:

> The imprimatur of certain critics associated with ... elite literary circles indicated which literary novels were good literature and identified those who read those novels as participants in high culture. It also limited the ability of people outside those circles to claim cultural distinction simply because they read books — or even wrote them. ... Educated, elite men were to prevail.
> (Tuchman and Fortin, 1989, p.69)

Lovell's research provides further evidence to support the view that the organization of the author-function was gendered. She shows that one important use of the author-function in the early nineteenth century was in establishing that the work did address an ideal or 'implied' male reader. She concludes that, 'A condition of literary canonization [i.e. inclusion of the work in the canon of 'great literature'] … may have been not so much that the author must be male, as that the work must be addressed to men and read by them, and not addressed exclusively to women' (Lovell, 1987, p.830).

The application of the author-function also had significant consequences for the kinds of activity which were deemed appropriate for the audience. The use of the author-function was linked to

George Meredith and Thomas Hardy, canonized as writers of 'great literature'; Mrs Oliphant and Charlotte Yonge

specialized techniques of giving attention, for it required that the reader or viewer immerse him- or herself in the text in a contemplative fashion, showing a respect for the text's internal narrative order, and interpreting the text as an expression of authorial sensibility. In this way, the audience's activity was tied to the perceived intentions of the author and the potentially multiple meanings of the text were restricted. Moreover, as pointed out earlier, to participate in this form of literary culture, even as a reader, required submission to a lengthy period of education, in which not simply technical literacy, but learning or 'cultivation', was taught.

The regulation of access to this level of literacy, and its exclusive association with the qualities of sensitivity and appreciation, thus contributed to the maintenance of internal hierarchies within the audience, and to the distinction between popular fiction and literature. Certainly, the outcome of the failure to apply the author-function equally to all writing is that much fiction is defined negatively as 'that which is not literary'. Indeed, it can be argued that institutional support for the author-function contributed to the strengthening of the already hierarchical distinction between high culture and popular culture which was related to the development of exclusive elements of lifestyle in aristocratic groups — especially the development of a notion of refinement or cultivation. High culture was distinguished by its ability to offer 'aesthetic' experience through different art forms in a particularly intense and powerful way, and had its own clear principles of selection and discrimination. Most popular culture, from this point of view, was either banal or trivial.

However, popular culture is not simply that which is not high culture, but needs to be seen in relation to its own principles of selection and evaluation and its own techniques of interpretation. What these might be has only recently begun to be studied. Popular culture is conventionally equated with mass culture or the production of cultural objects in a standardized fashion. As part of this view (commonly held by most cultural critics until the mid-twentieth century) the standardized manner of such objects' production is seen to obviate any need for analysing them on an individual basis: they are seen as little more than formulas for escapism. The audience is assumed simply to absorb uncritically the entertainment which is directed at it. More recently, in opposition to this rather elitist view, a number of writers have developed an approach to the study of popular culture which challenges this negative definition and stresses the active role of the audience in developing techniques of interpretation. The sections which follow outline the ways in which this approach has been used to investigate a means of communication more recently developed than print — broadcasting, the whole of whose output is often understood to belong to popular culture.

6   BROADCASTING AS A MEANS OF CULTURAL PRODUCTION

There were several different ways in which broadcasting might have been implemented as a means of communication following its initial development at the beginning of the twentieth century. It might, for example, have been developed as a medium for interactive communal viewing in public centres. However, its actual implementation was as a system for the *centralized* transmission of images and sounds received in *privatized* circumstances. This development has been explained in terms of the wider social and political context surrounding its introduction, and as part of the processes of conflict and negotiation taking place between different social groups. Raymond Williams, for example, argues that the development of broadcasting in the early twentieth century should be related to a general social process which he calls 'mobile privatization'. He writes that this period was 'characterized by the two apparently paradoxical yet deeply connected tendencies of modern urban industrial living: on the one hand, mobility, on the other hand, the apparently more self-sufficient family home' (1974, p.26).

From this perspective, television is one of a large number of consumer items, such as telephones, cars, electric irons, fridges and cameras, that were produced at this time specifically for mass consumption in the domestic context. Clearly, the decision to develop broadcasting along the lines of a domestic utility has had very particular implications for its possible uses, locating it firmly in the context of everyday life, rather than in the specialized arena of high culture.

Broadcasting was easily accessible to the audience in another way too. Many of the skills involved in its reception are not restricted, as in the case with print, to those who have received specialized training; rather, they are already well developed in normal social interaction. The potential audience for this new means of communication was thus the whole of society. As a result, as Anthony Smith suggests, broadcasting, from its very beginning, had to face, 'the problems of ... what image it should contain within itself of the single and simultaneous manifestation of the mass audience' (Smith, 1976, p.46).

These problems can be seen to lie behind many of the conflicts between state and commercial interests over the development of broadcasting. The differences between 'public service' and 'commercial' models testify to the continuing importance of the disputes between state and market which Williams identified in relation to the development of print. The conflict concerns the sort of audiences that should be envisaged and served. For example: should the audience be regarded as consisting of customers in a market or citizens in the community? And how should the audience, whatever it consists of, be subdivided into specific audience segments?

This conflict is also evident in the histories of broadcasting in other nation states. In the United States, for example, commercial interests were particularly strong, and the early broadcasting networks were federations of manufacturers, who acquired production facilities only as a secondary operation. The finance for production was drawn wholly from advertising, in the two forms of sponsorship and spot insertion ('commercials'). These commercial networks, which began forming in the mid-1920s, went on to become the defining institutions of American radio and, later, television. A public service ethos only developed within a structure already dominated by commercial institutions. So, for example, it was only after 1944 that the U.S. Federal Communications Commission began to try to define the public interest in terms of standards of social usefulness, public fairness and public morality.

In contrast, the state and its associated institutions had a much greater role in defining the role of broadcasting as a means of public communication in Britain, and commercial television was introduced only after public service television had been able to establish its own conventions of operation. Stuart Hall (1986) explains this in terms of the relative strength of the British state, and, in particular, its effectiveness in defending the leadership of the dominant class-cultural formations in what was a period of social reconstruction. He suggests that the emergence of broadcasting in this period was of particular interest to the ruling groups because of the profound changes to the political sphere which were occuring at the time — changes which were related to the extension of the franchise first to working men and then to women. The 'problem' which faced the state was how to contain democracy while at the same time maintaining popular consent in circumstances of economic difficulty and intense international rivalry. Hall argues that the social and economic crisis was transformed into an issue of cultural and political authority, and that the state's interest in the new means of communication — a medium of potentially immense social and political power — should be seen as part of its increasingly active role in defining the 'general interest' for its citizens. He goes on to point out, however, that while the state intervened in the development of broadcasting to protect its position, it was itself transformed as a result of its intervention.

At a practical level, the state's decisive role in the development of broadcasting was facilitated by the fact that, even before the potential of broadcasting was realized, all transmitters and receivers initially had to be licensed by the Post Office. By the 1920s, the GPO was faced with over a hundred demands for permission to broadcast from wireless manufacturers who had begun to see the large-scale possibilities of the medium. However, rather than granting every applicant permission to broadcast, as had been done in the case of print, the government adopted the solution of encouraging the largest companies to form a consortium, perhaps because of the reasons identified by Hall. This consortium became the industrial base of the British Broadcasting Company. The significant elements of this agreement were the granting of a monopoly to the Company, and the decision to finance broadcasting by the sale of licenses for receivers. Once granted the elements of monopoly and guaranteed finance, the BBC was assured of the necessary continuity and resources to become a producer rather than merely a transmitter of broadcast material.

The terms of this decision were reaffirmed in 1925 when the Crawford Committee, which had been set up by the government to examine the future of broadcasting, explicitly rejected both unregulated broadcasting for profit and a service directly controlled and operated by the state. Instead, the Committee proposed that broadcasting be conducted by a public corporation acting as a trustee for the national interest, and consisting of a Board of Governors responsible for seeing that broadcasting was carried out as a public service. It further recommended that the British Broadcasting Company was a fit body for such a task, and the Company duly became a Corporation in January 1927. Its then Managing Director, John Reith, became the first Director General of what Stuart Hall calls an 'extraordinary hybrid beast': a broadcasting authority which was both independent from the state yet constituted as a state-protected monopoly (Hall, 1986, p.44).

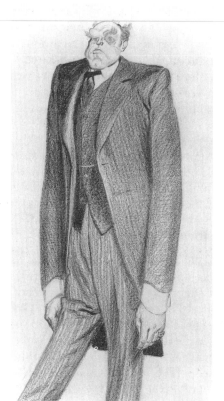

John Reith, first Director General of the BBC, and its home, Broadcasting House

Certainly, as a public corporation, the BBC was a new type of cultural institution; although, interestingly, the organizational form of the public corporation was to be widely used in the inter-war period, precisely because, while it was not subject to detailed state control, it was a state-sponsored and state-regulated system. While this arrangement is seen by many writers to have given the BBC a degree of operational autonomy, the extent of its independence has been much debated. It has been pointed out that, while the British state does not directly intervene in the running of the BBC as a matter of course, its influence is evident in a number of indirect practices. Moreover, following the introduction of commercial broadcasting systems in the mid 1950s, the BBC has had to compete for an audience large enough to legitimate its claim to be a public service.

Other writers have focused on the question of how the notion of 'public service' was interpreted by the BBC, even before such competition was introduced, suggesting that the Corporation's practice reveals the hidden limits of its autonomy. In general, very few explicit injunctions occur in the BBC's charter. For example, the BBC has never been directly required or directed to observe impartiality. Instead, as Stuart Hood notes:

> What has happened is that the Postmaster General has *desired* the Corporation 'as in the past' to refrain from broadcasting any expression of its own opinion on current affairs or on matters of public policy. The situation is therefore based on *trust* — on the belief, to quote the White Paper on Broadcasting published in 1946, 'that the Corporation would ensure that such subjects would be treated with complete impartiality'.
> (Hood, 1967, p.19)

Williams (1974) suggests that this reliance upon an assumed consensus was possible because of the strength of an already existing elite national culture. He points out that the constitution of the BBC permitted the emergence of an independent corporate broadcasting policy, in which the independence was real, but qualified by its definition in terms of a pre-existing cultural hegemony. Thus a consensus version of the public interest, closely linked with dominant political conceptions of the national interest, could simply be assumed and then imposed through a system of internal corporate controls.

Indeed, it seems that public service was initially defined, not by popularity or audience appreciation, but in terms of its congruence with dominant values. The BBC saw its purpose as giving authority to a particular set of elite cultural values, rather than as representing the general audience's interests. It did not aim to reflect public interests, but to educate, guide and shape taste and values towards 'higher things'. This aspiration was reflected, not only in specific standards for programmes, but also in a distinctive style of programming and an implied model of listening.

This model is best understood in relation to the mode of appropriation which had been developed in relation to the notion of a text. In most communications systems before broadcasting, the conditions of distribution and reception ensured that cultural goods were perceived as discrete, both spatially and temporally: that is, as texts. A book was taken and read as a specific item, a painting was seen in particular places at a particular time, as too were plays and even films. The BBC's early policy of programming and scheduling can be seen as attempts to reproduce these conditions of reception — to construct radio as an 'occasional resource'. So, for example, listeners were requested to be selective in their choice of programme. They were not to use the wireless to provide a continuous background of noise to the domestic round, but rather to explore the range of programmes on offer as discrete items. Programme continuity was arranged so as to inhibit 'lazy' non-stop listening; for example, there were sometimes minutes of silence between programmes to allow people to switch off or recompose themselves. In addition, there was a policy of mixed programming, in which different types of programme followed each other without reference to the likely routines of different groups of listeners. In this way, the BBC's understanding of public service was based on a particular set of cultural values, which not only structured the content of programmes, but also prescribed a particular relation between the listener and the programmes. As part of this implicit 'contract', the listener was expected to pay particularly intense attention to the internal form of the programme. The BBC could thus be said to have attempted to impose a mode of appropriation on its audience; a mode of appropriation with a strong resemblance to that of high culture.

However, this initial understanding of public service broadcasting did not last long. David Cardiff and Paddy Scannell (1991) suggest that this was because the BBC did not have the necessary autonomy or external support to pursue such an elitist policy. As Hall's argument (see above) implies, the balance of political and cultural forces was so uncertain that even the BBC's monopoly could not protect it from criticism. Cardiff and Scannell argue that, in order to convince the government of the authority of the BBC as a national institution, the BBC's personnel introduced a gradual shift away from its initial high culture conception of public service. What replaced this conception is less easy to identify, but Cardiff and Scannell suggest it can be characterized in terms of the development of an institutional voice speaking 'on behalf of' the nation.

As Cardiff and Scannell make clear, the shaping of the BBC as a national cultural institution was a complex process. However, it can be illustrated by reference to changes at a number of different levels: changes in particular kinds of programmes, changes in programming scheduling, and the development of an institutional identity or voice. Changes in programmes can be illustrated by the shift from an initial heavy dependence on outside broadcasts — i.e. material transmitted straight, without selection, framing or editing, from theatres, variety halls, churches, sporting events, public ceremonies and occasions — to programmes which employed conventions specific to broadcasting. In using such outside broadcast material the broadcasters did not at first restructure the material or adapt it to the conditions appropriate to broadcasting.

ACTIVITY 6

How has the handling of material from 'outside broadcasts' changed in contemporary broadcasting? Think, for example, of the broadcasting of events such as the World Cup, Live Aid, parliamentary debates and elections.

Even in presenting current affairs the BBC was initially dependent on external producers and already existing cultural forms. In fact, when it first began broadcasting the new company was allowed only to use news bulletins written and supplied by an external news agency, namely, Reuters. It was only in 1930 that the BBC secured the right to edit and write its own news bulletins, and even then a coherent approach to radio news was slow to develop. And it was not until the 1950s that distinctively new formats for documentary and current affairs coverage began to appear, both in radio and television. An important feature of these new formats was the prominent role given to the programme presenter: more particularly, the personality of the commentator provided a device through which events were mediated. This form of televised current affairs, which combined objectivity with personalization to dramatize public events, represented the beginnings of a cultural form — in the sense of a relationship between broadcaster and listener — specific to broadcasting. It did so by providing a symbolic means of 'representing' the public through the personality of the commentator. In this and other ways, the BBC can be seen to have developed programme styles which embodied its understanding of public service as speaking on behalf of the audience.

More generally, from the 1930s onwards, a new programming policy began to take shape, an important aspect of which was the increased routinization of schedules. A key element of this was the recognition that the audience for radio typically did not listen to discrete programmes, but would listen for a sustained period of time as part of their everyday routine. The routinization of schedules was also linked to the development of many new programmes with a weekly serial or series format. A further aspect of this broad change was the increase in the number of programmes directed at specific sections of the audience, such as women or young people, or covering particular interests such as sport. These took items which had earlier been scattered among individual programmes and packaged them together in a style appropriate to a fragment of the national audience. New styles of presentation were also implemented, with a systematic separation out of 'serious' and 'popular'.styles of presentation and production, once again suggesting that producers were coming to terms with the idea of a differentiated public with specific kinds of tastes and levels of education.

Paddy Scannell points to one particular aspect of this realization of broadcasting as a public service in his discussion of 'Radio Times: the temporal arrangements of broadcasting in the modern world' (Scannell, 1986). He shows the ways in which the new broadcasting schedules of radio and television helped to sustain both patterns of day-to-day life — playing a significant role in the organization of the rhythms of work and leisure — and created a sense of an annual order or calendar through the relay of a series of public occasions. Through the regularity of such broadcasts and the predictability of the broadcasting schedule, he suggests, the timing of broadcasting created and maintained certain kinds of continuity for the audience. In doing this, it provided a reassuring response to the large-scale displacements and readjustments of modern industrial societies. In all these ways, then, the BBC acted as a focus for the creation and mobilization of a sense of national identity in which, although the social and political differences between different groups were recognized, divisions were contained within an imaginary community.

The separation out of streams of broadcasting was formalized after the Second World War via the use of three channels with distinct programming policies: the Light Programme, the Third Programme, and the Home Service. This represented a decisive move away from the assumption that programmes are separate coherent items towards the view that the flow of programming is what is significant. It also implies a shift from a view of society as an aggregate of individuals towards a concept of particular groups with separate interests. Furthermore, these groupings persist today, with BBC Radio 2, 3 and 4 approximating to the three channels identified above; the introduction of Radio 1 marking the emergence of young people as a recognizable market for radio. Significantly, the emergence of targetted channels also meant that competition was introduced between various parts of the Corporation. It has been argued that this internal reform was a more important stage in the history of broadcasting than the competition later offered by commercial radio (and television) since it meant that representing the public's interests had become central to the Corporation's plan.

ACTIVITY 7   List the different ways in which contemporary radio channels target segments of the audience.

Although the new importance attached to the audience's own interests can in some ways be seen as an essentially democratic modification of the notion of public service broadcasting, as Ien Ang (1991) notes, the representation of the audience is indirect and is always a matter of interpretation or mediation by the profession of broadcasters. In its actual technological and social form, broadcasting is essentially one-way: the audience's experience of broadcasting is constrained by relations of re-presentation in which the listener is fixed at the end of a chain of mediation that runs through the medium of broadcasting into the home. The implications of this deep contradiction between producers and audience in broadcasting, both public service and commercial systems, have been the subject of much of the analysis of both its specificity as a mass medium and its significance for popular culture.

7 BROADCASTING AS A DOMESTIC MEDIUM

Certainly, the domestic context for the reception of broadcasting has been seen by a number of writers as a very important factor in its development. In his book *Visible Fictions*, John Ellis points out that the assumed audience for broadcasting was households organized as 'families', and that the internalization of the audience in this form shaped programming policy. He writes,

> 'The home' and 'the family' are terms which have become tangled together in the commercial culture of the twentieth century. They both point to a powerful cultural construct, a set of deeply held assumptions about the nature of 'normal' human existence. The family is held to consist of a particular unit of parents and children: broadcast tv assumes that this is the basis and heart of its audience.
> (Ellis, 1982, p.113)

Happy family listening to the radio: inside page of early issue of Radio Times

In looking at the reasons for this, including the arguments developed by Hall and Williams, Ellis suggests that the notion of the masses, a term which signified the potential threat posed by the newly franchised groups in society, was actively re-defined during the mid twentieth

century in terms of a particular conception of the family. It was both as
a consequence and a cause in this redefinition of what it meant to be a
good citizen that the family entered into the development of
broadcasting as the appropriate focus for its distribution; the notion of
mass was effectively redefined in terms of multiple private receivers.

For Ellis, this internalization of the mass audience in terms of an
assumed 'normal' family can be related to the emergence of the
characteristic cultural forms of both radio and television; that is, it
shapes their modes of address. It helps to explain the concentration of
fictional representations of the family — including, for example, its
predominance in situation comedies (*The Cosby Show* and *Bread* are
contemporary examples) and in soap operas (ranging from *The Archers*,
to *EastEnders* to *Dallas*) — the frequent use of direct address to 'you'
the viewer, and the confirmation of a position of domestic isolation for
this viewer. This argument is developed in relation to television in
particular:

> Television confirms the domestic isolation of the viewer, and
> invites the viewer to regard the world from that position. The
> viewer is therefore confirmed in a basic division of the world
> between the 'inside' of the home, the family and the domestic, and
> the 'outside' of work, politics, public life, the city, the crowd.
> (Ellis, 1982, p.166)

Ellis also argues that the domestic circumstances within which
broadcasting is received means that it tends to engage the look or the
glance rather than the concentration of the gaze. He thus suggests that it
is its context of use which explains why television has a relatively low
degree of sustained concentration from its viewers in comparison with,
for example, cinema. Putting these two points together, Ellis concludes
that the process of delegating 'looking' to television leaves the viewer in
a position of isolation from, rather than involvement with, the events
shown.

This understanding of television is developed by Margaret Morse (1985)
who argues that the television transmission offers itself to us as a quasi-
subject addressing us personally and directly as a 'you'. She argues, on
the basis of an analysis of contemporary American broadcasting, that
the impression of television as a subjective presence is fostered at
several levels:

> 1   The television itself occupies three-dimensional space with us;
> it speaks to us as a voice embodied by the box. An electronic arm
> of the space of production is with us in the simultaneous present
> of 'liveness', showing us the world as it happens. The television is
> situated like a partner in a conversational circle, like the centre of
> a proscenium arch in the theatre, i.e. part partner, part spectacle.
>
> 2   The programming of television is accompanied by the constant
> discursiveness of a story-teller holding the flow of miscellaneous
> images together. The coherence of television is largely due to this

continuous self-referential subjectivity. Within and between programmes there are constant relays of words and looks between narrators, of graphics over images, frames and wipes for sequential shifts of scene or story and a continual use of narrative images in the trailers which precede a programme or in the recaps which follow the story itself. … Furthermore, programming is constantly interrupted by the foreign material of commercials. Discursive intrusions over and between story space are a pervasive feature, no matter what the genre, and are interpreted as 'live' or spoken in the present.

3   There is also a highly articulated chain of looks and denial of looks between narrators, characters of a story and the viewer which separates the space 'in' the tube into *story* and *audience space*. The chain of articulations differs by genre and even stylistically by programme.
(Morse, 1985, pp.5–6)

In these ways, she suggests, the audience is apparently, or *virtually* incorporated into television; its presence is acknowledged through a 'virtual form of direct address' (Morse, 1985, p.4).

ACTIVITY 8   Analyse a chat show, such as *Wogan* or *The Oprah Winfrey Show* in terms of these three dimensions of address. How are you, as a member of the broadcast audience, made to feel included? How does this inclusion differ across types of programmes?

The coherence provided by this fiction of discourse — of talking to 'you at home' — within the television transmission has become ever more important as public service broadcasting has been challenged in recent years by the state-prompted introduction of market-led interpretations of the audience into broadcasting, the increasing globalization of programme production and distribution, and the intensification of links between television and other media such as cinema, music, advertising and magazines. All these processes have undermined the professional and, some would say, self-understanding of the audience as a national public, and replaced it with the notion of the audience as a market, or rather series of markets made up of isolated individuals. Indeed, many of the current debates about the quality of broadcasting, among professional broadcasters, within the press and the academy, can be seen in terms of the uncertainty about who currently makes up the audience for television, and how they watch. So how does the audience for broadcasting actually understand its own activities?

Ellis's and Morse's arguments provide sophisticated examples of an approach to the study of the institutions and technologies of the mass media which seeks to explore their cultural impact without contrasting them negatively with high cultural forms. Nevertheless, an alternative approach to the study of television as a domestic medium suggests that the kinds of conclusions presented so far are misleading in so far as they make use of arguments which look at the development of broadcasting from the point of view of producers alone. This alternative approach suggests that the most important aspect of the development of television as domestic medium is the way in which it deepened the asymmetry between producers and the audience. This asymmetry, it is suggested, is so great in the case of broadcasting that the audience's interpretations of its output are likely to diverge considerably from those intended by its producers.

While this line of argument has recently been taken up in relation to broadcasting, it was developed in general terms by Walter Benjamin in his article 'The work of art in the age of mechanical reproduction' (1970b). This article, written as the potential reach of broadcasting systems was just beginning to be realized, has provided the starting point for many accounts of modern popular culture which stress the ways in which people are not passive, but active users of mass-produced cultural goods, appropriating and transforming their meaning in the context of everyday life. What is significant about Benjamin's argument from our point of view is that he argues that the radical potential of the mass reproduction of cultural goods is made possible by the new cultural technologies — including photography and cinema as well as broadcasting.

ACTIVITY 9   Now read **Reading C, 'The work of art in the age of mechanical reproduction'**, by Walter Benjamin. What is the significance of these new technologies for Benjamin?

Benjamin suggests that the most immediate consequence of these new technologies is the mass reproducibility of cultural goods which they make possible. This is seen by Benjamin to result in the detachment of the work of art from what he calls the aura of its singular presence, that special sense of 'here and now' which confers on the unique work of art its authenticity. But rather than seeing the decline of aura as a loss (as you might have thought he would from his analysis in 'The storyteller' discussed earlier), its demise is presented in a positive light as the detachment of the work of art from the mystifying and elitist processes of ritual and tradition. As a result of the technologies of mass reproduction, copies of the cultural object are newly mobile, they can be received in 'situations which would be out of reach of the original itself'. He thus suggests that the application of the new technologies will lead to the insertion of the artwork into social life in new ways. For Benjamin then, popular culture represents the set of cultural activities in which mass-produced cultural goods are transformed and given new meaning in the context of the audience's everyday life; popular culture is the site of negotiation, transformation and creativity.

However, as we have seen with the example of the novel, this mobility is not in itself a sufficient condition for the removal of the constraints of ritual and tradition; indeed, it may simply provide the basis for the invention of new traditions, as with the creation of what has come to be known as the 'literary canon' during the early twentieth century, a tradition which defines what counts as Great Literature. Nevertheless, the significance of reproducibility for Benjamin is that it allows the possibility that the cultural object can be a part of the ordinary and commonplace; in being detached from its originating context, the cultural object can potentially enter into the realm of the mundane or 'profane'. The implication of this argument is that the use of the technologies of mass communication within the mode of appropriation associated with the formation of high culture is only one possibility, and that they have the potential to support another mode or modes in which the audience is located in a new position of independence in relation to the producers of cultural goods. Arguably, the likelihood of this potential being realized has been enhanced by the greater accessibility of reception afforded by audio-visual communication. For example, the availability of audio- and video-cassette recorders gives greater independence to the audience.

ACTIVITY 10   But is this the case with broadcasting? Do you think audiences have the power to define the meaning of programmes in opposition to producers?

Much of the work that has been discussed so far in this chapter has developed its arguments through some kind of combination of institutional and textual analysis. Thus, the section on broadcasting combined analysis of the different modes of regulation (public service/commercial) with shifts in the BBC's mode of address to its audience. While this is obviously important, it has not considered the place of the audience other than as it is *assumed* in the practices of the producers. In order to investigate the activity of the actual audience, it is necessary to turn to an approach which has been developed by researchers in cultural studies, linguistics, and literary theory as well as the social sciences to study the nature of media reception. This approach focuses attention on the audience member as a social subject, that is, as an individual who lives in a particular social formation and is constituted by a complex social and cultural history. Much of this work asks not only 'what does this mean?' for particular viewers, but also 'how does it come to mean this'? For writers such as Michel de Certeau, consumption — in its broadest sense — is not 'something done by sheep progressively immobilized and "handled" as a result of the growing mobility of the media as they conquer space' (1984, p.165); rather it is productive. This re-evaluation of the practices of reception (from passive to active) has led to the use of ethnographic techniques as a way of studying television through viewers' interpretations, some researchers adopting an observational technique and others looking at viewers' verbalizations of their responses to television in everyday situations.

Such television ethnographers have begun to study 'audiencing': that is, the ways in which individuals become audiences, including the ways in which television is interpreted within the culture of the home, since they believe that it is in the processes of reception that the meaning of its programmes are fixed. They agree with Williams, Scannell and Ellis that television is essentially a domestic medium, but they take this argument a stage further and suggest that an investigation of its cultural significance requires an exploration of the activities of the viewer. Their conclusions stress the heterogeneity of the audience, and indicate that different groups within the audience find different and plural meanings and pleasures in television. In general terms, however, this research suggests that individual members of the audience are always situated in a cultural milieu which is in turn largely determined by the individual's position in the social structure, from which they draw cultural resources with which to 'decode' media messages.

So, for example, research by David Morley (1986), Ien Ang (1985) and David Silverstone (1990), suggests that patterns of viewing are part of the domestic routines by which home life is organized, and that domestic routines are reworked and given new meaning in patterns of viewing. It also provides evidence to suggest that viewers can and do employ a number of different styles of watching: they may watch television as a primary activity; they may reluctantly give it second place while they do something else; or they may have it on in the background while they read the paper, have a conversation or do homework. Viewers may even switch from one style of watching to another during an evening spent 'watching' the television, sometimes moving from one style to another within the course of a single programme.

This research also suggests that the meaning of a programme is not necessarily fixed at the moment of watching, but can be defined and redefined following a programme's transmission. Studies have identified the importance of talk about television — at school or work, as members of clubs or other social organizations — as a key practice in which the viewing experience is made meaningful and pleasurable. It is argued that this incorporation of programmes into domestic and local cultures is an active and creative process: the audience participates in the meanings of a programme in a way that the programme's producers can neither foresee nor control. This kind of research thus suggests that the meaning of programmes is negotiable, and that it is very often discursive, in the sense that it is constructed in and through talk with others. In other words, it seems that the fiction that a discourse is taking place in the television transmission, as discussed by Morse (1985) is made real in its reception.

The changes in the relationship between cultural production and reception associated with these new means of cultural production have led to the suggestion that a process of cultural re-integration is occuring.

So, for example, some researchers have concluded that the meaning of 'mass reproduced' cultural goods such as television programmes is primarily a product of the social context of their reception: it is suggested that the meanings of cultural objects are now once again being defined primarily in relation to the general pattern of social relations. But this suggestion assumes that the meanings produced by the audience would have lost any 'practically useless, imaginative element' and any distance from socially prescribed ends. Such an assumption seems unjustified given the complexity, range and diversity of interpretations indicated by the research that has been carried out. The paradox identified at the beginning of the chapter remains, although it may be taking a new social form.

Michel de Certeau's work offers one basis for a preliminary investigation of this thesis; that is, that while the cultural and the social spheres are still distinct, their differentiation now has a novel organization. He argues that, on the one hand, the social, economic and political spheres are increasingly colonized by the cultural, through the use of advertising, design, and the ever-increasing significance attached to the visual, resulting in what he describes as a 'semiocratic' society: that is, one in which the practice of signification becomes increasingly important. On the other hand, everyday life itself retains a dynamic and creative essence that escapes subordination to the established order. He writes:

> To describe these everyday practices that produce without capitalizing, that is, without taking control over time, one starting point seemed inevitable because it is the 'exorbitant' focus of contemporary culture and its consumption: *reading*. From TV to newspapers, from advertising to all sorts of mercantile epiphanies, our society is characterized by a cancerous growth of vision, measuring everything in its ability to show or be shown and transmuting communication into a visual journey. It is a sort of epic of the eye and of the impulse to read. The economy itself, transformed into a 'semiocracy' encourages a hypertrophic development of reading. Reading (an image or a text), moreover, seems to constitute the maximal development of the passivity assumed to characterize the consumer, who is conceived of as a voyeur ... in a 'show biz society'.

> In reality, the activity of reading has on the contrary all the characteristics of a silent production: the drift across the page, the metamorphosis of the text effected by the wandering eyes of the reader, the improvization and expectation of meanings inferred from a few words, leaps over written spaces in an ephemeral dance. But since he is incapable of stockpiling (unless he writes or records), the reader cannot protect himself against the erosion of time (while reading, he forgets himself and he forgets what he has read) unless he buys the object (book, image) which is no more than a substitute (the spoor or promise) of moments 'lost' in reading. He insinuates into another person's text the ruses of

pleasure and appropriation: he poaches on it, is transported into it, pluralizes himself in it like the internal rumblings of one's body. ... A different world (the reader's) slips into the author's place.

This mutation makes the text habitable, like a rented apartment. It transforms another person's property into a space borrowed for a moment like a transient. Renters make comparable changes in an apartment they furnish with their acts and memories; as do speakers, in the language into which they insert both the messages of their native tongue and, through their accent, through their own 'turns of phrase,' etc., their own history; as do pedestrians, in the streets they fill with the forests of their desires and goals. ...

Reading thus introduces an 'art' which is anything but passive. ... Imbricated within the strategies of modernity (which identify creation with the invention of a personal language, whether cultural or scientific), the procedures of contemporary consumption appear to constitute a subtle art of 'renters' who know how to insinuate their countless differences into the dominant text.
(de Certeau, 1984, pp.xxi–xxii)

De Certeau puts forward a view of culture as a battleground, in which the tactics of everyday life are an expression of resistance to discourses of discipline and surveillance. He argues that the procedures and narratives of everyday life — speaking, shopping, cooking, dressing and watching television, all of this he sees as forms of reading — encroach on and subvert the proper space and strategy of the powerful. He makes use of a diversity of metaphors — poaching, renting, hunting and travelling — in an attempt to catch the intricacies of these arts of making, arts of doing, or arts of making do. The meanings of these practices of reading are not to be deduced from their products, but rather from their ways of using products. He stresses that these arts transform the products which are used: for de Certeau, to assume these activities leave the object untouched is to misunderstand the nature of consumption: 'This misunderstanding assumes that "assimilating" necessarily means "becoming similar to" what one absorbs, and not "making something similar" to what one is, making it one's own, appropriating or reappropriating it.' (1984, p.166).

He further argues that these tactics help define our individual and social identities; they link together to form what he calls *lignes d'erres,* wandering lines through the structures, the 'rocks and defiles', of the established order. De Certeau establishes the inventiveness of everyday practices, but he also stresses the transience and indeterminacy of such activities. He emphasizes their contextual contingency: that is, their embeddedness in social life. Nevertheless, his work does suggest that there is still a specificity to the cultural sphere. Indeed, it may be precisely the arbitrary, fragmentary and temporary nature of the existence of these everyday practices which ensures their critical, utopian or aesthetic aspect.

8 CONCLUSION

The chapter has suggested that cultural differentiation is an aspect of modernization, and has tried to identify the distinctive characteristics of this sphere. In developing the idea that the cultural sphere can be understood in terms of the historical emergence of a 'field of forces' this chapter has suggested that the sphere can be seen to have its own logic and its own internal hierarchies. It has been suggested that it is through the analysis both of the hierarchies within this sphere and of its changing relationship with the economic, political and social spheres that the paradoxical links between cultural practices and power relations can most usefully be explained. A number of different ways of looking at this field were identified with this end in mind, including investigating its history, its definition, its means of production, the relations of political and commercial forces within it, and its (changing) modes of appropriation.

This last concept in particular has allowed us to consider the field of forces as unstable, and to consider the shifting nature of the relationship between cultural production and reception from one historical period to the next. The arguments presented here suggest that reproducibility is one of the more important distinguishing characteristics of the modern cultural sphere in this respect. It was suggested that while there have been definite limits of a commercial, political and social kind placed upon cultural reproduction, the mobility of cultural objects made possible by the newer means of communication undermines, to some extent at least, the effectivity of these restraints and underpins the specificity of modern cultural life.

REFERENCES

Ang, I. (1985) *Watching Dallas: Soap Opera and the Melodramatic Imagination*, London, Methuen.

Ang, I. (1991) *Desperately Seeking the Audience*, London, Routledge.

Benjamin, W. (1970a) 'The storyteller', in *Illuminations*, London, Jonathan Cape.

Benjamin, W. (1970b) 'The work of art in the age of mechanical reproduction' in *Illuminations*, London, Jonathan Cape.

Cardiff, D. and Scannell, P. (1991) *The Social History of British Broadcasting, Volume 1; 1922–1939: Serving the Nation*, Oxford, Blackwell.

Curran, J. (1986) 'The impact of advertising on the British mass media', in Collins, R. *et al.* (eds) *Media, Culture and Society: A Critical Reader*, London, Sage.

de Certeau, M. (1984) *The Practice of Everyday Life*, Berkeley and Los Angeles, University of California Press.

Eisenstein, E. (1979) *The Printing Press as an Agent of Change*, Cambridge, Cambridge University Press.

Ellis, J. (1982) *Visible Fictions. Cinema, Television, Video*, London, Routledge.

Foucault, M. (1979) 'What is an author?' in Harari, J.V. (ed.) *Textual Strategies: Perspectives in Post-Structuralist Criticism*, Ithaca, New York, Cornell University Press.

Hall, S. (1986) 'Popular culture and the state', in Bennett, T. *et al.* (eds) *Popular Culture and Social Relations*, Milton Keynes, Open University Press.

Hall, S. and Gieben, B. (1992) *Formations of Modernity*, Cambridge, Polity Press.

Hood, S. (1967) *A Survey of Television*, London, Heinemann.

Laqueur, T. (1976) 'The cultural origins of popular literacy in England 1500–1850', *Oxford Review of Education*, vol. 2, 3, pp. 255–75.

Levi-Strauss, C. (1969) *Totemism*, Harmondsworth, Penguin.

Lovell, T. (1987) *Consuming Fictions*, London, Verso.

McLuhan, M. (1962) *The Gutenberg Galaxy: The Making of Typographic Man*, London, Routledge.

McLuhan, M. and Fiore, Q. (1967) *The Medium is the Message*, Harmondsworth, Penguin.

Morley, D. (1986) *Family Television: Cultural Power and Domestic Leisure*, London, Comedia.

Morse, M. (1985), 'Talk, talk, talk', *Screen*, vol.26, no.2, pp.2–15.

Mulhern, F. (1980) 'Notes on culture and cultural struggle', *Screen Education*, no.34, pp.31–6.

Murdock, G. (1980) 'Authorship and organisation', *Screen Education*, no.30, pp.51–67.

Silverstone, D. (1990) 'Television and everyday life: towards an anthropology of the television audience' in Ferguson, M. (ed.) *Public Communication: the New Imperatives*, London, Sage.

Scannell, P. (1986) 'Radio Times: the temporal arrangements of broadcasting in the modern world', paper presented to the 1986 International Television Studies Conference.

Smith, A. (1976) *The Shadow in the Cave: The Broadcaster, the Audience and the State*, London, Quartet Books.

Tuchman, G. and Fortin, N.E. (1989) *Edging Women Out: Victorian Novelists, Publishers and Cultural Change*, London, Routledge.

Williams, R. (1974) *Television: Technology and Cultural Form*, London, Fontana.

Williams, R. (1981) *Culture*, London, Fontana.

READING A MEANS OF CULTURAL PRODUCTION

Raymond Williams

The invention and development of the material means of cultural production is a remarkable chapter of human history, yet it is usually underplayed, by comparison with the invention and development of what are more easily seen as forms of material production, in food, tools, shelter and utilities. Indeed a common ideological position marks this latter area off as 'material', by contrast with the 'cultural' or, in the more common emphases, the 'artistic' or the 'spiritual'.

Yet ... whatever purposes cultural practice may serve, its means of production are unarguably material. Indeed, instead of starting from the misleading contrast between 'material' and 'cultural', we have to define two areas for analysis: first, the relations between these material means and the social forms within which they are used (this is of course a general problem in social analysis, but the discussion is limited, here, to cultural means and forms); and, second, the relations between these material means and social forms and the specific (artistic) forms which are a manifest cultural production. ...

We can make, first, an important general distinction ... between (i) that class of material means which depends wholly or mainly on inherent, constituted physical resources, and (ii) that other class which depends wholly or mainly on the use or transformation of non-human material objects and forces. No history of the arts can be written without full attention to both. The arts of spoken poetry, of song and of dance are obvious examples of the former, as are painting and sculpture of the latter. And then what is interesting is that whatever their exact priority (which may perhaps never be determined) each of these kinds is very early indeed in human culture. Moreover each kind has continued to be important; it is not a simple question of successive stages. ...

Development of inherent resources

The achievement of language, in any full sense, lies within the complex transition from the evolutionary to the social. The development of species-inherited 'non-verbal communication' (postures, gestures, facial expressions) into cultural forms and variations of these basic possibilities is within the same complex transition. But even if the 'social' stage is moved forward (tendentiously) to the point at which these developed resources can be said to 'already' exist, it is impossible to overlook the extraordinary social history of the institution of systems for their further cultural development.

Dance, song and speech

There is, for example, the amazing social development of all the forms of dance, over a range from complex traditional forms to prolonged pro-

Source: Williams, R. (1981) *Culture,* London, Fontana, pp.87–95, 98–100.

fessional training. There is the same remarkable development in ways of using the human voice in singing and in certain specifically formal kinds of speech. We can observe a familiar transition from a relatively general training, in these highly valued skills, to degrees of specialization and professionalization in more complex societies, but some forms of specialization seem to be remarkably early and, on the other hand, there are probably no societies in which relatively general training in forms of these basic skills is not attempted.

This relative generality of development is of great sociological importance, by contrast with the much more uneven and often specialized and exclusive development of forms of cultural production which depend on the use or transformation of non-human resources. In complex societies there is a significant and often decisive unevenness, as the systems which train these inherent and constituted resources become more professional and more masterly. But (the more so while elements of the most general training persist) certain crucial human and social connections, or potential connections, are still there, in the shared resources of which these are developments. It is then not at all surprising that dancing and singing, in their most general forms, have been and have remained, in complex as in simple societies, the most widespread and popular cultural practices.

Uses of non-human means

It is when we turn to practices based (in whole or in part) on the use or transformation of non-human material objects and forces that the social relations become much more complex and variable. We can begin with a preliminary distinction of types of such practice, as follows:

1   *combination* of the use of external objects with the use of inherent physical resources, over a range from the use of paint, masks and costume in dance to the use of masks, costume and scenery in acted drama;

2   *of instruments* of new kinds of performance, as notably in musical instruments;

3   selection, transformation and production of *separable objects,* which then carry cultural significance, as in the use of clay, metal, stone and pigment in sculpture and painting;

4   development of *separable material systems of signification*, devised for cultural significance, as most notably in writing;

5   development of *complex amplificatory, extending and reproductive technical systems,* which make possible new kinds of presentation of all the preceding types, but also new kinds of presentation of practices still otherwise based on the use of inherent and constituted resources.

In the matter of social relations, the first three types are relatively continuous with those based on inherent resources, while the fourth and fifth types introduce problems of relationship of quite new kinds.

Problems of access

There is usually some generality of access to at least some of the techniques involved in the first three types. Where this is so, the relation between some form of general training and highly developed specialist training is not necessarily more difficult than in the comparable relation in the training of inherent physical resources. On the other hand, as a culture becomes richer and more complex, involving many more artistic techniques developed to a high degree of specialization, the social distance of many practices becomes much greater, and there is a virtually inevitable if always complex set of divisions between participants and spectators in the various arts. These important divisions affect the character of modern cultures, to the point where the social relations between artists and ('their') spectators or 'publics' can seem the only kind that needs to be considered.

Yet ... the form of division between 'artist' and 'public' need not be at all of a damaging kind; it is often in practice a willing and serious interchange between professionals and those interested in the highest development of these skills. The very different case of a generalized division, between 'creators' and 'spectators', may in part be influenced by such relations, but is not fully generated or confirmed there. Indeed it is only, or at least primarily, in the development of material techniques of the fourth and fifth types that what is at first not much more than a relatively open specialization and diversity of attention becomes a formative and even determining set of *divisive* social relations. ...

Writing

... While anyone in the world, with normal physical resources, can watch dance or look at sculpture or listen to music, still some forty per cent of the world's present inhabitants can make no contact whatever with a piece of writing, and in earlier periods this percentage was very much larger. Writing as a cultural technique is wholly dependent on forms of specialized training, not only (as became common in other techniques) for producers but also, and crucially, for receivers. Instead of being a development of an inherent or generally available faculty, it is a specialized technique wholly dependent on specific training. It is then not surprising that for a very long period the most difficult problems in the social relations of cultural practice revolved around the question of literacy.

Social relations of writing

The earliest forms of writing were developed by and confined to very limited specialist (usually official) groups; they were later somewhat extended in continued urban development and in merchant trade. The general cultural problem was not at this stage acute, for writing was still primarily a technique of administration, record and contact. It was in the next stage, when writing came to carry an increasing proportion of law, learning, religion and history, previously carried in oral forms, that very marked cultural divisions, already socially present in preliterate societies, became, as it were, technically stabilized.

In the further powerful development of all these uses, and even when some other social relations were changing, this form of stratification of access became more and more important. Increasingly, also, the oral 'literature' of preliterate or marginally literate societies was, through many complex stages, transferred to this new material technique, and further developed through it. Writing moved from (i) a supporting and recording function, in societies in which oral composition and tradition were still predominant, through (ii) a stage in which this function was joined by written composition for oral performance and (iii) a further stage in which composition was additionally written only to be read, to (iv) that later and very familiar stage in which most or virtually all composition was written to be silently read, and was at last, for this reason, generalized as 'literature'.

The great advantages of writing, with its enormous expansion of newly possible kinds of continuity and access, have been counterpointed, throughout, by the radical disadvantages of its inherent specialization of the faculty of reception. It is only in the last hundred and fifty years, in any culture, that a majority of people have had even minimal access to this technique which already, over two millenia, had been carrying a major part of human culture. The consequences of this long (and in many places continuing) cultural division have been very great, and the confusion of developments beyond it, in societies at last becoming generally literate, is still very much with us. ...

Relations between social and cultural production and reproduction

The most important theoretical indication ... is that of the *variable degrees of symmetry* between cultural production and general social and cultural reproduction. For all practical purposes we can designate such relations in the earliest productive modes as wholly symmetrical. There is an effectively full parity between the purposes of cultural production and this more general social and cultural reproduction. But in some of the early stages of the technical reproduction of cultural production, as most notably in the political empires and the related imposition of religious systems, elements of asymmetry begin to appear, in the relations between dominant and subordinated cultures. In the massively reproductive social orders of the feudal and medieval periods these elements are still evident, and can at times be clearly perceived as asymmetries of a class kind.

Asymmetries

But it is in the new period of widely available physical reproduction of cultural artefacts, within already diversifying social relations, that asymmetries of a more complex kind than those of domination and subordination begin to appear. Many of the leading relations are still of course quite symmetrical, as in the case of the production of religious prints and texts. Indeed in some respects the new technologies of standardized and widely distributed reproduction made certain forms of social and cultural reproduction very much more effective, over a wider range, and in modes distinguishable from direct domination and subordination. But in printing especially — in literature and learning but also in scientific texts, in which accurately reproducible illustration played a crucial part — there was soon an evident asymmetry between the received and relatively rigid forms of social and cultural reproduction and this newly diverse and mobile cultural production and distribution. Many of the most important problems of the social relations of culture take their origin from the appearance of this effective if always variable asymmetry.

Three types of asymmetry

This general condition of asymmetry can be examined in three major areas of tension, conflict and struggle, within which the fact of asymmetry is always a major element. These areas are (i) the organization of licensing, censorship and other similar forms of control, and the struggle against these; (ii) the organization of the market, both in its aspect as a trading area whose purposes, in expansion and profit, may often be in conflict with otherwise dominant political and cultural authorities, and its aspect as a mechanism for commodities in this especially sensitive field, where inherent calculations of profit and scale may impose tensions with other conceptions of art and, at a different level, impose its own new forms of commercial controls; and (iii) the uneven and changing relations between a received and always to some extent recuperated 'popular' (largely oral) culture and the new forms of standardized and increasingly centralized production and reproduction.

READING B WHAT IS AN AUTHOR?

Michel Foucault

Let us analyze [the] 'author function'. ... In our culture, how does one characterize a discourse containing the author function? In what way is this discourse different from other discourses? If we limit our remarks to the author of a book or a text, we can isolate four different characteristics.

First of all, discourses are objects of appropriation. The form of ownership from which they spring is of a rather particular type, one that has been codified for many years. We should note that, historically, this type of ownership has always been subsequent to what one might call penal appropriation. Texts, books, and discourses really began to have authors (other than mythical, 'sacralized' and 'sacralizing' figures) to the extent that authors became subject to punishment, that is, to the extent that discourses could be transgressive. In our culture (and doubtless in many others), discourse was not originally a product, a thing, a kind of goods; it was essentially an act — an act placed in the bipolar field of the sacred and the profane, the licit and the illicit, the religious and the blasphemous. Historically, it was a gesture fraught with risks before becoming goods caught up in a circuit of ownership.

Source: Foucault, M. (1979) 'What is an author?', in Harari, J.V. (ed.) *Textual Strategies: Perspectives in Post-Structuralist Criticism,* Ithaca, Cornell University Press, pp.108–19.

Once a system of ownership for texts came into being, once strict rules concerning author's rights, author–publisher relations, rights of reproduction, and related matters were enacted — at the end of the eighteenth and the beginning of the nineteenth century — the possibility of transgression attached to the act of writing took on, more and more, the form of an imperative peculiar to literature. It is as if the author, beginning with the moment at which he was placed in the system of property that characterizes our society, compensated for the status that he thus acquired by rediscovering the old bipolar field of discourse, systematically practicing transgression and thereby restoring danger to a writing which was now guaranteed the benefits of ownership.

The author function does not affect all discourses in a universal and constant way, however. This is its second characteristic. In our civilization, it has not always been the same types of texts which have required attribution to an author. There was a time when the texts that we today call 'literary' (narratives, stories, epics, tragedies, comedies) were accepted, put into circulation, and valorized without any question about the identity of their author; their anonymity caused no difficulties since their ancientness, whether real or imagined, was regarded as a sufficient guarantee of their status. On the other hand, those texts that we now would call scientific — those dealing with cosmology and the heavens, medicine and illnesses, natural sciences and geography — were accepted in the Middle Ages, and accepted as 'true', only when marked with the name of their author. 'Hippocrates said', 'Pliny recounts', were not really formulas of an argument based on authority; they were the markers inserted in discourses that were supposed to be received as statements of demonstrated truth.

A reversal occurred in the seventeenth or eighteenth century. Scientific discourses began to be received for themselves, in the anonymity of an established or always redemonstrable truth; their membership in a systematic ensemble, and not the reference to the individual who produced them, stood as their guarantee. The author function faded away, and the inventor's name served only to christen a theorem, proposition, particular effect, property, body, group of elements, or pathological syndrome. By the same token, literary discourses came to be accepted only when endowed with the author function. We now ask of each poetic or fictional text: From where does it come, who wrote it, when, under what circumstances, or beginning with what design? The meaning ascribed to it and the status or value accorded it depend on the manner in which we answer these questions. And if a text should be discovered in a state of anonymity — whether as a consequence of an accident or the author's explicit wish — the game becomes one of rediscovering the author. Since literary anonymity is not tolerable, we can accept it only in the guise of an enigma. As a result, the author function today plays an important role in our view of literary works. (These are obviously generalizations that would have to be refined insofar as recent critical practice is concerned.)

The third characteristic of this author function is that it does not develop spontaneously as the attribution of a discourse to an individual. It is, rather, the result of a complex operation which constructs a certain rational being that we call 'author'. Critics doubtless try to give this intelligible being a realistic status, by discerning, in the individual, a 'deep' motive, a 'creative' power, or a 'design', the milieu in which writing originates. Nevertheless, these aspects of an individual which we designate as making him an author are only a projection, in more or less psychologizing terms, of the operations that we force texts to undergo, the connections that we make, the traits that we establish as pertinent, the continuities that we recognize, or the exclusions that we practice. ...

[In] modern literary criticism, ... the author provides the basis for explaining not only the presence of certain events in a work, but also their transformations, distortions, and diverse modifications (through his biography, the determination of his individual perspective, the analysis of his social position, and the revelation of his basic design). The author is also the principle of a certain unity of writing — all differences having to be resolved, at least in part, by the principles of evolution, maturation, or influence. The author also serves to neutralize the contradictions that may emerge in a series of texts: there must be — at a certain level of his thought or desire, of his consciousness or unconscious — a point where contradictions are resolved, where incompatible elements are at last tied together or organized around a fundamental or originating contradiction. Finally, the author is a particular source of expression that, in more or less completed forms, is manifested equally well, and with similar validity, in works, sketches, letters, fragments, and so on. ...

But the author function is not a pure and simple reconstruction made secondhand from a text given as passive material. The text always contains a certain number of signs referring to the author. These signs, well known to grammarians, are personal pronouns, adverbs of time and place, and verb conjugation. Such elements do not play the same role in discourses provided with the author function as in those lacking it. In the latter, such 'shifters' refer to the real speaker and to the spatio-temporal coordinates of his discourse (although certain modifications can occur, as in the operation of relating discourses in the first person). In the former, however, their role is more complex and variable. Everyone knows that, in a novel narrated in the first person, neither the first-person pronoun nor the present indicative refers exactly either to the writer or to the moment in which he writes, but rather to an alter ego whose distance from the author varies, often changing in the course of the work. It would be just as wrong to equate the author with the real writer as to equate him with the fictitious speaker; the author function is carried out and operates in the scission itself, in this division and this distance. ...

To conclude, I would like to review the reasons why I attach a certain importance to what I have said. ...

There are reasons dealing with the 'ideological' status of the author. The question then becomes: How can one reduce the great peril, the great danger with which fiction threatens our world? The answer is: One can reduce it with the author. The author allows a limitation of the cancerous and dangerous proliferation of significations within a world where one is thrifty not only with one's resources and riches, but also with one's discourses and their significations. The author is the principle of thrift in the proliferation of meaning. As a result, we must entirely reverse the traditional idea of the author. We are accustomed ... to saying that the author is the genial creator of a work in which he deposits, with infinite wealth and generosity, an inexhaustible world of significations. We are used to thinking that the author is so different from all other men, and so transcendent with regard to all languages that, as soon as he speaks, meaning begins to proliferate, to proliferate indefinitely.

The truth is quite the contrary: the author is not an indefinite source of significations which fill a work; the author does not precede the works; he is a certain functional principle by which, in our culture, one limits, excludes, and chooses; in short, by which one impedes the free circulation, the free manipulation, the free composition, decomposition, and recomposition of fiction. In fact, if we are accustomed to presenting the author as a genius, as a perpetual surging of invention, it is because, in reality, we make him function in exactly the opposite fashion. One can say that the author is an ideological product, since we represent him as the opposite of his historically real function. (When a historically given function is represented in a figure that inverts it, one has an ideological production.) The author is therefore the ideological figure by which one marks the manner in which we fear the proliferation of meaning.

In saying this, I seem to call for a form of culture in which fiction would not be limited by the figure of the author. It would be pure romanticism, however, to imagine a culture in which the fictive would operate in an absolutely free state, in which fiction would be put at the disposal of everyone and would develop without passing through something like a necessary or constraining figure. Although, since the eighteenth century, the author has played the role of the regulator of the fictive, a role quite characteristic of our era of industrial and bourgeois society, of individualism and private property, still, given the historical modifications that are taking place, it does not seem necessary that the author function remain constant in form, complexity, and even in existence. I think that, as our society changes, at the very moment when it is in the process of changing, the author function will disappear, and in such a manner that fiction and its polysemous texts will once again function according to another mode, but still with a system of constraint — one which will no longer be the author, but which will have to be determined or, perhaps, experienced.

READING C   THE WORK OF ART IN THE AGE OF
MECHANICAL REPRODUCTION

Walter Benjamin

> Our fine arts were developed, their types and uses were established, in times very different from the present, by men whose power of action upon things was insignificant in comparison with ours. But the amazing growth of our techniques, the adaptability and precision they have attained, the ideas and habits they are creating, make it a certainty that profound changes are impending in the ancient craft of the Beautiful. In all the arts there is a physical component which can no longer be considered or treated as it used to be, which cannot remain unaffected by our modern knowledge and power. For the last twenty years neither matter nor space nor time has been what it was from time immemorial. We must expect great innovations to transform the entire technique of the arts, thereby affecting artistic invention itself and perhaps even bringing about an amazing change in our very notion of art.
> (Valéry, 1964, p.225)

... I

In principle a work of art has always been reproducible. Man-made artifacts could always be imitated by men. Replicas were made by pupils in practice of their craft, by masters for diffusing their works, and, finally, by third parties in the pursuit of gain. Mechanical reproduction of a work of art, however, represents something new. Historically, it advanced intermittently and in leaps at long intervals, but with accelerated intensity. The Greeks knew only two procedures of technically reproducing works of art: founding and stamping. Bronzes, terra cottas, and coins were the only art works which they could produce in quantity. All others were unique and could not be mechanically reproduced. With the woodcut graphic art became mechanically reproducible for the first time, long before script became reproducible by print. The enormous changes which printing, the mechanical reproduction of writing, has brought about in literature are a familiar story. However, within the phenomenon which we are here examining from the perspective of world history, print is merely a special, though particularly important, case. During the Middle Ages engraving and etching were added to the woodcut; at the beginning of the nineteenth century lithography made its appearance.

With lithography the technique of reproduction reached an essentially new stage. This much more direct process was distinguished by the tracing of the design on a stone rather than its incision on a block of wood or its etching on a copperplate and permitted graphic art for the first time to put its products on the market, not only in large numbers as hitherto, but also in daily changing forms. Lithography enabled graphic art to illustrate

Source: Benjamin, W. (1970b) 'The work of art in the age of mechanical reproduction', in *Illuminations*, Jonathan Cape, pp.219–226.

everyday life, and it began to keep pace with printing. But only a few decades after its invention, lithography was surpassed by photography. For the first time in the process of pictorial reproduction, photography freed the hand of the most important artistic functions which henceforth devolved only upon the eye looking into a lens. Since the eye perceives more swiftly than the hand can draw, the process of pictorial reproduction was accelerated so enormously that it could keep pace with speech. A film operator shooting a scene in the studio captures the images at the speed of an actor's speech. Just as lithography virtually implied the illustrated newspaper, so did photography foreshadow the sound film. The technical reproduction of sound was tackled at the end of the last century. These convergent endeavours made predictable a situation which Paul Valéry pointed up in this sentence: 'Just as water, gas and electricity are brought into our houses from far off to satisfy our needs in response to a minimal effort, so we shall be supplied with visual or auditory images, which will appear and disappear at a simple movement of the hand, hardly more than a sign' (Valéry, 1964, p.226). Around 1900 technical reproduction had reached a standard that not only permitted it to reproduce all transmitted works of art and thus to cause the most profound change in their impact upon the public; it also had captured a place of its own among the artistic processes. For the study of this standard nothing is more revealing than the nature of the repercussions that these two different manifestations — the reproduction of works of art and the art of the film — have had on art in its traditional form.

II

Even the most perfect reproduction of a work of art is lacking in one element: its presence in time and space, its unique existence at the place were it happens to be. This unique existence of the work of art determined the history to which it was subject throughout the time of its existence. This includes the changes which it may have suffered in physical condition over the years as well as the various changes in its ownership. The traces of the first can be revealed only by chemical or physical analyses which it is impossible to perform on a reproduction; changes of ownership are subject to a tradition which must be traced from the situation of the original.

The presence of the original is the prerequisite to the concept of authenticity. Chemical analyses of the patina of a bronze can help to establish this, as does the proof that a given manuscript of the Middle Ages stems from an archive of the fifteenth century. The whole sphere of authenticity is outside technical — and, of course, not only technical — reproducibility. Confronted with its manual reproduction, which was usually branded as a forgery, the original preserved all its authority; not so *vis à vis* technical reproduction. The reason is twofold. First, process reproduction is more independent of the original than manual reproduction. For example, in photography, process reproduction can bring out those aspects of the original that are unattainable to the naked eye yet accessible to the lens, which is adjustable and chooses its angle at will. And photographic reproduction, with the aid of certain processes, such as enlargement or slow motion, can capture images which escape natural vision. Secondly, technical reproduction can put the copy of the original into situations which would be out of reach for the original itself. Above all, it enables the original to meet the beholder halfway, be it in the form of a photograph or a phonograph record. The cathedral leaves its locale to be received in the studio of a lover of art; the choral production, performed in an auditorium or in the open air, resounds in the drawing room.

The situations into which the product of mechanical reproduction can be brought may not touch the actual work of art, yet the quality of its presence is always depreciated. This holds not only for the art work but also, for instance, for a landscape which passes in review before the spectator in a movie. In the case of the art object, a most sensitive nucleus — namely, its authenticity — is interfered with whereas no natural object is vulnerable on that score. The authenticity of a thing is the essence of all that is transmissible from its beginning, ranging from its substantive duration to its testimony to the history which it has experienced. Since the historical testimony rests on the authenticity, the former, too, is jeopardized by reproduction when substantive duration ceases to matter. And what is really jeopardized when the historical testimony is affected is the authority of the object.

One might subsume the eliminated element in the term 'aura' and go on to say: that which withers in the age of mechanical reproduction is the aura of the work of art. This is a symptomatic process whose significance points beyond the realm of art. One might generalize by saying: the technique of reproduction detaches the reproduced object from the domain of tradition. By making many reproductions it substitutes a plurality of copies for a unique existence. And in permitting the reproduction to meet the beholder or listener in his own particular situation, it reactivates the object reproduced. These two processes lead to a tremendous shattering of tradition which is the obverse of the contemporary crisis and renewal of mankind. Both processes are intimately connected with the contemporary mass movements. Their most powerful agent is the film. Its social significance, particularly in its most positive form, is inconceivable without its destructive, cathartic aspect, that is, the liquidation of the traditional value of the cultural heritage. This phenomenon is most palpable in the great historical films. It extends to ever new positions. In 1927 Abel Gance exclaimed enthusiastically: 'Shakespeare, Rembrandt, Beethoven will make films … all legends, all mythologies and all myths, all founders of religion, and the very religions … await their exposed resurrection, and the heroes crowd each other at the gate.' (Gance, 1927, vol.2, pp.94–5.) Presumably without intending it, he issued an invitation to a far-reaching liquidation.

III

… The concept of aura which was proposed above with reference to historical objects may usefully be illustrated with reference to the aura of natural ones. We define the aura of the latter as the unique phenomenon of a distance, however close it may be. If, while resting on a summer after-noon, you follow with your eyes a mountain range on the horizon or a branch which casts its shadow over you, you experience the aura of those mountains, of that branch. This image makes it easy to comprehend the social bases of the contemporary decay of the aura. It rests on two circum-stances, both of which are related to the increasing significance of the masses in contemporary life. Namely, the desire of contemporary masses to bring things 'closer' spatially and humanly, which is just as ardent as their bent toward overcoming the uniqueness of every reality by accepting its reproduction. Every day the urge grows stronger to get hold of an object at very close range by way of its likeness, its reproduction. Unmistakably, reproduction as offered by picture magazines and newsreels differs from the image seen by the unarmed eye. Uniqueness and permanence are as closely linked in the latter as are transitoriness and reproducibility in the former. To pry an object from its shell, to destroy its aura, is the mark of a perception whose 'sense of the universal equality of things' has increased to such a degree that it extracts it even from a unique object by means of reproduction. Thus is manifested in the field of perception what in the theoretical sphere is noticeable in the increasing importance of statistics. The adjustment of reality to the masses and of the masses to reality is a process of unlimited scope, as much for thinking as for perception.

IV

The uniqueness of a work of art is inseparable from its being imbedded in the fabric of tradition. This tradition itself is thoroughly alive and extremely changeable. An ancient statue of Venus, for example, stood in a different traditional context with the Greeks, who made it an object of veneration, than with the clerics of the Middle Ages, who viewed it as an ominous idol. Both of them, however, were equally confronted with its uniqueness, that is, its aura. Originally the contextual integration of art in tradition found its expression in the cult. We know that the earliest art works originated in the service of a ritual — first the magical, then the religious kind. It is significant that the existence of the work of art with reference to its aura is never entirely separated from its ritual function. In other words, the unique value of the 'authentic' work of art has its basis in ritual, the location of its original use value. This ritualistic basis, however remote, is still recognizable as secularized ritual even in the most profane forms of the cult of beauty. The secular cult of beauty, developed during the Renaissance and prevailing for three centuries, clearly showed that ritualistic basis in its decline and the first deep crisis which befell it. With the advent of the first truly revolutionary means of reproduction, pho-tography, simultaneously with the rise of socialism, art sensed the approaching crisis which has become evident a century later. At the time, art reacted with the doctrine of *l'art pour l'art* ['art for art's sake'], that is, with a theology of art. This gave rise to what might be called a negative theology in the form of the idea of 'pure' art, which not only denied any social function of art but also any categorizing by subject matter. (In poetry, Mallarmé was the first to take this position.)

An analysis of art in the age of mechanical reproduction must do justice to these relationships, for they lead us to an all-important insight: for the first time in world history, mechanical reproduction emancipates the work of art from its parasitical dependence on ritual. To an ever greater degree the work of art reproduced becomes the work of art designed for reproducibility. From a photographic negative, for example, one can make any number of prints; to ask for the 'authentic' print makes no sense. But the instant the criterion of authenticity ceases to be applicable to artistic production, the total function of art is is reversed. Instead of being based on ritual, it begins to be based on another practice — politics.

V

Works of art are received and valued on different planes. Two polar types stand out: with one, the accent is on the cult value; with the other, on the exhibition value of the work. Artistic production begins with ceremonial objects destined to service in a cult. One may assume that what mattered was their existence, not their being on view. The elk portrayed by the man of the Stone Age on the walls of his cave was an instrument of magic. He did expose it to his fellow men, but in the main it was meant for the spirits. Today the cult value would seem to demand that the work of art remain hidden. Certain statues of gods are accessible only to the priest in the cella ['the inner chamber of a temple']; certain Madonnas remain covered nearly all year round; certain sculptures on medieval cathedrals are invisible to the spectator on ground level. With the emancipation of the various art practices from ritual go increasing opportunities for the exhibition of their products. It is easier to exhibit a portrait bust that can be sent here and there than to exhibit the statue of a divinity that has its fixed place in the interior of a temple. The same holds for the painting as against the mosaic or fresco that preceded it. And even though the public presentability of a mass originally may have been just as great as that of a symphony, the latter originated at the moment when its public presentability promised to surpass that of the mass.

With the different methods of technical reproduction of a work of art, its fitness for exhibition increased to such an extent that the quantitative shift between its two poles turned into a qualititative transformation of its nature. This is comparable to the situation of the work of art in prehistoric times when, by the absolute emphasis on its cult value, it was, first and foremost, an instrument of magic. Only later did it come to be recognized as a work of art. In the same way today, by the absolute emphasis on its exhibition value the work of art becomes a creation with entirely new functions, among which the one we are conscious of, the artistic function, later may be recognized as incidental. This much is certain: today photography and the film are the most serviceable exemplifications of this new function.

References

Valéry, P. (1964) 'The conquest of ubiquity', in *Aesthetics*, New York, Pantheon.

Gance, A. (1927) 'Le Temps de l'image est venu' *L'Art Cinématographique*, Paris.

CHAPTER 9   METROPOLIS: THE CITY AS TEXT

James Donald

CONTENTS

1   INTRODUCTION

1.1   PROLOGUE

London. Michaelmas term lately over, and the Lord Chancellor sitting in Lincoln's Inn hall. Implacable November weather. As much mud in the streets, as if the waters had but newly retired from the face of the earth, and it would not be wonderful to meet a Megalosaurus, forty feet long or so, waddling like an elephantine lizard up Holborn Hill. Smoke lowering down from chimney-pots, making soft black drizzle with flakes of soot in it as big as full-grown snowflakes — gone into mourning, one might imagine, for the death of the sun. Dogs, indistinguishable in mire. Horses, scarcely better; splashed to their very blinkers. Foot passengers, jostling one another's umbrellas, in a general infection of ill temper, and losing their foot-hold at street-corners, where tens of thousands of other foot passengers have been slipping and sliding since the day broke (if this day ever broke), adding new deposits to the crust upon crust of mud, sticking at those points tenaciously to the pavement, and accumulating at compound interest.

Fog everywhere. Fog up the river, where it flows among green aits and meadows; fog down the river, where it rolls defiled among the tiers of shipping, and the waterside pollutions of a great (and dirty) city. Fog on the Essex Marshes, fog on the Kentish heights. Fog creeping into the cabooses of collier-brigs; fog lying out on the yards, and hovering in the rigging of great ships; fog drooping on the gunwales of barges and small boats. Fog in the eyes and throats of ancient Greenwich pensioners, wheezing by the firesides of their wards; fog in the stem and bowl of the afternoon pipe of the wrathful skipper, down in his close cabin; fog cruelly pinching the toes and fingers of his shivering little 'prentice boy on deck. Chance people on the bridges peeping over the parapets into a nether sky of fog, with fog all around them, as if they were up in a balloon, and hanging in the misty clouds.

Gas looming through the fog in divers places in the streets, much as the sun may, from the spongey fields, be seen to loom by husbandman and ploughboy. Most of the shops lighted two hours before their time — as the gas seems to know, for it has a haggard and unwilling look.
(Dickens, 1853)

This is the opening of Charles Dickens's novel *Bleak House*, published in 1853 (Penguin edition, 1971). What is it doing here? Shouldn't a chapter dealing with the city in a series of books entitled *Understanding Modern Societies* get straight into questions of demography, social relations, work and leisure, housing, sub-cultures and the like? These are certainly important questions for an urban sociology, and they all have a vital role to play in determining the shape and nature of a city. But remember that the focus in the latter part of this Book is *culture*. That is to say, we are dealing with questions about the creation and dissemination of meaning, about modes of perception, and about the formation of individual and collective identities. The particular 'take' on the city in this chapter reflects my concern with these aspects of modernity: it is about the different meanings of, not a history of the modern city.

My argument is that attempts to describe Western cities in the nineteenth and twentieth centuries tell us a great deal about ways of understanding modernity more generally. The city has become a sort of metaphor for modernity itself. Reading accounts of what makes cities tick, how and why they changed, and what it was like to live through those changes can show us how modern ways of seeing and modern ways of making sense came into being. The search for categories and images adequate to the metropolis is evident not only in government reports and social scientific analysis, but also in literary and artistic conventions, and in the perceptions and practices of everyday life. The borders of these spheres are much fuzzier and more permeable than we often assume and, in the course of the chapter, I shall be drawing on this varied range of sources

So why the Dickens? Well, the passage I have quoted suggests to me not only that the city is one of the key images of modernity, but also why it should be so.

ACTIVITY 1   Read the opening of *Bleak House* again. What aspects of nineteenth-century London does Dickens mention? What analogies does he draw in order to convey an impression of what it was like? What metaphors are at work here?

Dickens conveys a powerful impression of the *feel* of the metropolis, and so of the city dweller's psychological response to this new and apparently chaotic landscape. By emphasizing the mud, the November fog, and the soot, he recreates the disturbing, even terrifying impact of what the poet James Thompson called 'the city of dreadful night'. And, by his reference to the Megalosaurus, he seems to imply that these signify something 'monstrous' about the city — a barely controlled nature that always threatens to shatter the veneer of civilization that holds it in check.

What are the constituents of that metropolitan civilization? Again, Dickens stresses the physical reality of crowds of strangers, always on the move, jostling the observer, their anonymity emphasized by their umbrellas. But he also looks beyond the apparent randomness of all this bustle and begins to identify the institutions and social interactions that bind the city together: the law, money (here linked to the capital accumulation of mud), and trade (embodied not only in London's shops but also in international shipping). He also mentions the new technology of gas lighting that both contributes to the general filth and impenetrability of the city, but also allows a fitful illumination.

London fog drawn in 1847 for the Illustrated London News, six years before the publication of *Bleak House*

In *Bleak House*, Dickens treats London as a labyrinth in which the form of social relations befogs or obscures the reality that links a rich aristocratic landowner to an impoverished and doomed crossing sweeper. Through the courts, the law colludes in this obscurantism. But it was also in this novel that Dickens introduced that other figure of the law, the detective who can disentangle these hidden connections and see through the London fog.

To summarize, Dickens sees the metropolis as an extraordinarily complex and initially indecipherable set of relationships welded together by networks at once symbolic and economic or administrative. In *Bleak House*, these are the networks of the law and money. In *Dombey and Son*, it is the railways, in *Our Mutual Friend* dust heaps, and prisons in *Little Dorrit* (Sharpe and Wallock, 1987, p.17). These interconnecting structures are not self-evident: they have to be inferred or read. Through the fog, Dickens identifies what makes the city run. And in representing those processes in the narratives and imagery of his novels, he also helped to disseminate certain techniques of reading the city that we now take for granted — our common sense about cities, if you like. As the architect Kevin Lynch has observed, 'Dickens helped to create the London we experience as surely as its actual builders did' (1981, pp.147–50).

You might suspect that this sort of approach works only in a special case like that of Dickens. To suggest how pervasive this sort of representation of the city has been, here is another novelist describing a different city almost a century after Dickens, in 1949. This example is drawn from American popular culture: from W.R. Burnett's gangster thriller *The Asphalt Jungle*, which was turned into a successful film in 1950. The novel is set in an unnamed American city, though it is clearly Chicago.

ACTIVITY 2   Note again the structure and references Burnett uses to convey not just an atmosphere, but a state of mind. Are there echoes of Dickens here? What differences are there between the two passages?

A dark, blustery night had settled down like a cowl over the huge, sprawling Midwestern city by the river. A mistlike rain blew between the tall buildings at intervals, wetting the streets and pavements and turning them into black, fun-house mirrors that reflected in grotesque distortions the street lights and neon signs.

The big downtown bridges arched off across the wide, black river into the void, the far shore blotted out by the misty rain; and gusts of wind, carrying stray newspapers, blew up the almost deserted boulevards, whistling faintly along the building fronts and moaning at the intersections. Empty surface cars, and buses with misted windows, trundled slowly through the downtown section. Except for taxis and prowl cars, there was no traffic.

River Boulevard, wide as a plaza and with its parkways and arched, orange street lights stretching off into the misty horizon in diminishing perspective, was as deserted as if a plague had swept the streets clean. The traffic lights changed with automatic precision, but there were no cars to heed or disobey them. Far down the boulevard, in the supper-club section of the city, elaborately glittering neon signs flashed off and on to emptiness. The night city, like a wound-up toy, went about its business with mechanical efficiency, regardless of man.

Finally the wind died down and the rain began to fall steadily all over the huge city: on the stacks of the steel plants in Polishtown; on the millionaires' mansions in Riverdale; on the hilly regions of Tecumseh Slope, with its little Italian groceries and restaurants; on the massed tenement apartments along the upper river, where all the windows had been dark for hours and men would start awake cursing as the alarm clocks blasted at five a.m.; on the fanned-out suburban areas to the north and east, where all the little houses and the little lawns looked alike; and finally on the dark and unsavory reaches of Camden Square and its environs, the immense downtown slum beyond the river, where there was at least one bar at every intersection, prowl cars by the dozens, and harness bulls working in pairs.

A taxi pulled up at a dark store front near Camden Square, and the driver turned to speak to his fare.

'You sure you know where you're going, buddy?'
(Burnett, 1950)

There are a number of rhetorical and thematic similarities between this and the opening of *Bleak House*: the reference to the effect of the weather on the different districts of a metropolis; the sense of the city as somehow alien and of civilization as mechanically sophisticated but fragile; the weaving in of the technologies and forces that constitute the life of a city — transport, lighting, police, and so forth. Two features of Burnett's description of Chicago may register the differences in time and place from Dickens's London. One is the double-take on the city as both a *machine* ('The night city, like a wound-up toy, went about its business with mechanical efficiency, regardless of man') and yet also a strange, even magical place (the wet pavements become 'fun-house mirrors that reflected in grotesque distortions the street lights and neon signs'). This is a characteristic modern ambivalence to which we shall be returning. The other is the commonsense awareness of the class and ethnic differences consolidated in the various districts of the metropolis. Burnett's 'urban ecology' of his 'sprawling Midwestern city' is strikingly close to that devised by the influential Chicago school of sociologists. (You might check the *Penguin Dictionary of Sociology:* CHICAGO SCHOOL; URBAN ECOLOGY) I have no idea whether Burnett knew their work. Intended or not, this is another example of the migration of images and ways of understanding across genres of writing: here between academic sociology and popular fiction.

1.2 'THE CITY' AS IMAGINED ENVIRONMENT

The point I am making by starting with *Bleak House* and *The Asphalt Jungle* is that 'the city' does not just refer to a set of buildings in a particular place. To put it polemically, there is no such *thing* as a city. Rather, *the city* designates the space produced by the interaction of historically and geographically specific institutions, social relations of production and reproduction, practices of government, forms and media of communication, and so forth. By calling this diversity 'the city', we ascribe to it a coherence or integrity. *The city*, then, is above all a representation. But what sort of representation? By analogy with the now familiar idea that the nation provides us with an 'imagined community', I would argue that the city constitutes an *imagined environment*. What is involved in that imagining — the discourses, symbols, metaphors and fantasies through which we ascribe meaning to the modern experience of urban living — is as important a topic for the social sciences as the material determinants of the physical environment.

Given that premise, in the rest of this chapter I shall focus on three questions.

1   What concepts, images and metaphors have reformers and planners used to make sense of the city?

2   How have these been translated into plans and policies for rationalizing and managing its immensity and apparent chaos?

3   In what terms have people experienced, imagined and envisioned the city forms which have resulted?

As you will see from these questions, my emphasis is primarily on what the city *means*. (My approach could therefore be termed *semiotic*, in the sense outlined in the *Penguin Dictionary of Sociology*: SEMIOTIC.) Both planners and people, I suggest, make sense of the city as if it were a text to be read in a 'quest for urban legibility' (Sharpe and Wallock, 1987, p.17). But, however much planners have tried to impose a single, definitive meaning to be found beneath all its interactions and social relations, the city — like a novel or poem — remains open to many competing interpretations. Part of my concern is therefore to discover how certain *forms of analysis*, discourses about the city, become authoritative, and to identify moments at which their authority is undermined and new paradigms of representation and interpretation emerge.

These concerns determine the structure of the chapter. I begin by looking at some of the concepts used by social observers and reformers in the nineteenth century. *Organic* and *mechanical* metaphors in particular shaped an emerging urban discourse. The problems of an industrial city like Manchester were seen as a disease in one part of a body needing to be cured before the whole was affected, or as a faulty part making a machine inefficient. These readings of the city determined the nature of urban policies. Taking Paris as an example, however, I argue that, when implemented, such rationalizing plans had unexpected and unintended consequences. One was an emerging aesthetic of modernism: that is, a distinctively new sensuous perception or experience of metropolitan life that was formalized in new techniques of representation and new — modern — artistic movements. These often revealed the products of the reformed cities to be, not just more efficient, but also phantasmagoric, grotesque, and even inhuman.

This ambivalence of the modern metropolis meant that, by the turn of the twentieth century, debates about urban planning and architecture inevitably entailed *aesthetic* and *psychological* considerations as well as social and political ones. This argument is exemplified by a debate about the modernization of Vienna. Then, after a reading of Georg Simmel's classic essay on 'The city and mental life', I consider the extent to which such aesthetic and ideological ideas affected twentieth-century urban life by looking at the utopian schemes of modernist architects and town planners like Le Corbusier and Ebenezer Howard.

Finally, and more speculatively, I try to identify some of the concepts, metaphors and images that inform the regulation and experience of today's 'world cities'. My argument is that the old organic and mechanical images have given way to ideas of *movement* and *flow*: the migration of people, for example, and the flows of information associated with recent developments in wealth production and communication technologies. This raises the question whether the old modernist terminology of urban planning and urban sociology is becoming outmoded.

2   CAPITALIST CITY

2.1   POLICING A POPULATION: MANCHESTER

This section presents my first example of how ways of reading the landscape and social relations of modern cities move in a circuit from observation and interpretation through the discourses and practices of urban government and back into the experience of everyday life. I show how a number of nineteenth century reformers could only make sense of this new urban phenomenon in terms of images and paradigms that were already familiar to them, and yet also how these paradigms were transformed in the act of reading the city to produce new discourses and new practices of urban planning and government.

In the early decades of the nineteenth century, many British towns and cities were radically transformed. So were the ways in which they were perceived and represented. The emergence of industrial modes of production was accompanied by unprecedented population growth. At the same time, there was massive migration of rural populations into urban areas. This combination of factors led to the establishment of new class relations and new patterns of urban segregation in terms of work, residence, class, occupation and ethnicity.

Who were the first chroniclers of this unprecedented urban environment? Not novelists like Dickens, but rather two groups of investigators groping towards techniques for governing industrial towns and cities. This required new techniques of analysis and conceptualization. The city had to be understood if it was to be governed and managed. But how? The perspectives and explanations of these urban critics drew on existing analogies and concepts from natural theology, physiology and political economy, but combined them in new ways and added distinctly new elements. For the most part, they worked within an *organic* paradigm. That is, they saw the city as a *natural* system, and made sense of it in terms of interrelated ideas about the universe, the human body, and the body-politic (Davison, 1983, pp.349–50).

The metaphor of divine order

The first group adapted and extended the 'natural theology' of the eighteenth century theologian William Paley (1743–1805) to the study of political economy and the urban environment. He had conceived of the universe as a benignly ordered *system*, with 'each part either depending on other parts, or being connected with other parts by some common law of motion or by the presence of some common substance'. In the 1830s, in his *Introductory Lectures* as the Professor of Political Economy at Oxford, Richard Whately illustrated this principle by the example of how London's population was fed. Imagine being a head commissionary responsible for this task, he suggested. The size of the city, the range of commodities, fluctuations in demand and the variability of supply would render the task impossible. And yet, he observed:

> ... this object is accomplished far better than it could be by any effort of human wisdom, through the agency of men, who think each of nothing beyond his own interest. ... In the provisioning of London, there are the same marks of contrivance and design, with a view to a beneficent end as we are accustomed to admire (when our attention is drawn to them by the study of Natural Theology) in the anatomical structure of the body, and the instincts of brute creation.
> (quoted in Davison 1983, p.354)

Such ideas clearly derived from Adam Smith's conception of the 'invisible hand' of the market. Those who espoused them belonged principally to the liberal section of the Church of England or the conservative wing of Dissent, and addressed themselves to 'the higher and more intelligent classes'. They seemed for the most part impervious to the brutal reality of poverty, crime and disease: these were generally treated as inevitable, if unfortunate, facts of nature (Davison, 1983, p.369).

The medical paradigm

Less complacent (perhaps because more marginal socially) were an emergent group of professional administrators and reformers: men like Edwin Chadwick (1800–90), who produced the influential *Report on the Sanitary Condition of the Labouring Population of Great Britain* in 1842, Thomas Southwood Smith, and Neil Arnott (1788–1874). Their strongest religious and philosophical affinities were with Unitarians and Benthamites; they had learned their economics from Malthus and took their model of society from contemporary physiology. They perceived urban ills as a disease — a more serious threat to the health of the body-politic than the 'natural historians' — and they believed in the power of human intelligence to diagnose and cure them. This group of investigators and reformers therefore devised new techniques of social observation and political calculation to tackle the perceived problems created by urbanization (Davison, 1983).

Typical of these new administrators was a Manchester doctor, James Phillips Kay (1804–1877). (He later became Sir James Kay-Shuttleworth; I shall refer to him in this form.) He came from a nonconformist background in the industrial bourgeoisie; his family's capital was in cotton, calico, printing, and blacking. He was a founder-member of the Manchester Statistical Society, became the city's chief public health officer, and, later, an Assistant Poor Law Commissioner. When he first moved to London he worked with Chadwick and, from 1839, he took on perhaps his most influential post, as the Secretary of the newly formed Committee of Council on Education.

Manchester from Kersall Moor painted by William Wyld around 1850

From the start, he had set his medical researches in the context of broader political questions. He realized that the causes of infection and disease, especially among the working classes, were linked to economic, social and environmental factors. In his 1877 autobiography, he justified his approach to social intervention in terms that suggest how important these reformers were in defining the terms and approaches of later social science:

> I came to know how almost useless were the resources of my art to contend with the consequences of formidable social evils. It was clearly something outside scientific skill or charity which was needed. ... Very early therefore, I began to reflect on this complex problem. Were this degradation and suffering inevitable? Could they only be mitigated? Were we always to be working with palliatives? Was there no remedy? Might not this calamity be

traced to its source, and all the resource of a Christian nation
devoted through whatever time, to the moral and physical
regeneration of this wretched population? Parallel therefore with
my scientific reading I gradually began to make myself acquainted
with the best work on political and social science, and obtained
more and more insight into the grave questions affecting the
relations of capital and labour and the distribution of wealth, as
well as the inseparable connection between the mental and moral
condition of the people and their physical well-being.
(quoted in Mort, 1987, pp.19–20)

In 1832, Kay-Shuttleworth was senior physician at the Ardwick and
Ancoats dispensary in a district of Manchester inhabited mainly by Irish
labourers and textile workers. Early that summer, the cholera epidemic
that had swept much of Europe reached the city, and Kay-Shuttleworth
became the secretary of a special committee that coordinated the work
of several boards of health to deal with it. This led him to investigate
the social conditions of the slums, and he reported his findings in his
influential pamphlet *The Moral and Physical Condition of the Working
Classes Employed in the Cotton Manufacture in Manchester*. Note in
this brief extract (1) how he sets up his narrative as a journey to the
heart of darkness; (2) how an impoverished environment and political
discontent are yoked intimately together; and (3) his use of an organic
imagery.

He whose duty it is to follow in the steps of this messenger of
death [cholera], must descend to the abodes of poverty, must
frequent the close alleys, the crowded courts, the overpeopled
habitations of wretchedness, where pauperism and disease
congregate round the source of social discontent and political
disorder in the centre of our large towns, and behold with alarm,
in the hot-bed of pestilence, ills that fester in secret, at the very
heart of society.
(quoted in Mort, 1987, p.21)

Although many evils afflicting the poor might 'flow from their own
ignorance or moral errors', Kay-Shuttleworth refused to dissociate these
from appalling living conditions, wretched diets, inadequate or non-
existent sanitation, the supposedly 'pernicious' moral example of Irish
immigrants, and the 'prolonged and exhausting labour' which
resembled 'the torment of Sisyphus' and deadened their minds. These
ills he attributed less to the commercial and manufacturing system as
such than to urbanization. He believed that the natural tendency of
capitalist industry was 'to develop the energies of society, to increase
the comforts and luxuries of life, and to elevate the physical condition
of every member of the social body'. This is why a pastoral or welfare
strategy was not only ethically necessary, but also offered a rational
means of preventing potential damage to that system.

However conventional Kay-Shuttleworth's work may have been in its emphasis on the maintenance of social order, its proposed solutions were strikingly novel. Here it is possible to see the formation of those discourses and techniques which eventually produce the modern conception of society as a knowable and governable object. Indeed, that concept only became a possibility within these new techniques of observation, calculation, and writing. The city as a problem of administration had to be rendered as 'text' — in pamphlets like his, but increasingly in official reports and commissions — to bring it into the ambit of government. How was this translation achieved?

It required a method of reading the city that produced a type and a scale of knowledge which could form the target of this emerging political rationality. Again, the analogy is with medical diagnosis. By attempting to isolate symptoms of disease in the 'social body', reformers like Kay-Shuttleworth created both new techniques of investigation, based primarily on the collection of statistical information about the urban population, and new administrative apparatuses designed to impose norms of conduct on that population. That is why Kay-Shuttleworth was concerned, not just with the good order of the working class, but with the details of their health, literacy, sentiments, domestic life, temperance, criminal propensities and sexuality — and with the statistically significant relations he discerned between them. The problem, and the solution, came to be defined in terms of *social welfare.*

This sphere involved both techniques of information-gathering and administrative agencies. These divided up the city into a grid of regulated spaces and, in doing so, identified both new 'social problems' and new objects of government. In his autobiography, Kay-Shuttleworth explains how these techniques were developed in Manchester at the time of the cholera outbreak.

> Boards of Health were established, in each of the fourteen districts of Police, for the purpose of minutely inspecting the state of the houses and streets. These districts were divided into minute sections, to each of which two or more inspectors were appointed from among the most respectable inhabitants of the vicinity, and they were provided with tabular queries, applying to each particular house and street.
> (quoted in Hunter, 1988, pp.55–6)

The diagnostic map of the 'social body' that emerged from this collection of statistics not only enabled the reformers to promote norms of individual conduct, but — perhaps more effectively — norms for public health, decency, cleanliness and sanitation. Urban government became a question of welfare as well as surveillance and discipline. It attempted to manipulate the urban environment so as to remove the sources of infection and corruption.

Unhealthy urban environment in nineteenth-century Leeds: from the Leeds
Insanitary Areas Collection

The logic of 'police'

To grasp what this new logic entailed, it is useful to spell out a little
more fully a term that Kay-Shuttleworth uses in the quotation above:
that is, the notion of 'police'. In the eighteenth century, this had had a
broader meaning than the one we normally associate with it; it also
prefigured many of these later reforms.

In a 1979 lecture, Michel Foucault explained the type of rationality
implemented in the exercise of power by modern states. This is
determined by the need to articulate two elements: political power
wielded over legal subjects and pastoral power wielded over live
individuals (Foucault, 1988, p.67). Its rationale was formulated in two
sets of doctrine from the sixteenth century onwards. One was concerned
with *reason of state*, the other with the *theory of police*.

Reason of state concerns those arts of governing which are concerned
not with enhancing the power a prince can wield over his domain, but
with reinforcing the state and its institutions as such. This therefore
entailed the need for concrete, quantifiable and precise information
about the strength of the state. The generation of this knowledge was
then called political *statistics* or *arithmetic*.

This shades into what was meant by 'the police'; that is, a technology of
government which defined the domains, techniques and targets of state
intervention. It involved cataloguing the resources of a state, both

material and human, in minute detail. It identified a new object: a population, whose geographical distribution, rates of fertility and mortality, and susceptibility to contagion could be quantified. Within that population, it paid unprecedented attention to the conduct of individuals — in terms of their capacities, their morals, their well-being, and so forth. Foucault refers to *Elements of Police,* a work by the German author Von Justi, to draw out the central paradox of this combination of surveillance and welfare.

> The police, he says, is what enables the state to increase its power and exert its strength to the full. On the other hand, the police has to keep the citizens happy — happiness being understood as survival, life, and improved living. He perfectly defines what I feel to be the aim of the modern art of government, or state rationality: viz., to develop those elements constitutive of individuals' lives in such a way that their development also fosters that of the strength of the state.
> (Foucault, 1988, p.82)

This approach then produces:

> ... a grid through which the state, i.e., territory, resources, population, towns, etc., can be observed. Von Justi combines 'statistics' (the description of states) with the art of government. *Polizeiwissenschaft* is at once an art of government and a method for the analysis of a population living on a territory.
> (Foucault, 1988, p.83)

If you read Kay-Shuttleworth's pamphlet on Manchester — or perhaps even more Chadwick's *Sanitary Report,* with its combination of statistical tables of mortality and disease and its first-hand reports from doctors and medical officers — it is just this combination of analysis and policy prescription that you will find. What the reformers' emphasis on quantifying the urban environment meant in practice was that statistical *norms* increasingly became or were translated into *governmental* definitions of the normal and the pathological, and hence also social self-understandings.

The underlying logic of the nineteenth-century strategy was by no means unique to Britain. The 1832 cholera epidemic had much the same effect in Paris. It provoked a more rigorous analysis of the urban milieu, focusing on *conditions de vie* (conditions of life) that included local biological and social variables. Although the attempt to imagine, implement, and co-ordinate macro- and micro-reforms was initially ineffective, it provided the catalyst for the emergence of an apparatus of finely grained observation of the social body: supervised by physicians, aided by architects, and backed by the police, in the service of the health of the population and the general good (Rabinow, 1989, p.39).

In his Foucauldian history of these developments, Paul Rabinow also suggests how this statistical grid of investigation produced a new social scientific conception of society that in turn informed the physical structure of the city.

> Society was becoming an object *sui generis*, with its own laws, its own science, and eventually its own arts of government. If the individual's normality and pathology were a function not of his independent moral state but rather of his place within a social whole, then it made little sense to try to reform him separately from reforming the social milieu within which his actions were formed and normed. ... The use of statistical approaches to social problems posed the problem of finding forms through which to present this understanding, just as the century-long search for new architectural forms was perplexed about the norms of modern society that these forms were supposed to embody and represent. (Rabinow, 1989, p.67)

The nineteenth-century emergence of strategies for social welfare and administrative reform was given a different inflection in different contexts. In Britain, it bore the marks of nonconformism, Benthamite utilitarianism, and the medical metaphors of the body-politic and the city. In France, the intellectual impetus came from the rationalism of Saint-Simon and his followers. (For an account of this rationalism, see Book 1 (Hall and Gieben, 1992), Chapter 1; see also *The Penguin Dictionary of Sociology:* SAINT-SIMON.)

Structural determination

We have seen that both the natural theologians and moral environmentalists like Kay-Shuttleworth and Chadwick used *organic* analogies when interpreting urban life. The former saw society as another aspect of divinely ordained nature, the latter as a functioning body whose manifest ills needed to be cured. Both were therefore concerned to identify the universal laws or mechanisms that governed its workings. In their emphasis on a statistical understanding of the population, for example, the reformers were attempting to identify norms of behaviour and systematic patterns of interaction between different characteristics and dispositions. This required a more refined observation and surveillance of the urban population. In the remedies they proposed, they sought to ensure the welfare of the working classes as a prerequisite for the efficient functioning of society as a whole. Increasingly, then, their plans shaded into what we would call *social engineering*: that is, a deliberate attempt to subject the flux of social life to the rule of reason. In doing so, they began to shift from an organic analogy (social development reflecting the unfolding of natural laws) to a mechanical analogy (the manipulation of the environment as a way of imposing norms of conduct).

Just ten years after Kay-Shuttleworth's pamphlet, another account of Manchester was published which saw the city less as an organism to be modified than as a historical phenomenon to be interpreted. It attempted to synthesize Kay-Shuttleworth's commitment to detailed empirical observation with a much more explicit interpretive framework based on the dynamics of social and economic relations. Its author was a young German businessman sent by his father to learn the cotton trade in England — Friedrich Engels (1820–95). Although Engels was a diligent student of British writers like Kay-Shuttleworth, Chadwick and Southwood Smith, he identified not with these Benthamite reformers but with the poor and the working classes. He respected their research, and drew on it widely in *The Condition of the Working Class in England in 1844* (Engels, 1892). Nevertheless, he rejected not just the idea of the virtues of capitalism or a providential social order but also their representation of the city as an organism or a natural system (Davison, 1983, p.368). Instead, Steven Marcus has argued, he managed to read the 'illegible' industrial city by showing that its 'apparently unsystematic and possibly incoherent' form could be 'perceived as a total intellectual and imaginative structure' (Marcus, 1973, p.258).

ACTIVITY 3   Now read **Reading A, 'The great cities: Manchester'**, by Friedrich Engels, which you will find at the end of this chapter.

Ideally, I would like you to read Engels' account of Manchester and its inhabitants twice: the first time to grasp his analysis of the social relations governing the layout of the city, the second time concentrating on *how he reads* the signs of the city and *how he represents* that interpretation.

Make sure, in any case, that you have a clear sense of both his argument and his rhetorical style: his language, his metaphors, and the forms of explanation he uses.

Engels begins by mapping out the overall shape of the city. In doing so, he outlines an interpretation of the relation between districts in terms of a determining but implicit social dynamic. He describes how Manchester's commercial heart, with its offices and warehouses, is linked by new and efficient roads to its prosperous suburbs: an arrangement that leaves the surrounding working-class slums discreetly hidden from the view of those who live off this poverty. In contrast to someone like Kay-Shuttleworth, however, he does not see this poverty as a sickness to be cured or a malfunction in the machinery of production. On the contrary, he sees it as a necessary consequence of the forms of production that produce this spatial organization. It is what makes the display of wealth possible.

Having identified this coherence at the level of the city's macro-structure, Engels records his explorations of its micro-structures.

Starting at the twelve o'clock position on the compass, he works around the city in a clockwise direction, systematically penetrating the screens behind which increasingly squalid courtyards and back alleys fester. This method confers a spatial and narrative unity on his analytic reading of this 'unplanned wilderness'.

Engels repeatedly attempts to pre-empt accusations of exaggeration by insisting that his words are inadequate to the reality he discovered. It is not the passion with which he denounces the conditions in which people are forced to live that is new, however, nor his narrative structure of a journey to the lower depths. Where he differs from an investigator like Kay-Shuttleworth is in the explanation he begins to offer of why these conditions exist.

On the one hand, he sees confident wealth. On the other, at the heart of darkness he finds the poorest of the working class living in the midst of filth and excrement. What is the link? Engels explains these urban social relations neither in terms of an organism nor of a machine, although he invokes elements of both. Rather, he discerns a *structure* which functions as a complex, concrete totality, and whose parts have meanings that are only decipherable in relation to all its other parts. The key insight is that this structure is a *dynamic* one. The whole thing is in motion. This movement does not represent the unfolding of divine or natural laws, but the interaction between the forces and the social relations of production. It was this dual focus on deciphering a systematic *economic structure* to urban social relations and interpreting it *historically* that was the powerful Hegelian insight in Engels' chapter (Marcus, 1973, p.263).

I have emphasized the semiotic power of Engels' reading of Manchester: in many ways it was more revealing and certainly more sophisticated conceptually in its explanation of why the city was like it was than Kay-Shuttleworth's. Engels' approach to the problems of industrial cities also implies different definitions of what solutions might be desirable or possible from those of a Chadwick or a Kay-Shuttleworth. The dangers of translating a totalizing analysis like Engels' into a political strategy for cities will become clearer when we look at the ideas of Le Corbusier in the twentieth century.

In this section, I have argued that the problems posed by urbanization provoked new techniques for investigating, mapping, and administering the city and its population. I have identified three main perspectives.

1   The first was based on natural theology and the invisible workings of the market. This makes most sense in terms of classical economics.

2   In the work of a new class of social scientists and administrators it is possible to discern a new conception of 'the social'. Its characteristic mode of investigation was empirical and statistical; the strategies it proposed involved a combination of surveillance and welfare provision. The later work of Michel Foucault provides valuable insights into its history and logic.

3   Engels' analysis of Manchester prefigures a Marxist urban sociology
      more concerned with deciphering structures than with imposing
      grids of observation. In contrast to the urban reformers, it offers
      little in the way of plans or blueprints for change. Rather, it sees the
      improvements they proposed as part of the same dynamic structure
      that produced the problems of industrialization and urbanization in
      the first place.

These competing perspectives underline once again the importance of
the concepts and metaphors through which we perceive 'the city', not
only as an object of thought and study but increasingly as an object of
government. What is evident in the examples in this section is a search
for ways of formulating a problem in terms that render it soluble. The
perspectives are produced in the quest for urban legibility: that is, in the
process of interpreting the city and rendering it in discourse.

This emphasis on the emergence of 'the city' as an effective *concept* in
the discourses of government, social administration and social science,
however, is only part of the story. It does not tell us how the new forms
of social regulation, increasingly embodied in the concrete form of
architecture and planning, were experienced by those who lived in
these cities.

2.2   THE CONCEPT OF THE CITY AND THE EXPERIENCE OF THE CITY

Although it breaks the sequence of my narrative, it is vital to grasp the
distinction between the way that the city is conceptualized and the way
that the city is experienced.

The feel of what is at stake in these two ways of reading the city is
beautifully captured in a passage from Doris Lessing's novel *The Four-
Gated City* (1969). The protagonist, Martha Quest, is an intellectual and
a newcomer to London. She is no urban reformer, but she tries to make
sense of the city in rational, analytic terms. For Iris, on the other hand,
her neighbourhood is textured and animated by histories and memories.

> Iris, Joe's mother ... knew everything about this area, half a dozen
> streets for about half a mile or a mile of their length; and she knew
> it all in such detail that when with her, Martha walked in a double
> vision, as if she were two people: herself and Iris, one eye stating,
> denying, warding off the total hideousness of the whole area, the
> other, with Iris, knowing it in love. With Iris, one moved here, in a
> state of love, if love is the delicate but total acknowledgement of
> what is. [...] Iris, Joe's mother, had lived in this street since she
> was born. Put her brain, together with the other million brains,
> women's brains, that recorded in such tiny loving anxious detail
> the histories of windowsills, skins of paint, replaced curtains and
> salvaged baulks of timber, there would be a recording instrument,
> a sort of six-dimensional map which included the histories and

lives and loves of people, London — a section map in depth. This
is where London exists.
(Lessing, 1969)

What is at stake in that ambivalence? Why is it so important? In a
chapter on 'Walking in the city', the French theorist, Michel de Certeau
proposes a dual perspective for mapping urban space that may help us
to understand it.

First, he identifies the 'concept city' embodied in 'utopian and
urbanistic discourse'. This is what we found in reformers like Kay-
Shuttleworth: the desire for a perspective both god-like and voyeuristic
that can encompass all the diversity, randomness and dynamism of
urban life in a single panorama or a neat collection of statistics. This
urbanistic discourse, suggests de Certeau, must start by producing *un
espace propre'* — a phrase that in French suggests both 'its *own* space'
and 'a *pure* space'. That this ambiguity is deliberate is clear from de
Certeau's comment that 'rational organization must thus repress all the
physical, mental and political pollutions that would compromise it' (de
Certeau, 1984, p.94). So, for example, by imagining the city as an
organism the urban reformers could represent disease, death, and
deviance, not as the inevitable consequences of social and economic
relations but as 'pollutions' or malfunctions. They should not happen.
Utopian schemes to banish these ills can thus be seen as a form of
repression.

De Certeau's second perspective emphasizes that the *fact* of any city is
always more diverse, more messy and more active than reformers find
comfortable or comprehensible. The *concept* of the city can never get its
full measure: an accurate representation would require something more
like the experiential 'section map in depth' described by Doris Lessing.
'Beneath the discourses that ideologise the city,' writes de Certeau, 'the
ruses and combinations of powers that have no readable identity
proliferate; without points where one can take hold of them, without
rational transparency, they are impossible to administer' (de Certeau,
1984, p.95).

That is a daunting sentence, but it is saying something important: that
discourses have limits and blind spots. The urban reformers imposed an
interpretive grid on the city and reduced its social life to a number of
human capacities, vices and virtues which allowed them to extrapolate
a fixed pattern of statistical relationships. In doing so, they subjected
the population of the city to observation, amelioration and discipline.
But could all the activities of the populations of Manchester or London
— 'the histories and lives and loves of people' — really be captured in
this neat categorization? Many of the things people got up to simply
would not fit the categories: they are too unpredictable, inventive and
devious for that. This is why de Certeau says that their 'ruses and
combinations of powers' have '*no readable identity*'. And if the
administrators cannot read them, if they do not have a six-dimensional
recording machine, then they cannot regulate them.

When we walk the city streets, de Certeau suggests, we are engaged in 'illegible' improvisations. It is like using language. In both cases, we operate within a constraining structure — the streets and buildings of the city on the one hand, grammar on the other — but we adapt it to our own creative purposes. Such negotiations produce a different space. This is not the physical environment manipulated by social administrators, but a symbolic order. It is not a representation of space, but a representational space (Lefebvre, 1991). De Certeau calls it 'an "anthropological", poetic and mythic experience of space'. The urban text he is interested in is the opaque one inscribed by the bustling journeys of people going about their business: 'a *migrational*, or metaphorical, city thus slips into the clear text of the planned and readable city' (p.93).

Let me relate de Certeau's ideas to more conventional sociological arguments. You will know that this series of books on *Understanding Modern Society* has as its framework the narrative of the Enlightenment project: that is, the attempt to bring ever more areas of life under the rule of reason (see Book 1 (Hall and Gieben, 1992), Introduction and Chapter 1). This is the story of Western modernity usually attributed to Max Weber. In this version, the eighteenth and nineteenth centuries witnessed the triumph of abstract, formal rationality as the organizing principle not only of structures of production, markets, and state bureaucracies, but also of cultural forms such as music and law. It was inevitably accompanied by the demythification and disenchantment of the social world. This account of modernization can certainly make sense of the sort of demographic, industrial and administrative changes that we identified in nineteenth-century Manchester. This is the logic that de Certeau captures in his idea of the 'concept city'.

But does it tell the whole story of the metropolis? The analysis of nineteenth- and twentieth-century cities by the German critic Walter Benjamin (1892-1940) suggests that it does not; and that it does not because it fails to acknowledge the other, darker, more magical side of the Enlightenment project. Benjamin would probably not have disputed the general validity of Weber's observations. But, he insists, at the same time as the social and cultural institutions of Western cities became more and more rationalized in form, on an unconscious 'dream' level — the symbolic order of de Certeau's 'illegible' improvisations and resourceful journeys — the new urban-industrial world was being fully *re-*enchanted. These were two sides of the same process. That, at least, is what Benjamin tried to show in his work on nineteenth-century Paris. He wanted to recapture the newness and strangeness of living there and then. In the representational spaces of Paris, the 'threatening and alluring face' of myth was alive and everywhere: in the new shopping arcades that were the main focus of Benjamin's study, in department stores, in the giant new advertising hoardings. Myth even whispered its presence in the most rationalized urban plans that, 'with their uniform streets and endless rows of buildings, have realized the dreamed-of architecture of the ancients: the labyrinth' (Buck-Morss, 1989, pp.253–4).

A Paris department store,1910: the main hall of the Galeries Lafayette

It would be wrong to suggest that de Certeau and Benjamin are making exactly the same point. Nevertheless, their arguments, when taken together, do suggest that one reason why urban plans and people's experience are never quite in rhythm is that the rationality of the 'concept city' inevitably undervalues the mythical element of city life. To illustrate this point, let us look at Benjamin's example of nineteenth-century Paris.

2.3 RATIONALITY AND ENCHANTMENT: PARIS

Modernity is inherently both rational and mythical. Nowhere is this more evident than in the modern city. This ambivalence between the rational 'concept city' of the reformers and people's everyday urban improvisations is exemplified by two emblematic figures central to Benjamin's vision of nineteenth-century Paris: the planner Haussmann and the poet Baudelaire.

Haussmann

The great modernizer of Paris in the second half of the nineteenth century was Baron Haussmann (1809–1891), Napoleon III's prefect of the Seine. In seventeen years he was responsible for a thorough-going transformation of the city. By 1870 one-fifth of the streets in central Paris were his creation, and the acreage of the city had been doubled by annexation. At the height of the reconstruction, one in five Parisian workers was employed in the building trade. In the name of slum clearance, some 350,000 people (on Haussmann's own estimation) were displaced from the *quartiers* of old Paris to make way for his new boulevards, parks and 'pleasure grounds'. These provided the illusion of social equality, but the practical effect — as in Engels' Manchester — was to raze working-class neighbourhoods and shift the eyesores and health hazards of poverty to the suburbs.

Although the boulevards, with their uniform facades interspersed with national monuments, created unprecedented urban vistas, equally important was the creation of the physical infrastructure to sustain them. A hundred miles from Paris, aqueducts were laid to improve the city's tap-water supply. New lenses were fitted on the gas lamps. The great collector sewer and a new morgue were opened. An outer circle of railways surrounded the city, and a ring of stations acted as city gates. Haussmann broke the monopoly of the cab company in 1866, and promoted that of the makers of street lamps in 1856. (Clark, 1984, pp.37–8; Buck-Morss, 1989, pp.89–90.)

What were the purposes of this 'Haussmannization'? They were, of course, complex and sometimes contradictory. There was certainly an element of Saint-Simonian utopianism in the 'concept city' of Haussmann and Napoleon III. They wanted to create a clean, light and airy city protected by policemen and night patrols; they wanted to provide trees, schools, hospitals, cemeteries, bus shelters, and public urinals (for men at least). But the logistics of state power and economic calculation were equally powerful motives. The city was redesigned to allow the most efficient circulation of goods, people, money, and troops: the boulevards provided the shortest routes between the barracks and working-class districts.

Haussmann's schemes reflected the logic of the stock market and commerce — they fuelled a boom in property speculation — rather than that of the factory and its disciplines. They were based on a static, and therefore already archaic, conception of both urban space and the social relations of the city (Rabinow, 1989, p.77). Although he could understand the political, economic and technological problems of Paris, Haussmann did not think in the emerging social terms of technocratic and administrative rationality: the concerns with the welfare, morality and efficiency of an urban population that we identified in our study of Manchester.

This may explain the ambivalent outcomes of Haussmann's carefully planned upheavals. Many Parisians complained that he had created an artificial city where they no longer felt at home. The boulevards, parks, and other new public spaces created a backdrop against which the worlds of rich and poor — supposedly cordoned off from each other — became all the more visible to each other, if no more legible. Even his 'strategic beautification' proved of limited value when barricades appeared across his boulevards in the Paris Commune of 1870.

Baudelaire

The displacements brought about by Haussmannization may have lent a specially fantastic and elusive quality to life in the city. It was, in any case, in this changing, reinvented Paris that the poet Charles Baudelaire (1821–1867) coined the term *modernity* to identify a pervasive and disturbing experience of *newness*. He located this modernity not in grand schemes or epochal changes, but in representational spaces characterized by '*le transitoire, le fugitif, le contingent*': what is transitory, fleeting, and contingent. The task of the modern artist was therefore to capture 'the ephemeral, contingent newness of the present'. What becomes apparent in Baudelaire are a consciousness and an aesthetic based on those resourceful negotiations of the mythical and metaphorical city which de Certeau presents as the other side of the rational 'concept city'.

Baudelaire used various analogies to express this new way of seeing. Above all, he presented himself as the *flâneur*: the strolling observer of 'the landscapes of the great cities'. The *flâneur's* natural milieu was the anonymous ebb and flow of the urban crowd. This enabled him, in Baudelaire's words:

> To be away from home and yet to feel oneself everywhere at home; to see the world, to be at the centre of the world, and yet to remain hidden from the world. The spectator is a *prince* who everywhere rejoices in his incognito.
> (quoted in Frisby, 1985, pp.18–19)

The *flâneur* combined the passionate wonder of childhood with the analytic sophistication of the man of the world as he read the signs and impressions of 'the outward show of life'. Amongst the other perspectives — or guises — that Baudelaire adopted were those of the dandy, the whore, and the rag-picker. In these marginal, despised figures, living on their wits and for whom reading the signs of the city rightly could be a matter of life or death, Baudelaire saw an image of the modern poet's social location and role.

In his own work, Walter Benjamin attempted to recreate Baudelaire's mythical Paris. He wanted to show how this other side of the modern metropolis — its transformation into a spectacle, a phantasmagoria — was as closely linked to the logic of capitalism as the 'concept city' of the rationalist planners and reformers. His central image was that of the arcades: glass-covered, gas-lit 'fairy grottoes' that prefigured today's shopping malls. These Benjamin saw as 'the original temple of commodity capitalism'. Their shop windows displayed luxurious commodities like icons in niches. Food, drink, roulette and vaudeville shows were abundantly on offer, and, in the first-floor galleries, sexual pleasures could be bought: 'The windows in the upper floor of the Passages are galleries in which angels are nesting; they are called swallows' (quoted in Buck-Morss, 1989, p.83).

The Passage Choiseul, Paris, in the nineteenth century

During the Second Empire of Napoleon III, this urban phantasmagoria burst out of the confines of the original arcades and spread throughout Paris. Commodity displays became ever more grandiose, especially in the new department stores. This ostentation reached its peak in the world expositions that, in the wake of London's Crystal Palace in 1851, were held in Paris in 1855, 1867, 1889 and 1900. Industrial products and machine technologies were displayed like artworks. They were set off against ornamental gardens, statues, and fountains. Military canons were juxtaposed with fashion costumes in a dazzling fantasy world. The fairs also left permanent traces on the city landscape: the Grand Palais, Trocadero, and the Eiffel Tower were all built for them.

In these international fairs Benjamin saw the origins of a 'pleasure industry' and advertising techniques in which spectacle and fantasy were skilfully calibrated to the tastes and dreams of a mass audience. In

L'Exposition Universelle by Edouard Manet, 1867

The 1900 Universal Exhibition, Paris

La Tour Eiffel by Robert Delaunay, 1910-11

a magnified version of the *flâneur's* window shopping, their message was: 'Look, but don't touch.' The crowds were taught to derive pleasure from the spectacle alone. At these fairs, buying and selling were less significant than their phantasmagoric function as 'folk festivals' of capitalism. Here mass entertainment itself became big business (Buck-Morss, 1989, pp.83–6).

The contrast between Haussmann's Concept-Paris and Baudelaire's phantasmagoric Paris indicates an emerging modernist ambivalence around the city that marks a shift from the investigative, reforming programmes of the first generation of urbanists. From the second half of the nineteenth century onwards, the modernization of the great Western metropolises was characterized, physically, by the spectacular redesign of city centres and the growth of residential suburbs. Equally significant were the perceptual and psychological changes that accompanied this development. Modern consciousness became urban consciousness; the landscape, rhythms and dynamism of the city became internalized (Sharpe and Wallock, 1987, p.13; Williams, 1973, p.235).

On the one hand, planners attempted to reorganize and regularize space in order to manage the conduct and welfare of a potentially insurrectionary urban population. On the other hand, *flâneurs*, artists and anonymous but inventive crowds were devising ways of reading these social constructs as a comic parade or a hellish dream-world. On the one hand, modernizers sought to impose the rationality of the 'concept city' on urban life; on the other, modernists developed an expressive aesthetic which systematically re-enchanted it.

2.4   RATIONALISM AND HISTORICISM: VIENNA

One consequence of this dualism was that the old images of urbanism had to change. Just as the medical paradigm had given way to the metaphor of social engineering, now a purely mechanical conception of planning was itself in question. Two new variables became evident in any 'concept city': the cultural and aesthetic values expressed in an architectural style or an urban plan, and their supposed psychological impact on the population.

This change can be seen in a debate about architecture and planning that raged in Vienna right at the end of the nineteenth century (Schorske, 1980). When liberals won control of the Austrian capital in 1860, they had reshaped the city in their own image. The centrepiece of this version of Haussmannization was the Ringstrasse, a sweeping circular boulevard of municipal buildings and private dwellings that separated the old city centre from its suburbs. Typically, its creators had attempted to combine a historicist grandeur of style with rationality and efficiency in function. When Austrian intellectuals turned against the culture and values of liberalism, the Ringstrasse became the symbolic focus of their critique. Most relevant are the polemics of two pioneers of modern thought about the city and its architecture. One, Camillo Sitte (1843–1903), was a nostalgic communitarian; the other, Otto Wagner (1841–1918), a thoroughgoing modernist and rationalist.

The Ring, Vienna

Sitte's objection to the Ringstrasse was that, although traditionalist in its aesthetics, traditional values were betrayed to the exigencies of modern life. By 'modern' in this context he meant the technical aspects of city building — 'traffic, hygiene, etc.' — whereas he was interested in what makes certain forms of spatial organization picturesque and psychologically satisfying. Against the geometric grids favoured by both speculators and rationalist planners, he exalted the irregular streets and squares of ancient and medieval cities, and set out to recreate by deliberate artistic planning what earlier eras had achieved by spontaneous slow growth. Inspired by the idea of opera as a total work of art and committed to the traditions of artisanship, he envisaged the modern city planner as an inspired creator who remakes our lives by redesigning our environment (Schorske, 1980, pp.62–72).

Otto Wagner's attack on the Ringstrasse was diametrically opposed to this. He denounced the masking of modernity and its functions behind the stylistic screens of history. Whereas Sitte evoked visual models from the communitarian past to counteract the anomie of modern urbanism, Wagner sought new aesthetic forms to express the values of the hectic capitalist urbanity he joyfully embraced. He wanted to celebrate new materials and the functional rationality of buildings. 'Art,' he proclaimed, 'has the task of adapting the face of the city to contemporary humanity.' Architects and city planners should therefore 'make visible our better, democratic, self-conscious and sharp-thinking essence, and do justice to the colossal technical and scientific achievements as well as to the fundamentally practical character of modern mankind' (Schorske, 1980, pp.73–4).

How does this Viennese dispute illuminate our history of the metaphors through which people have made sense of the city? As a traditionalist, Sitte saw the city in organic terms, although now as a historically evolving organism: an entity with a natural process of growth that can be stunted or perverted by insensitive attempts at planning and social engineering. Wagner, in contrast, saw modern man as a radically new, self-created being and therefore sought progressive styles of architecture and city planning adequate to this machine age. Sitte wanted to recapture the human scale of the past, Wagner to create the city of the future. In both cases, the old explanatory metaphors had been rearticulated as architectural and urban *aesthetics*. They no longer merely provided a guide to reading the city, but principles for redesigning it. The competing claims to authority of the nostalgic and progressive models were now based on assumptions about how the urban environment affects people's psychic well-being. Elements from the organic and mechanical metaphors were still very much in play. But the city had also become a work of art and a human laboratory.

3 UNREAL CITY

3.1 THE METROPOLIS AND MENTAL LIFE

Just as an aesthetic dimension became integrated into urbanism, so — as we saw in Baudelaire's conception of the modern artist — the city and the metropolitan experience were at the heart of modernism as an aesthetic movement. 'The forces of the action have become internal,' Raymond Williams observes of the Irish novelist James Joyce's great modernist novel about Dublin, *Ulysses* (1922); 'in a way there is no longer a city, there is only a man walking through it' (Williams, 1973, p.243). The frenetic rhythms and fragmented perspectives of the metropolis not only became a theme of modernist works; they also determined formal experiments in literature, painting and film. Modernism was, of course, highly differentiated. There were different national schools and traditions, different political affiliations, and radically opposed judgments on metropolitan culture in the machine age. Some variants of modernism celebrated its novelty and energy; others emphasized the psychic costs of its alienation and lack of meaning. In one of the most important and influential of modernist poems, *The Wasteland* (1922), T.S. Eliot, like Dickens, invokes London's fog and river and its anonymous crowd. But here the city has become purely a state of mind. It is *unreal*.

> Unreal City,
> Under the brown fog of a winter dawn,
> A crowd flowed over London Bridge, so many,
> I had not thought death had undone so many.
> Sighs, short and infrequent, were exhaled,
> And each man fixed his eyes before his feet.
> Flowed up the hill and down King William Street,
> To where Saint Mary Woolnoth kept the hours
> With a dead sound on the final stroke of nine.
> (Eliot, 1922)

Of the first generation of sociologists, the one most in tune with this ambivalence of modernity was the German writer Georg Simmel (1858–1918). Like Baudelaire, he was alert to the possibilities of self-creation and sensitive to the city's parade of impressions. Above all, Simmel stressed the *psychological* impact of social existence in his definition of modernity.

> The essence of modernity as such is psychologism, the experiencing [*das Erleben*] and interpretation of the world in terms of the reactions of our inner life and indeed as an inner world, the dissolution of fixed contents in the fluid of the soul, from which all that is substantive is filtered and whose forms are merely forms of motion.
> (quoted in Frisby, 1985, p.46)

ACTIVITY 4 Now read **Reading B, 'The metropolis and mental life'**, by Georg Simmel.

As you read, bear in mind Simmel's definition of modernity and the emphasis in the previous sections on the perceptual and psychological impact of changes in the structure and experience of Western capitals.

At the same time, focus on the following questions.

1   Can you identify the metaphors or paradigms through which Simmel 'reads' the city? Does he use an organic, historic, or semiotic approach to the city, a combination of some of these, or none of them?

2   What is his object of study? Does he discuss, for example, the physical fabric of the city, the general welfare and habits of its population, or the institutions that make up its infrastructure? Or is he more concerned with the city as a state of mind?

3   What techniques of social scientific investigation does he use? Are there any statistics, reports, interviews, or detailed descriptions here? In short, how would you characterize his sociological method?

Simmel is clearly not someone who saw the metropolis in terms of an urbanistic 'concept city'. He was no planner, trying to cure the city's ills or make the machine run more smoothly. Rather, he was interested in de Certeau's other city space: the representational space within which a mass of transitory, fleeting and fortuitous interactions take place, and the ways in which these are translated into an inner, emotional life. Rather like Baudelaire before him or Benjamin after, he presents the metropolis as the location of the everyday experiences of modernity, as a complex, interwoven web or *labyrinth* of social relations. Like Baudelaire, too, he therefore uses an *impressionistic* method to record the psychological impact of modern city life (Frisby, 1985, p.268).

Most metropolitan interactions, he suggests, require only fragments of the individual personality to be involved. The bombardment of the senses with an almost cinematic stream of impressions and the constant juxtaposition to anonymous individuals produces an accentuated nervousness. Individuals — and Simmel deals very much with an 'ideal type' of the sensitive bourgeois, presumably not unlike himself — therefore resort to stratagems of inward retreat and social distance. The indifference of the blasé attitude is one such defence.

At one level, then, Simmel was concerned — rather as a modernist poet like Eliot — with the impact of the city on the individual; or, perhaps, with how 'the individual' is formed within and by an urban world. Simmel has been called the first sociologist of the emotions and the senses. But (like Benjamin) he was equally interested in the determinants of the modern metropolis, which he explains primarily in terms of the money economy. The rationality of the city is not just something imposed by planners: the emphasis on time, transport and communication is an inevitable consequence of this form of economic organization.

3.2 TOTAL MODERNISM

I have identified two contrasting types of urban critic: the *flâneurs* and the planners. Simmel's sociology of a modern urban mentality can be read as a formalization of the *flâneur's* perspective. In Vienna, his contemporaries like Sitte and Wagner were establishing the new breed of specialist urbanists. These planners incorporated into their totalizing discourse — their 'concept cities' — not only Simmel's concern with the psychological impact of cities, but also historical and aesthetic considerations. By the turn of the twentieth century, the discipline of urbanism — the management of urban populations — combined spatial planning with political power and social scientific knowledge.

For the first half of the century, it was undoubtedly progressivists like Wagner rather than traditionalists like Sitte who defined the terms and set the tone of urbanism. The archetypal figure here was Le Corbusier (1887–1965), who poured forth models for ideal cities. (In this account, I draw primarily on Holston, 1989, Chapter 2, and Choay, 1986: the quotations from Le Corbusier appear in these two sources.)

Underlying all Le Corbusier's plans and polemics was a conception of modernity, but this was the *modernity* of Haussmann and Otto Wagner rather than of Baudelaire. The first machine age — the age of the Industrial Revolution — had in the nineteenth century created dehumanized and chaotic cities. In the new machine age, the progessivists argued, architecture would solve that problem. It would not do so by turning back to pre-modern values and urban landscapes. Le Corbusier was scathing about such archaeological nostalgia: 'The cult of the donkey-path has just been created. The movement originated in Germany, and is the result of a work by Camillo Sitte.' On the contrary, architecture would create a more orderly, more efficient and more egalitarian metropolitan fabric by adapting modern industrial techniques and avant-garde aesthetics: 'The machine, that vast modern event, will be seen for what it really is, a servant and not a ruler, a worker and not a tyrant, a source of unity and not of conflict, of construction and not of destruction.'

Despite this assertive modernism, Le Corbusier's critique was often expressed in familiar metaphors and images. The slums of industrial cities were 'cesspools' of tuberculosis and cholera, spreading 'contagiously' and destroying the surrounding countryside 'like a disease'. In place of the strong skeleton of a 'healthy organism', the sprawling metropolis displayed morbid symptoms: its circulation clogged, suffocating for lack of air, its tissues decaying in their own noxious wastes (Holston, 1989, p.44).

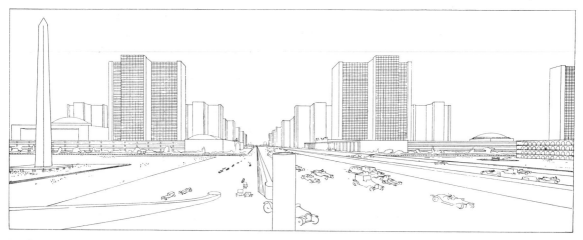

Le Corbusier's conception of the modern city

Le Corbusier admired Haussmann as a 'surgeon' who had tried to decongest the arteries of Paris and to endow the city (in Haussmann's own words) with 'space, air, light, verdure and flowers, in a word, with all that dispenses health'. The modernist planners went further than Haussmann in two decisive ways, however. One was in proposing new forms of public expropriation of land in order to allow planners a free hand and to disentangle regeneration from speculation. The other, more relevant here, was again at the level of metaphor.

Although Le Corbusier used organic metaphors of disease when describing existing cities, his prescriptions were always couched in terms of the city as machine. For architects like him, this was not just a metaphor. They proposed, quite literally, to organize and recreate the city as a machine, as 'a working tool'. They therefore adopted a functionalist, engineering approach. According to *The Athens Charter*, in which many of the progressivists' principles were laid down: 'The keys to city planning are to be found in the four functions: housing, work, recreation (during leisure) and traffic'. The retooling of the city would entail the reconceptualization and reorganization of these functions. Each was to be specifically catered for so that it would mesh smoothly with the others to make the machine-city hum.

This was why Le Corbusier wanted to 'green' the city, de-densifying it by substituting for the old rows of houses detached high-rise 'units' set in sunlight and greenery. Whereas in the old cities housing and other buildings were interspersed by parks and public spaces, in the progressivist city space would become the background in which vertical settlements would be set. Le Corbusier's aim was that: 'The city will gradually be transformed into a park.'

Pedestrians were to be completely separated from vehicles. This, along with the disappearance of old forms of low-rise housing, pointed to the abolition of the street, and with it the type of crowd and the range of activities associated with it. The urbanism charted by Baudelaire was now regarded as a barbaric anachronism. In the modern master plan, residence, work, commerce, and recreation were to be separated off into designated zones. Right down to 'coffee-houses, restaurants, shops ... remaining vestiges of the present street', everything must be 'given form or set in order, in a condition of full efficiency. Concentrated places for strolling and socializing'. These different zones were to be linked by new highways, themselves determined only by the terrain and 'perfectly independent of the edifices or buildings which happen to be in greater or lesser proximity' — another radical departure from the old idea of the street, here seen as 'the symbol in our era of the chaos of transportation'.

Behind all this social engineering lay an ambition far more audacious than the desire to manage the urban population that guided much nineteenth-century reformism. It was nothing less than the construction of a new framework of experience that would determine any possible social behaviour, and so create a new type of person. Like many avant-garde artists, their aim was to 'de-familiarize' the city, to make it strange and so to negate previous expectations (Holston, 1989, p.55). Such changes in perception were a prerequisite for the imposition of a new urban order.

It is here that the brilliance of the progressivists' critique of the capitalist city and the heroic radicalism of their alternative vision is vitiated by a dangerous naivety. Dangerous, because their style of total social engineering can often turn out in practice to be, simply, totalitarian. Naive, because they fell into the trap of aesthetic formalism. They believed not only that their 'concept city' could provide the basis for a more rational spatial organization, but also that it could exhaustively determine how people would experience and respond to the city. From the premise that the built environment plays an important role in shaping and constraining how we live, they made the unwarranted deduction that *planned* changes in that environment would be sufficient to produce *predictable* changes in people's perceptions, mental life, habits and conduct. They took their metaphors at face value, and mistook them for achievable states. 'On the day when contemporary society, at present so sick, has become properly aware that only architecture and city planning can provide the exact prescription for its ills,' predicted Le Corbusier, 'then the time will have come for the great machine to be put in motion.' There was simply no room in that vision for de Certeau's other urban space, the representational space of experience, symbol, myth and fantasy. 'Nothing is contradictory any more' in Le Corbusier's utopia; 'everything is in its place, properly arranged in order and hierarchy.' Everything, that is, apart from the ruses and stratagems of everyday life. (All quotations in this section were drawn from Holston, 1989, Chapter 2, and Choay, 1986.)

3.3   MIDDLING MODERNISM

In very few cases were the total plans of Le Corbusier and other progressivist architects put into practice wholesale. Generally they had to work at the level of single buildings or groups of buildings like housing estates. In the process, their vision was often not only scaled down, but rendered less heroic and more prosaic in the name of political and economic expediency. The result is what Paul Rabinow calls *middling modernism*: the version of modernism that came into existence in the middle ground between the apocalyptic prophecies of a Le Corbusier and the representational spaces of everyday life, between the public space of *la cité* and the rationalized, regulated, anonymous space of the urban *agglomération* (Rabinow, 1989, p.322).

In Britain, this middling modernism was perhaps at its most influential in the period of reconstruction after the Second World War. The ideas of Le Corbusier and other modernist architects provided a framework and often an inspiration for engineers, politicians, builders, and developers who saw themselves as not only repairing the physical devastation caused by the war, but as planning a welfare state and decent housing in unpropitious circumstances.

The potentially totalitarian and authoritarian aspects of Le Corbusier's version of rational planning were further tempered in their adaptation to the priorities of the welfare state by more communitarian and culturalist values: less Sitte's taste for medieval and Baroque towns, for the most part, than the vision of 'garden cities' pioneered by Ebenezer Howard (1850–1928), and embodied in the development of new towns like Letchworth (1903) and Welwyn (1920). Howard's 'gas-and water' socialism (public provision of basic amenities), along with his nostalgic ruralism, were embodied in Britain's town and country planning legislation. 'Green belts' restricted the spread of suburbanization, and post-war new towns like Milton Keynes still reflect his vision of planning. In the renewal of the old cities, however, the high-density blocks of flats derived from Le Corbusier's model often proved more economically attractive, especially as industrialized construction systems were adopted.

The growing conflict between the principles of the welfare state and rational planning, on the one hand, and political constraints on central and local government expenditure, on the other, played a decisive role in shaping Britain's urban landscape in the nineteen-sixties and seventies. This proved far from utopian. Today, its failures and shortcomings have taken on their own demonic dimensions in journalistic representations and political debates. *Any* idea of planning now tends to be associated with what one urban sociologist describes as 'a stereotypical concoction of high-rise barracks, children without childhood, family disruption, noise, pollution, unemployment, crime, blackness and organized vice' (Mellor, 1989, p.246). The solution, in short, has become the problem.

4 GLOBAL CITY

Metaphors and analogies are ways of reducing the infinite complexity of urban social relations to intellectually manageable proportions. By representing the city as an organism or a machine, we provide ourselves with a model of how it works, and how its various parts fit together. The choice of metaphor is a conscious act. But, as we saw in the schemes of reformers from Kay-Shuttleworth to Sitte or Le Corbusier, the use of urban metaphors often reveals not only political presuppositions and a calculated utopianism, but also unconscious fantasies about purity, order and what constitutes the good life.

Although, when articulated in plans and laws, such metaphors do have real effects, they remain only one element in determining the texture of urban space. Both the urbanist's 'concept city' and the lived, mythical world of everyday life (in de Certeau's useful distinction) are in part responses to, and in part contingent on, an organization of urban space which is beyond the control of either of these two metaphors. Among the important determinants of this organization of urban space, some — like the terrain on which a city is built and the climate — are natural. Others are aspects of modern societies which are discussed elsewhere in this series of books: the organization of production, work and commerce; strategic defences against potential enemies, both external and internal; the form taken by households and gender relations; networks of communication, both physical (roads, railways, canals, airports) and semiotic (newspapers, cinemas, broadcasting); the form of political institutions and conceptions of citizenship; the symbolic and cultural forms of the sacred, the profane and the obscene embodied in the disposition of churches, national monuments, football stadiums, and red-light districts.

Metaphors, analogies and images are the means by which we make that historically produced and increasingly unrepresentable urban space intelligible and psychically negotiable.

4.1   DEPENDENT METROPOLIS

Today we are entering a third phase of development in the modern city, comparable to the emergence of the industrial city in the early nineteenth century and the split between the spectacular metropolitan centres and spreading suburbs that appeared at the end of the century and the beginning of the twentieth century. This new city is characterized by the three Gs of *globalization, gentrification,* and *ghettoization.*

It is no longer enough to identify the networks that operate within a city. Metropolitan centres like London, New York, Los Angeles and Tokyo have themselves become international enclaves locked into a global network of highly sophisticated telecommunications technologies as the processing of information becomes a key to capital accumulation. This leads Manuel Castells to argue in *The Informational City* that we are witnessing 'the historical emergence of the space of flows, superseding the meaning of the space of places' (Castells, 1989, p.348). Increasingly, the spatial organization, politics and social relations of global cities depend on decisions made outside national boundaries (King, 1990, p.145). This global restructuring, claims Castells, is producing a new disjunction in the experience of the city: 'People live in places, power rules through flows' (1989, p.349).

How might a new Dickens read the networks of our globalized London? What would he see in its cityscapes and riverscapes and how would he dramatize them? The old skyline of his time was shaped largely by London's position in an imperialist world economy, when it operated as a trading and political control centre in a colonial mode of production (King, 1990, p.143). Today, looking towards the City, he would see a skyline dominated by new skyscrapers similar to those to be found in any other business district of a major city.

Tokyo's traffic control and surveillance system

This 'architectural Manhattanization' is one outward sign of London's full entry into the information-based world economy when its financial markets were reorganized and deregulated in the 'Big Bang' of October 1986. Despite earlier predictions, the new technologies have not produced a de-centred urban space. It is true that much manufacturing industry has left the old metropolitan centres (and often the old imperialist nations), and that many corporations for whom it is not essential to be in central business districts have moved to suburban areas. Many middle-class residents have also moved out of the city centres, whether driven by choice, the cost of housing or the location of employment. At the same time, however, there has been an even greater concentration of advanced corporate activity in the central business districts of metropolitan nodes in the global network. This reflects the logic of information processing, which is to consolidate both sophisticated telecommunications and élite personnel in offices that themselves become, so to speak, part of the computer.

In London, the arrival of multinational financial houses created a demand, not merely for more space in and around the City, but for a different type of space. As the *Financial Times* (4 July 1986) noted, 'American conglomerates moving into London have little interest in rabbit warren Victorian blocks or older glass towers but rather, want layers of dealing floors buried in wide efficient structures' (quoted in King, 1990, p.98). This pressure provoked a spate of speculative new building, both in the City itself and in the old docks area of riverside East London.

So, looking down river to the east of the City, our new Dickens would see a transformation in the skyline of docks and cranes that symbolized London's role in the networks of imperial trade. Docklands is a particularly flamboyant example of *gentrification* or what Peter Williams and Neil Smith call *social Manhattanization*: 'the agglomeration of corporate and corporate-related activities at the centre leads to a further agglomeration of upper-income residential neighbourhoods and of lavish recreation and entertainment facilities' (Williams and Smith, 1986, p.212). Docklands was not conceived in terms of environmental reformism or welfarist urban planning. On the contrary, at least at the level of rhetoric and to a large extent in practice, it represented a return to a principle that we last encountered in the natural theology of the early nineteenth century: that is, the belief that *the market* offers an adequate and efficient principle of regulation.

Gone was the modernist idea of the city as a total system. No longer shaped to needs and functions defined by a wider conception of 'the social', urban space became simply parcels of land for sale and architectural design a matter of individual taste and whim. The result in Docklands has been, for Bill Schwarz (1991, p.86), a chaotic and ultimately unimaginative urban Disneyland, where the gleam and glitter of corporate offices cannot hide an inadequate infrastructure and often jerry-built, if superficially stylish, private residences.

Socially, the influx of highly paid young City workers into Docklands marginalized or uprooted the working-class population of the Isle of Dogs, which had grown up around the now defunct docks industry. ('Like Manchester or Haussmannization all over again', Engels might mutter to Dickens.) There is no evidence of the investment in the riverside schemes, spreading or 'trickling down' to other parts of the East End. Rather, it has coincided with the continued immiseration of many parts of Tower Hamlets and Newham. These are often centres for first-generation migrants from the low-income countries of the Commonwealth — the West Indies, India, Pakistan, and, particularly in these cases, Bangladesh — and their British-born children.

In the post-war period, this international flow of people to London's inner-city areas initially indicated a need for 'replacement labour' in poorly paid service occupations, transport, and 'dirty' jobs in industries that were becoming economically obsolescent in global terms. Since the nineteen-sixties, the collapse of industry and the increasing specialization of London's functions in the global economy have often left such groups trapped, with limited employment opportunities (other than in the low-paid servicing of City firms as cleaners, caretakers, security staff, and so forth), a declining quality of education, and decreasing social welfare provision. This tendency to *ghettoization*, although still less marked in London than in New York or Los Angeles, is the other side of social Manhattanization. ('Do you really think this is your city any longer?' the racist mayor of New York imagines asking his complacent white constituents in *The Bonfire of the Vanities*, Tom Wolfe's 1988 novel about Manhattan and Manhattanization. 'It's the Third World down there!')

At the same time, London's position as a financial centre in the global economy and its strategic importance for international investment and capitalist accumulation require the presence of personnel from the world's richest nations, and also rich investors from poorer countries. Thus, not only office space but residential accommodation has been bought up by firms and individuals from Japan and the United States in particular, but also from Saudi Arabia and other Gulf states. London's global position thus attracts people from the richest and the poorest countries. As Anthony King notes, however, 'the historical economic, class, spatial, and built-environment divisions, between the West End and East End, which divided rich and poor in the Imperial City, continue to keep both groups apart' (King, 1990, p.145).

In the global, Manhattanized city, it is not so much a case of 'the West and the Rest' (see Book 1 (Hall and Gieben, 1992), Chapter 6), as of 'the Rest in the West'.

4.2   THE REST IN THE WEST

Today, therefore, Baudelaire might add another peripheral but revealing perspective on the city to his repertoire of the *flâneur*, the dandy, the rag-picker and the whore: that of the migrant. Defending Salman Rushdie's controversial novel *The Satanic Verses* (1988) as a celebration of 'the hybrid hotchpotch of the mongrel postmodern novel with "black, brown and white leaking into each other" in tropicalized *Ellowen Deeowen* (L-o-n-d-o-n) or *Mumbai* (bastardized Bombay)', the critic Homi Bhabha suggests that migration may have become the key metaphor for understanding the metropolis of the nineteen-nineties. 'The historical and cultural experience of the western metropolis *cannot* now be fictionalized without the marginal, oblique gaze of its postcolonial, migrant populations cutting across the imaginative metropolitan geography of territory and community, tradition and culture' (Bhabha, 1990, p.16).

This certainly ties in with Castells's argument that the global city is increasingly defined by the space of flows, and with London's growing ethnic and linguistic diversity (172 languages were spoken by children in its schools at the last count). But, as Castells also insists, people still live in places. It is the conflict between urban flux and the fixity of place that seems to have created a crisis in the anthropological experience and representational spaces of the city.

In his account of London's East End in the nineteen-eighties, for example, Bill Schwarz notes how radical social and cultural changes, on the one hand, coincided with the phenomenal success of the new television soap opera *EastEnders* on the other:

> ... just as in 1960 *Coronation Street* brought to a national public the culture of a particular working-class formation — two-up-two-downs, football and the dogs, the corner pub and so on — at the very moment when it had all but disappeared as a dominant form, so perhaps in the 1980s the media construction of *EastEnders* cultivates a curiously anachronistic idea of a collective identity, in which Albert Square casts a magical spell of cohesion on all its otherwise diverse inhabitants.
> (Schwarz, 1991, pp.79–80)

He also records how a BBC executive justified the risk of a soap opera set in the south of England: it was specifically the East End that could offer 'roots ... identity ... an attractive folklore and a sense of history' (Schwarz, 1991, p.79). In the oblique, postcolonial perspective on modern Britain — the migrant's view — the sometimes hysterical desire to fix history as *heritage, narrative* and *spectacle* in the nineteen-eighties appears as a response to the flux of community and economic globalization. In such ways, the everyday perceptions and representational spaces of the city are populated with images provided by another key network, the mass media; and these images have become increasingly *racialized*.

This process was one central theme in the study of 'mugging' and urban politics by Stuart Hall and his colleagues in *Policing the Crisis* (Hall *et al.*, 1978). They focused not on planning, housing and community development, but on crime, the stereotypes of black youth disseminated through the mass media and the judiciary, and the movement to a 'law-and-order' state. They explored the social consequences of urban metaphors and symbols: journalistic constructions of the inner city as an 'infectious' environment, for example (Hall *et al.* 1978, p.115). Presaging both the social logic of the period of Thatcher government and the uprisings in Brixton, Handsworth, Liverpool and Bristol in the nineteen eighties, *Policing the Crisis* showed how all the perceived failings of urban planning and the welfare state, as well as the vulnerability of urban populations to crime, were condensed into the demonic symbol of the black mugger (Hall *et al.*,1978), and later the black rioter (Mellor, 1989, p.246).

The migrant metaphor also suggests possibilities for urban politics and regeneration. Like *Policing the Crisis*, for example, Paul Gilroy's *There Ain't No Black in the Union Jack* (1987) starts from the premise that ' "race" and "racism" come to denote the urban crisis'. Drawing in part on the earlier work of Manuel Castells, however, Gilroy argues that 'race' has also become 'a marker for the activity of "urban social movements" ' capable of challenging state institutions (Gilroy, 1987, p.229). He is therefore more interested in the capacities of 'collective identities spoken through "race", community and locality' (p.247) than in images of the nation imposed through the mass media or normative definitions of heritage. In place of the Enlightenment language of rights and obligations, he insists on the cultural and political importance of localized urban spaces.

This idea then ties in with another emerging discourse of urban regeneration. In its critical revival of earlier urban metaphors, the city is depicted not as market, nor as diseased organism, nor as machine, but as a *public domain* — a sphere of communal life and free communication. This recognizes the importance but also the limits of strategic planning, and tries to formulate a new vocabulary for it that is sensitive to the complex texture of urban space. It treats community not as a known, fixed, unitary identity but as an aspiration, as always to be formed in confused and conflictual negotiations. Franco Bianchini and Hermann Schwengel insist that planning must therefore involve *re-imagining* the city.

> Planning will have to be much more rooted in the understanding of how cities are *lived*, and of the place the locality occupies both in national and international markets and in popular consciousness. ... Planning, in short, will have to concentrate more on *users* and less on uses, more on *ends* and less on *means*, and will have to recognize the usefulness of moral-practical and expressive-aesthetic forms of knowledge, rather than just cognitive-instrumental.
> (Bianchini and Schwengel, 1991, pp.231–2)

Does this suggest a possible 'concept city' that, by acknowledging its own limits, allows space for the ruses and combinations of everyday, popular urban ways of life? Or does it offer an admittedly more populist and democratic version of the republican city idealized in Enlightenment thought without taking on the full force of objections to the exclusions and marginalizations built into that tradition? It looks as though such questions may form the agenda for impending debates about the politics of the city and about the role of the state in planning.

5   CONCLUSION

The city is an imagined environment. It is an environment shaped by the interaction of practices, events and relationships so complex that they cannot easily be visualized. That may be why it is an environment imagined in metaphors (the diseased city, the city as machine), animated by myth, and peopled by symbols such as the *flâneur*, the prostitute, the migrant, the mugger.

My argument has not been that it is wrong to use metaphors. We cannot think without them: hence the need to be sensitive to their limitations and blind-spots, and alert to their possible consequences. This caveat applies equally to the metaphor I have been using, that of the city as text. This metaphor has the virtue of avoiding the functionalism inherent in organic and mechanical images, and it underlines the interpretive aspects of both urban experience and social analysis. It makes the point that we 'read' the city. Consciously or not, we make sense of a host of complex signs and signals.

The city-as-text analogy is comparatively weak, however, when it comes to identifying and understanding the economic and political forces that determine the shape and rhythms of the city. It also risks underplaying the multi-layered and often contradictory *texture* of the city, and overemphasizing the interpretive role at the expense of the *agency* of urban experience. Henri Lefebvre makes the objection like this:

> Rather than signs, what one encounters [in urban space] are directions — multifarious and overlapping instructions. If there is indeed text, inscription or writing to be found here, it is in a context of conventions, intentions and order (in the sense of social order versus social disorder). That space signifies is incontestable. But what it signifies is dos and don'ts — and this brings us back to power. ... Activity in space is restricted by that space; space 'decides' what activity may occur, but even this 'decision' has limits placed upon it. Space lays down the law because it implies a certain order — and hence also a certain disorder (just as what may be seen defines what is obscene).
> (Lefebvre, 1991, pp.142–3)

Lefebvre's insistence on *how* urban space signifies is important: we experience the city less as a novel or even as an image than as the embodiment of possibilities and prohibitions.

If urban space lays down the law, however, does that mean we all negotiate its 'dos' and 'don'ts' in the same way? Allow me one last set of analogies.

Policemen uphold and impose the law. Social relations have to be subjected to reason. A population has to be disciplined and protected. Rotten elements have to be driven out. Isn't this the logic of many urban reformers from Kay-Shuttleworth to Le Corbusier, with their dreams of a purified and rationalized city?

The detective, in contrast, starts not from the dictates of reason but from the inherently enigmatic nature of reality. The comforting serenity of the 'concept city' will always be disrupted by surprising events. It is not the police who solve the mysteries of a befogged London, but Sherlock Holmes. He does so by identifying clues, and deducing from them the sequence of events and combination of forces that produced the initially baffling circumstance. The *flâneur* has often been equated with the detective, but in some ways Engels fits the model better — or at least the Engels who patiently pursues his investigation by reading the apparently illegible clues of Manchester's topography. (He also risks the danger of detective stories, which is to explain away all the mysteries as the machinations of a single master criminal — whether capitalism or Professor Moriarty.)

The *flâneur* certainly shares something of the detective's claim to be able to unravel, and so master, the complexity of the modern city. But Baudelaire's adoption of different guises — mostly of those figures on the edge of the law — suggests a different analogy. This returns us to *The Asphalt Jungle*, and to the figure of the gangster, at least as characterized in Robert Warshow's essay 'The Gangster as Tragic Hero'.

The gangster is the man of the city, with the city's language and knowledge, with its queer and dishonest skills and its terrible daring, carrying his life in his hands like a placard, like a club ... for the gangster there is only the city; he must inhabit it in order to personify it: not the real city, but that dangerous and sad city of the imagination which is so much more important, which is the modern world.
(quoted in McArthur, 1972, p.28)

Between this street-wise machismo and Doris Lessing's description of the London that exists in women's brains, can we begin to get a sense of how people experience and act in the city?

What these gaudy analogies from crime fiction suggest are different relationships to the city: the policeman trying to control it, the detective trying to explain it, the gangster trying to survive and exploit it. There are elements of all three in the perspective of the social scientist. Finally, then, I hope that this chapter will enable you — and encourage you — to see the metropolis in a new light and to read the signs in the streets a little differently in future. Watch out for the lamp posts.

REFERENCES

Abercrombie, N., Hill, S. and Turner B.S. (eds) (1988) *The Penguin Dictionary of Sociology*, 2nd edn., Harmondsworth, Penguin.

Bhabha, H. (1990) 'Novel metropolis', *New Statesman and Society*, 16 February.

Bianchini, F. and Schwengel, H. (1991) 'Re-imagining the city', in Corner. J and Harvey, S. (eds) *Enterprise and Heritage: Crosscurrents of National Culture,* London, Routledge.

Buck-Morss, S. (1989) *The Dialectics of Seeing: Walter Benjamin and the Arcades Project,* Cambridge, Mass., MIT Press.

Burnett, W.R. (1950) *The Asphalt Jungle*, London, Macdonald.

Castells, M. (1989) *The Informational City: Information Technology, Economic Restructuring and the Urban-Regional Process,* Oxford, Basil Blackwell.

Choay, F. (1986) 'Urbanism in question', in Gottdiener, M. and Lagopoulos, A.Ph. (eds) *The City and the Sign,* New York, Columbia University Press.

Clark, T.J. (1984) *The Painting of Modern Life: Paris in the Art of Manet and his Followers,* London, Thames and Hudson.

Davison, G. (1983) 'The city as a natural system: theories of urban society in early nineteenth century Britain', in Fraser, D. and Sutcliffe, A. (eds) *The Pursuit of Urban History*, London, Edward Arnold.

de Certeau, M. (1984) *The Practice of Everyday Life,* Berkeley, University of California Press.

Dickens, C. (1971) *Bleak House*, Harmondsworth, Penguin. First published in 1853.

Eliot, T.S. (1922) *The Wasteland,* London, Faber (paperback edn 1972).

Engels, F. (1892) *The Condition of the Working Class in England in 1844*, London, Allen and Unwin. First published in 1845.

Foucault, M. (1988) *Politics, Philosophy, Culture* (ed. L.D. Kritzman), New York, Routledge.

Frisby, D. (1985) *Fragments of Modernity*, Cambridge, Polity Press.

Gilroy, P. (1987) *There Ain't No Black in the Union Jack,* London, Hutchinson.

Hall, S., Critcher, C., Jefferson, T., Clarke, J. and Roberts, B. (1978) *Policing the Crisis: Mugging, the State, and Law and Order*, London, Macmillan.

Hall, S. and Gieben, B. (eds) (1992) *Formations of Modernity*, Cambridge, Polity Press.

Holston, J. (1989) *The Modernist City: An Anthropological Critique of Brasilia,* Chicago, University of Chicago Press.

Hunter, I. (1988) *Culture and Government: The Emergence of Literary Education,* London, Macmillan.

King, A. (1990) *Global Cities: Post-Imperialism and the Internationalization of London,* London, Routledge.

Lefebvre, H. (1991) *The Production of Space*, Oxford, Basil Blackwell.

Lessing, D. (1969) *The Four-Gated City*, New York, Alfred A. Knopf.

Lynch, K. (1981) *The Image of the City,* Cambridge, Mass., MIT Press.

McArthur, C. (1972), *Underworld USA*, London, Secker and Warburg.

Marcus, S. (1973), 'Reading the illegible', in Dyos, H.J. and Wolff, M. (eds) *The Victorian City: Images and Realities,* London, Routledge and Kegan Paul.

Mellor, R. (1989) 'Urban sociology: a trend report', *Sociology*, vol. 23, no. 2.

Mort, F. (1987) *Dangerous Sexualities: Medico-moral Politics in England since 1830,* London, Routledge and Kegan Paul.

Penguin Dictionary of Sociology: see Abercrombie *et al.* (1988).

Rabinow, P. (1989) *French Modern: Norms and Forms of the Social Environment,* Cambridge, Mass., MIT Press.

Schorske, C. (1980) *Fin-de-Siécle Vienna: Politics and Culture*, London, Weidenfeld and Nicolson.

Schwarz, B. (1991) 'Where horses shit a hundred sparrows feed: Docklands and East London during the Thatcher years', in Corner, J. and Harvey, S. (eds) *Enterprise and Heritage: Crosscurrents of National Culture,* London, Routledge.

Sharpe, W. and Wallock, L. (eds) (1987) *Visions of the Modern City*, Baltimore, Johns Hopkins University Press.

Simmel, G. (1950) *The Sociology of George Simmel* (ed. K. Wolff, trans. H.H. Gerth), New York, Macmillan/The Free Press.

Williams, P. and Smith, N. (1986) 'From "renaissance" to restructuring: the dynamics of contemporary urban development', in Smith, N. and Williams, P. (eds) *Gentrification of the City*, Boston, Allen and Unwin.

Williams, R. (1973) *The Country and the City*, London, Chatto and Windus.

Wolfe, T. (1988) *The Bonfire of the Vanities*, London, Cape.

READING A   THE GREAT CITIES: MANCHESTER

Friedrich Engels

Manchester ... is peculiarly built, so that a person may live in it for years, and go in and out daily without coming into contact with a working-people's quarter or even with workers, that is, so long as he confines himself to his business or to pleasure walks. This arises chiefly from the fact, that by unconscious tacit agreement, as well as with out-spoken conscious determination, the working-people's quarters are sharply separated from the sections of the city reserved for the middle-class; or, if this does not succeed, they are concealed with the cloak of charity. Manchester contains, at its heart, a rather extended commercial district, perhaps half a mile long and about as broad, and consisting almost wholly of offices and warehouses. Nearly the whole district is abandoned by dwellers, and is lonely and deserted at night; only watchmen and policemen traverse its narrow lanes with their dark lanterns. This district is cut through by certain main thoroughfares upon which the vast traffic concentrates, and in which the ground level is lined with brilliant shops. In these streets the upper floors are occupied, here and there, and there is a good deal of life upon them until late at night. With the exception of this commercial district, all Manchester proper, all Salford and Hulme, a great part of Pendleton and Chorlton, two-thirds of Ardwick, and single stretches of Cheetham Hill and Broughton are all unmixed working-people's quarters, stretching like a girdle, averaging a mile and a half in breadth, around the commercial district. Outside, beyond this girdle, lives the upper and middle bourgeoisie, the middle bourgeoisie in regularly laid out streets in the vicinity of the working quarters, especially in Chorlton and the lower lying portions of Cheetham Hill; the upper bourgeoisie in remoter villas with gardens in Chorlton and Ardwick, or on the breezy heights of Cheetham Hill, Broughton and Pendleton, in free, wholesome country air, in fine, comfortable homes, passed once every half or quarter hour by omnibuses going into the city. And the finest part of the arrangement is this, that the members of this money aristocracy can take the shortest road through the middle of all the labouring districts to their places of business, without ever seeing that they are in the midst of the grimy misery that lurks to the right and the left. For the thoroughfares leading from the Exchange in all directions out of the city are lined, on both sides, with an almost unbroken series of shops, and are so kept in the hands of the middle and lower bourgeoisie, which, out of self-interest, cares for a decent and cleanly external appearance and *can* care for it. True, these shops bear some relation to the districts which lie behind them, and are more elegant in the commercial and residential quarters than when they hide grimy working-men's dwellings; but they suffice to conceal from the eyes of the wealthy men and women of strong stomachs and weak nerves the misery and grime which form the complement of their wealth. ... I know very well that this hypocritical plan is more or less common to all great cities; I

Source: Engels, F. (1892) *The Condition of the Working Class in England in 1844*, London, Allen and Unwin, pp.45–54. First published in 1845.

know, too, that the retail dealers are forced by the nature of their business to take possession of the great highways; I know that there are more good buildings than bad ones upon such streets everywhere, and that the value of land is greater near them than in remoter districts; but at the same time I have never seen so systematic a shutting out of the working-class from the thoroughfares, so tender a concealment of everything which might affront the eye and the nerves of the bourgeoisie, as in Manchester. And yet, in other respects, Manchester is less built according to a plan, after official regulations, is more an outgrowth of accident, than any other city; and when I consider in this connection the eager assurances of the middle-class, that the working-class is doing famously, I cannot help feeling that the liberal manufacturers, the 'Big Wigs' of Manchester, are not so innocent after all, in the matter of this sensitive method of construction.

I may mention just here that the mills almost all adjoin the rivers or the different canals that ramify throughout the city, before I proceed at once to describe the labouring quarters. First of all, there is the Old Town of Manchester, which lies between the northern boundary of the commercial district and the Irk. Here the streets, even the better ones, are narrow and winding, as Todd Street, Long Millgate, Withy Grove, and Shude Hill, the houses dirty, old, and tumble-down, and the construction of the side streets utterly horrible. Going from the Old Church to Long Millgate, the stroller has at once a row of old-fashioned houses at the right, of which not one has kept its original level; these are remnants of the old pre-manufacturing Manchester, whose former inhabitants have removed with their descendants into better-built districts, and have left the houses, which were not good enough for them, to a working-class population strongly mixed with Irish blood. Here one is in an almost undisguised working-men's quarter, for even the shops and beerhouses hardly take the trouble to exhibit a trifling degree of cleanliness. But all this is nothing in comparison with the courts and lanes which lie behind, to which access can be gained only through covered passages, in which no two human beings can pass at the same time. Of the irregular cramming together of dwellings in ways which defy all rational plan, of the tangle in which they are crowded literally one upon the other, it is impossible to convey an idea. And it is not the buildings surviving from the old times of Manchester which are to blame for this; the confusion has only recently reached its height when every scrap of space left by the old way of building has been filled up and patched over until not a foot of land is left to be further occupied. ...

The south bank of the Irk is here very steep and between fifteen and thirty feet high. On this declivitous hillside there are planted three rows of houses, of which the lowest rise directly out of the river, while the front walls of the highest stand on the crest of the hill in Long Millgate. Among them are mills on the river, in short, the method of construction is as crowded and disorderly here as in the lower part of Long Millgate. Right and left a multitude of covered passages lead from the main street into numerous courts, and he who turns in thither gets into a filth and disgusting grime, the equal of which is not be found — especially in the courts which lead down to the Irk, and which contain unqualifiedly the most horrible dwellings which I have yet beheld. In one of these courts there stands directly at the entrance, at the end of the covered passage, a privy without a door, so dirty that the inhabitants can pass into and out of the court only by passing through foul pools of stagnant urine and excrement. This is the first court on the Irk above Ducie Bridge — in case any one should care to look into it. Below it on the river there are several tanneries which fill the whole neighbourhood with the stench of animal putrefaction. Below Ducie Bridge the only entrance to most of the houses is by means of narrow, dirty stairs and over heaps of refuse and filth. The first court below Ducie Bridge, known as Allen's Court, was in such a state at the time of the cholera that the sanitary police ordered it evacuated, swept, and disinfected with chloride of lime. Dr. Kay gives a terrible description of the state of this court at that time.[1] Since then, it seems to have been partially torn away and rebuilt; at least looking down from Ducie Bridge, the passer-by sees several ruined walls and heaps of *débris* with some newer houses. The view from this bridge, mercifully concealed from mortals of small stature by a parapet as high as a man, is characteristic for the whole district. At the bottom flows, or rather stagnates, the Irk, a narrow, coal-black, foul-smelling stream, full of *débris* and refuse, which it deposits on the shallower right bank. In dry weather, a long string of the most disgusting, blackish-green slime pools are left standing on this bank, from the depths of which bubbles of miasmatic gas constantly arise and give forth a stench unendurable even on the bridge forty or fifty feet above the surface of the stream. But besides this, the stream itself is checked every few paces by high weirs, behind which slime and refuse accumulate and rot in thick masses. Above the bridge are tanneries, bone mills, and gas-works, from which all drains and refuse find their way into the Irk, which receives further the contents of all the neighbouring sewers and privies. It may be easily imagined, therefore, what sort of residue the stream deposits. Below the bridge you look upon the piles of *débris,* the refuse, filth, and offal from the courts on the steep left bank; here each house is packed close behind its neighbour and a piece of each is visible, all black, smoky, crumbling, ancient, with broken panes and window-frames. The background is furnished by old barrack-like factory buildings. On the lower right bank stands a long row of houses and mills; the second house being a ruin without a roof, piled with *débris;* the third stands so low that the lowest floor is uninhabitable, and therefore without window or doors. Here the background embraces the pauper burial-ground, the station of the Liverpool and Leeds railway, and, in the rear of this, the Workhouse, the 'Poor-Law Bastille' of Manchester, which, like a citadel, looks threateningly down from behind its high walls and parapets on the hilltop, upon the working-people's quarter below.

Above Ducie Bridge, the left bank grows more flat and the right bank steeper, but the condition of the dwellings on both banks grow worse rather than better. He who turns to the left here from the main street, Long-

---

[1] 'The Moral and Physical Condition of the Working-Class employed in the Cotton Manufacture in Manchester.' By James Ph. Kay, M.D. 2nd Ed. 1832.

Dr. Kay confuses the working-class in general with the factory workers, otherwise an excellent pamphlet.

Millgate, is lost; he wanders from one court to another, turns countless corners, passes nothing but narrow, filthy nooks and alleys, until after a few minutes he has lost all clue, and knows not whither to turn. Everywhere half or wholly ruined buildings, some of them actually uninhabited, which means a great deal here; rarely a wooden or stone floor to be seen in the houses, almost uniformly broken, ill-fitting windows and doors, and a state of filth! Everywhere heaps of *débris*, refuse, and offal; standing pools for gutters, and a stench which alone would make it impossible for a human being in any degree civilized to live in such a district. The newly-built extension of the Leeds railway, which crosses the Irk here, has swept away some of these courts and lanes, laying others completely open to view. Immediately under the railway bridge there stands a court, the filth and horrors of which surpass all the others by far, just because it was hitherto so shut off, so secluded that the way to it could not be found without a good deal of trouble, I should never have discovered it myself, without the breaks made by the railway, though I thought I knew this whole region thoroughly. Passing along a rough bank, among stakes and washing-lines, one penetrates into this chaos of small one-storied, one-roomed huts, in most of which there is no artificial floor; kitchen, living and sleeping-room all in one. In such a hole, scarcely five feet long by six broad, I found two beds — and such bedsteads and beds! — which, with a staircase and chimney-place, exactly filled the room. In several others I found absolutely nothing, while the door stood open, and the inhabitants leaned against it. Everywhere before the doors refuse and offal; that any sort of pavement lay underneath could not be seen but only felt, here and there, with the feet. This whole collection of cattle-sheds for human beings was surrounded on two sides by houses and a factory, and on the third by the river, and besides the narrow stair up the bank, a narrow doorway alone led out into another almost equally ill-built labyrinth of dwellings. ...

Such is the Old Town of Manchester, and on re-reading my description, I am forced to admit that instead of being exaggerated, it is far from black enough to convey a true impression of the filth, ruin, and uninhabitableness, the defiance of all considerations of cleanliness, ventilation, and health which characterize the construction of this single district, containing at least twenty to thirty thousand inhabitants. And such a district exists in the heart of the second city of England, the first manufacturing city of the world. If any one wishes to see in how little space a human being can move, how little air — and *such* air! — he can breathe, how little of civilization he may share and yet live, it is only necessary to travel hither. True, this is the *Old* Town, and the people of Manchester emphasize the fact whenever any one mentions to them the frightful condition of this Hell upon Earth; but what does that prove? Everything which here arouses horror and indignation is of recent origin, belongs to the *industrial epoch.* The couple of hundred houses, which belong to old Manchester, have been long since abandoned by their original inhabitants; the industrial epoch alone has crammed into them the swarms of workers whom they now shelter; the industrial epoch alone has built up every spot between these old houses to win a covering for the masses whom it has conjured hither from the agricultural districts and from Ireland; the industrial epoch alone enables the owners of these cattlesheds to rent them for high prices to human beings, to plunder the poverty of the workers, to undermine the health of thousands, in order that they *alone*, the owners, may grow rich. ...

READING B   THE METROPOLIS AND MENTAL LIFE

Georg Simmel

... An inquiry into the inner meaning of specifically modern life and its products, into the soul of the cultural body, so to speak, must seek to solve the equation which structures like the metropolis set up between the individual and the super-individual contents of life. Such an inquiry must answer the question of how the personality accommodates itself in the adjustments to external forces. ...

The psychological basis of the metropolitan type of individuality consists in the *intensification of nervous stimulation* which results from the swift and uninterrupted change of outer and inner stimuli. Man is a differentiating creature. His mind is stimulated by the difference between a momentary impression and the one which preceded it. Lasting impressions, impressions which differ only slightly from one another, impressions which take a regular and habitual course and show regular and habitual contrasts — all these use up, so to speak, less consciousness than does the rapid crowding of changing images, the sharp discontinuity in the grasp of a single glance, and the unexpectedness of onrushing impressions. These are the psychological conditions which the metropolis creates. ... In order to accommodate to change and to the contrast of phenomena, the intellect does not require any shocks and inner upheavals; it is only through such upheavals that the more conservative mind could accommodate to the metropolitan rhythm of events. Thus the metropolitan type of man — which, of course, exists in a thousand individual variants — develops an organ protecting him against the threatening currents and discrepancies of his external environment which would uproot him. He reacts with his head instead of his heart. In this an increased awareness assumes the psychic prerogative. Metropolitan life, thus, underlies a heightened awareness and a predominance of intelligence in metropolitan man. ...

The metropolis has always been the seat of the money economy. Here the multiplicity and concentration of economic exchange gives an importance to the means of exchange which the scantiness of rural commerce would not have allowed. Money economy and the dominance of the intellect are intrinsically connected. They share a matter-of-fact attitude in dealing with men and with things; and, in this attitude, a formal justice is often coupled with an inconsiderate hardness. The intellectually sophisticated person is indifferent to all genuine individuality, because relationships

Source: Simmel, G. (1950) *The Sociology of Georg Simmel*, ed. Kurt Wolff, trans. H.H. Gerth with the assistance of C.Wright Mills, New York, Macmillan/The Free Press.

and reactions result from it which cannot be exhausted with logical operations. In the same manner, the individuality of phenomena is not commensurate with the pecuniary principle. Money is concerned only with what is common to all: it asks for the exchange value, it reduces all quality and individuality to the question: How much? All intimate emotional relations between persons are founded in their individuality, whereas in rational relations man is reckoned with like a number, like an element which is in itself indifferent. Only the objective measurable achievement is of interest. Thus metropolitan man reckons with his merchants and customers, his domestic servants and often even with persons with whom he is obliged to have social intercourse. …The money economy dominates the metropolis; it has displaced the last survivals of domestic production and the direct barter of goods; it minimizes, from day to day, the amount of work ordered by customers. The matter-of-fact attitude is obviously so intimately interrelated with the money economy, which is dominant in the metropolis, that nobody can say whether the intellectualistic mentality first promoted the money economy or whether the latter determined the former. …

In certain seemingly insignificant traits, which lie upon the surface of life, the same psychic currents characteristically unite. Modern mind has become more and more calculating. The calculative exactness of practical life which the money economy has brought about corresponds to the ideal of natural science: to transform the world into an arithmetic problem, to fix every part of the world by mathematical formulas. Only money economy has filled the days of so many people with weighing, calculating, with numerical determinations, with a reduction of qualitative values to quantitative ones. Through the calculative nature of money a new precision, a certainty in the definition of identities and differences, an unambiguousness in agreements and arrangements has been brought about in the relations of life-elements — just as externally this precision has been effected by the universal diffusion of pocket watches. However, the conditions of metropolitan life are at once cause and effect of this trait. The relationships and affairs of the typical metropolitan usually are so varied and complex that without the strictest punctuality in promises and services the whole structure would break down into an inextricable chaos. Above all, this necessity is brought about by the aggregation of so many people with such differentiated interests, who must integrate their relations and activities into a highly complex organism. If all clocks and watches in Berlin would suddenly go wrong in different ways, even if only by one hour, all economic life and communication of the city would be disrupted for a long time. … Punctuality, calculability, exactness are forced upon life by the complexity and extension of metropolitan existence and are not only most intimately connected with its money economy and intellectualistic character. These traits must also color the contents of life and favor the exclusion of those irrational, instinctive, sovereign traits and impulses which aim at determining the mode of life from within, instead of receiving the general and precisely schematized form of life from without. …

The same factors which have thus coalesced into the exactness and minute precision of the form of life have coalesced into a structure of the highest impersonality; on the other hand, they have promoted a highly personal subjectivity. There is perhaps no psychic phenomenon which has been so unconditionally reserved to the metropolis as has the blasé attitude. The blasé attitude results first from the rapidly changing and closely compressed contrasting stimulations of the nerves. From this, the enhancement of the metropolitan intellectuality, also, seems originally to stem. Therefore, stupid people who are not intellectually alive in the first place usually are not exactly blasé. A life in boundless pursuit of pleasure makes one blasé because it agitates the nerves to their strongest reactivity for such a long time that they finally cease to react at all. In the same way, through the rapidity and contradictoriness of their changes, more harmless impressions force such violent responses, tearing the nerves so brutally hither and thither that their last reserves of strength are spent; and if one remains in the same milieu they have no time to gather new strength. An incapacity thus emerges to react to new sensations with the appropriate energy. This constitutes that blasé attitude which, in fact, every metropolitan child shows when compared with children of quieter and less changeable milieus.

This physiological source of the metropolitan blasé attitude is joined by another source which flows from the money economy. The essence of the blasé attitude consists in the blunting of discrimination. This does not mean that the objects are not perceived, as is the case with the half-wit, but rather that the meaning and differing values of things, and thereby the things themselves, are experienced as insubstantial. They appear to the blasé person in an evenly flat and gray tone; no one object deserves preference over any other. This mood is the faithful subjective reflection of the completely internalized money economy. By being the equivalent to all the manifold things in one and the same way, money becomes the most frightful leveler. ... The self-preservation of certain personalities is bought at the price of devaluating the whole objective world, a devaluation which in the end unavoidably drags one's own personality down into a feeling of the same worthlessness.

Whereas the subject of this form of existence has to come to terms with it entirely for himself, his self-preservation in the face of the large city demands from him a no less negative behavior of a social nature. This mental attitude of metropolitans toward one another we may designate, from a formal point of view, as reserve. If so many inner reactions were responses to the continuous external contacts with innumerable people as are those in a small town, where one knows almost everybody one meets and where one has a positive relation to almost everyone, one would be completely atomized internally and come to an unimaginable psychic state. Partly this psychological fact, partly the right to distrust which men have in the face of the touch-and-go elements of metropolitan life, necessitates our reserve. As a result of this reserve we frequently do not even know by sight those who have been our neighbours for years. And it is this reserve which in the eyes of the small-town people makes us appear to be cold and heartless. Indeed, if I do not deceive myself, the inner aspect of this outer reserve is not only indifference but, more often than we are aware, it is a slight aversion, a mutual strangeness and repulsion, which will break into hatred and fight at the moment of a closer contact, however caused. The whole inner organization of such an extensive communicative life rests upon an extremely varied hierarchy of sympathies, indifferences, and aversions of the briefest as well as of the most permanent nature. The sphere of indifference in this hierarchy is not as large as might appear on the surface. Our psychic activity still responds to almost every impression of somebody else with a somewhat distinct feeling. The unconscious, fluid, and changing character of this impression seems to result in a state of indifference. Actually this indifference would be just as unnatural as the diffusion of indiscriminate mutual suggestion would be unbearable. From both these typical dangers of the metropolis, indifference and indiscriminate suggestibility, antipathy protects us. A latent antipathy and the preparatory stage of practical antagonism effect the distances and aversions without which this mode of life could not at all be led. The extent and the mixture of this style of life, the rhythm of its emergence and disappearance, the forms in which it is satisfied — all these, with the unifying motives in the narrower sense, form the inseparable whole of the metropolitan style of life. What appears in the metropolitan style of life directly as dissociation is in reality only one of its elemental forms of socialization.

This reserve with its overtone of hidden aversion appears in turn as the form or the cloak of a more general mental phenomenon of the metropolis: it grants to the individual a kind and an amount of personal freedom which has no analogy whatsoever under other conditions. ... Metropolitan man is 'free' in a spiritualized and refined sense, in contrast to the pettiness and prejudices which hem in the small-town man. For the reciprocal reserve and indifference and the intellectual life conditions of large circles are never felt more strongly by the individual in their impact upon his independence than in the thickest crowd of the big city. This is because the bodily proximity and narrowness of space makes the mental distance only the more visible. It is obviously only the obverse of this freedom if, under certain circumstances, one nowhere feels as lonely and lost as in the metropolitan crowd. For here as elsewhere it is by no means necessary that the freedom of man be reflected in his emotional life as comfort.

Cities are, first of all, seats of the highest economic division of labor. ...City life has transformed the struggle with nature for livelihood into an interhuman struggle for gain, which here is not granted by nature but by other men. For specialization does not flow only from the competition for gain but also from the underlying fact that the seller must always seek to call forth new and differentiated needs of the lured customer. In order to find a source of income which is not yet exhausted, and to find a function which cannot readily be displaced, it is necessary to specialize in one's services. This process promotes differentiation, refinement, and the enrichment of the public's needs, which obviously must lead to growing personal differences within this public.

All this forms the transition to the individualization of mental and psychic traits which the city occasions in proportion to its size. There is a whole series of obvious causes underlying this process. First, one must meet the difficulty of asserting his own personality within the dimensions of metropolitan life. Where the quantitative increase in importance and the expense of energy reach their limits, one seizes upon qualitative differentiation in order somehow to attract the attention of the social circle by playing upon its sensitivity for differences. Finally, man is tempted to adopt the most tendentious peculiarities, that is, the specifically metropolitan extravagances of mannerism, caprice, and preciousness. Now, the meaning of these extravagances does not at all lie in the contents of such behaviour, but rather in its form of 'being different', of standing out in a striking manner and thereby attracting attention. For many character types, ultimately the only means of saving for themselves some modicum of self-esteem and the sense of filling a position is indirect, through the awareness of others. In the same sense a seemingly insignificant factor is operating, the cumulative effects of which are, however, still noticeable. I refer to the brevity and scarcity of the inter-human contacts granted to the metropolitan man, as compared with social intercourse in the small town. The temptation to appear 'to the point', to appear concentrated and strikingly characteristic, lies much closer to the individual in brief metropolitan contacts than in an atmosphere in which frequent and prolonged association assures the personality of an unambiguous image of himself in the eyes of the other.

The most profound reason, however, why the metropolis conduces to the urge for the most individual personal existence — no matter whether justified and successful — appears to me to be the following: ... the metropolis is the genuine arena of a culture which outgrows all personal life. Here in buildings and educational institutions, in the wonders and comforts of space-conquering technology, in the formations of community life, and in the visible institutions of the state, is offered such an overwhelming fullness of crystallized and impersonalized spirit that the personality, so to speak, cannot maintain itself under its impact. On the one hand, life is made infinitely easy for the personality in that stimulations, interests, uses of time and consciousness are offered to it from all sides. They carry the persons as if in a stream, and one needs hardly to swim for oneself. On the other hand, however, life is composed more and more of these impersonal contents and offerings which tend to displace the genuine personal colorations and incomparabilities. This results in the individual's summoning the utmost in uniqueness and particularization, in order to preserve his most personal core. He has to exaggerate this personal element in order to remain audible even to himself.

ACKNOWLEDGEMENTS

Grateful acknowledgement is made to the following sources for permission to use material in this text:

Chapter 1

Readings

Reading A: Lockwood, D. *The Blackcoated Worker,* 1958, Unwin University Press. Reproduced by permission of Harper Collins Publishers Limited; *Reading B:* Braverman, H. *Labor and Monopoly Capital*, 1974, Monthly Review Press. Copyright © 1974 by Harry Braverman. Reprinted by permission of Monthly Review Foundation; *Reading C:* Amos, V. and Parmar, P. 'Challenging imperial feminism', *Feminist Review 17*, 1984, Routledge; *Reading D:* Cockburn, C. 'Women and technology: opportunity is not enough', in Purcell, K., Wood, S., Waton and Allen, S. (eds) *The Changing Experience of Employment*, 1986, Macmillan Press Ltd. Reprinted by permission of the author, the British Sociological Association and the publishers.

Tables

Tables 1.2 and 1.6: reproduced by permission of the Controller of Her Majesty's Stationery Office; *Table 1.8:* Brown, C. *Black and White Britain*, 1984, Heinemann Educational. Reprinted by permission of the Policy Studies Institute.

Figures

Figures 1.1 and 1.2: reproduced by permission of the Controller of Her Majesty's Stationery Office.

Illustrations

p.16: Photo by Paul Cranham/Copyright Gerry Cranham Photo Library; *p.18:* Courtesy CBI News; *p.40:* Barry Lewis/Network; *p.45:* David Hoffman; *p.48:* Copyright Asadour Guzelian.

Chapter 2

Readings

Reading A: Elliot, F.R. 'The family: private arena or adjunct of the state?', *Journal of Law and Society,* vol.16, no.4, 1989, Basil Blackwell Ltd; *Reading B:* Yeatman, A. 'Domestic life and sociology', in Gross, E. and Pateman, C. (eds) *Feminist Challenges: Social and Political Theory*, 1989, Allen and Unwin; *Reading C:* Mitchell, J. *Psychoanalysis and Feminism*, 1990, Penguin Books. Copyright © 1974 Juliet Mitchell; *Reading D:* Coward, R. 'Female desire and sexual identity' in Diaz-Diocaretz, M. and Zavala, I. (eds) *Women, Feminist Identity and Society in the 1980s*, 1985, John Benjamins Publishing Company. Reprinted by permission of the author and publisher.

Figures

Figures 2.1, 2.2 and 2.3: Keirnan, K. and Wicks, M. *Family Change and Future Policy*, 1990, Family Policy Study Centre with the Joseph Rowntree Memorial Trust (York).

Illustrations

p.76: Hulton Deutsch Collection; *p.78:* Hulton Deutsch Collection.

Chapter 3

Readings

Reading B: Mort, F. 'Boy's Own? Masculinity, style and popular culture', in Chapman, R. and Rutherford, J. (eds) *Male Order: Unwrapping Masculinity*, 1988, Lawrence and Wishart; *Reading C:* Miller, D. *Material Culture and Mass Consumption*, 1987, Basil Blackwell.

Tables

Tables 3.3 and 3.4: reprinted by permission of the Controller of Her Majesty's Stationery Office.

Illustrations

p.125: Bildarchiv Preussischer Kulturbesitz; *p.134:* Bedfordshire Photographic Services; *p.141:* Hulton Deutsch Collection; *p.143:* Courtesy of Levi Strauss and Shilland & Co.; *p.145:* The Adverstising Archives; *p.150:* The Anthony Blake Photo Library; *p.152:* Pillitz/ Network.

Chapter 4

Readings

Reading A: Parsons, T. 'Social structure and dynamic process: the case of modern medical practice', in *The Social System*, 1951, Routledge. Reprinted by permission of Routledge and The Free Press, a Division of Macmillan, Inc. Copyright © 1951, copyright renewed 1979 by Talcott Parsons; *Reading B:* Goffman, E. *Asylums: Essays on the Social Situation of Mental Patients and Other Inmates*, Copyright © 1961 by Erving Goffman. Reprinted by permission of Doubleday, a division of Bantam Doubleday Dell Publishers Group, Inc.; *Reading C:* Foucault, M. *Madness and Civilization: A History of Insanity in the Age of Reason*, 1967, Tavistock. Reprinted by permission of Routledge.

Tables

Table 4.1: Busfield, J. *Managing Madness: Changing Ideas and Practice,* 1986, Unwin Hyman.

Figures

Figure 4.1: Raynes, N. and King, R. 'Residential care for the mentally retarded', *First International Congress for the Scientific Study of Mental Defiency,* 1967, reprinted by permission of the authors.

Illustrations

p.177: An ALEX strip from *The Independent* of March 13 1991. The ALEX annual volumes are available through Penguin Books; *p.187 (top):* Mary Evans Picture Library; *p.187 (bottom):* Collection Viollet; *p.190:* Punch; *p.195:* Copyright 1966 by David Levine.

Chapter 5

Readings

Reading A: Vance, C.S. 'Social construction theory: problems in the history of sexuality', in van Kooten Nierkerk, A. and van der Meer, T. (eds) *Homosexuality, Which Homosexuality?*, 1989, GMP Publishers. Reprinted by permission of Schorerstichting, Amsterdam; *Reading B:* Davidoff, L. 'Class and gender in Victorian England', in Newton, J.L., Walkowitz, J.R. and Ryan, M.P. *Sex and Class in Women's History,* 1983, Routledge. Reprinted by permission of Routledge and International Thompson Publishing; *Reading C:* Plummer, K. ' Going gay: identities, life cycles and lifestyles in the male gay world', in Hart, J. and Richardson, D. (eds) *The Theory and Practice of Homosexuality*, 1981, Routledge. Reprinted by permission of Routledge and International Thompson Publishing.

Illustrations

p.223: Mary Evans/Sigmund Freud Copyrights; *p.225:* Photo Jacques Robert/Copyright Gallimard; *p.234:* Mary Evans Picture Library; *p.236:* Reproduced by kind permission of the Master and Fellows of Trinity College, Cambridge; *p.238:* Joanne O'Brien/Format; *p.245:* Sunil Gupta/ Network; *p.254:* Brenda Prince/Format.

Chapter 6

Readings

Reading A: Green, A. *Educational and State Formation*, 1990, Macmillan Press Ltd; *Reading B:* Bowles, S. and Gintis, H. 'The correspondence principle', in Cole, M. (ed.) *Bowles and Gintis Revisited*, 1988, Falmer Press; *Reading C:* Collins, R. 'Some comparative principles of educational stratification', *Harvard Educational Review*, vol.47, no.1, 1977, reprinted by permission of the President and Fellows of Harvard College.

Text

'History and Thatcher', *Caribbean Times,* 8 September 1989, reprinted by permission of Hansib Publishing Ltd; Judd, J. 'Thatcher changes course of history', *The Observer*, 20 August 1989; 'Dangers of changing the course of history', *The Voice*, 19 September 1989; 'Chewing over history's core', *The Independent*, 11 August 1989; Plentie, D. 'Why should black history by taught in schools?', *The Voice*, 14 February 1989.

Tables

Table 6.1: adapted from Department of Education and Science's *Statistical Bulletin 1/90: Educational and Economic Activity of Young People Aged 16–18 Years in England from 1975–1989*; reprinted by permission of the Controller of Her Majesty's Stationery Office.

Figures

Figure 6.1: Moore, R. 'The correspondence principle and the Marxist sociology of education', in Cole, M. (ed.) *Bowles and Gintis Revisited*, 1988, Falmer Press.

Illustration

p.288: John Walmsley.

Chapter 7

Readings

Readings A and B: Gerard, D. 'Religious attitudes and values', in Abrams, M., Gerard, D. and Timms, N. *Values and Social Change in Britain*, 1985, Macmillan Press Ltd in association with the European Value Systems Study Group; *Reading D:* Beckford, J. *Religion and Advanced Industrial Society,* 1989, Unwin Hyman.

Illustrations

p.326: Barry Lewis/Network; *p.334:* Peter Marlow/Magnum; *pp.337, 339, 345 and 347:* Press Association.

Chapter 8

Readings

Reading A: Williams, R. *Culture*, 1981, Fontana, reprinted by permission of Harper Collins Publishers; *Reading B:* Foucault, M. 'What is an author?', in Harari, J.V. (ed.) *Textual Strategies: Perspectives in Post-Structuralist Criticism*, 1979, Cornell University Press, Ltd; *Reading C:* Benjamin, W. 'The work of art in the age of mechanical reproduction', in *Illuminations*, 1970, Jonathan Cape, reprinted by permission of the Random Century Group and Harcourt Brace Jovanovich.

Illustrations

p.372: British Library; *p.379:* British Library; *p.382:* F. Dodd *Virginia Woolf* (1908) National Portrait Gallery, London; *p.384 (top left):* W. Strang *Thomas Hardy* (1893) National Portrait Gallery, London; *p.384 (top right):* G.F. Watts *George Meredith* (1893) National Portrait Gallery, London; *p.384 (lower left):* Janet Oliphant *Mrs Oliphant* (1895) Scottish National Portrait Gallery; *p.384 (lower right):* George Richmond *Charlotte M. Yonge* (1844) National Portrait Gallery, London; *p.388 (left):* David Low *Lord Reith* (1933) National Portrait Gallery, London; *p.388 (right):* BBC Photograph Library; *p.393:* Radio Times.

Chapter 9

Readings

Reading B: Simmel, G. *The Sociology of Georg Simmel*, ed. Kurt Wolff, trans. H.H. Gerth with the assistance of C. Wright Mills, Macmillan, Inc/ The Free Press.

Illustrations

p.420: Mary Evans Picture Library; *p.426:* Windsor Castle, Royal Library. Copyright Her Majesty the Queen; *p.429:* From the Leeds Insanitary Areas Collection, The Brotherton Library, Leeds University; *p.437:* Studio Chevojon, Paris; *p.440:* Photothèque des Musées de la Ville de Paris/Musée Carnavalet. Copyright Musées de la Ville de Paris by SPADEM 1991; *p.441 (top):* Copyright Nasjonalgalleriet, Oslo/Photo: Jacques Lathion; *p.441 (bottom):* Collection Viollet; *p.442:* Emanuel Hoffman-Foundation, Kunstmuseum Basel; *p.443:* Historisches Museen der Stadt Wien; *p.448:* Copyright DACS 1991; *p.451:* London Transport Museum; *p.453:* Richard Kalvar/Magnum.

INDEX